The Canterbury and York Society

GENERAL EDITOR: DR P. HOSKIN

ISSN 0262–995X

PETITIONS TO THE CROWN FROM ENGLISH RELIGIOUS HOUSES c. 1272–c. 1485

CANTERBURY AND YORK SOCIETY VOL. C

Petitions to the Crown from English Religious Houses

c. 1272–c. 1485

EDITED BY

GWILYM DODD and ALISON K. McHARDY

with the assistance of LISA LIDDY

The Canterbury and York Society

The Boydell Press

2010

First published 2010
Reprinted in paperback and transferred to digital printing 2012

A Canterbury and York Society publication
Published by The Boydell Press
PO Box 9, Woodbridge, Suffolk IP12 3DF, UK
and of Boydell & Brewer Inc.
668 Mt Hope Avenue, Rochester, NY 14620, USA
website: www.boydellandbrewer.com

ISBN 978-0-90723-9-76-5

A CIP catalogue record for this book is available from the British Library

Details of previous volumes are available from Boydell & Brewer Ltd

This publication is printed on acid-free paper

Printed in Great Britain by
4edge Ltd, Hockley, Essex

CONTENTS

This volume is published with the help
of grants from the late
Miss Isobel Thornley's Bequest
to the University of London
and from
the Lincoln Record Society

For our greatly valued friend and colleague

W. Mark Ormrod

PREFACE

In the course of planning and completing this volume the editors have incurred numerous debts of gratitude. It now gives us great pleasure to thank the individuals and institutions that helped us bring our work to fruition. In the first place, we should like to thank the British Academy whose award of a Larger Research Grant in March 2007 provided the essential funding necessary for the project. We very much hope this volume is worthy of the faith and commitment given to us by this funding body. We should like to acknowledge the support of the Canterbury and York Society, under whose auspices this volume is published. We are also indebted to the University of Nottingham, and especially to our colleagues in the School of History and to the staff of the Hallward Library for their help and support. The School of History has kindly helped in meeting the costs of the front cover. Gwilym, in particular, has benefited from study leave made possible by the University of Nottingham's Dean's Fund (Faculty of Arts). The National Archives has generously given us permission to use the contents of its Catalogue entries as the basis for many of the summaries of petitions provided in the volume, and to use some images of the petitions for publicity purposes.

Of the individuals involved in the project we should firstly like to thank Professors Chris Given-Wilson, Barrie Dobson, Michael Prestwich, Robert Swanson, Tony Pollard and the late Jeff Denton for their initial support of our application. The editors are also indebted to Brother Anselm (Dr Joseph Gribbin), Dr Martin Heale and Dr Richard Goddard for generously reading drafts of parts of the Introduction, and to Dr Julia Barrow, Dr Nicholas Bennett, Professor Anne Hudson, Dr Maureen Jurkowski and Mrs Jennifer Thorp who provided assistance in various other ways. We owe particular thanks to Mrs Lisa Liddy, our researcher, for her meticulous work on the transcriptions and notes for each petition, and for the good humour and resourcefulness with which she tackled the numerous challenges which the project raised. Dr Pippa Hoskin has fulfilled her role as General Editor of the Canterbury and York Society with consummate skill, combining tact, diplomacy and endless patience in her efforts to coax us over the finishing line. She also provided invaluable assistance in the developmental phase of the project. Finally, we would like to pay particular tribute to Professor Mark Ormrod, who has done more than anyone to nurture and encourage our endeavours. We dedicate this volume to Mark in recognition of the great debt that we, and the historical profession in general, owe to him. Thank you.

November 2009

Gwilym Dodd
Alison K. McHardy

ABBREVIATIONS

BRUC	A. B. Emden, *A Biographical Register of the University of Cambridge to 1500* (Cambridge, 1963)
BRUO	A. B. Emden, *A Biographical Register of the University of Oxford to AD 1500*, 3 vols (Oxford, 1957–9)
CChR	*Calendar of Charter Rolls*
CCR	*Calendar of Close Rolls*
CCW	*Calendar of Chancery Warrants*
CFR	*Calendar of Fine Rolls*
CIM	*Calendar of Inquisitions Miscellaneous*
CPR	*Calendar of Patent Rolls*
C&Y	Canterbury and York Society
EHR	*English Historical Review*
ERY	East Riding of Yorkshire
HC	J. S. Roskell, L. Clark and C. Rawcliffe, *The House of Commons 1386–1421*, History of Parliament, 4 vols (Stroud, 1992)
Heads of Houses II	D. M. Smith, *The Heads of Religious Houses, England and Wales, II. 1216–1377* (Cambridge, 2001)
Heads of Houses III	D. M. Smith, *The Heads of Religious Houses, England and Wales, III. 1377–1540* (Cambridge, 2008)
JEH	*Journal of Ecclesiastical History*
LAO	Lincolnshire Archives Office
MRH	D. Knowles and R. N. Hadcock, *Medieval Religious Houses, England and Wales* (London, 1971)
NRY	North Riding of Yorkshire
ODNB	*Oxford Dictionary of National Biography*, Oxford University Press, online edition (2007)
PRO	Public Record Office
PROME	*The Parliament Rolls of Medieval England*, ed. C. Given-Wilson et al. (Leicester, 2005), CD-Rom version
RP	*Rotuli Parliamentorum*, 6 vols (London, 1767–77)
Sainty, *Judges*	J. C. Sainty, *The Judges of England, 1272–1990: a List of Judges of the Superior Courts*, Selden Society, Suppl. Ser., 10 (1993)
SR	*Statutes of the Realm*, 11 vols (London, 1810–28)
TNA	The National Archives
VCH	*Victoria County History*
WRY	West Riding of Yorkshire

Unless otherwise stated, all unpublished documents are in London, The National Archives (TNA).

INTRODUCTION

Introduction

The petitions contained in this volume are all drawn from The National Archives, series SC 8, commonly known as 'Ancient Petitions'.[1] This class, containing over 17,000 separate requests, is an entirely artificial creation, the consequence of misguided attempts by nineteenth-century record-keepers to rearrange the medieval archives of central government into a regularised, homogeneous collection of records containing similar types of documents. The result was a large collection of petitions which satisfied their nineteenth-century keepers but which has been seriously detrimental to historical research. For example, readers will notice that few of the petitions printed here can be dated precisely. This is a consequence of the nineteenth-century reordering, when many petitions were separated from writs which would otherwise have provided a secure date for the case, because petitions did not contain a dating clause, and the crown's responses (usually endorsements) were rarely dated. The reordering also, in many cases, destroyed the provenance of the petitions, so that it has often proved difficult to establish where, and to whom, they were presented. Petition **161** in this volume nicely illustrates these difficulties, for without the fortuitous note-taking of Clemens Reynerus, who viewed the petition in its original file or 'bundle' in the seventeenth century, before it was rearranged, we would have no ready means of identifying it as a petition presented in the parliament of March 1330. This, however, is a rare exception. The twin problems of dating and provenance are important in explaining why the SC 8 petitions have been relatively underused in modern scholarship. Only recently have their importance and potential become fully appreciated, as a result of a project funded by the Arts and Humanities Research Council to publish detailed descriptions of their contents via The National Archives' on-line Catalogue and to provide free digitised images of the originals through its DocumentsOnline facility.[2] This volume is one of the fruits of the project's endeavours.

The volume has two basic aims. First, to demonstrate the great variety, and remarkable richness, of petitions as a source which illuminates the life and circumstances of religious houses in late medieval England; and second, to show the significance of petitions for the history of late medieval monasticism, especially the relations between the religious and the outside world. It has long been

1 See now, G. Dodd, *Justice and Grace: Private Petitioning and the English Parliament in the Late Middle Ages* (Oxford, 2007). See also, *Medieval Petitions: Grace and Grievance*, ed. W. M. Ormrod, G. Dodd and A. Musson (York, 2009).

2 'Medieval Petitions: A Catalogue of the "Ancient Petitions" in the Public Record Office', AHRC Resource and Enhancement Scheme. The principal investigator was Professor W. Mark Ormrod, University of York. See http://www.nationalarchives.gov.uk/cataglogue/ and http://www.nationalarchives.go.uk/documentsonline/

known that religious houses addressed petitions to the crown, but the subject has usually been studied in connection with precise types of request; this volume illustrates the whole range of cases. Petitions formed an important link between the religious – as subjects – and the crown, yet for practical reasons have been comparatively little studied,[3] in contrast to such areas as the demarcation lines between royal and ecclesiastical jurisdictions,[4] and the collective grievances which the clergy occasionally aired.[5] The following introduction is a survey of some key areas necessary for understanding how petitions can be used, and their usefulness for English monastic history between the late thirteenth and the mid-fifteenth centuries – the period in which most petitions in this volume were presented. Though in theory the religious had small cause to utilise the petitionary mechanism, in practice there was significant disparity between the monastic ideal of contemplative isolation, and the reality of monastic dealings with the outside world.[6] The documents printed here show us the religious in a variety of roles: as subjects of the English crown – immune neither to fiscal nor to political pressures – and as landowners, neighbours, and landlords. They also appear as groups of quarrelling men, whose relative isolation bred festering disputes. Contrariwise, they sometimes found the English crown a place of last resort in matters of discipline and development.

Although petitions to the crown in parliament would not appear *prima facie* to be 'records of the English church', these documents do, in fact, represent a remarkable convergence of influences. Underlying all petitioning were the theological concepts of justice and mercy; these were given practical expression during the twelfth and thirteenth centuries as popes sought to enhance their authority by encouraging petitions (supplications) from all over Christendom. Petitions, therefore, already played an important role in medieval church government before they were utilised by secular rulers. Indeed, there are indications that the English crown looked to the example of the papacy when opening parliament to large-

3 The principal exception is the unpublished research of J. H. Tillotson, 'Clerical Petitions 1350–1450: A Study of Some Aspects of the Relations of Crown and Church in the Later Middle Ages', unpublished D.Phil. thesis, Australian National University (1969). There is a useful study on bills presented in chancery by R. L. Storey, 'Ecclesiastical Causes in Chancery', in *The Study of Medieval Records: Essays in Honour of Kathleen Major*, ed. D. A. Bullough and R. L. Storey (Oxford, 1971), pp. 236–59, and more recently, Dodd, *Justice and Grace*, pp. 243–54. Even the use of the common law by the religious is relatively unexplored, though an exception is F. J. Pegues, 'A Monastic Society at Law in the Kent Eyre of 1313–1314', *EHR* 87 (1972), 548–64.

4 W. R. Jones, 'Relations in the Two Jurisdictions: Conflict and Cooperation in England during the 13th and 14th Centuries', in *Studies in Medieval and Renaissance History* 7, ed. W. M. Bowsky (Lincoln, NE, 1970), pp. 77–210; and J. H. Denton, 'The Making of the "*Articuli Cleri*" of 1316', *EHR* 101 (1986), 564–95.

5 W. R. Jones, 'Bishops, Politics, and the Two Laws: The *Gravamina* of the English Clergy, 1237–1399', *Speculum* 41 (1966), 209–45.

6 For which see J. G. Clark, 'The Religious Orders in Pre-Reformation England' (pp. 3–33), and B. Thompson, 'Monasteries, Society and Reform in Late Medieval England' (pp. 165–95), in *The Religious Orders in Pre-Reformation England*, ed. J. G. Clark (Woodbridge, 2002); and more recently, M. Heale, 'Introduction' to his *Monasticism in Late Medieval England, c. 1300–1535* (Manchester, 2009), pp. 6, 33–4.

scale petitioning at the end of the thirteenth century.[7] Thus, the clergy in general, and the religious especially, were already accustomed to using supplications as a means to further their own interests before the English crown constructed an elaborate petitionary apparatus of its own. During the later Middle Ages the two mechanisms, royal and papal, coexisted, and in some disputes were employed concurrently. Good discipline and good order were desirable ends for civil and spiritual rulers alike, and cooperation was more common than confrontation between the two powers.

The petitions

Petitions were an established part of the political, administrative and legal framework of late medieval England. Although petitioning could be done orally, this discussion concerns written requests which provided the essential means for higher authority to be formally canvassed by an individual or community wishing to secure assistance and support. Petitions to the crown were usually presented for one of two reasons: to secure justice against wrongdoing, or to gain favour. In both contexts, the act of petitioning implied an underlying acceptance by the supplicant of the superior authority of those who were being petitioned. Petitions played an important role in almost every branch of royal government, from the exchequer, chancery and central courts of justice, to the royal council and the king himself; there are also indications that petitions proliferated at a local level, in towns and local and baronial courts, though inevitably far fewer of those cases have survived.

Most petitions in SC 8 were intended for the king's personal consideration. Research into the earlier arrangement of these documents suggests that most were presented in a parliamentary context, and so were sent to the king at times when parliament was in session.[8] In technical terms, then, they are what parliamentary historians would describe as 'private petitions'; that is to say, supplications presented by individuals or corporations about matters which related to their own particular circumstances. This explains why there is a particular concentration – in this volume, as in the whole SC 8 series – of petitions dating to the first decades of the fourteenth century, the high water-mark of parliamentary petitioning, a period when few other routes were available to subjects seeking redress from the crown. The parliamentary context of the petitions invites one important qualification: although the king (or 'king and council') was usually the addressee of these supplications, and although in practice he undoubtedly gave his personal attention to large numbers of requests, parliament had, from its inception, developed mechanisms which helped alleviate the immense burden which the king and his councillors would otherwise have had to shoulder alone. Thus, it was not uncommon for some petitions to be processed without receiving

7 Dodd, *Justice and Grace*, pp. 36–7; B. Bombi, 'Petitioning between England and Avignon in the First Half of the Fourteenth Century', and P. Zutshi, 'Petitions to the Pope in the Fourteenth Century', in *Medieval Petitions*, ed. Ormrod, Dodd and Musson, pp. 64–81, 82–98.

8 G. Dodd, 'Parliamentary Petitions? The Origins and Provenance of the "Ancient Petitions" (SC 8) in the National Archives', in *Medieval Petitions*, ed. Ormrod, Dodd and Musson, pp. 12–46.

the king's personal consideration; committees of triers, comprising leading ecclesiastics, nobles, lawyers, and senior king's clerks, were instituted from an early period to discharge the more routine matters brought to parliament, and later, from the mid-fourteenth century, petitioners increasingly sent their requests to the Lords or Commons, in the hope of gaining their support before the case was presented to the king (many later requests were explicitly addressed to the Lords or Commons). When religious houses presented their petitions in parliament, therefore, they were petitioning not only the king but very often, in both principle and practice, the broader political community.

Petitions addressed to the king, whether inside or outside parliament, normally raised matters which required the bestowal of royal grace. The term, and concept, of royal grace is useful in explaining why kings in the fourteenth and fifteenth centuries continued to be showered with requests by their subjects to pay special regard to their individual circumstances, and instigate actions to alleviate distress or to enhance their interests. Grace, in the context of petitioning, describes the use of power which only the king could exercise, or delegate; it was an expression of the royal prerogative and it allowed a king to overturn judgements and to ignore due process, according to his conscience. An act of grace was by its nature entirely voluntary; the king was under no obligation to show such favour, unless minded to do so. Yet grace was an important attribute of medieval kingship, and there was an expectation that a king should respond generously to his subjects' appeals.

Only a proportion of the petitions addressed to the king fell into this category, however. Others were more straightforward requests for justice, and therefore appealed less clearly for royal grace, but more to the king's sense of equity and natural justice, attributes which could be shared and offered by royal ministers, councillors and justices acting for him. In these cases, the crown, and specifically the monarch, had a widely acknowledged responsibility to ensure that victims of wrong-doing gained redress. Still other petitions were directed to the king because they concerned particular actions or decisions which he had taken, or because they concerned the household or the royal patrimony. Yet others arose from the specific tenurial relationship existing between king and suppliant; this category was especially relevant to petitions presented by religious houses of royal patronage. Finally, some petitions may have been presented in parliament because they raised matters which had particular relevance to the activity of that assembly, or because the supplicants hoped to attract broader support for their request from the political community. The single most important requirement for a petition to parliament was that the matter could be resolved nowhere else. Theoretically, this meant that a petitioner had exhausted all other avenues, especially the common law courts, before resorting to parliament.

A final point should be made: the petitions presented by religious houses seeking special dispensation or justice were quite distinct from the requests found in the collection of 'Ecclesiastical Petitions' in TNA series C 84. These latter served the specific administrative function of gaining royal approval following the election of a new abbot or prior.[9] Such approvals were routine matters of administration, for by the later thirteenth century the crown was (with very rare

9 The process is described by B. Dobson, 'The Election of John Ousthorp as Abbot of

exceptions) no longer concerned with the promotion of particular individuals within religious houses.

The selection and arrangement of the petitions

In making their selection of material for this volume the editors have been guided by two considerations: one, to ensure that the full range of subjects raised by petitions from religious houses is represented; and two, that each petition has intrinsic interest. This means that its content stands out either in fullness or detail as an example of a particular type of request, or because this petition raises particular points of interest. Many of the petitions from religious houses to the crown were essentially routine and uncontentious. A representative sample of such cases is included at the start of the volume to give a flavour of the business which constituted the 'bread and butter' of supplicatory traffic between the religious and the crown, from the late thirteenth to the late fifteenth century (Part I: **1–13**). These examples cover such matters as requests for the repayment of loans, for charters of pardon, and for licences to go on pilgrimage. These are, mainly, requests for crown favour. The remaining, non-routine, petitions show a much higher proportion of complaints. These are grouped into five further sections, arranged thematically according to the kind of action which the petition sought. This arrangement has the benefit of highlighting the chief ways in which the king could intercede on behalf of a religious house, whilst at the same time providing a framework round which the petitions are grouped according to the nature of their request.

Thus, in Part 2 are all those petitions where the nature of the grievance placed the crown under a direct obligation to provide a remedy. Most arose from errors or transgressions committed by agents of the crown, more rarely by the king himself, which required amendment as a matter of course, in accordance with the principles of natural justice and good conscience. In Part 3 are those petitions in which the remedy was more clearly a matter for royal discretion or 'grace'. In these cases, the petitioners placed themselves at the king's mercy by asking for dispensations or favours which they could not automatically expect to receive. Part 4 contains petitions which required the crown to intercede or arbitrate between the religious house and a third party. Very often, these petitions were presented at times when a community was in conflict, either within itself or with its neighbours, and it sought the crown's help in restoring its fortunes. Part 5 is a small but important category of 'collective grievances', which were presented by several houses or whole religious orders acting collectively, raising matters very different from the requests presented by individual houses. Finally, Part 6 contains complaints or requests about monasteries from non-religious petitioners, included to provide balance by showing that a religious house could be as much the architect of ill-fortune as its victim. These cases illustrate the sorts of occasions when the crown was invited by petition to act against a religious house.

Selby in 1436', *Yorkshire Archaeological Society* 42 (1967), 31–40; and R. M. Haines, *Ecclesia Anglicana: Studies in the English Church of the Later Middle Ages* (Toronto, 1989), pp. 15–25.

LANGUAGE AND RHETORIC

The petitions presented to the crown by religious houses were generally no different in appearance or language from petitions presented by the king's other subjects. They broadly conformed to a set of diplomatic conventions which ensured a high level of standardisation in the tone, vocabulary and structure of almost all petitions put before the king and his ministers. Hence petitions from religious houses were almost always written in Anglo-Norman French, the language *par excellence* of complaint and request in secular legal and political contexts. Its predominance can be attributed to two important factors: first, the emergence of French in the thirteenth century as a language immutably associated with, and suited to, legal process, especially pleading (of which petitioning was a written form); and second, the use of French by the English political elite – the recipients of the petitions – as its main language for much of the period in which the petitions were presented. A handful of very early petitions from religious houses and other petitioners, dating to the first years of Edward I's reign, were drafted in Latin (e.g. **178**),[10] but very quickly French came to be adopted universally, and it did not lose its predominance until the middle decades of the fifteenth century, when English began to be more widely used (e.g. **53**, **120**, **135**, **213**, **214**).

Although most petitions addressed to the English crown in the later Middle Ages were written in Anglo-Norman French, their form and structure, and their underlying principles, owed much to the Latin petitions which the clergy had addressed to the papacy during previous centuries. Formulaic, and often obsequious, opening addresses and concluding appeals; the use of the third person; and an emphasis on brevity and economy of expression were essential characteristics of the petitionary form. The principles of equity, natural justice, conscience and benevolence which underpinned the authority with which petitions were dispatched in parliament, chancery and elsewhere, and which petitioners often implicitly invoked in the rhetoric of their requests to these institutions, were concepts firmly rooted in theological writing and in canon law.[11] The right of an individual to appeal to higher authority against an injustice was similarly deeply embedded in the legal culture and structures of the Church.[12] Indeed, there would have been an underlying familiarity with the petition simply by virtue of the fact that it drew on the language and imagery of prayer: like God, the king received supplications from his subjects and responded to those which he consid-

10 Requests for the confirmation of heads-elect continued to be written in Latin: *A Formula Book of English Official Historical Documents, Part I: Diplomatic Documents*, ed. H. Hall (Cambridge, 1908), pp. 88–90.

11 H. Coing, 'English Equity and the *Denunciato Evangelica* of the canon law', *Law Quarterly Review* 71 (1955), 223–41; M. Beilby, 'The Profits of Expertise: The Rise of the Civil Lawyers and Chancery Equity', in *Profit, Piety and the Professions in Later Medieval England*, ed. M. Hicks (Gloucester, 1990), pp. 73–4; and G. R. Evans, *Law and Theology in the Middle Ages* (London, 2002), pp. 85–90, 105–19.

12 Ibid., pp. 159–61.

ered deserving, as an act of grace.[13] The king's grace directly equated with the grace of God, on whose behalf the king ruled and judged his people.

These petitions were thus drafted in accordance with a well-defined set of linguistic and rhetorical conventions, and they followed a standard type of structure. Each began with an opening address which identified both the recipient – usually the king, council or Commons in parliament – and the petitioner, whose name was usually expressed in the third person. Then followed the main narrative; this initially described the misfortune which had befallen the supplicant, before outlining what the king could do to remedy these circumstances. Every petition ended with a formulaic concluding clause, typically asking for a remedy 'for God and for the sake of charity'. Although the length of petitions could vary greatly, depending on the amount of detail contained in the main narrative part, petitions throughout this period adhered to this basic outline.

Yet one great advantage of this volume is the opportunity it presents to show how the form and style of petitions evolved over a period of two hundred years. Readers will note that early petitions, dating to the late thirteenth and early fourteenth centuries, tend to employ fairly utilitarian vocabulary and are generally of relatively short length: the opening address, for example, is usually free of excess verbiage and identifies the king, or the king and council, as the recipients of the request in a very straightforward manner: e.g. *A nostre seyngnur le roi prie* (**1**) or *A nostre seingnur le roi e a soen consail prie* (**2**). As time passes, however, and especially from the mid-fourteenth century, petitions deployed language with increasing elaboration. The changes are particularly noticeable in the address clauses which, besides retaining their obvious practical function, were now also used by the supplicant to express their regard and reverence for the higher status of those to whom the petition was directed. A petition presented by Christ Church, Canterbury, in 1397, for example, began *A treshaut, tresexcellent, tresredoute seignur nostre seignure le roy* (**48**), whilst one handed in by the nuns of Henwood in 1411 was even more obsequious: *A treshaut, trespuissant, tresgracious et tresredoute seignur, nostre seignure le roy* (**82**). The changes to affect the style and tone of petitions across the later medieval period were symptomatic of broader developments in writing techniques within the royal secretariat. These have been traced to the early fourteenth century and have been characterised as a particular form of administrative writing style (later to be adapted for a literary context) known as 'curial' or 'clergial' prose.[14]

Whilst petitions from religious houses were generally little different from other petitions, there were still some characteristics which marked them out as requests from this source. Within the narrowly defined diplomatic conventions of the petitionary form there was still scope for petitioners to individualise their requests by drawing on rhetorical strategies which had particular relevance to their circumstances. In this respect, religious houses were no different from other petitioners. So, the power and prestige of the king and his ministers, and the wisdom and discretion of the Lords or Commons, was usually contrasted with descriptions by the religious communities themselves of their weak and impoverished condi-

13 G. Koziol, 'The Early History of Rites of Supplication', in *Suppliques et Requêtes: le Gouvernement par la Grâce en Occident (XIIe–XVe Siècle)*, ed. H. Millet (Rome, 2003), pp. 29–31.

14 J. D. Burnley, 'Curial Prose in England', *Speculum* 61 (1986), 593–614.

tion. It was commonplace for religious houses to describe themselves as the king's *poveres oratours* (e.g. **10**), or more elaborately, as the king's *povrez chapelleins et continuelx oratours* (e.g. **13**). Devotion and religiosity were attributes considered worth emphasising: many petitions in this volume describe the inhabitants of the religious house as the king's *humbles et devoutz chapelleins* (**17**), *devoutes oratrices* (**81**), and in the case of a petition presented in the name of an abbot, *son devout chapeleyn* (**38**). The term *oratour* – usually prefixed with the qualifier *continuelx* or *perpetuel* – is noteworthy, for although the description of a petitioner in these terms was not exclusive to monasteries, it had particular resonance when used in this context because of the double meaning it carried, as a description of the religious house both as supplicant to the king, and more generally as an intercessor on behalf of the king to God.

Rhetoric worked on other levels in these petitions. As already indicated, most petitioners, both secular and religious, couched their requests formulaically, often by aligning their supplication with the will of God and by appealing to the king's sense of charity, but the particular quality which religious houses possessed as centres of spiritual life meant that the formulaic clauses, which either introduced or concluded the part of the petition that specified what the king could do to help, were particularly prone to elaboration or embellishment. In 1384, for example, the Dominicans of Dunwich rather grandly invoked the king's 'high majesty' (*haute mageste*) and asked for licence to obtain lands *pur Dieu et pur les almes de son tresnoble pere et de ses autres progenitours* (**64**). Two years earlier, in 1382, the Benedictine nuns of Shaftesbury, finding themselves in severe financial straits, asked the king for sustenance *pur l'amour de Dieu et da sa douce* [sweet] *mere Sainte Marie et del glorious corseint* [body of] *Seint Edward le Martyr, vostre noble progenitour qi en vostre dit maison gist canonizez* (**81**). In this instance the petitioners cleverly incorporated the association of the abbey with Edward, King and Martyr (962–79), whose relics were held by the community, as an additional mark in their favour. A similar tactic was deployed in a petition presented jointly by the bishop of Ely and prior of Ely, in which they enjoined the king to grant their request for custody of the goods forfeited by convicted rebels *al reverence de Dieu et de Saint Auldree* (**63**). It did not harm one's cause to remind the king of the great spiritual heritage enjoyed by a religious house and its association with a saint (in the case of Ely, its founding saint) who hailed from a distant Anglo-Saxon past. In the case of a petition from Avebury priory, it was the crown rather than the petitioners who made such a connection, when it was stated that the request was granted partly out of reverence for the patron of the house, St George (**79**). A tactic of a different order was used by the abbot and convent of Tupholme who attempted to ingratiate themselves to Edward II by declaring their support for him at a time of great political turmoil (**76**). They were pleading for financial relief, and asked the king to provide a remedy *s'il vous pleise, treschier seignur, Dieu vous doynt bone vie et longe et victorie de voz enemys.*

In all the these instances the underlying purpose of the invocation of God, the alms of king's progenitors and even the personal wellbeing of the king himself, was to establish common ground between the petitioner and the king. Whereas the address of a petition deliberately emphasised the fundamentally unequal status of those who presented petitions in comparison to those who adjudicated on them, these turns of phrase highlighted the degree of mutuality that existed by securing for a petition a favourable outcome. The king was urged to respond positively to the request not so much to satisfy the personal or private interests of the petitioner, but for the sake of the souls of his ancestors and to please God. This was an immensely powerful strategy for any petitioner to use, but in petitions presented by religious houses, such entreaties obviously carried additional weight. It was a particularly effective means of putting moral pressure on the king to use his conscience to reach a just decision in their favour. For the clergy a degree of reciprocity could also be offered in the form of prayers. The prior of Harmondsworth asked to be allowed new copies of charters and relief from his rent *si q'il puisse viver et Dieu servir et prier pur nostre seignur le roy et son bone consail et les almes de touz sez progenitours* (**80**). A similar offer was made by the abbot of Bury St Edmunds in 1454 when he asked to be exempt from attendance of parliament (**53**). At the end of his request was written the promise (in English): *And he shall pray to God for you.* The words '... if you grant the petition' were not inserted, but the contractual nature of the abbot's pledge to offer prayers for the king would have been quite plain to see.

Religious houses sometimes placed emphasis on the practical aspects of their spiritual vocation, stressing the danger that these would be affected if resolution of the petition were not forthcoming. Thus, in 1403, the Carthusian prior of Axholme petitioned for the return of the alien priory of Monks Kirby (Warwicks.), arguing that its possession would ensure *la augmentacioun et encrece de divine service et autres oevres de charite alors abeisez*, as well as the sustenance of the prior and seven monks who would be able to celebrate mass and pray for the soul of their patron, Thomas Mowbray, earl of Nottingham (**49**). The abbot of Buckfast was rather more direct in a petition of Henry VI's reign in which he implored the king to release him from an obligation to attend law suits before the royal council, and *to suffre the said besecher to goone home to his said hous for the rule there of, and to attende dyvyne servys there as his profession axith* (**51**). In a declaration that builds to an impressive and perhaps improbable rhetorical climax, the prior of Bath declared in 1418 that unless resolution to his complaint was found – this related to a dispute with the inhabitants of the town over the ringing of bells – *les ditz priour et convent ne purrount ester ables ne disposes a faire et dire lour divinez services solonc lour reule et fundacione, au contempt de nostre sovereigne seignur le roy, grande damages del dit priour, final destuccione del esglise cathedrale suisdite* ... (**131**).

The interruption of divine service was a particularly useful rhetorical device which worked on several different levels for a religious house. First, it provided a very tangible and emotive illustration of the damage to befall the religious community as a result of the wrong which their petition aimed to right; second, it reminded the king and his ministers of the petitioners' unimpeachable religious and moral virtue, since their overarching concern was the restoration of the proper functioning of religious observance within the community; and third, it reinforced the notion that the main *raison d'être* of religious communities was to pursue a spiritual life, and that their engagement in the secular world, which their petition represented, was the consequence of circumstances which lay outside their control. This generated a sense that they were reluctant petitioners whose hand had been forced by the ill-wind of fate, or by injustices perpetrated by law-breaking third parties. It was, in short, a useful device to suggest that the supplicants were innocent victims. There was, however, another aspect to these persuasive strategies, for references to the disruption of divine service implied that the king had both an interest and also an obligation to protect and sustain the clergy because of their importance to the moral fabric of the kingdom. Indeed, by citing the damage caused to the spiritual life of the religious community, there was a tacit acceptance that spiritual welfare was a royal responsibility, and that the king and his advisors ought to be informed if the monastery was not playing its spiritual role effectively. This upheld a view of monasteries where they were regarded in essentially proprietary terms, from the point of view of the laity, as institutions whose activities were directed overwhelmingly to serve the spiritual needs of their founders, the king and the wider kingdom.[15]

Appeals to the past are also a particular feature of our petitions. These were commonly references to the house's founder or to the reigns of past kings in which charters had been issued delineating the freedoms and privileges which it should enjoy – often, in the case of royal foundations, these were the same thing. These were no mere semantic tools of persuasion, since much petitionary business emanating from religious houses concerned disputes over rights and customs which could often be resolved only by looking to the past for clarification. And, by invoking ancient charters and customs, religious houses were tapping into a familiar leitmotif of medieval thinking in which particular regard was held for long-held custom and historical continuity.[16] This especially applied to a legal context, since common law derived its authority from its claim to embody 'established custom'.[17] Such was the power of precedent that some monasteries which could not prove their rights and privileges by charter, nevertheless emphasised that their current condition had remained unchanged for as long as could be remembered. For example, in three separate places in their petition of 1384, for confirmation of their franchise in Mostowe Hundred, the Benedictine nuns of Wherwell pointed out that they had enjoyed these rights *de temps dont y n'y'ad memoire* ('time out of mind') (**18**).[18] Other communities could be more specific and boast of a long and prestigious lineage. St Augustine's Canterbury was able to point out that a tithe of all rents and profits from the manor of Milton had been granted to them by *le bon Roy Willeam, conquerour d'Engleterre, par devocion et par sa charge* (**32**).

15 B. Thompson, 'Laity, the Alien Priories and the Redistribution of Ecclesiastical Property', in *England in the Fifteenth Century: Proceedings of the 1992 Harlaxton Symposium*, ed. N. Rogers (Stamford, 1994), pp. 19–41, esp. pp. 20–2, 26–8; and C. Burgess, 'St George's College, Windsor: Context and Consequence', in *St George's Chapel Windsor in the Fourteenth Century*, ed. N. Saul (Woodbridge, 2005), pp. 63–96, esp. pp. 65–71.

16 A. G. Remensnyder, *Remembering Kings Past: Monastic Foundation Legends in Medieval Southern France* (Ithaca, 1995), esp. chpt. 6; and M. Innes, 'Introduction: Using the Past, Interpreting the Present, Influencing the Future', in *The Uses of the Past in the Early Middle Ages*, ed. Y. Hen and M. Innes (Cambridge, 2000), pp. 1–8.

17 J. Catto, 'Andrew Horn: Law and History in Fourteenth Century England', in *The Writing of History in the Middle Ages*, ed. R. H. C. Davies and J. M. Wallace-Hadrill (Oxford, 1981), pp. 367–91; and A. Musson, 'Appealing to the Past: Perceptions of Law in Late-Medieval England', in *Expectations of the Law in the Middle Ages*, ed. A. Musson (Woodbridge, 2001), pp. 165–79.

18 For discussion of the meaning and significance of the phrase, which effectively placed a legal decision beyond reproach of living memory, see P. Brand, '"Time out of Mind": The Knowledge and Use of the Eleventh- and Twelfth-Century Past in Thirteenth-Century England', *Anglo-Norman Studies XVI* (Woodbridge, 1994), pp. 42–52.

Other religious communities could point to precedents stretching back even further. In disputes with its tenants, Chertsey Abbey claimed in 1378 to have held certain manors as servile tenure *puis la fundacion du dit abbeye, quel fust founde par Frithewold et Seint Erkenwolde, q'est a present translate en l'esglise cathedrale de Seint Poule de Londres, et cele fundacion du dit abbee fuist en l'an del incarnacion nostre Jesus Crist DCCxxij* (**140**). The reference to the recent translation of the saint's relics to St Paul's may be regarded as an attempt to capitalise on a close association with a religious figure whose cult was then the focus of court enthusiasm.[19] The Augustinian canons used a similar tactic in the early 1420s when they asked to be granted land in Oxford to establish a college, in reverence to God, Our Lady *et de Seint Johan de Bridelynton', qi jadis fuist du dit ordre* (**174**).[20] In 1406 Evesham Abbey similarly invoked the distant past to suggest that the weight of history supported their request; in seeking clarification of the status of manors whose farm the king had recently granted to Sir John Cornwall and his wife Elizabeth, the petition included references to no fewer than seven previous monarchs, stretching far back to the early eighth century: Coenred, king of the Mercians (704–c.709), Edward the Confessor, William I, John, Henry I, Henry III and Edward III (**21**). In the absence of royal authority, the generosity of aristocratic founders was invoked. Thus, Shrewsbury Abbey declared that it had been granted a fair by its founder, *Counte Roger de Belem, qui veint ove le Conquerur Rey William*, which charter had been confirmed by every king since this time (**122**). St Mary's York, in describing the terms of its endowment, gave its founder as *Estevene nadgeirs duc de Bretaigne* (**42**). If this was incorrect, as it almost certainly was, the monks are hardly to be blamed since the founder's identity is elusive.

References to the distant past lent an air of legitimacy and authenticity to monastic claims, and, though reliance on ancient charters to prove ownership and privilege was not unique to religious communities, it was an especially common feature of those petitions about disputes over lands or revenues. Since religious corporations never died they had the advantage of stability and continuity over laymen – both individuals and families – and were better-placed to provide documentary support for their case in property disputes. In this, the charter reigned supreme. Petitions which enclosed copies of ancient charters to provide tangible and seemingly incontestable evidence in support of the abbey's cause (e.g. **32**, **34** and **36**); other supplications which pleaded for royal intervention because charters or deeds relating to an abbey's possessions had been lost or stolen (**80**, **116** and **148**); and yet other instances in which the crown appeared to make the outcome to a request dependent on the production of relevant charters and muniments (**101**, **110** and **146**), all bear testimony to the great emphasis

19 P. Wormald, 'Earconwald (*d.* 693)', *ODNB*. Chertsey Abbey, St Paul's and Barking Nunnery had each claimed to possess the saint's body. The phrase *a present* in the petition suggests that the abbey had not yet given up the possibility that the remains would sometime be handed over to their custody. See A. Thacker, 'The Cult of Saints and the Liturgy', in *St Paul's: The Cathedral Church of London 604–2004*, ed. D. Keene, A. Burns and A. Saint (New Haven and London, 2004), pp. 114–15. St Erkenwald's relics were translated to a new shrine in St Paul's in 1326: *The Saint of London: The Life and Miracles of St Erkenwald*, ed. and trans. E. Gordan Whatley (New York, 1989), pp. 66–7.

20 Michael J. Curley, 'John of Bridlington (*c.*1320–1379)', *ODNB*.

that was placed on the apparently unimpeachable authority of the written word, especially when it recorded ancient custom and rights.[21]

Whilst the petitions in this volume, as in the whole collection of 'Ancient Petitions', suggest that considerable store was placed on the need to conform to the structural and diplomatic norms of supplicatory writing, we should not assume that petitions were the product of a bland, unimaginative administrative culture. More work is needed before we fully understand the many different levels at which the rhetoric deployed in these petitions worked, and it is hoped that, by providing full transcriptions of a large selection of material, the volume will assist this enquiry. Moreover, there are many instances in which petitions deviated from these standard forms, or otherwise used language and rhetoric in a less conventional way, which carry additional interest. One example was presented by the Benedictine nuns of Lyminster in 1302 (**70**). Its unusual form suggests that, although the nuns were conscious of the general structure that a petition should take, they were ignorant of the precise use of language in this context; they both addressed and concluded their request in a way which only approximated to the common linguistic formulae then current. There is, also, the petition from the abbot of Clairvaux's proctors, who, in 1333, evidently felt that their case against John of Charlton, lord of Welshpool, would be significantly strengthened if they reported the precise words he allegedly uttered, to underline the scandalous and outrageous nature of his oppression of the abbey's commissary: *Je suis papes, je suis roys et evesques et abbes en ma terre* (**104**). It is also possible that the petition of the prior of Llanthony Secunda (c. 1326), in which the king's keeper of the priory's manors, Adam Helnak, was called Adam Halfnaked (an obsolete form), was a mischievous attempt to ridicule their opponent (**27**).

Religious houses and the crown

The largest group of petitions arose from the religious orders' dealings with the crown, and that is not counting the many cases which arose, directly or indirectly, from political events or court factions. The religious made many complaints against royal officials, whether local (**22**–**33**) or central (the exchequer: **38**, **40**, **46**, **52**, **69**, **71**); in this they were no different from kings' other property-owning subjects. Numerous petitions from 'alien priories', both Benedictine cells of French abbeys, and Cluniac houses, arose from the crown's policy of seizing them during periods of Anglo-French warfare. Complaints about the exactions of farmers of such houses (e.g. **20**, **31**, **79**) were one phase of the story; problems arising from their denization, or the redirection of their endowments to other foundations (**21**, **33**, **49**) came later. Complaints against royal policies or royal officials were generally treated fairly by the crown. Two cases brought against the king's ministers, with the resulting documentation, printed here, show with what care the government of Edward II, in the period of his fullest power, responded to the abbots of Byland and Bury St Edmunds (**25**, **26**). These sets

[21] M. T. Clanchy, *From Memory to Written Record: England 1066–1307* (Oxford, 1979, repr. 1993), pp. 294–327; R. Britnell, 'Pragmatic Literacy in Latin Christendom', in *Pragmatic Literacy, East and West, 1200–1330*, ed. R. Britnell (Woodbridge, 1997), pp. 5, 19–30, 12–16.

of documents are particularly valuable in showing how the machinery of royal government, both locally and at the centre, could be mobilised on behalf of a petitioner – this was a common feature across the late medieval period. They are also important from an archival perspective, showing how petitions were often the first in a long line of documents generated at various stages in the course of having a case brought to a satisfactory conclusion. After the rationalisation of SC 8 in the nineteenth century, intact 'paper trails' such as these are now rare.

Several petitions remind us that 'church-state relations' involved not just crown and Church, but the papacy too. Hence we find travel to Rome (**8**), papal taxes (**74**), debts to the pope (**3**), papal power in routine matters (**56**), and appeals to Rome (**105**) mentioned in petitions. In other cases appeals to the curia were less evident, yet more important (**147**, **182**). The impression is of cooperation (**171**) rather than competition between these two authorities, and when the prior of Eye (Suffolk) complained that the pope had been negligent (**14**) the response was that the crown would expedite matters.

Popes and kings were, however, in competition in raising money from the English clergy. Direct taxation of the Church was important to the crown throughout the period, and produced grievances in laity (**197**, **198**) and clergy alike. The handful of tax-related petitions printed here are but a small part of the material relating to clerical taxation to be found in crown records. The TNA series E 179, which has its own database,[22] is the main source, along with E 359 (Enrolled Accounts). Petitions about taxation from religious houses were of two kinds: requests for respite and exemption, and release from the position of collector. In 1294, the notorious 50% tax rate prompted the very rich Westminster Abbey to request that all the debts for which the exchequer was pursuing it should be respited, and a friend at court, Walter Langton, ensured a favourable response (**68**). The usual way for a house to gain exemption from a particular tax was through its diocesan. This mechanism was sparingly used but always respected, and the nuns of Lyminster (**70**) and canons of St Denys, Southampton (**88**), who received the replies 'perhaps' and 'no', respectively, would have been better advised to apply to their bishops.

It was bishops, too, who appointed the collectors of clerical taxes. This was an unpopular chore, and could leave the house, at least temporarily, out of pocket (**78**).[23] The problem of choosing collectors became acute in times of high taxation,[24] and the underhand – as the collectors saw it – practices which bishops resorted to prompted the heads of religious houses, collectively, to petition the crown against them in 1422 (**173**). Next year the Carthusians petitioned Henry VI's administration for complete exemption from clerical tenths (**175**). It is no coincidence that these two petitions followed the years of unprecedented taxation imposed by Henry V in his bid to win the throne of France, and form part of the reaction against the crown's demands which was not confined to the clergy. Another financial imposition by the crown came in the form of corrodies

22 http://www.nationalarchives.gov.uk/E179/

23 For discussion, see E. W. Kemp, *Counsel and Consent* (London, 1961), pp. 120–34.

24 A. K. McHardy, 'Clerical Taxation in Fifteenth-Century England: The Clergy as Agents of the Crown', in *The Church, Politics and Patronage*, ed. R. B. Dobson (Gloucester, 1984), pp. 168–92.

which kings apparently expected to be given, without payment, to their (usually) retired servants, seeing them as a cost-free way of providing pensions. Houses regarded corrodies with disfavour, for obvious reasons, and resisted them vigorously. 'Ancient Petitions' contains some of their responses, both individual (**17**, **75**, **76**, **91**, **201**), and collective (**168**), but many more are found in TNA series C 270 (Chancery: Ecclesiastical Miscellanea), files 1–6.

The needs to ensure that religious houses were well-disciplined and financially sound, able to receive corrodians, and whose heads would make suitable tax collectors, were just two of the reasons why the crown took an active role in the administration of those which fell into serious disarray. Three houses, Shaftesbury (nuns) in 1382 (**81**), St Denys, Southampton, in 1388 (**91**), and Henwood (nuns) in 1411 (**82**), all effectively asked to be taken into protective custody because of their financial misfortunes. Llanthony Secunda (**27**), and Abbotsbury (**157**), had complaints against the keepers, but both houses had been in turmoil before outsiders took them in hand. These five examples are a small proportion of the houses taken into royal administration, especially during the fourteenth century, and most cases appear in the patent rolls.[25]

The question of how far either the crown or the religious were influenced by royal patronage of religious houses must await systematic investigation of this archival class, and only brief observations are appropriate here. An analysis of the religious houses represented in this volume, where they are separated into different categories of patron (i.e. royal, lay or ecclesiastical), indicates that a surprisingly large proportion of supplications was presented by houses of royal patronage. Of the ninety monasteries included in our sample, which are also listed in Karen Stöber's survey of monastic patrons, the king was patron of no fewer than 36 (40%), while the laity were patrons of 39 (43%), and ecclesiastical patrons accounted for the remaining 15 (16%).[26] This presents a striking contrast to the respective share of all known patrons of religious houses calculated by Susan Wood; that is to say, houses of royal patronage account for 25%, lay patronage 68%; and ecclesiastical patronage 6%.[27] Even allowing for some distortion in our figures, because of the restricted nature of the data, the extent of this disparity is so pronounced as to clearly suggest that monasteries of royal patronage were more predisposed to petitioning the crown than those with non-royal patrons. This was no doubt symptomatic of their particular circumstances, and the greater probability that the rights and obligations which attended their close ties with the crown created conditions which made petitioning the king a more likely occurrence. It may also reflect the disproportionately greater wealth and influence which many religious houses of royal patronage possessed, and the increased chance that their ownership of lands and rights would bring them into conflict with third parties and even the crown itself; circumstances which again made petitioning a more likely course of action. On the other hand, the number of cases brought to the king's attention by other monasteries is not without signif-

25 K. L. Wood-Legh, *Church Life under Edward III* (Cambridge, 1934), pp. 1–37.

26 K Stöber, *Late Medieval Monasteries and their Patrons: England and Wales c.1300–1540* (Woodbridge, 2007), Appendix.

27 S. Wood, *English Monasteries and their Patrons in the Thirteenth Century* (Oxford, 1955), pp. 6–7.

icance, for these demonstrate the limitations of patronal lordship in the localities, and the extent to which royal jurisdiction effectively superseded the seigneurial power of lay and ecclesiastical patrons by offering the only ready means to obtain redress or resolution.

On the other hand, in our sample it is clear that kings did not hesitate to demand corrodies from houses in royal and non-royal patronage alike, for neither Tupholme (**76**) nor Hatfield Regis (**189**) were in royal patronage. Both cases date from Edward II's reign, when the crown was notoriously greedy in its demand for corrodies.[28] But this was a long-enduring burden for monasteries, as the joint petition of c. 1377 from the chaplains, abbots and priors of England, against corrodies imposed on houses *ne tiegnent del roi ne sount de sa fundacioun*, testifies (**168**). There is also a mixed picture in respect of royal administration of religious houses. In three cases raised by petitioners the crown was the patron: Shaftesbury, St Denys, Abbotsbury (**81**, **91**, **157**). But Llanthony had an aristocratic patron (**27**), and Henwood was in the abbot of Westminster's patronage (**82**), which could explain why the Henwood nuns suggested that the prior of Coventry, another Benedictine house, should be one of their keepers. Neither case invalidates Dr Wood-Legh's finding that Edward III only took houses into his administrative care if he was the patron.[29] Royal selectivity is evident in Edward III's response to the petition about problems of indiscipline and misgovernment among Cluniacs; he gave one answer for the houses in his patronage, but washed his hands of the rest (**161**).

Petitioners occasionally played the 'patronage card' in an effort to engage crown support. Bromholm Priory claimed, in 1305, to be of the king's patronage (**144**), as did the cathedral priory of Bath in c. 1418 (**131**), though in both cases this was untrue.[30] The prior of Hatfield Regis pointed out that his house was in the patronage of the earl of Oxford, then (1378) a minor in royal wardship (**128**). In 1384 another patron and royal ward needed help to combat the machinations of the prior of Walsingham (**205**). It was fairly common for royal houses to insert into the preamble of their requests a reminder that they were a royal foundation and of the king's patronage (e.g. **24**, **81**, **88**, **129**). This was a useful mechanism to imply a special relationship with the crown and to suggest added obligation to ensure that the petition received a favourable hearing. The religious were generally more keen to stress their independence from episcopal authority than to be concerned with their relationship to the crown, except in situations which cost them money and effort; reluctance to become parliamentary abbeys is notable, and the attempts by St Mary's York and Beaulieu (Hants) to have their houses deleted from the parliamentary lists (**42**, **43**) should be read alongside the excuses for non-attendance of individuals contained in TNA SC 10 (Parliamentary Proxies), files 1–51. A preliminary conclusion is that the patronage of abbeys was of less importance to the crown than their good governance, sound finance,

28 J. H. Tillotson, 'Pensions, Corrodies and Religious Houses: An Aspect of the Relations of Crown and Church in Early 14th Century England', *Journal of Religious History* 8 (1974), 127–43.

29 Ibid., p. 4. Nor does the case of Bardney Abbey, taken into administration under Edward II (**147**), which was in the patronage of the earls of Lancaster.

30 Stöber, *Late Medieval Monasteries*, Appendix.

and harmonious relationship with their lay neighbours, since these ensured spiritual excellence, order, and taxable wealth. Patronage was surprisingly changeable, given the fragility of noble families,[31] sometimes obscure, and could be divided between local laymen and distant abbots,[32] nor was the crown's interest in exercising patronage rights consistent.[33]

A provisional conclusion to be drawn from the selection of petitions printed here is that royal power over the religious tended to increase through the period, but that this was less a matter of direct policy than the result of Anglo-French wars which forced kings of both countries to exploit the resources of the Church to support military effort (e.g. **164**). At home, the rise of the king-in-parliament contributed to a widening of the governmental remit as its members demanded action in social and economic matters. Petitions from the Dominicans in 1390 (**170**) and Augustinian canons in 1422–3 (**174**) that the crown interfere in educational matters, could be seen as part of the same process. The amount of business which petitions generated for crown administration could account for the relaxed attitude towards ecclesiastical courts exemplified by the response to **60**. Conversely, the inconvenience, uncertainty and expense of taking cases to the *curia* explains why the religious might turn to the crown in what seemed to be matters of internal discipline (**161**). Petitions provided a mechanism to draw individual religious houses more firmly into the orbit of royal authority, whether or not they were of royal patronage. They helped define more clearly the subject status of the English religious orders in relation to the English crown. One of the most intriguing questions is the extent to which petitions helped forge collective identities among the religious themselves. The majority of the examples in Part 5 (**161–75**) show religious houses acting in concert, defining themselves by a set of common grievances that affected or concerned the religious order (in England) as a whole. Although small in number they deserve due consideration, alongside the better known *gravamina* of the whole clergy and the common petitions of the secular elite, as important expressions of cooperation and common purpose.

Religious houses and their secular neighbours

There were many other cases in which the crown was not directly involved as an interested party, but was instead called upon to act as final arbiter in disputes involving the rights, jurisdictions, or even security of a monastery. The religious could not ignore the world beyond their monastic enclosures, for a house's survival as an effective centre of contemplation usually depended on the vigorous, even aggressive, defence of its economic interests. Thus, whether they were poor and surrounded by more powerful neighbours, or possessed of wealth which attracted envy – yet lacking the means of physical defence – religious houses, in their role of property-owners, turned to the crown for assistance. Yet the religious were not always the victims of injustice. Here we also consider petitions presented

31 Ibid.

32 In Cluniac houses, for example.

33 A. K. McHardy, 'Patronage in Late Medieval Colleges', in *The Late Medieval English College*, ed. C. Burgess and M. Heale (York, 2008), pp. 89–109, esp. 107–9.

against religious houses (Part 6), to demonstrate that the ruthless and apparently unprincipled actions of secular neighbours towards houses might be more than matched by the uncompromising or highly questionable acts by religious intent on upholding or enhancing their own interests. The petitions in this volume provide numerous examples of strained relations between monastic communities and the laity. Two types are examined here: the often turbulent relations between monastic landlords and their tenantry; and between monasteries and their neighbouring urban communities. The following discussion places these requests into a broader historiographical context, highlighting the ways in which they add to existing debates and point to new approaches to the way monasteries interacted with the laity.

These petitions do, however, raise an important question: to what extent do complaints, whether by or against religious houses, represent the normal state of relations between religious orders and lay neighbours? Evidence of friction between religious and the laity abounds, in SC 8 as elsewhere. This is a natural consequence of the fact that large numbers of petitions are essentially about conflict resolution. Taken in isolation and at face value, they generate a misleading picture of unmitigated struggle between clearly defined and homogeneous social and economic groups. This has particular resonance in those cases involving monasteries and tenants which appear to endorse a traditional Marxist interpretation of medieval tenurial relationships, based on mutual feelings of antagonism and hostility.[34] But the management of ecclesiastical estates did not inevitably result in conflict,[35] while many religious houses were demonstrably both valuable for, and valued by, the laity – not least for providing education, welfare and charity.[36] The petitions should therefore be treated with caution. They contain a wealth of detail to illustrate the causes of intractable local problems, but they represent only one factor in a much larger and more complex set of considerations which determined the nature of their interaction with the outside world.

Tenants

Nowhere is the scenario of a powerful and unscrupulous religious community flexing its muscles over less powerful neighbours better played out than in its dealings with the tenants and serfs who worked on its lands. A religious house, like any other landlord, depended on the income from its estates as the main source for its economic wellbeing. There was a natural incentive for a landlord to

34 For a critique of the Marxist approach, see J. Hatcher and M. Bailey, *Modelling the Middle Ages: The History and Theory of England's Economic Development* (Oxford, 2001), pp. 66–120. The complexities involved in assessing the nature of landlord-peasant relations are considered in *Rodney Hilton's Middle Ages: An Exploration of Historical Themes*, ed. C. Dyer, P. Coss and C. Wickham (Oxford, 2007), contributions by Dyer and Müller.

35 G. Rosser, *Medieval Westminster 1200–1540* (Oxford, 1989), pp. 226–48; and M. Bonney, *Lordship and the Urban Community: Durham and its Overlords, 1250–1540* (Cambridge, 1990), pp. 230–3.

36 For example, see E. Jamroziak, *Rievaulx Abbey and its Social Context, 1132–1300: Memory, Locality, and Networks* (Turnhout, 2005), chpt. 2; and M. Heale, *The Dependent Priories of Medieval English Monasteries* (Woodbridge, 2004), chpt. 5.

maximise productivity by putting himself in as favourable a position as possible in relation to the peasants who worked the lands. From the late twelfth century, ecclesiastical landlords were particularly assiduous in working towards this goal, by seeking to tighten the legal definition of servile status and tenure.[37] It was inevitable, in a system that was so heavily weighted in favour of landlords, that peasant discontent would result in conflict, and although the Peasants' Revolt of 1381 was the clearest and most dramatic expression of this discontent – much of it aimed at religious houses – conflict between ecclesiastical landlords and their tenantry was a common localised phenomenon throughout the late Middle Ages.[38]

In this collection three petitions presented in quick succession by the abbey of Bec Hellouin in the early 1330s highlight how troubled landlord-peasant relations could be before the Black Death transformed the economic and social climate (**136–38**). All relate to the apparent contumacy of the abbey's serfs in its bailiwick of Ogbourne (Wilts.) which incorporated a set of manors where customary service was rigorously imposed.[39] The tenants were accused of having withdrawn their rent, services and customs and, if the petitions are to be believed, they had also taken up arms against the abbot's men to prevent proceedings from taking place against them in the manorial court; in a separate petition presented by the people of Ogbourne, the monks of the abbey, for their part, were accused of beating them, destroying their houses, and withholding for thirty years the alms to which they were entitled from the king.[40] A more graphic illustration of the impact of a monastery's determination to impose its seigneurial rights on its tenantry is provided by William Mervyn's complaint of 1273 that, in the abbot of St Albans' campaign to force Mervyn to accept villein status, many crimes had been committed against him, including theft, assault, imprisonment and fraud (**176**).[41]

In both instances, the basis of the tenants' case was that the lands they worked had originally belonged to the royal demesne, which protected them

37 E. A. Kosminsky, *Studies in the Agrarian History of England in the Thirteenth Century*, ed. R. H. Hilton, trans. R. Kisch (Oxford, 1956), pp. 103–16; C. Dyer, *Making a Living in the Middle Ages: The People of Britain 850–1520* (New Haven and London, 2002), pp. 140–5; R. Britnell, *Britain and Ireland, 1050–1530: Economy and Society* (Oxford, 2004), pp. 232–3. For the concentration of villeinage on the manors of aristocratic and major ecclesiastical landlords, see M. Bailey, 'Villeinage in England: A Regional Case Study, c.1250–c.1349', *Economic History Review* 62 (2009), 430–57, esp. pp. 431–2.

38 Z. Razi, 'The Struggles between the Abbots of Halesowen and their Tenants in the Thirteenth and Fourteenth Centuries', in *Social Relations and Ideas: Essays in Honour of R. H. Hilton*, ed. T. H. Aston, P. R. Coss, C. Dyer and J. Thirsk (Cambridge, 1983), pp. 151–67; and R. H. Hilton, 'Popular Movements in England at the End of the Fourteenth Century', in idem, *Class Conflict and the Crisis of Feudalism* (London, 1990), pp. 85–6.

39 M. Morgan, *The English Lands of the Abbey of Bec* (Oxford, 1946), p. 86.

40 For an outline of the dispute see ibid., pp. 106–10. The petition from the people of Ogbourne, not included in this volume, is SC 8/63/3133.

41 A discussion of the relations between the abbey and its tenants is in R. Faith, 'The Class Struggle in Fourteenth Century England', in *People's History and Socialist Theory*, ed. R. Samuel (London, 1981), pp. 50–60.

from customary services and other feudal exactions.[42] As landlords increasingly tightened the feudal ties which their tenants owed, the tenants for their part increasingly sought ways of resisting these impositions: one of the commonest legal strategies was to claim ancient demesne status in the hope that the rights and privileges which extended to such land would offer protection from increased rents and labour services. Tenants in this position did not usually have a ready body of records to demonstrate the tenurial history of their manor, so it was common practice to invoke the Domesday Book in the belief that this provided an authoritative and irrefutable statement of the villein labour services that ought to hold good for every manor in the kingdom (e.g. **183**).[43] But this faith in the authority of the Domesday Book was misplaced, or very optimistic, because fourteenth-century lawyers drew a distinction between the tenurial status of a manor in the eleventh century – which Domesday faithfully recorded – and the rights and privileges of its tenants, which could not so easily be verified using this record.[44] Thus, tenants' appeals against their ecclesiastical landlords were usually unsuccessful. In the struggles between religious houses and their tenants, the odds were weighted heavily in favour of religious houses, essentially because their interests as landlords coincided closely with the broader landed interests of the ruling secular elite.[45] This convergence of purpose is neatly epitomised in the answer given to the first petition of the abbot of Bec Hellouin in 1331 (**136**), where it was stated that the dissent of the tenants was 'in impairment of the peace and an affray of the people and also to the damage of the king and his heirs' (*... en enblemissement de la pees et affray du poeple et auxint au damage du roi et de ses heirs ...*). The endorsement further stated that if the abbot's tenants were found to be of villein status, he could count on 'the help of the king and his court to bring justice to his said villeins as their lord' (*... le dit abbe par le roi et sa court eide a justicer ses ditz villeins a faire ali ceo qe faire deveront come a leur seigneur*).

This common purpose is shown even more strikingly by the petition of the abbot of Chertsey which was presented in the parliament of October 1377 complaining about the rebellious acts of the abbey's tenants on four of its Surrey manors (**140**). This is important evidence for the 'Great Rumour' of 1377, when tenants of many manors across southern England, apparently acting in concert, withheld their services and dues from their landlords in the belief that 'exemplifications' – or extracts – obtained in chancery from Domesday Book proved that they were exempt from performing them.[46] The petition was remarkably successful, for it evidently informed, and may even on its own have prompted, the parliamentary Commons into presenting a more general complaint to the crown about the withholding of labour services, on the grounds that the lordships of

42 M. K. McIntosh, 'The Privileged Villeins of the English Ancient Demesne', *Viator* 7 (1976), 295–328, esp. pp. 303–4; idem, *Autonomy and Community: The Royal Manor of Havering, 1200–1500* (Cambridge, 1986), chpt. 1, esp. pp. 42–9.

43 R. Faith, 'The "Great Rumour" of 1377 and Peasant Ideology', in *The English Rising of 1381*, ed. R. H. Hilton and T. H. Aston (Cambridge, 1984), pp. 43–73.

44 M. A. Barg, 'The Villeins of Ancient Demesne', in *Studi in Memoria di Federigo Melis*, 5 vols (Rome, 1978), I, 213–37 (summarised in Faith, '"Great Rumour"', pp. 50–1).

45 See R. H. Hilton, *The Decline of Serfdom in Medieval England* (London, 1969), pp. 27–9; and idem, 'Peasant Movements in England before 1381', in idem, *Class Conflict*, p. 58.

46 Faith, '"Great Rumour"', pp. 43–7.

'Holy Church as of lay lordships … loose and have lost large profits … bringing about their disinheritance and injury to their estate'.[47]

For reasons which will now be apparent, religious houses were particularly hard hit in the Peasants' Revolt of 1381.[48] St Albans and Bury St Edmunds are the best known abbeys to have suffered at the hands of the rebels, but there were numerous other monasteries which were affected. Henry Knighton's chronicle gives a vivid description of an attack by the tenants of Peterborough Abbey, and their brutal suppression at the hands of Henry Despenser, bishop of Norwich.[49] The petition subsequently submitted by the abbot of Peterborough, after the rebellion subsided, provides a valuable insight into the sense of shock, as well as the desire for retribution, which many landlords felt once control had been regained (**141**). The abbot explained how, out of fear for their lives, he and his fellow monks had been forced to agree to the demands of the rebels to have 'diverse franchises, articles and redress against the common law'. He must have felt on safe ground admitting to these concessions given that the king himself had been faced with a similar situation when confronted by the mass of rebels at Mile End, and had reacted in the same way. His anxiety, though, was to ensure that the abbey's interests were not passed over in the wave of the judicial retribution which the crown exacted in the wake of the revolt.[50] His request to be granted the 'correction of his tenants' (*la correction de ses tenantz*) or otherwise to have 'such a remedy ordained that the abbot and abbey would not in future be destroyed or burnt by rebels' is particularly revealing. It hints at harsh reprisals, but it also points to the deregulated and self-sufficient nature of the judicial processes which followed the rebellion.[51]

Our final selection of petitions in this category highlights the continuing problems encountered by religious houses into the fifteenth century. The wholehearted support which the crown gave landlords after the Peasants' Revolt did nothing to arrest the underlying social and economic forces which impelled tenants to resist the services which their lords felt they had the right to impose on them. Ecclesiastical landlords, in particular, appear to have spearheaded this 'seignurial reaction'.[52] The essential problem was that income from the land was diminishing, so in order to make up the shortfall landlords looked to reintroduce or increase the 'incidences of villeinage' (i.e. customary dues, fines and

47 *PROME*, parliament of October 1377, item 88.

48 R. Hilton, *Bondmen Made Free: Medieval Peasant Movements and the English Rising of 1381* (London, 1973, repr. 1995), p. 167.

49 Cf. *The Peasants' Revolt*, ed. R. B. Dobson (London, 1970, repr. 1983), pp. 237–8.

50 J. G. Bellamy, *The Law of Treason in England in the Later Middle Ages* (Cambridge, 1970), pp. 103–5.

51 A. Prescott, '"The Hand of God": the Suppression of the Peasants' Revolt of 1381', in *Prophecy, Apocalypse and the Day of Doom*, ed. N. Morgan (Stamford, 2004), pp. 317–37.

52 R. H. Britnell, 'Feudal Reaction after the Black Death in the Palatinate of Durham', *Past and Present* 128 (1990), 28–47; P. V. Hargreaves, 'Seignorial Reaction and Peasant Responses: Worcester Priory and its Peasants after the Black Death', *Midland History* 24 (1999), 53–78; E. B. Fryde, *Peasants and Landlords in Later Medieval England* (Stroud, 1996), chpt. 8 ('After the Peasants' Revolt: General trends, c.1381–c.1430'); R. Britnell, *Britain and Ireland, 1050–1530: Economy and Society* (Oxford, 2004), pp. 431–4.

amercements) on their tenants.[53] A petition presented in 1426 by the prior of Ely provides a particularly vivid picture of the way conflict could arise, when it described how the common bell of the village of Haddenham had been rung to rally villagers against the prior's men who were attempting to levy £8 from them, as part of the fine due upon the vacancy of the bishopric of Ely (**142**). Over two hundred men, armed with 'swords, shields, bows, arrows, sheaves of arrows and pitchforks', were said to have rebelled against the prior and imprisoned the prior's servant, John Prior, for a day and night and stole money from his purse.

For religious houses, the impositions made on their tenants were entirely legitimate, lawful and moral; challenges against their authority, such as the one which took place in Haddenham, represented a 'disinheritance' of their rights and an affront to the natural social order. For the tenants, the impositions were unfair and unjust, and especially objectionable when many lords were improving tenants' working conditions and lives. But their scope for legal action was limited: ancient demesne status was no guarantee of freedom – though this did not deter petitioners, then and later, from making such claims[54] – and the right of landlords to impose feudal dues, fines and amercements usually had the backing of historical record, in particular the Hundred Rolls of the late thirteenth century, together with plea rolls and other legal and theoretical treatises of the same period. So petitions from peasants against their ecclesiastical landlords – when these did not question the underlying basis of their villein status – usually related to *ad hoc* or irregular impositions which resulted from the house's position of feudal overlordship. The basis of the complaint rested on a prevailing sense of the inviolability and unchangeable nature of tenurial custom, as defined in a past age when the manor had once belonged to the royal patrimony. The petitions appealed to the king on the basis of broken precedent rather than broken law.[55]

The petition of the tenants of Chertsey is particularly illuminating in this respect (**210**). Presented in 1410, it complained that the abbot had recently imposed tallages on them every year which they never used to pay, and those who refused payment were being distrained and pursued by the abbot and his ministers.[56] It is interesting that the tenants felt themselves to be in a position to seek the crown's intervention against their abbot even though, as we have seen, their case had been so emphatically rejected thirty years previously when they had sought exemplifications from the crown. The intervening period saw a new abbot, a new generation of tenants and a new political regime, all of which provided fresh impetus to the campaign to have the abbey's impositions curbed. But the tenants' complaint in 1410 was rather different from the campaign which their forebears had waged in the 1370s. In 1410 the tenants did not invoke the authority of the Domesday Book to support their cause, nor describe themselves as tenants of the ancient demesne; rather they drew upon the authority

53 See Hilton, *Decline of Serfdom*, pp. 32–43.

54 See discussion on the troubled relations between Barnwell Priory and its tenants in, G. Dodd, 'Thomas Paunfield, the "heye Court of rightwiseness" and the Language of Petitioning in the Fifteenth Century', in *Medieval Petitions*, ed. Ormrod, Dodd and Musson, pp. 222–41.

55 J. Hatcher, 'English Serfdom and Villeinage: Towards a Reassessment', *Past and Present* 90 (1981), 3–39, pp. 21–6, 38–9; Bailey, 'Villeinage in England', pp. 452–3.

56 For background on tallage, see Bailey, 'Villeinage in England', pp. 449–51.

of historical precedent to challenge the abbey's rights to impose a new or novel tallage. They claimed that this violated the terms of the grant made by King Edgar to the abbey when the manors had originally come into the latter's possession. Thus, their complaint was not that they were unjustly treated as customary tenants, but that the abbey was making impositions which lay outside the normal and accepted boundaries of seignurial jurisdiction.

Towns

In many ways the distinction between this section and the previous section is artificial, since disputes between monasteries and their tenants could as easily occur in urban settings, where monasteries might be the largest landlords, as in the countryside. Many causes of conflict in the countryside, such as disputes over obligations and discontent arising out of social and economic disparity, were mirrored in towns. There is also the underlying point that, like manorial disputes, conflict was usually initiated by the townsmen who wished to alter a *status quo* which favoured the religious house. But there were differences which are worth exploring in some detail. Perhaps the most important is that frequently a monastery was located in or near the urban centre against whose citizens it found itself in dispute. Often it was this proximity which was itself the cause of conflict, as the religious and secular worlds competed with each other to control the town's economic output. More often than not this revolved around basic questions of jurisdiction: the right of the monastery to levy tolls or customs (**124**, **181**), to hold markets or fairs (**132**), to enjoy salvage rights from wrecks (**133**), to control the local land market (**192**), and so on.[57] Whilst disagreement over these matters was usually the initial cause of the resentment of townsmen towards their monastic neighbours, conflict could also be underpinned by a deeper sense of mistrust and suspicion born out of a perception that a religious house was – in spite of its physical proximity – somehow separate and distinct from the urban community: a monastery was often surrounded by high walls; its monks followed a way of life which clearly removed them from the norms of secular life; and, perhaps most importantly, some of the monks were recruited from further afield, which added to a sense in which they were regarded as strangers or 'outsiders', whose interests were incompatible with those of the town.[58] (On the other hand, the complaint of the inhabitants of King's Langley (**213**), about the fraternisation of the members of its neighbouring Dominican priory with certain 'suspect persons', and their resort to *myslyveng women of their bodyes*, shows that there were expectations by the laity that the religious *ought* to live separate lives and must

57 Detailed case studies are G. Rosser, 'Conflict and Political Community in the Medieval Town: Disputes between Clergy and Laity in Hereford', in *The Church in the Medieval Town*, ed. T. R. Slater and G. Rosser (Aldershot, 1998), pp. 20–42; and P. Fleming, 'Conflict and Urban Government in Later Medieval England: St Augustine's Abbey and Bristol', *Urban History* 27 (2000), 325–43.

58 Though it is true to say that a majority of monks in a religious house were probably recruited locally: R. B. Dobson, *Durham Priory 1400–1450* (Cambridge, 1973), pp. 58–61; J. Greatrex, 'Who were the Monks of Rochester?', in *Medieval Art, Architecture and Archaeology at Rochester*, British Archaeological Association, Conference Transactions 28 (2006), 205–17.

be held accountable if their actions did not meet the highest moral standards in accordance with their religious vocation.)[59]

There were other important differences. Partly in consequence of the physical closeness of many urban and monastic communities, disputes between the two were often far more serious, more bitter and more protracted than conflict on manors. At least from the point of view of monasteries, the inhabitants of towns were usually more serious adversaries than recalcitrant village tenants because of the resources townsmen could mobilise in support of their campaigns: there were more people to threaten physical violence and there was more money to fund litigation and attract powerful patrons or protectors. From the point of view of townsmen, monasteries were similarly formidable opponents, usually well-connected and often averse to compromise.[60] Townsmen usually considered themselves to have, or to be entitled to have, greater parity of status and authority than manorial tenants, whose main objective was merely to reduce the burden of lordship imposed on them. Conflict between towns and monasteries, in contrast, often centred on the form and scope of urban government and how much share of the rule over townsmen a religious house ought to be allowed to have (e.g. **184**, **190**). In monastic, indeed all, boroughs townsmen tended to hold their tenements by burgage tenure which meant that, even if the town as a whole was subject to seigneurial control, the inhabitants themselves were free and therefore had greater expectations of constitutional and commercial self-determination.

Almost every major conflict between a town and a monastery resulted, at some point, in at least one petition being presented to the crown by one side or the other, making these documents not simply interesting, but essential, sources for such disputes. They do, however, present a number of challenges, not least in the terminology used to describe on whose behalf they were presented. We may describe these as petitions from religious or urban communities, but this term was as much a matter of convenience to contemporaries as it is to modern historians. Much of the rhetorical strength of a petition rested on the representative and inclusive quality it projected. Behind the façade of unity and solidarity presented in a petition from a community was almost certainly a more complex and mixed set of allegiances and loyalties.[61] Some townsmen may have sided with a monastery in an urban conflict because they were employed as bailiffs or tithing men or because they benefited from commercial arrangements or from the monk's charity; equally, though, some monks may have been sympathetic to the grievances of their urban neighbours because they were local men. Very rarely do petitions reveal these complex webs of social and political loyalty within a town or religious house.

The petitions in this category can be divided into two groups. The first contains petitions relating to monastic boroughs – towns which had originally been established by a religious house or came under its jurisdiction as a result of the provi-

59 This is a theme addressed in the works cited above, note 15.

60 See the comments by S. Reynolds, *An Introduction to the History of Medieval English Towns* (Oxford, 1977), pp. 115–16.

61 C. Dyer, 'Small-Town Conflict in the Later Middle Ages: Events at Shipston-on-Stour', *Urban History* 19 (1992), 183–210.

sions incorporated into its original foundation.[62] There were over thirty monastic boroughs by the thirteenth century, almost all ruled over by Benedictine monasteries.[63] A number are included in this volume: Abingdon (**111**, **126**, **127**), Bury St Edmunds (**26**, **129**), Coventry (**30**, **192**), Dunstable (**207**), Faversham (**124**), Peterborough (**141**) and St Albans (**176**, **184**, **190**). Monastic boroughs, like those boroughs which were governed by lay lords, were closely akin to manors, in the sense that they were subject to the seigneurial overlordship of the monastery. In practical terms, this meant that the monastery was complete master of the town by virtue of its control over the main civic offices (such as bailiffs, sub-seneschals, and aldermen) and its right to exercise jurisdiction in assizes, recognisances and pleas of the crown, and to oversee views of frankpledge.[64] It was also entitled to take a share of the wealth of the town by imposing taxes, tolls and tithes and, in some cases, it could benefit from additional feudal 'incidents', such as the requirement for townsmen to use the monastery's mill to grind their corn (and to pay for the privilege of doing so). Not surprisingly, conflict tended to focus on the economic and legal relationship between the town and monastery, but occasionally other matters could bring relations to crisis point: a petition from the burgesses of Dunstable dating to 1392, for example, shows how the use of shared space within a church, between the priory on the one hand and the parish community on the other, could become a matter of contention (**207**).[65] Whilst modern work has rightly indicated that conflict between urban communities and their religious overlords should not be regarded as inevitable,[66] it is true that the particular condition of a town which was subject to monastic overlordship made conflict more likely, as the control which the monastery exercised and jealously guarded over the town's government and economic output – and spiritual life – was often at odds with the aspirations of townsmen wishing to expand their commercial activity and have a greater say in running their own affairs.[67] In this volume a number of petitions illustrate the particularly troubled nature of some of the most famous monastic boroughs.

One of the better known, but also more unusual, cases was the dispute involving the inhabitants of Abingdon against their monastic overlord, Abingdon Abbey, at the end of Edward III's reign. While scholarship has focussed on the

62 The classic work is N. M. Trenholme, *The English Monastic Boroughs: A Study in Medieval History* (Columbia, 1927).

63 J. Burton, *Monastic and Religious Orders in Britain, 1000–1300* (Cambridge, 1994), p. 243. For a complete list see M. Beresford and H. P. R. Finberg, *English Medieval Boroughs: A Handlist* (Newton Abbot, 1973), p. 46, with addendum in *Urban History Yearbook* 8 (1981), 59–65.

64 For a good summary of the powers and privileges which could be exercised within a monastic borough by an abbey, see R. S. Gottfried, *Bury St Edmunds and the Urban Crisis: 1290–1539* (Princeton, 1982), pp. 167–72.

65 Trenholme misdates this episode to the 1350s (*Monastic Boroughs*, pp. 48–9). For further detail, see *VCH Bedfordshire*, III, 360. For more general discussion, see M. Heale, 'Monastic-Parochial Churches in Late Medieval England', in *The Late Medieval English Parish*, ed. E. Duffy and C. Burgess (Donington, 2006), pp. 54–77. See also **128**.

66 See above, note 35.

67 D. Postles, 'The Austin Canons in English Towns, c.1100–1350', *Historical Research* 66 (1993), 1–20, p. 17; Dyer, 'Small-Town Conflict', pp. 207–9.

broader constitutional and legal significance of this episode, and in particular the attempts of the citizens to prosecute the abbey by impeachment, the two documents in this collection provide important new context to the dispute itself, showing how deep the lines of division between the monks and townsmen ran and how the conflict developed locally whilst the case was still pending at the centre.[68] They show, in particular, the abbey in a state of acute vulnerability. The first (**126**), a record of a royal writ, urges the sheriff and keepers of the peace of the county to extract assurances from the townsmen that the abbot and monks would remain unmolested; and the second (**127**) suggests that this had very little effect: some inhabitants refused to guarantee their good behaviour and were duly imprisoned by the justices, only then to escape and further threaten the 'life and body' of the abbot's servants. In its petition the abbey was keen to emphasise the seriousness of the actions of these townsmen and so constructed the petition as a complaint against the citizens who had rebelled and shown disobedience towards royal justices, rather than a complaint about the wrongdoings they themselves had suffered. They are pointedly described as 'rebels'.[69] This was an interesting and probably purposeful counterpoise to the rhetoric deployed by the 'commons of Abingdon' in the petition they presented in 1363, which described the abbey as acting against the law, the king's crown and dignity and of accroaching royal power to itself.[70]

The dispute between the abbot and townsmen of Abingdon was unusual because the townsmen were remarkably successful in securing crown support for their cause. This was because the status of the town of Abingdon was uncertain, and the abbey's claim to exercise lordship could not be proved conclusively. Few other towns of this type were as fortunate or resourceful as Abingdon, so the struggles between monastic boroughs and their religious overlords tended to unfold in the same way as the struggles on manors, with the crown ultimately siding with the religious house. Even at Abingdon the monastery eventually carried the day: the crown changed its position, and in 1372 agreed that Abingdon was a monastic borough after all, offering the townsmen the empty gesture that they could sue at common law if any felt themselves unduly aggrieved.[71] Other cases followed a similar pattern. A vivid example is offered by the petition presented by Bury St Edmunds in April 1384 which solicited crown support for the abbey's campaign of repression against the town's inhabitants following the town's violent rebel-

68 G. Lambrick, 'The Impeachment of the Abbot of Abingdon in 1368', *EHR* 82 (1967), 250–76.

69 Similar language was used in a petition presented in the early 1390s when the same abbot, Peter of Hanney, complained that the townsmen were seeking papal dispensation to have their dead buried in the cemetery of the church of St Helen, Abingdon, rather than in the abbey's cemetery: SC 8/88/4392. In his complaint, the abbot reminded the king of the town's record of civil disturbance, citing the year 1327 when they had robbed and burnt the abbey as well as the 'recent insurrection of the villeins and tenants' – possibly a reference to the events of the late 1360s. He also pointed to their continuing 'wickedness' (*malvestees*) as a result of their 'confederacy, conspiracy and oaths sworn between them, with [their] riots and companies'. For a slightly later petition relating to the same episode, see SC 8/21/1042.

70 SC 8/88/4370 (*contre la ley, votre coronne et dignete acrochant a eux seigneurie roial*).

71 Lambrick, 'Impeachment of the Abbot of Abingdon', p. 260.

lion against the abbey in 1381 (**129**).[72] In their request, the abbot and convent asked for recognisances from the townsmen that they would keep the peace. They attached a schedule to their petition suggesting the form that the surety should take (£10,000 to be forfeited upon future riot or rebellion).[73] The result was an unqualified success for the abbey: both petition and schedule were enrolled on the parliament roll, and the recognisance itself effectively became a parliamentary ordinance.[74] The crown's wholehearted support for the abbey's request was recorded in the unusually full response to the petition, which specified that the recognisance was to be made 'both to the king and to the abbot and convent'.

The second group of urban petitions is a more disparate collection and arose less from constitutional considerations than from the problems created simply by the presence of a religious house close to an urban settlement. Examples include the petition from the Franciscans of Bury St Edmunds in 1302 which asked for the courthouse of Cattishall to be rebuilt away from their house, because in wet weather people attending court used the friars' church to shelter themselves and their horses, and the general commotion caused by this 'press of people' prevented the friars from saying mass (**54**); and the petition from the prioress of Clerkenwell complaining that Londoners attending miracle plays and wrestling matches trampled her crops (**121**). Petitions were not necessarily the most effective means of resolving urban disputes because they were inevitably partisan and, if granted, there was a danger that the antagonism felt by the opposing (and losing) party might lead to further unrest. The crown needed to treat such disputes carefully, tempering an urge to act decisively with the need to ensure lasting peace by imposing a settlement that was agreeable to both sides.[75] Its handling of the dispute between St Mary's Abbey and the city of York in the early 1350s, over the status of the district of Bootham, is an excellent case in point (**125**). The king chose not to respond to the abbey's petition immediately, but put the case on hold until, some years later, a settlement was reached which gave the city control of Bootham but provided protection to the monks of the abbey from arrest within its boundaries. Sometimes, ironically, the crown itself was the cause of conflict. In 1309 Shrewsbury Abbey complained that the burgesses of the town were claiming the right to hold a fair on the feast of St James (25 July) for three days (**122**). This seriously threatened the viability of its own fair which, the petition alleged, had been held every year on 1 August since its foundation by Roger of Bellême in the eleventh century. But the situation arose from Edward II's grant of a charter to the townsmen of Shrewsbury in June 1309.[76] In the event, the petition made little headway, for the townsmen themselves were petitioning ten

72 *The St Albans Chronicle, Volume I: 1376–1394*, ed. J. Taylor, W. R. Childs and L. Watkiss, pp. 480–2 and nn.; *Peasants' Revolt*, ed. Dobson, pp. 243–56; Gottfried, *Bury St Edmunds*, pp. 231–6.

73 For discussion of this surety, see M. D. Lobel, 'Some Additions to André Réville's Account of Events at Bury St Edmund's Following on the Revolt of 1381', *Proceedings of the Suffolk Institute of Archæology and Natural History* 21 (1931–3), 208–14.

74 *PROME*, parliament of April 1384, item 19.

75 L. Attreed, 'Arbitration and the Growth of Urban Liberties in Late Medieval England', *Journal of British Studies* 31 (1992), 205–35, esp. pp. 208–12, 224–9, discusses a dispute between the city and cathedral of Exeter.

76 *CChR 1300–26*, p. 127.

years later for the fair to be moved to 22 September, and it was not until the beginning of Edward III's reign that it was finally moved to St Matthew's day (21 September).[77]

In Bath a different kind of dispute arose in the early fifteenth century, when the prior and convent took exception to the ringing of bells by the townsmen in the parish churches of the town (**131**). The priory claimed that it had long been the custom that no bell in the town or suburbs was rung after the curfew had been sounded by the cathedral church, and none was sounded before the first ringing of the cathedral bells the next morning. Yet the mayor and townsmen persisted in breaking this custom, specifically by tolling their bells (this is described in Middle English as *knollyng*, and is helpfully explained in the petition as involving ringing a bell 'without any other sound') to enable the townsmen to go to their matins before the monks had risen. The obstinacy of the townsmen on the matter was made worse by the fact that the bells of the parish churches were said to sound louder in the cathedral church than in the parish churches themselves, so that the monks claimed to be prevented from 'performing and saying their divine service according to their rule and foundation'. This was more than a dispute about timing and noise. Bells not only provided parishes with their identity;[78] they also symbolised and reflected the authority of those who rang them. They therefore provided a means for the townsmen to challenge the position claimed by the abbey as the hub of spiritual life with the town of Bath.

Conflict of a different order, but no less intriguing, existed in the parish of Plympton in c. 1440 (**135**). There was a history of tension between the town and prior over the status of the secular chapel which stood in the priory's grounds.[79] In the petition, the prior described in graphic detail a shocking, even macabre, series of assaults by the townsmen, aimed at preventing the prior from asserting the chapel's dependence upon the priory. Although the petition does not say so, what was at stake was whether St Mary's held the status of the community's parish church. If it did, the inhabitants of Plympton would no longer have been obliged to pay offerings and tithes to the priory, nor to attend services at the priory church. What happened here was a phenomenon repeated in many other parishes across the kingdom, especially from the late fourteenth century when the desire of parishioners to exert more control over the spiritual life of their parish led to the rights of mother churches being challenged and increasingly resisted.[80] In 1441 the priory and men of Plympton reached an accord over the

77 A petition dating to 1325 is transcribed and printed in *RP*, I, 434–5. It lists a series of requests, including a plea to have their fair moved from the feast of St James to 22 September. For the eventual grant, see *CChR 1327–41*, p. 6. See also H. Owen, *A History of Shrewsbury*, 2 vols (London, 1825), I, 158 and 161; and the *Gazetteer of Markets and Fairs in England and Wales to 1516*, available online at http://www.history.ac.uk/cmh/gaz/gazweb1.html.

78 K. L. French, *The People of the Parish: Community Life in a Late Medieval English Diocese* (Philadelphia, 2001), pp. 146–7.

79 A. D. Fizzard, *Plympton Priory: A House of Augustinian Canons in South-Western England in the Late Middle Ages* (Leiden, 2008), pp. 169–72. Fizzard does not mention this petition.

80 R. N. Swanson, *Church and Society in England in the Later Middle Ages* (Oxford, 1993), p. 219; and B. R. Kemp, 'Monastic Possession of Parish Churches in England in the Twelfth Century', *JEH* 31 (1980), 133–60.

use of the chapel: from this point on it would be recognised as a parochial chapel subject to the conventual church of St Peter and St Paul.[81] The priory thus had its formal position upheld as ultimate spiritual authority within the parish, but the concessions made to the parishioners – these included the right to receive sacraments in St Mary's, to process around the chapel on Palm Sunday (with no obligation to attend the procession, sermon or any other office of the prior) and to be buried in the chapel – were tantamount to recognising the chapel as the focal point of parish life.[82]

These and other episodes printed here illustrate that no aspect of religious life was immune to the tensions and conflicts that occurred between religious houses and their neighbours.[83] They are a useful reminder that religious service, processions, burials and the ringing of bells – all uses of space in churches – were not simply seen as acts of religious devotion, but also as expressions of power and authority. The way in which people were permitted to express their religiosity free of imposition from unwanted external interference could be as much a source of conflict and contention as the imposition on communities of more obviously secular burdens such as tallages or suits of court. In particular, petitions concerning disputes about the use of church space show how the practice of religion could be as important in generating parish identity and fostering a sense of local community as it was in fulfilling the underlying spiritual needs of the members of that community. In this respect these petitions indicate a significant gap between the laity and religious in regard to lay expectations of what religious houses should do for their parishioners.

Conflicts among the clergy

The religious came into conflict not only with the laity, but with other members of the clerical estate, clashing – among seculars – with all ranks, from parochial clergy (**98**, **208**) to archbishops (**96**, **182**). The bad relations between Holy Trinity Priory, York, and the vigorous Archbishop Romeyn (**96**) are especially well-documented. Romeyn, having received his temporalities on 16 April 1286, quickly (18 June) gave notice that he intended to conduct a visitation of the city of York on 1 July, and would be based in Holy Trinity Priory. On 26 August 1286 he cited twelve religious houses to appear before him on 2 October to show by what right they had appropriated certain churches; in Holy Trinity's case these were Leeds and Bilbrough (WRY). By late September 1287 the house had incurred Romeyn's wrath by claiming 5 marks a year from Malton Priory, and, having lost its claim in the court Christian, was preparing to pursue it

81 *The Register of Edmund Lacy, Bishop of Exeter, 1420–1455*, ed. G. R. Dunstan, C&Y 62 (1967), III, 244–56.

82 R. N. Swanson, 'Parochialism and Particularism: The Dispute over the Status of Ditchford Friary, Warwickshire, in the Early Fifteenth Century', in *Medieval Ecclesiastical Studies in Honour of Dorothy M. Owen*, ed. M. J. Franklin and C. Harper-Bill (Woodbridge, 1995), pp. 214–57, esp. p. 243.

83 For a very useful consideration of these key points see K. L. French, 'Competing for Space: Medieval Religious Conflict in the Monastic-Parochial Church at Dunster', *Journal of Medieval and Early Modern Studies* 27 (1997), 215–44.

in the court of King's Bench. Meanwhile, Holy Trinity was defying the archbishop by claiming exemption from his jurisdiction. By October 1293 Romeyn had excommunicated the prior for contumacy, a fact publicised by letter patent the following January, and he signified this, under the mechanism for using the lay power to arrest persistent excommunicates, to the crown on 9 May 1294.[84] Romeyn died in 1296, and despite the prior's claim in 1298 that he was still being persecuted there is no record of this dispute in the registers of either Henry Newark (1298–9) or Thomas Corbridge (1300–4).

The religious also clashed with each other: house clashed with house, over rights (**144**, **148–9**), roads (**146**), recruitment (**150**), and recalcitrant individuals (**145**, **151**). A few petitions are indistinguishable from the significations, to the lay power, of religious apostasy contained in TNA series C 81;[85] the apostate canon of Hastings, who is the subject of **158**, has eluded detection so far. The strange case of Thomas Eyton, former subprior of Tutbury who was kidnapped by servants of Selby Abbey while travelling to York as the new prior of Holy Trinity (**195**), defies obvious classification. These categories are not necessarily watertight or mutually exclusive; attacks on a house by local laymen, and disputes over internal control were probably often connected (**103–4**, **106–7**, **112–15**).

The true cause of friction is not always apparent from a single petition. One illustration of this is the complaint of c. 1301 (**182**) by the people of Faversham (Kent) against St Augustine's Abbey, Canterbury. Far from being a little local difficulty, this was part of a long-running struggle with an international dimension.[86] St Augustine's enjoyed the twin advantages of crown patronage and of being directly under papal – and thus exempt from diocesan – control, and from the twelfth century it had tried to decrease archiepiscopal authority over its appropriated churches. Abbot Thomas de Fyndon (elected 1283) determined to extend the house's powers, and clashed first, though inconclusively, with Archbishop Pecham; but the vacancy between Pecham's death (December 1292) and Winchelsey's consecration (September 1294) gave Fyndon the chance to renew his scheme. His goal was to create a substantial peculiar: three rural deaneries, containing some forty churches. Had he been successful the archdiocese of Canterbury would have been virtually bisected.[87] The ensuing struggle is densely documented – and not only in Winchelsey's register or the history of St Augustine's by the monk William Thorne.[88]

Faversham was a flash-point in this dispute because its vicar, Peter de Milstede, had been instituted by Pecham, was loyal to archiepiscopal authority, and evidently carried his congregation with him; but it was not the only place where the struggle was carried out by force. The violence at Faversham was

84 *The Register of John le Romeyn, Archbishop of York 1286–1296*, ed. W. Brown, Surtees Society, 123 (1913), I, 50, 59–60, 133, 138, 164–5, 233; F. D. Logan, *Excommunication and the Secular Arm in Medieval England* (Toronto, 1968), p. 125 n. 38.

85 F. Donald Logan, *Runaway Religious in Medieval England, c.1240–1540* (Cambridge, 1996).

86 R. Graham, 'The Conflict between Robert Winchelsey, Archbishop of Canterbury, and the Abbot and Monks of St Augustine's, Canterbury', *JEH* 1 (1950), 37–50. This article was prompted by Miss Graham's work editing Winchelsey's register for C&Y, vols 50–1, 1950, 1956.

87 J. H. Denton, *Robert Winchelsey and the Crown 1298–1305* (Cambridge, 1979), pp. 180–3.

88 Ibid., p. 180 n. 13 lists some sources which have not been fully exploited.

only a small part of a dispute which involved Edward I, to whom Fyndon made effective representations when the king stayed at St Augustine's, which he did whenever he went to Canterbury, but which was played out mainly at the *curia*, to which both sides sent learned counsel – and bribes. Boniface VIII gave a definitive ruling in March 1303, in favour of Winchelsey. Six months later he was attacked at Anagni, and died shortly after.

Disputes among the members of a single house were among the most difficult cases for the authorities, of both church and state, to solve. An example of this was the dispute at Bardney, a case whose complexity and bitterness is masked by the two petitions sewn together which constitute **147**. Much about this matter is still obscure[89] but at the heart of the conflict was Robert de Wainfleet, who was already troublesome before his election as abbot in 1280. Wainfleet was deposed by John Dalderby, bishop of Lincoln in 1303, and between then and his resignation on January 1318 the conflict between abbot and bishop, and almost certainly between factions within the house, generated, in addition to these two petitions, another seven in 'Ancient Petitions' which relate to the case.[90] Another petition was written by Dalderby, but perhaps was never sent, though it was kept with his register.[91] In the course of this dispute the house was taken into crown management, which in turn generated disputes with lay officials. Wainfleet proved a doughty fighter; he appealed to the Court of Canterbury, which reversed his deposition. He then appealed to Rome, and Wainfleet went there in person, being *outre meer* in the first petition, and *en … absence* in the second. Between October 1305 and October 1317 Dalderby despatched no fewer than twenty-one messengers to the *curia* bearing letters about the Bardney case, but Wainfleet had the last laugh; he resigned the abbacy, citing age and infirmity, but did so only after receiving lavish provision for his retirement.[92]

Whether outside influences were at work at Bardney is not clear. They certainly were a century later at Newenham (Devon) when Philip Courtenay, scion of a comital family, intervened violently in the affairs of the house (**113–15**), and likewise at Bindon (Dorest) in the early 1330s (**153–5**). But monks were quite capable of creating mayhem by themselves, witness the sorry saga of Beaulieu (Hants) between 1393 and c. 1420[93] of which **116** is a small part. Much more detail is available about the strife at Abbotsbury (Dorset) in the 1350s (**157**). These and other entries indicate that disputes within individual houses were among the most toxic and intractable problems which petitioners brought before the crown. They also demonstrate, perhaps more than any other type of supplication, the regard which the religious had for the king, as the source of arbitration and the provider of protection, as much between themselves as between them and the laity.

89 Despite the detailed discussion of the case in *Heads of Houses* II, pp. 20–1.

90 SC 8/2/94; 9/440; 10/491; 181/9025; 201/10004; 195/9747; 331/15598.

91 LAO Reg. 3 (Dalderby, Memoranda), f. 118.

92 Provision for Wainfleet's retirement, 7 Jan. 1318; resignation of the abbacy and withdrawal of proceedings against the bishop, 11 Jan. 1318, ibid., ff. 377v–378.

93 *Heads of Houses* III, 265–6.

THE WIDER WORLD

The petitions provide a wealth of information showing how events of a more general nature could impact on the life and fortunes of a monastery. Often these were problems which had been caused by factors entirely outside the control of the community and which, in some instances at least, posed a serious threat to the very life and existence of the religious house. The religious communities of Dunwich, for example, faced the very real prospect of being swept away by the sea as a result of coastal erosion (**64**, **65**, **72**). Misfortune of a different order induced the abbot of the Premonstratensian canons of Croxton to petition the king in 1351, asking to be discharged from collecting the clerical tenth (**78**). In his supplication the abbot described how the community had been so desolated by the plague that few canons now remained and he was far too preoccupied in seeing to its recovery to spend time away. In 1382 it was not the mortality of members of the religious house, but instead the deaths of its tenants that induced the abbess of Shaftesbury to ask for the administration of the house at times of vacancy – a measure which avoided the often costly process of having the convent pass into the custody of the king's escheator (**81**).[94] Misfortune of positively apocalyptic proportions was said to have visited Avebury Priory in the 1350s, when it presented a petition asking for remission of its debts as a result of the poverty caused by flood, fire, plague, murrain, rent strikes and the heavy cost of repairs to its buildings (**79**).

War, alongside plague, was the other great dynamic of social and economic change in this period, though its impact on religious communities tended to be more selective, depending to a much greater extent on where the monasteries were positioned in relation to military activity. The petition included in this volume from the Gilbertines of York, dating to c. 1333, in which they asked for the value of their estates in the North Riding of Yorkshire to be reassessed for tax after the Scots had burnt their lands and driven their livestock away, highlights that it was not just the communities in the far north of the kingdom which suffered the effects of the war in the first half of the fourteenth century (**87**).[95] The request of the Augustinian canons of St Denys, Southampton, in c.1340 to be excused tax payments and the costs of equipping soldiers to defend the town after the great destruction caused by a recent French raid is another reminder of this same point (**88**).[96] War damage could also be inflicted from more unlikely quarters: the complaint of the Carthusians of Axholme, for example, against men who had attacked the priory after their return to England from campaign in France (possibly after the Agincourt campaign of 1415) hints at the sorts of problems created by the return of unruly and violent war veterans (**93**); another example is the complaint by the prior of Hexham in 1331 that his house had

94 For patrons' rights during vacancies, the best summary is Wood, *English Monasteries*, chpt. 5; and M. Howell, 'Abbatial Vacancies and the Divided *Mensa* in Medieval England', *JEH* 33 (1982), 173–92.

95 Other petitions from northern religious houses are calendared in C. Fraser, *Ancient Petitions Relating to Northumberland*, Surtees Society, 171 (1961), nos 159, 162, 170, 172, 173, 174, 175, 178, 179, 180, 182, 183; and idem, *Northern Petitions Illustrative of Life in Berwick, Cumbria and Durham in the Fourteenth Century*, Surtees Society, 194 (1981), nos 105, 109.

96 J. Sumption, *Trial by Battle, The Hundred Years War*, 1 (London, 1990), p. 248.

suffered greatly from the war, and that the king should have particular regard for the losses inflicted on them by the royal host at Haydon Bridge (**86**).[97]

The joint petition from the priors of Thetford and Bermondsey highlights an altogether different consequence of England's hostile relations with its neighbours (**92**). Thetford and Bermondsey, along with a number of other sister houses, had originally been set up as dependent priories of the Cluniac order. Subject to the authority of a 'foreign' mother house they were vulnerable to anti-alien sentiment generated as a result of the Hundred Years War.[98] In October 1377 parliament passed an ordinance banning all aliens from the realm, though the crown had managed to dilute the severity of its terms by having alien priories exempted, providing that their priors did not leave the country or receive messages from outside.[99] There were important practical considerations resulting from this policy, not least how the activities of the English Cluniacs were now to be overseen and what should happen in the event of a vacancy.[100] The petition describes a new framework of authority in which the English houses were now effectively to govern themselves, under the overall scrutiny of the archbishop of Canterbury in his capacity as papal legate. That the priors of Thetford and Bermondsey were in effect to act as the senior members of the Cluniac order in England, responsible, with the archbishop, not only for the visitation of the other houses but also for the general chapter of the order, underlines a further aspect to the Anglo-French conflict at this time. Both priories were among the dozen or so major houses of the Cluniac order in England, but the crucial qualification which marked out Thetford and Bermondsey was the English nationality of their priors, and the corresponding naturalisation or 'denization' of the priories themselves.[101] This was a critical factor because, following the Great Schism of 1378, the loyalties of the Cluniac order were divided along religious as well as political lines, and the Anglophile Roman pope Urban VI, and his successor Boniface IX,

97 For background, see R. Nicholson, *Edward III and the Scots: The Formative Years of a Military Career* (Oxford, 1965), pp. 29–30.

98 A. K. McHardy, 'The Effects of War on the Church: The Case of Alien Priories in the Fourteenth Century', in *England and her Neighbours 1066–1454: Essays in Honour of Pierre Chaplais*, ed. M. Jones and M. Vale (London, 1989), pp. 277–95, and references.

99 *PROME*, parliament of October 1377, item 91 (l). These measures were not formally enacted into statutory form. For background, see A. K. McHardy, 'The Alien Priories and the Expulsion of Aliens from England in 1378', in *Church Society and Politics*, ed. D. Baker, Studies in Church History, 12 (1975), pp. 133–41.

100 See R. Graham, 'The Papal Schism of 1378 and the English Province of the Order of Cluny', *EHR* 38 (1923), 481–95; D. Knowles, *The Religious Orders in England, Volume II: The End of the Middle Ages* (Cambridge, 1955), pp. 157–61.

101 Thetford was granted denization in 1376: *VCH Norfolk*, II, 367; Bermondsey received a similar grant in 1381: *CPR 1381–5*, p. 18. Financial considerations are likely to have been the main consideration compelling the Cluniacs to seek naturalisation. In its petition for denization in 1381 the prior of Bermondsey requested the king's grace on the grounds that alien priors had caused much damage to the house by granting outrageous corrodies and leases of their possessions: SC 8/93/4628. What the petition did not mention was that these burdens had arisen primarily as a result of the crown's policy of charging alien priories exceptionally high annual farms at the exchequer, for which see McHardy, 'Effects of War', pp. 281–4.

had every reason to prefer individuals whose allegiance lay unambiguously with the English crown. The petition thus shows how the new procedures to regulate the Cluniacs in England were recognised by the clergy as requiring the approval of the king. It is an important illustration of how war helped redefine the Church – and English monasticism – along nationalistic lines (see also **167**).

A particularly fine example of the involvement of the religious in domestic political affairs is given by a petition presented by two Dominican friars a few months after Edward II had been deposed in 1327 (**100**). The friars requested the aid of the young Edward III to have them released from prison following their arrest in Dunstable for conspiring to have Edward II rescued from Berkeley Castle. Although the whole tenor of the petition was aimed at rejecting these charges, it is interesting to note that the friars were actually committed to prison, to stay there at the king's pleasure. That two Dominican friars should have been singled out in this way should come as no surprise, for in June 1326 Edward had quite possibly been freed from captivity for a short time as a result of a conspiracy organised by the Dominican friar Thomas Dunheved, and other clerics.[102] It is possible that our two petitioners were acquainted with Dunheved, and they may even have been acting in accordance with his instructions.[103] The Dominicans were known to have been particularly favoured by Edward II, who had entrusted the body of his favourite, Piers Gaveston, into their hands after the latter's execution in 1312.[104] There is, moreover, a telling comment in a letter from the king's clerk John Walwayn, who had been instructed to investigate the attempted rescue of the king, that 'a great number of gentlemen in the county of Buckingham and in adjoining counties, have assembled for the same cause', namely, to free the king.[105] Dunstable – where the friars had been arrested – sits very close to Buckinghamshire's county border and it is significant that the friars, having first been incarcerated in Dunstable, were then transferred and imprisoned in the gaol at Aylesbury, the county town of Buckinghamshire. In the broader scheme of things this is a highly important petition, for whilst it does nothing to resolve the underlying mystery surrounding Edward's ultimate fate in Berkeley Castle in September 1327 (and the intense debate which this question has recently gener-

102 F. J. Tanquerey, 'The Conspiracy of Thomas Dunheved, 1327', *EHR* 31 (1916), 119–24; T. F. Tout, 'The Captivity and Death of Edward of Carnarvon', *Bulletin of the John Rylands Library* 6 (1921), 69–113, esp. pp. 81–8. Paul Doherty has argued more recently that the king was never in fact recaptured after the June raid: P. Doherty, *Isabella and the Strange Death of Edward II* (London, 2003), pp. 122–4, 224–5.

103 There is speculation that Dunheved was a member of Blackfriars, London, though this has no supporting evidence: *VCH London*, I, 499, citing C. F. R. Palmer, 'Fasti ordinis fratrum praedicatorum: or the Provincials of the Friar Preachers in England', *Archaeological Journal* 35 (1878), 134–65. It may be of some significance that Blackfriars was attacked by a London mob in October 1326, quite possibly because of its close connections with the king: J. Röhrkasten, 'Londoners and London Mendicants in the Late Middle Ages', *JEH* 47 (1996), 446–77, p. 452. There is no evidence to indicate where the petitioners were from, but Dunstable does lie on a main route north from the capital city.

104 R. M. Haines, *King Edward II* (Montreal, 2003), pp. 10, 86, 466 n. 22.

105 Tanquerey, 'Conspiracy of Thomas Dunheved', p. 120.

ated among modern day historians),[106] it nevertheless provides a measure of the atmosphere of political intrigue and suspicion that surrounded the circumstances of the king's imprisonment before this time, and gives substance to Walwayn's report that there were other plots that aimed to free the king from his captors.

Within some monastic contexts at least, life devoted to religiosity and spiritual contemplation was not deemed to be incompatible with showing an interest, and occasionally directly participating, in the kingdom's secular affairs. Although proportionately far greater numbers of bishops served the king in secular office, the heads of religious houses were not impervious to such activities, as the respective petitions of the abbots of Langdon and Rievaulx illustrate (**16**, **29**).[107] Both served the crown in a diplomatic capacity; in the case of the abbot of Langdon, by taking a leading role in arranging the marriage of Edward III's sister, Eleanor of Woodstock, to the duke of Guelders. Abbots and priors were also, of course, summoned to parliament on a regular basis. Here, however, attempts to emphasise their interest in the affairs of state flounder somewhat because only a small and, across the fourteenth century, diminishing number of mostly Benedictine abbots were called to attend parliament (note: priors were for the most part excluded from attendance) and very often those who received personal summonses did their utmost to release their houses from the obligation. The petitions of St Mary's York and Beaulieu are cases in point (**42**, **43**). Both appear to have petitioned in the early 1340s, almost certainly as a consequence of events in the parliament of April 1341 when the principle was articulated that a higher rate of taxation would be imposed on those clergy who had attended parliament, on the basis that they were tenants-in-chief who held their temporalities from the crown by barony.[108] The significant point is that whilst Beaulieu successfully secured for itself exemption from parliamentary attendance, St Mary's did not, even though it accurately pointed out that its lands were held in frankalmoign, or 'free alms', which theoretically denoted its freedom from secular services (including attendance at parliament) and lay jurisdiction.[109] This inconsistency reflected the imprecise, even confused, basis on which the crown decided which religious should be summoned to parliament.[110]

In other contexts, however, religious houses were sometimes the very vessels of political partisanship, when they became the focus of commemoration and veneration for particularly controversial deceased political figures. Thus, we learn

106 I. Mortimer, 'The Death of Edward II in Berkeley Castle', *EHR* 120 (2005), 1175–1214; J. S. Hamilton, 'The Uncertain Death of Edward II', *History Compass* 6 (2008), 1264–78.

107 See also H. Shaw, 'Cistercian Abbots in the Service of British Monarchs (1135–1335)', *Cîteaux: Commentarii Cistercienses* 58 (2007), 225–45.

108 H. M. Chew, *The English Ecclesiastical Tenants-in-Chief and Knight Service, especially in the Thirteenth and Fourteenth Centuries* (Oxford, 1932), p. 174.

109 Ibid., p. 176, and n. 5. See also E. G. Kimball, 'The Judicial Aspects of Frank Almoign Tenure', *EHR* 47 (1932), 1–11.

110 Knowles, *Religious Orders II*, pp. 306–7. In fact, precedent and the preference of crown, rather than type of tenure, appear to have been primary factors determining whether abbots should attend parliament. For detailed discussion, see A. M. Reich, *The Parliamentary Abbots to 1470*, University of California Publications in History, 17 (Berkeley, CA, 1941), esp. chpt 8.

that the Premonstratensian canons of Tupholme had been charged by Edward II to say mass for the soul of Piers Gaveston (**76**), and in their petition of 1327 we discover the important role which the Cluniac monks played in fostering the cult of Thomas of Lancaster at Pontefract, the scene of the earl's execution (**60**).[111] It is noteworthy that in both cases the motive for petitioning was financial: the canons at Tupholme pleaded poverty because they had to meet the expense of finding a chaplain to say mass for the royal favourite, and the prior of Pontefract asked to keep the offerings made at Lancaster's tomb to spend on repairing the fabric of the priory. Some religious houses evidently sought the benefits of political alignment in more dubious circumstances: witness Roger Birthorpe's complaint that Sempringham Priory had used its association with Hugh Despenser and Henry de Beaumont to challenge his claim to hold a prise, and to have legal proceedings taken out against him on false pretexts, which appears to be fundamentally true (**194**).[112]

Occasionally, an abbey could itself become the focus of a major political maelstrom. Two petitions included in this volume from the abbot of Westminster shed important new light on the infamous violation of the abbey's sanctuary early in Richard II's reign (**109**, **110**). The royal council, and in particular John of Gaunt, unofficial regent of England whilst the king was still a youth, were implicated in the outrageous murder of John Shakell who had taken refuge in the abbey from royal ministers after refusing to hand over a prisoner whom he and Robert Hawley had in their custody.[113] The great interest of the case lies in the resourcefulness of the abbey in its attempts to mobilise the support of the political community in defence of its liberties. From one contemporary account, the *Anonimalle Chronicle*, we know that the abbot of Westminster, Nicholas de Litlington, travelled up to Gloucester where parliament had been convened and there 'went before the Commons', where he put the case to them that his abbey had been gravely violated and 'begged them, for charity, for remedy by their good counsel'.[114] The chronicler was presumably reporting the contents of the petition in this volume (**109**). The document represents a most important watershed in the history of parliamentary petitioning, for it is one of the earliest, and may well be the very first, example of a private petitioner formally addressing his complaint to the Commons in parliament, rather than to the king and council or Lords as was usually the custom.[115] This innovation was evidently ill-received. According to the *Anonimalle Chronicle*, 'because he had laid these matters before the commons, the king and his council were very angry and greatly aggrieved

111 See J. M. Theilmann, 'Political Canonization and Political Symbolism in Medieval England', *Journal of British Studies* 29 (1990), 241–66, esp. pp. 249–52; and S. Walker, 'Political Saints in Later Medieval England', repr. in idem, *Political Culture in Later Medieval England* (Manchester, 2006), pp. 198–222, esp. pp. 202–3.

112 See further, J. Coleman, 'New Evidence about Sir Geoffrey Luttrell's Raid on Sempringham Priory, 1312', *The British Library Journal* 25 (1999), 103–28. In a royal mandate to the sheriff of Lincolnshire dating to 1317, the prior was noted as being 'indicted as a common conspirator and maintainer of felons, and disinheritor of many persons in that county': *CCR 1313–18*, p. 498.

113 See N. Saul, *Richard II* (New Haven and London, 1997), pp. 36–8.

114 *The Anonimalle Chronicle 1333–81*, ed. V. H. Galbraith (Manchester, 1927), p. 123.

115 Dodd, *Justice and Grace*, pp. 166–74.

towards the abbot and convent'.[116] Accordingly, John Wyclif was summoned to parliament not, it should be noted, to address the assembly in general, but rather to speak to the Commons specifically, to persuade them of the righteousness of the council's actions. How fitting and significant that it was an abbot who first fully and effectively solicited and then mobilised the parliamentary Commons behind his grievance. It took the political acumen of an abbot to demonstrate the possibilities and potential in having MPs act as formal lobbyists in parliament, by directly and deliberately sending their petitions in the first instance to the Lower House for endorsement. There is perhaps no better measure of the extent to which the religious could involve themselves in the affairs of the kingdom.

Conclusion

In setting out some of the main areas covered in petitions from religious houses, our intention has not been to make any overarching claims about the nature of late medieval monasticism or how monastic communities interacted with the outside world. In some respects generalisations of this type are difficult to come to, at least on the basis of the evidence presented by the petitions, since they cover such a broad range of different circumstances and scenarios. Thus, whilst some petitions can be used to demonstrate division and conflict within a religious house, others show unity of purpose and unwavering support among the monks for the leadership of their abbot or prior. Whilst some show monasteries in conflict with their lay neighbours, others highlight the convergence and mutuality of interest which existed with the secular world. Whilst some show the king readily exploiting monasteries by placing unreasonable burdens on their already overstretched resources, others highlight the crown's role in protecting and enhancing their fortunes. The point is that each petition, though it is written formulaically and adheres to a set of universally held diplomatic and legal conventions, nevertheless has its own story to tell. Each story is different, shaped by the circumstances of the religious house, the nature of the request and the predisposition of the crown to the request. In other words, petitions reflect the full panoply of experience which shaped the fortunes of English monasteries in the later Middle Ages. In this volume we have tried to capture the flavour of the material by selecting some of the most interesting and illuminating examples. As far as possible, context has been given to individual petitions in their respective notes, and to whole classes of request in the Introduction; but our endeavours necessarily represent only the preliminary groundwork in an area of study which offers considerable scope for further research. More detailed investigation into the petitions is required before their importance to monastic studies and more general considerations of church-state relations can be fully realised. Our hope is that, with the publication of this volume, petitions will now be assimilated more readily into these areas of study.

On one specific point, however, we would like to offer some preliminary thoughts. It strikes us that petitions shed valuable new light on the relationship

116 *Anonimalle Chronicle*, p. 123.

between religious houses and the English crown, and specifically on the readiness of the regular clergy to seek redress from the king and his ministers on matters directly affecting the life of the monastery. The great variety of subject matter represented in the petitions may make generalisations difficult for historians, but it does at the very least demonstrate the remarkable breadth of authority which the English crown held over monastic communities. Indeed, it is worth remembering that it was not just the richest and most powerful religious houses that placed themselves into the hands of the crown; petitioning opened up opportunities for even the humblest of religious communities to appeal directly to the king's grace. The widespread popularity of the process is shown by the remarkable range of foundations represented in this volume, and in the collection of 'Ancient Petitions' (TNA SC 8) more generally.

The key to understanding the significance of these petitions is to appreciate that they were *solicitations* for royal intervention, and that while they do indeed reveal the full extent of the king's jurisdiction over monastic houses, this was sought at the behest of the religious themselves and not as a result of an unwelcome intrusion into monastic life. The significance of this lies in the fact that the actions of monastic petitioners, in deliberately seeking the king's interference in the affairs of their community, were at odds with a deep-running strand of theological reformist thought which sought to assert the independence of ecclesiastical institutions from the claims of lay power.[117] Indeed, it could also be said that these petitions fostered a power dynamic with the crown that was fundamentally in opposition to the underlying purpose and sentiment of the clerical *gravamina* which were presented in parliament on behalf of the clergy as a whole and sought for the most part to limit secular encroachments upon the Church.[118] The petitions thus highlight the underlying paradox of the Church's conception of its own position in relation to the crown: as a unified body or collective identity it sought to uphold its independence from, and even its superiority to, the secular arm, but when its constituent parts operated singly, as separate 'private' entities, this drive for autonomy and sovereignty quickly dissipated. Individual religious houses, like any other private petitioner, made use of all possible means to safeguard or enhance their self-interest, even if this meant explicitly acknowledging and accepting the domination of the crown. There was thus a major disjuncture between what the Church aspired to be and the reality that its individual members were often forced to embrace, by virtue of the fact that the possession of temporalities automatically thrust them into the secular world where the crown was needed to provide protection and redress.[119]

We should not, however, envisage monasteries as reluctant petitioners of the crown, conscious that their actions were undermining the very foundation of the Church's claims to self-determination; such esoteric considerations were presumably lost in the more pressing and immediate business of ensuring the continued

117 B. Tierney, *The Crisis of Church and State 1050–1300* (Toronto, 1964, repr. 1996), pp. 193–4, 199–200; and J. Canning, *A History of Medieval Political Thought 300–1450* (New York, 1996, repr. 2005), pp. 137–48.

118 Jones, 'Bishops, Politics, and the Two Laws', passim.

119 B. Thompson, '*Habendum et Tenendum*: Lay and Ecclesiastical Attitudes to the Property of the Church', in *Religious Belief and Ecclesiastical Careers in Late Medieval England*, ed. C. Harper-Bill (Woodbridge, 1991), pp. 197–238, esp. pp. 199–203.

welfare and prosperity of the religious community. Their readiness to call upon the crown underscores the emphasis of more recent scholarship, that monastic communities were not isolated enclaves of religious contemplation, but were integrated into society and were fully conscious of, and prepared to use, the political and legal systems of secular government for their own ends.[120] This integration cut two ways, for the petitions show not only how the religious acted like any other landowner with rights and liberties to defend; they also indicate how they were treated like any other landowner, their religious vocation being no barrier to acts of hostility or aggression. Perhaps it was the very success of monasteries in mobilising the crown to meet these threats, and especially in exploiting their status as royal foundations, that contributed to feelings of anti-clericalism across the fourteenth and fifteenth centuries. The prominence of the religious as petitioners underlined the disparity between the monastic ideal of religious contemplation and a reality in which abbots and priors often proved themselves more than capable of engaging in the cut and thrust of competition to secure royal favour for the enhancement of their material wellbeing. Given the general levels of suspicion and resentment that seem to have been attached to the notion of the Church possessing land, the spectre of religious communities (and other members of the Church) regularly seeking recourse in parliament to preserve these temporalities cannot but have fuelled the desire to see them subjected to the same taxes and other impositions of the state as were endured by the laity.[121]

The crown's willingness to receive and act on petitions presented by the clergy, and specifically by religious houses, could be regarded as one manifestation of the king's fulfilment of his coronation oath in which he pledged to protect and preserve the rights of the Church.[122] However, it is more indicative of the overarching power that late medieval English kings exercised over the clergy in England. When, in 1351, the Statute of Provisors stated in its preamble that 'the church of England was founded in an estate of prelacy by the king and his ancestors, by the earls, barons and nobles and their ancestors to instruct the people concerning the law of God, to provide hospitality, alms and other works of charity' this was not a claim to propriety over the Church; it was a statement of fact.[123] By the time large numbers of petitions survive, from the end of the thirteenth century onwards, the crown's pre-eminence over the temporal affairs of the Church was already well established.[124] The self-assurance of the crown in this respect is indicated by the fact that its responses to petitions were not always emphatic statements of royal power: sometimes the crown referred disputes back into the provinces and it was not unusual for senior clergymen – regular or secular – to be brought in to arbitrate or settle matters. This usefully underlines the point

120 Thompson, 'Monasteries, Society and Reform'.

121 K. B. McFarlane, *John Wycliffe and the Beginnings of English Nonconformity* (London, 1952), pp. 45–6; M. Aston, '"Caim's Castles": Poverty, Politics and Disendowment', in *The Church, Politics and Patronage in the Fifteenth Century*, ed. R. B. Dobson (Gloucester, 1984), pp. 45–81; P. McNiven, *Heresy and Politics in the Reign of Henry IV: The Burning of John Badby* (Woodbridge, 1987), pp. 30–1, 72–7.

122 H. G. Richardson, 'The English Coronation Oath', *Speculum* 24 (1949), 44–75.

123 *SR*, I, 316–17.

124 This is summarised by Thompson, '*Habendum et Tenendum*', esp. pp. 204–12.

that the conjunction of the religious and secular worlds in a jurisdictional context need not necessarily be considered only in terms of competition, antagonism and separation: an imperative to find the most practical and workable solution was usually the first priority which governed the terms of the crown's responses to supplications. This could entail upholding episcopal authority or the rights of a patron as much as it could involve having the case decided by a royal minister or judge. Royal power was always, however, implicitly upheld.

Some years ago Denys Hay made the case for considering the Church in late medieval England as the Church *of* England, on the basis that the 'English clergy had a spiritual leader in the pope; they had a master in the king'.[125] Hay did not directly draw on petitions to support his case. Had he done so his arguments would have been further strengthened, for the petitions illustrate the impressive degree to which the crown was the focus of the hopes and aspirations of religious communities. They demonstrate in particular the highly integrated nature of the English polity and the remarkably centralised makeup of royal government. But the king figured so prominently in the fortunes of monasteries not simply because he was the sovereign head of this government, and was the ultimate source of royal justice and grace, but also because in a great number of cases he was also the monastery's patron. This provided him with a whole package of powers and rights which pertained to the running of the religious house, but it also encumbered him with a particular duty to offer his support and protection. Did monasteries of royal foundation and patronage petition the king as their sovereign or as their patron? Perhaps too strict a distinction is ill-advised, but the patronal aspect is undoubtedly important in understanding the motivation of many monasteries in seeking the assistance of the king in their affairs. This important context to large numbers of petitions helps explain why so many of the issues which they raised concerned matters which were generated from a relationship with the crown that was defined by more than the simple fact that the religious house possessed temporalities which were subject to secular jurisdiction. It explains why in a good many cases the crown was invited to adjudicate on matters which directly affected the spiritual life of the community. This made parliament, where the majority of petitions in this volume were presented, more than a facet of the medieval English sovereign state; it highlighted the assembly's role as a vessel of the king's personal suzerainty and underlined his obligation to show good lordship to his monastic subjects.

125 D. Hay, 'The Church of England in the Later Middle Ages', *History* 53 (1968), 35–50, quotation from p. 49.

EDITORIAL METHOD

Each petition and supporting document in this volume and has been presented *in extenso*, even if it has been printed elsewhere. Where a document is large and comprised of clearly defined sections these have been demarcated by numerical subdivisions. A summary translation has been provided for all the documents and a date ascribed. Editorial comments and additions are in square parentheses. Standard abbreviations in the Latin and Anglo-Norman have been extended and the original spelling retained, although *i* has been treated as *i* when a vowel and *j* when a consonant, and *u* is used as a vowel and *v* as a consonant. The letters *c* and *t* are used as in the original. In English thorn (þ) has been kept in its runic form; yogh (ȝ) did not appear within these documents. In Latin and Anglo-Norman the tironian *7* and ampersands have been rendered as *et* (and as *and* in English). Place names retain their original suspended form with the apostrophe marking this in the Latin, but have been expanded in the Anglo-Norman and English, usually through the addition of a final *e*. Christ's name has been extended as *Cristus* and not *Christus*. Abbreviated forms of denominations of money and numerals have been retained. Capital letters have been retained only for the beginnings of sentences, all personal and place names, the Deity, months, saints' days and religious festivals. Punctuation has been modernised throughout for clarity. Unless otherwise stated, the endorsement is written on the dorse of the petition or document.

Conjectural reading and supplied material appear in square parentheses, and an ellipsis (...) denotes missing text, and also the length of such missing text. Deletions made within the text have been noted in footnotes. Interlineations appear between inverted parentheses (\.../). The dates supplied are given in the New Style. Dates of office for abbots, abbesses, priors and prioresses are from the three volumes of *Heads of Houses*; dates of office for others (such as chancellors, treasurers and bishops) are from E. B. Fryde et al., eds, *Handbook of British Chronology*, 3rd ed., Royal Historical Society Guides and Handbooks no. 2 (Cambridge, 1986), unless otherwise stated.

Where petitions were enrolled on the parliament roll, references are to the most recent edition of this record (i.e. *PROME*). References to *Rotuli Parliamentorum* (i.e. *RP*) occur only in cases where petitions were not enrolled. (Many 'unenrolled' petitions were included by the eighteenth-century editors of *RP* from original files of petitions or other miscellaneous collections; for the most part, these cases were not subsequently transcribed in the appendices of *PROME*.) Other transcriptions of petitions can be found in TNA PRO 31/7, a set of early nineteenth-century volumes compiled in preparation for the publication of *Parliamentary Writs*. Unless otherwise stated *Heads of Houses* (vols 1 and 2) have been used to identify abbots and priors.

PETITIONS

PART ONE

ROUTINE CASES

1

Lilleshall, Shropshire (? 1285)
Augustinian canons
(SC 8/123/6121)
(permission to enclose land/confirmation of charters)

The abbot and convent of Lilleshall petition the king for permission to enclose land in their wood near Lubstree, and for confirmation of a charter granted to them by King John.

Suplicant domino regi suo abbas et conventus de Lylleshull' qui sunt de fundacione predecessorum suorum, regum Anglie, quod cum quemdam boscum ab antiquo habant inclusum qui est extra vastum regardum foreste qui vocatur Lebyrsty, quod possint in bosco predicto incluso de speciali gracia domini predicti regis feras habere \et/ optinere pacifice per litteras suas patentes.
Iidem suplicant domino rege confirmacioni cuiusdam carte qua habent ex dono et concessione domini Johannis bone memorie quondam regis Anglie, pro salute anime sue et antecessorum et successorum suorum.

No endorsement

? 1285. On 7 June 1285 Lilleshall Abbey was granted confirmation of its charters (*CChR 1257–1300*, p. 292). There is no definitive link between that confirmation and this petition, but the handwriting seems consistent with this date. If the dating is correct, the petitioner is Ralph of Shrewsbury, abbot of Lilleshall 1284–91. For a transcript of this petition see no. 157 of PRO 31/7/93.

2

Dorchester, Oxfordshire (c. 1285–c. 1310)
Augustinian canons
(SC 8/106/5282)
(licence to buy land)

The abbot and convent of Dorchester petition the king for a licence to purchase from Nicholas Heved rent in Clifton (Oxon.) and land in Ashendon (Bucks.), from William of Aston land in Dorchester (Oxon.), and from Thomas, son of William le Clerk, land in Burcott (Bucks.).

Endorsed: *Oxfordshire.*
Let them have a writ of inquiry.

A nostre seyngnur le roy prie le abbe de Dorkecestre e le covent ke de sa grace voylle graunter ke yl puisse de sun cungee purchascer v soudees e deus derrees de rente de Nichole Heved en Cliftone, e ke yl eyt grante a purchascer deus vergees e quatre acres de terre de Nichole Heved en Assendene de sun fie demeyne, e de deus acres de terre a purchascer de Willam de Astone en Dorkecestre, e de une acre de terre a purchascer de Thomas fiz Willam le Clerk en Birdecote de fie le dit abbe. E ke yl voylle pur sauvaciun de sa alme e pur charite fere graunter le grace avantdite.

Endorsed: Oxon'.
Fiat breve de inquisicione.

c. 1285–c. 1310. The petition is assigned, on the basis of the hand, to c. 1285–c. 1310. Had this petition been successful the grant of ı mortmain licence should have been recorded on the patent roll, which was not done. See E. D. Jones, 'Three Benedictine Houses and the Statute of Mortmain, 1279–1348', *Journal of British Studies* 14 (1975), 1–28.

3

Merton, Surrey (c. 1302)
Augustinian canons
(SC 8/127/6318)
(repayment of £500 loan)

The prior of Merton petitions the king and council, requesting the repayment of £500 loaned to the king, as the prior owes the money to the pope.
Endorsed: *Before the king.*
He should come to the exchequer before the treasurer and barons, and show the king's letters which he has. And he is to be allowed all that he owes to the king in that debt, and concerning the rest it is to be treated with him of another form so that the king be discharged.

A nostre seingnur le roi e a soen consail prie le priour de Mertone pres de Loundres q'il li voille restorer et sauver des damages en paies e en allouaunces D livres, les queux il est tenuz a l'apostoille par ces lettres obbligatoures pur nostre seingnur le rei, e ceo par soen comaundement, des queux deniers il ad paie les deus parties e de la tierce partie ad il jour taunt qe a la Paske, le quel jour il covient q'il tiengne suz peine de escumenge et de entredit, e pur Dieu, Sire somegnez vous de nous qe nous soyoms sauvez de damage.

Endorsed: Coram rege.
Veniat ad Scaccarium coram thesaurario et baronibus, et ostendat litteras regis quas inde habet. Et si quid debeat regi allocetur ei in isto debite, et de residuo tractetur cum eo de aliquo certa forma ad exoneracione regis.

c. 1302. Confirmation of the assignments for the repayment of this £500, issued on 1 March 1303, states that the prior granted the loan on 25 April 1286, and the charter of assignment was issued on 4 October 1302 (*CPR 1301–7*, pp. 119–20). The petition dates from between the two, but presumably shortly before the assignment was granted in 1302.

The petitioner is Edmund of Herriard, prior 1296–1305. The pope is Boniface VIII. The tax is presumably that originally levied in 1274.

4

Newstead, Nottinghamshire (c. 1307)
Augustinian canons
(SC 8/218/10887)
(to be allowed to enjoy lands peaceably)

The prior of Newstead petitions the king, requesting that he be allowed to enjoy peaceably his lands in the hay of Linby in Sherwood Forest, granted to him by the king, and not be required to pay tithes to the prior of Felley, who has been granted such tithes in Linby, as the lands were not in the king's hands on the date of the grant to Felley.
Endorsed on face: *These are the words of the king's charter: We grant to the prior and convent of Felley all tithes pertaining to our assarts in the hay of Linby assarted in our time.*
Endorsed: *He holds his lands according to the king's grant, and if anyone disturbs him of his tithes he should defend himself in court Christian.*

A nostre seignur le roi mostre le priour de Novel Leu en Shirewode qe com nostre seignur le roi long temps passe li aveit par sa charter done cent et quatre .... acres de wast en la foreste de Shirewode, \cest assaver/ dedenz la haye de Lyndeby, pur une summe d'argent q'il dona avaunt meyn, issint q'il poeit les dites acres enclore e cultiver, e issint les tenir a li e a ses successurs a tutz jours, reddaunt de ceo par an al Escheker iiij li. E nostre seignur le roi ore cest an eit grauntee au priour de Felleye les dymes des assartz le roi en la haie susdite en son temps assartez, e mesmes celi priour de Felleye par encheson de cel graunt demaunde la dyme de la dite terre le priour de Novel Leu. Prie a nostre seignur le roi q'il puisse sa dite terre en pees tenir sant dime doner au dyt priour de Felleye, desicom la dite terre ne fust mie en la meyn le roi jour du graunt fait a priour de Felleye, mes fust le demeyne le dyt priour de Novel Leu par la dite chartre le roi cel jour e graunt temps avaunt.

Endorsed on face: Hec sunt verba carte regis: Concessimus priori et conventui de Felleye omnes decimas provenientes de assartis nostris in haya de Lyndeby nostro tempore assartatis.
Endorsed: Teneat terram suam secundum quod rex ei concessit eam, et si aliquis eum inquietet de decimis defendat se in curia Cristiania etc.

c. 1307. Dated on the guard to c. 1307. Other petitions on this matter also appear to date to this period (SC 8/1/44; SC 8/131/6530). On 15 April 1305 Felley Priory was granted all tithes of assarts in the hays of Linby, Roomwood and Willey in Sherwood Forest (*CPR 1301–7*, p. 333). On 30 March 1307 Newstead was granted certain wastes in Sherwood, including 60 acres at Linby hay, with tithes (ibid., p. 513). The petitioner is Richard of Grangia, prior 1293–1324. The prior of Felley is William of Toton (c. 1295–1315). For other related petitions see SC 8/60/2954 and SC 8/111/5543.

5

Bicknacre, Essex (1320)
Augustinian canons
(SC 8/4/168)
(request for an inquest)

The prior of Bicknacre petitions the king and council, requesting that good men who are not corruptible by gifts be appointed to take an inquest into the lands and tenements alienated from the priory to the disinheritance of the king. The sub-escheator who is currently to take the inquest is considered too disposed to the tenants of the priory.
Endorsed: *Justices are to be assigned in chancery who are reliable and in no way suspect to enquire of the contents of the petition.*

A nostre seignur le roi et a son conseil mustre son povre chapeleyn priour de Bykenacre qe come de la grace nostre seignur le roi comande feust brief d'enquere des terres et tenementz alienez de la dite meson en desheritance le dit nostre seignur le roi, \et/ de qui avoerie la dite priorie est, la quele enqueste, par vertue du dit brief, serroit prise par le suzeschetur de ce pais qi est, nienz vuillant as ascuns des tenantz des dites terres q'il n'est a la dite meson ou al dreit nostre seignur le roi meintenir, et ensi serroit nostre dit seignur le roi et sa povre meson deceuz ...... partie s'il ne plust a li de comander qe la dite enqueste feust prise par ascuns sages et loiaux de ses places. Dont il prie, pur Dieu et pur seinte charite, qe auqune bones gentz qi ne sont pas corumpables de dens y soient assignes pur cele enqueste prendre, et qui vuillent et soievant sauver et meyntener l'estat et le droit nostre seignur le roi en touz pointz.

Endorsed: Assignentur in Cancellaria justiciarii sufficientes et in nullo suspecti ad inquirendum de contentis in peticione.

1320. A Latin summary of this petition is included on the parliament roll for October 1320: *PROME*, parliament of October 1320, item 78 (84). The petitioner is Robert of Ramesden *alias* Burre, prior 1315–20.

6

Hyde, Winchester, Hampshire (c. 1320–60)
Benedictine
(SC 8/167/8332)
(complaint against keepers of forest)

The abbot and convent of Hyde by Winchester petition the king and council for remedy, stating that, as rectors of the parish of Alton in Hampshire, they ought to have all tithes within that parish. However, the keepers of Alice Holt Forest have recently disturbed them from their rights, preventing them from taking the tithes of pannage and venison within the forest.
Endorsed: *Declare if he has title, and if he or his predecessors as parson were so seised.*

A nostre seignur le roi et a sun consail se pleignent ses chapeleyns l'abbe et le covent de la Hide juxta Wyncestre qe come il sunt parsones del eglise de Aultun en le counte de Sutht', et deyvent aver de resun les dismes deinz les boundes de lour paroch, la viegnent les gardeyns de la foreste de Alschesholte et les destourbent q'il ne poyent aver les dismes de pannage et de venisun pris en mesme la forest. Dount il prient remedie.

Endorsed: Declare s'il eit title, et si lui et ses predecessours parsones eit eient este seisiz.

c. 1320–c. 1360. Dated to the period c. 1320–c. 1360 on the basis of the handwriting. The petitioner is Walter of Fifehead, abbot 1319–62. For another petition from Hyde, cut from the same piece of parchment, see SC 8/166/8252.

7

Leiston, Suffolk (1345)
Premonstratensian canons
SC 8/227/11331
(pardon)

Peter of Brewes petitions the king for a grant of a charter of pardon to the abbot of Leiston for all manner of oppressions etc. for the time that he was an officer or minister of the king.
Endorsed on face: *This petition was granted by the king at the suit of Peter of Brewes.*

Plese a nostre seignur le roi de sa grace especial graunter sa chartre de pardoun al abbe de Leyston' de toutes maners oppressiouns, extorsiouns, damages, grevaunces, trespas, deficites, cooncelementz, excesses, dettes et de toutes demaundes dount nostre seignur le roi luy porra chalenger de temps q'il estoit officer ou ministre la roi. Dount yl ad fait gree en l'Eschekere.[1]

Endorsed on face: Iste peticion fut graunte par le roy a la sute Peres de Brewes.

1345. On 8 October 1345 a pardon was granted to the abbot, after the payment of a £50 fine (*CPR 1343–5*, p. 559). 'Abbot John' was abbot of Leiston from 1344 until 1399. Peter de Brewes kt, king's yeoman, also petitioned on behalf of the prior and convent of Pentney (Norf., Augustinian), 28 July 1345, *CPR 1343–5*, p. 538. He was later a chamber knight from at least 1360 until 1377, C. Given-Wilson, *The Royal Household and the King's Affinity* (Yale, 1986), p. 160.

8

Merton, Surrey (1350)
Augustinian canons
(SC 8/246/12268)
(permission to travel to Rome)

John of Cockington and John of Middleton, canons of Merton Priory, petition the king for letters of licence for them and three others to travel to Rome on pilgrimage.
Endorsed on face: *We have approved this petition and will that our chancellor make them writs of passage.*

A tresredote seignur Sire Edward, par la grace de Dieu roi d'Engleterrre et de France, prient les seons liges chapeleins Johan de Cokyngtone et Johan de Middel-

1 This sentence is written in a different hand.

tone, chanoignes de sa meson de Mertone, qe yplese au sa reale seignurie et de sa grace graunter, pur eaux et treis altres parsones, une lettre de licence pur passer la mier en pelrinage vers la cite patriarchal et imperial de Rome d'enquerre la indulgence et remission de noz prechez par divine auctorite grauntez en cest present an as visitauntz les apostres Saint Piere et Saint Paul en la dite cite. Ceste devoute requeste, tresredote seignur, prioms pur salve de noz almes, en oepre de charite et pur l'alme vostre piere. Et si vous grauntoms, treshonure seignur, part de tut nostre travail et prieroms ades especialment pur vous come nous sumes tenuz.

Endorsed on face: Nous avons ottroiez ceste peticion et volont qe nostre chanceller lour face avoir brief de passe.

1350. Protection and safe-conduct were granted to the petitioners on 8 September 1350 (*CPR 1348–50*, p. 561). It has been claimed that this endorsement is written in Edward III's own hand (V. H. Galbraith, *Kings and Chroniclers: Essays in English Medieval History* (London, 1982), p. 103 n. 47), although the clerical hand suggests that the king dictated his response to a clerk.[2]

9

Bridge End, Lincolnshire (c. 1353–7)
Gilbertine
(SC 8/115/5748)
(request grant of pontage)

The prior of St Saviour, Holland Bridge (Bridge End) petitions the king, requesting grants in order to pay for the upkeep of the bridge at Holland Bridge. His lands are insufficient to meet the 100s per year cost, and he therefore requests a grant of pontage, and fairs to be held at the feast of St Mary Magdalene and the feast of St Philip and St James.
Endorsed: *He shall have pontage for five years on account of his poverty by the oath and testimony of good and loyal men, and this ...*

A son trexcellent [*sic*] seignur le rey prie son povre chapeleyn le priour de Seint Savieour de Holandbrigge qe come le dit priour est charge annuelement en cent soutz a payer a reparacioun del dit pount, et totez les terres et tenementz apurtenauntz a la dite priourie sount devenuz de petite value, c'est a saver fors a la value de x li x d par an, et ceo ne puet sufficer [a maintenir] le dit priour et son compaignon et a lour servauns. Par quei pleyse a son dit seignur le roy en oevere de charite graunter au dit priour et a ces successours pountage del dit pount .... susteynener la dite charge de cent soutz, et ceo serroit graunt aumoyne et nule damage au dit seignur le roy. Et pleyse a son dit seignur le roy qe le dit priour puisse .... avaungraunte a deux festes, c'est a saver a la feste de la Maudeleyn treiz jours et a la fest Seint Philip et Seynt Jake treiz jours et saunz fin dener.

Endorsed: Eyt pountage par cynk ans par cause de sa poverte par le sermawnt et tesmoignance des bones gentz et loialx, et ceo ...

2 Thanks to W. M. Ormrod for pointing out this distinction.

c. 1353–57. Two grants of pontage for five-year periods were made to the prior around this time, the first in October 1353 (*CPR 1350–4*, p. 491; *CPR 1354–8*, p. 597). A fair, to be held at the feast of St Mary Magdalene, was granted on 30 June 1356, and larger fairs at both St Mary Magdalene and St Luke were granted on 12 August 1357 (*CChR 1341–1417*, pp. 148, 155). On 7 November 1357 the prior was granted an aid of 40s yearly for five years for the sustenance of the charges of the priory (*CPR 1354–8*, p. 631). The identity of the petitioner is unknown. The right-hand edge of this petition is faded and illegible. For an earlier related petition see SC 8/177/8810. Private landowners were not allowed to levy tolls on the king's highway, so could not make money from bridges. After the public Anglo-Saxon duty of repairing bridges fell into disuse it was eventually replaced by royal grants of pontage, A. Cooper, *Bridges, Law and Power in Medieval England, 700–1400* (Woodbridge, 2006), esp. p. 132. Other petitions from this priory are SC 8/71/3504, SC 8/87/4317 and SC 8/340/16046.

10

Bristol, Gloucestershire (1374)
Franciscans
(SC 8/226/11300)
(pardon for trespass)

The friars minor of Bristol petition the king, requesting a pardon of the trespass that they did in entering the piece of land that Joan Lydiard, widow of John Lydiard of Bristol, granted by Edward I to the friars' use, together with the spring on the land and the conduit to the house of the friars in the suburbs, as they believed that they did not need a further licence. They request that they may hold it without further impeachment to Lydiard's intent, namely two masses annually.
Endorsed: *This bill was granted by the king.*

A nostre tresredoute seignur le roi supplient ses poveres oratours freres menours de Bristuyt qe come une Johane de Lydiard qe jadis feust la femme Johan de Lydiard de Bristuyt jadis dona par sa chartre a touz jours a noble Roi Edward, filz a Roy Henri, vostre progenitour, au oeps des freres menours de mesme la ville en perpetuele almoigne, une rode de terre ensemblement ove la fonteyn del ewe vive et la conduit as ditz freres en les suburbes de Bristuyt, a avoir et tenir pur chanter chescun an deus messes pur l'alme du dite Johane et les ancesters nostre seignur le roy, les queles freres, adonqes supposantz le dit doun estre seure et sufficeant, entrerent mesme la terre et tenement par vertue del dit chartre, et issint ils et lour successours ount tenuz et occupez les dites terres et tenementz depuis en cea saunz autre licence ou garante. Par quoi plese a vostre tresnoble et tresgraciouse seignurie graunter as ditz freres une chartre de pardoun del dit trespas, et outre q'ils puissent tenir meisme la terre et tenementz a eux et a lour successours pur priere pur vous et vos progenitours et pur la dite Johane solonc l'entente du dit feffement saunz empeschement a touz jours, en oevere de charite.

Endorsed: Ceste bille fust grante par nostre seignur le roy.

1374. On 14 August 1374 the petitioners were pardoned and it was granted that they might retain the property (*CPR 1370–4*, p. 471).

11

Writtle, Essex (c. 1381)
Hospital
SC 8/223/11102
(exemption from tax)

Nicholas, master of the hospital of Writtle, petitions the king, requesting that the 34s for which he has been assessed by the sheriff of Essex for the last subsidy be cancelled and annulled, as the hospital has always been exempt from such charges from the time of King John.
Endorsed on face: *The king has granted this.*
Oxford.

A trespuissant seignur le roy moustre vostre povre oratour Frere Nichol, mestre del nostre hospitall de Writell, qe come le dit hospitall fuit quitz et deschargez de touz maners talages et taxes avaunt cez hoeurs, del temps de vostre predecessour Johan, roy d'Engleterre, tanqe a vostre temps, et ore le viscont del counte d'Essex ad destreint le dit Frere Nicholl pur paier xxxiiij s a luy pur la derrein subsidie a vous, tresexcellent seignur, graunte. Plese a vostre tresexcellent seignur, et pur l'alme de vostre tresnoble piere, qe Dieux assoille, comaunder a vostre chaunceler qe voet deliverer vostre brief direct ala viscount susdit de suircesser et relesser au dit Frere Nichol de la subsidei avauntdit, mez qe defaut qe poet provere la contrarye susditz, pur Dieu et en oevre de charite.

Endorsed on face: Le roy la graunte.
Oxenford.

c. 1381. Dated on the guard to c. 1385, with reference to close roll entries relating to Master Nicholas of Aquila who was master after 1376 (*VCH Essex*, II, 201) and before 1390 (New College, Oxford, archives, N.C. 13,901:W.417). The subsidy probably relates to one of the poll taxes levied between 1377 and 1380, and perhaps that granted in December 1380. 'Oxenford' refers to Robert de Vere, earl of Oxford who was chamberlain of the household from January 1381.

12

Launde, Leicestershire (? 1383)
Augustinian canons
(SC 8/122/6052)
(request for writ of *nisi prius*)

The prior of Launde petitions the king, requesting that a writ of nisi prius be granted in his case against John, rector of Arnold (Notts.). The case has been delayed because of the non-appearance of jurors.

A nostre seignur le roy supplie soun chapeleyn le priour le Lande de counte de Leyc' qe par la ou le dit priour ad suy un bref de adm[esur]ment devaunt justices de la comune bank devers Johan, parson del esglise de Arnale en le counte de Notyngham, et process taunt suy tanqe le dit parson vient ov tiel issu de ple entre lez parties susditz est joint, issi qe l'enquest est agarde sibien par le pays de counte de Leyc' come par le pays de counte de Notyngham, et les queux countes sount adjoynez ensemble, puis quel temps le dit priour ad este et unquore est longement delaye de soun droit par non venue des jurours, a cause qe lez ditz justices ne vorroient grauntier as ditz parties un *nisi prius*. Par quoy pleise a nostre dit seignur comander as ditz justices de graunt un *nisi prius* al suite le dit priour d'estre pris en la confyn dez ditz countes, pur Dieu et en oevre de charite.

No endorsement

? 1383. Dated on the guard to ? 1383, but no evidence is cited. If the date is correct, the petitioner is Thomas Colman of Lichfield, prior 1376–88. For a transcript of this petition see no. 53 of PRO 31/7/107.

13

Beauvale, Nottinghamshire (1403)
Carthusian
SC 8/229/11417
(letters patent)

The prior and convent of Beauvale petition the king, requesting the grant of letters patent dated to the same day as earlier letters patent granted to them by the king of the alien priory of Bonby (Lincs.), as these earlier letters have been of no use to them as the place is the rectory with the church of Bonby and not the priory.

A tresexcellent et tresredoute seignur nostre seignur le roi suppliount humblement voz povrez chapelleins et continuelx oratours lez priour et covent de Beauvale en le countee de Notyngham qe come le quartre jour d'Apprill darrein passe de vostre grace especial grauntastez as ditz suppliauntz par vostre lettres patentes la priorie de Bondeby alien ove lez appurtenauntz en le countee de Nichol, a avoir as ditz suppliauntz et a sez successours a toutzjours, lez queux lettres patentes ne puissent estre vaillablez as ditz suppliauntz acause qe mesme le priorie est \ seisez/ en voz mayns par noun del rectorie ove l'esglise parochiel de Bondeby et nemy par noun del priorie de Bondeby. Qe please a vostre roial mageste et a tresgraciouse seignurie degraunter as ditz suppliauntz voz autrez lettres patentes portantz daie del quarte jour d'Apprill suisdit solonc la forme, purport et effect entierment d'un autre bille a yceste bille annexe, lez queux rectorie et l'esglise parochiel de Bondeby ove lez pensions, porcions, rentes et autrez commoditees en la dite bille especifiez ne passent la value de xviij marz par an, saunz fyn ou graund fee de vostre graund seal ent paier a vostre oeps, pur Dieu et in oevre de charitee.

No endorsement

1403. The petition dates to 1403 as both grants of the rectory were made on 4 April, though the letter in response to this petition was probably made later in the year in July or August (*CPR 1401–5*, pp. 217, 270). The name of the petitioning prior is not known. Confusion as to the exact nature of alien property under consideration was quite common. See A. K. McHardy, 'The Effects of War on the Church: The Case of the Alien Priories in the Fourteenth Century', in *England and her Neighbours 1066–1453: Essays in Honour of Pierre Chaplais*, ed. M. Jones and M. Vale (London, 1989), p. 280. For an earlier petition by the same petitioners requesting the grant of Bonby, see SC 8/229/11416.

Part Two

ROYAL INTERCESSION: THE OBLIGATION OF THE CROWN

2.0 General

14

Eye, Suffolk (1327–30)
Benedictne (alien)
(SC 8/17/836)

The prior and convent of Eye petition the king and council stating that they have long sued to the king, both during parliament and outside parliament, for the return of the advowsons of Thorndon and Mellis, which they gave the late king in exchange for the appropriation of the church of Laxfield, which the king would arrange at the Roman Curia. *However, despite the king's letters, the pope has not done anything on this, and the advowsons are in the king's hand. They request that they might have either the appropriation, or the two advowsons, as the entire great council was informed at the last parliament at Westminster, in response to the prior's petition, that if the advowsons were given for this reason, the king should return them, or otherwise give them satisfaction.*
Endorsed: *It pleases the king to write specially to the bishop of Norwich and to the chapter, to appropriate the church of Laxfield, and he intends to expedite the matter; and if he does not, he will do justice to them concerning the other advowsons.*

A nostre seignur le roi et son conseil moustrent ses chapeleins priour et covent de Eye qe come ils ont longement suy devers nostre seignur le roi, auxi bien en parlementz come hors de parlementz, de reavoir les avoesones des eglises de Thorndone et Melles queles le dit priour dona au roi qi mort est, pere nostre seignur le roi q'ore est, c'est assavoir par tiel cause et en tiel manere qe le dit roi le pere manderoit a la Court de Rome et ferroit avoir a leur meson de Eye l'apropriacion del eglise de Laxfeld a toz jours; et tot soit qe les avantdites avoesones fusseint par tiel cause et nemye par autre donez, et sur ce lettres le dit roi de priere mandez a l'apostoil, jadumeins l'apostoil rien n'ad fait ne ne voet faire, et issint ont celes avoesones demorez en la mein le roi puis la mort le dit roi, par quei prie humblement le dit priour a nostre seignur le roi qe, pur salvacion de s'alme et del alme son pere, vulle faire avoir a sa dite meson de Eye l'avantdit apropriacion solonc la cause et l'entencion du doun et la volunte le dit roi, son pere, ou rebaillir a eux leur dites avoesones issi qe la dite povre \meson/ ne soit si voluntrement sanz reson et peccherousement desherite, et dissicome avis fust a tot le grant conseil en le derrein parlement a Westmostre par respons fait a la peticion le dit priour qe si les avoesones estoient donez par la cause susdite, qe le roi leur dett faire restitucion our autrement leur gre.

Endorsed: Il plest au roi descrivre especialment al evesqe de Norwicz et au chapitre, d'approprier la dite esglise de Laxfeld, et il entend bien d'esploiter; et en cas q'il ne porra esploiter, le roi fra droit a lui des autres avoesons.

1327–30. On 12 January 1326 the advowsons of Thorndon and Mellis came into the king's hand (*CCR 1323–7*, p. 539), and on 10 December 1330 were granted to John of Eltham, earl of Cornwall, in fee tail (*CPR 1330–4*, p. 51). This petition must date from between 1326 and 1330, probably towards the end of this period; the petitioner is Robert Morpayn, prior 1323–48, and the bishop of Norwich is William Ayermine (1325–36). The 'derrein parlement a Westmostre', at which the prior's previous petition (*RP*, II, 31, no. 1) was presented, is likely to be the parliament of February 1329. For an earlier edition of the petition, see *RP*, II, 414a, no. 200. The case is discussed in *VCH Suffolk*, II, 74. A contributing factor to Eye's impoverishment was the right of bishops of Norwich to take a large cut of the revenue from Laxford each time there was a vacancy: *The Register of William Bateman, Bishop of Norwich, 1344–1355*, ed. P. Pobst, C&Y 90 (Woodbridge, 2000), II, no. 1466.

15

Burton Lazars, Leicestershire (1330)
Hospital
(SC 8/266/13294)

To the king and council from the master and brethren of the hospital of Burton Lazars requesting payment of the money due to them by tally for wheat taken from them for Roger Mortimer by John Appleby, his purveyor, when the king was last at Nottingham.
Endorsed: *Before the king.*
The king holds the chattels of traitors and felons so freely that he does not have to acquit their debts.

A nostre seignur le roi et son consail prient ses povres religious le maistre et les freres del hospital de Seint Lazar de Burtone qe come Sir Roger de Mortimaer, par Johan de Appelby, purveour de son hostiel, avoit pris, la dereyne foitz qe nostre seignur le roi fuit a Notingham, xv quartiers et demy de furment de veuz greigne par taille pris de chescun quartier vj soutz, et vj busseux des veuz peise, de quele prise rien lour fuit paie, a graunt empovericement et damage del dit hospital, par ount ils prient a nostre seignur le roi qe luy pleise, par Dieu et par oevre de charite, de ceo avoir regard et comander qe les ditz maistre et freres de la prise avantdite puissent estre servies.

Endorsed: Coram rege.
Le roi tient les chateux des treitres et felons si franchement q'il n'est mie tenuz a acquiter lour dettes.

1330. The petition was amongst those transcribed by Hale and ascribed a date of 1330, being a petition presented to the November parliament held at Westminster in that year (*RP*, II, 51a, no. 82). The petitioner is either William Ty or Tye, who is recorded as master of Burton Lazars between 1324 and 1327 (*VCH Leics.*, II, 38), or his successor, William Daumenyl, who is recorded as master in 1331 (*CCR 1330–3*, p. 327). Parliament was summoned to meet at Nottingham in October 1330, but on 19 October Edward III and his friends staged a coup, seizing Mortimer, who was executed in London on 29 November 1330. The financial results of this episode continued for decades, see *Royal Writs addressed to John Buckingham, Bishop of Lincoln*, ed. A. K. McHardy, C&Y 86 (1997), nos 126, 149. For general background on the hospital of Burton Lazars, the principal preceptory of the order of St Lazarus in England, see D. Marcombe, *Leper Knights: The Order of St Lazarus of Jerusalem in England, c. 1150–1549* (Woodbridge, 2003), index.

16

Langdon, Kent (1336)
Premonstratensian canons
(SC 8/56/2795)

The abbot of Langdon petitions the king that the treasurer, barons and chamberlains of the exchequer be ordered to pay his expenses or make a convenient assignment in lieu. The king and council recently assigned him to discuss, in the company of Eleanor, the king's sister, the performance and completion of her espousal to the duke of Guelders. After the matter was completed he returned to England and accounted at the exchequer for his expenses in the journey (£19 15s 8d), for which he was assigned payment from the receipts of John Mauger, late sheriff of Herefordshire, by the treasurer, who gave him a tally to deliver, but he has still not been paid because the sheriff had not the means and is now dead, and the petitioner cannot levy from his goods and chattels.
Endorsed: *He should explain the petition, as the sheriff had lands and tenements when he was in his office.*

A nostre treshonurable seignur le roi moustre, si lui plest, son chapellein abbe de Langedone qe come il fust nadgares assigne par le dit nostre seignur le roi et son conseil d'aler en la compaignie Alianore, seoz nostre dit seignur le roi, de parfourmer et parfaire les asposailles entre le duc de Gelre et la dite \Alianore/, et il y alast par cele cause et apres la busoigne espleiste revint en Engleterre et acompta en l'Escheqier le dit nostre seignur le roi de les resceites et despenses q'il avoit fait en la vyage avauntdit. Par quelx acompte lui furount duez dys et neof livres, quinzse souldz et eyt deners, si come par meisme la compte peust apparer. Sur quei il fust assigne de receyvre meisme la summe de Johan Mauger, adunqe viscounte de Hereford, par le tresorer qe adunqe fust, et une taille ent levez et tout eit le dit abbe ..... defaire levir la dite summe del dit Johan, il ne poast unqes rien avoir par resoun de la noun suffisauncie meisme celui Johan et il est ja mortz, et n'avoit biens ne chateux de quei rien ne peust estre leve, issint qe le dit abbe n'ad rien resceu de Johane avauntdite. Par quei il prie a nostre dit seignur le roi qe lui plese, en eovre de charite, commander a tresorer, barouns et chaumberleins de le Escheqiere defaire paier au dit abbe la summe avauntdite, ou lui faire assignement en lieu covenable la ou il peust estre servy.

Endorsed: Soit la peticioun declare, si le viscount avoit terres ou tenemenz au temps q'il feust en son office.

1336. 'William, abbot of Langdon' occurs in the period 1302–45. John Mauger, sheriff of Herefordshire, left office in January 1336. On 25 January 1337 the treasurer and barons of the exchequer were ordered to receive his attorneys to render his account for the time he was sheriff. He had been unable to appear on the preceding morrow of Hilary, the day originally given him, since he was then detained in the Tower of London. For the marriage of Eleanor of Woodstock to Reginald II duke of Guelders (1332), see A. K. McHardy, 'Paying for the Wedding: Edward III as Fundraiser 1332–3', in *Fourteenth Century England IV*, ed. J. S. Hamilton (Woodbridge, 2006), pp. 43–60, and references. The lavish ceremonies and equipment for this wedding have left a considerable mark on TNA series SC 8, since religious houses bore the brunt of the financial burden: 13/620 (Darley), 106/5284 (West Dereham), 124/6192 (Markby), 129/6434 (Newhouse), 182/9053 (Launde), 191/9547 (Chester).

17

St Swithin (Winchester Cathedral Priory), Hampshire (c. 1348)
Benedictine
(SC 8/257/12828)

To the king and council from the prior and convent of church of St Swithin, Winchester, stating that, at the request of Edward II, they provided a corrody for Menald of Fountz, servant of Edward II, and in return were granted a charter that they and their house would not be charged by the king or his heirs with finding any more corrodies. Then at the request of Edward III they provided a corrody for Henry Hwyff, his servant, of their own free will, and were granted another similar charter. Now a master John of Mildenhall has come to have the same corrody that Menald of Fountz had, and is suing to the king for it. They ask that their charters might have their force.
Endorsed: *When the prior is led in response and produces his charters in his defence, he shall have justice.*

A nostre seignur le roy et son conseil moustrent ses humbles et devoutz chapeleins priour et covent de l'eglise de Seint Swithon de Wyncestre qe come ala priere de nostre seignur le roy, qe mort est, piere a nostre seignur le roy q'orest, graunterent a un Menald de Fountz, son vallet, sa sustenance dedeinz lour meson pur terme de la vie le dit Menald, pur le quel graunt l'avantdit nostre seignur le roy graunta par sa chartre qe les ditz priour et covent mes ne serroient chargez de nulle sustenance trover a nul des soens ne la dite maison charge pur lui ne pur ses heirs, come piert par sa dite chartre. Et puis nostre seignur le roy q'orest pria par ses lettres as ditz priour et covent qe a sa priere vouzissint graunter a Henri Hwyff, son vallet, sa sustenance dedeinz lour meson pur terme de sa vie, la quele priere les ditz priour et covent graunteri de lour franche volunte, pur le quel graunt nostre dit seignur le roy graunta par sa chartre qe mes n'en chargerent les ditz priour et covent ne la maison de nulle sustenance pur nul des soens, come piert par sa chartre. Et ore est un Mestre Johan de Mildenhale venuz au dit priour d'avoir mesme la sustenance qe l'avantdite Menald de Fountz avoit, et fait sa suyte devers nostre seignur le roy pur mesme l'estat avoir. Dont ils prient remedie et qe les chartres puissent avoir lour force.

Endorsed: A quelle houre qe le priour soit mevee en respouns et mette avant ses chartres en defens de lui, et eit droit.

? 1348. This petition is printed in *RP*, II, 198a, no. 86, where it is included with petitions from the parliament of January 1348. The corrody was originally granted to Fountz on 24 March 1323 (*CCR 1318–23*, p. 704). Master John Mildenhale was a king's serjeant from June 1316 (*CPR 1313–17*, p. 486), and king's yeoman from June 1335 (*CPR 1334–8*, p. 114). He received grants for good service to the king and queen in August and October 1340 (*CPR 1340–3*, pp. 23, 38), and perhaps the corrody was given at about the same time. In May 1345 a commission was issued 'to make inquisition in Berkshire touching the persons who wickedly killed John de Mildenhale at Hungerford and all the circumstances of his death' (*CPR 1343–5*, p. 508). The victim may have been this corrodian. The petitioner is probably Alexander Herierd, prior 1328–49.

18

Wherwell, Hampshire (1384)
Benedictine (nuns)
(SC 8/224/11191)

The abbess and convent of Wherwell petition the king for confirmation of their franchise in the hundred of Mostowe in Hampshire, whereby Gilbert Joseph, the abbess's provost, has seized the goods of Henry Harold, who has fled to sanctuary in their church after killing his wife Isabel. The matter had been tried by the judges of the King's Bench, and the king was found to have no right to such chattels except during any vacancy, but judgement was not rendered due to a difference between the justices.

A nostre tresredoute et tresgraciouse seignur nostre seignur le roi moustrent les poveres noneynes l'abbesse et covent de Wherewelle, qe sont de vostre patronage et de la fundacion de voz progenitours, qe come eux et leurs predecessours, de temps dont y n'y'ad memoire, ont ew un hundred apelle Mostowe Hundred, deinz quel hundred eux ont ew et usee diverses franchises entre anex eux ount ew chatel de futif parmy tut mesme le hundred a seisir par lour ministres du temps dont y n'y'ad memoire, si la qe presente fuit nadgairs en Bank le Roy qe un Henry Harold de Wherewelle occist Isabelle, sa femme, a Wherewelle, q'est deinz mesme le hundred, a cause de quel felonie il s'enfuist a la esglise de Wherewelle, et qe certeins biens et chateux le dit Henry, a la value de xxxv li iiij s et viij d, deviendrent as mains la dite abbesse, par cause de quel presentment la dite abbesse vient en le dit Bank et alleggea qe ele et ses predecessours du temps dont y n'y'ad memoire avoient ew chatel de futif par my tut le dit hundred a seisir par lour ministres d'ymesne, et qe par la cause suisdite ele avoit seisi les ditz chateux deinz le dit hundred par Gilbert Josep, adonqes provost la dite abbesse, et qe nostre seignur le roi ne nul de ses progenitours furent unqes seisiez de tieux chateux deinz mesme le hundred, sinoun en temps de vacacion del abbeie de Wherewelle, et coment qe ce soit trie par enquest et trove pur la dite abbesse en le Bank suisdit juggement ent arendre ad penduz lengement pur diversitee des opynyons des justices, et uncore peut. Par quoi supplient les ditz abbesse et covent qe plese a vostre hautesse de approver lour possession de dite franchise, et grauntier q'eles et lour successours a toutz jours la poent aver et user deinz le hundred suisdit, et q'eles ne soient enpeschez sur lour possession de mesne la franchise nient pluis de temps passee qe de temps avenir, et qe brief soit maunde as justices du dit Bank d'alower la dite franchise en le cas suisdit, pur Dieu et en oevre du charitee.

No endorsement

1384. The petitioner is Cecily of Lavington, abbess 1375–1412. On 5 December 1384 it was granted that the abbess should be entitled to such franchises (*CPR 1381–5*, p. 488).

19

Michelham, Sussex (c. 1385)
Augustinian canons
(SC 8/125/6229)

The prior of Michelham petitions the king and council in parliament, stating that the king had granted him the keeping of the alien priory of Wilmington for the duration of the war. The prior undertook this despite the great costs, which have been borne by his house. However, the king has now granted the farm of the priory to James Berners, and the prior has been ousted, to his great loss. He therefore requests that the patent to Berners be repealed, and the same patent be re-granted to him.

A nostre seignur le roy et a soun sage counseil de parlement moustre soun humble et povre chapeleyn le priour de Michylam qe come nostre dit seignur le roy graunta par sez lettres patentz a dit priour la garde de la priorie de Wylmyngtone aliene durant la guerre, rendant ent par an C li au dit roy et paiant al piour [*sic*] de mesme la priorie xx marcz par an pur sa susteinance, lez queux xx marcz serront en encresce a la dite ferme a nostre dit seignur le roy et a sez heirs apres la mort du dit priour outre lez ditz C li, fesauntz divines services, almoignes, oevres de charite, sibien come pur lez progenitours nostre dit seignur le roy come pur lez fundours, et toutz autres charges avaunt usez et custumez, quele priorie de Wylmyntone n'est de la priorie de Michilham qe deux leuez, a quele cause, et pur exchuer la ruine et damage del dit priorie de Wylmyngtone qe poet avoir avenue si ele eust este es meins dez seculers, le dit priour la prist a ferme et ad mys en ces graundez costages, sibien en reparacions dez maisons come en deffences du meere et en tut autre manere. Et ore tarde la dite priorie de Wylmyngtone est graunte a Monsire James de Berners, chivaler, par une patent de la Chauncellarie a terme de sa vie, si la guerre atant dure, en allouance de C li par an sanz rien rendre, a cause de quele patent le dit priour est ouste encontre la ley, a grand damage et perdre de lui et de sa maisoun s'il n'est de ceo remedie. Sur quoi supplie le dit priour qe la dit patent graunte a dit Monsire James soit repelle sanz garnisement afaire envers le dit Monsire James, ou autre delai alouer, par moustrance de la patent a dit priour, et qe nulle graunte soit fait desore, a contrarie de mesme la patent, et qe, si pleast a roy, qe lez C li reservetz par mesme la patent soient assignez a dit Monsire James en l'allouance susdite, pur Dieux et en oevre de charite.

No endorsement

c. 1385. The petitioner is John Leme, prior of Michelham c. 1377–1415, who on 3 February 1378 was ordered to find fit sustenance for Thomas Auncel, prior of Wilmington c. 1375–c. 1388 (*CFR 1377–83*, p. 68). James Berners was appointed keeper of the alien priory of Wilmington on 6 October 1385 (*CPR 1385–9*, p. 27), and on 19 December 1385 the prior of Michelham was granted the disposal of all the goods which belonged to that priory before Berners' appointment, in order to pay his farm (*CPR 1385–9*, pp. 70, 72). It is not clear that the grant to the prior was prompted by this petition, since it related to the prior being distrained for his farm by summons of the exchequer which is not mentioned. James Berners was a king's esquire in 1378, became a chamber knight in 1382, and was executed during the Merciless Parliament, 1388: C. Given-Wilson, *The Royal Household and the King's Affinity* (Yale, 1986), pp. 119, 162–4, 247, 282. For an earlier transcript of this petition, see no. 67 of PRO 31/7/109.

20

Eye, Suffolk (c. 1402–3)
Benedictine (alien)
(SC 8/110/5476)

The prior and convent of Eye petition the king for redress in the matter of the farm of the town of Dunwich. From time out of mind the men of Dunwich have paid the petitioners alms of £12 yearly from their fee farm, until 1346 when Edward III reduced the amount to £9 10s 9d. On 23 April 1357, by his letters patent, Edward III granted the farm of the vill of Dunwich to the burgesses of the same, making no mention of the said alms, because of which the barons of the exchequer of Richard II would make no allowance to the burgesses in their farm for money paid to the prior and convent for the said alms. The petitioners have sued writs directed to the sheriff of Suffolk to levy the arrears of the alms from the burgesses, and he has done so, but John Bussy, now deceased, at the instigation of the burgesses, ordered the sheriff not to pay the arrears to the petitioners. They request that letters of privy seal be directed to the bailiffs and burgesses of Dunwich to pay them the said £9 10s 9d yearly with arrears, as well as to the treasurer and barons of the exchequer to make allowance to the said bailiffs and burgesses for such payments made out of their fee farm.
Endorsed: *They should sue to the king's council, and when the barons of the exchequer have been called there, justice will be done.*

A nostre tresexcellent et tresredoute seignur nostre seignur le roi supplient humblement vos poveres oratours lez priour et covent de Eye qe come ils et lour predecessours en temps de pees, et lez fermers de le dit priorye de Eye en temps de guerre, de temps dount memorie ne court, ount prisez et ewez xij li annuelment de la fee ferme de la ville de Donewych par lez mains de lez hommes du dite ville, quex pur le temps furent al temps qe la dite ville fust en lour garde a ferme, et auxi par lez mains de lez approvours de voz tresnobles progenitours al temps qe la dite ville fust en lour garde, pur ent acompter come frank almoigne de voz tresnoblez progenitours, servauntez as moignes de Eye, tanquil'an du regne le Roi Edward tierce vintisme, qe Dieu assoille, devaunt quel an lez hommes de mesme la ville paieront par an lxv li pur la ferme de la dite ville, et a cause qe vostre dit aiel fuist pleineint enfourme qe la dite ville fust a poy destruit, issint qe lez profitz provenantz de la dite ville dont la dite fee ferme seloit estre leve, la somme de xiiij li x s ix d ne passeront de sa grace especial, le vint et tierce jour d'Aprill l'an de son regne xxxj, par sez lettres patentz, graunta as burgeises et prodhomes le mesme la ville l'avauntdite ville ove lez appurtenancez, a avoir de luy et et [*sic*] sez heirs a ferme, rendant ent par an a son Escheker d'illoeqes lez xiiij li x s ix d avauntditz, nient fesant ascun mencioun es ditz lettres patentz de l'almoigne avauntdite, a cause de quele lez barouns de l'Escheker le dit Richard nadgairs roi d'Engleterre ne voillant faire ascun allowance as ditz burgeisez en lour dite ferme de xiiij li x s ix d ou d'ascun denier par eaux paie as ditz priour et covent del almoigne avauntdite, pur qoi lez ditz priour et covent ount pursuez diversez briefs hors del dit Escheker directz al viscounte de Suff' de lever lez biens et chatelx dez ditz burgeisez toutz lez arrerages de ix li x s ix d avauntditz, le quel viscounte, par vertu dez ditz briefs, avoit leve toutz lez ditz arreragez et lez avoit en sez mains, sur qoi Johan Busshy, qe mort est, par procurement dez ditz burgeisez, comanda a dit viscounte q'il ne paieroit riens as ditz suppliantz dez arreragez avauntditz, a cause de quel comand le dit viscounte riens ne voilloit paier de lez ditz arreragez, as graundez damagez dez ditz suppliantz. Plese a vostre gracious hautesse graunter voz gracious lettres de prive seal directz as baillifs et burgeys de la dite ville pur paier annuelment as ditz suppliantz lez ditz ix li x s ix d et toutz lez arreragez, et auxi de graunter autrez lettres as ditz tresorer et barouns de faire allowance as dit baillifs et burgeys de toutz lez paiementz par eux as ditz suppliantz faitz ou a faire par celle cause de lour dit ferme de xiiij li x s ix d, pur Dieu et en oevere de charite.

Endorsed: Sue au conseil du roy, et illeoqes appellez les barons de l'Escheqer, soit droit fait as parties.

c. 1402–3. On the dorse, in an early modern hand, is written '*petitiones parliamenti anno 4*', which indicates that this is part of a (now dispersed) file of parliamentary petitions. Internal evidence indicates that this must be the fourth year of Henry IV, since the petition refers to Richard II as the late king. Thus, the petitioner is probably Thomas of Fakenham, who was appointed as prior in 1391, with the next known successor not being appointed until 1431. For John Bussy, executed in 1399, see *HC*, II, 449–454.

21

Evesham, Worcestershire (1406)
Benedictine
(SC 8/23/1105)

The abbot and convent of Evesham petition the king and Lords in parliament because they, and also John Cornwall and Elizabeth, his wife, question the validity of the king's gift to John and Elizabeth, and to Hugh Vertot, proctor of the abbey of Fécamp in England, of the wardship of all the lands and tenements formerly belonging to Fécamp in England, as concerning certain manors in Salmonsbury hundred in Gloucestershire, which seems to be undermined by certain words in an agreement made in the time of Henry III to resolve the competing claims of the monasteries of Evesham and Fécamp in this hundred. They ask the king in this present parliament, and with the advice of the Lords present, to clarify these words.

Endorsed: *It is agreed by the king and the Lords Spiritual and Temporal in parliament that this petition should be sent into chancery, and that the chancellor, calling to himself the justices, the parties and other necessary people, is to have power, by authority of parliament, to do justice to the parties, as seems best to him.*

Whereupon the chancellor, having called the parties before him in chancery, and having heard their arguments in the presence of the justices, with the aforesaid authority and the advice and assent of the justices, has declared and adjudged that the lands, tenements and possessions contained in this petition are sufficiently amortised by licence of the king, without other licence being necessary from the abbot of Fécamp, or John Cornwall or his wife, or Hugh Vertot; and concerning the clause mentioned in this petition, in the agreement between the abbots of Fécamp and Evesham and their convents – that if the hundred of Salmonsbury should at any time be removed from the abbot and convent of Fécamp, the agreement would become invalid until it is returned to them – the chancellor, having carefully examined this clause, has declared and adjudged that the agreement remains valid, notwithstanding the said clause, because the clause is not relevant, as all Fécamp's possessions are in the king's hand as of the right of the abbot and convent, because of the wars between England and France, during these wars, and for no other reason, the chancellor, with the aforesaid authority and the advice and assent of the justices.

A nostre tresredoute et tressovereign seignur le roy et a toutz les seignurs espirituelx et temporelx de cest present parlement supplient voz oratours l'abbe et covent de Evesham qe come eux et lour predecessours ont heue diverses manoirs, c'estassavoir Seint Edward Stowe, Bradewelle, Donintone, Malgaresbury, Tadlesthorpe, Bourghtone, en la contee de Gloucestre, du temps dont memoire ne court, de doune et feoffement de Kenrede, nadgairs roy, vostre progenitour, et la dite abbey est de la fundacioun de voz tresnobles progenitours et de vostre patronage, et les quels manoirs sont dedeins le hundrede de Salomonsbury. Et puis le Roy Henry le primer par sez lettres patentz granta al abbe q'adonqes fuist abbe d'Evesham, en perpetuel almoigne, entre auters libertiez, qe le dit abbe et moignes eiont et tiegnont toutz lour terres et possessions en toutz lieux ou ils eiont terres, bien et en pees, quitement et franchement, come sook et saak, tolle et theam, enfongonthefe, descharge franchement et quitement \de/ shirez et hundredez, plees, quarels, geldez et denegeldez et hidagez, taillage et d'overeigne de chastelx, vivers et pontez, de murdre et de cariage, et de tout manere seculer service et overeigne servyle et d'escuage, savant ent a dit roy et sez heirs iiij fees de chevalers et demy en expedicion le roy present. Et auxint granta as ditz abbe et moignes q'ils eient a Edward Stowe susdite port et merchandise le joefdy checun semaigne. Et qe la dite esglise d'Evesham eit toutz custumez et libertiez a soun eux qeux le dit \Roy/ Henry avoit en toutz sez portz et burghs, come en la dite chartre pleinement est contenuz. Et la quele chartre le Roy Henry, fitz a Roy Johan, vostre tresnoble progenitour, par sa chartre ad ratifie et conferme, l'an de soun regne xxv, come par la dite chartre pleinement apierte. Et puis mesme le Roy Henry, par sa chartre l'an de soun regne xxvj^{me}, graunta a Richard, abbe d'Evesham, et moignes illeoqes Dieu serviantes, et lour successours, q'ils eiont ceste libertie, qe ils par lour mayns, ou par lez mains de lour baillifs, resceivont de toutz lour terrestenantz hommes en queconqes lieux ou ils soient, toutz deniers qeux viscontz ou hundreders, ou lour baillifs, de dit Roy Henry resceiver solent, si bien pur eaide de viscontz, hundreders et baillifs come pur view de franchiplegge, suytz de countez, hundredez, veillez et auters custumes et demandez as viscontz \et/ hundreders, ou \a lour/ baillifs, pertenantz, par lour mayns a dit Roy Henry et sez heirs ent respoignont a l'Escheqer, issint qe viscontz le dit Roy Henry, ou hundreders, ou lour baillifs du dit Roy Henry, ne de sez heirs, n'eient nulle entre en terres ou tenementz le dit abbe, ou sez successours, ne en lour hommes, ne en nulle ent eux entremettont. Par force des quels chartres les ditz suppliantz et lour predecessours ont este seisez peisiblement des fraunchises avauntditz. Et ont heue un baillif a Seint Edward Stowe suisdite pur garder les fraunchisez avauntditz, et les profitz ent provenantz a resceiver, et ent accompter de ceo q'est due a nostre seignur le roy en soun Escheqer, et del remenant as ditz suppliantz et lour predecessours, puis lez confeccions des chartres avauntditz. Et la ou vostre tresnoble progenitour Edward tierce, nadgairs roy d'Engleterre, par sez lettres patentz graunta licence a Johan Whitchirche, pur un fyn qe William abbe, par noune abbe d'Evesham, fist au dit Roy Edward, qe le dit Johan Whitchirche j mees, j carue et j verge de terre, vj acres de pree, xviij s de rent, ove les appurtenancez, en Donintone, Hodecote et Burtone, doner purroit et assigner a dit abbe, par noune \de/ abbe d'Evesham, et soun covent, a tenir as ditz abbe et covent et lour successours en perpetuite. Et dona licence a dit abbe et covent qe eux les avauntditz mees, terre, pree et rent, ove les appurtenantz, de levauntdit Johan Whitchirche resceiver purrent, et tenir a eux et lour successours en perpetuite, par sa chartre de licence de la date le xxvj[me] jour de Septembre l'an de soun reigne quart. Par force de quele grant et licence, le dit Johan Whitchirche dona les ditz mees, terre, pree et rent a dit abbe et covent, a eux et lour successours, dont les ditz suppliantz et lour predecessours puis en cea ont este seisez peisiblement par force de licence et doune avauntditz, et les ditz villez de Donintone et Burtone sont deins le hundrede de Salomonsbury suisdite. Et par la ou le dit Roy Edward, par sez lettres patentz, graunta licence a William Somerville, clerc, pur un fyn qe le dit William, par noune abbe d'Evesham, fist ove le dit Roy Edward qe le dit William Somerville j mees, xv acres et j rode de terre, ij acres de pree, j darre de rent et le rent d'une rose, ov les appartenantz, en Tadlesthorpe, doner purroit et assigner as ditz abbe, par noun de dit abbe et covent de mesme le lieu, a aver et tenir a eux et lour successours en perpetuite. Et dona licence a dit abbe, en noune de dit abbe et covent, qe eux les avauntditz mees, terre, pree et rent, ove les appartenantz, de levauntdit William Somerville receiver purrent, et tener a eux et lour successours en perpetuite, par sa chartre de licence de la date le xij[me] jour de Mars l'an de soun regne xij[me]; par force de quel licence le dit William Somerville dona les ditz mees, terre, pree et rent a dit William, par noun abbe d'Evesham, et covent, a eux et lour successours, dont les ditz suppliantz et lour predecessours puis en cea ont este seisez pesiblement, par force de licence et doune avauntditz, et la dite ville de Tadlesthorpe est en la dit hundrede de Salomonsbury. Et come le dit Roy Henry fitz le Roy Johan, puis les grauntiez des liberties avauntditz par le \dit/ Roy Henry fitz Johan et auters de ses progenitours faitz as predecessours les ditz suppliantz, dona en escheange al abbe et moignes de Fyscampe les manoirs de Chiltenham en la counte de Gloucestre, ove les hundredez et auters appartenantz, et de Sloughtre en mesme la contee, ove le hundrede de Salomonsbury avauntdit, ove les appurtenantz, et de Navesby en la contee de Nicolle, saunz aucune retient, a avoir et tenir as ditz abbe et moignez de Fyscampe en perpetuite, ensi franchement et quitement come devaunt tenoient Wynchelse et le Rye, par cause de doune a eux fait de Seint Edward, et conferment puis heue a William et Henry, nadgairs roys d'Engleterre, de la terre de Stannyngg, ove les appartenantz, entre qeux Wynchelse et la Rye furent rehercez. Et en la chartre du dit William, nadgairs roy d'Engleterre, furent contenuz tieux liberteez, c'estassaver qe les ditz abbe et moignes de Fyscampe eiont la dite terre de Stannyngg, ove toutz les appendantz, et ove toutz leyes et liberties, et frank custumez, quitances, plees, querels, causes qe sont ou purront estre, sanz aucune diminucion de checun seclar ou jugge poair, sicome chose *ad fiscum dominicum pertinentes*. Et qe les ditz abbe et moignes de Fyscampe et lour ministers eiont tout manere roial libertie et custume, et toutz justices de toutz chosez et causez qe en la dite terre viegnent ou purront avener, ne ascun si noun par eux soi ent entremet, dont la date de la dite chartre est l'an du regne le Roy Henry fitz Johan susdites lj. Et puis le dit Roy Henry fitz Johan dona as ditz abbe et moignes de Fyscampe vj li ix s vj d qeux l'abbe d'Evesham soloit paier adevaunt a dit Roy Henry fitz Johan, par viewe de franchiplegge, tethyngpeny, veillez et auters choses assisez en les manoirs du dit abbe d'Evesham en le dit hundrede de Salomonsbury, des qeux les viscontz de Gloucestre solent respondre au roy, a cause qe apartenerent a la ferme du countee de Gloucestre; et unqore le dit abbe d'Evesham ad un baille de respondre au roy de toutz chosez qe sont duez a luy en l'Escheqer annuelment quaunt le viscont de Gloucestre soun accompt rende illeoqes. Et puis, non obstant qe les predecessours les ditz suppliantz furont quitz de shirez et \de/ hundredez, de plees et de querels, et auxi qe null viscont, hundreder, baille, ne lour ministrez, n'averont nulle entre en lour terres, tenementz, ne lour hommes en ascun chose ent soy ne entremetterent, come desuis est declare par les chartres desuis especifiez, un debate estoit moeve entre William, abbe de Fyscampe, et soun covent d'une part et Thomas, abbe d'Evesham, et soun covent d'autre part, de pleez et purchasez de terres, tenementz, et les hommes du dit abbe et covent d'Evesham en le dit hundrede de Salomonsbury provenantz, et de paiement des ditz vj li ix s vj d d'argent pur terres, tenementz et hommes deinz le dit hundrede de Salomonsbury, contenantz en mesme la manere d'avoir les ditz vj li ix s vj d de doune de roy come furont paiez en l'Escheqer a Westm' par les predecessours du dit abbe d'Evesham. Et les ditz parties ent accorderont en temps de Roy Henry fitz Johan suisdite par composicion, c'estassaver qe le dit Thomas, abbe d'Evesham, et soun covent duissent paier annuelment a dit William, abbe de Fyscampe, et soun covent les ditz vj li ix s vj d as deux termes del an, c'estassaver la moite al Hockeday et l'autre moyte al fest de Seint Michelle, et pur plees, querels et perquisitz de terres, tenementz et hommes, de levauntdit abbe d'Evesham et soun covent en le dit hundrede de Salomonsbury provenantz xx s par an, as termes suisdites, issint qe le dit abbe de Fiscampe ne soun covent ne sez successours des ditz terres, tenementz et hommes en temps avener rien duist demander, sinoun les ditz vj li ix s vj d, et pur les ditz plees, querels, perquisitz, les ditz xx s, des qeux vj li ix s vj d et les xx s lez abbe de Fyscampe et sez predecessours ont este seisez peisiblement puis la dite composicion tanqe toutz les possessions qe le dit abbe de Fiscampe ad en Engleterre sont seisez en voz mayns, tresredoute seignur, par cause de guerre moeve entre vous et ceux de France, et en la dite composicion est tiel clause contenuz: 'Et si aveigne le dit hundrede de Salomonsbury a mains de levauntdit abbe et covent de Fyscampe *aliquo tempore diverti*, la dite covenant et composicion doit cesser, tanqe le dit hundrede de Salomonsbury as mains du dit abbe et covent de Fyscampe, ou a lour successours, reverte.' Et puis vous, tresredoute seignur, avez graunte a Johan Cornewaille, chivaler, Elizabeth sa femme et Hugh Vertot, moigne et procutour [*sic*] en vostre roiaume d'Engleterre del abbey de Fyscampe en Normandie, la garde de toutz les terres, tenementz, possessions et libertiez, ove lez appartenantz, qe sont de l'avauntdite abbey en vostre roiaume, forspris le manoir de Bury en les mains le count d'Arundelle esteant, dont Sloughter en le hundrede de Salomonsbury suisditz sont parcelle, a aver a terme de lour vies durant la guerre entre vous et ceux de France, rendant \ent/ a vous et voz heirs solonc ceo q'est contenuz en voz lettres patentz sur ceo faitz. Et puis les ditz Johan Cornewaille et Elizabeth, supposant la purchace faite par la licence le Roy Edward tierce, vostre tresnoble progenitour, as predecessours le dit abbe d'Evesham, ore suppliant, des mees, terres, prees, rentz, ove les appartenantz, en les ditz villes de Donintone, Burtone et Tadlesthorpe estre de meins value, a cause qe la dite licence duist avoir este graunte par l'abbe de Fyscampe suisdite, ent tant qe les ditz villes sont deinz le hundrede de Salomonsbury, es qeux abbe de Fyscampe avoit roial libertie, coment qe les ditz tenementz ne soient tenuz de dit abbe de Fyscampe, issint qe sanz avoir licence de luy tiel amortisment ne purroit estre fait effectuel par la ley, come ils supposent, et en tant qe la dite libertie est seise en les mains de roy et comys as ditz Johan Cornwaille, Elizabeth et Hugh, en manere come desuis est dit, les ditz Johan Cornwaille et Elizabeth ont seisez les ditz tenementz come forfaitz pur defaute de licence du dit abbe de Fyscampe, ou le dit abbe n'avoit nulle tiel libertie, ne purroit par la chartre le dit Roy Henry fitz Johan, a cause qe l'estatut de religiouses puis en cea fuist fait en temps le Roy Edward fitz le dit Roy Henry, l'an de soun reigne septisme, et auxint qe en la dite composicion est la dite clause, c'estassaver 'Et si aveigne le dit hundrede de Salmonsbury a mains de levauntdit abbe et covent de Fyscampe *aliquo tempore diverti*, la dit covenant et composicion doit cesser, tanqe le dit hundrede de Salmonsbury as mains du dit abbe et covent de Fyscampe, ou a lour successours, reverte.' Les quels materes ont este tretez et debatuz entre les ditz abbe d'Evesham et Johan Cornwaille et Elizabeth avauntditz, les ditz suppliantz, et auxi les ditz Johan Cornwaille et Elizabeth, vous enpriantz de vostre roial majeste defaire en cest present parlement, par advys de les seignurs de dit parlement, adeclarer la dite clause et l'effect d'icelle solonc ceo qe la ley voet, en eaide de voz ditz oratours, et pur peser les ditz debatez, si les ditz licences faitz et grauntez par vostre tresnoble progentiour, le dit Edward le tierce, des tenementz en les ditz villes de Donintone, Burtone et Tadlesthorpe, en manere come desuis est declare, soient suffisantz sanz avoir licence du dit abbe de Fyscampe, ou noun, en plein declaracion de vostre regalie. Et auxint coment le dit abbe d'Evesham ad heue un baille de Stowe avauntdit de tout temps, en manere come desuis est dit, et la clause en la composicion avauntdit, c'estassaver 'Et si aveigne le dit hundrede de Salomonsbury a mains de levauntdit abbe et covent de Fyscampe *aliquo tempore diverti*, la dit covenant et composicioun doit cesser, tanqe le dit hundrede de Salomonsbury as ditz abbe et covent de Fyscampe, ou a lour successours, reverte.' Par quel clause aucuns sont en opinioun qe la dit composicion serra voide en celle parcelle, en tant qe fuist seise en voz mains par cause de guerre ou le frank tenement nientmeins est continue tout temps en les mains du dit abbe de Fyscampe. Et auxi le dit Hugh Veritot, moigne, est un d'eux q'ad la possessioun, et ascuns, nient obstante cest clause, et les maters avauntditz, tiegnont la dite composicioun bone et effectuel. Que plese auxint a vostre roial mageste de faire en cest present parlement, par advys de les seignurs du dit parlement, adeclarer la dite clause et l'effect d'icelle solonc ceo qe la ley voet, en eade et tranquillite de voz ditz oratours, et pur peser les batez avauntditz pur toutz jours, pur Dieu et en oevre de charitee.

Endorsed: Accordez est par le roy et les seignurs espirituelx et temporelx en parlement qe cest peticioun soit envoiez en la Chancellerie, et eit le chanceller, appellez a luy les justices et auxint les parties et auters qe sont a appeller en celle partie, poair par auctorite de parlement de faire droit as dites parties selonc ceo qe mielx luy sembler en le cas.
Sur quoy le dit chanceller appelluz devaunt luy en la Chancellerie les parties suisdites, et oiez et entenduz lour raisons en presence des ditz justices, de l'auctorite suisdite et de l'advis et assent de mesmes les justices, ad declarrez, adjuggez et agardez, et declare, adjugge et agarde, qe les terres, tenementz et possessions amortisez comprisez en cest peticioun sont sufficientment et duement amortisez par licence du roy, sanz autre licence avoir ou suir de l'abbe de Fyscampe, ou de Monsire Johan Cornwaille, ou de sa compaigne, ou de Hugh Veritot, moigne

et procuratour du ditz abbe de Fiscampe deinzescriptz. Et touchant la clause comprise en ycest peticioun de la composicioun fait parentre l'abbe de Fiscampe et soun covent et l'abbe d'Evesham et soun covent – qe s'il adviegne le hundrede de Salmonsbury as mayns de l'avauntdit abbe et covent de Fiscampe *aliquo tempore diverti*, la dite covenant et composicioun doit cesser tanqe le dit hundrede de Salomonsbury as mayns du dite abbe et covent de Fiscampe, ou a lour successours, reverte – le dit chanceller diligealment examinez la dite clause de *diverti*, par tant qe la dite clause n'est pas en le cas pur les ditz abbe et covent de Fiscampe, a cause qe toutz les possessions de mesmes les abbe et covent de Fiscampe sont as mayns de nostre seignur le roy come en droit des ditz abbe et covent de Fiscampe, a cause des guerres moevez parentre les roiaumes d'Engleterre et de France durantz mesmes les guerres, et par nulle autre voie, le dit chanceller, de l'advys et assent des ditz justicez et par l'auctorite suisdite, ad declarez, adjuggez et agardez, et declare, adjugge et agarde, la dite composicioun bone sufficiente et vaillable pur les ditz abbe et covent de Evesham, non obstante la dite clause de *diverti* comprise en ycelle composicioun, come en ycest peticioun pluis pleinement est contenuz.

1406. Sir John Cornwall (Cornwaile), Henry IV's brother-in-law, had, along with the monks' bailiff in England, acquired all Fécamp's English lands in 1403, and when the bailiff died in 1409 he wrote, apparently in his own hand, to the abbot of Fécamp proposing to lease the house's English lands for 100 or 120 years. In 1414 Henry V founded Sheen Priory (Carthusian), endowing it with the reversion of Fécamp's lands then held by Cornwall: D. Matthew, *Norman Monasteries and their English Possessions* (Oxford, 1962), pp. 123, 124, 127, 164–5; for general background ibid., pp. 120–33. On 12 July 1406 an exemplification was granted which incorporated the tenor of this petition, the agreement, mentioned within it, between Thomas, then abbot of Evesham, and William, abbot of Fécamp, concerning lands in Salmonsbury hundred, and the king's response to the petition (*CPR 1405–8*, p. 212). The petition, therefore, must have been presented at the parliament of March 1406 by Roger Zatton, abbot 1379–1418. Abbot Richard was Richard le Gras (1236–42), and Abbot William was William of Chiriton (1316–44). Thomas, abbot of Evesham was either Thomas of Marlborough (1230–36) or Thomas of Gloucester (1243–55). The earl of Arundel was Thomas Fitz Alan (1400–15). Thomas Langley was the chancellor at this time. An earlier edition of the petition is printed in *RP*, III, 561–3, no. 5.

2.1 The king's ministers

22

Owston, Leicestershire (1279–1300)
Augustinian canons
(SC 8/133/6620)

The abbot of Owston petitions for a remedy concerning Ralph Malore, keeper of the forest of Rutland, and others concerning the manor of Withcote, which the abbot holds of the king. Malore prevents the abbot from having his issues and profits from the woods pertaining to the manor, cuts down and sells his brambles, prevents the abbot from using the king's mill, cuts down the hedges surrounding the manor's fields, has wrongly imprisoned the abbot's men of Withcote and has taken sheep from the abbot's common, amongst other things.

Ce ... mustre le abbe de Osulvestone ke la ou il prist le maner de Wytekok ov les apurtenances ke est de le demeine le roys a terme, rendant a le Chekere plus au duble ke unkes ne soleyt rendre par le bayl Sire Ricar de Holebroc e tus les fermers un ou la garde del boys apurtenant au maner, e tus lez issues e profis deu boys, cum de cabys, paunage, noyz e autre plusurs choses Rauf Maulure, forester de Roteland, tuz les choses avant nomes issant du boys lur desturbe e de force en cuntre la furme du bayl le roys, a grant damage de le abbe.
Derichef meme le Rauf abati e vendi en la vandist boys le roys arables espines e autre fust dunt il ad esleve grant argent au damage le roys.
Derichef memes celi Rauf desturbe le abbe de aver franche entre e issue au molin le roys, pur le quel le abbe pae sa ferme, e le abbe ne put aver poer due molyn garder, dunt le molyn est dechaet par sa desturbance e le merin enporte, a damage le roys e le abbe.
De autre part il cravente e abat les hays en tur les champs le avantdist maner ke tus jurs unt este pur les blez sauver par unt checun an sunt destrus, a grant damage le abbe.
Meme celi forester prent les gent le abbe en Wytekok s.. mis enditement e les en prisdune e le reynt sa volunte ke a peyne qe nul demorer ilekes.
Meme celi Rauf prent les motouns le abbe en sa commune, e lez tent en cuntre ley, e uncore retent partie.
Meme celi Rauf prit les chens le abbe en sa cusyne dens sa abbey ke est hors de la foreste. E fit arder a tort le porcherye le abbe ki il tuz jurs ad en hors de la foreste. E fet fourner se chivaus e sez genz cuntre le estatut en le abbey avantdite.

No endorsement

1279–1300. Edward I granted custody of the forest of Rutland for life to Ralph Malore on 15 November 1279 (*CPR 1272–81*, p. 335); he retained custody until 1300, when it was granted to another (*CPR 1292–1301*, p. 533). The identity of the petitioner cannot be established as a succession of six men held the office of abbot of Owston during these years.

23

Westminster (1310–24)
Benedictine
(SC 8/149/7411)

The abbot and convent of Westminster petition the king and council, stating that in the time of Richard of Ware, formerly abbot of Westminster and treasurer of England, the abbey used to provide bread and ale for the clerks in the exchequer and the receipt as a courtesy, and that they have since claimed this as a right, to the great harm of the abbey. They request a good inquisition into this, as they claim that it never happened before Richard of Ware's time, and was only a courtesy in his day.
Endorsed on face: *William of Bereford, John of Benstead and John of Foxley.*[3]
Endorsed: *The treasurer and barons of the exchequer are to be ordered that, having called before them the justices of the Bench, they are to inquire into the contents of the petition, and*

3 Possibly part of the petition rather than of the endorsement.

whether the aforementioned bread and ale was first granted out of the pure liberality of the aforesaid abbot, for a certain period of his will, or whether the aforesaid bread and ale should be given out of duty or not; and if from duty then by whose grant, and from when, and by what right and in what way; and if from grace, then by whom was this grace given and when and by what right and in what way. And they are to inform the king of what they find.

A nostre seignur le roi et a son conseil prient l'abbe et le covent de Weystmouster qe come Richard de Ware jadis abbe de Weystmouster et tresorer nostre seignur le roi, qi mort est, eust plusurs foitz de an corteysie taunt come il fuit tresorer fit liverer hors du celer de la dite maison payn et cervoise pur les divers des clerks del Escheqer et de la Rescite, et les clerks ...s meismes les places par reson de cel cortoisie ount puis chalenge de droit certeyne livere de payn et cervoise, c'est assaver duex payns et trois galons de bon cervoise checun jour pur lour diners, et l'ount resceu et unqore resceivount par extorsion et par destresce en l'Escheqer des busoignes des dite abbe et covent en grant prejudice et damage de la dite meison, plese a nostre seignur le roi et a son conseil comaunder qe bon en quest soit pris sur cest bosoigne qe cele livere cesse et seit sustrete desicome atient le temps le dit Abbe Richard unqes ne fu donee ne en son temps fors par cortoisie ne puis fore par excepsion et destresce come avaunt est dit.

Endorsed on face: Sire William de Bereford, Sire Johan de Benestede et Sire Johan de Foxle.
Endorsed: Mandetur thesaurio et baronibus de Scaccario quod, assumptis sibi justiciis de Banco, inquirend' sur contentis in peticione, et utrum panis et cervisia infrascripta primitus concessi fuerunt ex mera liberalitate predicti abbatis per aliquid tempus pro voluntate sua percipiend', vel quod panis et cervisia predicti ex debito solui debent nec ne; et si ex debito, tunc per cuius concessionem, et a quo tempore et qualiter et in quo modo; et si ex gracia, tunc per quem, huius-modi gracia concessa fuerit, et a quo tempore et qualiter et quo modo. Et de eo quod invenerint certificent regem.

1310–24. The petition must date to before the deaths of John of Foxley in 1324 and of John of Benstead in c. 1323, and probably after the appointments of Foxley as baron of the exchequer, of Benstead as justice of Common Pleas, and of Bereford as chief justice of Common Pleas all in 1309. Since the petitioner describes himself as abbot, rather than abbot-elect, the petition cannot have been presented before 1310 when Richard of Kedynton, alias of Sudbury, was confirmed as abbot. Either he or his successor, William of Curtlyngton, abbot 1315–33, is the petitioner. Richard Ware was abbot of Westminster 1258–83, and occurs as treasurer of England 18 June 1280. SC 8/78/3881 is a duplicate of this petition with a different endorsement which reads: 'The treasurer and barons of the exchequer are ordered to call before them the ministers of the exchequer referred to in the petition, in the presence of the abbot, as to whether bread and ale was given of old, or more recently introduced. The king is to be certified upon this.' For an earlier transcript of this petition, see no. 101 of PRO 31/7/95.

24

Battle, Sussex (1318–27)
Benedictine
(SC 8/32/1558)

The abbot of Battle petitions the king and council, complaining that the keepers of the king's market and the keepers of the alnage have entered the franchise of his abbey at Wye to perform their office there, and by distraint have levied fines and amercements from his men, contrary to the charters granted to the abbey by the king's ancestors and confirmed by the king, and without regard for the abbot's challenge or the king's command to respect the abbot's franchises.
Endorsed: *He is to have a writ pleadable before the king against the clerk of the king's market and alnager, to answer there why, contrary to the tenor of the charters, they have entered the abbot's liberty to exercise their office, contrary to the king's command, and why they do not let him have the amercements of his men etc.; and justice is to be done to him there.*
Before the great council.

A nostre seignur le roy e a son consail mustre le abbe dela Bataille qe come les auncestres nostre seignur le roy qe ore est par leur chartres eyent grauntez al eglise Seyn Martyn dela Bataille q'ele eyt sa court par tout e reale fraunchise e custume, a treter de ses bosoigne e a tenir droit par eux meismes, e qe yl seyent quites de totes manere des servitutes, e qe nule justice ne nul ministre nostre seignur le roy se entremettent ses terres, possessions nes des hommes dela dite eglise, e qe le dit abbe eyt les amerciementz de luy e de ses hommes, fyns e redempciouns de touz ses hommes, les queux fraunchises nostre seignur le roy qe ore est ad conferme, les gardeyns del marche nostre seignur le rey e les gardeyns des aunages encountre les poynts des fraunchises susdites entrent la fraunchise le dit abbe a Wy, fesantz leynz leur office, e par destresce ount levez fyns e amerciementz des hommes le dit abbe, nyent eyantz regard au chalenge le abbe ne al maundement nostre seignur le roy a eux fait qe eux la fraunchise le abbe allouatent.

Endorsed: Habeat breve placitabile coram rege versus clericum de mercato et ulnatorem regis, ad respondendum ibidem quare, contra tenorem cartarum, ingressi sunt libertatem abbatis ad officium suum excercendum, \contra mandatum regis/, et quare non permittant ipsum habere amerciamenta hominum suorum etc.; et ibidem fiat ei justicia.
Coram magno consilio.

1318–27. On 4 October 1312 Edward II confirmed the abbot of Battle's charter: *CChR 1300–26*, p. 195. On 6 July 1318 the abbot of Battle was granted cognisance of all assizes and juries within the house's liberty (*CCR 1313–18*, p. 556). Taking the references to the confirmation of charters in 1312 and to the grant of cognisance in 1318 as limiting it to the reign of Edward II, this petition must date to 1318–27. Thus the petitioner is either Roger of Pevensey, abbot 1318–24, or Alan of Retlyng, abbot 1324–51. Other related petitions from the abbot of Battle, concerning Wye, are SC 8/15/737 and SC 8/34/1658 (below, **37**).

25

Byland, NRY (1322)
Cistercian
(SC 8/204/10190)

The abbot and convent of Byland petition the king and council for remedy. They have had and used the liberty of the chase of Middlesmoor, and have had a forester to keep the venison with the forester of Lord Mowbray, according to a fine made in the king's court, and were peaceably seised of this until the death of John of Mowbray, by whose forfeiture the forest has come into the king's hand, and now they are disturbed by Richard of Cardel and John of Kilvington, the king's bailiffs and keepers of the forest of Nidderdale.

A nostre seyngur le roy e a soen counseil mustrunt l'abbe e le covent de Beylaund qe come eux \devient e/ solaynt avoir e user fraunche chace en Middelismore denz la forest de Nidderdale pur chacer e fair chacer a lour volunte, e de avoir lour forester gardaunt la veneysone en meisme la forest ove le forister le seingnurs de Moubray, solom ceo q'est contenue en une fine leve en la curt le roy, sicome apirt par le tranescrit \de la fin/ atache a cest present peticion, de quele choses les avauntditz abbe e covent unt este peysablement seysez toutz jours puis la sesauns de l'avaundit fine tank apres la mort Johan de Moubray, \par qi forfetour la dite foreste devint en la mein le roi/, qe eux sunt desturbez par Richard de Cardel et Johan de Kilvingtone, baillifs e gardeins \en nom nostre seignur le roi/ de la forest avandist, dunc eux prient remedie.

No endorsement

1322. The petitioner, John of Myton, was elected abbot of Byland on 11 July 1322. This petition was probably one of his first acts as abbot, as all the associated documents, except the fine, date to August 1322 (SC 8/204/10192–6) and Kilvington was ordered to deliver the forest to the abbot on 9 August 1322 (*CCR 1318–23*, p. 588). For the endorsement to this petition, see SC 8/204/10191, below. John of Mowbray was an adherent of Thomas of Lancaster, was captured at the battle of Boroughbridge and hanged at York on 23 March 1322: R. E. Archer, 'Mowbray, John (I), second Lord Mowbray (1286–1322)', *ODNB*. He was a descendant of Roger de Mowbray, who founded the abbey at Byland in 1177: *MRH*, pp. 116–17. John Mowbray confirmed the abbey's right to pasture in Middlesmoor in April 1321: *The Cartulary of Byland Abbey*, ed. J. Burton, Surtees Society 208 (Woodbridge, 2004), no. 660.

(SC 8/204/10191)

Copy of a final concord, made in the third week of Michaelmas 1245 at Westminster before Roger of Thirkleby, between Henry, abbot of Byland, and Roger of Mowbray, whereby Mowbray acknowledges the forest of Middlesmoor to be the right of the abbot and his church as that which the abbot's predecessors had of the gift of Mowbray's father, to hold with rights to assart and build, saving Mowbray's rights to hunt in the same.
Endorsed: *They should show the fine in chancery, and the king should be certified concerning the manner and cause of the impediment, and if necessary the truth of the matter should be enquired into, and justice done.*

Hec est finalis concordia facta in curia domini regis apud Westm' a die Sancti Michaelis in tres septimanas anno regni Regis Henrici xxx^{mo} tercio coram Rogero de Thurkelby etc., inter Henricum, abbatem de Bella Landa, querentem, et Rogerum de Moubray, deforciantem, de foresta de Middelesmor' in Nidderdale cum pertinenciis, unde placitum convencionis summonitum fuit inter eos in eadem curia, scilicet, quod predictus Rogerus recognoverat totam predictam forestam cum pertinenciis, tam subtus terram quam supra terram, esse jus ipsius abbatis et ecclesie sue de Bella Landa ut illam quam predecessores predicti abbatis et ecclesia sua predicta habuerunt ex dono Willelmi de Moubray, patris predicti Rogeri, cuius heres ipsi est, habendum et tenendum eidem abbati et successoribus suis et ecclesie sue predicte de predicto Rogero et heredibus suis imperpetuum. Ita quod bone licebit eidem abbati et successoribus suis predictam forestam assartere et arare et in eadem edificare ubicumque voluerit, salvis eidem Rogero et heredibus suis feris in eadem foresta capiendis, ita quod possent venari in eadem foresta ad omnimodas ferias in ea capiendas quibus modis voluerint. Et quod habeant unum forestarium tantum in eadem foresta ad venacionem custodiendam una cum forestario ipsius abbatis vel successorum suorum, et abbas et succesores sui facient venari in predicta foresta quando et quibus modis voluerint ad omnimodas feras capiendas. Et sciendum quod nullus se intromittet de venacione in predicta foresta custodienda tanquam forestarius nisi forestarius predicti Rogeri et heredum suorum et forestarius predicti abbatis vel successorum suorum. Ita quod si canes predicti abbatis vel successorum suorum aliquam feram prosequti [*sic*] fuerint extra metas predicte foreste sue de Midelesmor' usque in forestam ipsius Rogeri vel heredum suorum bene licebit eidem abbati et successoribus suis canes suos revocare ore e tornu usque ad metam foresti sue de Middilesmorr', et idem Rogerus et heredes sui warantizabunt, aquietabunt etc.

Endorsed: Ostendant finem in Cancellaria, et certificetur rex super modo et causa impedimenti, et si necesse fuerit inquiratur veritas, et ulterius fiat justicia etc.

Henry of Battersby was abbot of Byland from 1230 to1268. Roger of Mowbray was John of Mowbray's paternal grandfather; William of Mowbray was Roger's father and John's great-grandfather.

(SC 8/204/10192)

Writ of Edward II, dated 1 August 1322, to William of Herlaston and Richard of Aldeburgh assigning them to hold an inquisition by jury into the complaint made by petition by John, abbot of Byland, concerning the forest of Middlesmoor in Nidderdale, which he and his predecessors have held since the gift of William of Mowbray, and by fine of Roger of Mowbray until the forfeiture of John of Mowbray when the forest was taken into the king's hand.

Edwardus, Dei gracia rex Anglie, dominus Hibernie et dux Aquitanie, dilectis et fidelibus suis Willelmo de Herlaston' et Ricardo de Aldeburgh salutem. Monstravit nobis dilectus nobis in Cristo Johannes, abbas de Bella Landa, per peticionem suam coram nobis et consilio nostro exhibitam, quod cum Rogerus Moubray dudum per finem in curia domini Henrici, quondam regis Anglie, avi nostri, anno regni sui tricesimo tercio coram tunc justiciis suis de Banco, inter Henricum, tunc abbatem de Bella Landa, querentem, et predictum Rogerum, deforciantem, de foresta de Middelesmore in Nitherdale cum pertinenciis, levatum recognovisset predictam forestam cum pertinenciis, tam subtus terram quam supra terram, esse jus ipsius tunc abbatis et ecclesie sue de Bella Landa ut illam quam predecessores predicti abbatis et ecclesia sua predicta habuerunt ex dono Willelmi de Moubray, patris predicti Rogeri, cuius heres ipse fuit, habendum et tenendum eidem abbati et successoribus suis et ecclesie sue predicte de predicto Rogero et heredibus suis imperpetuum. Ita quod bene liceret eidem abbati et successoribus suis predictam forestam assartare et arare et in eadem edificare ubicumque voluerint, salvis eidem Rogero et heredibus suis feris in eadem foresta capiendis, ita quod possint venari in eadem foresta ad omnimodas feras in ea capiendas quibus modis voluerint. Et quod habeant in eadem foresta tam unum forestarium ad venacionem custodiendam una cum forestario ipsius abbatis vel successorum suorum, et quod idem abbas et successores sui facerent venari in predicta foresta quando et quibus modis vellent ad omnimodas feras capiendas. Et quod nullus se intromitteret et de venacione in predicta foresta custodienda tanquam forestarius nisi forestarius predicti Rogeri et heredum suorum et forestarius predicti abbatis et successorum suorum. Ita quod si canes predicti abbatis vel successorum suorum aliquam feram prosecuti fuissent extra metas predicte foreste sue de Middelesmore usque in forestam ipsius Rogeri vel heredum suorum bene liceret eidem abbati et successoribus suis canes suos revocare, ore et tornu usque ad metam foreste sue de Middelesmore, prout in fine predicto plenius continetur. Et licet predictus Johannes, abbas, et predecessores sui, abbates eiusdem loci, semper hactenus a tempore levacionis finis predicti de predicta foresta de Middelesmore pacifice seisiti fuerint, et idem abbas et predecessores sui predicti libera chacea in eadem foresta usi fuerint, et feras ibidem ad voluntatem suam ceperint, ac forestarium suum in foresta illa ad venacionem custodiendam una cum forestario predicti Rogeri et heredum suorum habuerint et ministri tamen nostri parcium illarum nuper per forisfactum Johannis de Moubray dictam forestam de Middelesmore, ac si eiusdem Johannis fuisset cum non fuerit una cum terris et tenementis que fuerunt eiusdem Johannis ceperunt in manum nostram et ipsum abbatem libera chacea sua predicta uti, seu feras ibidem capere, aut forestarium suum ibidem habere, prout ibidem habere debet juxta tenorem finis predicti, nullatenus permittentes in ipsius abbatis dispendum non modicum et exheredacionis ecclesie sue predicte periculum manifestum super quo nobis supplicavit sibi remedium adhiberi. Nos igitur, super premissis certiorari volentes, assignavimus vos ad inquirendum per sacramentum proborum et legalium hominum de comitatem Ebor' per quos rei veritas melius sciri poterit in presencia custodis nostre foreste predicte per vos super hoc premuniendi utrum prefatus abbas et predecessores sui predicti seisinam suam de predicta foresta de Middelesmore pacifice continuaverint, et libera chacea sua ibidem usi fuerint, et feras ad eorum voluntatem ibidem ceperint, ac forestarium suum ibidem in forma predicta habuerunt, a tempore levacionis finis predicti usque ad tempus dicte captionis in manum nostram nec ne, et si sic tunc qualiter et quo modo, et si idem abbas vel predecessores sui predicti statum suum in premissis post levacionem finis predicti, in aliquo mittaverint nec ne, et si sic tunc in quibus et qualiter et quo modo et quo tempore dicta foresta capta fuit in manum nostram, et per quem et ex qua causa et de aliis articulis premissa contingentibus plenius veritatem. Et ideo vobis mandamus quod ad certos diem et locum quos ad hoc provideritis inquisicionem illam facere, et eam distincte et aperte factam sub sigillis vestris et sigillis eorum per quos facta fuerit sine dilacione mittatis. Et hoc breve mandamus enim vicecomite comitatis predicti quod ad certos diem et locum quos ei scire faciatis, venire faciat coram vobis tot et tali probos et legales homines de balliva sua per quos rei veritas in premissis melius sciri poterit et inquiri, et custodi nostro predicto quod ad eosdem diem et locum capcioni inquisicionis illius intersitis ad proponend' in hac parte quod pro nobis fore viderit proponendum. In cuius rei testimonium has litteras nostras fieri fecimus patentes. Teste me ipso apud Novum Castrum super Tynam primo die Augusti anno regni nostri sextodecimo.

No endorsement

(SC 8/204/10193)

Writ of Edward II, dated 1 August 1322, to the sheriff of Yorkshire ordering him to empanel a jury to be before William of Herlaston and Richard of Aldeburgh at a day and place that they will make known to him for an inquisition into the complaint made by petition by John, abbot of Byland, concerning the forest of Middlesmoor in Nidderdale, which he and his predecessors have held since the gift of William of Mowbray, and by fine of Roger of Mowbray until the forfeiture of John of Mowbray when the forest was taken into the king's hand.
Endorsed on face: *By petition of the council.*
Endorsed: *It was mandated to the bailiff of Claro that he render by jury the attached writ.*

Edwardus, Dei gracia rex Anglie, dominus Hibernie et dux Aquitanie, vicecomiti Ebor' salutem. Monstravit nobis dilectus nobis in Cristo Johannes, abbas de Bella Landa, per peticionem suam coram nobis et consilio nostro exhibitam, quod cum Rogerus de Moubray dudum per finem in curia domini Henrici, quondam regis Anglie, avi nostri, anno regni sui tricesimo tertio coram tunc justiciis suis \de/ Banco, inter Henricum, tunc abbatem de Bella Landa, querentem, et predictum Rogerum, deforciantem, de foresta de Middelesmore in Netherdale cum pertinenciis levatum recognovisset totam predictam forestam cum pertinenciis, tam subtus terram quam supra terram, esse jus ipsius tunc abbatis et ecclesie sue de Bella Landa ut illam quam predecessores predicti abbatis et ecclesia sua predicta habuerunt ex dono Willelmi de Moubray, patris predicti Rogeri, cuius heres ipse fuit, habendum et tenendum eidem abbati et successoribus suis et ecclesie sue predicte de predicto Rogero et heredibus suis imperpetuum. Ita quod bene liceret eidem abbati et successoribus suis predictam forestam assartare et arare et in eadem edificare ubicumque voluerint, salvis eidem Rogero et heredibus suis feris in eadem foresta capiendis, ita quod possint venari in eadem foresta ad omnimodas feras in ea capiendas quibus modis voluerint. Et quod habeant in eadem foresta tam unum forestarium ad venacionem custodiendam una cum forestario ipsius abbatis vel successorum suorum, et quod idem abbas et successores sui facerent venari in predicta foresta quando et quibus modis vellent ad omnimodas feras capiendas. Et quod nullus se intromitteret et de venacione in predicta foresta custodienda tanquam forestarios nisi forestarius predicti Rogeri et heredum suorum et forestarius predicti abbatis et successorum suorum. Ita quod si canes predicti abbatis vel successorum suorum aliquam feram prosecuti fuissent extra metas predicte foreste sue de Middelesmore usque in forestam ipsius Rogeri vel heredum suorum, bene liceret eidem abbati et successoribus suis canes suos revocare ore et tornu usque ad metam foreste sue de Middelesmore, prout in fine predicto plenius continetur. Et licet predictus Johannes, abbas, et predecessores sui, abbates eiusdem loci, semper hactenus a tempore levacionis finis predicti de predicta foresta de Middelesmore pacifice seisiti fuerint, et idem abbas et predecessores sui predicti libera chacea in eadem foresta usi fuerint, et feras ibidem ad voluntatem suam ceperint, ac forestarium suum in foresta illa ad venacionem custodiendam una cum forestario predicti Rogeri et heredum suorum habuerint, et ministri tamen nostri parcium illarum nuper per forisfactum Johannis de Moubray dictam forestam de Middelesmore, ac si eiusdem Johannis fuisset cum non fuerit una cum terris et tenementis que fuerunt eiusdem Johannis ceperunt in manum nostram et ipsum abbatem libera chacea sua predicta uti, seu feras ibidem capere, aut forestarium suum ibidem habere, prout ibidem habere debet juxta tenorem finis predicti, nullatenus permittentes in ipsius abbatis dispendum non modicum et exheredacionis ecclesie sue predicte periculum manifestum super quo nobis supplicavit sibi remedium adhiberi. Nos igitur, super premissis certiorari volentes, assignavimus dilectos et fideles nostros Willelmum de Herlaston' et Ricardum de Aldeburgh' ad inquirendum per sacramentum proborum et legalium hominum de comitatem Ebor' per quos rei veritas melius sciri poterit in presencia custodis nostri foreste predicte per ipsos Willelmum et Ricardum super hoc premuniendi utrum prefatus abbas et predecessores sui predicti seisinam suam de predicta foresta de Middelesmore pacifice continuaverunt, et libera chacea sua ibidem usi fuerunt, et feras ad eorum voluntatem ibidem ceperunt, ac forestarium suum ibidem in forma predicta habuerunt, a tempore levacionis finis predicti usque ad tempus dicte captionis in manum nostram nec ne, et si sic tunc qualiter et quo modo, et si idem abbas vel predecessores sui predicti statum suum in premissis post levacionem finis predicti, in aliquo mittaverint nec ne, et si sic tunc in quibus et qualiter et quo modo et quo tempore dicta foresta capta fuit in manum nostram, et per quem et ex qua causa et de aliis articulis premissa contingentibus plenius veritatem. Et ideo tibi precipimus quod ad certos diem et locum quos iidem Willemus et Ricardus tibi scire faciant, venire facias coram eis tot et tales probos et legales homines de balliva tua per quos rei veritas in premissis melius sciri poterit et inquiri. Et habeas ibi hoc breve. Teste me ipso apud Novum Castrum super Tynam primo die Augusti anno regni nostri sextodecimo.

Endorsed on face: Per peticionem de consilio.
Endorsed: Mandatum fuit ballivo de Clarhou qui respondit per panellum huic brevi attachiato.

The writ is addressed to Simon Warde, sheriff of Yorkshire from 1318 to 1323.

(SC 8/204/10194)

Writ of Edward II, dated 1 August 1322, to the keeper of the forest of Middlesmoor in Nidderdale that, at the day and place to be made known to him by William of Herlaston and Richard of Aldeburgh, he should attend the inquisition to say what is to the king's best interest concerning the complaint made by petition by John, abbot of Byland, concerning the forest of Middlesmoor in Nidderdale, which he and his predecessors have held since the fine of Roger of Mowbray until the forfeiture of John of Mowbray when the forest was taken into the king's hand.
Endorsed on face: *By petition of the council.*

Edwardus, Dei gracia rex Anglie, dominus Hibernie et dux Aquitanie, dilecto sibi custodi foreste de Middelesmore in Netherdale in manu nostra existentis salutem. Cum asignavimus dilectos et fideles nostros Willelmum de Herlaston' et Ricardum de Aldeburgh' ad inquirendum per sacramentum proborum et legalium hominum de comitatu Ebor' per quos rei veritas melius sciri poterit utrum Johannes, abbas de Bella Landa, et predecessores sui, abbates eiusdem loci, seisinam suam de predicta foresta de Middelesmore quam clamat tenere sibi et successoribus suis per finem inde in curia domini Henrici, quondam regis Anglie, avi nostri, anno regni sui vicesimo tercio coram tunc justiciis suis de Banco, inter Henricum, tunc abbatem de Bella \Landa/, predecessorem predicti Johannis abbatis, querentem, et Rogerum de Moubray, deforciantem, de predicta foresta de Middelesmore \ac pertinenciis/ levatum pacifice continuaverunt, et libera chacea \sua/ ibidem usi fuerunt, et feras ad eorum voluntatem ibidem ceperunt, ac forestarium suum in eadem foresta ad venacionem custodiendam una cum forestario predicti Rogeri et heredum suorum habuerint, a tempore levacionis finis predicti usque ad tempus quo dicta foresta de Middelesmore nuper per forisfactum Johannis de Moubray, ac si eiusdem Johannis fuisset cum non fuerit una cum terris et tenementis que fuerunt eiusdem Johannis capta fuit in manum nostram, et si sic tunc qualiter et quo modo, et si idem abbas vel predecessores sui predicti statum suum in premissis post levacionem finis predicti, in aliquo mittaverint nec ne, et si sic tunc in quibus et qualiter et quo modo et quo tempore dicta foresta capta fuit in manum nostram, et per quem et ex qua causa et de aliis articulis premissa contingentibus plenius veritatem, vobis mandamus quod ad certos diem et locum quos isdem Willelmus et Ricardus vobis scire faciant, capcioni inquisicionis illius intersitis ad proponendum in hac parte quod pro nobis fore videritis proponendum. \Et habeatis ibi hoc breve./ Teste me ipso apud Novum Castrum super Tynam primo die Augusti anno regni nostri sextodecimo.

Endorsed on face: Per peticionem de consilio.

(SC 8/204/10196)

Writ of Edward II, dated 1 August 1322, to John of Kilvington, keeper of the forest of Nidderdale, commanding him to certify the manner and cause of the taking of the forest of Nidderdale into the king's hand.
Endorsed on face: *Knaresborough.*
Endorsed: *Thomas of Burgh, the king's escheator, seized the forest of Nidderdale that was John de Mowbray's and the chace of Middlesmoor into the king's hand because he was given to understand that the chace was the right of Mowbray. Burgh delivered it to Kilvington by writ of the king and the forest and chace remain in the king's hand.*

Edwardus, Dei gracia rex Anglie, dominus Hibernie et dux Aquitanie, dilecto \sibi/ Johanni de Kilvyngton', custodi foreste de Niderdale in manu nostra quisbusdam de causis existentis, salutem. Quia quibusdam certis de causis certiorari, volumus super modo et causa capcionis foreste abbatis de Bella Landa de Midelesmore per vos in manum nostram facte ut dicitur, vobis mandamus quod nos super modo et causa predictis sub sigillo vestro distincte et aperte sine dilacione reddatis certiores hoc breve nobis remittentes. Teste me ipso apud Novum Castrum super Tynam primo die Augusti anno regni nostri sextodecimo.

Endorsed on face: Knaresburgh'.

Endorsed: Thomas de Burgh', eschaetor domini regis, seisivit totam forestam de Niddersdal quod fuit Johannis de Mowbray in manum domini regis, et dictam chaceam de Middelsmores, quia intellexit quod dicta chacea de Middelsmor fuit jus ipsius Johannis, et dictus Thomas, per breve domini regis et per indenturam mihi liberavit predictam chaceam de Nidderdal simil cum predicta chacea de Middelsmore, et sic retinui in manum domini regis predictam chaceam quousque habui aliud mandatum a domino rege.

(SC 8/204/10195)

Inquisition taken at Kirkby Malzeard on 9 August 1322 before William of Herlaston and Richard of Aldeburgh, by a jury who say that Henry, late abbot of Byland, was seised of the forest of Middlesmoor from the time of the levying of a fine between him and Roger of Mowbray, and that he and his successors were seised of it until the forest was taken into the king's hand by the escheator after the death and forfeiture of John de Mowbray, and that the king's ministers impeded the abbot in his enjoyment of the same.

Inquisicio capta apud Kyrkeby Malsart coram Willelmo de Herlaston' et Ricardo de Aldeburgh', assignatis per commissionem domini regis, in presencia Johannis de Kylvyngton', capitalis custodis foreste de Midelesmore in Niderdale, die dominica in octaba Sancti Petri ad Vincula anno regni predicti domini regis sextodecimo, secundem tenorem brevis predicti domini regis huic inquisicioni consuti, per sacramentum Willelmi de Aldefeld, Johannis le Warner, Willelmi de Casteley, Willelmi de Casteley junioris, Willelmi de Sunnyng, Thome de Wynkeslay, Roberti de Quixlay, Johannis de Cukewald, Ricardi filii Johannis, Willelmi de Kyrkebye, Johannis Warde et Thome Litster, qui dicunt super sacramentum suum quod Henricus, quondam abbas de Bella Landa, seisitus fuit de foresta de Midelesmore in Niderdale tempore levacionis cuiusdam finis inter ipsum Henricum, querentem, et Rogerum de Moubray, deforciantem, de eadem foresta et eciam de libera chacea in eadem, habenda ad omnimodas feras quandocumque et quibus modis vellet capiendas, et de uno forestario suo ad venacionem ibidem custodiendo una cum forestario dicti Rogeri. Et quod idem Henricus, abbas, et successores sui a tempore levacionis finis predicti, videlicet anno regni Regis Henrici, filii Regis Johannis tricesimo tercio, continue seisiti fuerunt de predicta foresta, chacea et forestario, habenda in eadem foresta sicut predictum est, juxta tenorem finis predicti absque mutacione, status sue interrupcione aliqua, usque post mortem Johannis de Moubray quod eadem foresta una cum terris et tenementis que fuerunt eiusdem Johannis per forisfactum suum capta fuit per Thomam de Burgo, escaetorem domini regis, in manum eiusdem domini regis, a quo tempore abbas qui nunc est et ministri sui super premissis per ministros domini regis fuerunt inpediti et adhuc existunt. In cuius rei testimonium huic inquisicioni juratores predicti sigilla sua apposuerunt. Dat' die, loco et anno supradictis.

No endorsement

26

Bury St Edmunds, Suffolk (1326)
Benedictine
(SC 8/234/11700)

The abbot and convent of Bury St Edmunds petition the king, making two requests:
(1) They state that by the charters of the king's progenitors they have had the franchise that no secular person or minister of the king should interfere in the borough of Bury St Edmunds or with its inhabitants, or hold any pleas there, but that some of the king's ministers are disputing this. They ask that there might be an inquiry into whether they have had and used this franchise, and that this might be clarified in their charters.
(2) They state that they have had chattels of felons and fugitives, year and waste, and all other forfeitures from their tenants in the 8½ Hundreds, as can be seen from records of various allowances made in the exchequer. They ask the king to grant by his charter that they might have these chattels, year, waste and forfeitures, without being challenged in Eyre.
Endorsed: *A writ is to be issued to inquire into the contents of this petition, and when the inquisition has been returned the king will speak his will on the matter.*

A nostre seignur le roi moustrent ses humbles chapeleyns l'abbe el covent de Seint Edmond qe tut soit issint qe graunte lour soit par chartres voz progenitours nostre dit seignur le roi qe nule seculere persone ne ministre nostre seignur le roi se melle del Burgh Sinte Edmond ne des gentz, leyntz menauntz ne illoeqes sete pur ascuns plez tener, quele franchise l'abbe el covent avantditz et lour predecessours ount use de la confectioun des chartres avantdites jesqes en cea nepurquant ascuns des ministres le roi mettent debat ore denovel, dount il prient a nostre seignur le roi qe lui plese comander d'enquere coment ils ount use, et ceo qe trove soit par l'enqueste q'ils ount use clerement, q'il voille par sa chartre esclarsir et mettre en especialte.
Item, pur ceo qu'eux et lour predecessours ount eu et usee chateux de felons et des futyfs, an et wast, et totes autres feofaitures de touz les reseaunz deinz lour Ouyt Hundrez et demy de qi feez ou tenauntz q'il soient et des touz lour tenauntz demene de quel part q'il eient terres ou tenauntz, dount ils vouchent record des diverses allouances faites a eux en l'Escheqer nostre dit seignur le roi. Priont de recheif qe plese a nostre seignur le roi par ja charge grantier q'ils puissent par lour ministres les chateux, an, wast et forfaitures avant nomeez ocuper et retener apres q'ils soient forfaitz saunz estre chalenge en Eire.

Endorsed: Fiat breve de inquirendo super contentes in peticione, et inquisicionem retornatum, dicat rex inde voluntatem.

1326. The petitioner is Richard of Draughton, abbot 1312–35. A string of documents which relate to this petition follow below. On 4 March 1326, in response to the petition, a writ was issued to the treasurer and barons of the exchequer asking them to investigate the second request (SC 8/234/11698), to which a schedule was attached (SC 8/234/11699). Two days later Giles of Wachesham, sheriff of Suffolk from June 1323 to February 1327, was ordered to investigate the first request (SC 8/234/11694), and William of Bereford, chief justice of Common Pleas 1309–26, was asked to search the rolls for evidence of the abbot's jurisdiction (SC 8/234/11696); Bereford's answer is at SC 8/234/11697. Also on 6 March letters patent were directed to John of Mutford, John of Whelnetham and John Claver, asking them to hold an inquisition *ad quod damnum* into the abbot's claim (SC 8/234/11695). On 23 March 1326 the inquisition was held, finding in favour of the abbot and convent of Bury St Edmunds (SC 8/234/11693). As a result of the inquisition the abbey's liberty was confirmed by charter dated 20 April 1320: *CChR 1300–26*, pp. 487–8. For discussion of St Edmund's liberty and the abbey's attempts to defend it from royal encroachment, see L. J. Redstone, 'The Liberty of St Edmund's', *Proceedings of the Suffolk Institute of Archaeology* 15 (1914), 200–11; R. S. Gottfried, *Bury St Edmunds and the Urban Crisis: 1290–1539* (Princeton, 1982), pp. 167–72; and A. Gransden, 'John de Northwold, Abbot of Bury St Edmunds (1279–1301) and his Defence of its Liberties', in *Thirteenth Century England III*, ed. P. R. Coss and S. D. Lloyd (Woodbridge, 1991), pp. 91–112.

(SC 8/234/11698)

Writ of Edward II, dated 4 March 1326, to the treasurer and barons of the exchequer, in response to a claim by the abbot of Bury St Edmunds to have the chattels of felons and fugitives, year and waste, and all other forfeitures from all residents in the 8½ Hundreds of Bury St Edmunds, and all his men and tenants, asking them to examine the rolls and memoranda of the exchequer for evidence as to whether these liberties were allowed to the abbot there or not.
Endorsed: *Enrolled in Easter term in the nineteenth year, in the first roll.*
The rolls have been searched concerning the contents of this writ, as can be seen from the schedule sewn to this writ.
Abbot of St Edmunds.

Edwardus, Dei gracia rex Anglie, dominus Hibernie et dux Aquitanie, thesaurario et baronibus suis de Scaccario salutem. Quia dilectus nobis in Cristo abbas de Sancto Edmundo, per cartas progenitorum nostrorum quondam regum Anglie et confirmacionem nostram, asserit se habere, debere et ipsum et predecessores suos abbates loci illius hucusque habuisse catalla felonum et fugitivorum, annum et vastum, et omnes alias forisfacturas de omnibus residentibus infra octo hundreda sua et dimidia de Sancto Edmundo \et omni hominium et tenencium suorum in regno nostro/, et quod libertates predicte coram vobis in eodem Scaccario ante hec tempora eidem abbati et predecessoribus suis allocate fuerunt. Nos volentes certiorari si predicte libertates prefate abbati et predecessoribus suis allocate fuerunt ut predictum est nec ne, si sic tunc in qua forma, quo tempore et qualiter et quo modo, vobis mandamus quod scrutatis rotulis et memorandis Scaccarii predicti nobis de eo quod inde inveneritis reddatis sub sigillo eiusdem Scaccarii distincte et aperte sine dilacione certiores hoc breve nobis remittentes. Teste me ipso apud Leycestre quarto die Marcii anno regni nostri decimo nono.

Endorsed: Irrotulatur termino Pasche anno xix^{o}, rotulo primo.
Scrutati sunt rotuli super contentis in brevi ut patet in cedula huic brevi consuta.
Abbas de Sancto Edmundo.

(SC 8/234/11699)

Extracts from the great roll of the exchequer from the reigns of John (1203/4), Henry III (1225/6) and Edward I (1290/1, 1292/3), concerning the claim of the abbot of Bury St Edmunds to have the chattels of felons and fugitives, year and waste, and all other forfeitures from all residents in Bury St Edmunds and all his men and tenants:

Amercements in 5 John in Northamptonshire: 12s from Godfrey's chattels to the abbot of St Edmund by liberty of charters.

In 10 Henry III in Essex: 44s from Peter of la Burne's chattels to the abbot of St Edmund by liberty of the king's charters.

In 19 Edward I in Norfolk: ½ mark from Henry FitzNicholas for defaults before justices; 1 mark from Robert of Horkesleye for the same; ½ mark from Jordan of Langemere; 15d from John Pane and Nicholas Knoc; 40d from Giles and Juliana of Harehoures, Gerberda and Alice of Theford; 20d from Henry Grul; £26 8s 4d from the men within the liberty of St Edmunds; and £6 14s 7d from the liberty of St Edmunds in Suffolk; in total £34 17s 11d to the abbot of St Albans by liberty of his charters and by the king's writ.

In 19 Edward I in residue in Norfolk: the abbot of St Edmunds rendered account of £655 7s 4d from various debts of men of the liberty of St Edmunds for various years, of which he has paid £6 14s 7d. He owes here £648 12s 9d from the men of his liberty. He rendered account of the same debt. And to the same abbot £548 12s 9d by liberty of his charters and by the king's writ.

In 21 Edward I in Norfolk: the abbot of St Edmunds rendered account of £19 5s 4d for William of Redham, former sheriff, from chattels of the abbot's men. To the same abbot £19 5s 4d by liberty of the king's charters.

In magno rotulo de anno quinto Regis Johannis in North' sub titulo de amerciamentis per Simonem de Pateshull et socios suos continetur' sic:
Simon de Pateshull reddit compotum de xij s de catallis Godefridi. In thesaurario nul. Et in perdon' abbati Sancti Edmundi xij s per libertatem cartarum. Et quietus est.

In rotulo decimo Regis Henrici tercii in Essex sub titulo de amerciamentes de itinere Simonis de Hal et socii eius annotatur sic:
.... reddit compotum de xliiij s de catallis Petri de la Burne suspens'. In thesaurario nul. Et abbati Sancti Edmundo xliiij s per libertatem cartarum regis. Et quietus est.

In rotulo xix Regis Edwardi filii Regis Henrici in Item, Norff' annotatur sic:
Idem vicecomes reddit compotum de dimidia marca de Henrico filio Nicholai de Sancto Edmundo pro pluribus defaltis coram Willelmo de Gysleham et Willelmo de Pageham, justiciis assignatis anno xviij. Et j marca de Roberto de Horkesleye pro eodem ibidem. Et dimidia marca de Jordano de Langemere de Chardatr' et sociis suis que non habent ibidem. Et xv d de Johanne Pane et Nichola Knoc que non habet coram rege anno xvij. Et xl d de Egidio de Harehoures et Juliana, uxore eius, Gerberda filia Johannis de Theford et Alicia, sorore eius, que non sunt presente coram Willelmo de Gysleham et sociis suis, justiciis assignatis anno xix. Et xx d de Henrico Grul de Sancto Edmundo per plegios, sicut continetur ibidem. Et xxvj li viij s iiij d de amerciamentis hominum infra libertatem Sancti Edmundi quorum nominibus propono hoc signum Sancti Edmundi. In rotulo de amerciamentes diversorum comitatuum et de libertate Sancti Edmundi in comitatu Suff' de Banco anno xvij et xviij. Et vj li xiiij s vij d de catallis diversorum et vasto domorum et terra diversorum \sicut infra continet/. In Thesaurio nichil. Et abbati de Sancto Edmundo xxxiiij li xvij s xj d per libertatem cartarum suarum et per breve regis allocatam abbati infra et sic allocata est eidem abbati in rotulo x Regis Henrici. Et quietus est.

In rotulo xix Regis Edwardi filii Regis Henrici in residuum Norff' post Wygorn' annotatur sic:
Abbas de Sancto Edmundo reddit compotum de DClv li vij s iiij d de pluribus debetis, sicut continetur in rotulo principali, videlicet, vj li xiiij s vij d de cas diversorum et vasto domorum et terrarum diversorum, sicut continetur in rotulo xxiij Regis Henrici et CCCxiiij li xvj s iij d de debitis pluribus que sunt de numeris hominum villarum decennarum et hundredi infra libertatem Sancti Edmundi pro Hamo Hauteyn, quondam vicecomite, sicut continetur in rotulo xvjjj, et CCvj li xiiij d de consuetudinibus numeris hominum villarum et hundredi pro Roberto Sauvage, quondam vicecomite, sicut continetur in rotulo xxxix, et viij li xvj s viij d de consuetudinibus numeris hominum pro Willelmo de Swyneford, quondam vicecomite, sicut continetur in rotulo xlj, et Cxiij li xviij s viij d de consuetudinibus numeris hominum villarum et hundredi infra libertatem ipsius abbatis et non de feodo suo pro Roberto de Norton', quondam vicecomite, sicut continetur in rotulo liij, et C s pro defalta, sicut continetur in rotulo vij. De quibus responsis in Item Norff' de vj li xiiij s vij d de catallis diversorum et vasto domorum et terrarum diversorum ubi dicta catalla allocantur. Et debet hic DCxlviij li xij s ix d qui sunt de numeris hominum villarum decennarum et hundredi infra libertatem ipsius abbatis. Idem reddit compotum de eodem debito. In Thesaurio nichil. Et eidem abbati DCxlviij li xij s ix d per libertatem cartarum suarum et per breve regis adhuc inter communia de anno xx, in quo continetur quod rex anno xviij per breve suum adhuc inter communia de eodem anno xviij mandavit thesaurario et baronibus de Scaccario quod omnes cartas quibuscumque prelatis vel magnatibus a progenitoribus regis, regibus Anglie, super quibusdam libertatibus factas que xviij anno Regis Henrici, patris regis nunc, allocate fuerit ad Scaccarium facerent in eodem Scaccario pariter, et omnes cartas de precedenti tempore perquisitas allocari, et quod rex accepit ex insumacione prelatorum et magnatum regni sui quod carte ipsorum prelatorum et magnatum tam per regem quam dictum patrem suum et alios progenitores suos predictos facte in singulis articulis suis juxta concessiones regis et progenitorum suorum predictorum per thesaruarium et barones in Scaccario predicto non sunt allocate. Super quo rex, volens salubre remedium adhiberi, providit, concessit et firmiter precepit quod omnes carte que fuerunt allocate in predicto Scaccario dicte xviij anno Regis Henrici, patris regis nunc, et eciam omnes carte quecumque tempore, tam tempore regis quam progenitorum suorum, concesse manuteneantur et allocentur decetero in singulis articulis suis contentis in eisdem, secundum quod prelati et magnates eisdem usi sunt licet compertum fuerit quod carte ille juxta tenorem earumdem in suis articulis in eisdem continentis tempore preterito non fuerunt eisdem allocate, dum tamen articulis illis usi fuerunt extra amerciamentis quoscumque pro consideracionem curie regis pro propriis delictis suis qui quietanciam inde per cartas huiusmodi clamant habere, de quibus amerciamentis rex suam intendit facere voluntatem prout coram rege et consilio suo fuerit alias ordinatas, videlicet, quod prelati et magnates qui per cartas regis et progenitorum suorum, regum Anglie, clamant habere amerciamenta sua propria ad que in quibuscumque curia regis fuerunt amerciati pro propriis dilectis suis habeant omnia amerciamenta sua propria in que inciderunt ante festum Pasche anno xiij Regis Henrici juxta tenorem cartarum earumdem. Et quod predicti prelati et magnates omnia amerciamenta sua propria in que inciderunt pro propriis dilictis suis post predictum festum Pasche anno xiij regi ad Scaccarium

persolvant decetero et de satisfaciant, non obstantibus aliquibus libertatibus seu concessionibus dictis prelatis et magnatibus de huiusmodi propriis amerciamentis suis habendis per cartas regis seu progentorum suorum quorumcumque factis. Qua quidem libertate percipiendi amerciamenta predicta idem abbas usus est, sicut apparet per rotulos supradictos, ubi idem abbas olatur de eisdem amerciamentis pro eo quod ea recepta sicut senescalli libertatum eiusdem abbatis recognoverunt, sicut continetur ibidem. Et quietus est.

In rotulo xxj Regis Edwardi filii Regis Henrici in Norff' annotatur sic:
Abbas de Sancto Edmundo reddit compotum de xix li v s iiij d pro Willelmo de Redham, quondam vicecomitate, de catallis diversorum hominum ipsius abbatis, sicut continetur in rotulo xij. In Thesaurio nichil. Et eidem abbatis xix li v s iiij d per libertatem cartarum regis et sicut allocata est eidem in rotulo xix in hoc comitatu. Et quietus est.

No endorsement

This document was produced in response to SC 8/234/11698, dated 4 March 1326. The extracts go back as far as 5 John (1203/4). William of Gisleham, justice, lived c. 1230–93 (P. Brand, 'Gisleham, Sir William of (*c.*1230–1293)', *ODNB*). The dates for the sheriffs of Norfolk are as follows: Hamo Hauteyn (1258–60); Robert Savage (1249–55); William de Swyneford (1255–58); Robert de Norton (1267–70); William de Redham (1278–81 and 1290–94). The document is partly illegible due to gall stains.

(SC 8/234/11694)

Writ of Edward II, dated 6 March 1326, to the sheriff of Suffolk, in response to a petition from the abbot of Bury St Edmunds asking that all his liberties in respect of being free from the interference of justices or other ministers of the king in Bury St Edmunds might be set down and granted to him specifically, asking him to hear all, or two of John de Mutford', John de Whelnetham and John Claver, who have been ordered to assemble a jury for an inquisition into whether the abbot had held these liberties, and whether it would be to the harm of the king or anyone else, or would lessen the farm of the county to grant them to him, to give their findings.
Endorsed on face: *By petition of the council.*

Edwardus, Dei gracia rex Anglie, dominus Hibernie et dux Aquitanie, vicecomiti Suff' salutem. Sua nobis peticione coram nobis et consilio nostro exhibita supplicavit dilectus nobis in Cristo abbas de Sancto Edmundo quod cum inter ceteras libertates eidem abbati et conventui loci predicti, per cartas progenitorum nostrorum, quondam regum Anglie, quas per cartam nostram confirmavimus, concessas, concessum sit eis quod nulla secularis persona aut minister regis se intromittat de Burgo Sancti Edmundi aut hominibus in eo manentibus nisi iidem abbas et conventus et eorum ministri, et licet idem abbas et predecessores sui, abbates eiusdem loci, a tempore confeccionis earumdem cartarum et confirmacionis hucusque pretextu dictorum verborum generalium infra Burgum illum habere consueverint libertates subscriptas, videlicet cogniciones omni placitorum tam ipsum abbatem quam homines et tenentes Burgi illius contingencium tam videlicet placitorum terrarum, tenementorum, convencionum, contractuum, transgressionum et querelarum quam aliorum quorumcumque infra Burgum illum quoquo modo emergencium, videlicet tam de placitis per brevia nostra et dictorum progenitorum nostrorum coram quibuscumque justiciariis et aliis ministris nostris et ipsorum progenitorum nostrorum quam sive huiusmodi brevibus qualitercumque motis, absque eo quod aliqui justiciarii sive ad placita coram nobis seu ipsis progenitoribus nostris tenendas sive ad assisas capiendas, gaoles deliberandas, felonias aut transgressiones aliquas audiendas et terminandas assignati sive justiciarii de Banco seu itinerantes sive senescalli, marescalli, clerici mercati hospicii nostri seu ipsorum progenitorum nostrorum escaetores, vicecomites, taxatores, collectores ulnarii aut alii quicumque ministri nostri seu ipsorum progenitorum nostrorum ad quecumque officia facienda assignati se de predicto Burgo aut hominibus in eo manentibus in aliquo intromiserunt seu infra eundem Burgum ad aliqua placita ibidem tenenda, inquisiciones capiendas aut alia facienda hucusque sederunt nichilominus pro eo quod libertates predicte in cartis illis specificate non existunt idem abbas super eisdem libertatibus per quosdam de eisdem justiciariis et ministris nostris pluries impetitus existit velimus omnes et singulas libertates predictas per cartam nostram specificare et eas sic specificatas eidem abbati concedere, habendas sibi et successoribus suis imperpetuum in forma supradicta. Nos eius in hac parte supplicacioni annuere et ea occasione super premissis certiorari volentes assignavimus dilectos et fideles nostros Johannem de Mutford', Johannem de Whelnetham et Johannem Claver, vel duos eorum quorum Johannem de Mutford' alterum esse, volumus ad inquirendum per sacramentum proborum et legalium hominium de comitatu predicto, per quos rei veritas melius sciri poterit, in presencia tua per prefatos Johannem, Johannem et Johannem, vel duos eorum quorum prefatum Johannem de Mutford' alterum esse, volumus super hoc premuniendum si predictus abbas et predecessores sui predicti omnes cogniciones predictas modo quo predicitur habere consueverint, absque eo quod aliqui justiciarii seu ministri predicti se de Burgo aut hominibus predictis in aliquo intromiserunt seu ibidem sederunt nec ne, et si sic ad dampnum seu prejudicium nostrum aut alterius cuiuscumque, seu diminucionem firme comitatis predicti, si nos cogniciones omnium placitorum predictorum prefato abbati per cartam nostram pro nobis et heredibus nostris concedamus, habendas sibi et successoribus suis abbatibus loci predicti in forma predicta imperpetuum. Ita quod huiusmodi justiciarii vel alii quicumque ministri nostri vel heredum nostrorum ad quecumque officia facienda deputati sive assignati, sive in presencia nostro et ipsorum heredum nostrorum sive in absencia se de Burgo illo aut hominibus in eo manentibus aliqualiter non intromittant nec in eodem sedeant ad aliqua officia ibidem facienda, et si sit ad dampnum vel prejudicium nostrum aut aliorum seu diminucionem firme predicte, tunc ad quod dampnum et quod prejudicium nostrum, et ad quod dampnum et quod prejudicium aliorum, et ad quam diminucionem firme predicte, et qualiter et quo modo, et de premissis omnibus et singularis et aliis articulis premissa contingentibus plenius veritatem. Et ideo tibi precipimus quod ad certos diem et locum quos iidem Johannes, Johannes et Johannes, vel duo eorum quorum prefatum Johannem de Mutford' alterum esse, volumus tibi scire facient, venire facias coram eis, vel duobus eorum quorum prefatum Johannem de Mutford' alterum esse, volumus tot et tales probos et legales homines de balliva tua per quos rei veritas in premissis melius sciri poterit et inquiri. Et habeas ibi hoc breve. Teste me ipso apud Leycestre vj^{o} die Marcii anno regni nostri decimo nono.

Endorsed on face: Per peticionem de consilio.

(SC 8/234/11696)

Writ of Edward II, dated 6 March 1326, to William de Bereford, wishing to know whether the abbot of Bury St Edmunds had cognisance of all pleas touching the abbot and his tenants of Bury St Edmunds or not, and if these liberties have been allowed before William and his colleagues of Common Pleas, and asking him to search the rolls and memoranda of Common Pleas for evidence.

Edwardus, Dei gracia rex Anglie, dominus Hibernie et dux Aquitanie, dilecto et fideli suo Willelmo de Bereford' salutem. Quia quibusdam certis de causis [certiorari] volumus utrum abbas de Sancto Edmundo cogniciones omnium placitorum ipsum abbatem et homines et tenentes Burgi Sancti Edmundi contingencium de ...., videlicet coram vobis in Banco predicto motis habuerit sicut dicit nec ne, et si huiusmodi libertates ei coram vobis in eodem Banco allocate fuerit nec ne, vobis mandamus quod scrutatis rotulis et memorandis de Banco predicto nos de eo quod inde inveneritis reddatis in .... nostra, distincte et aperte sine dilacione, certiores hoc breve nobis remittentes. Teste me ipso apud Leycestre vj[to] die Marcii anno regni nostri decimo nono.

No endorsement

(SC 8/234/11697)

Pleas at Westminster before William of Bereford and his fellow justices of the King's Bench one month after Easter 1315 (Roll 231).
Suffolk: Amabilla, Emma, Sarah and Alice, daughters of Hugh the Taverner, seek against William of Marlow concerning a messuage in the suburbs of Bury St Edmunds which should be theirs as their father's heirs. The bailiffs of the liberty of the abbot of St Edmunds appeared and were told to show the court if they had a deed from the king or his ancestors proving their right to such liberties. Thereupon the same bailiffs proffered a writ by Edward II, dated 3 March 1315, to the justices of his Bench verifying the abbot's claim to the liberty.
When asked if the liberties were allocated to the abbot or his predecessors in the time of the king's ancestors, they said that the liberties had always belonged to the abbot. And after inspecting several rolls, it was found that the abbot was allocated the liberties in a plea of 33 Edward I between the abbot and Robert of Brandon, merchant, and in another between the abbot and William le Chaloner.

Placita apud Westm' coram Willelmo de Bereford' et sociis suis, justiciariis domini regis de Banco a die Pasche in unum mensem anno regni Regis Edwardi filii Regis Edwardi octavo. (Rotulo CCxxxj)
Suff': Amabilla filia Hugonis le Taverner, Emma, Sarra et Alicia, sorores eiusdem Amabille, per Henry de Lyvermere, attornatum suum, petunt versus Willelmum de Merlawe una mesuagia cum pertinenciis in suburbis ville de Sancto Edmundo ut jus et hereditatem suam. Et in quod idem Willelmus non habet ingressum nisi per Hugonem le Taverner, patrem predictarum Amabille, Emme, Sarre et Alicie, cuius heredes ipse sunt, qui illud ei dimisit dum infra etatem fuit etc.
Et Willelmus, per Edmundem de Caldecotes, attornatum suum, venit. Et super hoc venient ballivi libertatis \abbatis/ de Sancto Edmundo et petunt inde cur'

libertatis sue Sancti Edmundi de Sancto Edmundo. Et dictum est eis quod ostendant cur' hic si quod habeant factum de domino rege aut progenitoribus suis per quod talis libertas eis allocari debeat. Et super hoc iidem ballivi proferunt hic breve domini regis nunc clausum justiciariis suis hic directum in hec verba:

'Edwardus, Dei gracia etc. justiciariis suis de Banco salutem. Quia ex parte dilecti nobis in Cristo abbatis de Sancto Edmundo nobis est ostensum quod ipse cogniciones omnium placitorum per brevia nostra, tam tenencium quam alia quecumque tangencium infra libertatem suam de Burgo de Sancto Edmundo emergencium habere debet ipse que et predecessores sui, abbates loci predicti, semper hactenus a tempore quo non extat memoria huiusmodi cogniciones ibidem habere consueverunt, et que coram justiciariis dicti Edwardi, quondam regis Anglie, patris nostri, et aliorum progenitorum nostrorum, quondam regum Anglie, de Banco et alibi eidem abbati et predecessoribus suis predictis ut dicit allocate fuerunt, vobis mandamus quod ipsum abbatem cogniciones huisumodi infra libertatem suam predictam absque impedimento habere permittatis prout eas habere debet, et ipse et predecessores sui predicti eas ibidem semper hactenus habuerunt. Teste me ipso apud Westm' tercio die Marcii anno regni nostri octavo.' Et quesitum est a prefatis ballivis si huiusmodi libertas ipsi abbate aut predecessoribus suis allocata fuit tempore progenitorum domini regis nunc, dicunt revera quod huiusmodi libertas semper hucusque allocata fuit ipsi abbati et predecessoribus suis cum petita fuerit tempore competenti etc. Et quia inspectis rotulis Radulfi de Hengham de Banco hic termino Sancti Michaelis anno regni Regis Edwardi, patris domini regis nunc, tricesimo tercio, compertum est quod huiusmodi libertas ipsi abbati allocata fuerit in quodam placito inter Robertum de Brandon, mercatorem, querentem, et abbatem de Sancto Edmundo, Fratrem Rogerum de Cheventon' et Ricardum le Messer, de placito detencionis unius jumenti. Et similiter, in quodam alio placito inter Willelmum le Chaloner de Sancto Edmundo, querentes, et abbatem de Sancto Edmundo, Fratrem Rogerum de Cheventon' et Ricardum le Messer, de placito detencionis unius equi, ut patet CCij rotulo eiusdem termini Sancti Michaelis. Ideo predictus abbas habeat curiam suam in placito isto. Et ballivi prefixerunt diem partibus apud Sanctum Edmundum die mercurii in septimana Pentecostes. Et dictum est eis quod partibus celerem justiciam exhibeant alioquin etc.

No endorsement

(SC 8/234/11695)

Letters patent from Edward II, dated at Leicester on 6 March 1326, to John of Mutford, John of Whelnetham and John Claver in response to a petition from the abbot of Bury St Edmunds asking that all his liberties in respect of being free from the interference of justices or other ministers of the king in Bury St Edmunds might be set down and granted to him specifically. He asks them, or two of them provided John of Mutford is one, to hold an inquisition by the oaths of good loyal men of Suffolk into whether the abbot has always held these liberties without interference from the king's justices or ministers, and whether it would be to the harm of the king or anyone else, or would lessen the farm of the county, to grant them to him. He also orders them to inform the sheriff of their findings.

Endorsed on face: *By petition of the council.*

Edwardus, Dei gracia rex Anglie, dominus Hibernie et dux Aquitanie, dilectis et fidelibus suis Johanni de Mutford, Johanni de Whelnetham et Johanni Claver salutem. Sua nobis peticione coram nobis et consilio nostro exhibita supplicavit dilectus nobis in Cristo abbas de Sancto Edmundo quod cum inter ceteras libertates eidem abbati et conventui loci predicti, per cartas progenitorum nostrorum, quondam regum Anglie, quas per cartam nostram confirmavimus, concessas, concessum sit eis quod nulla secularis persona aut minister regis se intromittat de Burgo Sancti Edmundi aut hominibus in eo manentibus nisi iidem abbas et conventus et eorum ministri, et licet idem abbas et predecessores sui, abbates eiusdem loci, a tempore confeccionis earundem cartarum et confirmacionis hucusque pretextu dictorum verborum generalium infra Burgum illum habere consueverint libertates subscriptas, videlicet cogniciones omnium placitorum tam ipsum abbatem quam homines et tenentes Burgi illius contingencium, tam videlicet placitorum terrarum, tenementorum, convencionum, contractuum, transgressionum et querelarum quam aliorum quorumcumque infra Burgum illum quoquo modo emergencium, videlicet tam de placitis per brevia nostra et dictorum progenitorum nostrorum coram quibuscumque justiciariis et aliis ministris nostris et ipsorum progenitorum nostrorum quam sive huiusmodi brevibus qualitercumque motis, absque eo quod aliqui justiciarii sive ad placita coram nobis seu ipsis progenitoribus nostris tenendas sive ad assisas capiendas, gaoles deliberandas, felonias aut transgressiones aliquas audiendas et terminandas assignati sive justiciarii de Banco seu itinerantes sive senescalli, marescalli, clerici, mercati, hospicii nostri seu ipsorum progenitorum nostrorum escaetores, vicecomites, coronatores, taxatores, collectores ulnarii aut alii quicumque ministri nostri seu ipsorum progenitorum nostrorum ad quecumque officia facienda assignati se de predicto Burgo aut hominibus in eo manentibus in aliquo intromiserunt seu infra eundem Burgum ad aliqua placita ibidem tenenda, inquisiciones capiendas aut alia facienda hucusque sederunt nichilominus pro eo quod libertates predicte in cartis illis specificate non existunt idem abbas super eisdem libertatibus per quosdam de eisdem justiciariis et ministris nostris pluries impetitus existit velimus omnes et singulas libertates predictas per cartam nostram specificare et eas sic specificatas eidem abbati concedere, habendas sibi et successoribus suis imperpetuum in forma supradicta. Nos eius in hac parte supplicacioni annuere et ea occasione super premissis certiorari volentes assignavimus vos et duos vestrum, quorum vos prefate Johannes de Mutford' alterum esse, volumus ad inquirendum per sacramentum proborum et legalium hominium de comitatu Suff', per quos rei veritas melius sciri poterit, in presencia vicecomitis nostri eiusdem comitatis, per vos vel duos vestrum, quorum vos, prefate Johannes de Mutford', alterum esse, volumus super hoc premuniend' si predictus abbas et predecessores sui predicti omnes cogniciones predictas modo quo predicitur habere consueverunt, absque eo quod aliqui justiciarii seu ministri predicti se de Burgo aut hominibus predictis in aliquo intromiserunt seu ibidem sederunt nec ne, et si sic ad dampnum seu prejudicium nostrum aut alterius cuiuscumque, seu diminucionem firme comitatis predicti, si nos cogniciones omnium placitorum predictorum prefato abbati per cartam nostram pro nobis et heredibus nostris concedamus, habendas sibi et successoribus suis abbatibus loci predicti in forma predicta imperpetuum. Ita quod huiusmodi justiciarii vel alii quicumque ministri nostri vel heredum nostrorum ad quecumque officia facienda deputati sive assignati, sive in presencia nostro et ipsorum heredum nostrorum sive in absencia se de Burgo illo aut hominibus in eo manentibus aliqualiter non intromittant

nec in eodem sedeant ad aliqua officia ibidem facienda, et si sit ad dampnum vel prejudicium nostrum aut aliorum seu diminucionem firme predicte, tunc ad quod dampnum et quod prejudicium nostrum, et ad quod dampnum et quod prejudicium aliorum, et ad quam diminucionem firme predicte, et qualiter et quo modo, et de premissis omnibus et singulis et aliis articulis premissa contingentibus plenius veritatem. Et ideo vobis mandamus quod ad certos diem et locum quos vos, vel duo vestrum, quorum vos, prefate Johannes de Mutford', alterum esse, volumus ad hoc provideritis inquisicionem illam facietis, et eam distincte et aperte factam nobis sub sigillis vestris vel duorum vestrum, quorum vos, prefatum Johannes de Mutford', alterum esse, volumus et sigillis eorum per quos facta fuerit sine dilacione mittatis, et hoc breve mandavimus vicecomite comitatis predicti quod ad certos diem et locum quos vos, vel duo vestrum, quorum vos, prefate Johannes de Mutford', alterum esse, volumus ei scire facietis, venire faciat coram vobis vel duobus vestrum, quorum vos, prefate Johannes de Mutford', alterum esse, volumus tot et tales probos et legales homines de balliva sua per quos rei veritas in premissis melius sciri poterit et inquiri. In cuius rei testimonium has litteras nostras fieri fecimus patentes. Teste me ipso apud Leycestre vj° die Marcii anno regni nostri decimo nono.
Endorsed on face: Per petitcionem de consilio.

(SC 8/234/11693)

Inquisition held before John of Mutford and John Claver by the king's writ in the presence of the sheriff of Suffolk at Henhowe Heath on the Thursday following the close of Easter [March 23] 1326, by the oaths of William of Langham, Thomas of Wridewelle, William Kenne, Henry of Langham, Thomas of Ayssh, Nicholas of Prato, Robert of Saxham, Richard of Mastone, William Mariot, David Scot, Robert atte Hel and Richard of Langham, jurors, who say on their oath that the abbot of Bury St Edmunds and his predecessors have had cognisance of all pleas touching the abbot and his men and tenants of Bury St Edmunds, and of all pleas arising in any way in Bury St Edmunds, without interference from the king's justices or ministers. They also say that it is not to the harm of the king or anyone else, or to the diminution of the farm of the sheriff of Suffolk, if this cognisance is granted to the abbot by charter.

Inquisicio capta coram Johanne de Mutford' et Johanne Claver per quoddam breve domini regis patentem eis directum in presencia vicecomitis Suff' ad hoc premuniti apud Hennowe, die jovis proxima post clausum Pasche anno regni Regis Edwardi, filii regis Edwardi, decimo nono, per Willelmum de Langham, Thomam de Wridewelle, Willelmum Kenne, Henricum de Langham, Thomam de Ayssh', Nicholaum de Prato, Robertum de Saxham, Ricardum de Manstone, Willelmum Mariot, Davyd Scot, Robertum atte Hel et Ricardum de Langham, juratos, qui dicunt super sacramentum suum quod abbas de Sancto Edmundo et predeccessores sui, abbates loci predicti, a tempore quo non extat memoria hucusque habere consueverunt cogniciones omnium placitorum tam ipsum abbatem quam homines et tenentes Burgi Sancti Edmundi contingencium tam videlicet placitorum terrarum, tenementorum, convencionum, contractuum, transgressionum et querelarum quam aliorum quorumcumque infra burgum illum quoquomodo emergencium, videlicet tam de placitis per brevia regis et progenitorum suorum coram quibuscumque justiciariis et aliis ministris regis et progenitorum suorum quam sive huiusmodi brevibus qualitercumque motis, absque eo quod aliqui justiciarii sive ad placita coram rege seu progenitoribus suis tenenda, sive ad assisas capiendas, gaolas deliberandas, felonias aut transgressiones aliquas audiendas et terminandas assignati, sive justiciarii de Banco seu itinerantes sive senescalli, marescalli, clerici mercati hospicii regis seu progenitorum suorum, eschaetores, coronatores, taxatores, collectores ulnarii aut alii quicumque ministri regis seu progenitorum suorum ad quecumque officia facienda assignati se de predicto burgo aut hominibus in eo manentibus in aliquo intromiserunt, seu infra eundem burgum ad aliqua placita ibidem tenenda, inquisiciones capiendas aut alia facienda hucusque sederunt. Dicunt eciam quod non est ad dampnum seu prejudicium regis aut alterius cuiuscumque, seu diminucionem firme comitatis Suff', si dictus rex cogniciones omnium placitorum predictorum et omnes et singulas libertates predictas per cartam suam specificare, et eas sic specificatas prefato abbati per cartam suam pro se et heredibus suis concedat, habendas predicto abbati et successoribus suis, abbatibus loci predicti, in forma predicta imperpetuum. Ita quod huiusmodi justiciarii vel alii quicumque ministri regis vel heredum suorum ad quecumque officia facienda deputati sive assignati sive in presencia regis et [ipsorum heredum] suorum sive in absencia se de Burgo illo aut hominibus in eo manentibus aliqualiter non intromittant nec in eodem sedeant ad aliqua officia ibidem facienda. In cuius rei testimonium dicti juratores sigilla sua apposuerunt presentibus.

No endorsement

27

Llanthony Secunda, Gloucester (c. 1326)
Augustinian canons
(SC 8/56/2787)

The prior of Llanthony Secunda petitions the king and council for damages of £200 for the time that the king's keeper of the petitioner's manors, Adam Halfnakede, abused his office in the manor of Alvington, and of £20 for his taking of a palfrey from the same manor. Halfnakede continues to levy revenue from the said manors by colour of his office contrary to the terms of his warrant from the king.
Endorsed: *He should have a writ of trespass of the one and the other.*

A nostre seignur le rei et a son consail moustre le prior de Lanthoni jouste Gloucestre, qe est de la fondacion counte de Herford, qe com nostre seignur le roi aveit assigne nagers Adam Halfnakede gardeyn de la dite priorie de Lanthoni, saunz rien prendre ou aporter des chateux ou des issues de la dite priorie [ou] de leur maners apportenaunt, la vintk le dit Adam par colour de sa garde en le maner le dit prior de Alvyngton' et illoqe prist le palefrey le dit prior, pris de xx li, et la mena la bieau lui futz et uncore le de tintk. Ensement le vauntdit Adam, countre la forme et le garaunt q'il avoit du roi, leva deversse issues en les maners le vauntdit prior ala quittaunce de CC li, et uncore les de tintk de ver lui, de quei le dit prior prie remedie.

Endorsed: Eit bref de trespas del un et del autre.

c. 1326. The dispute referred to ran from 1324 to 1326, with the petition dating from shortly after William of Penbury's reinstatement as prior in 1326. Penbury had first resigned as prior in 1324, but the canons could not agree on his replacement. So, on 24 May 1324, Edward II gave the custody of the monastery to his servant, Adam of Helnak, and bade him dispose of the revenues of the house with the counsel of the sub-prior (*CPR 1321–4*, p. 419). For two years the convent was without a head. In 1326 rival candidates agreed to submit their claims to John Stratford, bishop of Winchester, who decided in favour of Penbury because his resignation had been made under duress, while imprisoned. For a full account, see *VCH Gloucester*, II, 89. Adam Halfnakede was probably from Halnaker, a hamlet within the parish of Boxgrove, Sussex. The forms 'Halfnaked' and 'Halfnakede' were common during the thirteenth and fourteenth centuries: A. Mawer and F. M. Stenton, *The Place-Names of Sussex*, Part I, English Place-Name Society, 6 (1929), p. 67. For the background to this story of internal strife see R. Graham in *VCH Gloucester*, II, 88–9 and nn.; and TNA C 270/9/44.

28

Leicester, Leicestershire (1331)
Augustinian canons
(SC 8/242/12077)

The abbot of Leicester petitions the king that the treasurer and barons of the exchequer be ordered to cease their demands on him for money and florins that they allege that he has in his keeping that belonged to Simon of Bereford, as he has delivered these goods, and an inquisition has confirmed this, but they continue to make demands and distrain him grievously.

A nostre seignur le roi prie le seon chapeleyn abbe de Leycestre qe come il fust empeche en l'Eschekir nostre seignur le roi, devant le tresorer et les barons, de deners queux il dust avoir en garde de Sire Simond de Bereford, sur quoi il vint en le dit Eschekir et conust q'il avoit en garde ij coupes, ij eweretz et florins enseales en un puche du seal le dit Sire Simond, et les rendi au tresorer al oeps nostre seignur le roi illoeqes, et a ceo ad acquitance, et tut soit il qe le dit abbe n'avoit deners ne autres biens et chateux qe furent au dit Sire Simond le jour q'il fust atteint en sa garde, solonc ceo qe torne est par enqeste prise a Leycestre devant le chaunceller nostre seignur le roi et Mestre Henri de Cliff a ceo assignes, et auxint par serment q'il ad fuit devant eux sur la foialte q'il dois au roi. Nepurquant les ditz tresorer et barons par proceis del Eschekir sount de novel demander du dit abbe C et lx marcs d'esterlinges et florins, par ount le dit abbe est grevousement destreint. Q'il pleise a nostre seignur le roi avoir regard a la coniceance qe le dit abbe fist de coupes, eweretz et florins avantditz, dont il ne fust pas a donqes empeche, et auxint a la dite enqueste qe acorde a sa dite coniceance et a son dit serment, et comander as ditz tresorer et barons q'ils sursecent de la dite demande et ent lui ac quitent.

No endorsement

1331. The privy seal warrant with which this petition was formerly enclosed is dated 6 October 1331 (no. 4839 of C 81/184). The petitioner is Richard Tours, abbot 1318–45. On 10 October 1331 it was ordered that the abbot be discharged from £75 13s 4d of £109, it having been found by inquisition that Simon of Bereford delivered the £109 to the abbot, who delivered the same to William Pyk of Surrey. The abbot was to pay the residue in instalments (*CFR 1327–37*, pp. 276–7).

29

Rievaulx, NRY (1334)
Cistercian
(SC 8/69/3430)

The abbot of Rievaulx petitions the king and council, stating that his predecessor, John of Reynton, was often sent on diplomatic missions to Scotland, both in the twentieth year of the king's father, and in his own time, and that, because he rode so hard between Scotland and London and elsewhere on these missions, he lost all his horses, the king gave him three Hainault horses in compensation. However, 40 marks are now being demanded for these horses in the exchequer, as if Abbot John had bought them. The present abbot asks that he might be discharged this sum, in consideration of his predecessor's labour, expenses and diligence in the king's service.
Endorsed: *Because it is attested before the council that the said abbot lost several of his horses in the king's service, and that the said present king gave him the said three horses as a gift, in compensation for his horses, the treasurer and barons of the exchequer are to be ordered to cease from the demand they are making on the said abbot for the aforesaid reason, and to make him quit and discharged of it.*

A nostre seignur le roi et son conseil mo[ustrent son] chapeleyn l'abbe de Ryvaux qe come l'abbe Johan de Reynton', son predecessour, en l'an du regne piere nostre seignur le roi vintisme, par commandement nostre seignur le roi q'ore est et de son conseil, et puis sovent en temps nostre seignur le roi q'ore est, par lui et par son conseil, feust charge d'aler en Escoce od autres bones gentz a ceo assignez pur treter et finalment faire les choses contenuz en lour commissiouns. Et pur ceo qe le dit Abbe Johan se hasta taunt par commandement nostre seignur le roi en alaunt et returnaunt a nostre seignur le roi a Londres et aillours issint q'il perdist touz ses chyvaux, nostre seignur le roi comanda a Sire Robert de Wodhous, adonqes gardeyn de la garderobe, q'il liverast au dit Abbe Johan treis chyvaux Henuers en alowaunce de ses chyvaux issint perduz en son service, pur queux chyvaux sont ore demandez hors de la Pipe de l'Escheqer quaraunt mars auxicome le dit Abbe Johan les eust resceu de achat, dont le dit abbe q'ore est prie q'il soit descharge, pur Dieu et en alowaunce del graunt travail, despense et diligence qe le dit Abbe Johan, son predecessour, fist en tiel manere, par comandement nostre seignur le roi et son conseil avantdit.

Endorsed: Pur ceo q'il est tesmoigne devant le conseil qe le dit abbe perdy plusurs de ses chivaux en le service le roi, et qe le dit roi q'ore est lui doner le ditz trois chivaux de son donu en restorance de ses chivaux, soit mande as tresurer et barons del Escheker q'ils sursessent de la demande q'ils font au dit abbe par la cause avantdite, et lui facent ent quites et discharge.

1334. On 4 March 1334 the treasurer and barons of the exchequer were ordered to supersede the demand for payment for the horses, in response to this petition (*CCR 1333–7*, pp. 213–14). The petitioner is probably William of Ingleby, who occurs as abbot of Rievaulx from at least 1322 until 1333 (his successor was apparently William of Langton who was not elected until 1335). Robert Woodhouse was keeper of the wardrobe 20 October 1323 – 1 November 1328: T. F. Tout, *The Place of the Reign of Edward II in English History* (Manchester, 1936), p. 316. The petition presents new evidence for the existence of John de Reynton as abbot of Rievalux at the end of Edward II's reign. An abbot 'John' is noted to have occurred in 1327 in *Cartularium abbathiae de Rievalle*, ed. J. C. Atkinson,

Surtees Society, 83 (1889), pp. c and 421, but refuted in *Heads of Houses II*, p. 302 n. 26. His abbacy appears to have interrupted Ingleby's term in office. Reynton's diplomatic service was probably used in connection with the negotiations which led to the Treaty of Northampton/Edinburgh in Spring 1328: E. L. G. Stones, 'The English Mission to Edinburgh in 1328', *Scottish Historical Review* 28 (1949), 121–32; ibid., 'The Anglo-Scottish Negotiations of 1327', *Scottish Historical Review* 30 (1951), 49–54. An earlier edition of this petition is printed in *North Riding Records III: The Honor and Forest of Pickering*, ed. R. B. Turton (London, 1896), pp. 254–5.

30

Coventry, Warwickshire (1335)
Benedictine
(SC 8/99/4926)

The prior of Coventry petitions the king and council, stating that William Erneys, escheator of Warwickshire, out of malevolence towards the prior and convent, and in agreement with other malevolent people of Coventry, accused the prior of acquiring lands and tenements in Coventry after the statute and without permission from the king, forging false inquisitions on this matter, and taking the tenements into the king's hand. The prior was able to prove that these accusations were false, and the king ordered a new inquisition and that his hand be removed, but the escheator put the same people on the new inquisition, with the result that the prior and his house are on the point of being disinherited. He requests a new and full inquisition, to be held in the presence of one or two of the most loyal knights or sergeants of the country as well as of the escheator, and with a new jury.
Endorsed: *A writ is to be sent to the escheator containing the result of this petition, that he is to take with him Roger la Zouche and John of Peyto the elder and hold a new inquisition with people who are not suspected, in the presence of the said prior or of his attorney; and he is to return the inquisition in chancery. And a writ is also to be sent to the aforesaid Roger and John, that they are to attend the holding of the said inquisition.*

A nostre seignur le roi et a son consail prie, si lour plest, le priur de Coventre qe come William Erneys, eschaetour nostre seignur le roi en le counte de Warrewyk, q'est mauveullauntz a la meson de Coventre par mauveise coveigne entre li et ascuns autres de la ville de Coventre, mauveullauntz a la dite meson, eust surmis au dit priur q'il avoit purchace divers terres et tenementiz en la dite ville de Coventre puis statut et saunz congie du roi nostre seignur ou de ses progenitours, et de ceo forgierent enquestes ne mie verrers, par queux il prist plusours tenementz du dit priur en Coventre en la mein nostre seignur le roi. Et sur cele cause ne mie verrere \par le dit eschetour/ retourne en Chauncellerie par bref de modo, et causa qe de ceo li vint le dit priur fist sa sugestioun coment partie des ditz tenementz estoit purchace a sa dite meson devaunt statut, partie puis statut par chartres de licence des rois, partie par voie d'eschete, et partie edefi en leur soil propre, come bien lour leust, issint qe a toutz les tenementz avauntditz issint prises en la mein nostre seignur le roi par le dit eschaetour le dit priur et ses predecessours sount avenuz par bon title et saunz offens faire au ditz statut, empriaunt au roi nostre seignur qe de ceo li pleust comaunder sa main estre ouste, par quoi divers brefs li estoient grauntes au dit eschaetour d'enquerer de la verite de ses susgestiouns avauntdites. Et le dit eschaetour, pur sa malice avauntdite, continuer et meintenir ne voleit soefrir autres qe ceaux qi en la primere enqueste prise de office maliciousement passerent contre le dit priur ou la secunde enqueste prise a la sute le dit priur estre mis, issint qe de partie des tenementz avauntditz ils ount autre foez fait faux sermentz countre le dit priur, nient eyaunt regard as chartres, munimentz ne evidences depar le dit priur a eux de ceo moustre, parount le dit priur et sa dite meson sount en point d'estre desherite si autre remedie de ceo ne soit fait. Qe pleise a nostre seignur le roi et a son consail sus les pointz avauntditz derechief graunter bref de pleinement enquere la verite des pointz avauntditz et joyndre au dit eschaetour un ou deux des plus loiaux chivalers ou sergiauntz du pais de ver et assentir qe cours de lei en reson son fait au dit priur en icele busoigne, et q'il puisse avoir enquest d'autres qe de ses nusours avauntditz, issint qe sa esglise susdite ne seit desherite.

Endorsed: Soit bref fait a l'eschetur contenant l'effect de ceste peticion, q'il preigne od lui Monsire Roger le Zouch et Johan de Peyto l'eysne, et q'il face de novel enquere par genz nient suspecionouse en presence du dit priour ou de son atturnez, et q'il retourne l'enquest en Chancellerie. Et auxi soit bref mande a les avantditz Roger et Johan q'ils soient entendantz a la prise de la dite enqueste.

1335. On 26 June 1335, as a result of this petition, and after a second inquisition held before William Erneys and Roger la Zouche found that the prior had indeed acquired the lands legally, the king's hand was ordered removed from the tenements mentioned within (*CCR 1333–7*, p. 411). The first commission to investigate the charges against the priory was issued on 30 March 1334 (*CPR 1330–4*, p. 574). The petitioner can be identified as either Henry of Leicester (1294–?1342) or Henry Irreys (occurs 1328); these may, in fact, be the same person, and references to Prior Henry continue until the next prior's appointment in 1342. The statute referred to is the Statute of Mortmain, enacted in 1279 (*SR*, I, 51), for which see E. D. Jones, 'Three Benedictine Houses and the Statute of Mortmain, 1279–1348', *Journal of British Studies* 14 (1975), 1–28. For further background, see note to **192** below. Additional context is provided by R. Goddard, *Lordship and Medieval Urbanisation: Coventry, 1043–1355* (Woodbridge, 2004), pp. 34–5, 282–3. For an earlier transcription of this petition, see no. 35 of PRO 31/7/104.

31

Boxgrove, Sussex (1339)
Benedictine (alien)
(SC 8/160/7959)

The monks of Boxgrove petition the council for a writ out of chancery to the treasurer and barons of the exchequer to remove their hand from the house and not to intermeddle further, as they have not been taken into the king's hand because of war with France before this time. However, their house has now been taken into the king's hand because the prior is an alien preferred by the pope.
Endorsed: *Because it is found by many certifications of the exchequer returned into chancery that the priory has never been taken into the king's hand in time of war with France, the prior and monks ought to have a pardon of the farm for being taken into the king's hand because it was an alien house and have restitution of the temporalities and goods, because the prior was an alien and preferred by the pope.*

Au conseil nostre seignur le roi prient les povres moygnes de Boxgrave en Sussex qe come ils soient Engleys et de temps dont memorie .... chescun vacacion de la dite priorie eslyre priour deux mesmes et al diocesan del lieu presenter, le quel soleyt estre conferme, institut et .... par le diocesan avandit, par cause de lour priour q'ore est, qi est aliene le quel le Pape Johan fist en priour, lour dit meson est seisye en la meyne nostre seignur le roi entre terres des alyens, la ou ils paient lour disme come altre religious Engleys a nostre seignur le roi. E sur peticion de ditz moignes, qu'ils unt avant ces houres longement suy au dit conseil nostre seignur le roi, trove est par certificacion des roulles del Escheker retourne en la Chauncellerie par mandement nostre seignur le roi qe unqes en temps des progenitours le roi le dit meson ne fust pris en meyne le roi fors en temps le priour q'ore est une foitz en temps le roi le pier et altre foitz a ore, dont ils sont malement grevez et empovrez. Par qei ils vous prient, pur Dieu en oever de charite, q'ils puissent estre demys et aver lour dit meson hors de la meyn nostre seignur le roi, qe nous avons taunt suy qe nous ne poyum plus, et si ore n'avons graces il nous covent toutz l'oostell deguerpier et aler mendiant, nostre payn priaunt come altre beggauns, par my le pays. Par qai ils vous priont q'il eiont brief hors de la Chauncelerie au tresorer et barons del Escheker q'il ostont la mayn et mes ne entremettont de la dit meson.

Endorsed: Pur ceo qe trovez est par diverses certificacions de l'Escheqer retournes en la Chauncerie par mandement du roi qe la priorie ne feust unks prise en le mains de progenitours nostre seignur le roi entre les possessions des aliens, par reson de nulle guerre q'ad este entre lez deux roialmes avant le oytisme jour d'Octobre l'an du regne nostre seignur le roi, piere le roi q'ore est, dys et oytisme, ne qe les ditz progenitours ne furent responduz des issues de mesme la priorie en lour temps. Et sur ceo tesmoignez est par prelatz et autres grantz en plein parlement qe la priorie est de la fundacion des progenitours les seignurs de Seint Johan, et qe apporte ne soleit ne deveroit ent estre fait, ne qe ele est suggette a nulle maison de religion pardela, et q'ele soleit tut temps passez avant le temps le priour q'ore est, q'est alien et nez del poair de France et qi fu prefect par le pape, et qe la dit priorie soleit tut temps estre governee par prior Engleis, si est assentuz et acordez en plein parlement par les ditz prelatz et grantz qe le priour et moignes de meisme la priorie eient pardon de la ferme quele est demaundee d'eux, par cause qe la priorie fu prise en la main le roi entre les possessions des aliens de ceux de France ensemblement od les arrerages de meisme la ferme, et auxi de la fin si nul soit fait par cause d'aver la garde avant autres, et q'ils eient restitucion des temporaltez et biens appurtenances a la dite priorie ensemblement od fez et avoesons, et qe le roi ent ouste sa main, et qe mes la priorie \ ne/ soit prise en la main le roi entre les tenemenz des aliens par encheson de le parsone le priour q'ore est, qi fu nez la outre et qi fu ensi prefect par le pape, et qe sur ceo soient lettres et briefs faitz en due manere.

1339. The prior was John of Wareng (c. 1322–48). A pardon was issued in accordance with the response to this petition on 25 October 1339 (*CPR 1338–40*, p. 325). A full edition of a similar petition presented at either the January or March parliament of 1348, with accompanying text of a patent letter, is printed in *RP*, II, 206, no. 6. See *VCH Sussex*, II, 57. A later petition on the same subject is **33**.

32

St Augustine's, Canterbury, Kent (1343)
Benedictine
(SC 8/256/12797)

To the king and council from the abbot and convent of St Augustine, Canterbury, making two requests:
(1) They state that William the Conqueror granted them a tithe of all rents and profits from the manor of Milton, except for the rent of honey and the tithe of rent called pennygavel, and that his charter for this, a copy of which is sewn to this petition, has been confirmed by later kings, and that they have been peacefully seised of this until the third year of the present king, who granted the manor to John of Florence for term of life. John lived for four years after that, and withheld the tithe of rent, cheese and pannage from them; and then Benedict of Fulsham, who is the queen's farmer for the manor, has also withheld them. They ask that they might be paid the arrears from the time of John of Florence, and that Benedict of Fulsham might be ordered to pay them the arrears from his time, and to pay them their tithe in future.
(2) They state that they have had the correction of bread and ale, by presentment of their tenants in their court of Newington, from time immemorial and by claim in various eyres, and which the king's father confirmed to them specifically by point of charter in the sixth year of his reign, but that Benedict of Fulsham is now distraining the tenants to present infringements of the assize of bread and ale in the hundred court of Milton, to the detriment of their franchise. They request a remedy.
Endorsed: *[To the first] This petition is to be sent into chancery and the certification, of which a transcript is sewn to this petition, is to be searched for there; and when the certification has been examined, together with the charter of the said abbot, and when the said Benedict, farmer of the manor of Milton, and other necessary people have been summoned, justice and reason are further to be done there.*
[To the second] He is to have a writ in chancery on his charter.

A nostre seignur le roy et a son counsail moustront ses umbles chapeleins abbe et covent de Augstin de C[ant'] qe come le bon Roy Willeam, conquerour d'Engleterre, par devocion et par sa charge lour granta et dona entre aultres ...... a dismes des totes ses rentes et des touts aultres profits aportenants a son manoir de Middiltone forqe ..... de rente de meel et la disme de rente apelle penygavel, come piert par sa dite chartre dount la copie de la dite est tosne a ceste peticion, la quele chartre pus est confermee par chartres des mults des roys, issint qe eus ount este peysiblement servi de x li come de la disme de C li de rente assise aportenant au dit manoyr de Midd' et de viij peyse de formage de certein parau et de pannage et des aultres profits du dit manoyr en noun de disme du temps le Roy Willeam avantdit tauncqe a tierce an du rengne nostre seignur le roy qe ore est, qe Deux gard, qi granta a Mestre Johan de Floronce le dit manoyr a terme de sa vie, li quel Mestre Johan vesqu.. apres quatre aunts et lour detint la avantdite disme de rente et de formage et de pannage tout cel temps. Et pus Beneit de Fulsham, qi est fermer ma dame la reyngne du dit manoyr, lour ad detenu la avantdite disme de rente et de formage et de pannage du temps qe Mestre Johan donia tauncqe a ore qe amountez a quatre a... et plus de temps le dit Beneit, dount les avantdits abbe et covent prient a lour treshonurable seignur Edward, par la grace de Deux noble roy d'Engleterre, qe ly plese, par pite et par regard de charite, comander a ses ministros qe les arrerages du temps Mestre

Johan avantdit lour seient payes et qe ly plese comander a Beneit de Fulsham avantdit qe il lour paye les arrerages de la dite disme de son temps qe amounze a quartre a... et plus et que eus en temps avenir prissent estre peysiblement servi de la dite disme en temps nostre seignur le roy qe ore est, come eus unt este en temps de ses progenitours.
Auxint moustrent les avantdits abbe et covent a nostre seignur le roy et a son counsail qe come eus eyent en et ul............ dount il ni ad memorie et par cleyme de fraunchise aloue en le Eyre Hervy de Stantone et en aultres Eyres devant de aver amendes de pain et de cerveyse par presentement de lour tenants en lour court de Newentone sount nostre seygnur le Roy Edward, piere nostre seignur le roy qe ore est, lour ad grauntes confirmacion par point de chartre entre altres franchises en l'an de son rengne sisme par les paroles qe son suent: Et in manerio de Newentone emondas assise panis et cervisie fracte, ore vient Beneit de Fulsham, fermer ma dame la reyngne du manoyr de Middiltone, et destreint atort les tenantes les avantdits abbe et covent de Newentone de presentier en la hundred de Middiltone la assise enfreinte de pain et de cervoyse en Newentone a defesaunce de la dite fraunchise alouue al abbe et covent avantdits, dount eus prient remedie.

Endorsed: [To the first] Soit cest peticion mande en Chancellarie et la certificacion, dont le transescript est coseu a ceste peticion, illeoqes serche et vewe mesme la certificacion ove la chartre le dit abbe, et apelez le dit Beneyt, fermer du manoir de Middeltone, et autres, qe busoigner soit illeoqes fait outre droit et reson.
Endorsed: [To the second] Eyt bref en Chancellarie sur sa chartre.

1343. This was part of a lawsuit starting at the exchequer in March 1338 and ending in chancery in April 1343, and which was recorded in *William Thorne's Chronicle of St Augustine's Abbey Canterbury*, trans. A. H. Davis (Oxford, 1934), pp. 490–502. This petition and its endorsement are printed on pp. 493–4. See also chancery warrant 1 April 1340 (C 81/263, no. 12711), SC 8/88/4376, and British Library Stowe Ms. 541 f. 115. The petitioner was Thomas Poucyn, abbot 1334–43; the queen was Philippa of Hainault.

33

Boxgrove, Sussex (? 1383)
Benedictine (alien)
(SC 8/94/4690)

The prior and convent of Boxgrove petition the king in the present parliament for a remedy and for confirmation of their letters patent, as they have been impeached before the barons of the exchequer that the priory ought to be taken into the king's hand because of the war, though they have letters patent of the king's grandfather making them denizen, and because their house was badly damaged by fire and they are impoverished, which matter is not allowed before the barons of the exchequer.

A nostre tresredoute seignur le roi en son present parlement supplient ses poverez oratours le priour et covent de Boxgrove, dount tout la covent est Engleis, qe par la ou le dit priour est empeche devant les barons en son Eschequer de ceo qe sa dite priorie serreit prise et seisie es meyns nostre dit seignur le roi a cause de cest present guerre entre luy et son adversarie de Fraunce, qe pleise a sa roiale majeste considerer qe la dite priorie est de la fundacioun des auncestres des seignurs de Seint Johan et qe les priours de la dite priorie sount coventuels et electifs et del institucion et induccion de l'evesqe de Cicestre et de sa visitacion, et par luy deposables si ascun prior soit trove en defaut, et qe l'evesqe del dite eveschie presentera par *lapsum temporis* et qe le dit priour nul aport ne fait ne ne doit a nulle maison pardela la mier, et qe a sa venue en Engleterre fut testimoigne par lettres du roi de Navarre q'il estuyt et est de son power et par sa testimoignance fut accepte et fist sa foialte en la Chauncellerie quant l'evesqe de Wyncestre q'ore est estoit chaunceller a Roi Edward, son aiel, et devient son lige homme, et issint demoert lige a sa seignurie et nulle defaute trove en luy, et la dite priorie tout \temps/ tenuz et ajugge denisein et nemye alien, come piert par lettres patentez de son dit aiel, portaunt date le xxv jour d'Octobre l'an de son reigne xiij^{me}, grauntez a un son predecessour en son parlement tenuz a Westm' a meisme le temps del assent de touz ses prelatz, countz, barons et altres illoeqes assemblez, et qe nostre seignur le roi ne nul de ses progenitours en le .... unqes ne fuirent respounduz des issues de lour posessions entre altres aliens en temps de guerre, forqe un foitz en temps du dit roi l'aiel et son piere qe fuirent restituez a son dit predecessour a le dit parlement ensemblement ovesqe fyns et altres profitz qe le dit roi aiel et son peire avoient resceux par lour seisine, come piert par meismes les lettres patentez. Et ore en brief temps passe les maisons del dite priorie estoient wastez, destruitz et abatuz par arseurs et l'esglise descovert, issint q'ils sount grauntement endettez, et qe les profitz des posessions de la dite priorie entre les charges issauntz sount meyns suffisauntz pur le dit priour et son covent, la quele matere le dit priour ad declare devant les ditz barons de son Eschequer et ne poet illoeqes estre allowe come ses predecessours ount estez saunz comaundement de conseil. Dount il prie remedie, et qe plese a sa treshaute seignurie de sa grace especiale, en oevre de charite, les ditz lettres patentz de son dit aiel renoveler, ratifier et confermer.

No endorsement

? 1383. It is likely that this petition prompted a confirmation on 12 February 1383 of letters patent issued to the priory under Edward III, at which point the priory's temporalities were also returned, having been seized into the king's hands as a result of the war (*CPR 1381–5*, p. 228). Thus, the petitioner was John of Lunda, prior 1369–c.1383. The bishop of Winchester was William Wykeham, chancellor 1367–71, and the king of Navarre was Philip III (1328–43). Earlier petitions on the subject are **31** and *RP*, II, 206, no. 6. See also *VCH Sussex*, II, 57. For an earlier transcript of this petition, see no. 51 of PRO 31/7/106.

Part Three

ROYAL INTERCESSION: MATTERS REQUIRING THE KING'S GRACE

3.0 General

34

Battle, Sussex (1280–1300)
Benedictine
(SC 8/312/E6)

The abbot of Battle petitions the king that he be granted his livery according to the purport of his charter.
Copy of a charter of William I granting that the abbot and two monks should receive liveries of rye-bread and candles at Pentecost and Christmas.
Endorsed: *At the exchequer, and the seisin and the time should be considered there, and similarly if the rent was ever released to the king or his progenitors, or recompense made in any way.*

Willelmus rex Anglie Lanfranco, archiepiscopo Cant', et omnibus baronibus suis Francis et Anglis per Angliam constitutis, salutem. Sciatis me concessisse et confirmasse regali auctoritate quod abbas ecclesie de Bello, quam fundavi ex voto ob victoriam quam michi Deus ibidem contulit, cum aliis abbatibus regni mei in tribus festis, Pasches scilicet et Pentecostes et nativitatis Cristi, ex parte regis ad curiam venire summonitus habeat liberationem de curia sibi et duobus monachis suis, panes scilicet duos simillagines de dominico et alios duos panes similagines de communi et unum sextarium vini de dominico et alium sextarium vini de communi et de pisce aut de hoc quod erit in curia, abbati tria fercula et duobus monachis suis alia tria fercula honorifice et duos cereos et decem frusta candele; similiter si alio tempore a rege summonitus curiam adierit, hanc liberationem habeat quamdiu ibi fuerit. Testibus Lanfranco, archiepiscopo Cant', Willelmo filio Osberti, apud Wyndesores.

A nostre seygnur le rey prye le abbe de la Batayle ke il ly voylle graunter sa lyveree solom le porpert de la charte desusescrite.

Endorsed: Ad Scaccarium, et videatur ibi de seysina et de tempore, et similiter si unquam redditus ille relaxabatur domino regi aut progenitoribus suis, vel pro recompensacione eis facta in alia aut quocumque alio modo.

1280–1300. Tentative dates based upon the hand. The charter dates to 1070: Lanfranc, the addressee, was archbishop of Canterbury 1070–89; William Fitz Osbern, earl of Hereford, close counsellor of William I and witness to the charter, left England for Flanders in 1070, and was killed in battle there in 1071. A full transcript of the charter in a subsequent confirmation of Edward II, dated 4 October 1312, appears in *CChR 1300–26*, p. 196.

35

Thorney, Cambridgeshire (? 1290)
Benedictine
(SC 8/75/3739)

The abbot of Thorney petitions the king and council, complaining that the hundred of Normancross, which he and his predecessors held, was taken into the king's hand because of the withholding of 20s rent, although these 20s were from the abbot of Peterborough's vills of Alwalton and Fletton, and were allowed to the sheriff in the time of Richard I when the abbot produced charters of franchises for the vills. He asks for the king's grace in this matter, and that his house might remain in the same estate as it was in the time of his predecessors.
Endorsed: *Before the king.*

A nostre seygnur le rey e a sun counseil moustre le abbe de Nostre Dame \e de Sent Botolf/ de Thorneye ke la ou meymes cely abbe e ses predecessurs tyndrent le hundred de Normancros a fe ferme, rendaunt C s par an par la mein le viscunte de Huntedone par chartre des predecessurs nostre seygnur le rey ke ore est, e cele ferme feseient tut tens deke al tens le Rey Richard, a quel tens le abbe de Burg Seynt Pere mist avant chartres de fraunchises al Escheker ke ses dous viles, cest a dire Waltone et Flettone, ke soleyent rendre xx s al avantdite ferme, les quels xx s alowe furent a un Richard le Engleis, viscunte en cel tens, par les chartres de fraunchises avantdites, les queles les predecessors le abbe de Burg Seynt Pere al Escheker avant mistrent, sicom pert par roulle del Escheker l'an del Rey Richard quynt, e pur co ke il semble al abbe de Thorneye ke une duresce ly fu fete kaunt l'avantdit hundred fu prys en la meyn nostre seygnur le rey quant il fu aresone de la sustrete del avantdite ferme de xx s e rien ne aveit pur ly for soul la alowaunce aroulle al Escheker fete [par] Rychard le Engleys, viscunte de Huntedone, par les fraunchises de Burg Seynt Pere kar ... ne poeyent aver par la reson ke il ne aveit mie entre meyns les chartres de fraun[chises], les queles furent en les meyns le abbe de Burg Seynt Pere, e memes celes chartres [de] fraunchises puys botees en pleyn Escheker e enroullez l'an del avantdit Rey Richard premer. Dount il prie a nostre seygnur le rey sa grace de le hundred, e ke sa mesoun, ke est sa fraunche aumone, seit meyntenue en tel estat cum ele fust en soun tens e en tens de ses predecessurs.

Endorsed: Coram rege.

? 1290. This is probably the petition which was summarised in a parliament roll ascribed to the Easter parliament of 1290 by H. G. Richardson and G. O. Sayles (*The English Parliament in the Middle Ages* (London, 1981), XIX, pp. 146–7) – see *PROME*, Edward I, Roll 2, item 92 (74). However, the hundred was not restored to the abbot and convent until 1 February 1292 (*CPR 1281–92*, p. 473), where it is mentioned that it was taken into the king's hand in 15 Edward I (1286/7), so there remains a possibility that this is in fact another petition on the same subject. On a different roll for the same parliament is an entry detailing the ownership and farm of the hundred of Normancross, prohibiting any grant of it to the abbot of Peterborough or the abbot of Thorney for two or three years (*PROME*, Edward I, Roll 1, item 58). On 28 June 1290 Queen Eleanor was appointed to the custody of the hundred, recently recovered by the king (*CPR 1281–92*, p. 369). The grant of the hundred of Normancross to the abbot of Thorney is included on the 1292 parliament roll (*PROME*, Edward I, Roll 5, item 16 (14)). The petitioner was William of

Yaxley, abbot 1261–93. Richard Anglicus (or English) was sheriff of Cambridgeshire and Huntingdonshire from Michaelmas 1191 to Michaelmas 1192.

36

Burnham, Buckinghamshire (1300–1)

Augustinian nuns
(SC 8/191/9503)

The nuns of Burnham petition the king for confirmation of [a charter of] Edmund, earl of Cornwall, the transcript of which is sewn to this petition.
Endorsed: *The king has granted the confirmation of his special grace, without a fine.*

A nostre seignur le roy prient ses povrez noneines de Burnham qe, pur Dieu e l'alme sez ancestores, voille granter la confermacioun .... qe Edmund, conte de Cornwaill lor fist, dont le transcrite est atach a ceste peticion.

Endorsed: Rex concessit confirmacionem de gracia sua speciali, absque finem.

(SC 8/191/9504)

Copy of a charter dated at Ashridge in 25 Edward I (1296/7) from Edmund of Almaine, earl of Cornwall, granting the nuns of Burnham in Lincoln diocese permission to elect an abbess without licence from him or his heirs, and granting the diocesan of the place permission to confirm the election. He stipulates that he and his heirs, and their ministers, will not have entry into the convent or its lands and tenements during a vacancy.

[Omnibus] Cristi fidelibus ad quos presens scriptum pervenerit, Edmundus, [clare] memorie Ricardi regis Almannie filius, comes Cornubie [salutem in domino. Quia non nunquam] ecclesiis ex earum morosa vacacione dampnum non modicum pervenerit et gravamen nos indempnitati monasterii [monialium] de Burnham, Linc' diocesis, super hoc prospicere cupientes eisdem monialibus ob salutem \animarum/ patris nostri et matris nostre concessimus quod [quocien]scumque per cessionem aut decessionem abbatisse earum[4] contigerit earum monasterii pastoralis solacio desolari. Liceat ipsis monialibus earum successoribus, absque licencia nostri seu heredum nostrorum, dicti monasterii patronorum, obtenta seu petita aliqua sibi in abbatissam canonice, prout eisdem spiritus sanctus inspiraverit eligere. Liceatque loci diocesano earum sic ecclesiam confirmare et ipsis abbatissam preficere patroni super hoc assensu minime requisito. Nec volumus quod, vacante quovismodo monasterio supradicto, nos vel heredes nostri seu ministri nostri aut heredum nostrorum, in dicto monasterio seu in aliquibus terris et tenementis ad illud pertinentibus, in posterum habeamus ingressum. Nec de ipsis aliqualiter intromittemus quominus terre et tenementa predicta tam temporibus vacacionum quam aliis in manibus dictarum monialium libere valeant et integre remanere. In cuius rei testimonium presenti scripto nostro sigillam nostram duximus apponendam. Dat' apud Asscherugg' anno regni Regis Edwardi vicesimo quinto.

4 This word may be deleted.

No endorsement

1300–1. Edward I confirmed this charter (SC 8/191/9504) as requested in the petition (SC 8/191/9503) on 27 March 1301 (*Collectanea Topographica et Genealogica* 8, ed. J. G. Nichols (1843), p. 123). The abbess of Burnham at this time was Joan of Ridware (1274–1314). The first three lines of the charter are partially illegible, due to excessive use of ox-gall; very tenative readings have been taken from an edition of the charter published in *Collectanea Topograpica* (p. 123), in which the charter is dated to 4 November 1297. Edmund, earl of Cornwall (1249–1300), was the son of Richard, first earl of Cornwall and king of Germany (1209–1272), who founded the abbey in 1266: *MRH*, p. 279.

37

Battle, Sussex (1309–26)
Benedictine
(SC 8/34/1658)

The abbot of Battle petitions the king and council, stating that he had impleaded Robert Bridge and others before the justices of the Bench that they took and carried away the abbot's goods and chattels to the value of £20 at Dungeness. Bridge and the others responded that the place where the abbot stated that the trespass took place was within the liberty of the Cinque Ports according to the letters close of Edward I, and they should not answer. The abbot said that they should not be excused by this, and that Dungeness pertained to their manor of Wye by their charter of William I, and was not within the liberty. The abbot requests that the letters close should not undo the charter of William I.
Endorsed: ....*to William Bereford* ....*of this business at W[estminster]* ....*feast of the Nativity of the Blessed Mary* ....
Afterwards in the presence of William of .... *before the council it was agreed* .... *chancellor, justice[s] of the Bench that* .... *aforesaid procede* ... *in the said words at the request of the parties to do [justice according to] the law and custom of the realm etc.*

[A nostre seignur] le roy e a son conseil moustre son chapeleyn l'abbe de la Bataille qe come il emplede Robert atte Bregge de .... autres devaunt les justices du Baunk de ceo qe eux biens e chateux a la value de xx li a Dengemareys k'est .... de Wy trovez pristrent e enporterent e l'avantdit Robert e les autres eient respunduz devant les justices q'il .... des Cink Portz, e qe l'avantdit leu de Dengemareys ou l'abbe se pleint le trespas estre fiat est mem .... Romenale denz la fraunchise avauntdite, e sor ce mistrent avant les lettres overtes le Roy Edward, piere nostre seignur [le roy qe ore est], par les queux il graunta a les barons de Dengemareys, le quel il dit estre membre du port de Romenale, ascunes .... et l'avauntdit abbe dit qe par ce la ne soroient excusez q'il ne covendrunt respoundre car il dist qe Dengemareys est .... du maner de Wy comme est susdit, quel maner od ses membres est hors de la fraunchise de Cink Portz e en le geldable ....nte, e sor ce mist avant la chartre le Roy William le Conquerour, par la quele il dona a l'abbe e al covent de la Bataille .... [m]aner de Wy ove Dengemareys et autres ses membres en cele chartre moteez, e qe touz jours puis la confeccion de cele chartre [le dit] abbe e le covent unt tenu le dit maner ove ses membres hors de la fraunchise de Cink Portz, e en geldable dit conte, e ceo .... prest feust et uncore est d'averrer par quant qe la court agardera. E por ceo qe la dite chartre e les lettres overtes sunt contraries en eux .... les justices ne les voillent pas juger ne nul averrement receivre contre eux sanz conseil nostre seignur le roy, mes unt .... au treis semeins de Seint Michel, e qe enter ci e la sue en parlement de saver la volunte le roy. Par qei prie [nostre dit seignur le roi et so]n conseil qe desicomme il semble qe les lettres overtes grauntees par le roy qe .... askunes gentz ne devient pas defere la chartre le Roy William le Conquerour qe touz jours .... maundie as justices, qe non contresteant les choses susdites aillent avant en le proces afaire .... et usage du reaume.

.... abbe emplede Esteven Gale, Johan Coly e autres devaunt les meismes justices du Baunk d'un autre tres .... [avan]tdit leu de Dengemareys d'une prise de vj chivaux e de xxiiij porcz, pris de xx li, par mesmes tiel proces .... nostre seignur le roy e a son conseil qe soit ensement sor ce comaunde as ditz justices qu'il aillent avaunt .... ley e usage du roiaume.

Endorsed: ....[W]illelmo de Bereford .... istius negocii apud W[estm'] .... festum Nativitatis Beate Ma[rie] .... Postea, presente domino Willelmo de .... coram consilio predicto, concordatum .... cancellerar', justic' de Banco quod ....rtis predictis proced..... in loquelis predictis ad instanciam partibus faciend' .... legem et consuetudinem regni etc.

1309–26. The petition, which is largely illegible, dates to the reign of Edward II since it refers to Edward I as the king's father. William Bereford was chief justice of the Common Pleas 1309–26. Other related petitions from the abbot of Battle, concerning Wye, are SC 8/15/737, SC 8/32/1558 (above, **24**) and SC 8/312/E6 (above, **34**).

38

St Osyth, Essex (1322)
Augustinian canons
(SC 8/7/326)

The abbot of St Osyth petitions the king for remedy. The constables of the hundred of Stow in Suffolk, at the sheriff's command, have seized into the king's hand the abbot's manor of Stowmarket and his other possessions in that hundred, until he has satisfied them for the sum with which they have assessed him for not swiftly sending men at arms to the king's aid at Burton-upon-Trent, although he had sent an allowable excuse to the king's court, and the promise to give satisfaction and to do what he could. Now, on the sheriff's authority, they have assessed him with finding men at arms to send to the king's aid at Newcastle-upon-Tyne, and will not let his people work on his manor or his other possessions in Suffolk until he has given them security that he will send men to the king's summons at the octave of Trinity next.
Endorsed: *With regard to the seizure of the manor etc., it is to be ordered that if it is for that reason and no other, it is to be released etc.*

With regard to the summoning of men for Newcastle-upon-Tyne, that is an act of the common council in parliament.

A nostre seignur le roi et a son conseil moustre son devout chapeleyn l'abbe de Seinte Osithe qe come il tiegne auscunes terres, tenementz et rentes en le contee de Souff', du doun des auncestres nostre seignur le roi et autres bones gentz, par leur chartres et par le conferment nostre seignur le roi q'ore est, qi Dieu gard, en franche, pure et perpetuele almoigne, les conestables del hondred de Stowe en le dit contee de Suff', par comandement du visconte auxi come les conestables dient, ont pris a seisis le manur le dit abbe de Stowemarket, et quant q'il avoit en le dit hundred, en la mein nostre seignur le roi, desqes atant q'il eust fait gre ovesque les ditz conestablez de l'agistement q'il firent seur lui, pur ceo q'il ne mandast pas hastivement gentz as armes en eide de nostre seignur le roi a Burton' seur Trente, tout feust issi q'il mandast a la court nostre dit seignur sa escusacion alowable par reson, et ensement a faire son gre a son poer. Et outre ceo, les ditz conestables, ore de novel, par autorite du dit visconte, ont agiste le dit abbe a trover certeines gentz as armes a envoier en eide nostre seignur le roi a Nouel Chastel seur Tyne, ne en nule manere ne volient soeffrir le dit abbe ne ses gentz meynoverir en son dit manoir, ne en ses terres, ne en ses tenementz, ne en ses rentes, en le contee avandit, desqes atant q'il eust trove grant sourte de envoier certeines gentz as armes en eide de nostre seignur le roi a la somonse qe feust faite as oytaues de la Trinite proschein avenir. Dont le dit abbe prie, pur Dieu et seinte charite, qe en regard as enchesons avantdites, et au grant qe nostre seignur et son conseil ent ont ore fait, remedie lui ent soit grante des grantz deurtes et grevances avantditz.

Endorsed: Quant a la prise du maner etc., seit maunde qe si par cel encheson et par nul autre seit deliveres etc.
Et quant a la cuillette pur gentz vers Neof Chastel, ceo est de fet par commun conseil en parlement.

1322. The patent rolls contain several items, dated early June 1322, relating to a summoning of men in late July (*CPR 1321–4*, pp. 130–2); however, this is rather later than the octaves of Trinity mentioned here. The name of the abbot of St Osyth is unknown. The episode is discussed in G. Dodd, *Justice and Grace: Private Petitioning and the English Parliament in the Late Middle Ages* (Oxford, 2007), pp. 249–50. An earlier transcript of this petition is printed in *RP*, I, 413, no. 153.

39

Waverley, Surrey (1326)
Cistercian
(SC 8/275/13716)

Letter to the king, dated 13 July 1326, from William, the abbot, and the convent of Waverley requesting that, because of various misfortunes that their house has suffered, the house be taken into the protection and keeping of Hugh Despenser, earl of Winchester.

A tresexcellent prince e lour trescher seignur Monsire Edward, par la grace de Deux tresnoble roy d'Engleterre, le suens chapelayns Frere Willeam, abbe de Waverle, e le covent de meme le leu honurs e reverences. Pur ceo, trescher seignur, qe vostre dite meson de Waverle est molt abassee par diverses cheances par defaute de blez en les dures anees, par morine de bestes, par diverse pleez, par oppressions, duresces e charges, par qei la dite meson ne puet suffrer la charge ne la grace de hospitalite, prient le dit abbe e covent qe vous pleise de vostre espiciale grace prendre la dite meson en vostre protection, e la bailler en la garde Monsire Hugh Despenser, counte de Wincestre, treis anz qe ele puisse le mayn tepus [*sic*] estre qite de pleez e de qereles, e meyntenue e relevee par la dite protection e la bond garde le dit counte. Escrit a Waverle le tressime jour de Juyl l'an de regne le Roy Edward vintisme.

No endorsement

1326. This William was abbot of Waverley from at least 1313 until 1328. The request was granted on 18 July 1326 (*CPR 1324–7*, p. 304).

40

Tilty, Essex (1328)
Cistercian
(SC 8/264/13193)

To the king and council from the abbot and convent of Tilty requesting that whereas the abbot's predecessor made a recognisance in the king's court to the Riccardi of Lucca in a debt of £64 and half a mark, and then, not knowing that in 1296 Edward I had seized into his hand the goods and debts of the merchants of the said company, paid the entire debt to the merchants, this debt has been demanded of them in the exchequer, for which they have often sued for remedy in parliament. The treasurer and barons of the exchequer were ordered by writ to certify to the king and council the reason why allowance of the debt was not made to the abbot and convent, to which it was answered that it was because the acquittance of £64 and half a mark was made after the confiscation of the merchants' goods and debts. They ask that the king consider the poverty of their house and the damage to the same if they have to pay the debt again, and allow them the debt and that they may be quit and discharged of the same.
Endorsed on face: *Certification was returned in chancery after Christmas last.*
Endorsed: *Certification should come before the council.*
Because the great poverty of the house was testified in full parliament, they should have a writ and letters to pay by instalments of 40s yearly at the usual terms at the exchequer until the debt is paid.

A nostre seignur le roi et a son conseil moustrent ses povres chapeleins l'abbe et le covent de Tileteye en Essex qe com un abbe de la dite meson, lour predecessour, feust tenu par conissance faite en la court le roi a la compaignie de Richardyns de Lukes en une dette de lxiiij li et demi marka paie a le bon Roi Edward, ael nostre seignur le roi q'ore \est/, l'an de son regne xxiiij, fist seisir en la mayn touz les biens et chateux dez marchauntz de la dite compaignie, ensemblement od totes les dettes qe homme lour devoit en son poair, apres la pris des queux biens, chateux et dettes issint faite, meismes celui abbe, lour predecessour, nonsachant de la dite prise, paia as ditz marchantz tote la dette susdite, de qoi ils firent bone acquitance al abbe et le covent de la meson susdite. Jadumeins, la dite dette par somons de l'Escheqer ad coru et uncore court en demande sur l'abbe et le covent susditz, et coment q'ils eient suy en parlement plusour foitz d'avoir remedie et alleggeance par peticion de la dette susdite, sur quoi mande feust as tresorer et barons de l'Escheqer par bref du grant seal q'ils certifiassent nostre seignur le roy et son conseil la cause pur qoi l'allowance de la dite dette n'est fait as ditz abbe et covent sur l'aquitance avantdite, a qoi est respondu par la certificacion qe demoert en la Chauncellerie qe pur ce qe la dite acquitance de lxiiij li et demi marc feust faite puis le temps de la prise des biens et dettes des ditz marchantz en la mein le roi, come desus est dit, est sursis de faire allowance as ditz abbe et covent de meisme la dette. Par qoi ils prient, pur Dieu et pur oevre de charite, qe nostre seignur le roi de sa grace, eaunt regarde a la poverte de la dite meson et a l'arerissement d'ycele si la dite dette soit autrefoitz paie, qe Dieu defend, plese comander as ditz tresorer et barons d'allower as ditz abbe et covent la dite dette et de ce faire quites et deschargez come droit et bone foi demand.

Endorsed on face: Retornata fuit certificatio in Cancellaria post festum Natalis Domini ultimo preteritum.
Endorsed: Veniat certificacio coram consilium.
Por ceo qe tesmoigne est \en plein parlement/ la graunte poverte de la meson, eient bref et lettres d'estallement a paier quarant soltz par an as termes usuels a l'Escheqer tanqe la dette seit perpae.

1328. On 12 May 1328 licence was granted to the abbot of Tilty in accordance with the petition (*CPR 1327–30*, pp. 268–9). The petitioner was probably Simon, who occurs as prior on 14 January 1328. Earlier petitions on the matter, alluded to in this request, are SC 8/144/7153 and SC 8/145/7201. Presented in the parliament of January 1327, the endorsement to the second of these petitions states that the receipt for repayment was obtained by the abbot after the seizure with intent to defraud the king. The Riccardi of Lucca was an Italian banking house whose assets were confiscated by Edward I in 1294 (not 1296 as claimed in the petition) after it failed to supply him with adequate funds: see R. W. Kaeuper, *Bankers to the Crown: The Riccardi of Lucca and Edward I* (Princeton, 1973), pp. 220–7.

41

Robertsbridge, Sussex (1332)
Cistercian
(SC 8/234/11668)

The abbot and convent of Robertsbridge petition the king, stating that Edward II granted them permission by his charter to acquire £100 of land or rent in compensation for their losses to the sea along the coast of Sussex; and that they have acquired the advowsons of the churches of Salehurst, Udimore and Mountfield, prebends of the king's chapel of Hastings, finding a vicar to serve there: something that is not mentioned in their charter. They ask that the charter might be confirmed and expanded to include the words 'prebends of his free chapel of Hastings'; saving the rights of the king and his chapel.

A nostre seignur le roy prient ses povres chapeleyns le abbe et le covent de Pount Roberd qe come nostre seignur le roy Edward, excellent prince, vostre piere, lour eust graunte par sa chartre qe eux, pur la graunte perte de lour terres perdeus et surundees par la costere de la mere en le counte de Sussex, pusent purchacer cent liverez de terre ou de rente en reconpensacioun del dit damage. Et de peus eux ount purchace par le conge le dit nostre seignur le roy le piere de Sire William de Echingham les avouesounes des eglises de Salhurste, Odymere et Mundefeld, a tenir en propres eus come en la dite chartre, dount le transecrit est a ceste peticioun acosne plus pleinement pert, qeles eglises sount prebendeles en la chapele nostre seignur le roi de Hastynges atrover un vikere de servir en la dite chapele, de qele chose lour dite chartre ne fait pas mencioun. Qe lui plese de sa grace especiale lour dite chartre de conge confermer, et de sa grace especiale en largir de ceste parole 'prebendeles de sa fraunche chapele de Hastynges'; le dreit nostre seignur le roi et de sa dite chapele tous jours a lui salve.

No endorsement

1332. The petitioner was John of Lamberhurst, abbot c. 1323–33. Edward II originally granted licence to the abbot and convent of Robertsbridge to appropriate these churches on 20 May 1309 (*CPR 1307–13*, p. 159). This was to offset damage caused to other lands belonging to the abbey as a result of the inundation of the sea: *VCH Sussex*, I, 72. However, the abbey was to be involved in many years of legal wrangling before the advowsons were finally secured. It was not until 26 November 1332, in response to this petition, that the licence was reissued and the petitioners were able to appropriate the churches, notwithstanding that they were prebends of the king's free chapel of Hastings (*CPR 1330–4*, p. 371). An account of this legal wrangling, with accompanying documents, is in C. S. Perceval, 'Remarks on Some Charters and Other Documents Relating to the Abbey of Robertsbridge', *Archaeologia* 45 (1880), 427–61, esp. pp. 430–42. For a copy of the letters patent of Edward II granting permission for the appropriation of these churches, see SC 8/234/11669. Hastings had been claimed as a royal free chapel only from the start of Edward I's reign, and 'there are no adequate grounds for including Hastings ... in a list of "genuine" royal free chapels'; J. H. Denton, *English Royal Free Chapels 1100–1300* (Manchester, 1970), pp. 114–16.

42

St Mary's, York, NRY (c. 1341)
Benedictine
(SC 8/280/13975)

The abbot of St Mary's, York, whose predecessors have held in pure and perpetual alms since the abbey's foundation by Stephen, late duke of Brittany and earl of Richmond, petitions the king and council that whereas he was summoned to parliament because it was found in the roll of parliament that his predecessors had been summoned since Abbot Simon was first summoned 80 years ago, that he and his successors not be charged to come to parliament by such summons since the acts of the predecessor should not be put on the successor.
Endorsed: *It is enrolled in chancery who are bound to come to parliament, and therefore he should sue to the chancellor that justice be done to him.*

A nostre seignur le roi et son counseil prie son humble chapellein abbe Nostre Dame d'Everwyk qe come le dit abbe tient grant q'il ad en pure et perpetuel esmoigne de la fundacioun Estevene, nadgeirs duc de Bretaigne et counte de Rychemond, et retenz par baronie, come plus pleinement peirt en l'Escheqer, la est le dit abbe somouns de venir au parlement par resoun q'ils trovount en roule du parlement qe ses predecessours ont venuz par somons, ou l'Abbe Simond fuist le primer qe unqes vient au parlement par somons, et ceo fuist deinz ces iiij[xx] anz, q'il pleise au nostre dit seignur le roi, en oevre de charite, granter q'il ne soit mes chargee ne ses successours de tieux somons de venir au parlement desicome les fait le predecessour ne poet pas charger le successour la ou il est descharge de droit.

Endorsed: Enroule est en Chauncellerie queux sount tenuz de venir au parlement, et pur ceo sue vers le chaunceller qe droit ly sont fait.

c. 1341. Simon of Warwick was abbot 1258–96. The abbot of St Mary's York was among those summoned to Simon de Montfort's parliament (1265), which suggests that this petition dates from c. 1341 (see A. M. Reich, *The Parliamentary Abbots to 1470*, University of California Publications in History, 17 (Berkeley, CA, 1941), Appendix 1; also discussion in Introduction, pp. xxv–xxvi and xliv). Despite this plea, the abbots of St Mary's continued to receive summonses to parliament, and to appoint proctors to represent them. St Mary's was probably founded in William I's reign, when the connection between the honour of Richmond and the counts (later dukes) of Brittany was established. The likeliest candidate for founder is Count Alan Niger (d. 1093), but during the twelfth century St Mary's continued to attract grants from this Breton family, who were earls of Richmond by 1100. Count (never duke) Stephen was a generous benefactor to the house from c. 1093 until his death in 1135–6. His gift of the soke of Gate Fulford, two miles south of York, would have made him prominent in the monks' consciousness: *Early Yorkshire Charters, IV: The Honour of Richmond, part 1*, ed. C. T. Clay, Yorkshire Archaeological Society, Record Series, Extra Series, 1 (1935), pp. 3, 4, 8–10, 39, 84, 86.

43

Beaulieu, Hampshire (1341)
Cistercian
(SC 8/161/8017)

The abbot of Beaulieu petitions the king and council that he and his successors be discharged of coming to parliament, as none but his immediate predecessor have been summoned, and no abbot of his order is summoned. He also requests that he be discharged of paying the ninth on wool and other charges which he is charged because he is summoned to parliament, since he was not present at the parliament when the grant was made, and has paid his tenths when others of his condition have.

A nostre seignur le roi et a son conseil prie le seon povere chapeleyn abbe de Beaulieu qe come il tient quant q.................................... almoigne, et rien ne tient du roy en chief par quoi il soit mys d'estre somons al parlement, ne nul de ses pred[ecessours] .... somons al parlement, forsqe son darrein predecessour qi primes fut somons en temps le roi piere nostre seignur le roi ...., plese avoir regard a cestes choses et a ceo qe nul autre abbe d'Engleterre q'est de meisme l'ordre est somons al parlement .... et commander q'il et ses successours soient desore deschargez de venir au parlement et a conseil nostre dit seignur le roi as touz jours ... qe le dit abbe puisse estre deschargez del la neofisme levies et autres charges dont il \est/ charge pro cause q'il est somons, et coment q'il ...... pas present ne pro procuratour quant les grantz se firent des tieles charges et outre ceo la eit paie ses dismes come autres ...... ount qui sount de sa condicioun.

No endorsement

1341. The petitioner was William of Hameldon, abbot 1340–c.1349. The chancery warrant with which this petition was probably enclosed is dated 12 June 1341 (no. 14147 of C 81/277). On 15 July 1341 the abbot and his successors were granted discharge from attending parliament (*CPR 1340–3*, p. 243). The top right-hand corner of this petition is damaged. The petitioner was less than honest about his predecessors' attendance in parliament: Beaulieu was summoned five times under Edward I, twenty times under Edward II, and eighteen times under Edward III. It has been conjectured that the grant of a ninth by parliament in 1341 prompted seven houses, including Beaulieu, to seek exemption from attending: A. M. Reich, *The Parliamentary Abbots to 1470: A Study in English Constitutional History*, University of California Publications in History, 17, no. 4 (Berkeley, CA, 1941), pp. 346–8, 363. See the Introduction, pp. xxv–xxvi and xliv.

44

Bradwell, Buckinghamshire (1375–6)
Benedictine
(SC 8/333/E1095)

To the prince and his council from the monks of Bradwell requesting letters to the bishop of Lincoln that he will make to Ralph of Kington, monk of Bradwell, ... to settle this business of the election of a prior as they are the prince's tenants in the honour of Wallingford and are greatly damaged by such unreasonable wrongs. The office of prior has been long vacant because of the great oppression by Richard Bitesle, who makes himself patron of the house and will make a prior of his own will without the assent of the convent. They have elected Kington, but they are prevented from having this confirmed by the bishop by the actions of Bitesle.

A nostre tresnoble et tresredoute seignur le prince et a soun sage counseill supplient humblement ses poveres chapellains moynes del meisoun de Bradewell vacaunt coment ils ont grant oppression par une Richard Bitesle, qe se face patroun de dite meisoun voillant faire un priour a sa vollunte .... commune assent du covent et a tort come lour semble, et sur ceo ils ont fait lour eleccion en acord de un Rauf de Kyngton, commoigne, qe grante ad........................... pursuyte de soun eleccion devers l'esvesqe de Nicole pur pursuyte l'avauntdit Richard, et auxint pur favour fait a lui par continuance et delayes, a tresgrant des........................... Qe pleise a vostre tresnoble seignurie, en overe de charite, granter vos graciouce lettres au dit evesqe de Nicole q'il voille faire au dite Rauf l'avauntdite .... esploit de ces bosoignes touchant la dite elecciooun, a cause q'ils sont voz oratours et povere tenantz en la honour de Walongford, issint qe le dit meisone .... greve n'endamage pur tiel nounresonable tort, issint a vous declarre qe Dieu vous doigne bone vie et longe.

No endorsement

1375–6. The petition comes from an original file of petitions addressed to the Black Prince (Edward of Woodstock, prince of Wales) and/or his council dating to 1375–76. No reference to Ralph of Kington as abbot of Bradwell has been found. On 18 August 1375 a commission was appointed to administer the goods of the priory *sede vacante* (LAO, Register 12 (Buckingham, Memoranda), f. 42v). The next recorded abbot occurs in 1388: *VCH Bucks.*, I, 34. The bishop of Lincoln was John Buckingham (1363–98).

45

Eynsham, Oxfordshire (1377–99)
Benedictine
(SC 8/212/10587)

The abbot and convent of Eynsham petition the king and council, giving an account of the history of tax relief at Tilgarsley in the time of Edward III, and requesting that the abbot be confirmed as exempt from paying lay taxes there.
Endorsed: *Order for instructions to the treasurer and barons of the exchequer to inquire into the matter.*

A nostre seignur le roy et son counsail supplient l'abbe et covent de Eynesham qe come ils ount terres et tenementz en la ville de Tylgarsley en le countee de Oxenford, lez qeux terres et tenementz sont parcell de la fundacion de lour dit abbeye et fust devant la Conquest et continuelment puis en cea, et pur qeux terres et tenementz lez predecessours le dit abbe, l'an xx le Roy Edward fitz le Roy Henry, fust taxe entre lez clers et continuelment puis en cea, qant x[e] ou autre taxe fust grantes a nostre seignur le roy ou a cez progenitours le dit abbe et sez predecessours ont este taxe entre lez clers pur lez ditz terres et tenementz, et le dit abbe n'ad autres terres ne tenementz en la dite ville, quelz terres et tenementz suisditz et lez quels terres et tenementz lez predecessours le dit abbe lesseront a lour neifs demesne a tenir a lour volunte, et nient contresteant cella Johan Whitfeld et sez compaignouns, coillours de la xv grante a aiel nostre seignur le roy, qi Dieux assoille, l'an de son regne xxxj, distreineront le dit abbe pur paier la xv pur lez ditz terres et tenementz en la dite ville, pur qoi le dit abbe fist pleint devers le dit Johan et sez compaignouns pur la dite distresse torcinousment pris devant lez barouns del Escheqier le dit aiel, l'an de son regne xxxiij, et le dit Johan et sez compaignouns justifieront la pris de la distresse par tant qe, l'an oeptisme le dit aiel, lour ditz neifs tenantz furont demurantz en la dite ville de Tylgersley, lez qeux furont taxez et assiz de peier qatre liveres qatorze soldz et neof deniers a la xv[e] a le dit aiel, le dit an oeptisme, et lez terres et tenementz qeux lez ditz tenantz issint tiendront en la dite ville a la volunte le dit abbe et covent revindrent a lez mains del dit abbe par la mort dez ditz tenantz neifs et unqore pur defaute dez tenantz remayngnent, et tout dys puis en cea ount demurez, es mayns mesme l'abbe et covent, qe le dit abbe alleggea, empledant qe lez ditz tenantz furont sez neifs et lez terres et tenementz, lez qeux eux avoient le dit an oeptisme ou puis en la dite ville, tiendrent de ly et de cez predecessours en bondage come parcell de sez temporaltez, et lez qeux terres et tenementz, le dit an xx[e] le dit Roy Edward fitz a Roy Henry et continuelment puis en cea qant x[e] ou autre taxe fust grantee a nostre seignur le roy ou a sez progenitours par lez clers, feust taxe entre lez clers, et qe par cause qe touz lez ditz neifs mureront l'abbe occupia lez ditz terres et tenementz come parcell de sez temporaltez, annexez a sez spirtualtez, nient mayns la dite matiere allegge pur la dite abbe lez ditz barouns agarderount noun resonablement qe le dit abbe pur lez ditz terres et tenementz serroit de la xv[e] devers le dit aiel charge, nient obstant q'il fust charge entre lez clers pur mesmes lez terres et tenementz et continuelment puis le dit juggement qant x[e] ou xv[e] ont estez grantez a nostre seignur le roy ou a son aiel le dit abbe ad este taxe entre lez clers et lez laies pur lez ditz terres et tenementz, et issint il ad paie pur eux double taxe, a grand damage de dit abbe. Qe plese de anuller le dit juggement et ordiner qe le dit abbe soit descharge de porter taxe pur lez ditz terres et tenementz entre lez laiez, ou descharger de porter taxe pur eux entre lez clers, issint qe le dit abbe et sez successours ne porterant double taxe pur lez ditz terres et tenementz, pur Dieux et en oevre de charite.

Endorsed: Soit brief mande as tresorers et barons de l'Escheqer, lour doignant en mandement qe serchez les accomptes des coillours des dismes et quinzismes en dit conte del dit temps, renduz al dit Escheqer, si par inspeccion d'icelles, ou par enquest ent a prendre, ou en autre resonable manere purra apparoir qe la suggestion des ditz abbe et covent en ceste bille compris contient pleinie verite, adonqes il deschargent les ditz suppliantz de paier la quinszisme pur lour ditz terres issint esteantz parcell de lour fundacioun fait devant le Conquest, et dont ils paient lour dismes come dessuis est dit, et q'ils surseant outre vient de la demande de mesme la quinzisme de lour dite possession, nient contresteant le juggement renduz en dit Escheqer envers les ditz suppliantz a contraire.

1377–99. The petition dates to the reign of Richard II, since it refers to events of the thirty-first year of the reign of the king's grandfather, who must be Edward III. The petitioner was either Geoffrey of Lambourne, abbot 1351–88, or Thomas Bradingstock, abbot from 1388 until at least 1409. Tilgarsley, otherwise known as Twelve Acres, lay within the parish of Eynsham.

46

Hospitallers in England (1383)

(SC 8/20/986)

The prior of the hospital of St John of Jerusalem in England petitions the king, stating that he is distrained in the exchequer for 15s for the farm of two forges built by the Templars in the middle of the high road of Fleet Street, which were lately completely destroyed by the insurrection (of 1381), so that the prior has not been able to have any profit from them, nor can he nor will he be able to have such profit, because they cannot be rebuilt. He requests release and pardon of the farm, which is due only to the king and leviable by the sheriffs of London.
Endorsed: *The prior is to sue urgently, as he ought, to have permission to rebuild the sites where the forges were, and when they have been rebuilt, he is to be obliged to pay the due rent; but in the meantime he and his successors are to be discharged of the said 15s.*

A nostre tresredoute seignur le roy supplie le priour del hospital de Seint Johan Jerusalem en Engleterre qe come il soit destreint en l'Escheqer pur xv s de la ferme de duez forges jadis leve par les Templers en my le haut rue de Fletstrete, les queux forges furent ore tard tout outrement abatuz par les insurrectours, issint qe le dit priour null ferme ne profit des dites forges prist de puis en cea ne unqore poet prendre ne unqes prendra par cause qe les dites forgez ne purrent en null manere estre relevez, qe plese a vostre roiale mageste relessez et pardoner al dit priour et ses successours a touz jours la dite ferme ou rent de xv s par la cause avantdite, la quele ferme est tantsolement due a nostre dit seignur le roy et levable par les viscontes de Londres.

Endorsed: Face le dit priour pursuit effectuelment, et son devoir, pur avoir congie de reedifier les dites plaices ou les forges furent, et celles reedifier, delors soit tenuz de rendre le rent due; mais toutes voies en le muen temps ent soit le dit priour et ses successours deschargez de lors xv s avauntditz.

1383. The petitioner was John Raddington, who succeeded the murdered prior Robert Hales in 1381 and remained in office until at least 1395. Despite writs of *supersedeas* directed to the exchequer to cease demands for the farm temporarily (6 July 1383, 6 December 1384, *CCR 1381–5*, 390, 593–4), the matter was not settled quickly. There were further petitions in 1383 (SC 8/20/986), 1384 (SC 8/20/987), 1404 (SC 8/216/10787, 10788), and 1439 (SC 8/27/1322, 1323). The house was finally successful in c. 1442 (SC 8/118/5871), see **52**. Forges erected in the highway were unpopular because they caused obstruction and blocked light to neighbours (see *London Assize of Nuisance 1301–1431: A Calendar*, ed. H. M. Chew and W. Kellaway, London Record Society, 10 (London, 1973), nos 483, 547–8, 617) which would explain why this structure was a target in the Peasants' Revolt.

47

Tortington, Sussex (1385)
Augustinian canons
(SC 8/251/12503)

The prior and convent of Tortington petition the king for confirmation of their possession of a house and appurtenances in London and the advowson of the church of St Swithin in Candlewick Street, granted to them by Robert Aguillon in the time of Edward I. These were taken into the hands of Edward III after it was adjudged that the gift breached the statute of mortmain, and were granted to the earl of Arundel, but he and his son have re-granted possession to the prior.

A tresexcellent et tresredoute seignur le roi supplient voz poveres oratours les priour et covent de Tortyngtone qe come un Robert Agwylon, chivaler, par son testament proeve et enroulle en le Hustyng en la Gildehalle de Loundres tenu le lundy proschein apres le mescredy de Ceindres l'an du regne le Roi Edward, fitz le Roi Henry, xiiij^{me}, devisa a la dite priourie sa mansioun en la cite de Loundres ove toute sa court, gardin et patronage de l'esglise de Seint Swithin en Candelwikstrete, ove toutz les appurtinantz et ovesqe toutz rentes queux a l'avantdit Robert apartiendrent, par quele devise le priour a celle temps de Tortyngtone, apres la mort le dit Robert, entra et prist possessioun en toutz les tenementz et rentes queux feurent au dit Robert a temps de sa moriant deinz la dite cite, forsprise une place appelle *aream tentoriorum*, les queux priour et covent ont este en peisible possessioun de toutz les tenementz avantditz del an suisdit tanqe al an xlj du regne le Roi Edward, aiel a nostre seignur le roi q'ore est, qe par un *mandamus* direct a Johan Lovekyn, mair et eschetour en la dite cite, fuist trovee et en la Chauncellarie retourne qe l'avantdit Robert avoit devise sanz licence de nostre seignur le roi, countre la forme de l'estatuit de terres et tenementz nient d'estre mys a morte maine fait al priour et covent de Tortyngtone et lour successours par soun dit testament tout soun dit tenement, ove les appurtinantz, ove la patronage de l'esglise avantdite, par quoi apres la mort le dit Robert les ditz priour et covent entreront en toutz les tenementz queux feurent au dit Robert a soun moriant, forsprise une place appelle *aream tentoriorum*, sur quele matiere un scire facias fuist suy devers le priour a cele temps de Tortyngtone direct al viscounte de Loundres et retourne en la dite Chauncellarie a certein jour, a quel jour le dit priour vient et a l'autre jour apres qe luy fuist done de aparer en court fist defaute, par quoi toutz les tenementz et rentes, ensemblement ove la patronage suisdit, queux feurent au dit Robert a temps de sa moriant, forsprise la place appelle *aream tentoriorum*, feurent seisiz en la maine nostre seignur le roi a cele temps. Et apres nostre dit seignur le roi, aiel a nostre seignur le roi q'ore est, par sez lettres patentz, dona a tresnoble counte d'Arundell, qe Dieux assoille, le tenement avantdit ove les appurtinantz et le dit avowesoun, a avoir a luy et a sez heirs a toutz jours, par force de quel doun le dit treshonure counte fuist seisy de toutz les tenementz et rentes et la dite avowesoun queux feurent au dit Robert a temps de sa moriant, forsprise la place avantdite. Et puis nostre dit seignur le roi, par sez autres lettres patentes, dona licence pur luy et sez heirs au dit tresnoble counte q'il purroit doner et assigner le tenement avantdit ove les appurtinantz et la dite avowesoun a les priour et covent de Tortyngtone et a lour successours a toutz jours, sicome en les dites lettres patentes puis pleinement est contenuz, le quel tresnoble counte devant le feoffament de ceo fait as ditz priour et covent murruist, par quoi le tresnoble counte d'Arundell q'ore est entra et seisist toutz les tenementz et rentes et l'avowesoun avantdite queux feurent au dit Robert deinz la dite cite a soun moriant, forsprise la dite place, come fitz et heir au dit tresnoble counte, soun piere, et puis nostre seignur le roi q'ore est de sa grace especiale, reherceant les douns et grauntes et la licence faitz au dit tresnoble counte le piere du dit tenement ove les appurtinantz et l'avowesoun come avant est dit dona et graunta licence au dit tresnoble counte le fitz, q'il purroit doner et assigner le dit tenement ove les appurtinantz et la dite avowesoun a le priour et covent de Tortyngtone et lour successours a toutz jours. Le quel tresnoble counte dona par force de dite licence le dit tenement ove les appurtinantz et l'avowesoun suisdite as ditz priour et covent et lour successours a toutz jours, par quel doun ils feurent et sont seisiz de toutz les tenementz et rentes et l'avowesoun queux feurent au dit Robert a temps de sa moriant en la dite cite, forsprise la dite place. Please a vostre tresexcellent majeste roiale considerer la possession des ditz priour et covent des tenementz, rentes et avowesoun suisditz, ew par longe temps, et les douns et grauntes faitz as ditz tresnobles countes et lour possessioun de toutz les tenementz et rentes et dite avowesoun queux feurent au dit Robert a temps de sa moriant en la dite cite, forsprise la dite place, confermer et ratifier l'estat de les ditz priour et covent a toutz jours, sibien en toutz les tenementz et rentes queux le dit Robert avoit a sa moriant en la dite cite, forsprise la dite place, come en le tenement ove les appurtinantz et avowesoun suisdite queux ils avoient de doun le dit tresnoble counte par la licence avantdite, et grauntier q'ils ne serront empechez par vous ne vos heirs par nul manere de title ne a cause d'ascune amorticement de les ditz tenementz fait as ditz priour et covent encontre l'estatuit des terres et tenementz a morte maine nient d'estre mys fait, pur Dieu et en oevre de charite.

No endorsement

1385. The chancery warrant with which this petition was formerly enclosed and the requested confirmation are dated 11 June 1385 (no. 3673 of C 81/489; *CPR 1381–5*, p. 578). John Lovekyn was mayor of London 1348–9, 1358–9 and 1366–7. The earl of Arundel to whom Edward III granted the tenement was Richard FitzAlan, earl of

Arundel 1330–76. After his death Richard FitzAlan, his son and heir, became earl of Arundel (1376–97). The identity of the prior of Tortington at this time is unknown. See also Helena M. Chew, 'Mortmain in Medieval London', *EHR* 60 (1945), 1–15, esp. p. 12, and E. D. Jones, 'Three Benedictine Houses and the Statute of Mortmain, 1279–1348', *Journal of British Studies* 14 (1975), 1–28. In 1392 Tortington owned several properties in London, the most valuable being worth £14 10s 8d, close to St Swithin's church; *The Church in London 1375–92*, ed. A. K. McHardy, London Record Society, 13 (London, 1977), nos 166, 418, 513 and especially 515.

48

Holy Trinity (Christ Church), Canterbury, Kent (1397)
Benedictine
(SC 8/253/12642)

To the king from the prior of Holy Trinity requesting that, for the relief of the works of his church, for the space of five years, no two of John Brian, his mason, John Brown, his plumber, and John Pirye, his surveyor, be put on juries or the such like, nor appointed to offices in the city or to other offices against his will.
Endorsed on face: *This petition is granted by the king.*

A treshaut, tresexcellent, tresredoute seignur nostre seignur le roy supplie humblement vostre perpetuel oratour et chappelleyn le priour de l'esglise de la Trinitee de Canterbirs qe please a vostre treshaut seignurie grauntier, pur relevacione dez oeveraynngnez du dite esglise, a Johon Brian, masoun, Johon Brone, plomer, servauntz et oeverours de vostre dite esglise, et Johon Pirye, surveyour et clerk dez oeveraynngnez susditz, tiel liberte a terme de cynk aunz proschenz ensuauntz qe nul deux soit mys en assises, jurres, attintz, enquerrez ou reconusauncez qeconqes coment q'ils touchent vous ou vos heirs, et qe nul deux soit fait bailly, alderman ne jurre de citee, coroner, conestable, collectour, taxour, assessour, surveiour, contrerollour de dismes et quinzismes ne autre subside, quote ou charge a vous ou a vos \heirs/ grauntes ou agrauntiers, custoumer, aulner ne autre bailif, officer ne ministre de vous ou vos heirs en countre lour volunte, pur Dieux et en oevere de charitee.

Endorsed on face: Ista peticio concessa est per dominum regem.

1397. The petitioner was Thomas Chillenden, prior of Christ Church 1391–1411. The requested exemptions were granted on 27 February 1397 (*CPR 1396–9*, p. 79). The second phase of the rebuilding of the nave of Canterbury Cathedral Priory began in 1391: J. Harvey, *Henry Yevele: The Life of an English Architect* (London, 1944), p. 80.

49

Axholme, Lincolnshire (1403)
Carthusian
(SC 8/178/8871)

The prior of the Charter House in the Isle of Axholme petitions the king that he be granted full restoration of the priory of Monks Kirby (Warwicks.), which had been granted to them after it

was taken into the late king's hand as an alien priory, to support the work of the house which will be destroyed otherwise. The priory was subsequently granted to Brother John Godinier, a Frenchman, and his monks, who ousted the petitioner and have lived dissolutely without observance. Following the prior's plea against Godinier the priory of Monks Kirby has been taken into the king's hand. He further requests that a writ of de procedendo *be commanded in the plea that he has pending, notwithstanding the taking of the priory into the king's hand.*
Endorsed: *On 6 May in the 4th year etc., the council agreed that the chancellor should call to him in chancery the king's justices and sergeants and, after the evidences and letters patent mentioned in the petition have been examined, if it seems that a writ de procedendo is grantable in the case, the chancellor should make the writ addressed to the justices of the King's Bench to proceed in the plea.*

A nostre tresredoute et tressoverain seignur le roy supplie humblement le priour del measoun de Chartuse deinz l'Isle de Axiholme qe come Richard, nadgairs rey d'Engleterre le seconde apres le conquest, a la compleint et request de Thomas, nadgairs counte de Notyngham et mareschall d'Engleterre, nadgairs patrone et advoe de le priori de Kirkeby des Moignes en le countee de Warr', considerant de certein science qe mesme le priorie, alors esteant es maine le dit nadgairs roy par resoun de guerre entre luy et sez adversairs de France, moene estoit malement governe, encountre l'ordinance et bone volunte de les foundours icell priorie, et mesme le priorie, et les manoirs et autres possessiouns a dit priorie appurtenantz, degaster et destrutz, et le divine service, et autres oevres de charite queux soloent estre faitz en mesme le priorie pur lez almes des auncestres le dit counte, sustretz, graunta par sez lettres patentz, le vij jour de Juyll l'an de soun regne dys et neofime, a dit priour et sez successours le dit priorie de Kirkeby ove les appurtenantz, a avoir et tenir ovesqe toutz maners possessions espiritelx et temporelx, fees des chivalers, advoesons des esglises et toutz autres choses, et rendont a dit priorie regardantz ou appurtenantz pur toutz jours, sanz riens ent rendre ou paier a dit nadgairs roy ou a sez heirs en temps de la dite guerre ou de pees, sicome en dite lettre est contenuz pluis au plein. Par force des queux lettres le dit priour fuist seise pesibilement du dit priorie ove toutz sez appurtenantz, et puis cella, trespuissant seignur, vostre hautesse nient enformez des ditz lettres ne del droit del dit priour, le xxix jour de Decembre l'an de vostre regne primer, graunt estez par voz lettres patentz mesme le priorie ove les appurtenantz a Frere Johan Godimer, Frauncеys, a avoir et tenir a luy ove les fees des chivalers, advoesons des esglises et autres choses a mesme le priorie regardantz et appurtenantz, sicome en mesmes les lettres est contenuz pluis au plein. Par force des quels lettres le dit Johan le dit priorie ove les appurtenantz, puis le \dit/ xxix jour tanq'ensa, ad occupie et unqore occupie, et les issues ent et profitz en le mesne temps ad pris a soun oeps, et le dit priour de la Chartuse del dit priorie de Kirkeby outrement ouste, par quoi mesme le priour puis cella ad suye en vostre court en Bank le Roy par brief de scire facias envers le dit Johan Godimer de repeller les ditz lettres patentz ensy faitz a mesme le Johan encontre la ley, en le quel suyt et plee le dit Johan vous ad prie en eide par force de mesmes les lettres patentz, le quel eide per agard de vostre court a luy estoit graunte. Et combien qe vostre chaunceller et justices de l'un Bank et de l'autre estoient ore tarde accordez pur avoir grauntes brief de procedendo a voz justices de Bank le Roy pur aler avant en le plee come la ley demande, ils ne purront a ore proceder en mesme le plee par resoun de les ordinances faites en cest darrein parlement des priories alienes pur estre reseisez es toz meyns, a tresgraund meschief le dit suppliant. Qe plese a vostre hautesse considerer de pitee coment le dit priorie de Kirkeby estoit avue incorporate et annexe au dit measoun de la Chartuse parmy les ditz lettres patentz le dit nadgairs roy, del assent et voluntee del dit counte, alors patrone et advoe d'icelle priorie de Kirkeby, et par auctorite del seint pier le pape, pur la augmentacioun et encrece de divine service et autres oevres de charite alors abeisez, et pur la entier sustenance d'un priour et vij moignes perpetuelement a celebrere et prier pur les almes suisditz en la dit measoun de la Chartuse, q'est a present en poynt d'estre desolate et anientez par defaut de sustenance, la ou ne feurent a plus en le dit priorie qant il estoit es mayns des moignes Franceys qe troys moignes vivantz dissolutement sanz observance de lour religioun, granter pur tant plein restitucioun al dit priour de le dit priorie de Kirkeby, a avoir ovesqe les appurtenantz d'icelle priorie regardantz solonc l'effect des lettres patentz suisdit a mesme le priour ent faitz, ovesqe les issues d'icelle puis le xxix jour de Decembre suisdit tanq'ensa, et enoutre comandre brief de procedendo en le plee unqore pendant parentre le dit suppliant et le dit Johan Godimer de mesme le priorie ove les appurtenantz devant voz justices de vostre bank, come la ley demande, noun obstant la dite reseisyn en voz mayns del dit priorie oves les appurtenantz par assent de vostre parlement, pur Dieu et en eovre de charites.

Endorsed: Le vj jour de May l'an etc. quart, presens en le counsail messires l'ercevesqe de Cantirbirs, le chaunceller, tresourer, l'evesqe de Roucestre, le garden du privie seal, le Sire de Louvell, Monsires Hugh Waterton et Johan Norbury, assentez est qe mon dit seignur le chaunceller face appeller a lui en la Chauncellerie les justices et sergeantz du roy a la ley, et y veues et examinees les evidences et lettres patentes desqueles mencion est faite en ceste peticion, si leue semble que brief de procedendo soit grauntable en le cas, adonques face mon dit seignur le chaunceller tiel brief estre adressez as justices du Banc du Roy pur proceder avant en le plee pendant devant eux sur la matire cy dedeinz comprise.

1403. The alien cell at Monks Kirby was granted to Axholme in 1396, but restored to Angers, its mother house, in 1399, and finally granted back to Axholme by Henry V in 1414. This petition (as well as SC 8/128/6364) is concerned with the aftermath of Henry IV's grant of 1399. On 20 January 1403 justices were ordered to proceed with the case in response to this petition, naming the petitioner as John Moreby (*CCR 1402–5*, p. 38). Thomas Mowbray was the earl of Nottingham (1383–99) at whose request the king had granted the priory to Axholme. Those present in the council when this petition was endorsed were Thomas Arundel, archbishop of Canterbury, Henry Beaufort, bishop of Lincoln and chancellor, Guy Mone, bishop of St David's and treasurer, John Bottlesham, bishop of Rochester, Thomas Langley, keeper of the privy seal, John Lovell, fifth Lord Lovell of Titchmarsh, Hugh Waterton and John Norbury. Monks Kirby, a cell of St Nicholas, Angers, had been founded by one of Mowbray's ancestors, hence his choice of its property, valued at over £200 p.a., as part of the endowment of his new house. See R. Graham in *VCH Lincs.*, II, 158–60.

50

Guisborough, NRY (1405)
Augustinian canons
(SC 8/113/5645A)

The prior and convent of Guisborough petition the king that their tenants be pardoned their rebellions, for which many are indicted, and that they be pardoned their forfeitures of their goods and chattels. The tenants, believing they were to join the king's son, went with John Fauconberg to Cleveland and Allerton, not knowing his purpose or intent. Afterwards they made their way to Sir John at Berwick at their own costs.
Endorsed on face: *The king, willing that he be* ....

A nostre tressoverain et tresgracious seignur, nostre seignur le roy, suppliount voz humblez liges chapeleins et oratours lez priour et covent de Gisburne qe come Johan Fauconberge, chivaler, par lettre de vostre honourable fith et treshonoure seignur Sire Johan, fist lever .... et tenauntz dez ditz priour et covent, a l'effect et entent d'aler ovesqe lour ditz seignur Sire Johan ou luy plerroit, sur quel colour le dit Johan Fauconberge, chivaler, eux amesna ovesqe luy en Cleveland et Allertone en sa cumpanye, eux nient sachauntz de soun purpose ne entent, et en apres lours ditz servauntz et tenauntz travaleront ovesqe lour dit seignur Sire Johan en .... taunqe a Berwyk a lour propre cost. Que plese a vostre mageste roiall de vostre grace espesiall pardoner a lez ditz servauntz et tenauntz dez ditz priour et covent generalment un chartre de insurreccioun, rebelleouns, tresons ou felonies dount ils, ou ascune d'eux, sount ou est endite, erette ou blame, lez nouns dez queux sount anexez en un cedule a cell bille, de vostre pluis habundant grace, pardoner as ditz suppliantz toutz lez forfaitures de lour biens et chateux a vous appertenauntz par le cause suisditz, saunz fyn fair ou fee ..... solement le fee pur un chartre, pur Dieu et en overe de charite.

Endorsed on face: Roy voulons qu'il soit ..... sanz .... en nostre servyce puis .... en prisone \............................./ .... dit priour avant vous ....

(SC 8/113/5645B)

List of names of indicted tenants, formerly appended to SC 8/113/5645A.

Johannes Hebson, Petrus Mark, Johannes Hobsthorke, Willelmus Swynburn, Willelmus Slake, Johannes Osebern

No endorsement

1405. The petition and list were clearly made in the aftermath of the Scrope rebellion, in which Faunconberg became one of the leaders of the rising in Cleveland: P. McNiven, 'Fauconberg, Sir Thomas (1345–1407)', *ODNB*. John Fauconberg's head was sent to be placed on the pillory of Guisborough on 22 July 1405 (*CPR 1405–8*, p. 69). The prior at this time was William Lasingby (Lasyngby) who, like Walter Skirlaw bishop of Durham, supported Scrope's rebellion. Guisborough Priory was a regular stopping-place for Skirlaw on journeys south to his Yorkshire manors, and the two men had been associates since 1402, TNA SC 10 (Parliamentary Proxies), file 41, no. 2012; J. H. Wylie, *History of England under Henry IV*, 4 vols (London, 1884–98), I, 355; II, 256, 263. The right-hand edge of the petition is damaged, and most of its endorsement is illegible.

51

Buckfast, Devon (1434–40)
Cistercian
(SC 8/93/4642)

Thomas, abbot of Buckfast, petitions the Commons of the present parliament that he may return home to his house and be discharged from the council, for he has had to stay in attendance on the council for two years because of many malicious suits made against him by Nicholas Brendon, Richard and William Easton and others, as this attendance is to the impoverishment of his house. The suits were made because the abbot sued against them for damage they did to his land at Buckfast.
Endorsed on face: *By the chancellor, 2 March. Let it be sent to the Lords.*

To the full wyse comunes of this present parlement besechith mekely Thomas, abbot of Bukfast in the counte of Devenshire, that for as myche as late Nicholl Brendone, Richard Eston, William Estdone and other persons yn grete nombre riotersly comen yn to the several wode and medwe of the said besecher at Bukfast forsaid, and there mynyd and overturnyd his ground by dyvers days, ayen the leve and comaundment of the same besecher, where thurgh he lese and yit lesith the profite of the same ground, for whiche trespasse the same besecher hath swid actions yn the kyng'is court at comune lawe ayen dyvers of the said misdoers, by cause of which actions the same misdoers have swid dyvers billis to the kyng oure sovereyne lord and to the lordis of his counceile, comprehendyng oonely mater determynable by the comune lawe, as it may appere by the copeis of the same billis annexid herto; where uppone the said besecher hath be send fore by letters under the kyng'is privy seal and writtis sub pena, and made to appere before the kyng'is counceile, and thanne ajournyd froe day to day to appere before the same counceile, and so holden and kepte here the more parte of al this ij yere, and yit is here evne dismysid or dischargid froe the said counceile ayen the comune lawe of this land and the goode statutis yn like case purveyd, to his importable cost and ynpoverysshyng of his hous, which is of the foundacione of the progenitouris of oure said sovereyne lord, and yn lettyng of devyne servis there to be done for oure seid sovereyne lord and his noble progenitouris, theire founders. Hit like youre wisdoms to praye oure said sovereyne lord that it like his noble grace to suffre the said besecher to goone home to his said hous for the rule there of, and to attende dyvyne servys there as his profession axith, and to have hym dismyssid and dischargid froe the said counceile as for this cause fro this tyme fourthward, for the love of God and yn the way of charite.

Endorsed on face: Per cancellarium, ij die Marcii. Soit baille as seignurs.

1434–40. The petitioner was Thomas Roger, abbot 1432–40. The earlier petitions referred to by those who were maliciously suing the abbot are SC 8/93/4643 and SC 8/93/4644.

In the former, Nicholas Brendon asked that the abbot surcease all executions against him and his tinners, and that they be allowed to work the mine at Hawkmoor. In the latter, Brendon and the Eastons requested a writ directing the abbot to appear before the council to be examined on the ousting of the petitioners from the tin workings near the abbey by the abbot and many others by force and arms. They also asked that they should be able to continue to work, and that the abbot find surety to keep the peace towards them. This petition appears to be the earliest of the three and can be dated to 1434, or later, since it mentions events of the Tuesday before the Conversion of St Paul in the twelfth year of the king's reign (19 January 1434). All three petitions have the following note written on their face, 'By the chancellor, 2 March.'

52

Hospitallers in England (c. 1442)
(SC 8/118/5871)

The prior of St John of Jerusalem in England petitions the Commons that he and his successors be acquitted of all outstanding and future rent due for two forges, which once stood in Fleet Street in London. The forges were destroyed during the Peasants' Revolt and not re-built, but the sheriffs of London are again being charged with it in their account. He asks that the rent be cancelled, and the king take the land and do with it as he sees fit.
Endorsed on face: *Let it be sent to the Lords.*
Endorsed: *Let them be respited until the next parliament.*

To the right wyse comunes of this present parlement, plesith it your right wyse discrecions to consider that where the predecessours of the priour of the hospitall of Seint John Jerusalem in Englond late were sesed of ij forges that were somtyme stondyng in the hegh strete of Fletestrete in the subburbes of London', for the wheche ij forges they paied, by the handes of the sherrefs of London' for the tyme beyng, yerely to the progenitours of our sovereyn lord the kyng, kynges of Englond, in her Escheker xv s, the wheche ij forges, atte the tyme of insurrecione of the comunes in King Richard daies seconde, were drawen doune and utterly destroied by the said comunes, for wheche cause the priour that nowe ys and alle his predecessours from that tyme in to this tyme have bene respited in the Escheker of the said rent, that it lyke yowe, the premises considered, and that the said forges mowe not be reedified for cause of streityng, noiaunce, cumbraunce and blemesshyng of the said strete, ne the said priour, his predecessours or successours myght or may in eny wyse eny profitz take for the soile where the said forges stode, to pray unto our soverain lord the kyng that it wolde lyke hym, wyth the advyse and assent of the lordes spirituelx and temporalx, and by auctorite of this present parlement, to descharge alswell the seid priour as the said sherrefs of the said rent and of all the arrerages therof to hym in enywyse longyng, and also to descharge alswell the said priour and his successours as the sherrefs aforesaid for the tyme beyng of the said rent for evermore, and that oure said soverain lord, by auctorite of this said parlement, mowe take into his handes the soil where the forsaid forges stoden to approwe hym ther of as it best semeth to his gracious lordshipe.

Endorsed on face: Soit baille as seignurs.
Endorsed: Respectuetur usque proximum parliamentum.

c. 1442. The petitioner was either Robert Mallory, occurs 1435, 1439, or Robert Botyll, occurs 1444, 1467: *Heads of Houses II*, 165. This petition brought to a successful conclusion a matter of grievance which had been going on since 1383: see above, **46**. The rent and arrears were cancelled on 4 December 1445 (*CPR 1441–6*, p. 447), during the penultimate session of the 1445–6 parliament. This would suggest this petition was presented to the previous parliament, held in January–March 1442. Other petitions have been identified which seem to date from the preceding parliament, held in 1439–40 (SC 8/27/1322–3). The earliest petitions presented on this matter, in 1383 and 1384 respectively, are SC 8/20/986 (above, **46**) and SC 8/20/987. Another petition, endorsed on 29 November in the sixth year of Henry IV (1404) is SC 8/216/10787, to which a writ of supersedeas was issued in response (SC 8/216/10788).

53

Bury St Edmunds, Suffolk (1454)

Benedictine
(SC 8/28/1386)

To the king and council from the abbot of Bury St Edmunds requesting writs or letters of the privy seal to the treasurer and barons of the exchequer ordering them to surcease the levying of £40 from him for not attending this current parliament. He states that at the time the parliament was summoned he was only abbot-elect and did not receive a summons.
Endorsed: *Memorandum that on the 15 April 1454 the king, by the advice of the Lords Spiritual and Temporal in parliament, considering the petition, granted the bill just as it is petitioned; and a writ of execution should be had.*

To the kynge oure sovereign lorde and to his discrete counsell, plees youre roiall mageste, by þ'avice of youre discrete counsell, to direct your writs or lettres of prive seale to your treasorer and barouns of your Eschequer commaundyng þem to surcesse of ony processe makynge ageyns the abbot of Bury for xl li of money to be leved of hym for his nounbeynge at þis your present parlement, and outterlie to discharge hym and his successours, abbotts of Bury, of þe seid xl li, eny acte of parlement made in þat behalf not withstondyng, in asmuch as he was elect abbot of Bury after the seid parlement somond and hadde never writte of parlement ne was nather somond ne called to cume to the seid parlement, as it was knowen and considered by tho wisdomes of the lordes of your seid parlement. And he shall pray to God for you.

Endorsed: Memorandum quod quintodecimo die Aprilis anno regni domini Regis Henrici sexti post conquestum tricesimo secundo, idem dominus rex, de avisamento dominorum spiritualium et temporalium in parliamento ipsius domini regis tunc congregatorum, consideracione infrascripta ibidem intellecta, voluit et concessit istam billam prout infra petitur; et quod haberentur super eadem brevia executoria.

1454. The petitioner is John Boon, abbot 1453–70. An earlier edition of this petition is printed in *RP*, V, 335a–b, no. 13.

3.1 Permission

54

Bury St Edmunds, Suffolk (1302)
Franciscan
(SC 8/1/21)

The friars minor of Bury St Edmunds petition the king, requesting that the courthouse of Cattishall, which is to be removed by the procurement of certain people, should not be rebuilt to the damage and nuisance of the friars, as William of Sutton, then sheriff of Norfolk and Suffolk, had been ordered. If the courthouse is built in the place decided by the people, it will be to the great harm and damage of the friars because when it is rainy or stormy people seek refuge for themselves and their horses in the friars' church; at other times when they are assembled the friars are unable to say mass because of the noise and press of the people. The friars request, so that their masses not be disturbed, that the king command by his letters that the courthouse, if it is removed, be rebuilt closer to the town so that the people may have more convenient recourse to it.
Endorsed: *The king orders that if they wish to build that hall, they should set it up in such a place that it should not be to the damage of the friars.*

A nostre senyur le rey priunt les povre freres menurs de Seint Edmund ke de sa grace volie cumaunder qe la sale de plez de Catteshale, qe serra remue par procurement de aukune genz, qe co ne seyt plaunte a damage ne a nuysaunce de le freris, si cum autre fez le cumaunda a Sire Wyliam de Suttone dunke vescunte de Norf' e de Suffouc. Kar si ele seit plaunte par la u aukune genz unt purw e ordine, co serra a freris graunt grevaunce e damage par la reisun ke si pluye avenye u tempeste le genz ne averunt refu ne pur eus ne pur lur chivaus for qe a le eglise de freris, si cum autre fez est avenu qaunt assembles i unt est entaunt ke le freres en lur eglise lur messes dire ne poeynt ne autre byen fere pur noyse e presse de genz. E pur co, Sire, pite ws prenye de le freris e ne suffret qe les vreisuns e le messes qe le freres dirrunt pur vus par taunt seunt desturbes. Mes Sire, si pleisir ws seit, volyet cumaunder par vostre lettre qe, si la mesun avauntdite serra remue, qe ele seit plaunte de autre part plus prede la vile par la u le genz purrunt plus prestement aver recest a la vile qe a freris.

Endorsed: Rex mandabit quod, si velint construere aulam illam, quod plantent illam in tali loco quod non sit ad nocumentum fratrum.

1302. This petition was discovered in an original file of petitions belonging to the parliament of Summer 1302 (*PROME*, Edward I, Petition 2, item 18). This case arose from a request by the abbey of Bury St Edmunds to move the courthouse at Cattishall. It appears that no action was taken until the abbey renewed its request in 1305: on 4 April the sheriff of Suffolk was ordered to enquire into the matter, and specifically whether the place for hearing royal pleas arising within the abbey's liberty could be moved from Cattishall to Henhowe, near Bury (no. 13 of C 143/52). On 19 June 1305 the king granted the abbey its request (*CPR 1301–7*, p. 367). These buildings had been completed and were in use by December 1306, when an oyer and terminer was granted concerning the people who entered into the houses at Henhowe, which Thomas of Tottington, the abbot, had built for holding the pleas arising in his liberty (*CPR 1301–7*, p. 472). For the presence of the Franciscans in Bury, see R. S. Gottfried, *Bury St Edmunds and the Urban Crisis: 1290–1539* (Princeton, 1982), pp. 220–2. The petition is also printed in *Select Cases in the Court of King's Bench under Edward I*, ed. G. O. Sayles, Seldon Society 57 (1938), II, cxxxvi–cxxxvii.

55

Bridlington, ERY (1305)
Augustinian canons
(SC 8/265/13217)

To the king and council from the prior of Bridlington requesting that a new road be made beside the sea from Bridlington to Kingston-upon-Hull. Such a road did exist, by which the prior, his men and other men of the country used to travel from Bridlington to the king's market at Hull, the town of Hedon and all other towns of Holderness where there are markets, but it has been destroyed by the influx of the sea, and those who have their lands there adjoining the sea are unwilling to allow the prior and his men, or anyone else of the country, to pass over their lands beside the sea as they used to do.
Endorsed: *John of Lisle, Lambert of Threekingham and Richard Oysel are to be assigned to hear and determine etc., or two of them etc. And if the road is not sufficient they should create another road to the least harm of the men of those parts, so that the king will satisfy those whose lands are assigned for that road for the value of the said lands.*

A nostre seyngur le roy et a son counsayl moustre le priour de Bridelingtone, pur ly et pur la comunalte del pays, qe la ou une vaye solait estre sur la marine dela mere de Bridelingtone jekes a Kyngestone sur Hulle, par quele vaye levandist priour et ses genz et les autres genz del pays solaint aler apee et a cheval, a char et a charet, de Bridelingtone tanke al marche nostre seyngur le roy en Kyngestone sur Hulle avantdist, et la vile nostre seigur [*sic*] le roy de Hedone, et a totez les autres viles de Heudrenesse ou marche est, la quele vay par refoule de la mer est defete, et ceus qe unt lur teres illokes joynaunt la marine ne voylent soffrir qe le priour ne sez genz ne nule autre del pays peussent illokes outre lure teres sur la marine passer com il solaynt fere, par quey le roy perde de eus son tonue et autres avauntages, qe par resone de marche a ly acrestre purraint, et la comunalte del pays en ad graunt damage. E de ceo levantdist priour, pur li et pur la comunalte, prye a nostre seyngur le roy qe vay lur sayt fete com estre solayt, si ly plest.

Endorsed: Assignentur Johannes de Insula, Lambertus de Trikingham et Ricardus Oysel ad audiendum et terminandum etc., et quod duo procedant si omnes interesse non possint etc. Et si via non sit sufficiens, dicti assignati ordinent aliam viam ad minus gravamen hominum partium predictarum, ita quod rex satisfaciat hiis quorum terre assignabuntur ad dictam viam de valore dictarum terrarum.

1305. The petitioner was Gerard of Burton, prior 1293–1315. Editions of this petition are printed in *Memoranda de Parliamento*, ed. F. W. Maitland (London, 1893), pp. 32–3, no. 29 and *PROME*, Edward I, Roll 12, Appendix no. 29, where it is noted that the second half of the endorsement (from 'Et si via...') was added later on the parliament roll during the same parliament (*PROME*, Edward I, Roll 12, item 176 (170)). The entry on the parliament roll specifies that it was Thomas of Munceaus who would not let the prior and community have passage over his lands to Hull (*PROME*, Edward I, Roll 12, item 29 (49)).

56

St Albans, Hertfordshire (1309)
Benedictine
(SC 8/240/11979)

The abbot-elect of St Albans petitions the king for his grace on seven matters:
(1) He requests the king's letters to the pope to put the confirmation of his election into effect, after he has received that confirmation at court.
(2) He requests the king's letters to the cardinals to expedite this business.
(3) He requests letters of permission to go overseas with two monks of St Albans and his people, and that no other monk of St Albans or its cells might pass without the king's special permission.
(4) He asks that when he has been advanced, the king might give permission to the treasurer to advance him if he is abroad.
(5) He asks the king to assign the keeping of the gate of St Albans to Thomas Brown, servant of the abbey of St Albans, to keep in the king's name, provided that he does not have charge of guests until the abbey has re-established itself.
(6) He requests letters to the prior of St Albans, asking him to receive whatever monk the abbot assigns to his company, to guard and watch over everything concerning the abbey, with the aid and counsel of the steward, until his return.
(7) He states that the king gave him his commission to survey his manors and the manors of the Templars on this side of the Trent, and asks to be absolved of the manors of the Templars, so that he might survey his own manors only, because he has told the pope that he has been in the king's service. And he requests his letters attesting this.
Endorsed: *To William of Melton, from Robert of Wingfield. All the petitions contained in this schedule are granted.*

Ces sunt les articles pur quels l'eslit de Seint Auban pri la grace sire seigneur le roy, si ly plest:
Primerement, de puis qe ly avient aler a la court pur avoer sa confirmacion, voeille, si ly plest, graunter ses lettres especiales a nostre seint pere le pape pur sa confirmacion graciousement parfourmir;
De autre part, pri sa grace, si ly plest, qu'il deigne graunter ses \lettres/ especiales as cardinals pur ayder graciousement de la dite bosoigne esploitier.
De autre part, pri sa grace qu'il ly voeille doner congie par ses lettres de passer sauvement, ove deus moynes de Seint Auban et ove ses gentz, et qe nul autre moyne de la meson ne de les celles de Seint Auban passe saunz especial congie nostre seigneur le roy, si ly plest.
Quare pri la grace nostre le roy qe quant il serra esploite ove le ayde de Dieu et de ly voeille granter, si ly plest, qe le tresorier le puisse esploitier si nostre seignur le roy soit en autre pays.
Estre ceo, pri la grace nostre seignur le roy qe ly doigne assignier la garde de la porte de Seint Auban a Thomas Broun, sergeaunt de la meson, a garder en noun nostre dit seignur le roy, issint qe y ni eit charge de survenauntz tant qe la meson seyt releve, si ly plest.
De autre part, prie la grace nostre seignur le roy qe ly deigne escrivre al priour de Seint Auban qe il accepte a receive quel moyne qe il voudra assignier en sa compaignie a garder et surveer totes les choses touchanz la dite meson, ove le ayde et le conseille le seneschal de la meson, tantqe a son retournier.
Estre ceo, par la ou nostre seignur le roy dona sa commission a le eslit a sour-

veer ses manieres et manieres des Templiers de ca Trente, pri sa grace qe il soit assenz de manieres du Templiers et qe sa commission soit chaunge et demoerge, si ly plest, sourveir de ses propres manieres pur ce qe il ad maunde a l'apostoill devant ces houres qe il ad este en son service et ceo, si ly plest, deigne encore tesmonier par ses lettres.

Endorsed: Domino Willelmo de Melton' per dominum Robertum de Wyngefeld. Concedunter omnes peticiones in ista cedula contente.

1309. Hugh of Eversden, the cellarer, was elected abbot 28 February × 27 April 1309; confirmed in Rome 11 February 1310, *Heads of Houses II*, 63. Despite his proctors expending *expensas horribiles ... in donis variis* at the curia, and despite the supplications of both king and queen, Hugh was informed that only an appearance in the papal presence would secure his confirmation, news which Eversden received with alarm, due to his weakness in Latin. The confirmation was finally secured after yet more expenditure, the whole process costing over £1,000: *Gesta abbatum monasteri sancti Albani*, ed. H. T. Riley, Rolls Series 28, 3 vols (1867–9), II, 113–14. This petition was apparently formerly enclosed with a chancery warrant containing instruction to make suitable letters for the petitioner, 7 October 1309: *CCW 1244–1326*, p. 300. Useful context for elections at St Albans is given by R. Vaughan, 'The Election of Abbots at St Albans in the Thirteenth and Fourteenth Centuries', *Proceedings of the Cambridge Antiquarian Society* 47 (1954), 1–12.

57

Vale Royal, Cheshire (1312)
Cistercian
(SC 8/145/7247)

The abbot and convent of Vale Royal petition the king, making six requests:
(1) They ask that the executors of John of Berwick be ordered to pay them the arrears of a sum devised to them by the king's mother for work on the abbey and to found a chantry there; and that they might be able to use this money to buy lands and tenements to the value of £20 annually to support the chantry, as the queen wished.
(2) They ask that the money from fines from indictments in eyres against the abbot and convent or the people of their fees might be put towards the work on the abbey.
(3) They ask that they might have the mills and fishery of [Chester] bridge after the death of Richard Lenginnour, who holds them for term of life, paying what he does.
(4) They ask for some convenient form of payment for the arrears of the money granted to them by Edward I for work on their abbey.
(5) They request the fishery of Hatch Mere in Delamere Forest.
(6) They ask that they might be able to move the house where they make glass for their abbey, as they burn alder-wood for the glass, and the burning of such dead wood would not harm the king; and because they can only pay their workmen in glass, they request permission to do so.
Endorsed: *With regard to the first petition: the testament of Lady Eleanor, formerly queen of England, is to be examined, and likewise the account of John of Berwick, so that from inspection of the testament it might be clear whether she bequeathed the said sum to them or not, and from inspection of the account what and how much of the sum mentioned in the petition has been paid to the said abbot and convent. And it is further to be seen how much money Berwick owed the king on the day he died; and then they are to wait until the king has levied from Berwick's goods the money that he owed the king on the aforesaid day, as has been said above.*

With regard to the second: the king is to do his will, but it does not seem to the council that it is to be done in the form requested.
With regard to the third petition: he is to wait for the death of the present farmer, if it pleases the king.
With regard to the fourth: if it pleases the king it can be done.
With regard to the fifth: the justice of Chester is to be ordered to inquire if it is to the harm or prejudice of the king or of anyone else if the king grants the said fishery to them, and how much it is worth annually etc.; and he is to inform the king.
With regard to the sixth: the justice of Chester is to be ordered to inquire if it is to the harm etc., and to what harm etc., and he is to inform the king.

A nostre seignur le roi priere ses chapelains l'abbe et le covent de Vaureal qe lui pleise comaunder as executors del testament Sire Johan de Berewik qe il lour facent paer C et vj li xiij s iiij d qe arert sount du CCCL marcs qe la dame la reyne vostre meire, qe Dieus assoille, devisa pur les overaines del abbeie de Vaureal, et pur une chanterie trover illoqes perpetuele de deus moignes pur s'alme, la quele chanterie se fet de jour en autre et atouz jours fra, si Dieu plest, et qe lui pleise de sa grace graunter qe des ditz deners le dit abbe poisse purchacer terres et tenementz en eide de la dite chanterie, alamontaunce de xx li par an, come la deraine volonte la dame vostre meire de cel devis estoit.
Item, prient les ditz abbe et covent qe com divers enditementz par diverses causes soient prises et fetes en Eyres en le counte de Cestre use s'il aviegne qe le dit abbe, ou nul de son covent, ou auqune de ses gentz denz ses feez, soient enditez de auqune trespas pur quei fin deveit feere, q'il pleise au dit nostre seignur le roi qe de sa bone grace voille graunter qe les deners de teles finz soient liverez as gardeinz des overaines de sa dite abbaie de Vaureal, queles overaines le dit nostre seignur le roi fet feere a ses custages demene taunt qe [les] distz overaines soient chevis, ou taunt qe lui plerra.
Item, prient les ditz abbe et covent q'il pleise au dit nostre seignur le roi graunter les molins et la pescherie de pount de C[estre], les queux nostre seignur le roi vostre ere graunta a Mestre Richard Lenginnour aterme de sa vie pur un certain rente, au aver et tenir les ditz molyns et la pescherie apres la mort le dit Richard ala volonte nostre seignur le roi, rendaunt p....... com le dit Richard eurent ore.
Item, prient les ditz abbe et covent qe com le Roi Edward vostre pere, qe Dieus assoille, dona ete assigna a ses overaines de [dite] abbaie M li, dequeux CCCC et ix li sount arere, qe vous voillet de vostre especiale grace graunter et assigner pur l'alme de son dit pere et pur la dite overaine avauncer auqune chose de quei il peussont de toux CCCC et ix li estre covenablement paiez, desicom l'overaine de la dite eglise par defaute de ceux deners est mout areri, et la volonte vostre cher pere .... acompli.
Item, priont les ditz abbe et covent q'il voille de sa grace et aumone a eux graunter la pescherie de Hachedemere en la foreste de la Mare de queei vous memes Sire ne nul de vos auncestres rien pristront onqes profit.
Item, priont les ditz abbe et covent q'il voille de sa grace graunter reinowement de lour meison un il fount lour verrure, desicom il ne ardont fors qe aunay afere verrure al overaine del eglise avauntdite, et desicome riens in descrest au ... par reison de arson de tel mortbois, et pur ceo qe pur charge de lour overaignes et autres meschef, il ne pount fere gre as overours du ver pur lour overaigne si noun du ver meismes, il prient qe nostre seignur le roi lour voile doner conge ..... ver qe

il ferrount fere il pusent fere gre as overours du ver meismes pur lour overayne, sanz chalange ou pechement du roi ou de ses ministres.

Endorsed: Quo ad primam peticionem: videatur testamentum Domine Alianore, quondam regine Anglie, et similiter videatur compotum Domini Johannis de Berewyco, ut per inspeccionem dicti testamenti appareat ac dictam summam legaverit eisdem nec ne, ac per inspeccionem dicti compoti quid et quantum dictis abbati et conventui de summa in petitione contenta sit solutum. Et ulterius videatur in qua summa pecunie dictus dominus Johannes de Berewyco tenebatur regis die quo obiit; et tunc expectent quousque rex levaverit de bonis ipsius Johannis pecuniam quam rege debuit die predicto, ut predictum est.
Quo ad secundam: faciat rex voluntatem suam, set non videtur consilio quod sit faciendam sub forma petita.
Quo ad terciam peticionem: expectat tempus mortis illius qui nunc est firmarius, si placit regem.
Quo ad quartam: si placeat rego fieri potest.
Quo ad quintam: mandetur justicio Cestr' quod inquirat si quod ad dampnum vel prejudicium regis aut ulterius si rex concedat sibi dictam piscariam, et quantum valet per annum etc., et certificet regem.
Quo ad sextam: mandetur justicio Cestr' quod inquirat si sit ad dampnum etc., et ad quod dampnum etc., et certificet regem.

1312. The future Edward I vowed to found a large Cistercian abbey during a rough sea crossing in the winter of 1263–4, but before the building was completed or the endowment sufficient his interest had waned and his generosity was much reduced (see J. Denton, 'From the Foundation of Vale Royal Abbey to the Statute of Carlisle: Edward I and Ecclesiastical Patronage', in *Thirteenth Century England IV*, ed. P. R. Coss and S. D. Lloyd (Woodbridge, 1992), pp. 123–37, esp. p. 128). The result was a string of petitions (SC 8/316/E208, SC 8/241/12014, SC 8/277/13843, SC 8/279/13916, SC 8/327/E827) by which the abbey sought to complete its buildings and secure its finances. This petition from John Hoo (abbot 1305–15) concerns specifically the legacy of 350 marks left by Eleanor of Castile (died 1290), to fund a chantry of two monks, and support the building work. Vale Royal's early years are particularly well-documented: R. Allen Brown, H. M. Colvin, A. J. Taylor, *History of the King's Works I: The Middle Ages* (London, 1963), pp. 248–57. The right-hand edge of this petition is damaged. For an earlier transcript, see no. 103 of PRO 31/7/96.

58

Gloucester, Gloucestershire (c. 1322)
Benedictine
(SC 8/114/5670)

The abbot and convent of St Peter, Gloucester, petition the king for permission to appropriate from the spiritual and temporal possessions to the value that pleases the king, to relieve the damages that they suffered when the Contrariants resided there.
Endorsed: *They should specify what they demand, and the king will be advised.*
Before the king.

A nostre seignur le roi prient ces chapeleins l'abbe e le covent de Seint Piere de Gloucestre q'il de sa grace lur voille graunter par sun fait q'il pussent aproprier de espirituaulte ou de temporaulte a lur eglise a la vailaunce de quele summe qe luy plerra de deinz lur fee demeigne, en eaydement de relever de lez grauntz mauls et pertes qe eaux aveyent nadgueres par la demeore de lez Contrariauntz lur dit seignur le rey, qe eaux e lur homages destrureit e tiel meschiefs e si bas, par quei eaux ount fiat moultz dures chevisaunces come de vende, dez livereisons, e maners e eglises mettre a ferme, de avoir lur vivre, a lur moult graunt arerisement pur temps avenir.

Endorsed: Mostrent en certein ceo q'il demandent et le roi s'avisera.
Coram rege.

c. 1322. The Contrariants were those in rebellion against Edward II in 1321–2: see N. Fryde, *The Tyranny and Fall of Edward II 1321–1326* (Cambridge, 1379), chpts 4–6, and further references in index. They occupied Gloucester in 1321–2 (see below, **59**). Thus the petitioner was John Thoky, abbot 1306–28. This was a time of great political upheaval, when the kingdom was in a state of virtual civil war, and when the Severn valley in particular had become the likely location for a clash of arms between the Marcher lords, led by Humphrey de Bohun, earl of Hereford, and Adam de Orleton, bishop of Hereford, and the king, Edward II. The town of Gloucester held particular strategic importance as a crossing point for the Severn and it was taken by the Contrariants as part of a strategy to deny the king access to the southern marches of Wales. The abbey itself was an obvious location to provide the king's opponents with shelter and sustenance, facilities they would no doubt have availed themselves of with relish given the abbey's royalist connections. See J. R. Maddicott, *Thomas of Lancaster 1307–1322: A Study in the Reign of Edward II* (Oxford, 1970), p. 304. For an earlier transcript, see no. 54 of PRO 31/7/97.

59

Gloucester, Gloucestershire (c. 1322)
Benedictine
(SC 8/114/5690)

The abbot and convent of St Peter, Gloucester, petitions the king and council for permission to appropriate one of their churches, as their estate has suffered considerable damage when the king's enemies resided there for several weeks, so that they have nothing to live off and to perform the alms for the king and his progenitors, or provide hospitality. The Contrariants took the town with force and arms on 18 December 1321 and stayed there for seven weeks, and each day took goods and chattels from the abbey and its surrounding manors, paying nothing.
Endorsed: *Before the lord king.*
They should advise which church and where, or another thing which is not in distress of the king, and the king will be advised.

A nostre seignur le roi e a sun consail moustrent ces chapeleins l'abbe e le covent de Seint Piere de Gloucestre qe par la ou lez Contrariauntz nostre seignur le roi vindrent en la ville de Gloucestre, a force e as armes ove lur gentz a pee e a chival, Galeys e aultres come saunz noumbre, en countre la pees nostre seignur le roi, e de guerre, le vendredi proschein apres la feste de Seint Lucie en l'an de nostre seignur le roi desusdit xv, e la dite ville pristrent e ileok demorerent par vij simaignes proscheinz ensuwauntz, e de jour en jour duraunt cel temps lez biens e lez chateux de lez avauntditz abbe e covent hors de lur abbeye e de lur maners ileok environ pristrent e enporterent, saunz rien payer, e lur homage dez ditz maners pleinement destrurent, par quei lez uns vient ore mendenauntz e lez uns en exil pur tous jours, en alesement del estat de lez avauntditz abbe e covent, q'il ne pount lur rentes ne lur services avoir come il soleyent en eide de lur vivre, e outre ceo lur rentes q'il aveyent en la ville de Gloucestre de maisons louwes, dez queus il soleyent prendre par an x li de rent, abatirent tut a tere, e le merym enportirent e ardirent, e auxi lur graunges e lur boveryes e aultrez maisons deinz lur maner de La Bertone jouste Gloucestre ardirent tut acendres, a lur graunt damage de MDCCCxxxviij li xviij s vij d, sicome il seient demoustrer, si pleise a nostre seignur le roi escoter, dount lez avauntditz abbe e covent sount si empoveriz e si bas mis q'il n'ount ore dount vivre, e lez aumoignes q'il soleyent faire pur nostre seignur le roi e ces progenitours sustenir, ne houspitaulte tenir. Dez queux mauls e damages prient a nostre seignur le roi lez avauntditz abbe e covent qe, si lui pleise, voille pur eaux ordiner de sa grace en eide de relever lur dite maisun en apropriacioun de acune eglise de lur avouwerie demeigne, ou autrement auxi come plerra a sa seiynurie.

Endorsed: Coram domino rege.
Se avisent quele eglise et ou, ou autre chose qe ne soit pas en destres du roi, et le roi se avisera.

c. 1322. See note to **58**. The Contrariants' occupation is precisely described as 18 December 1321 – c. 5 February 1322. On 18 February 1322 Abbot John was granted licence to appoint attorneys for life for the affairs of himself and his house, and on 4 March 1322 a burgess of Gloucester was pardoned a fine for communicating with the Contrariants when they were in Gloucester (*CPR 1321–4*, pp. 78, 79).

60

Pontefract, WRY (c. 1327)
Cluniac
(SC 8/66/3283)

The prior and convent of Pontefract petition the king that lay people are receiving and spending the offerings made at the hill where the earl of Lancaster died, which is in prejudice of them and against the estate of Holy Church. They ask that they might be able to have free administration of these offerings, as of right of their church, and they will guarantee that the building works they have undertaken will be expedited swiftly, and that the money will be spent on these.
Endorsed: *He is to sue in Court Christian if he is prevented from receiving offerings within his parish.*

A nostre seignur le roi priont ses chapellans le prior et le covent de Pontfreynt qe come gentz lors resceyvont et despendont les offrandes venauntz au tertre ou le count de Lancastre morust, quele chose est en prejudice de eux et encontre l'estat de seynte esglise, il luy pleyse ordiner par son bon consail qe les ditz prior et covent puissont avoir franche administracion des dit offrandes come du droit de lour esglise, et ils enprendront qe l'overaigne illoqes qe ad pris si grant delay serra covablement hastee, et les offrandes dument desponduz sur l'overaigne avantdite.

Endorsed: Sue en Court Cristiene s'il soit destourbe des offerandes dedeinz sa paroche.

c. 1327. The petitioner was Stephen of Cherobles, prior 1322–c.1349. Thomas, earl of Lancaster, a leader of baronial opposition to Edward II, was captured at the battle of Boroughbridge, and executed on 22 March 1322 near Pontefract Castle. On 3 February 1327 Robert of Werington was ordered not to interfere further with offerings to the priory church of Pontefract (*CCR 1327–30*, p. 21). For discussion of the cult of Thomas of Lancaster and its focus in Pontefract, see D. Piroyansky, *Martyrs in the Making: Political Martyrdom in Late Medieval England* (Basingstoke, 2008), pp. 23–30.

61

St Helen's, Bishopsgate, London (c. 1351)
Benedictine (nuns)
(SC 8/45/2211)

The prioress and nuns of the convent of St Helen's, Bishopsgate, London, petition the king that he grant and ratify Edward I's charter granting them a market and fair in their manor of Brentford, which have fallen into disuse because they are enclosed and cannot pursue their business.
Endorsed: *Because the abbot of Westminster, which is of the king's foundation, is lord of the vill, and has all manner of franchises in the said vill, the abbot is to be called to show his arguments against this before anything is done.*

A nostre seignour le roi moustrent les poveres recluses, prioresse et ses nonaignes de la mesoun de Seinte Eleine en Loundres, qe come lui noble Roi Edward, aele a nostre dit seignur le roi q'ore est, qi Dieux assoille, avoit done, graunte et par sa chartre conferme a prioresse et nonaignes et a les successours de la dite mesoun en lour manoir de Braynford el countee de Midd' une marchee chescune semaigne en le jour de marsdy et une feire illeoqes chescun an en la veille et en la jour de Seint Laurence et par qatre jours proscheins ensuantz, les queux marche et feire eueient este desusez par cause qe les dites poveres nonaignes sount recluses et ne poent lours busoignes pursurer. Par quei plese a vostre tresredoute seignurie, en eovre de charite et pur les almes de voz progenitours, grauntier et ratefier la dite chartre, qe les avauntdites poveres recluses puissent avoir et user les dites marches et feires come ils fuissent de vostre dit aele grauntez.

Endorsed: Purceo qe l'abbe de Westm', qest de la fundacione nostre seignur le roi, est seignur de la ville, et ad totes maneres des franchiseis en la dite ville, soit l'abbe appelle a moustrer ses resouns a l'encountre avant qe rien soit fait.

c. 1351. In 1350 Pope Clement VI granted the nuns an indulgence for their difficulties following the Black Death, which may indicate a date for this attempt to recover their market and fair (*VCH London*, I, 458). No. 26 of C 49/7 suggests that this petition was presented in c. 1351. Thus, the petitioner is Margery of Honilane, who occurs as prioress from 1349 until 1368. The abbot was Simon Langham (1349–62). The right to hold a fair at Brentford was originally granted by Edward I in 1306: M. Reddan, 'St Helen's, Bishopgate', in *The Religious Houses of London and Middlesex*, ed. C. M. Barron and M. Davies (London, 2007), pp. 72–3. The petition is printed in *RP*, II, 403, no. 138.

62

Peterborough, Northamptonshire (1375–6)
Benedictine
(SC 8/333/E1079)

The abbot of [Peterborough] petitions the prince and his council that he may have the keeping and marriage of [the heir of Hugh of Northborough], and enjoy it in peace without debate from the prince or his ministers. He states that Northborough at his death held …, Thurlby and Northborough from him, by which the wardship should pertain to him.

A nostre seignur le prince et son bon et sage conseil moustre son chapellein l'abbe de Burgh .... [Hugh de] Northburgh qe mort est, qe Dieux assoille, tient de lui le jour de son moriant par service .... en le contee de Norht' et auxint le manoir de Thurleby en le contee de Nichole .... verge de terre et dimy en Northburgh en le contee de Norht', par quele cause le dit abbe .... le dit Mesire Hugh issint ad le dit abbe droit d'avoir la garde et mariage du dit heir .... q'il puisse avoir et joier en pees sanz debate son dit seignur ou ses ministres ...

No endorsement

1375–6. The petition comes from an original file of petitions addressed to the Black Prince and/or his council dating to 1375–6. The petitioner was Henry of Overton, abbot 1361–91. SC 8/333/E1076 is a schedule of land held by Northburgh on the day of his death from Lady Wake (Joan of Kent), and was probably formerly enclosed with this petition. The right-hand side of this document is completely illegible.

63

Ely, Cambridgeshire (1383)
Benedictine
(SC 8/183/9108)

Thomas, bishop of Ely, and the prior and convent of Ely petition the king that they may receive all the lands, tenements, goods and chattels of men in their franchises who have been condemned to death for their part in the Peasants' Revolt. This property has been seized into the king's hands by the escheators. They also request confirmation of their rights in such cases.
Endorsed: *On 3 August in the 7th year, the lords of the council assembled at Nottingham Castle agreed that the bishop, prior and convent shall have all goods, chattels, lands and tenements forfeited due to the insurrection of the commons in the manner requested in this bill, and that they have in perpetuity all manner of forfeitures made in the future in connection with that insurrection, and that no person should be made to appear before royal justices on this matter.*

A tresredoubte et tresexcellent seignur nostre seignur le roy supplient humblement ses chapellains Thomas, evesqe d'Ely, et priour et covent de mesme le lieu qe come les nobles progenitours nostre dit seignur le roy, par lour chartres par lui confermees, eiont grante a Dieu et a Saint Auldree d'Ely et as predecessours les ditz evesqe, priour et covent toutes maners des forfaitures escheantz deinz l'Isle d'Ely et deinz le hundred et demy de Mitford et deinz les cynk hundredz et demy de Wykelowe, Trillyngum et Wynestone, si bien des hommes et tenantz d'autres fes come des hommes et tenantz de lour seos propres, et oie en la darreine surrexion des comunes ascuns des hommes et tenantz les ditz evesqe, priour et covent et hommes et tenantz d'autry deinz les ditz seignuries furent mys a mort par justices en diverses commissions, par quoi les eschetours des conties de Cantebr', Norff' et Suff' ont saisiz lour terres et tenemenz, biens et chateux come forfaitz a roy, queux terres et tenemenz, biens et chateux les ditz evesqe, priour et covent clayment avoir par vertue des ditz paroles generales en les chartres susdites comprises. Qe plaise a nostre dit tresredoubte et tresexcellent seignur le roy, de sa grace especiale et pour les almes de ses nobles progenitours susditz, grantier par ses lettres as ditz evesqe, priour et covent toux les avantditz biens et chateux ensi saisiz ou forfatiz ensemblement ovesqe les avantditz terres et tenemenz, a avoir et tenir a eux et a lour successours en perpetuel almoigne a toux jours, et outre ceo, pour declaracion des ditz paroles generales al reverence de Dieu et de Saint Auldree, grantier par sa chartre as ditz evesqe, priour et covent et a lour successours a toux jours toute manere des forfaitures en chescun caas de perdicion touchantz surrexions ou levees des comunes forsiblement a feoz de guerre, fausours de monoie et contrefaitoures du seal le roy, ou autre quecumqe perdcicion done la forfaiture au roy ou a ses heirs en ascune manere pourra appereteneir, deinz le dit Isle perpetuelement a seisir et a prendre par lour ministres a lour oeps demesne, sanz ce qe ascun ministre du roy se entremelle, et qe les ditz evesqe, priour et covent ne nul autre persone pur les ditz terres et tenemenz, biens et chateux, ne pur occupacion d'iceles, ne soient empechez ou mys a response devant nul juge en temps avenir, maes q'ils et les eschetours en soient quites et deschargees a toux jours.

Endorsed: Le tierce jour d'Augst l'an septisme, les seignurs du conseil le roy assembles a chastel de Notyngham assentierent qe l'evesqe, priour et covent deinz especifiez eient touz les biens et chateux seisiz en forfaitz par cause del insurrectioun des comunes faite encontre la roiale mageste et heirz deinz escriptz, et auxint les terres et tenemenz seisiz a forfaitz par mesme la cause illoqes, a eux et a lour successours en perpetuele almoigne en manere q'ils par ceste bille ont demandez, et en outre qe mesmes l'evesqe, priour et covent et lour successours eient en perpetuele almoigne touz maneres des forfaitures qe purront escheer a cause d'acuns tiles insurrexioun ou levee des comunes forsiblement en temps avenir et appertener au roy ou a ses heirs deinz l'Isle d'Ely deinz escriptz, a seiser et prendre par lour ministres a lour eops de mesne, sanz ce qe aucun ministre du roy s'entremelle, et qe les ditz evesqe, priour et covent ne nule autre persone pur les ditz terres, tenemenz, biens et chateux, ne pur occupacion d'icelles, ne soient empeches ou mys a response devant nule juge en temps avenir, mes q'ils et touz autres ent soient quitz et deschargez envers le roy et ses ministres a touz jours.

1383. The chancery warrant with which this petition was formerly enclosed is dated 21 July 1383 (no. 3 of C 81/1340). On 3 August 1383 the king granted the request, incorporating the text of the endorsement (*CChR 1341–1417*, pp. 288–9). The petitioners are Thomas Arundel, bishop of Ely 1373–88, and John Bukton, prior of Ely c. 1364–96. During the rebellion the court rolls of the priory at West Wratting were destroyed, captives in the bishop's prison were released, and a mob entered the cathedral church and declared from the pulpit what measures ought to be taken against the traitors of the king: E. Powell,

The Rising in East Anglia in 1381 (Cambridge, 1896), pp. 46–8. For a similar petition from the abbot of Peterborough, see below, **141**.

64

Dunwich, Suffolk (1384)
Dominican
(SC 8/183/9121)

The Dominicans of Dunwich petition the king for licence for Robert of Swillington, knight, to grant them certain lands in Blythburgh for the building of a new friary. They state that much of Dunwich has been destroyed by the sea, and their house is now in great peril. They also request licence to sell their land in Dunwich if possible.

Al tresexcellent et tresgracieux seignur nostre seignur le roy supplient les povers freres prechours de la ville de Donewys en le countee de Suff' qe come les ditz freres ount un covent en la dite ville, de quele ville la greindre parte est gastee et destruite puis la grande pestilence par la mier, et la mansion des ditz povers freres serra en brief auxi gastee par la mier, issint qe leur entent q'ils changent leur maison en aillours, sur quoy Monsire Robert de Swelyngtone, chivaler, pur pite q'il ad d'eulx, est en bone voluntee a douner a eulx de sa aulmoigns dix acres de terre et quatre acres de mareys pur leur edifier en la ville de Blibourgh, q'est presde la dite ville de Donewys, quele terre et mareys sont parcelle de son manoir de Blibourgh q'est tenuz de nostre dit seignur le roy. Q'il plese a sa haute mageste, pur Dieu et pur les almes de son tresnoble pere et de ses autres progenitours, douner licence d'amortiser yceulx terres et mareys as ditz povers freres perpetuelment pur leur edifier illeoqes, et q'ils purront translater leur maison en Donewys saunz impediment de nully et leur soil en Donewys vendre, apres les maisons enrases en aide des grands custages q'ils ferront entour leu dite edificacion, et ce saunz fyn fere, pur Dieu et en oevere de charite.

No endorsement

1384. The chancery warrant with which this petition was formerly enclosed is dated 23 November (no. 46 of C 81/1343), as is the requested licence (*CPR 1381–5*, p. 488).

65

Dunwich, Suffolk (1384)
Dominican
(SC 8/183/9126)

The Dominicans and chaplains of Dunwich petition the king for licence for Robert of Swillington, knight, to found a new friary for them at Blythburgh, and to grant them certain lands there. They state that much of Dunwich has been destroyed by the sea, and their house is now in great peril. They also request licence to sell their land in Dunwich if possible.

A tresexcellent et nostre tresredoute seignur le roi supplient sez povres freres prechiours et chapelleyns de la vile de Dunewyche en la counte de Suff', la soile de quele vile, ovesqe les mesons et esglises sure ycele esteauntz, est graunte partie destrute et trebuche en la mier, si qe la habitacioun de les dites freres illoqes est semblable par rage de la mier dienz brefe temps d'estre destrute, come autres habitacions et esglises sount en la dite vile sount, issint qe les dites povres freres coveint a fine force chaungier lour dite habitacion en aliours, sure qoi tresredote seignur, Robert de Swyllyngtone, chivaler, pur pite q'il ad de les dites freres, s'il plest a lour tresredote seignur le roi, est en volunte pur doner a eux de sa almoigne dise acres de terre et quatre acres de mareis en la vile de Blitheburgh pur eux eidifier et founder illoqes une novelle habitacioun en la dite vile de Blitheburgh pres Dunwyche, la quele vile de Blithburgh, ovesqe les dites dise acres de terre et quatre acres de mareis, sount tenuz de lour tresredote seignur le roi en chief come del corone. Qe plese a lour tresredote seignur de sa grace especiale grauntier licence al dit Robert q'il purra founder la dite novelle habitacioun del ordre des dites freres en la dite vile de Blitheburgh, et doner et graunter as mesmes les freres et a lour successoures perpetuelment les dites dise acres de terre et quatre acres de mareis en la dite vile de Blitheburgh en lour foundacioun, a tenire de le dit Robert et sez heires en pure et perpetuelle almoigne, et qe le dit Robert et sez heires teignent les dites dise acres de terre et quatre acres de mareis de lour tresredote seignur le roi et de sez heires come il tient la dite vile de Blitheburgh, non obstant la graunte ent affaire as dites freres et lour successours en fourme susdit, et qe mesmes les freres puissent resceyvere les dites dise acres de terre et quatre acres de mareis del doune et graunte le dit Robert en manere susdit, et auxint translater lour meisons de la dite vile de Dunwyche tanqe a la dite vile de Blitheburgh sauncz impediment de nulli, et q'ils purrount vendre lour soile en Dunwyche apres les meisons illoqes enracez, en eide des grauntez coustages q'ils covendra affaire entour lour novelle edificacioun, sauncz empechement de eux ou de ceux qe les achateront, sauncz fine ou fee pur icelles paier, pur Dieu et en eovre de charite.

No endorsement

1384. The chancery warrant with which this petition was formerly enclosed is dated 23 November (no. 47 of C 81/1343), as is the requested licence (*CPR 1381–5*, p. 529). Despite these grants, no move to a new site took place, and the house remained standing until the Dissolution: *VCH Suffolk*, II, 121–2.

66

Scarborough, NRY (1388)
Dominicans; Order of Friars Minors; Carmelites
(SC 8/224/11183)

The Dominican, Franciscan and Carmelite friars of Scarborough petition the king to allow an officer to travel freely within the town to pray for the souls of those buried within their houses and cemeteries, and the soul of Edward II, chief founder of the Carmelite friary in the town.

A tresexcellent et tresdoubte seignur nostre seignur le roy supplieunt humblement voz povers liges et devoutes oratours les frieres des ordres de prechours, menours et Carmes de ville de Scardeburgh en le counte d'Everwyk qe please a vostre treshaute et tresnoble seignurie de vostre grace especial grauntier a voz ditz oratours une chartre patente qe l'officer q'est soleez d'aler en la dite ville ove une sonet manuel a prier communement pur les almes de gentz enseayleez deinz seintuarie purteit, en mesme la manere, fraunchement et saunz destourbaunce, passer en la dite ville et prier pur les almes du quelles les corps reposerount et au present reposeount enterreez deinz les suisditz frieres, et par especial en les jours de leur creances, ensevilares et anniversaires, et pur l'alme du tresnoble et puissauntt seignur le Roi Edward Secounde apres le Conquest, chief et principal foundour de les frieres Carmes en la ville susdite, et pur toux autres foundours et avowez de les dites treis ordres, pur Dieu et en oevre de charite.

No endorsement

1388. The requested grant was made on 3 October 1388, but later revoked (*CPR 1385–9*, p. 513). Edward II granted two houses to the Carmelites, for an oratory and dwelling place, on 19 October 1319: *VCH York*, III, 279.

67

Sele, Sussex (c. 1396)
Benedictine (alien)
(SC 8/36/1757)

The prior and monks of Sele next to Bramber petition the king, stating that the bridges over the River Bramber, which pertain to them and bear a royal road, are ruined by great inundations of the sea and their great age. They request that the king grant them pedage and tronage to repair the bridges as their destruction would block the road so that none could pass, to the great damage of the commons of the country.

A tresnoble et tresexcellent prince nostre seignour le roy supplient ses povres chapellains priour et moines de La Selle jouste Brembre que comme les pons sur la eawe de Brembre dessus dite, qi pertenens au prioure, priour et moines du dit lieu de La Selle, soient destruis, gastes et roumpus, tant par les grans inundacions de la mer comme par la grant auncienete d'iceulles, quielx est le grant chemin royal, que pleise a vostre graciose seignourie, en aumosne et en pitie, douner et otroier de vostre benigne grace aucune aide et soucors de pedage et trenage pour les pons redroissier et reparer des bestes, chevaux, jumens, charretes et autres chargees passans et repassans par les ditz pons, ou autrement, par la destrucion d'eulx, le dit chemin royal seroit briefment en celle manere escoupe que nulle gent, ne a pie ne a cheval, ne y pourreit passer, la quelle chouse seroit en grief damage et desturbance de tout le comun du pays.

No endorsement

c. 1396. The petition is dated on its guard as being from between the reigns of Richard II and Henry VI. The absence of any reference to payment of an annual farm at the exchequer suggests that this petition post-dates 1396 when the priory became independent of its mother-house of St Florent-de-Saumur (*CPR 1391–6*, p. 721). The petitioner is therefore Stephen of Sens, prior 1378–1429. How many bridges were involved is not clear, but at least one was very ancient: on the bridge over the River Adur between Bramber and Beeding was the chapel of St Peter 'de Veteri Ponte' which was in the house's possession by 1150, *VCH Sussex*, II, 60. Pedage was a toll paid for passing through a place or country. Tronage, so-called because of the weighing of merchandise at the tron (scale, balance) was a charge upon goods so weighed and the right to levy such a toll.

3.2 Poverty

68

Westminster (1294)
Benedictine
(SC 8/201/10033)

The abbot and convent of Westminster petition the king and council for a year's respite from paying their debts, because they will have to give half their goods this year for the common grant of the clergy.
Endorsed on face: *The king granted us this thing on Sunday, at the request of Walter Langton.*

A nostre seignur le rey e a soen cunseil prient le abbe e le covent de Westmustre ke tuttes les dettes les quels current en demaunde sur eus par la somunse del Eschekere seient respiter, si luy plest, un an, pur ceo ke il paerunt cest \an/ al roy la meite de lour biens solunk le commun graunt de la clergie.

Endorsed on face: Ceste chose nous graunta le rey dymenge, a la requeste Sire Walter de Langetone.

1294. The petitioner is Walter of Wenlock, abbot 1283–1307. Walter Langton was keeper of the Wardrobe 1290–5 and treasurer 1295–1307, as well as being bishop of Coventry and Lichfield 1296–1321. This petition was a result of the tax grant of 50% of their income which Edward I, taking advantage of a vacancy at Canterbury, bullied the English clergy into conceding at a church council held 21–24 September 1294: J. H. Denton, *Robert Winchelsey and the Crown 1294–1313* (Cambridge, 1980), pp. 69ff.

69

Ellingham, Hampshire (c. 1290)
Benedictine (alien)
(SC 8/324/E611)

To the king and council from the prior of Ellingham requesting remedy as he and his two fellow monks only had as temporalities the church of Ellingham, worth 25 marks per annum, and had no other temporalities or spiritualities, but the king's ministers of the exchequer came and seized the church into the king's hand and take 20 marks annually so that the prior, monks and house have nothing to sustain them.

A nostre seyngnor le rey e a sun counseyl moustre le prior de Elyngham qe la ou nule manere de temporaute ne est apendaunt a sa priorie avauntdist fors soulement la eglise de la vile de Elyngham, la quele ne vaut par an fors xxv mars par dreit taxacion, ne autre chose ne ad de temporaute ne de espirituautee a sustenir luy e deus moyngnes ne sa priorie avantdiste fors soulement cel petite eglise, la venent les ministres le roy del Eschekere e unt seisi cele eglise en la meyn le roy, e pernent chescun an de cele eglise avantdiste xx mars al oes le roy, par quoy levantdist prior n'ad nule sustenance a luy ne a ses moyngnes ne a sa mesun sustenir, dont ses deus moyngnes sunt morz de meseyse, e ses mesons e ses graunges e ses bleez ars de ouan en la garde le roy, dont il prie remedie, pur Dieu e pur l'aume la royne.

No endorsement

c. 1290. Reference to the soul of the queen in the final clause of the document suggests that the petition was presented shortly after the death of Edward I's first wife, Eleanor of Castile, in 1290. Ellingham was a cell of the abbey of St Sauveur-le-Vicomte, Normandy.

70

Lyminster, Sussex (1302)
Benedictine (nuns)
(SC 8/315/E193)

The prioress of Lyminster requests grace as she is in arrears of the tax levied on her house because of the Gascon war, is unable to pay and has nothing with which to sustain the house, yet the sheriff of Sussex distrains them daily.
Endorsed: *To the exchequer. And they should have mitigation if it is considered that it ought to be done by the discretion of the treasurer and barons.*

Sire, por Deu la povere priuresse de Leministre \coste Arundel/ vos prie qe vous eiez merci de li, por ceo qe ele esteit taxe tote feiz puis la guere de Gaskonine ove les autre aliens, et amounce sa porcion a trente deus liveres a paier par an, qe les aveesont este febles en son pais de ble et de vente, de quei ele pur faut de nostre paiement de ceste an de doze marcs ne ne ad de quei paier tant qe ele le \pusse/[5] lever de ces dimes que sont avenir \e si n'ad ele/[6] neule manere de dimes for de garbes, ne neule manere de rente, ne de lai fe, ele se ad tant aforce por vos plere souz esperaunce de nostre grace qe ele ad ou promie plus qe touz lour biens ne valent, qe il ont \ressu a/ la anuitaunce de Lij mars, e si ne unt de quei rendre le ne de quei vivere, kar eles ne troevent gent qe plus lour voilont \a/ prester, e sour ceo une esterobes de quant qe eles averont de biens en lour meson, e ceo cest hom bien en lour pais la ou eles sont demorauntes, et le vicounte de Shutsex les destreint de jour en jour por les arrerages[7]avantdites \de/ dose mars. De quei, Sire, ele prie vostre grace de respit tant qe ele le prise lever. Ensement autre grace \q'il vous pleise fere a eux/[8] ou eles ne averient pouer de vivere en la manere, Sire, pur Deu, pite vos preingne de li \e/ de la duresse qe bailifs li font.

Endorsed: Ad scaccarium. Et fiat ibi mitigacio si viderint esse faciendam ad discrecionem thesaurarii et baronum etc.

5 In place of the deleted *ad.*
6 In place of the deleted ... *garbes kar ele ne ad.*
7 The letters *en* have been deleted.
8 In place of the deleted *qe vos lour plese fere.*

1302. The petition belongs to an original file of petitions returned to the exchequer from the summer parliament of 1302 (*PROME*, parliament of Summer 1302, Appendix). The petitioner was Agatha of la Poynte, who occurs as prioress from 1271 until November 1302. John Abel was the sheriff of Sussex (October 1298 – October 1302).

71

Prittlewell, Essex (1302)
Cluniac
(SC 8/315/E155)

To the king from the prior and convent of Prittlewell requesting that the £100 demanded of them be released as there are 18 monks in the house, and as the previous prior's fine in that sum, made by distress to the treasurer and barons of the exchequer for one year to the use of the king, has been fully paid. The house is only assessed at £150 and the treasurer and barons, through the sheriff and bailiffs, demand the same £100 each year to their great ruin.
Endorsed: *They should go to the exchequer and account for the manors of Eastwood and Rayleigh and then show the state of their house, and the treasurer and barons of the exchequer should do according to what by their discretion ought to be done.*

A nostre seygnur le roy prient le povre priour e le covent de Pritewelle qe pur ceo qe le priour qi fut devaunt cesty fist une fyn de centz livers par destresse a tresurer e as barons del Escheker \par un an/ al oes nostre seyngnur le roy, e cela fyn seyt pleynement paye, e la meson ne vaut par an qe vij[xx] x livers a haut estente, le tresurer avantdit e les barons del Escheker, par viscunte e baillifs, demandent uncore de an en an les avant dit C livers, e graunt partye en unt leve par grevouses destresces, dont lour meson est tant mys a defitez qe il ne se poent desoremes susteinier si nostre seignur le roi ne eyt mercy e pite de eaus. Pur quoi il prient com avant pur Dieu qe cele demande seyt relesse, desicom il sount bien xviij moynes en covent, et nul aport la outre ne peterent a cheef meson pleount unkes, mes tutz lur byens unt despenduz en Engleterre en lour meson demeyne, selonk la furme de lur chartres, q'il unt de Henri de Essex', lour fundur, e prient qe ceo seit enquis e de la value de lour possessions.

Endorsed: Adeant Scaccarium et computent de maneriis de Estwode \et Reylee/ et tunc ostendant statum domus sue, et faciant thesaurarius et barones secundum \quod/ par discrecionem suam viderint quod fuerit faciendum.

1302. The petition belongs to an original file of petitions returned to the exchequer from the summer parliament of 1302 (*PROME*, parliament of Summer 1302, Appendix). The petitioner was Peter of Montellier, prior from 1290 until at least November 1302. Henry of Essex, named as founder of the priory, has been identified as the son of Robert, son of Sweyn, the latter being the holder of Prittlewell in Domesday (*VCH Essex*, II, 138).

72

Dunwich, Suffolk (? c. 1305)
Hospital
(SC 8/328/E887)

To the king from Robert of Sefeld, warden of the king's house called the Maisondieu of Dunwich, requesting that he be able to receive and purchase land to the value of £20 for the

relief of the house, and for the chantry to sustain it. The house should sustain ten chaplains to sing for the souls of the king's ancestors but is so ruined by the sea that it is not worth twelve marks, as was found by inquisition, and the people of the town and country have made voluntary gifts to them to relieve their situation.
Endorsed: *They should identify the lands and who wishes to give them.*
In chancery.

A nostre seigneur le roi moustre Robert de Sefeld, gardeyn de la meeson le roi qe est apelle la meeson Dieu de Donewyz, qe la ou cele meeson soleit sustenir dys chapeleyns chauntanz pur les auncestres nostre seignur le roi, la est cele meeson si destrute e anientie par la meer qe la meeson ne vaut forsqe dous mars, sicome enquis est par comandement nostre seignur le roi, dont la estente est en sa Chauncelerye, par quei tuiz les chapeleyns qe leur furent sauve doens sont par poverte issuz, dont les gent de la \dite/ ville et du pais \unt grant pite e/ volontiers durreient de lur terres e lur tenementz pur la meeson relever. Dont il prie la grace nostre seignur le roi qu'il voille graunter qu'il pussent receyvere e purchacer a la value de xx li par an ou tant come il voudra de sa grace pur la meeson relever e la Chauncerie pur li e pur ses auncestres sustenir.

Endorsed: Nominent terras et qui dare voluerint.
In Cancellaria.

(SC 8/328/E888)

Schedule of lands for purchase for the relief of the Maisondieu, Dunwich, including land in Brampton, late of Haliwell Priory.

Robertus de Sefeaud: unum mesuagium et unam carucatam terre et duas marcatas redditus cum advocacione ecclesie de Bramton', que nuper fuerunt in domo de Halywell, London', et unum mesuagium et quatuor marcatas redditus in Donewyco.
Robertus atte Welle: unum messuagium et centum solidos redditus in Donewyco.
Paulus de Wytham: unum mesuagium, unum molendinum, quadraginta acras terre et quadraginta solidatos redditus in Donewyco.

No endorsement

? c. 1305. The petition and formerly enclosed schedule probably date to c. 1305, since on 22 March 1305 a mortmain licence was granted for the hospital's acquisition of several pieces of land and a mill (*CPR 1301–7*, p. 322), though these properties are not the same as the items and individuals recorded in the above schedule. At least ten years previously Sefeld had petitioned the king concerning his right to the land and advowson of Brampton (SC 8/326/E768). For the requirement to obtain a licence see E. D. Jones, 'Three Benedictine Houses and the Statute of Mortmain, 1279–1348', *Journal of British Studies* 14 (1975), 1–28.

73

Hastings, Sussex (c. 1307–27)
Augustinian canons
(SC 8/51/2502)

The prior and convent of Holy Trinity, Hastings, petition the king, stating that they have been ruined by flooding of the sea, so that their income from three churches in Hastings is greatly reduced, and they have also lost other rents, and ask that they might be able to approve £40 of land or rent annually for their sustenance.
Endorsed: *Concerning the acquisition of tenements, they are to come into chancery and have a writ there to inquire if it is to the [king's] harm.*

A nostre seignur le roy priont le pouvre priur de Hastynges de la meson de la Trinite e le covent de meme le leu ke auxi come eux sunt assis sus la marine e par la meer destrut, lur voile graunter de aproprier pur lur sustenaunce quarante lifrees de teres ou de rentes par an, kar eux solayent aver trays eglises en Hastynges que rendirent cent lifres par an ke ne valent pas par an mayntenant vynt soutz. E si unt perdu, par inundacion de la meer, vynt lefrees de rente assise par an en memes la ville, dont luy priont, pur le alme son pere e sa mere, ke luy voyle de lur sufferte e povrete suvenyr auxi com il porra par touz les bone gens de meme la ville de ceste chose la verite enquere.

Endorsed: De tenementis adquirendis, veniant in Cancellaria et ibi habeant breve de inquirendo si sit ad dampnum.

c. 1307–27. On 24 October 1339 it was ordered that the prior and canons of Holy Trinity, Hastings, be allowed a respite from the tithe for the churches of St Michael, St Peter and St Margaret, which had been burned by pirates (*CCR 1339–41*, p. 333), and on 18 May 1340 an inquisition was ordered into the damage done by the sea to the churches of St Michael, St Peter and St Margaret in Hastings (*CIM 1307–49*, no. 1709). This petition, however, seems much earlier, both from the hand and the Latin endorsement, and no mention is made of burning by pirates. It is almost certainly from the reign of Edward II.

74

St Leonard's, York, NRY (1312–22)
Hospital
(SC 8/153/7625)

The warden and brothers of St Leonard's hospital, York, petition the king for his letters to the pope to acquit them of the taxes and charges due to him, as they are quit of such charges to the king.
The hospital contains 103 men and 102 women in beds, 18 brothers and chaplains, 18 sisters, 15 orphans, and sometimes more. Each week they hand out 60 loaves of bread and potage at the castle, 40 loaves to the lepers, and also provide for any pilgrims stopping at the hospital. There are 80 men and women who work and live in the hospital. They also have to receive more prominent visitors, such as Lord Mowbray.
Endorsed on face: *This is not able to be done without parliament.*

A nostre seignur le roi priont, se li plest, ses devoutz chapelains guardeyn et freres de vostre hospital de Saint Leonard de Everwyk qe come touz les biens et les possessions de vostre dit hospital sount deputes pour la sustenance de povres et de lour ministres, qe mout ont este a meschief, et sont a present, des dismes et autres charges grantees de sainte eglise, par nostre saint pere le pape, et par la clergie, et par taxacions des temporautes. Que de vostre benigne grace il vous plaise granter qe desoremes il soient quites de toutes maneres de tieux dismes, charges et taxacions, et prier par voz lettres a nostre dit pere le pape \que/ tant comme ce appartient a la Court de Rome, il vueill granter qe ain siut soit, par reguart de charite, a la quiete de voz avant ditz povres et ministres, qe priont pur vous et pur touz leur bien faiteurs assiduelment nuit et jour.

Et fait assavoir qe en vostre dit hospital sont des avant ditz povres cent et trois hommes et cent et deux femmes en litz. Item, des freres et chapelains en habit et hors de habit xviij. Item, de seurs en habit et hors de habit xviij. Item, en la maison des orphannis xv, et aucunes foiz plus, selonc ce qe les enfantz sont getes. Item, a les prisons du chastiel lx panis la semaigne et potage. Item, a les Lazeres de Everwyk xl panis et a les povres pelerins passanz selonc ce qe il vienent et les biens de l'ospital poont suffire. Item, sont el service du dit hospital quatrevintz hommes et femmes qe vivont de lainz. Item, des autres survenanz, comme le seignur de Moubray et autres auxibien des genz de court comme du pays, as queux il convient fair honeur pur les biens faitz qe vostre dit hospital a receu de eaux et de leur auncestres et qe il font de jour en autre.

Endorsed on face: Ne poet estre fait sanz parlement.

1312–22. The Lord Mowbray, who had been a guest at the hospital, was probably John of Mowbray, 2nd Baron Mowbray (1286–1322). He was appointed keeper of the city and county of York in 1312 (*CPR 1307–13*, p. 479) and again in 1315 and 1316 (*Rotuli Scotiæ*, ed. D. Macpherson, 2 vols (1814–19), I, 135, 156). Since he is referred to in the petition as alive, the petition must date from after his appointment as keeper but before his execution in 1322. For the life and career of Mowbray, see Rowena E. Archer, 'Mowbray, John (I), second Lord Mowbray (1286–1322)', *ODNB*. It had been thought that the hospital catered for only women by the end of the thirteenth century: P. H. Cullum, *Cremetts and Corrodies: Care of the Poor and Sick at St Leonard's Hospital, York, in the Middle Ages*, Borthwick Papers, 79 (1991), p. 6.

75

Dover, Kent (c. 1315)
Hospital
(SC 8/43/2125)

The master and brothers of the hospital of the Maison Dieu (St Mary's hospital) of Dover, which was founded by the king's ancestors and other good people to receive poor people going overseas and coming from overseas at Dover, petition the king that whereas he recently asked them, by his writ, to find maintenance for life for John Lamb, his mariner of Dover, which they have done, he has now sent William son of Thomas the Carter of Grove and Henry of Oldington with similar writs. If they are to support all these people it will be a great drain on their resources, and harm their ability to provide the alms for which they were founded, and so they request a remedy which will enable them to sustain these alms.
Endorsed: *Before the king, whether he wishes to accept these excuses or not.*

A nostre seignur le roi et a son counseil moustrent le mestre et les freres del hospital de la Mesoun Dieu de Dovere, de si come la dite mesoun est founde par les auncestres nostre seignur le roi et d'autres bons gentz en pures e perpetuels et en certeynes augmoignes, a resceivre nuyt et jour continuement touz les povres venauntz de outre meer a vers la meer a Dovere pur passer, solom la primere fundacioun de la dite meesoun. Et sur ceo nostre seignur le roi qe ore est nadgeres passe maunda par son bref a lez auauntditz mestre et freres qi eux resceusent un Johan Lamb, son maryner de Dovere, de quel fu resceu a sa garison al terme de sa vie, qe est uncore en vye. Et ausint ore de novel un William le fiz Thomas le Charetter de Grove et un autre Henri de Oldyngton' sunt venutz ala dite meeson et portent bref nostre seignur le roi de avoir lour garisoun a terme de lour vyes, a graunt suscharge del augmoigne nostre seignur le roi et d'autres bones gentz. La quele meeson ne poet suffire saunz ceo qe les augmoignes establies par ses auncestres et autres bones gentz ne fuissent sustretes, qe serroit a graunt damage del povre poeple e amenusement des augmoignes et en contre la volunte des foundours. Par quoi le mestre e les freres avauntditz prient, pur Dieu e par charite, a nostre seignur le roie et a son counseil qe remedie sur cest chose sont faite, issint qe les augmoignes soyent tenues et mayntenues en lour primer estat pur les povres venauntz et alauntz si come desus est dit, et pur sustenir les voluntees des ditz foundours.

Endorsed: Coram rege, utrum velit acceptare huius excusaciones nec ne.

c. 1315. On 12 August 1314 William son of Thomas the Carter of Grove was ordered to the hospital of St John, Brackley (*CCR 1313–18*, p. 192). Henry of Oldington was first ordered to Dover on 26 March 1315 (*CCR 1313–18*, p. 220) and again on 6 January 1316 (*CCR 1313–18*, p. 319). On 17 November 1316 he was ordered to Barking Abbey (*CCR 1313–18*, p. 437). The petitioner was Henry of Herefeld, master of Dover hospital from 1305 (*CPR 1301–7*, p. 340) until his death in 1316 (*CPR 1313–17*, p. 551). For useful context, see S. Sweetinburgh, 'Royal Patrons and Local Benefactors: the Experience of the Hospitals of St Mary at Ospringe and Dover in the Thirteenth Century', in *Religious and Laity in Western Europe, 1000–1400: Interaction, Negotiation, and Power*, ed. E. M. Jamroziak and J. E. Burton (Turnhout, 2006), pp. 111–29. See also note to **189**.

76

Tupholme, Lincolnshire (c. 1317)
Premonstratensian canons
(SC 8/197/9804)

Letter to Edward II from the abbot and convent of Tupholme stating that the king has written to them asking them to give his servant, Robert of Crowland, sustenance in their house for life, or to explain to him why they have not done so in response to his previous request. They say that, although they would gladly obey him in all things, their very small income is already heavily burdened with the charge of finding a chaplain to say mass for the soul of Piers Gaveston, and they have further been impoverished by flooding, diseases of their livestock and buying corn and malt for their sustenance, so that they have fallen into debt. They therefore ask the king to excuse them from this charge, asking him to verify the truth of what they have said from their neighbours.
Endorsed: *To our lord the king, from his chaplains of Tupholme.*

A noble prince et lez treschier seignur lige mon sire Edward, par la grace de

Dieu roi d'Engleterre et seignur d'Irlande et duc d'Aquitaigne, les soens povers chapeleyns abbe et covent de Tupholm honurs et treschiers reverences, treshonurable seignur, nous receusives voz lettres neest geires, par les quieles vous nous requestes por Robert de Croulande, vostre servant, qe nous luy receusomes en nostre maison, et qe nous luy troessomes sa resonable sustenaunce en vivre et vestire en nostre dite mayson a terme de sa vie, enfeisaunte a luy de ceo noz lettres patentez seales souz nostre comune seal, ou qe nous assignissoms certeyn cause por quai nous n'avoms pas estez obeissauncez a vostre maundement, de ceo autrefoiz a nous maunde, trescher sire, voillez saver qe vostre requeste nous serra totes joures commaundement en totes choses qe nous puroms faire, mes chier seignur, voilez sovenire qe nous somes charges par vostre maundement de un chapelleyn chauntant en nostre maison pro l'alme Sire Pieres de Gaveston, jadis counte de Cornewaile, qe Dieu l'asoile, et a ceo faire somes nous obligez par noz lettres liverez a vous enseales de nostre commune seal et, treshonurable seignur, voillez entendre qe noz tropetites terres et rentes de temparautez et de spirituautez ne valent por resonable extent fors cynkant six livres seez souz et maile par an, et ceo est molt petit por la sustenaunce de nostre dite maisoun et de noz mesmes a la charge qe nous gist sur de aumosnes faire et de autres choses dont somes charges de noz fundours et noz fessorns, et a ceo, sire, somes nous tant enpoveriz par cretyn de eawe et morin de noz bestes et d'achat de ble et de brese por la sustenaunce de nostre pover maison, cestes cheires et mannaises autres qe nous n'avoms getres dont nous meismes eider mes vivoms sur creaunce et eide de noz veisines de an en an, issint qe nous somes tant endettes a divers gentz qe qantqe partint a nostre povere maison en quater aunz ne suffice mie d'aquiter noz dettes qe nous devoms, par quai, cher sire, nous prioms a vostre honurable seignurie, por l'amour de Dieu et por salu de vostre alme, qe il vous plaise aver regarde as dites meschiefs et aver nous par celes enchesons excusez qe nous ne poems a ceste foiz vostre dite maundement a complir, qar ceste nostre excusacioun contynt tote verite, et ceo prioms nous qe soit enquis par noz veisyns et gentz qe conoissent l'estat de \nostre/ maison, s'il vous pleise, treschier seignur, Dieu vous doynt bone vie et longe et victorie de voz enemys.

Endorsed: A nostre seignur le roi par ses chapeleyns de Tupholm.

c. 1317. On 12 May 1317 provision was made for the maintenance of Robert of Crowland at Reading Abbey (*CCR 1313–18*, p. 463). The identity of the petitioning abbot of Tupholme is uncertain, though was probably 'William', elected in 1310 and occurring in February 1317. Tupholme was a house of real and enduring poverty. In November 1380, for example, the bishop of Lincoln requested the house's exemption from royal taxation on the grounds of poverty, LAO, Reg. 12 (Buckingham, Memoranda), f. 214. See also note to **189**.

77

Chicksands, Bedfordshire (c. 1324)
Gilbertine
(SC 8/103/5127)

The prior of Chicksands petitions the king to cancel the excessive interest on his principal debt, or he cannot maintain his house etc. He shows that he keeps 160 nuns and sisters in his house,

together with 24 canons and five lay brothers, and for their maintenance in victuals took from Bartholomew Rik and his associates £370, for which he is bound in £1200 to be paid at certain times, namely: £830 of interest and £370 of principal debt, which has not yet been paid.
Endorsed: *This does not concern the king.*

A nostre seignur le roi moustre son chapelein, si lui plest, priour de Chikesond del ordre de Sempyngham q'ad en sa garde cent e seysaunte noneynes e sorours en la diste maisoun encluses, vint e quatre chanoines, e vint freres lays, qe por vitayles qe lui coveneyt a la sustenance de les avantditz prist d'aprest de Barth' Rik' e son compaignonz treys centz seysaunte e diz livres, por les queux il est oblige en mile e deuz centz livres a paier a certeyn termes assignez, c'est asavoir ouyt centz e trente livres d'acres outre les CCClxx livres la dette principale. E por ceo qu'il ne poet la diste dette totale paer soloinc la fourme entre eux taille, al dist Monsir Hugh prie le dist priour, pur Dieux, si lui plese, qu'il voille estre aydaunte vers nostre seignur le roy desicum il est succurs e eyde as autres e en hast, par la grace Dieux, serra avouue de la diste maisoun, qe la diste dette pusse estre estalle a tiel estallement qe la maisoun le pusse covenablement paier, e le dit covent avoir sustenance, eaunt regard si lui plese a la grant charge de la diste maisoun e al outraiouse acres outre la dette principale.

Endorsed: Non tangit regem.

c. 1324. The petitioner was John of Camelton, who occurred as prior from 1316 to November 1324. Bartholomew Rik' or Richi, a merchant of the Grimaldi of Chieri, Italy (*CCR 1323–7*, p. 567), appears frequently in the close rolls in the mid 1320s as a creditor of numerous religious houses (*CCR 1323–7*, pp. 165, 169, 200, 306, 635). On 14 May 1325 there was enrolled a deed, dated at Chicksands on St Peter ad Vincula 18 Edward II, made by John Puisaquila of Genoa, citizen and merchant of London, witnessing that the prior and convent demised to Richi and himself their manors called 'the chapel of St Thomas' in Meppershall and 'Hawengraunge' in Hawnes, for £200 p.a. to the prior and convent, and granted them the fruits of their church of Haynes for seven years, and sold them their woods called Appley and 'Inwode', and bound themselves to Richi and himself in 3,300 gold florins. In consideration of this, he and Richi granted by deed of agreement that if the prior and convent paid them £1,200, the demises, grant, sale and obligation would be annulled. The prior and convent had at this point paid only £300, a quarter of the debt, for which Puisaquila released to them all his debts and all his right and claim in the above. The prior of Chicksands at this time (the morrow of St Barnabas 18 Edward II) called himself Simon (*CCR 1323–7*, p. 293). The financial position of Chicksands had been serious since 1257, when fifty nuns and ten lay brothers had to be dispersed among other houses of the order. From the early fourteenth century successive priors borrowed extensively from Italian (Genoese and Florentine) merchants, and even from English fellow-religious, *VCH Bedfordshire*, I, 391. It is possible that the house suffered an influx of women, the dependants of Contrariants, after the battle of Boroughbridge (1322). For their savage treatment see Natalie Fryde, *The Tyranny and Fall of Edward II 1321–1326* (Cambridge, 1979), pp. 79, 111–15.

78

Croxton, Leicestershire (1351)
Premonstratensian canons
(SC 8/209/10410)

The abbot of Croxton petitions the council to be released from the office of collector of clerical tenths in Leicestershire, Northamptonshire and Bedfordshire, as the abbey of Croxton is greatly impoverished by the plague and the abbot preoccupied in its welfare.
Endorsed: *A writ should be sent to the bishop to discharge the said abbot because he is poor and exempt from the bishop's jurisdiction, and for the other causes contained in this bill, and that he restore the said patent in chancery.*

Au conseil nostre seignur le roi prie l'abbe de Croxtone qe come il soit exempt de chescun manere de jurisdiccion del evesqe de Nichole, et coment qe par la mortalite sa abbey soit desolat des chanouns qeux y estoient forpris le dit abbe et son priour et novices de novele reseuz nient meins le dit evesqe soi enforce de luy charger de la colleccion des dismes aore graunteez au roi en les counteez de Leyc', Norht' et Bed', en graunt oppression de le dit meison, qe lour pleise avoir regard al exempcion de lour eglise, et a ceo qe le dit abbe ne ad nul eyde de ses chanons aore pur lour invent, et qe le dit abbe mesmes est durement greve par maladie et sa abbeye assis en chaumpestre loyns de refust des gentz pur salvacion de la disme issint a coillier, et eyant regard qe la dit abbeye nadgairs estoit ars, luy voillent graunter d'estre descharge du colleccion des tiels dismes et sur teil condicion il pardurra a nostre dit seignur le roi dys marcz qeux il luy doit, et de ceo luy fra restitucion de la patentez nostre dit seignur le roi.

Endorsed: Soit brief fait al evesqe a descharger le dit abbe pur ce q'il est pour et exempt de jurisdiccion de dit evesqe, et pur les autres causes compris en cest bille, et pur tant q'il ad restitute le dit patent en la Chauncellerie a dampner.

1351. The identity of the abbot of Croxton at this time is unknown. On 16 November 1351 John Gynwell, bishop of Lincoln 1347–62, was ordered to replace the abbot of Croxton for two years as collector of the tenth granted by convocation in May 1351 (*CCR 1349–54*, pp. 335–6). As a result of fire and the destruction of its lands in the north by the Scots, the abbey already owed a debt of £2,000 in 1348. In 1363 the abbot obtained a papal dispensation allowing the ordination of twelve canons aged twenty-one years to compensate for the losses caused by the plague: *VCH Leics.*, II, 29–30.

79

Avebury, Wiltshire (1356–7)
Benedictine (alien)
(SC 8/195/9706)

The prior of Avebury petitions the king, listing the misfortunes which have befallen him through flood, fire, plague, murrain of sheep, rents withheld and expenses for repairs to his priory, and stating that he has petitioned the king to have a pardon for the arrears of his farm. Now a large sum of money has been assigned to John Brocas for the term of Easter last. He asks that this might not be levied until the king has ordained his grace.
Endorsed: *The prior owes £96 from arrears of his priory, for which he requests grace. He is*

to be pardoned £36 of the arrears which he owes from times past, and he will pay £40 now. And he will have respite of £20, to pay £10 next Michaelmas with his farm and £10 at the following Easter with his farm, of the king's grace, out of reverence for St George, patron of the house, and for their poverty; and letters are to be sent to the treasurer, barons and chamberlains.

Cez sount les meschiefs qe sount avenuz a l'oustiel de Avebury, c'est asavoir: un molyn ewestre et un colomber par merveillouse cretyne d'eawe abatuz; et une graunge ove touz les bledz et partie dez feyns d'un aan neyetz et porrtz, et le remenaunt esteaunt dehors en preez par mesme l'eawe enportez; et un molyn avent tut ruynous si qe nul homme ne la voet prendre a ferme pur le tonne. Item, la boverye ove xvj boefs et vaches ars et mortz, et plus de CCC de sez berbyz mort par moryne. Item, le dit priour ad mys en reparaciouns dez mesouns de sa priorie xl lyvres et plus, et altrement ils eussent toutz chenz, et unqore ils enbosignent molt plus d'amendement. Item, deux marchez de rente sustretz par ix aunz par ma dame la Countesse Mareschal et un Thomas Trett q'ount tenuz la priorie de Upavene a ferme, de la quele rente la dite priorie de Upavene est charge de payer annuelment a celuy qe serra priour de Avebury. Item, vj mies, xij cotages et vj vergez de terre ount gew voider et frischez puis la pestilence, qe soleynt rendre vj marcz et altres coustimez par aan, dount le dit priour n'ad ore rienz. Par cause de qeux meschiefs le dit priour de Avebury ad suy au roy par peticioun d'avoir pardoun dez les arrerages de sa ferme, q'amountent a qatre vynti et cesze lyvres, et quod sount lvj lyvre vj s viij d del terme de Pask darreyn passe assignez a Monsire Johan Brokas, la ou la ferme de celle terme n'est qe xviij li, dount il prie remedie et un supersedeas taunqe le roy eit ordyne sa grace.

Endorsed: Le priour doit des arrerages de sa priorales iiij^{xx} xvj li, dont il prie grace. Eyt pardoun de les arrerages q'il doit pur le temps passe de xxxvj li, et payere ore xl li. Et avera respite de les xx li, de paier ala Saint Michel proschein ovesqe sa ferme x li et ala Pasqe suyant x li ovesqe sa ferme, de la grace le roi, de la reverence de Saint George, avouwe de la maisone, et pur lour povertie; et soit lettres fait as tresurer, barons et chamberleins.

1356–7. The petitioner was Robert of Verretot, who was granted the keeping of the priory in 1354 and was prior until at least 1369. The Countess Marshal was Margeret Brotherton, countess of Norfolk (cr. 1338). On 20 January 1357 an order was issued to the treasurer and barons of the exchequer in accordance with the endorsement of this petition (*CCR 1354–60*, p. 293). Sir John Brocas (d. 1365) of Clewer and Windsor (Berks.) belonged to a Gascon family which prospered through service to English kings, in Gascony and England. Sir John served both Edward II and Edward III, and was effectively the latter's Master of the Horse, and constable of Guildford Castle. See M. Burrows, *The Family of Brocas of Beaurepaire and Roche Court* (London, 1886), and the biographies of Sir John's third son and eventual heir Bernard by H. Summerson, 'Brocas, Sir Bernard (*c.*1330–1395)', *ODNB*, and in *HC*, II, 359–62. Avebury was one of two English cells of the Benedictine abbey of St Georges de Boscherville near Rouen and was therefore in the fortunate position of being associated with a saint chosen by Edward III to be patron of the Order of the Garter: D. A. L. Morgan, 'The Banner-bearer of Christ and Our Lady's Knight: How God became an Englishman revisited', in *St George's Chapel Windsor in the Fourteenth Century*, ed. N. Saul (Woodbridge, 2005), pp. 51–61.

80

Harmondsworth, Middlesex (c. 1381–2)
Benedictine (alien)
(SC 8/116/5755)

The prior of Harmondsworth petitions the king and council for new copies of charters and relief from his rent. During recent disturbances, the commons had entered his house, threatening him and burning all his muniments. Also, disease had killed all their sheep, leaving the house in poverty.

A nostre seignur le roy et son bon conseil supplie le povre priour de Harmondesworth coment, en l'errour des comunes levetz, grant partie de eux vindrent a sa mesoun de Harmondesworth et lui firent grant injuriez en plusours maneres, toz jours lui manachantz de lui couper la teste et ardre ses mesons, et entreint sa chambre, et lui comanderent d'overer son cofer, le quele overt pristrent tout qe estoit dedeyns et ovesqe seu touz les chartres del fundacioun de sa meson et les custumere, registrez, rentals, roules de courtz et da countez, lettres da quitancez et touz altres munumentes tochanz sa meson, et luy et les ardirent tout a poudre, et entendanz qu'il avoit altres lettres a Weymostier, luy comanderent de les envoyer quere, suz peyne de C li ou de couper sa teste luy contreignancez de plegez de ceo, et lui baillerent a certainz gentz engard tanqe les lettres venissent, les queles venuitz les ardirentz et mistrent en cendre come les altres, a grant peyne, refreynantz, de la grace de Dieux, de lui tuer et ardre sez mesons. Et oveqe ceo, a ceste an ad perdu par moreyn pres qe touz sez berbyz, pur qoi la dite mesoun est destruyt atoz jours, si par nostre seignur le roy et son bone consail n'est purveu de remedie graciouse. Qe de vostre especial grace lui voilletz granter novelez chartres et confirmacions, si qe son hostel puis estre salve et lez custumes et franchisez del hostiel gardez coment ils furent devaunt cez heurez. Et pur lez damagez et desolacion suis ditz, vous plese lui fairre aloaunce de sa ferme du terme de Seint Michel darreyn passe, si q'il puisse viver et Dieu servir et prier pur nostre seignur le roy et son bone consail et les almes de touz sez progenitours.

No endorsement

c. 1381–2. The petitioner was the prior of Harmondsworth, who is usually identified as Robert de Bello Campo, or Beauchamp, allegedly prior from 1351 (though in 1381 the prior was called Richard: *The Church in London 1375–92*, ed. A. K. McHardy, London Record Society, 13 (London, 1977), no. 337). The episode referred to was the Peasants' Revolt of 1381, in which rebels targeted 'writings' especially, and attacked several religious houses. Harmondsworth was an alien priory, dependent upon St Catherine du Mont, Rouen, and like the other alien houses was then in the king's hands because of the Anglo-French war. Successive priors, as keepers, paid an annual farm at the exchequer; from 1338 to 1369 it was £80 p.a., but was reduced to 80 marks in 1369. The house was acquired in 1392 by William of Wykeham, as part of the endowment of his colleges at Winchester and Oxford which undertook to provide for the prior and his companion: J. Freeman, 'The Priory of Harmondsworth', in *The Religious Houses of London and Middlesex*, ed. C. M. Barron and M. Davies (London, 2007), pp. 304–6. For an earlier transcript of this petition, see no. 35 of PRO 31/7/107.

81

Shaftesbury, Dorset (1382)
Benedictine (nuns)
(SC 8/20/954)

The abbess and convent of Shaftesbury petition the king and council in parliament stating that, although their house was suitably endowed by the king's progenitors, their founders, they are so ruined by pestilences among their tenants, which have killed almost all of them, by murrain among their cattle at various times in all their possessions, and by other charges which necessity forces them to bear from day to day, that they will find it very hard to get to the end of the year without endangering themselves to their creditors. They request wardship and administration of their house, and its temporalities and possessions, in all vacancies for whatever reason, so that no escheator, sheriff or other minister of the king or of his heirs meddles with it in any way (except for the escheator to take a simple seisin in the king's name to save his right and lordship there), paying to the king the true value of their temporalities for however long the vacancy lasts, and saving to the king the fees and advowsons pertaining to the nunnery.
Endorsed: *It pleases the king that this petition be granted, on the advice of his council.*

A nostre tresgracious seignur le roy et son tressage et noble consail en ce parlement supplient humblement ses devoutes oratrices abbesse et convent de Shaftesbirs qe combien qe leur dite maison, q'est del fundacion des nobles progenitours nostre seignur le roy et del patronage nostre dit seignur le roy, soit covenablement donez en possessions par mesmes voz nobles progenitours, dont Dieux ait mercys toutes voies, voz dites oratrices sont einsi arrertz a jour de huy, quoy par les pestilences en queles lours tenantz sont trestoutz apoy mortz, et par murryne de lour bestaille a grant nombre et value, nemye tantsoulement a une place et a une foitz einz a diverses foitz en toutes lours places, quoy par autres grandes charges quelles lour convient a fine force de jour en autre porter et sustener, qeles ne purront si noun qe a moelt grant peine sanz lour endangerer a diverses bones gentz lours creditours mesner l'an a \bon/ fyn, qe vous plese, pur l'amour de Dieu et de sa douce mere Sainte Marie et del glorious corseint Seint Edward le Martyr, vostre noble progenitour qi en vostre dit maison gist canonizez, veullez en grant reliefment de mesme vostre maison lour granter qe la prioresse et convent de mesme vostre maisoun et lours successours aient desore la garde et administracion de mesme l'abbeye, et des quelconqes temporaltees et d'autres possessions a ycelles regardantz, a toutz les foitz ete si sovent come mesme l'abbeye par mort, cession, resignacion ou privacion del abbesse illoeqes, ou par autre manere qelconqe, serra voide apres cest heure, issint qe l'eschetour, viscont n'autre ministre du roy ou de ses heires ne se medler desore del dite abbeye ne de nulles des possessions d'ycelles a nulle tielle voidance, forsqe qe l'eschetour del lieu pur le temps esteant deinz la porte del dite abbeye tantsoullement a chesoun tielle voidance y preigne une simple seissine en noun du roy nostre seignur, en salvacion de son droit et seignurie illoeqes ete cele seisine par luy illoeqes pris tantost se departe d'illoeqes, sanz pluis soi ent medler ou faire illoeqes par manere qelconqe, rendant ent a nostre dit seignur le roy et a ses heirs a chescune tiel voidance, si par un an entier tielle voidance durrera, la verroy l'extentz de lours dites temporaltees. Et si par meindre temps durrera ycele voidance qe par un an come par demy an, ou par quarter del an, ou par demy quarter del an, ou par deux moys, ou par un moys entier, ou par meindre \ou greindre/ terme, solonc l'afferant del dit annuel extente et l'espace de cele voidance, et salvez toutes foitz a vous, nostre seignur, et a voz heires durantes mesmes les voidances les feez et advouesons appertenantz a l'abbeye desusdite, entendant, tresredoute seignur, qe parmy vostre grace en celle partie affaire grant reliefment, si Dieu plest, a amendement avendra a mesme vostre maison, et nul damage ent purra avenir a vous ne a voz heirs ne a nul autre forsqe soulement a voz ministres, les queux en temps de tieles voidances y sont acustumez defaire grandes destruccions et wastes et y prendre grantz et diverses profitz a lours propres oeps, dont rienz ne vient a vostre oeps, combien qe mesme la voidance ne dure si par petit temps noun.

Endorsed: Il plest au roi qe ceste peticion soit grantez, sur l'advis de son conseill.

1382. The petitioner was Joan Formage, abbess 1362–94, who probably presented this petition at the parliament of October 1382, since on 20 October letters patent of Edward III granting the nuns custody of the abbey, without rent during its next vacancy, were inspected and confirmed (*CPR 1381–5*, p. 177). For an earlier edition of the petition, see *RP*, III, 129, no. 11, which assigns this petition to 5 Richard II. One of the reasons for the financial difficulties confronting the abbey in the fourteenth century was the excessive number of nuns admitted to the community: *VCH Dorset*, II, 77.

82

Henwood, Warwickshire (1411)
Benedictine (nuns)
(SC 8/53/2635)

The prioress and convent of Henwood petition the king, stating that they have been ruined by bad governance, and are being overburdened with pensions, corrodies and other charges. They ask the king to take them and their possessions into his hand, and to grant their keeping to Richard, prior of Coventry, Roger Leche, John Weston and Thomas Buxton for seven years, according to the tenor of the letters patent granted to the prior of Coventry in a similar case. They also ask that they might be discharged from all pensions, corrodies and other charges in the meantime, and that the king might grant them his protection with the clause nolumus.

A treshaut, trespuissant, tresgracious et tresredoute seignur, nostre seignur le roy, supplient humblement voz poveres oratrices la prioresse et le covent de Hynwode que par l'ou la dite priorie est de fundacioun de voz progenitours et est de vostre patronage, pour default de bone governance de dit priorie en temps de diverses prioresses jadis la esteantz de toutz pensions, corrodies et autres diverses sommes de deniers estoit charge et endette, si qe la prioresse q'ore est et la covent sont ensi vexez, laborez et inquietez si qelles ne poient de lour possessions vivere et divine service come eles duissent excerser et user, que serroit semblable en finale destruccioun a dit priorie sic ne soit de vostre tresgracious seignurie eider [en] releve et succurre. Que plese a vostre tresgracious seignurie de vostre treshabundant grace, pour la conservacioun de dit priorie, des terres et tenementz et les possessions de dit priorie les prendre en vostre mayn ove les pensions et corrodies d'icell grantez, et de committer la garde de dit priorie et les possessions et facultes de dit priorie a Richard, le priour de Coventre, Roger Leche, Johan Westone et Thomas Buxtone, pour icelles governer, ordeiner et lesser pour le commun profit et relevacioun de dit priorie, en sustentacioun de dite prioresse et covent et de divine service illoeques a faire duement en manere et selonc la forme des lettres patententes [*sic*] par vous grantez a le priour de Coventre en cas semblable, pour sept ans adurer, et qe le dit priorie, terres et tenementz susditz en le mesne temps soient dischargez de toutz manere de corrodies, pensions et chargez tanqe le dit priorie soit releve, et que vous autrement ent averez, ordeignez et de prendre le dit priorie, terres, tenementz et possessions, biens, chateux d'iceux provenauntz en vostre proteccioun cum clausula *nolumus*, pour Dieu et en oevre et [*sic*] charitee.

No endorsement

1411. On 4 June 1411 a warrant was sent to the keeper of the great seal to grant the petitioners protection for seven years (no. 6900 of C 81/651). On 9 June 1411 the priory was committed to Richard Crosby, prior of Coventry (1398–1437), Roger Leche, John Weston and Thomas Buxton for seven years, releasing them from pensions and other charges, and granting protection, as requested in the petition (*CPR 1408–13*, pp. 294–5). The name of the petitioner is unknown.

3.3 War

83

Tavistock, Devon (c. 1298–1311)
Benedictine
(SC 8/75/3720)

The abbot and convent of Tavistock petition the king and council, stating that they hold certain isles in the sea between Cornwall and Ireland, of which the largest is called Scilly, to which ships come passing between France, Normandy, Spain, Bayonne, Gascony, Scotland, Ireland, Wales and Cornwall; and because they feel that in the event of a war breaking out between the kings of England and France, or between any of the other places mentioned, they would not have enough power to do justice to these sailors, they ask that they might exchange these islands for lands in Devon, saving the churches on the islands appropriated to them.
Endorsed: *An inquisition is to be held into the contents by Walter of Gloucester, the king's escheator, and by Thomas of la Hyde, so that the escheator inquires in person; and the inquisition is to be returned before the king's council.*

A nostre segnur le roi et a son counsail moustrent l'abbe et le covent de Tavistok qe come il ount ascunes ildes par entre Cornwaille et Irlaunde en milyn la meer, entre les queux il i ad une ilde q'est apele Sulleye, qe coment en sei environ jesqes a diz lyus et plus et les autres ildes sunt ascuns de cink lyus et ascuns de treis lyus environ, par entre les queus touz les neefs qe venent de Fraunce, Normandye, Espaygne, Bayone et de Gascoygne chescun an passent vers Escoce, Irlande, Gales et Cornwaille et des plusours autres terres, et illuk sovent demoerent et .... ters qe unkes mes ne soleynt, et il iad un port en l'ilde de Sulleye en le quel mile neefs poent bien et covenablement ariver et demorer de garder lur temps quele part q'il voillent aler, et les mariners apelent cele ilde leur erber, et celes ildes vallent au ditz abbe et au covent par bone extente lx liveres d'esterlyngs par an et plus, saunz les eglises qe leyns sunt et eux apropriez, et les ditz neofs peussent illuk estre destreyutz pur totes maneres de trespas faitz a nostre segnur le roi ou a son roiallme, et pur coe qe les ditz abbe et le covent sunt de petit poer a justicer celes neefs si ca avensist qe guerre feust par entre nostre dit segnur le roi et le roi de Fraunce, ou entre les segnurages des terres avaunt nomeez, qe Dieu defende, si prient le dit abbe and le covent a nostre segnur le roi q'il voille pur celes ildes eschaunger de ses terres en Deveneshire a la value des ildes avaunt nomez, pur son honur et pur le profit de son roialme, si pleisur lui, seit sauvez a eus lur eglises en les ildes avauntdites a eus et lur meson aproprietz.

Endorsed: Fait inquisicio super contentis per dominum Walterum de Gloucestre, excaetorem regis, et per Thomam de la Hyde, ita quod idem escaetor inquirat in propria persona et retonetur inquisicio coram consilio regis.

c. 1298–1311. The petitioner was Robert Champeaux, abbot 1285–1324. Walter of Gloucester was escheator south of the Trent between 26 May 1298 and 26 April 1311. Thomas of la Hyde, justice, appears frequently in the patent rolls in matters involving Cornwall from 1297 (*CPR 1292–1301*, p. 275) to 1314 (*CPR 1313–17*, p. 228) and was steward of Cornwall in 1306 (*CPR 1301–7*, pp. 419, 483). The abbey was granted the lands and churches in Scilly by Henry I in 1114; a dependent cell was established on the island of Tresco to manage these possessions. Nothing appears to have resulted from the inquiry that resulted from this petition. In later years, the abbot of Tavistock was not infrequently called upon by the crown to guard the south coast (*CCR 1374–7*, p. 497; *1381–5*, p. 270; and *CPR 1401–5*, p. 353). See H. P. R. Finberg, *Tavistock Abbey: A Study in the Social and Economic History of Devon* (Cambridge, 1951), index.

84

Healaugh Park, WRY (c. 1300–25)
Augustinian canons
(SC 8/65/3232)

The prior and canons of Healaugh Park petition the king and council, stating that they are impoverished and too poor to serve God in the number that was ordained at the time of their foundation, because modern people have less devotion to God than their predecessors and because most of their lands are in the north near Yarm where they have been destroyed by the Scots, and they ask that they might be able to acquire lands, tenements, rents or appropriation of churches to the value of £10 to support themselves.
Endorsed: *They are to have permission of the king's grace to acquire 10 marks worth, either in advowsons or in lands and tenements, except for lands and advowsons held of the king in chief.*

A nostre segnur le roi et son counseil prient ses povers chapelleyns priour et chanoignes de Park de Helagh qe come ils sont poverment foundouz et ne pount Dieu servire illoqes a noumbre q'ils furent ordeynez au temps de la fundacion de la dit Park, par qant qe les gen du secle n'ount mye tant devocion a ore vers gentz de religion come ils avoient adonqes, et tot la pluis de lour terres dont ils dusserent estre sustenuz sont en les parties de North' pres de Jarum ou les Escotz ont sovent ardz et destruz, q'il pleyse a nostre seignur le roi, de sa grace especiale et pur l'alme son pier, grantir as ditz priour et chanoignes q'ils puissent purchacer terres, tenementz, rentes ou appropriacion des esglises a la vayllaunce de x li par an, en eide de lour sustenance et en relevacion de lour povre estat, pur Dieu.

Endorsed: Habeant licenciam de gracia regis adquirere decem marcatas, vel in advocationibus vel in terra et tenementis, terra et advocationibus que de rege tenentur in caput exceptis.

c. 1300–25. Dated on the guard to 1334, but the reference is spurious and the petition is dated here notionally to the first quarter of the fourteenth century on the basis of the hand and the Latin endorsement. The damage done to lands at Yarm might be a reference to one of the great Scottish raids into northern England under Edward II, between 1314 and 1322: C. McNamee, *The Wars of the Bruces: Scotland, England and Ireland 1306–1328* (East Linton, 1997), pp. 72–122.

85

Gilbertines (c. 1307)
(SC 8/71/3546)

The priors and nuns of the Gilbertine order petition the king and council that sustenance be ordained for the wives and daughters of Scots placed with them.
Endorsed: *It is ordained by the council that the widow of Richard Seward at Chicksands, the widow of Christopher of Seaton at Sixhills, and the daughter of Robert Bruce, late earl of Carrick at Watton, should each receive 3d a day, and one mark per annum for a robe and other necessaries.*

A nostre seignur le roi et a son consayle prient les priouris e les nonaynes del ordre de Sempingham qe y voylent ordayner al estat e de la sustenaunce de les femmes de Escoces qi demorent en l'ordre avandite en abyt de seculer par maundement nostre seignur le roi encontre estatute de lour religione, ceo est asavoir, a Chykesand cele qe fu la femme Richard Seward le fiz e sa daumsele, a Sixsle cele qe fu la femme Cristopher de Setone, e a Wattone la fyle Robert de Brus jadis count de Karrige.

Endorsed: Ordinatum est per consilium quod quelibet istarum habeat per diem iij d et die ultime solucionis vadiorum eis facte, videlicet, uxori Ricardi Seward commoranti apud Chikesond solvantam iij d per diem per vicecomitem Bedef' et Buk' et per visum prioris loci eiusdem, et relicte Cristophori de Setone commoranti apud Sixle iij d per diem per vicecomitem Linc' et per visum prioris loci eiusdem, et filie Roberti de Brus comitis de Karrik commoranti apud Wattone iij d per diem per vicecomitem Ebor'. Et quelibet illarum habeat unam marcam per annum per manus vicecomitum predictorum pro robes et aliis necessariis suis.

c. 1307. On 15 March 1307 the sheriffs of Yorkshire, Bedfordshire and Lincolnshire were ordered to pay the sums as outlined in the response to the petition (*CPR 1301–7*, p. 503). A memorandum in this case specifies that Richard Seward's wife Elizabeth began her stay at Chicksands on 24 June 1306, and that Christopher Seton's widow Christina was received at Sixhills on the same day that Marjory was received at Watton, namely 3 November 1306 (no. 8 of C 81/1538). Christina and Marjory were daughters of Robert Bruce *alias* Robert I of Scotland. Enraged by Bruce's uprising, Edward I harshly punished those of Bruce's entourage who had fallen into English captivity and the Gilbertine nunneries were used, in effect, as places of 'house arrest' to hold these high-ranking Scottish noblewomen as hostages: C. J. Neville, 'Widows of War: Edward I and the Women of Scotland during the War of Independence', in *Wife and Widow in Medieval England*, ed. S. S. Walker (Ann Arbor, MI, 1993), pp. 109–39, esp. pp. 121–5. For a related petition see below, **194**.

86

Hexham, Northumberland (1331)

Augustinian canons
(SC 8/115/5749)

The prior and convent of Hexham petition the king for pardon of the remaining £63 10s of a debt of £71 10s owed to the king for victuals bought at Newcastle in the time of Edward II. They have suffered greatly from the war, and ask that the king have regard for the losses he himself inflicted on them at Haydon Bridge.
Endorsed: *It seems to the council that, if it pleases the king and on account of the great losses and destruction suffered by them as a result of the Scottish war, they should be pardoned the said sum.*
It pleases the king.

A nostre seignur le roi prient ses povers chapeleyns le priour et le covent de Hextildesham en le counte de Northhumberland sur l'entre de la marche d'Escoce qe la ou il ount este si sovent destrutz par la guerre d'Escoce qe aore sount en tiele estate et ensi enpoveriz par la dite guerre qe a peine purront il vivre, q'il pleise au dit nostre seignur le roi de faire \a eux/ sa bone grace de pardoun de lxiij li x s qe current sur eux par somonce del Escheker du remanant de une dette de Lxxj li x s, les queux il devoient ascoun temps a nostre seignur son piere, qi Deux assoile, pur vitailes achatez a Noef Chastel sur Tyne, et \ceo/ prient il pur l'ame le dit piere et de ses auncestres, eiaunt regard, si lui plest pur Dieu, a les grant perdes q'ils avoient par son hoste au Pounte de Haydone.

Endorsed: Il semble au conseil, s'il plest au roy, qe aumoigne serroit au roi, pur les grauntes pertes et destruccions q'il ount suffert par la guerre d'Escoce, de pardoner la dite summe.
Il plest au roi.

1331. The petitioner was Thomas of Appleton, prior 1328–49. The reference to Haydon Bridge refers to Edward III's military activities in Northumberland in 1327 (the 'Weardale campaign'): C. J. Rogers, *War Cruel and Sharp: English Strategy under Edward III, 1327–1360* (Woodbridge, 2000), chpt. 2. On 8 October 1331 the exchequer was ordered to discharge this debt (*CCR 1330–3*, p. 267), with similar pardons granted to Blanchland and Brinkburn (*CCR 1330–3*, pp. 266–7). A calendar of this petition appears in *Ancient Petitions Relating to Northumberland*, ed. C. M. Fraser, Surtees Society, 171 (1961), pp. 196–7, no. 174.

87

St Andrew outside York, NRY (c. 1333)

Gilbertine
(SC 8/46/2261)

The prior and convent of St Andrew outside York, of the Gilbertine order, petition the king:
(1) They ask for an allowance for 6 marks' worth of stone which they bought for work on their church, by the view of Richard of Worcester, master of works at York Castle during the late king's reign, who took that stone for work on York Castle, without paying.
(2) They state that, although their lands in the North Riding have been burnt by the Scots and their livestock driven away, greatly impoverishing them, both the tenth granted to the late king and the one granted to the present king are based on an assessment of their wealth before this

happened. They ask for a new assessment of their lands in the North Riding and the East Riding, and their rents in the city of York, and that they might be charged for that.
Endorsed: *With regard to the first petition: before the king and great council.*
With regard to the second: he is to have a writ to the archbishop of York, to re-assess the temporalities of the said prior, attached to his spiritualities.

A nostre seignur le roy priount le priour e covent de Seint Andreu hors d'Everwyk, del ordre de Sempingham, qe com il avoynt achate pere al overayn de lur eglise a la value de vj mars, par la vieu Sir Richard de Wyrcestre, chapplayn e maystur del overayn de son chastel d'Everwyk en le temps le roy qe mors est, lur sengnur, e cel pere prist a dit overayn de son chastel saunz rien payer dener ne mayl, plays il a nostre dit sengnur le roy qu'or est de sa grace comander au dit priour e covent alouanz de la dite pere, pur Dieu.
A nostre sengnur le roy prient le priour e covent de Seint Andreu hors d'Everwik, del ordre de Sempingham, qe com rien ount dount estre sustaynu fors petite chose en temperaute en maunays soylle, e sount ars en Northtridding par les Escos, e lur bestes enchasez, e taunt sount empoveriz e destruz q'il ne ount de lur dount estre sustaynu. E en checon dime dener graunte a lur sengnur le roy qe fuit e qu'or est sount en memes la demaund ore a payr com enz q'il furent ars e lur bestes enchasez fesoint. Qe nostre dit sengnur lur voyl graunter novel tax de lur beans en Northtridding e en Esttridding, e de lur rentes de denz sa cite d'Everwyk. E sour ceo soint charget a ors, pur Dieu.

Endorsed: Quant a la primer peticion: coram rege et magno consilio.
Quant a secunde: eyt bref a l'ercsevesqe d'Everwyk de [aceser] de novel les temporautes le dit priour aveyes a ses espirituautez.

c. 1333. The petitioner may be Prior Ralph, who occurs in early 1335. The archbishop of York is William Melton (1316–40). The commission for the inquisition into this matter was issued on 10 February 1333 (*CIM 1307–49*, no. 1365), and the inquisition was held on the following 22 February. The inquisition found that the money for the stone was still owed, and that the king could grant the convent a plot of land which had belonged to the Templars in compensation. For work done on York Castle in the early fourteenth century see R. Allen Brown, H. M. Colvin and A. J. Taylor, *The History of the King's Works: The Middle Ages* (London, 1963), II, 891–2. The damage done by the Scots might be a reference to their raid of 1327: R. Nicholson, *Edward III and the Scots: The Formative Years of a Military Career* (Oxford, 1965), pp. 26–41, and Rogers in note at **86** above.

88

St Denys, Southampton, Hampshire (c. 1340)
Augustinian canons
(SC 8/142/7079)

The prior and convent of St Denys near Southampton petition the king and council, stating that their rents and tenements in Southampton, from which they have the greater part of their sustenance, have been burnt and destroyed by enemies, and that their men are charged with finding men at arms and archers for the defence of the town, and with paying the tenths, so that they can scarcely find enough to live off. They ask that during their misfortunes they might be excused these tenths and the charge for men at arms and archers.

Endorsed: *With regard to their tenths, they cannot be discharged; and with regard to finding men at arms and archers, they are to wait for the response to the common petition.*

A nostre seignur le roy et seon consail prient ces povres chapeleins priour et covent de Seint Denys pres de Suthamptone, de vostre patronage, qe come lur rentes et tenementz en la ville de Suthamptone en queux estoit la greindre partie de lur sustenaunce sont par enemyes ars et destrutz, et auxint sunt par les gentz venantz pur la garde de la meyer grevousement chargez et artez a trover gentz d'armes et archiers pur garde de la dite ville et a paier lour dimes come devant, issint qe a peine pount avoir lur vivre et ceo cheytivement et a graund meschief q'ils puyssent durant lur meschief avantdit estre excuser, de la dymerie avant dit et de la charge des gentz armeez et archiers pur la garde de la dite ville en opre de charite.

Endorsed: Quant a leur disimes, ils ne poont estre descharger; et quant a gentz armez et archiers trover, attendent la response de la comune peticion.

c. 1340. The writ of respite for the petitioners, entered on the roll of the parliament of January 1340 (*PROME*, parliament of January 1340, item 45), mentions that it was granted because their houses had been burnt and destroyed; there is mention of another respite on the roll of the following parliament (*PROME*, parliament of March 1340, item 32). The prior of St Denys, as well as rectors of other churches in Southampton, were granted respite from paying taxation on 28 April 1340, as a result of the destruction of their property 'by certain pirates who had invaded the town': *CCR 1339–41*, pp. 402, 477–8. The petitioner was William of Warham, prior 1328–49. The priory of St Denys was at Portswood, on the west bank of the River Itchen, north of Southampton but still very vulnerable to sea-borne raiding. It also owned properties within the town. Southampton was sacked by the French in 1338: C. Platt, *Medieval Southampton: The Port and Trading Community, A.D. 1000–1600* (London, 1973), pp. 107–18. In 1340 the priory was still trying to recover from this; William de Wareham the prior leased to William de Bolt of Swathelyng, his wife Joan and their sons, for their lifetimes, a vacant plot outside the north gate of the town of Southampton, to be built upon and repaired at their own expense, and maintained in a suitable state: *The St Denys Cartulary*, ed. E. O. Blake, Southampton Record Society, 24–5 (1981), I, 44–5. See also **91**.

89

St Augustine's, Canterbury, Kent (c. 1375–87)

Benedictine

(SC 8/102/5094)

The abbot of St Augustine's, Canterbury, petitions the king for a full explanation as to whom certain prisoners and their goods belong by right and reason, considering that they seem to belong to him. He states that various boats of the French enemy advanced there on the sea to take and rob the king's lieges. One of the enemy boats was damaged on the stakes driven into the petitioner's land for the defence of the isle of Thanet in his lordship, and some of the enemy from the said boat swam and others assembled with their goods and prayed and swam until taken by the petitioner's servants and tenants of the said lordship. Some of the enemy then saved and taken have escaped and are at large spying on the coast in those parts for lack of safeguard.

Endorsed: *This bill should be sent into chancery, and the king's justices and sergeants summoned, and enough bachelors, men-at-arms and others; and when this matter and its circum-*

stances have been explained, full justice should be done to the king as for the petitioner, according to the law and custom of the land, good faith and conscience.

A nostre seignur le roi supplie vostre chapellein et oratour l'abbe de Seint Austyn de Canterbiers qe la ou diverses barges des enemys de France esteiantz sur la mere pur tuir et robber les liges nostre dit seignur le roi, et un barge de ditz enemys fuist debrusse sur les piles riches en la terre le dit abbe en defense del Ile de Tanet deinz sa seignurie, et ascunz des ditz enemys esteantz en la dite barge estoient neiez et les autres ensemblement ove lour biens en point d'estre periez et neiez, tanqe ils furent salvez et prises par les servantz et tenantz du dit abbe de sa dit seignurie, et ascuns des ditz enemys ensi salvez et prises ore sont alantz a large et espiont les costes du mere en celle partie pur defaut de salve garde, a cause qe plein declacione[9] n'est fait a qi les ditz prisons ove lour biens devoient de reson apertenir, qe plese a nostre dit seignur le roi fair ent plein declaracion a qi les ditz prisoners ensemblement ove lour breve devoient de droit et reson apertenir, considerantz qe les ditz biens et prisons pertinent a dit abbe come lui semble.

Endorsed: Soit ceste bille mande en la Chancellerie et illoeqes appellez les justices et sergantz le roi, et aucuns suffisantz bacheloers et gentz d'armes et autres queux y sont appellers; et illoeqes oiez et declarez ceste matire aver, les circumstances et dependences d'ycelle, plein droyt illoeqes ent soit fait, sibien pur nostre seignur le roi come pur la partie, solonc les loys et usages de la terre et bone foy et conscience.

c. 1375–87. The petitioner was probably Michael of Pecham, abbot of St Augustine's 1375–87. This possibly refers to the French raids of the summer 1377: see William Thorne, *Chronicle of St Augustine's Abbey, Canterbury*, trans. A. H. Davis (Oxford, 1934), p. 609, and Thomas Walsingham, *The St Albans Chronicle, Volume I, 1376–1394*, ed. and trans. J. Taylor, W. R. Childs and L. Watkiss (Oxford, 2003), pp. 162–5.

90

Holm Cultram, Cumberland (1385)
Cistercian
SC 8/20/994

The abbot and convent of Holm Cultram petition the king, stating that, to avoid being burnt down by the earl of Douglas and other Scots, they agreed to a ransom of £200 in English coin, but do not dare to pay this without the king's permission. They ask that they may have such permission, notwithstanding any common law, ordinance or statute to the contrary.
Endorsed: *Because they did it of necessity, the king has granted them a charter of pardon.*

A lour tresexcellent et tresgracius seignur le roi, supplie sez povres oratours abbe et covent Nostre Dame de Holmcoltram en le countee de Cumbr' qe come ils ount raunsone lour esglise et abbey, quele est del patronage nostre dit seignur le roi, a les Escoces pur un an entier pur CC li de money d'Engleterre, ou autrement lez ditz esglise et abbay ussent estez arcez par le counte de Douglays et autres Escoces et ennemys nostre dit seignur le roi, quele somme n'essent as ditz Escoces paier saunz conge du roi. Qy pleise graunter de sa grace especial, en

9 Sic, for *declaracion*.

salvacioun du dit esglise et abbay et covent, conge de paier a Monsire Archebald de Douglays le somme de lez CC li avauntditz, neyntcontresteant comun ley, ordeignance ou estatut fait al encontre.

Endorsed: Par cause q'ils l'ont fait de necessite, le roi lour ad grantee chartre de pardoun.

1385. On 6 November 1385 the abbot and convent of Holm Cultram (or Abbey Town) were pardoned for paying the ransom, in accordance with the endorsement of this petition (*CPR 1385–9*, p. 71). The identity of the abbot of Holm Cultram at this time is not known. The earl of Douglas was James, 2nd earl of Douglas (1358–88). The petition refers to one of two major raids launched by the Scots into northern England in the second half of 1385: A. J. MacDonald, *Border Bloodshed: Scotland, England and France at War 1369–1403* (East Linton, 2000), pp. 90–4. For an earlier edition of the petition see *RP*, III, 181, no. 22.

91

St Denys, Southampton, Hampshire (1388)

Augustinian canons
(SC 8/253/12634)

To the king from the prior and convent of St Denys by Southampton requesting that he take them and all their possessions into his protection, and warrant the keeping to certain persons in discharge of their corrodies until the priory is relieved of its oppressions and damages. They are on the verge of destruction because their property was burnt in the French raid, their livestock is destroyed by murrain and they are overburdened with corrodies.
Endorsed on face: *This is granted by the king.*
Let the keeping be entrusted to the earl of Nottingham, Peter of Barton, John Polymond and Hugh Craan.

A treshaut et tresredoute seignur le roy supplient humblement voz povres oratours le priour et le covent de Seint Denys juxte Suthamptone, qe sont de la fundacioun de voz tresnobles progenitours et de vostre patronage, qe come lour tenementz en la ville de Suthamptone susdite, qeux estoient la grendre partie de lour vivre furont nadgars arstez et destrutz par les Fraunces et autres voz enemys, et auxint aient sustenuz et portez les ditz suppliantz treschargantz custages et despens en murage, fossage et autres fortificacions de la dite ville, et tresgrantz destruccions et damages sibien par gentz d'armes demurantz sur le dit priorie et lour manoirs a lour passage outre le mer sovent foitz faitz devaunt ces heures come en moryne de lour bestes, issint qe par force de graunt necessite chiant sur eux, par cause de l'arsoun, costages, destructions et moryne susditz, fust le dit priore charge a diverses persones en corodies a la value de xl marcz par an, les queles corodiers ount resceu des biens de dit priore outre lour primer paiement CCC li et plus. Et issint par les causes susditz sont les ditz suppliantz en poynt d'estre perpetuelement destrutz et de mendyver lour sustenance s'il ne soit, par vostre tresgracious aide et seignurie, remedie ent purveu, qar ils ne ont rien dont vivre sinoun sur creance. Plese a vostre treshaute et tresredoute seignurie considerer les avauntditz allegeances, qeux sont en toutz vois et le perpetuel destruccioun de dit priorie, q'est de vostre patronage, si remedie ne soit le plustost ordene, et le prendre ove toutz lour possessions et appurtenantz en vostre protectioun especial, grantant la garde d'icelle a ascuns cereteyns persones en descharge des ditz corodies jesqe le dit priorie par tieux oppressions et damages soit relever amende, en le honour de Dieu et de seint charite.

Endorsed on face: Concessa est per ipsum regem.
Soit la garde comise a count de Notyngham, Piers de Bartone, clerc, Johan Polymonde, burgis de Suthampton, et Hugh Craan, citeseyn de Wynchestre.

1388. For background, see the notes to **88** above. The petitioner was Richard Staunford, prior 1349–91. The hospital was taken into royal protection and custody for two years on 28 April 1385, 13 February 1387 and 11 February 1389, with the same four custodians every time: *CPR 1381–5*, p. 556; *CPR 1385–9*, p. 277; *CPR 1388–92*, p. 8. Peter Barton was a greater clerk of chancery from 1376: B. Wilkinson, *The Chancery under Edward III* (Manchester, 1929), p. 205. For the career of John Polymond, *fl.* 1364–93, with references, see C. Platt, *Medieval Southampton: The Port and Trading Community, A.D. 1000–1600* (London, 1973), p. 255.

92

St Mary's, Thetford, Norfolk, and Bermondsey, Surrey (1390)

Cluniac
(SC 8/143/7133)

The priors of Thetford and Bermondsey petition the king, stating that the recent statute ordaining that all French in England should leave the realm had made an exception for conventual religious, for term of their lives, and that provision had been made for the visitation of houses of the Cluniac order by the archbishop of Canterbury and the priors of Thetford and Bermondsey, as these houses are outwith any episcopal jurisdiction. The priors now ask permission to make such a visitation.
Endorsed: *It is agreed that the supplicants may exercise the jurisdiction granted to them by the Holy Father during the schism, as the abbot of Cluny and the prior of La Charité would duly have done if there had been no schism, saving always to the king, and to the other founders and patrons of the alien and denizen priories and houses, their inheritances, rights, patronages and advowsons in them.*

A tresexcellent, treshaut et tresredoute nostre seignur le roi supplient treshumblement voz poverez oratours les priours de Thetford et de Bermundeseye del ordre de Cluny, del jurisdiccion de chescun ordinar[ie] toutoutrement exempt, qe come par un estatut nadgers fait y estoit ordeyne qe toutz les aliens Fraunceys serroient voidez le roialme, sibien religious mendinantz come autres religious, horspus les pri[ours] conventueles et autres parsones q'ount title a terme de vie en lour benefices ou offices et conuz pur bones parsons et loialx. Et a quele heure qe les ditz priours conventuelx et autres benefices et offices issint par title voiderent, par cesser ou decesse de ditz priours ou occupiours qe adonqe furent, ou en autre manere durant les guerres, qe honestes parsones d'Engleterre yserreient mys en lieux de eux pur accompler le divine service, et null des enemys suisdite. Et au fyn qe divine service soit custeim en les ditz priories aliens y fuist ordeyne qe cheschun evesqe en sa diocise a la presentacion des patrones e ..... de mesmes les priories serra acceptacioun, et mettre en ycelles autres parsones religious de mesons Engles ou bones et honestes chapellains seculers pur demeter et avoir covenable sustenance en les ditz priories affaire le divyne service en ycelles durant les guerres, jusqe a nombre q'est a present en chescun de ditz priories, come en le dit estatut est contenuz pluis aplayn. Et nostre treseint pier le pape, consideront le ordre de Cluny de chescun manere de jurisdiccioun ordinarie toutoutrement exempt soutz le reule et governayle l'abbe de Cluny estre, et par cause del scisme del esglise de Court de Rome en le roialme d'Engleterre tut dissolat, come il ne soit qe priories ou autre lieux de dit ordre en le dit roialme visiter, corriger ou parsones nient ables remoer et autres en lour lieux mettre poit deins le dit roialme, ad graunte al tresreverent piere en Dieux l'erchevesqe de Caunterbirs et les priours de Thetford et de Bermundeseye tout maner poer qe le dit abbe de Cluny .... de visiter, corriger, ordeyner et disposer des lieux et parsones de dit ordre deins le roialme d'Engleterre, et benefices et priories ent doner, come en bulle de dit treseint piere ent faites est pleynement compris. Qe please a vostre treshaute et tresgracious seignurie graunter qe les ditz erchevesqe et priours poent les ditz priories et autres lieu deins le roialme d'Engleterre visiter, ordeyner, disposer .... parsones nient ables enjoer et autres covenables des Engles en lour lieux mettre, solon le tenour de ditz bulles, nient obstaunt le dit estatut. Entendant, treshaut seignur, qe vostre dit graunte in null manere tourner en prejudice del effect de dit estatut, considere coment le dit ordre est hors de chescun jurisdiccioun ordinarie et ne poet par la ley de seint esglise estre ...., sinoun par l'abbe de Cluny ou autres deputez par le dit treseint piere le pape.

Endorsed: Accordez est qe les supplantz puissent user la jurisdiccion a eux graunte par le seint pier durant le scisme, en manere come l'abbe de Cluny et le prior de la Charite deveroient duement faire si null scisme y feusse, savant toutdis au roy, et as autres fondours et patrons des priories et mesons aliens et denzeins, lour enheritementz, droitures, patronages et avoesons d'ycelles.

1390. Cluny and La Charité were the parent houses of Thetford and Bermondsey respectively. On 26 November 1390 licence was granted for the priors of Bermondsey and Thetford and the archbishop of Canterbury to exercise jurisdiction over persons and places of the Cluniac order, apparently in response to this petition (*CPR 1388–92*, pp. 333–4). The petitioners were John of Fordham, prior of Thetford 1371–c.1411, and Richard of Dounton, prior of Bermondsey c. 1372–90. Days after the grant of this licence Dounton resigned, and by 3 December had been replaced as prior by John of Attilburgh (*CPR 1388–92*, pp. 332–3). The archbishop of Canterbury is William Courtenay (1381–96). The 'statute' was in fact a response to a common petition presented in the parliament of October 1377: *PROME*, parliament of October 1377, item 91 (l). No formal legislation was passed on the matter at this time. In the Good Parliament of 1376, the Commons asked the crown to ensure that the priors and monks of the Cluniac order in England should henceforth be English: *PROME*, parliament of 1376, item 128 (LXIX). This petition was based on a much less elaborate draft text which made no reference to the Cluniac order (below, **167**). See A. K. McHardy, 'The Alien Priories and the Expulsion of Aliens from England in 1378', in *Church Society and Politics*, ed. D. Baker, Studies in Church History, 12 (Oxford, 1975), pp. 133–41; also Introduction, pp. xlii–xliii. The right-hand edge of this petition is damaged. For an earlier transcript of this petition, see no. 54 of PRO 31/7/111.

93

Axholme, Lincolnshire (c. 1415–22)
Carthusian
(SC 8/116/5770)

The prior of Axholme petitions the king and council for remedy against William Colman, William Bosevyll, Robert Fox and others who attacked the priory of Monks Kirby when the king lately returned into England, destroying and stealing property, to the great damage of his house.
Endorsed: Charterhouse.

A tresexcellent et tresgraciouse seignur liege, nostre seignur le roy, e a soun tressage conseil du parliament supplie humblement vostre povere oratour le priour de measoun del ordre de Carteuse deinz l'Isle de Haxholme qe come il estoit nadgairs seisy en soun demesne come de fee del priorie de Monkeskirkeby en la contee de Warr', ovesqe toutz les terres et tenementz et autres choses qeconqes a mesme le priorie apurtiegnantz ou appendantz, come du droit de sa esglise de Nostre Dame de Haxholm, la William Colman, William Bosevyll et Robert Fox ove plusours autres, ore tarde puys vostre darrain venir, tresexcellent seignur, en Engleterre, et qe chivacherent ovesqe vous, forciblement ont entrez deinz la dite priorie de Monkeskirkeby et ent a foers de guerre ostez le dit suppliant et les profitz ent proveignantz levez et pris, et unqore tiegnent a force, encontre la proclamacion ore tard fait a contraire, et diverses biens et chateux a grande value et chartres, escriptz et autrez munimentz et auxint xxv li xij s j d en monoy nombre del dit suppliant illeoqes trovez pristrent et enporterent. Qe pleise a vostre roial mageste, tresexcellent seignur, et a vostre tressage conseil suisdite ent ordeigner remedie, pur Dieux et en oevre de charite, considerantz qe la dite priorie de Munkeskirkeby est la substance de la sustenance du dit suppliant et soun covent, et qe les ditz malfaisors ne sont pas suffisantz de faire restitucioun et duhes amendes s'ils soient suffertz de continuer lour torcenouse occupacioun avandite.

Endorsed: Chartheuse.

c. 1415–22. This petition dates to after Henry V's grant of Monks Kirby to Axholme in 1415, although probably to the reign of Henry V, given that it mentions the king's return to England (probably after the Agincourt campaign of 1415 or his invasion of Normandy and subsequent campaigning in 1417–20). The petitioner was either Thomas Selby, who occurred as prior 1415–17, or 'John', who occurred 1422–4.

Part Four

ROYAL INTERCESSION: PETITIONS INVOLVING THIRD PARTIES

4.0 General

94

Chichester, Sussex (1269–85)
Augustinian Friars
(SC 8/309/15418)

To the king from the Augustinian friars requesting a house at Portsmouth since disturbances by the earl of Cornwall and his bailiffs have made living in Chichester impossible.
Endorsed: *The king should not grant them a chapel or lands which belong to the crown.*

Pur coe ke les freres de Seint Austyn, pur desturbaunce ke le cunte de Cornwaille e ses baillifs lur funt, ne pount habiter a Cycestre, e la priere le roy ne lur puet valer, e prient les avauntditz freres au roy, si ly plest, ke pur l'alme le Roy Henri e pur les almes de ses auncestres, lur voillez graunter une place a Portesmue, dunt il memes commaunda fere une enqueste ke la place vaulist, e dunt il unt la enquest, e ke le roy veuwe cele enqueste, sur coe lur face sa grace.

Endorsed: Rex non concedet eis capellam nec terram que est de corona.

1269–85. The petition probably dates to the reign of Edward I since the only named soul to be prayed for is that of Henry III. Thus the earl of Cornwall is Edmund of Almaine (d. 1300). The house's existence was of very short duration. The Austin friars were conditionally given a site in Chichester after 1269, but this was granted to St Mary's hospital in 1285. No permanent house of the order was founded in Sussex before 1364; *MRH*, p. 246.

95

St Mary of Carmel, London (1290)
Carmelite
(SC 8/276/13792)

To the king from the prior and convent of St Mary of Carmel, London, requesting that William Gildel be ordered not to burn sea coal on his plot of land adjoining their house, because such a smell comes from its burning that they are unable to remain in their house or church, and people have stopped coming to their services.
Endorsed: *London.*
The petition of the prior and convent of St Mary of Carmel.
Before the king.
Dealt with before the king.

In this file are contained 58 petitions.
It is ordered before the king that they be removed.

Le priur et le covent del ordre Nostre Dame \de/ Carme en le suburbe de Londres prient la grace nostre seygnor le rey por coe ke Wiliam Gildel ad une place joinaunte a lor mesoun, en la quele place il ard de costome cauz \de carbon de mer/, dont une graunt puier leve ke eus ne pount ben en lor mesoun demorer ne en lor eglise por Deu servir, et mult de bone gent par cele reson se resteent de la venir et lor service ous, a graunt damage del prior et son covent et destorbaunce del service Deu, ke nostre seygnor le rey voille \de/ sa grace, al honor de Deu, comaunder ke tel mester de cauz arder ne seit desoreme ilokes use.

Endorsed: Lond'.
Peticio prioris et conventus Sancte Marie de Carme.
Coram rege.
Expedita coram rege.
In isto filacio continentur lviij peticiones.
Preceptum est per dominum regem quod et deponantur.

1290. The Carmelite priory was founded in the early 1240s: see, J. Röhrkasten, 'The White Friars', in *Religious Houses of London and Middlesex*, ed. C. M. Barron and M. Davies (London, 2007), p. 128. It was sited beside the Thames, in the western suburbs, south of Fleet Street, between the Temple and the bishop of Salisbury's inn. This is the kind of dispute between neighbours that from the early fourteenth century would have been dealt with under London the assize of nuisance. The petition was subsequently enrolled on the parliament roll: *PROME*, Edward I, Roll 2, item 231 (197).

96

Holy Trinity, York, NRY (c. 1293–6)
Benedictine (alien)
(SC 8/46/2258)

The prior of Holy Trinity, York, petitions the king, making four requests:
(1) Although he is exempt of ordinary jurisdiction by especial privilege of the court of Rome, the archbishop of York has excommunicated him and his sub-prior, sequestered the goods he needs for his support and to pay his tenth, and is taking away his right of reply by sending his letters to those whom the prior pleads before the justices in eyre at York, saying that he is excommunicated, and has purchased a writ of capias *against him and his sub-prior. He requests a remedy.*
(2) The prior has purchased a writ of right concerning the church of Barton against Henry of Grey, who is delaying the case by claiming that he holds the manor of Barton of the gift of Henry III, and that the gift can return to the king. He requests a remedy.
(3) He requests the return of his franchise, which has been withheld from him since the late war.
(4) He requests an inquiry into his claim that the king holds 3½ acres of arable land which ought to be held of him.

A nostre seigneur le roy supplie le priur de la Trinite de Everewyk que cume il soyt exempt de tote jurisdiction ordeneyre par especial privilege de la Curt de Rome, qui il ad de ceo ly ercevesque de Everewyk le dit priur e soen suppriur de jour en jour escomenye, e ses biens sequestre de quoy il deit vivre e de quoy

il diet soen dizime paer. Derichef il doune ses lettres a gens encontre qui le dit priur plede devaunt vos justices erranz a Everwyk que le dit priur est escomenge e ensi ly tolt respunse. Derichef il ad purchace bref de caption contre le dit priur e soen suppriur. Le dit priur prie remedie come il soit exempt e eit appele.
Derichef come le dit priur eit bref de droit purchace du patronage del eglise de Barton' en Ridale contre Sire Henry de Grey, e le dit Henry eit respundu qua ad le maner e la vile de Barton', ove les apurtenaunces, du doun le Roy Henry, pere nostre seignur le roi qui ore est, e que le doun devauntdit poet returner a nostre seigneur le roy e purceo ad ia en deus delays ne ne voet respundre, dunt le priur prie remedie.
Derichef de sa fraunchise reaver que lui ad este detenue puis la guere dareyne de quoy le priur ad pur lui le Domesday e les chartres de confermement des roys d'Engleterre, e especiaument la chartre le Roy Henry, pere nostre seignur le roy qui ore est. Prie le dit priur remedie.
Derichef nostre seigneur le roy tenet treys acres e demye de terre gaignable que devoyent estre tenues du dit priur, dunt le priur prie remedie e que la verite seit enquise.

No endorsement

c. 1293–6. The petition dates from between October 1293, when Archbishop Romeyne excommunicated the prior, and Romeyne's death in March 1296. The petitioner was John de Insula, prior 1283–1305. On 17 August 1298 a privy seal writ ordered a search of chancery records in connection with part one of the petition: *CCW 1244–1326*, pp. 95–6. The background to the dispute between the prior and Romeyne can be followed in *The Register of John Le Romeyn, Lord Archbishop of York 1286–1296*, part 1, Surtees Society, 123 (1913), pp. 50, 59, 133, 138, 164, 233. See also the references in *Heads of Houses II*, 217. A writ of *capias* was a writ addressed to the sheriff ordering the arrest of the person named. The case is further discussed in the Introduction, pp. xxxviii–xxxix. See also, F. D. Logan, *Excommunication and the Secular Arm in Medieval England* (Toronto, 1968), p. 125 n. 38.

97

Butley, Suffolk (c. 1300–17)
Augustinian canons
(SC 8/329/E942)

To the king and council from the prior of Butley requesting that the chancellor make a writ to John Botetourt or William Ormesby commanding them to receive the prior's attorney, as he is so ill and old. He needs an attorney because he is impleaded in the Bench by John of Chavent who demands by writ of what service the prior claims to hold his tenements in Butley.
Endorsed: *This is not able to be done because it is against the custom and law of the land.*

Suff'. Buttele. A nostre seignur le rei e soun consail moustre le priour de Buttele de ceo qe il est inpled devant justices en baunk ke par Mounsire Johan de Chavent' qe demand par bref par queus services le dit priour cleyme tenir ses tenementz en Buttele. Prie, pur Dieux et en salutz de s'alme, qe il de sa grace voille fere comaunder au chaunceller q'il face bref a Mounsire Johan Boutetourte u a Mounsire Williame de Ormesby deprendre attorne le priour avaunt dite, pur coe qe il est malangeus e issi chere en age qe il ne se peut ayder en travail.

Endorsed: Non potest fieri quia contra consuetudinem et legem terre.

c. 1300–17. The petition is speculatively dated on the basis of the hand. Ormesby was a justice of the King's Bench, 1296, 1298–1303; died 1317: Sainty, *Judges*, p. 23, s.n. Ormsby, and P. Brand, 'Ormesby, Sir William (*d.*1317)', *ODNB*. John Botetourt was a politically influential baron and an active soldier: R. Gorski, 'Botetourt, John, first Lord Botetourt (*d.*1324)', *ODNB*. Both Ormesby and Botetourt were influential landowners in East Anglia and were appointed to numerous judicial commissions in the region at the end of the thirteenth and beginning of the fourteenth century.

98

Castle Acre, Norfolk (? c. 1307)
Cluniac
(SC 8/173/8645)

The prior of Castle Acre petitions the king and council that since John Bozun, parson of the church of Whissonsett (Norf.), has no means of further remedy in a suit brought against him by the prior, the supersedeas that he obtained be repealed, and he be sent back to prison until he makes redress to the church. Bozun was excommunicated by the archbishop of Canterbury at the prior's suit and was imprisoned, but he came and alleged by a false allegation that he had appealed to the Court of Rome and had purchased a bull, and that the appeal was still pending there, though his appeal had been refused as he had not appealed in time, and he was without a remedy.
Endorsed: *He should sue to the archbishop of Canterbury for a new letter called a 'significavit'; and he should show in chancery how process was revoked, and have there a writ to retake Bozun.*

A nostre seignur le roy et a sun cunsel prie le priur de Chastelacre qe vous voliez faere remedie de coe qe Johan Bozun, parsone de la eglise de Wyssingset, qe est escomunge par auctorite le erceveske de Canturbr' par quoy il fuit en prisune\a la suyte de le dyt priur/ par un significavit qe le dyt erceveske maunda en Chauncelrie, vint meme ce ly Johan ow un faus suggestiun et fyt entendaunt a la curt ke il avoit appelle de cele sentence a la Curt de Rome et fulle purchace a sez juges delegas, devaunt quors juges sa cause fu pendaunt, u lez avantditez juges delegaz unt pronuncie en curter luy en la dite cause pur coe ke il ne fuyt point sun apel de enz le an ne vivant le Apostolie, par quoy il ne poyt aver remedie par ne cel apel ne par cele bulle, si cum lez juges delegas temoniunt par lur letteres patenz et par instrument pupplys, et le queus le dit priur \est/ prest de vaunt vous a mostre. Dount il vous pri, si vous plest, ke luy avant dit Johan par sa faus suggestiun plus ne eyt remedie mes ke sa supersedias seyt \repelle et/ defet et qe il soyt arere en prisune taunt kum il se volit redrescer a seynt eglise.
Et pur coe qe avauntdite Johan est excomenge par le auctorite le erceveske en deuz diverses causis par diverses enchesuns et nule apel fyt fors ke une cause sicum le erceveske certifie, il ne doy aver remedie de *supersedeas* de un apel.

Endorsed: Sequatur versus archiepiscopem Cant' pro nova littera que dicitur significavit habenda pro capcione dicti Johannis habenda iterato; et ostendat in Cancellaria qualiter processus delegatorum extiterat revocatus et habeat ibi breve super facto predicto ad recapiendum Johannem infrascriptum.

[Another endorsement, similarly instructing the petitioner to sue to the archbishop of Canterbury, has been deleted].

? c. 1307. The petition is dated to c. 1307 on the basis of a possibly related pardon granted to John Bozun (*CPR 1301–7*, p. 489). If correct, the petitioner was John of Acre, who occurred as prior of Castle Acre in June 1307 and January 1308, but also possibly from 1302 until 1311. The archbishop of Canterbury is Robert of Winchelsey (1295–1313). The use of the word 'purchace', for the process of obtaining the bull was surely intended to be derogatory; it described the action of a man whom the prior had excommunicated and reported to the crown as obdurate. The signification has not survived. Bozun was probably related to Sir Peter Botzoun of Wyssingsete who, on Tuesday 6 December 1323, granted the advowson of Yelverton church to Sir Geoffrey Wyth; TNA C 146/707.

99

Godstow, Oxfordshire (c. 1315)
Benedictine (nuns)
(SC 8/50/2473)

The abbess of Godstow petitions the king and council for a remedy. The king's ancestors granted a vaccary and pasture in Panshill to the abbey of Godstow, but Hugh le Despenser the elder, by colour of his office of keeper of the forest below the Trent, seized them into the king's hand without cause. He then extended the pasture at little value, delivering it to John of Handlo, his sub-keeper, by an arentment made in the exchequer, holding it at the king's will, from which pasture, called Lachemede, her predecessor was wrongfully ejected in the time of Edward I.
Endorsed: *She should sue at the common law.*

A nostre seignur le roi et son conseil prie l'abbesse de Godestowe qe come les auncestres nostre seignur le roi eient par lour chartres grantez et donez a la meson de Godestowe, en fundacion del eglise en pur et perpetuel almoyne, la vacherie ditz Panchehale ove la several pasture sicome les auncestres nostre seignur le roi en lour propre meyn la avoient come il piert par paroles des chartres, la quel several pasture Sire Hugh le Despenser le pere, quant il estoit gardein de la forest le roi de cea Trent, par sa seignurie et par colour de son office, seisit en la meyn nostre seignur le roi sanz cause, et quel pasture feust puis estendue a petite value par le procurement le dit Sire Hugh et livere a Sire Johan de Handlo, son southgardein de la forest, par arentement faite en l'Escheqier le roi, sicome le dit Sire Johan dist atener a la volunte le roi, de quele several pasture, \q'est appele Lacchemede/, feust sa predecessere \issint/ ostee a tort en temps le Roi Edward le pier, dount ele prie remedie.

Endorsed: Sequatur ad communem legem.

c. 1315. The date, though uncertain, is based on a number of suggestive entries in the chancery rolls, including a grant made to John of Handlo, then keeper of Bernwood forest (*CCR 1313–18*, p. 187), which concerned land in the king's wood at Panshill (*CFR 1307–19*, p. 229). In July 1315 a commission was charged to investigate the complaints of those from named counties (not including Oxon.) about the misdeeds of the keepers of the forests and the bearing of Hugh Despesner the elder: *CPR 1313–17*, p. 407. Also suggestive is the year's protection given to the abbey by the king in March 1316: *CPR 1313–17*, p. 446. The petitioner was either Matilda of Upton, abbess 1304–16, or Margery Dyve, abbess 1316–35. A translation and discussion of this petition is printed in *Parliamentary*

Petitions Relating to Oxford, ed. L. Toulmin Smith, Oxford Historical Society, XXXII (1896), pp. 110–11, no. 44. For a petition by Handlo, see SC 8/50/2494. For another petition on the same matter, see **101** below.

100

Dunstable, Bedfordshire (c. 1327)

Dominican
(SC 8/69/3444)

Brother John of Redmer and Brother John of Norton petition the king and council because when they were at Dunstable, to hear mass in the house of their order there, they were arrested by the bailiffs and community and thrown into prison, accused of conspiring to rescue Edward II from Berkeley Castle. The bailiffs were ordered to provide information on why they arrested the friars, and provided such information (a transcript of which is attached to the petition) that John and John can only be delivered before the king. They ask that they might be able to come before the king to stand to right according to the law of the land, as they have been in prison first at Dunstable and now at Aylesbury, and are at point of death as a result.
Endorsed: *The certification is to come before the council.*
The sheriff is to be ordered that if Brothers John and John have been arrested and held for the reason given in the petition and for no other, then he is to have the said Brothers John and John brought, at their own cost, before the king at the quinzaine of Easter next, wherever he is, to answer to the king concerning the things contained in the bailiffs' certification, and to do and receive what the court will decide. And then this petition, with the said certification, is to be sent before the king, under the foot of the great seal.

A nostre seignur le roi et a son conseil moustrent Frere Johan de Reddmere et Johan de Nottone qe come il vindrent passant parmy la ville de Dunstapel et decendirent as freres illoqes pur oier messe, les baillifs et la comunalte de la dite ville les firent espier et prendre et mettre en prisone, et les surmistrent qe eux furent entour de faire assemblez des gentz et alliance de rescovre le pier nostre seignur le roi hors del chastel de Berkeley. Et sur ceo feust mande par bref as ditz baillifs de certifier le roi sur la cause de la prise et detenue des avantditz Johan et Johan en la prisone avantdite, les queux baillifs certifaverent la cause avantdite et plusours autres causes contenues en lour certificatione, dount le transescrit est attache a ceste bille, par les queles il peert qe eux ne purront estre delivers si noun devant le roi. Par quei il prient, pur Dieu et pur l'alme le pier nostre seignur le roi, et pur estre allegge de la dure prisone ou il sount, q'il pleise a nostre seignur le roi et a son conseil comander qe lour corps ove lour attachement veignent devant le roi de esteer au droit haut et baas solonc ley de terre, qar il ount demore en prisone primes a Dunestaple et peus a Ailesbury, issint q'il sount en peril de mort pur durete de prisone et defaute de sustenance.

Endorsed: Veniat certificatio coram consilio.
Soit mande au visconte qe si Frer Johan et Johan soient pris et detenuz par l'encheson nome en la peticion et nemie par autre, adonqes face mevir les ditz frer Johan et Johan et leur custages devant le roi a la quinzeine de Pasche prochein avenir, ou q'il soit a respondre au roi des choses contenues in la certificacion des baillifs, a faire et receivre ce qe la court agardera. Et adonqes soit ceste peticion, ove la dite certificacion, mandez devant le roi, suth le pee du grant seal.

c. 1327. Although this incident took place at Dunstable, and involved the priory there, the petitioners were clearly from elsewhere. On 11 August 1327 the bailiffs of Dunstable were ordered to deliver the petitioners to the constable of Wallingford Castle, where they were to be kept safely and not delivered thence without the king's special order (*CCR 1327–30*, p. 156). While at Dunstable, Redmer and Norton were in the prison of the prior and convent; Aylesbury was the county gaol, R. B. Pugh, *Imprisonment in Medieval England* (Cambridge, corr. reprint, 1970), pp. 59, 77, 234, 254, 350. The transcript detailing the reasons why the petitioners were arrested is no longer attached to the petition. For further discussion, see Introduction, pp. xliii–xliv.

101

Godstow, Oxfordshire (c. 1327)
Benedictine (nuns)
(SC 8/16/774)

The abbess of Godstow petitions the king and council for a remedy. The king's ancestors granted by their charter to her and her house a tithe of venison in the forest of Wychwood, of which her predecessor, Mabel Wafre, was seised until Hugh Despenser the father, when he was keeper of that forest, prevented her from having it.
Endorsed: *She is to show her charter in chancery, and a writ is to be sent to the justice of the forest or his lieutenant etc., to institute an inquisition into whether the abbess's predecessors were seised of the tithe, and which of them was first ousted from it, and for what reason, and into all other necessary matters. And when the inquisition has been returned in chancery, it is to be shown to the king.*

A nostre seignur le roi et a son conseil prie l'abbesse de Godestowe qe come les auncestres nostre seignur le roi eient grante par lour chartres al abbesse et a la meson de Godestowe, en la fundacion del eglise, la disme de tut le venesoun qe a temps qe serroit pris en la foreste de Whichewode, par vertue de queu graunt la predecesseresse l'abbesse qe ore est estoit seisie tanqe Hugh le Despenser le piere, quant il fust gardein de la dite foreste, destourba Mabille Wafre, predecesseresse l'abbesse q'ore est, aprendre l'avandite disme, dount ele prie remedie.

Endorsed: Moustre la chartre en Chauncerie, et illoeqe soit mande bref a la justice de la foreste ou a son lieu tenant etc., q'il face enquere si les predecessers la dite abbesse furent seisiz de cel disme come la peticion purport, et quele de ses predecessers fust primers ouste, et par qi, et par quele cause, et de totes autres choses necessaires. Et retorne l'enqeste en Chauncerie, soit mostre au roi.

c. 1327. This probably dates to shortly after the fall of Despenser and clearly relates to **99** above. Thus, the petitioner is Margery Dyve, abbess 1316–35. Mabel Wafre was abbess 1283–95. Despenser had been justice of forests south of the Trent since 1297. An earlier edition of the petition is printed in *RP*, II, 402, no. 134.

102

Butley, Suffolk (c. 1330)
Augustinian canons
(SC 8/92/4572)

The prior of Butley petitions the king and council for remedy because Richard of Reynham, Adam the Selgravere, John the Bokeler, Adam the Blake, Thomas of Roulesham, John Fish, William the Latoner, Nicholas the Lyvers, William Fourwoukes and William his son, Geoffrey Miles, Robert Brownrobin, John the Sacker, John of Sabrichesworth and Laurence of Chayham have demolished the prior's houses in London and carried away the materials, and entered his church of St Olave and carried away the oblations, and by confederacy and malice have threatened the prior's proctor so that he cannot pursue his suit in the Guildhall, the bishop of London's court or the Court of Arches.
Endorsed: *The mayor and the sheriffs should be ordered to prevent such force and duress, and proclaim that no one is to be so presumptuous as to disturb the prior in any manner from pursuing his right in their court or any other. And if they find that after the proclamation anyone does disturb him, then they are to certify the king of their names.*

A nostre seignur le roi et son conseil moustre le priur de l'esglise de Nostre Dame de Buttele qe come nadgaiers Richard de Reynham, mercer de Loundres, Adam le Selgravere, Johan le Bokeler, Adam le Blake, hakeneyman, Thomas de Roulesham, chapellein, Johan Fisch, pursere, William le Latoner, Nicholas le Lyvere, William Fourwoukes, fevre, et William son fils, Geffrei Miles, Robert Brounerobyn, Johan le Sackere, Johan de Sabrichesworth et Laurence de Chayham les mesons meisme cesti priur en Loundres, nomeement une sale ove deux chaumbres d'estage, deux shopes, une quisine, une chaumbre basse, une bracine, une estable, debriserent et abatirent en terre, et le merin de ceux a la value de xl li emporterent, et ses pomers, perers, vynes en son gardin cressantz enracerent et emporterent, et sa esglise de Seint Olaf, quele il tent en propres us, entrerent et les oblacions, menues, dymes et les autres profitz de celle esglise, le lundi prochein apres la feste de Seint Luke l'Ewangelist l'an du regne nostre seignur le roi q'ore est tierz, pristrent et enporterent, et de cel jour jeske encea touzjours unt cel tort continue. Sure queles choses le dit priur, par ses attornez et procuratours, comencea de pursuyre par la ley et l'usage de la cite de Loundres en la Gyhaud son recovrir, et en la court l'evesqe de Loundres et en les Arches, quant as pointz touchantz offense de seinte esglise, les avantditz Richard et les autres entredonantz, par confederacion, fauxe alliance et cunspiracie entre eux et Roger Aeynes, Johan de Lyrestowe et Robert le Coupere et plures autres de la dite cite, et par poer et manaces de vie et de membre, rebukent et arusent les attornez et procuratours le dit priur q'il nosent ne poent pursuyre pur le dit priur en nul point et sont issi entrealliez ceux et autres de la dite cite par serment, qe le dit priur ne nul de par luy puysse pursuyre son recovrir ne nule sute pur luy faire, et en tieu manere destourbent qe la loy ne se puet faire en prejudice du roi and de sa corone et grant damage du dit priur, dont le dit priur humblement compleignant prie remedie.

Endorsed: Soit mande au mair et as viscontes q'il ostent tiele force et durece, et q'il facent criere qe nul soit si harde de faire force ne a destourber en autre manere le priour a pursuir son droit en l'une court ne en l'autre. Et s'il troessant apres la proclamacion faite nul qe face destourbance ou faire, q'il certifient au roi des nouns.

c. 1330. The violent incident took place on Monday 21 October 1329, so the petition probably dates from 1330 or soon afterwards. The petitioner was William Gayton, prior 1312–33. Butley Priory was patron of St Olave Old Jewry and the neighbouring St Stephen Coleman Street. Insofar as the miscreants can be identified they seem to have been highly respectable. See *Calendar of Letter Books of the City of London: Letter Book E*, ed. R. R. Sharpe (London, 1903), pp. 93, 94, 204, 216, 233, 241. Stephen Gravesend was bishop of London from 1318 to 1338. For an earlier transcript of this petition, see no. 10 of PRO 31/7/96.

103

Strata Marcella (Ystrad Marchell), Montgomeryshire, Wales, and Clairvaux, Champagne, France (1333)
Cistercian
(SC 8/239/11937)

Matthew, abbot of Strata Marcella, petitions the king and council, stating that he was made abbot in the church of Valle Crucis (Denbigh), in the presence of the abbots of Clairvaux, Cymmer and Valle Crucis, in order to avoid the interference of John of Charlton, lord of Welshpool, who claims to have the right to create the abbots of Strata Marcella, contrary to the statutes of the Cistercian order; but that John is refusing to allow the abbot and his convent to enter their abbey, and is preventing them by force. He asks that he and his convent might be restored to their abbey by the justices of the peace in Shropshire, John of Layburne and William Butler, and that when this has been done these people might guard and preserve them there, and prevent John of Charlton from interfering with them; and that if John wishes to advance any claim against them, that he might have a day before the king and council to do this according to the law.

A nostre seignur le et a son conseile moustre son povre chapeleyn, si luy plest, Matheus, abbe de Stratemarcel, que com le dit Matheu, en le presence le commissare l'abbe de Clarevaux, Piere, abbe de la dite maysone, l'abbe de Kymere et l'abbe de Vaule Crois, par l'ascent dil convente de la mesone de Stratemarcel avantdite, fuit cree en abbe en la eglise de Vale Crois, pour eschair l'empecschement de Sire Johan de Charletone, seignur de La Pole, qui, contre les statuz de nostre ordre, se wet entremettre de faire abbe en la dite eglise et de ordiner a sa volente tant dou temporel com de l'espirituel, la quele chose est ou grant et grief prejudice de nostre seignur le roy comme de son droit reaul, il doive avoir la souverainne garde de ses eglises especialment de l'ordre de Cystiaux seronc [sic] les bons status de son reaulme, et com le dit Sire Johan ne voille soffrir qe le dit abbe de Stratemarcel ne son convent entrient en leur dite abbeye qe il fait garder par ses gent et par force d'armes, qe l'office Deu qui doit estre fais par les diz abbe et convent en leur ditte abbeye, pour mon seignur le roy, pur ma dame la reine, pour ses enfans et pour le bon estat de son reaume, est ja demoreiz afair par l'espasse de xv jours ou de plus en la coupe dou diz Sire Johan. Por ce est qe le dit abbe requireit et prie pour Deu a nostre seignur le roy et a son consail qe le pourcione de remede soffisant afin q'il et ses convent soient restitue en leur dite eglise par vostre justice de la pes en le conte de Saloburs, Sire Johan de Layburne et Sire William Botillier, es quex wille commander nostre seignur le roy que, restaubliz les diz abbe et convent en leur abbeye, willent tenir et garder la dite abbeye en nom de nostre seignur le roy et deffandre au dit Sire Johan Charleton qe ne les empeesche des or enavant a faire le servise de vin et se li diz Sire Johan Charleton wet demander aucune choses au dit abbe, qe journe le soit dounee par devant monseignur le roy ou son conseil, et li diz abbes pairra droit en la court de nostre seignur le roy seronc [*sic*] la ley de li terre.

No endorsement

1333. On the death of Abbot Griffin of Strata Marcella in late 1332 or early 1333, 'Matthew was elected by the prior and convent of Strata Marcella at the abbey of Valle Crucis, as they did not dare to proceed with an election at Strata Marcella because of diverse threats of death and other damages made to them by John de Cherleton, lord of la Pole in Wales. John, upon Matthew's election being confirmed, entered the abbey of Strata Marcella by armed force whilst the prior and convent were at Valle Crucis' (*Heads of Houses II*, 313). This petition, along with SC 8/248/12354 (below, **104**) was formerly enclosed with a privy seal warrant dated 25 February 1333 (no. 6268A of C 81/198). On 28 February 1333 the king ordered Charlton to withdraw from the abbey and restore it to Abbot Matthew (*CCR 1333–7*, pp. 93–4). John Charlton was first Lord Charlton of Powys, soldier, administrator and prominent landowner in Shropshire: J. F. A. Mason, 'Charlton, John, first Lord Charlton of Powys (*d.*1353)', *ODNB*. The abbot of Valle Crucis at this time was Adam Atha (c. 1330–43). A calendar of this petition appears in *Calendar of Ancient Petitions Relating to Wales: Thirteenth to Sixteenth Century*, ed. W. Rees (Cardiff, 1975), pp. 400–1.

104

Strata Marcella (Ystrad Marchell), Montgomeryshire, Wales, and Clairvaux, Champagne, France (1333)
Cistercian
(SC 8/248/12354)

To the king from the chaplains, fathers, monks and commissaries of the abbot of Clairvaux, requesting that whereas John of Charlton, lord of Welshpool, will not allow the abbey's commissary to enter his land, and threatens him with loss of life or limb if he participates in the exercise of any jurisdiction of the order in his land, especially in the abbey of Strata Marcella which Charlton's men-at-arms guard, so that neither the abbot nor convent can enter there to do the service of Our Lord, that the abbey may be in the king's protection, and that the abbot and his convent may be re-established in their abbey, and that the commissary may have letters of protection from the king throughout his entire land, since he has great fear of Charlton, especially because he says: 'I am pope, I am king and bishop and abbot in my land.'

A nostre seignur le roy requient pour Deu en supplient ses povres chapelains, pierres, moines et commissaire de son humble chapelain l'abbe de Clerevaux que comme Sire Johans de Charleton, seignur de La Pole, ne voille soffrir qe le dit commissaire de l'abbe de Clerevaux entre sa terre, en seis le dit commissaire menace de pardu vie ou mambre se il s'entremest de exercer nulle juridicion de l'ordre en sa terre, especialment en l'abbeye de Stratemarcell, la quele le dit Sire

Johans fait garder par ses gens d'armes qe l'abbe ne le convent de la mesone ypuisser entrer pur parie le servise nostre seignur pur le bon estat de nostre seignuyr le roy, qui doit avoir la soveraine garde de ces eglise, especialment des abbeyes de l'ordre de Cistiaux. Si prie pour Deu li dix commissaires que la dite abbey soit en la protection de nostre seignur le roy, et qe l'abbe et son convent soient restaubli en lour abbeye, et que le dit commissaire ait lettres de nostre seignur le roy de sa protection par mi tante sa terre, se ille plait, en la reverence de Deu et de l'ordre de Cistiaux, quar il se doubte nient dou dit Sire Johan Charleton especialment pur ce qe il dit 'Je suis papes, je suis roys et evesqes et abbes en ma terre,' les qelles parloes sunt contre l'oneur de nostre seigur le roy et nostre, et contre toutz sainte eglise, si vous prie pour Deu li diz commissaires qe vous le voillier recevoir vostre sauve garde et protection et ma dame la reine autre si, se il li plait.

No endorsement

1333. This petition relates closely to SC 8/239/11937 (above, **103**). It is calendared in *Calendar of Ancient Petitions Relating to Wales: Thirteenth to Sixteenth Century*, ed. W. Rees (Cardiff, 1975), pp. 411–12.

105

Butley, Suffolk (? 1334)
Augustinian canons
(SC 8/263/13108)

To the king and council from the prior of Butley recounting that Gilbert of Dedham presented Nicholas Frauncеys, chaplain, to the church of Dedham (Essex) in the diocese of London, which church the prior and his convent have appropriated for over twenty years, and the prior, not knowing the presentment to be false, approved of Dedham's presentee, but the bishop refused to admit him. Whereupon Frauncеys appealed to the Court of Rome, where he has been for a long time, and now that his process against the bishop has been refused, he has sued the prior in the same court for the patronage and possession of the said church. And because a writ of prohibition to the party is worthless while he remains at the Court of Rome and has nothing in England, the prior requests that the king grant his letters to the pope that those things which concern his rights and laws should be pleaded in England and that the pope should not allow them to be pleaded before him.
Endorsed: *It should go to the king.*

A nostre seignur le roy et son conseil prie le priour de Buttele qe come Gilbert de Dedham presenta Nicholas Frаunceys de Bildestone, chapeleyn, al esglise de Dedham en le diocise de Loundres, la quele esglise le dit priour de Buttele et le covent tienent en propres us et unt ja tenutz par vint aunz et plus, et l'enqueste prise nounsachaunt, le dit priour a la presentement del dit Gilbert fausement procure dist de tout pur le dit Gilbert et pur son presente, mes l'esvesqe, sachaunt la dite appropriacioun par son registre et confirmaciouns suffisauntes par luy meismes et par ses predecessours et auxint par le chapitre de Seynt Paul de Loundres, refusa de admettre le dit presente. Sur quoi le dit presente appella a la courte de Rome et illoeqes est il ja longement, si ad meyntenaunt refuse son proces vers l'esvesqe et tret l'avauntdit priour en plee en mesme la court sur la voesoun del esglise avantdite auxi bien sur le dreit del patronage come sur le possessione. Et par encheson qe prohibicion a la partie ny poet valer q'il est demorant a la court de Rome et rien n'ad en Engleterre, plaise a nostre seignur le roi, pur l'amour de Dieu et sauvacion de son dreit et des leys de son reaume, graunter pur le dit priour ses lettres al apostoille qe ceo qe touche son dreit et selom ses leys soleit estre plede en son reaume ne soeffre estre plede devaunt luy en blemissement de sa corone.

Endorsed: Seuwe au roi.

? 1334. The petition probably belongs to either the March or September parliament of 1334 (an earlier edition dated to 5 Edward III is in *RP*, II, 82, no. 39). The petitioner is Matthew of Pakenham, prior 1333–53. The bishop referred to was Stephen Gravesend, bishop of London 1318–38.

106

Lapley, Staffordshire (1335)
Benedictine (alien)
(SC 8/45/2235)

Baldwin of Spinallo, prior of Lapley, petitions the king and council for a remedy, stating that he was ejected forcibly from his priory by Robert of Shareshull, his brother Adam, John of Robaston, Ralph of Barton of Lichfield and others, and afterwards reinstated by the sheriff of Staffordshire, through a writ of the king or his council at the last parliament at Nottingham; but now he fears that the abbot of St Remi, Reims, who has the right to present to Lapley and who presented him, is conspiring with one or other of the people he has named to abduct him and take him overseas, so that he does not dare to live in the priory.

A nostre seignur le roy et son conseil fait a savoir Danz Baudewyn d'Espynall, priour de Lappeleye perpetuel, par presentement l'abbe de Seint Remy de Reyns et par institucion et induccion del evesqe de Cestre, la quele priourie est de la fundacion le counte de Cestre, qe come le dit Danz Baudewyn fust de sa dite priourie enjete a force par Robert de Shareshull, Adam son frere, Johan de Robastone, Rauf de Bartone de Lichefeld et autres plusours conuz et nonconuz, et enapres, par brief nostre seignur le roy ou par son conseil au drein parlement qe fust a Notingham, fust par le visconte d'Estafford remys en sa dite priourie, mes se doute le dit Danz Baudewyn qe le dit abbe de Seint Remy de Reyns, par abettement le dit Robert de Shareshull et de ses autres malvoillantz, ne procure odvesqe luy un ou altre qe le dit Danz Baudewyn soit ravy et amene a force outre mier, pur quoy il n'ose a sa dite priourie demorer vel ne port en la manere q'il doit nostre seignur Dieu servir. Par quoy a nostre seignur le roy et son conseil avantditz prie et supplie le dit Danz Baudewyn qe sur co luy soit purveu de covenable remedie en tiele manere qe le dit Danz Baudewyn puisse en sa dite priourie sauvement demurrer et Dieu servir come il est tenuz et doit.

No endorsement

1335. The petitioner was granted protection for one year on 1 April 1335 at Nottingham (*CPR 1334–8*, p. 91), suggesting that the Nottingham parliament is that of March 1335. Further evidence is provided by the fact that on 14 February 1335 and on 5 June 1335 commissions of oyer and terminer were issued, resulting from complaints by the petitioner which mention all the malefactors named here (*CPR 1334–8*, pp. 136, 145). It thus seems likely that this petition was presented to the parliament held at York in May 1335. The petitioner is Baldwin of Spinallo, prior 1328–?1361. His position had been challenged by Gobert of Lappion who appears to have been the favoured candidate of Shareshull and his companions. In a letter of protection dated February 1335 Lappion was described as prior of Lapley; but in April, after his reinstatement by the sheriff, Spinallo was recognised as prior: *CPR 1334–8*, pp. 75, 91. For further details of this dispute and references, see *VCH Staffs.*, III, 341–2, and *Heads of Houses II*, 172. The bishop of Chester, or Coventry and Lichfield, is Roger Northburgh (1321–58). Robert (de) Shareshull of Wednesfield and Little Onn (Derbys.) belonged to a prominent Staffordshire gentry family and was a younger brother of William Shareshull, later (1350–61) chief justice of the King's Bench. For a brief biography of Robert see Bertha Haven Putnam, *The Place in Legal History of Sir William Shareshull* (Cambridge, 1950), pp. 10–11. He was one of the keepers of this alien priory, *CFR 1337–47*, p. 36; *CPR 1340–3*, pp. 590–1; *CPR 1343–5*, p. 80. Related petitions are SC 8/72/3568 and SC 8/123/6114 (**107**).

107

Lapley, Staffordshire (c. 1338)
Benedictine (alien)
(SC 8/123/6114)

The prior of Lapley petitions the king and council for remedy on a number of connected issues involving Robert of Shareshull:
(1) Shareshull and others broke into the abbey, stealing a variety of goods and muniments. The prior sued a writ in chancery, and the sheriff of Staffordshire and others were ordered to enquire into the matter. They found that the complaint was true, and that Shareshull and his companions should pay damages to the value of 110 marks, for which they have been indicted.
(2) When the priory was in the king's hands, Shareshull went to the bishop of Chichester and asked that he and Gobert of Lappion might have the wardship of the priory, and as a result the prior was ousted from his house. Shareshull then neglected the priory, to its great destruction, destroying the mill and cutting down the woods, and, when he was made proctor of the monks of St Remi, brought false cases against the prior.
(3) Shareshull had not paid sums owed for his time as keeper of the priory, and for this reason the people of Northamptonshire took goods worth £10 from the prior's estates in compensation for these unpaid debts.

A nostre seignur le roi et a son conseil moustre le seon povre chapellein le priour de Lapeleye qe come, le vendredy en la feste de Seint Fabian et Sebestien l'an du rengne nostre seignur le roi noefisme, vint Robert le Shareshulle, et ovesqes lui plusurs autres conuz et desconuz, a force et armes et encountre la pees nostre dit seignur le roi, et entra en sa dite priore encountre sa volente, et ses beins et ses chateux illeoqes trovez, c'est assavoir, divers bleez ala mountance de vij quarters prest et enporta, et ses bestes, c'est assavoir xxx boefs et vaches, vij^{xx} porcs, xv jumentz et chivaux, xxxiij baccine et iiij carcoys de boef s'aleez hors de sa priorie enporta, et sa chambre debruse et leinz entra et prist toutes ses monumentz et chartres, taillies et totes ses autres evidences tocheauntz sa priorie, et totes ses iceaux, si qe rienz ne remist et entra en son boys et leinz abaty iiij^{xx} x grosses chenes et peschea, viners et fosses et malers, en grant destruction et damage du dit priour et encontre la pees nostre dit seignur le roi, dount bref issy hors de la Chauncellerie pur le dit priour au viscount de Estafforde, Monsire Thomas de Alton et Roger Trowym d'enquire de la verite, et trove feust par xij bons et loialx du pays qe la chose feust veritable, et retourne en la Chauncellerie qe le dit Robert et sa compaignie avoient endamagez au dit priour et a sa priorie de C et x marcs, et de ceo furent enditez.

Item, se pleint le dit priour du dit Robert, qe come la dite priorie feust pris en la meyn nostre dit seignur le roi, vint le dit Robert al evesqe de Cicestre, adonqes chaunceller, et pria d'avoir la garde de la dite priorie ovesqe Gobert de Lapyone, moigne de Seint Remy de Reyns, le quel ne feust et n'avoit este deux anz avant en Engleterre einz amova un moigne estrange en lieu du dit Gobert en pleine Chauncellerie, le quel nul ne savoit qi il feust, et par cele collusion ousta le dit priour de sa priorie, come apiert par les roulles de la Chauncellerie. Par quei commission lui feust faite a lui et au dit Gobert, qi estoit en France, et par verite de cele comission entierement feust destruit sa priorie par le dit Robert, c'est assavoir, qe rienz ne remist en seler, barell, pichers ne hanaps, non la bracerie, vessel pur braser, et en mesme la manere en la pestrine, n'en la quisme il ne lessa potes ne peles, morters ne petasses, et en ses granges il ne lui remist tant come une poy de litere pur lui faire une lite pur lui cocher, et du ses viners il ad fait pasture, en graunt destruccion du dit priour et de sa priorie, et son molyn destruit qe quel le dit priour pert xl s de rent par an, et en le boys de la dite priorie entra et baty et emporta xx grosses chenes et de suiboys ala vailliantz de C s, et la ou le dit Robert se fait procuratour l'abbe et covent de Seint Remy de Reyms, il plede de jour en autre encontre eaux et manytient fauxs et maveys querels encountre la dite priorie.

Item, se pleint le dit priour du dit Robert, qe par la ou le dit Robert deust avoir paie a nostre seignur le roi pur le temps q'il avoit la garde de la dite priorie lv mars et rienz n'ad paie, vindrint les genz le counte de Northamptone et leverent taillie en l'Escheqiere sur le dit priour pur mesme cele dite, en noun des ditz priour et de Robert, et tout en defaute du paiement du dit Robert, et par voie de cele taillie batirent ses granges et pristrent ses bestes, en damage du dit priour de x li, la ou le dit priour n'est point en le dette nostre seignur le roy n'en joynt en nule comission ovesqe le dit Robert, come apiert par les roulles del escheqier serchez et provez en la presence del tresorer et des toutz les barons de la dite place. Par qei le dit priour \prie/ a vostre dit seignur le roi et a son consel qe des toutes cez choses remedie lui soit ordine.

No endorsement

c. 1338. This refers to events described in the previous petition (**106**). The bishop of Chichester was Robert Stratford, 1337–62, who was chancellor of England 1337–38 and 1340. The petition can be dated to after Stratford's removal from office on 6 July 1338. Lapley was seized into the king's hands as an alien priory after the outbreak of war in 1337; it had initially been given to Shareshull and Gobert as proctors of the abbot of St Remy, but was then returned into the possession of the petitioner in 1338: *VCH Staffs.*, III, 341–2. The date of Shareshull's attack is given as Friday in the feast of St Fabian and St Sebastian in the ninth year (20 January 1336). However, this is presumably an error for the eighth year (1335), as the feast fell on a Saturday in 1336, with the following Friday falling in the king's tenth year. The petitioner was Baldwin of Spinallo, prior 1328–?1361.

108

Whalley, Lancashire (? 1376)
Cistercian
(SC 8/149/7403)

The abbot of Whalley petitions the king and council because Alice, widow of John, son of Ralph of Holden, has brought a writ of appeal in Yorkshire against him and others for the death of her husband – of which he is not guilty, since he is over ninety years old, as will be attested by many at the present parliament. The writ is returnable now, at the octave of Trinity, and if he does not appear in person, and lay people are selected, he will lose the goods of his house. He asks, in consideration of the fact that he is too old and infirm to travel, that he might have an attorney in this case, or that some other remedy might be provided.

A son tresgraciouse seignur le roi et son consaile supplie l'abbe de Whalley qe vous pleise a entendre coment un Alice qe fust la feme Johan fitz a Rauf de Holden ad porte son brief d'appele vers le dit abbe et altres de la mort son baron en la counte de Everwyk, de quel [le] dit abbe est de rienz coupable, et le quel abbe est del age de iiij^{xx} x aunz et plus, com serra testmoigne par plusurz seignurs .... et escuierz de cest present parlement, et le dit brief d'appele est returnable ore a les octas de la Trynite, a quel jour si le dit .... viegne my et ley gentz soit agarde, il perdra les bienz de sa meison. Par quoi il pleist a vostre tresgraciouse seignury considerer le g.......... qe le dit abbe est si veile et nientpuissant qe il ne poet travailler saunz perile de mort, et granter qe il poet pleder par atturne en cest especial, ou qe il poet avoir ascun maner de remedi, pur Dieu et en oevre de charite.

No endorsement

? 1376. John, son of Ralph of Holden, was alive on 6 July 1375, when an order went out to arrest him (*CPR 1374–7*, pp. 158–9), and John Sotheren was pardoned for his death on 1 February 1377 (*CPR 1374–7*, p. 422). According to the note on the guard, the number 'xlix' written in a contemporary hand on the dorse corresponds to the equivalent entry on the fragmentary list of petitions probably for the 1376 parliament, now at C 49/43/10; that document is now too badly damaged and incomplete to verify this conclusively, although that entry certainly relates to a petition from an abbot. The petitioner was John of Lindley, who occurred as abbot from 1342 to 1377. The right-hand edge of this petition is damaged. For an earlier transcript of this petition, see no. 50 of PRO 31/7/105.

109

Westminster (1378)
Benedictine
(SC 8/18/896)

The abbot and convent of Westminster petition the knights, citizens, burgesses and commons of the counties, protesting that their right of sanctuary, which they have enjoyed since the time of Edward the Confessor, has been violated recently, when certain people entered the church by force, killed Robert Hawley, a fugitive, and a sergeant of the church, and removed John Shakell by force, molesting the monks and obstructing divine service. They request that the knights, citizens, burgesses and commons aid and counsel the Lords to ordain a suitable remedy and due compensation for this.
Endorsed on face: *Be it remembered that this bill was delivered to the clerk of parliament on behalf of the king to be filed etc., which bill was previously delivered to the king and his council on behalf of the Commons in the said parliament, to advise them on it etc.*

As chivalers, citesynes, burgeis et comunes des contees moustrent l'abbe et covent de Westmouster qe come ils eient diverses privileges et libertees, entre queux si est qe si aucun futyf y viegne deinz le purceint de leur eglise il y purreit estre sauf pur qeconqe cause, de quele manere condicion q'il soit, sanz empeschement de nullui, et de ceo ont est en paisible possession de temps Seint Edward, et les nobles rois, seignurs et comunes du roialme eantz conisance de ycelle, suffrantz et assentantz meisme la franchise, sibien pur dette come nulle autre cause, sanz nulle interrupcion en fait, mais ore tard les uns filz de lui malfez y entrerent a force la dit eglise et la tuerent Robert Haulee, futif, et un sergeant du meisme esglise, sanz cause qeconqe, et aussint pristerent et horsmenerent Johan Shakel, vif de la dite eglise, en molestunt greveusement les moignes et destourbant les divines services en ycelle, encontre les privileges et libertees la dite eglise, qe sont confermez par tresseint pieres apostoilles, et par les rois d'Engleterre tanqe en cea ratifiez, eiant nulle consideracion de les hydeuses censures qe partiegnent as touz les enfreignours des privileges susditz. Vous pleise estre eidantz \et/ conseilantz a les nobles seignurs du parlement, qe lour pleise d'ent ordeiner remedie covenable et due restitucion a la dite eglise, a salvacion des privileges et libertees grantez par les nobles roys Edgar, Seint Edward et autres roys, leur successours, seignurs et comunes du reyalme, si qe les divines services puissent estre celebrez en manere come attient, en l'onur Dieu, seint pier et Seint Edward, et de les reliqes qe reposent, et aussint pur les almes de lour nobles progenitours.

Endorsed on face: Fait aremembrer qe ceste bille estoit livere a clerc de parlement depar le roi nostre seignur pur mettre es fillaces etc., et la quelle bille estoit devant bailles a nostre seignur le roi et son conseil de par les comunes esteiantz en dit parlement pur lour ent aviser etc.

1378. The petition refers to the violation of the abbey's sanctuary in August 1378, in which Hawley and a sacristan of the abbey were killed. Hawley and his comrade-in-arms, John Shakell, had defied the wishes of the royal council by refusing to deliver a valuable foreign prisoner: N. Saul, *Richard II* (Yale, 1997), pp. 36–8. For their contumacy they were imprisoned in the Tower of London in October 1377, but in August 1378 they escaped and claimed sanctuary in Westminster Abbey. Sir Alan Buxhill, acting on the instructions of the council, attempted to arrest the pair and in the ensuing scuffle inside the abbey

Hawley and a sacristan were cut down and killed. The incident caused outrage and dominated proceedings in the next parliament, held at Gloucester on 20 October 1378, where this petition was presented. The petitioner is Nicholas de Litlington, abbot 1362–86. The endorsement indicates that the abbot succeeded in winning the support of the Commons. The archbishop of Canterbury, Simon Sudbury, also presented a petition on the abbey's behalf: *PROME*, parliament of 1378, item 27. For further discussion see Introduction, pp. xlv–xlvi. The story continues in the following item, **110**. Earlier petitions presented by Hawley and Shakell on the matter are: SC 8/18/893, 116/5787, 18/894 (also printed in *RP*, III, 50, no. 1), and 18/895 (also printed in *RP*, III, 50, no. 2) – these last two petitions were presented in the parliament of October 1377, when the crown took the decision to imprison them in the Tower of London: *PROME*, parliament of October 1377, item 35. For an earlier edition of this petition see *RP*, III, 50, no. 3

110

Westminster (1378)
Benedictine
(SC 8/18/897)

The right of sanctuary at Westminster Abbey is being greatly abused, and as a result of a petition complaining about this, the king has had the abbey's charters examined by masters of theology, doctors in both laws and justices, and other people learned in the laws of the realm, to see if this right applies to cases of debt and other personal actions. On their advice, and having heard the abbot's arguments, he is exercising his right to interpret his progenitors' charters, and has declared that no one should have right of sanctuary there for any such case, saving to Holy Church its franchise concerning felony. Nevertheless, out of love for the abbey, and reverence for the body of St Edward and its other relics, and for the bodies of his progenitors buried there, he will allow immunity there in certain genuine cases of debt.

Porce qe plusors grantz damages et meschiefs ont avenuz a plusours du roiaume par un privilege qe l'abbe et convent de Westm', par colour d'ascuns paroles generales contenues en certeines chartres de progenitours de nostre seignur le roi, ont claymez detard encea, cestassavoir qe ceux qi fuent a Westm' pur debte ou pur autres accions personels averoient immunytee en dit lieu, eux et lour biens. Et purce qe plusours ont este embaudiz et comfortez a faire et ymaginer fausetees sur fiance du recept q'ils averoient en dit lieu de Westm', paront les uns quant ils devoient grandz sommes, et aucuns quant ils voloient detenir les biens d'autry, ont alez illoeqes et demorez en dit lieu tant come il leur a pleu, et les uns a terme de lour vies, pur forbarrez ensi les pleintifs qe onqes n'ont seu aucun recoverir, et les uns ont cheviz et emprumtez tant come ils ont peu de diverses gentz, et ensi ont alez a dit lieu et vesquiz illoeqes, tanqe ceux asquelx ils estoient debtours voloient venir a eux, et par traitee leur pardoun la moitie ou la plus grande partie pur estre repaiez du remenant, la ou ils ont eeu assez de quoi paier toute l'entiere debte s'ils eussent valuz. Et auxi plusours servantz quant ils ont eeu en garde les biens de leur mesters ont alez au dit lieu ovec les ditz biens, et ont vesquiz illoeqes en lour pecche tantcome lour pleust, siqe ceux asqueux les ditz biens appertenoient n'en petient onqes avoir ascun recoverir. Pur les queles causes, et compleint d'auters qe soventfoiz sont avenuz par tieulx persones, qe trop longues serroient a escrire, nostre dit seignur le roi, considerant les griefs et domages qe a ses liges en sont avenuz par le temps passee contre reson, et qe vraisemblablement purroient avenir en avaunt si due remede n'y feust ordenez, et considerant auxi coment seinte esglise ne doit sustenir ne doner occasion a fausette ne pecche, et vuillant sur ce purvoir de remede convenable, sicome a lui est suppliez par peticion en ce present parlement, come celui q'est tenuz affere droit a chescun, ad fait veoir et examiner a grande deliberacion, tant par mestres en theologie et doctours d'ambedeux loys, come par ses justices et auters sages des lois de son roiaume, les chartres de ses ditz progenitours en les queles sont compris les generalx paroles avantdites, pur veoir si \par/ les dites paroles l'en deveroit pur debte et auters accions personeles avoir et rejoir immunytee en dit lieu de Westm', c'estassavoir une chartre du Roi Edgar et deux chartres de Seint Edward, et veues les dites chartres, et toutes les ditz paroles, et ois sur ce les resons et avis de touz les ditz sages, nostre dit seignur le roi, a qi de droit et par la loy appertient l'interpretacion des chartres de ses ditz progenitors, del avis de touz les ditz sages sovereinement, pur consideracion de justice, et pur oster toutes ambiguites et restreindre fausetee, en eese et quiete de ses ditz liges, et pur eschuire le general domage qe parmy tiele privilege purroit avenir a ses ditz liges en temps avenir, present le dit abbe, et oiz en ce q'il savoit dire pur li, ad declarez et interpretez qe par vertu ne colour de nulles paroles generales ne auters contenues en mesmes les chartres, nul ne doit avoir ne n'avera desore immunytee ne franchise nullepart dedeinz l'esglise, abbeie ou lieu de Westm' en nul tiel cas, come desus sont expressez, ne en nul autre semblable horspris et sauvez toudiz a seinte esglise toute sa franchise touchant felonie. Mes nientmeins, pur especial affeccion qe nostre dit seignur le roi ad au dit lieu de Westm' plus qe \a/ aucun auter leiu de son roiaume, et nomeement pur reverence du noble corps Seint \Seint/ [*sic*] Edward, et des auters grandz reliques qe y sont, et pur cause des nobles progenitours de nostre dit seignur le roi qe reposent illoeqes, est la volentee et entente de nostre dit seignur le roi, par l'advis desusdit, qe ceux qi par fortune de la meer, ou par fu, robberie ou autre meschief, sanz fraude ou collusion, serront ensi empoveriz q'ils ne puissent paier ce q'ils doyvent, et volront pur tiel meschief entrer en dit lieu de Westm' pur eschuire l'emprisonement de leur corps, puissent et soient soeffertz en tiel cas demorer sauvement et franchement en dit lieu, et y avoir immunytee de lour persones, a celle entente q'ils puissent \en/ le moyen temps estre relevez affere gree a ceux asquelx ils sont debtours.

No endorsement

1378. This directly relates to **109**, but it was prompted by a separate petition presented by an unspecified source requesting clarification of the abbot of Westminster's charters: SC 8/146/7263. Previous editions of both documents are printed in *RP*, III, 50–1, no. 4. John Wyclif was one of the experts brought in by the council to examine the abbey's charters. By exempting cases of debt, the schedule essentially signalled a defeat for the abbot, Nicholas de Litlington (1362–86), and the Commons and Spiritual Lords who had supported him. It probably formed the basis of a more detailed ruling recorded in the parliament roll in response to the archbishop of Canterbury's protest on the matter: *PROME*, parliament of 1378, item 28. It was not until the following parliament of April 1379, however, that the judgement was made into statutory legislation, though its terms were so far removed from the circumstances of the Hawley and Shakell affair that even Thomas Walsingham seems to have embraced them with unqualified enthusiasm: *SR*, II, 12 (iii); *St Albans Chronicle, Volume I, 1376–1394*, ed. J. Taylor, W. R. Childs and L. Watkiss (Oxford, 2003), pp. 272–3.

111

Abingdon, Berkshire (1396)
Benedictine
(SC 8/256/12757)

To the king from the abbot and convent of Abingdon stating that whereas King Edgar gave to Wulfstan and his heirs land in a certain place then called Whistley and now called the manor of Whistley and Hurst, and Richard I confirmed the same to the petitioners' predecessors forever, the foresters of Windsor pretend that they and their predecessors have always had in the manor of Whistley and Hurst a benefit called meat-home, which is the right to be supplied with two meals a week for themselves and their servants, contrary to the tenor of those charters. They ask that their estate in the manor might be confirmed, quit of this claim in accordance with their charters; and they ask that this might be done without paying fine or fee in chancery.
Endorsed on face: *This petition has been granted by the king.*

Excellentisimo et aretuendissimo domino regi: supplicant vestri humiles et subditi oratores abbas et conventus de Abyndon', de vestre patronatu et fundacione vestrorum nobilium progenitorum existentes, cum Edgarus, quondam rex Anglorum ceterarum que gencium, in circuitu persistencium gubernator et rector cuidam fideli suo nuncupato W[u]lfstan decem mansas perpetualiter concessisset in quodam loco, adtunc Wystelea vocato, que nunc manerium de Whysshelee et Hurst vocantur [sic], habendas eidem quamdiu vitalis spiritus aluerit corpus, et post sue dissolucionis diem cuicumque quem heredem dereliquerit se, ut predictum est, in eternam hereditatem, et quod predicta donacio foret ab omni mundali obstaculo libera cum ad se rite pertinentibus, campis, pratis, pascuis, silvis exceptis, istis tribus expedicione pontis, aras ve construccione. Ac postea, predecessoribus vestrorum dictorum oratorum in possessione dicti manerii existentibus, Dominus Richardus, nuper rex Anglie, unius progenitorum vestrorum, per cartam suam eis confirmavit omnes terras et omnes possessiones eis collatas sicut carte regum, predecessorum suorum, eis confirmarunt et aliorum donatorum, scripta tunc testaba [damaged ms] ac dicti vestri oratores dictas terras, per nomen manerii de Whisshelee et Hurst, sic jam optineant sibi et successoribus suis imperpetuum, et ipse et eorum predecessores a tempore cuius contrarii memoria non existit sic optinuerunt et habuerunt. Ac forestarii vestri foreste vestre de Wyndesore, cum eorum servientibus, pretendunt se et eorum predecessores, forestarios dicte foreste vestre, a tempore cuius memoria hominum non existit habuisse et habere debere ut de jure vestre tamquam vestri ministri, contra tenorem dictarum cartarum Edgari et Ricardi, in dicto manerio de Whysshelee et Hurst quoddam comedum sive beneficium vocatum Anglice *metehom*, videlicet, singulis septimanis duas refecciones alias nomine repastys tam cibi quam potus sibi ministrari. Quod placeat vestro regie majestati possessionem dicti manerii, cum pertinenciis, dictis oratoribus vestris et eorum successoribus ratificare et confirmare imperpetuum. Et ulterius considerare vestros dictos oratores, virtute dictarum cartarum suorum Edgari et Ricardi dudum regum, de huiusmodi onere per dictos ministros vestros exacto aliqualiter onerare non debere eosdem et eorum successores inde totaliter exonerare, tam erga vos et heredes vestros quam justiciarios, forestarios seu ministros quoscumque vestros vel heredum vestrorum foreste predicte possessione predicta dicte efeccionis seu alio jure vestro vobis inde in hac parte competente non obstantibus. Ac totum jus vestrum inde dictis vestris oratoribus et eorum successoribus penitur remittere et relaxare imperpetuum, et concedere quod vos et heredes vestri forestarii sue alii ministri vestri vel heredum vestrorum foreste predicte habemus *metehom*, recreacionem sive repastys aliqualiter infuturum habeatis, clametis vel exigatis aut exigere possitis, et inde vestros litteras patentes dictis oratoribus vestris inbere fieri, ob honorem Dei et pro tranquillitate dicte vestre domus de Abyndon', absque feodo vel fine in Cancellaria vestra solvendo vel faciendo.

Endorsed on face: Ista peticio concessa est per dominum regem.

1396. The petitioner was Peter of Hanney, abbot 1361–99. On 18 January 1396 the petitioners' estate in the manor of Whistley and Hurst was confirmed as being free and discharged of meat-home (*CPR 1391–6*, p. 669).

112

Abbey Dore, Herefordshire (c. 1398)
Cistercian
(SC 8/213/10624)

Jordan, abbot of Dore, petitions the king and council for remedy against the following grievances and horrible extortions and destructions done to him and his abbey by John ap Henry, Griffith ap Henry, Thomas of la Hay, John Oldcastle and Thomas ap John between 1396 and 1398.
(1) John ap Henry came with an armed force to the petitioner's manor of Morehampton and drove away his sheep there, and holds them as his own.
(2) John ap Henry came with force and arms to the same manor of Morehampton and drove away all the canons' cattle there.
(3) John ap Henry at various times came with force and arms to Treville and Knaudisknas and cut down 48 great oaks in the abbot's woods there for his own use.
(4) John and Griffith ap Henry forcefully entered all the petitioner's lands at Cantsely and have taken all the rents, issues and profits for their own use for the last three years, and still do, which lands are the greater part of the abbey's maintenance.
(5) Thomas of la Hay came with force and arms to the petitioner's manor of Godway and laid waste to the abbot's grange there, and carried away all its timber and stones to his own use.
(6) Thomas of la Hay at various times came with force and arms to Treville and Knaudisknas and cut down 22 great oaks in the abbot's woods there for his own use.
(7) John Oldcastle at various times came with a force of armed men to Treville and Cantsely and cut down 24 great oaks in the abbot's wood there for his own use.
(8) John and Griffith ap Henry sold a mansion called Shepcote, worth 200 marks, for £10 at the petitioner's manor of Trawscoed to John Hanard and John ap Meredith, who laid waste to the mansion and carried away all its timber and stones to their own use.
(9) The abbot does not dare to approach his abbey to celebrate divine service or govern his abbey and possessions for fear of being killed by John and Griffith ap Henry, Thomas of la Hay, John Oldcastle, Thomas ap John and others of their affinity.
(10) Griffith ap Henry and Thomas ap John came with force and arms to the abbey of Dore, and took Richard Madley, David Oswestry and Richard Clifford, monks of Dore, and imprisoned them for three days and nights at the wood called Snodhill. They then took them to the manor of Urishay where they imprisoned them for six days until Clifford made fine and ransom and was released on his oath that he would never obey the petitioner again, and then Madley and Oswestre were brought to the manor of Wendover and imprisoned there.

Endorsed: *Memorandum that on 6 November in the 22nd year by Lewis Byford, parson of Byford, and John Allerton of Kingston, Herefordshire, of satisfaction made.*

Les grevaunces et horribles extorciounz et destrucciounz faitez a Jordan, abbe de Dore et a sa abbacie:
A nostre trespuissaunt et tresredoute seignur le roy et soun tressage counseill moustre et sey compleint Jordan, abbe de Dore del counte de Herford, de Johan ap Henry, de ore qe le dit Johan vient ove force et armes enfourme de guerre, ove graunt multitude dez archers et plusours gentz harnisez en fourme de guerre, le venderdy proschein devaunt la feste de Seint Johan le Baptistre l'an du reigne nostre dit seignur le roy q'orest xxj, a Morhamptone al maneir du dit abbe, et illeoqes xiiij^{xx} owails le dit abbe illeoqes trovez, \pris/ de xx li, prist et enchasa, et de celle jour tanqe en cea les detientz a soun proprie oeps ove fort mayn, encountre le pees nostre seignur le roy, et en anientisement du dit abbe et soun mesoun, et as damages du dit abbe de xl li, dount il prie remedie etc.
Item, le dit Johan ap Henry vient ove force et armes enfourme de guerre a la maneir du dit abbe de Morhamptone, le venderdy proschein apres la feste de Seint Jake l'apostel, et illeoqes toutz les boefs de les chanons du dit abbe illeoqes trovez, c'estassavoir xxx boefs pris xxviij li, prist et enchasa, et les ditz boefs unqore detient ove fort mayn, en distruccion du dit abbe et soun mesoun, et a ces damages de xl li.
Item, le dit Johan ap Henry vient ove force et armes enfourme de guerre, par diversez temps parentre le feste del Purificacioun Nostre Dame l'an du reigne nostre dit seignur le roy q'orest xixme et le dit feste de Seint Johan le Baptistre la nostre dit seignur le roy vintisme second, a Tryvel et Knaudisknas, et illeoqes xlviij grauntz keynes le dit abbe dez meilliours queux furent en les boysz du dit abbe illeoqes, al value de xxiiij marcz, coupa, et les ent encaria a son oeps demesne, a graunt distrucioun dez bois du dit abbe avauntditz as toutz jours, et as damages du dit abbe de xl marcz.
Item, le dit Johan ap Henry et Gryffyt ap Henry, par lour graunt poiar, ove fort mayn ount entrez en toutz les terres et tenementz du dit abbe de Cantersely, les queux terres et tenementz vaillent annuelment aplus meyne estent iiij^{xx} marcz, et toutz maners rentes, comoditez, issuez et profitz des dites terrez et tenementz provenauntz par ces treis ans darrein passez ount pris a lour comune oeps, et unqore preignont, les queux terres et tenementz sount la greindre partie del susteignaunce de dit abbe et soun maisoun, dount le dit abbe est endamage en CC li.
Item, Thomas de la Hay vient ove force et armes enforme de guerre, le lundy proschein devaunt le fest de Seint George l'an du regne nostre seignur le roy q'orest xxj, a le manoir du dit abbe de Godewey, et illoques un graunge du dit abbe, pris de xl li, aracea et treia a la terre et la meresme et toutz maners piers du dit graunge encaria a soun oeps demesne, as damages du dit abbe de C marcz.
Item, le dit Thomas del Hay vient ove force et armes, par diverses temps parentre le fest de Purificacioun Nostre Dame l'an du regne nostre dit seignur le roy q'orest xix^{e} et le fest de Seint Pier Advincula l'an nostre dit seignur le roy xxij^{e}, a Tryvel et Knaudisknas, et illoqes xxij graundes keynes des plus melliours en les bois du dit abbe illoques esteauntz, pris x li, coupa et les encaria a soun oeps propre, as damagez du dit abbe de xx marcs.
Item, Johan Oldecastel vient ove force et armes, ove graunt noumbre des gentz

et enforme de guerre, par diverses temps parentre le fest de Purificacioun Nostre Dame l'an du regne nostre dit seignur le roy xix e et le fest del Assumpcioun Nostre Dame l'an nostre dit seignur le roy xxij[e], a Tryvel et Cantersely et illoques xxiiij grauntz keynes des melliours esteauntz illoqes en lez boys du dit abbe, pris xxiiij li, coupa et les encaria a soun propre oepes, a graunt destruccioun du dit abbe et soun mansoun et ces damages de xl li.

Item, les avauntditz Johan ap Henry et Gryffith ap Henry, de lour graund poair et fortesse, ount venduz a le manoir du dit abbe a Troscoit en Cantersely une graund maisoun appelle Shepcote, pris de CC marcz, a un Johan Hanard et Johan ap Meredith pur x li, les queux Johan et Johan, par force de lour de vent, ount aracez et treiez a la terre le dit Shipcote et le meresme et toutz maners des piers ont encariez a lour propre oepes, as damage du dit abbe de CCC marcz etc.

Item, le dit abbe suppliaunt n'ose approcher sa abbacie pur illoques divine service et la governaunce de sa abbacie et de ses possessiouns faire et ordiner, pur doute d'estre occys par le ditz Johan ap Henry, Gryffytz ap Henry, Thomas de la Hay, Johan Oldecastel et Thomas ap Johan, et autres par lour procurement et affinite, dount il prye remedie etc.

Item, l'avauntdit Griffitz ap Henry et Thomas ap Johan viendrount ove force et armes en fourme de guerre, le meskerdie proschein apres la feste de Seint Barnade la postre l'an du reigne nostre dit seignur le roy q'orest xxj[e], au dit abbacie de Dore et illeoqes un Richard Madley, David Oswestre et Richard Clifford, moignes du dit abbe illeoqes trovez, pristirunt et d'illeoqes les amesnerount tanqe a le boys appelle Snodhill, et illeoqes les ditz moignes par trois jours et noetz proschein ensuauntz emprisoneront en fort ferres, et ascun foith lez lierount illeoqes ove cordys et cheynez de ferres as arbres et les crucifierount, et lierount lour testes ove cordes, et puis lez ditz trois jours et noetz passetz, ils amesnerount les ditz moignes d'illeoqes tanqe a le manoir de Urshay, et illeoqes lez ditz moignes emprisonerount en cepps par vj jours, tanqe le dit Richard Clyfford illeoqes fist fyn et raunsoun ovesqe lez ditz Griffitz et Thomas a lour voluntee, et firrent le dit Richard, moigne, jurer in verbo sacerdocii q'il ne les discovereit jammes de son dit fyn et raunsoun, et qe ne serroit jammes de ceo enapris estre obedient ne entendaunt au dit suppliaunt, soun abbe, et d'illeoqes du dit manoir de Urshay amesnerount les ditz Richard Madley et David, les autres deux moignes, tanqe al manoir de Wendovere, et illeoqes eux mistrent en prisone force et dure, c'estassaver eux lierount ove cordys et penderount par les pees in un weole de plaustre lour pees paramount envers le fermement, et lours testes pendauntz a la terre, et issint endurrerount lours peynys par diverses temps iij jours et noetz en semble, en anientisement de les persons des ditz moignes, et en arrerisement de lour divine service a toutz jours, et as damages du dit abbe de M[l] marcz. Des qeux pointz le dit suppliaunt pria remedie en oevre de charitee, considerauntz \de/ voz tresgracious seignurs qe le dit suppliaunt est issint empoverez et distruit en toutz ses possessions, bienx et chateux q'il ne poet par la comune ley null remedie pursuyer ne avoir envers lez ditz maffesours dez extorciounz suisditz, ne le dit suppliaunt ne ses moignes ne ount nulle vivere, ne sustenaunce pur lour divine service en lour meason faire etc.

Endorsed: Memorandum quod sexto die Novembris anno etc. xxij[o] Magister Lodowicus Byford, parsona ecclesie de Byford, et Johannes Allerton' de Kingeston' in comitatu Hereford' assumpserunt pro abbate infrascripto quod ipse satisfaciet partibus infrascriptis \pro expensis suis/ in casu quo non probaverit intencionem suam etc.

1398. The petitioner was Jordan Bikeleswade, one of two men claiming to be abbot of Abbey Dore at this time, the other being John Holland whom Bikeleswade removed from his abbacy with force and arms; see SC 8/332/15772. Earlier in the same year, in an apparently unrelated incident, a commission of oyer and terminer was appointed, on complaint by the abbot, into an armed assault and robbery upon Abbey Dore and the abduction and imprisonment of a monk and several abbey servants, despite the abbey being in the king's special protection (*CPR 1396–9*, pp. 30, 362). This is an early reference to the future Lollard leader John Oldcastle: see J. A. F. Thomson, 'Oldcastle, John, Baron Cobham (*d.*1417)', *ODNB.*

113

Newenham, Devon (1402)
Cistercian
(SC 8/216/10798A)

Leonard, abbot of Newenham, petitions the council, recounting how John Legge, late abbot of Newenham, who committed many great offences concerning the goods of the abbey, lately resigned during a visitation from the abbot of Cleeve, and the petitioner, by the assent of the former abbot and all his fellow monks, was elected abbot and received his estate and possessions. These he held from the feast of the Trinity last until the morrow of the feast of John the Baptist last when Philip Courtenay sent 60 armed men arrayed for war who, at Courtenay's order and without reasonable cause, took the abbot from his house by force and brought him to Courtenay's manor of Bickleigh, where he was, and still is, imprisoned. The abbot requests that a writ be sent to Courtenay by a serjeant at arms ordering him to release the abbot from prison and allow him to go free, or to come before the council to certify the reason for the imprisonment.
Endorsed: *On 8 July in the third year (1402) at Westminster the council agreed that a writ under the great seal should be addressed to Courtenay ordering him to release the abbot of Newenham from prison, on pain of 1000 marks. And if Courtenay is not with the king, he should be before the council at Westminster on the morrow of St James next, and if he is travelling with the king, then within ten days of leaving the king's company, to answer in this matter. And a commission should be made to Robert Markeleye, serjeant at arms, to release the abbot and allow him to go at large.*

A tressage et tresnoble conseille nostre seignur le roy supplie Leonard, abbe de Niewenham el countee de Devenshire, qe come Johan Legge, jadis abbe illoeqes, pur plusours grandes offenses faitz encontre .... des biens de sa mesoun oretard en plein visitacioun fait par l'abbe de Clyve soun visitour de sa bone voluntee en plein chapitre cessa et resigna tout soun estat et luy delivera soun seal et qant appurte......................... qoi le dit Leonard, par due proces de ley et par assent le dit nadgairs abbe et toutz ses confrers, fuit eslu abbe illoeqes et mys en soun estat et possessioun, le quelle estat et possessioun il .... fest de la Trinite darrein passe tanqe al dymenge lendemain de le fest del Nativite de seint Johan le Baptistre darrein passee, qe moun sire Phelippe Courtenay enjoia une gra......................... et servantz a le nombre de lx, armez et arraiez affaire de guerre, de prendre le dit abbe et amesner a luy a Bykelegh, les queux par commandement le dit Monsire Phelippe le dit .... sanz cause resonable, pristront hors de soun dit mesoun a force et d'illoeqes luy amesneront a dit Monsire Phelippe a soun manoir de Bykelegh, et illoeqes l'avantdit Monsire Phelippe .... en prisoun tanqe encea, et uncore deteignont illoeqes, a grande prejudice et contempt nostre seignur le roi et damage le dit abbe. Plese a voz tresnobles et tresages discrecIOUNS ordeigner .... le dit abbe et qe brief nostre seignur le roi soit envoie a dit Monsire Phelippe par un sergeant d'armes luy commandant a deliverer le dit abbe hors de soun prisoun issint priz et ....nable et luy lesser aler a large, ou autrement d'estre devant vous a un brief jour par vous a limiter pur vous certifier la casue del dite emprisonement, pur Dieu et en [oevre de charite].

Endorsed: Fait aremembre qe le viij jour de Juilles l'an etc. tierz a Westmouster, presentz en le counsall messeignurs les evesques d'Exceter, chanceller, Baath, tresourer, Hereford et Roucestre, le gardein de prive seal, Johan Scarle, Prophete, Johan Doreward et Johan Frome, assentuz est qe brief souz le grant seal soit adressee a Monsire Phelip Courtenay deinz escrit q'il, sur peyne de mille marcs, face liverer hors de prisone Leonard, abbe de Newenham deinz escrit, et q'en cas que mesme celui Phelip ne soit aile devers le roy a present, q'adonques il soit devant le counsail cy a Westmouster lendemain de la Saint Jake l'apostre prochein venant, et en cas qu'il soit transportez devers le roy, q'adonques deinz dys jours procheins apres son departir de la compaignie du roy il soit devant le susdit conseil, sur la peyne dessus limitee, pur respoundre a la matire dedeinz escrite. Et que d'abundente une commission soit faite a Robert Markeleye, sargeant d'armes, pur desarester le susdit abbe, et lui soeffrir aler a sa large, adjoustez en mesme la commission clauses d'entendance necessaires en manere accustumee.

1402. John Legga became abbot of Newenham in 1391. His successor was Leonard Houndaller, the petitioner, but it is not known when he became abbot of Newenham, an office which he held until at least 1411. John, abbot of Cleeve, occurred from 1381 until 1406, and may, or may not, be Abbot John Mason who occurs in 1389 and 1394. For the colourful career of Philip Courtenay, see *HC*, II, 670–73. Those present in the council were Edmund Stafford, bishop of Exeter and chancellor, Henry Bowet, bishop of Bath and Wells and treasurer, John Trefnant, bishop of Hereford, John Bottlesham, bishop of Rochester, Thomas Langley, dean of York and keeper of the privy seal, John Scarle, John Prophet, John Doreward and John Frome. On 8 July 1402 Courtenay was ordered to release the petitioner (*CPR 1401–5*, p. 133; *CCR 1399–1402*, p. 537). The right-hand edge of this petition is missing. For subsequent petitions see **114** and **115**.

114

Newenham, Devon (1402)
Cistercian
(SC 8/216/10798B)

Leonard, abbot of Newenham, petitions the chancellor for remedy, since at his suit John Herle, sheriff of Devon, was ordered by the king's writ to stop Philip Courtenay from finding surety of peace on pain of £1000, and although the writ was delivered to Herle at Exeter on the Tuesday after the Assumption of Our Lady, he has not served it.

A tresreverent et tresgracious piere en Dieu chaunceler nostre seignur le roi supplie humblement Leonard, abbe de Newenham, qe par la ou Johan Herle, viscounte de Devon', fuist comaunde par brief de nostre seignur le roy al suyt de dit suppliaunt d'arester Phipp de Courtenay, chevaler, de trover suerte de pees sur pein de M[l] li al dit suppliaunt et as toutz autres lieges de nostre seignur le roy, le quele brief fuist a dit viscounte delivere le marsdy prochein apres le fest d'Assumpcioun de Nostre Dame darrein passe a Exestre, le quele viscounte n'ad paas le dit brief servy, dount le dit suppliaunt prie remedie, pur Dieu et en oevre de charite.

No endorsement

c. 1402. This petition must post-date the preceding petition, **113**, since the writ, which dates to 22 August 1402, is the one granted in SC 8/216/10798A. John Herle was sheriff of Devon from 8 November 1401 until 29 November 1402. Thus this petition dates to the second half of 1402, and the addressee was Edmund Stafford, bishop of Exeter and chancellor. See also **115**.

115

Newenham, Devon (1402)
Cistercian
(SC 8/126/6261)

Leonard, abbot of Newenham, petitions the Commons for remedy against Philip Courtenay, who he claims has attacked and imprisoned him, and against whom he can have no remedy at common law due to his great power in the county. He recounts that he was attacked in his abbey by Courtenay's men, and then taken to Honiton, where they demanded money from him. They then took him to Bickleigh, where he was imprisoned for 15 days. His friends sued writs before the council, summoning Courtenay to account, but he failed to appear. Courtenay was then ordered to keep the peace, but he again came to the abbey with a force, threatening the abbot and imprisoning two monks.
Endorsed on face: *Let it be pleaded to the king by the Lords.*
Endorsed: *This petition, and the record of it, is entered on the parliament roll.*

A les treshonurables et tressages comunes de cest present parlement supplie treshumblement Leonard, abbe de Newenham del counte de Devonshire, qe come le dit Leonard est et estoit abbe de dite abbeye, fait et eslieu duement par course de ley, quele estate et possessioun il continua peseblement en la pees de Dieu et de nostre seignur le roy del fest del Trinitee darrein passe tanqe demenge, lendemayn del fest del Nativite de Seint Johan le Baptistre adonqes prochein ensuant, qe Phelipe de Courteney, chivaler, ove tresgraunde multitude des gentz quelez par soun comandement, armes et araiez afuere de guerre, al nombre de lx, ove force et armes et encountre la pees nostre seignur le roy, assaut en le dit suppliant fisterent, et luy pristerent forceblement hors de son abbeye avaundite, et luy amesnerent et manesserent par groces paroles tanqe a ville de Honytoun, et illoeqes par manasse et grauntz paroles fisterent le dit suppliant pur paier pur lour costages encountre sa bone voluntee, et de illoeqes le dit suppliant amesnerent tanqe al maner de dit Phelipe de Bykelegh, et illoeqes le dit suppliant emprisonerent et en prisoun detenerent par xv jours proschein ensuantz; parount le dit suppliant fuist en despeire de sa vie. Et sur ceo le dit abbe, \par ses amyes/ suit diverses briefs hors du counseil nostre seignur le roy directez au dit Phelipe, luy chargeant et comandant de venir devaunt le dit counseil nostre seignur le roy, de respoundre a celle tort fait a dit suppliant, sur peine de M[l] marcs, a certeine jour limite par le dit brief; a quel jour le dit Phelipe ne venoit point. Et auxi chargeant et comandant q'il bone pees porteroit a dit suppliant et a ses servantz, et q'il ne destourberoit pur nulle rien le dit suppliant, ne soi entremelleroit del governance del dite abbie, ne de dit suppliant ne de ses comoygnes, et nient countresteant cela, ore puys cel temps, le dit Phelipe et graund numbre des gents armez et araiez, et encountre la pees nostre seignur le roy a son assignement, viendrent al dite abbeie, et illoeqes manasserent le dit suppliant, parount l'abbe de Beal lieu, son visitatour, ne osoit al dite abbeie pur son office faire aprochier, ne le dit suppliant en sa abbeie demurer ne par noet ne par jour, eyns en boys et en autres covertes pur son corps et sa vie garder. Et deux de ses comoygnes du dite abbeie deteignount, et eux fait chacers et fauconers encountre lour ordre, issi qe la seint esglise du dit suppliaunt n'est pas duement servy. Dount le dit suppliant est graundement empoverise, et destruitz et anientez, et grauntement travaillez et vexez, considerantz, treshonurables seignurs, qe le dit Phelipe est cy graunt de seignurie et de mayntenance en la dit countee qe le dit suppliant ne poet avoir envers \lui/ la comune ley saunz emportable charge et destructioun du dit suppliaunt et de sa mesoun avauntdit. Dount le dit suppliant treshumblement prie remedie, pur Dieu et en oevre de charite.

Endorsed on face: Soit ple a roy par les seignurs.
Endorsed: Ceste peticioun et le record d'icelle est entrez en rolle du parlement.

1402. As noted on the dorse, the details of this petition, and the response to it, are recorded on the roll for the parliament of 1402 (30 September – 25 November): *PROME*, parliament of 1402, items 19–21. Previous petitions on the matter are **113–14**. The abbot of Beaulieu, visitor to Newenham, was John Gloucester (see also the following petition, **116**).

116

Beaulieu, Hampshire (1405)
Cistercian
(SC 8/34/1664)

To the council from the abbot and convent of Beaulieu stating that because of the mis-governance of John Gloucester, late the abbot of the house, the king took the abbey and its possessions into his hand for the relief of the house. They request remedy because William Bray claims to have the farm of the manor of Tregonning and the church of St Keverne by Gloucester's lease, and has occupied and still occupies the same by force, taking the issues and profits and detaining them without title, with many charters and muniments of the house.
Endorsed: *On 20 December 1405, with the bishop of Bath, the chancellor and keeper of the privy seal present in council, it was agreed that a writ be directed to Bray that he be before the council at the quinzaine of St Hilary next on pain of £40 to answer the matters contained within the petition.*

A treshonurable et tressage conseil nostre seignur le roi, supplient les abbe et covent del abbecie de Beaulieu en le countee de Sutht', q'est del patronage nostre seignur le roi et del fundacion de ses nobles progenitours rois d'Eengleterre, esteant en tresgrande meschef, ruine et poverte par malveis governance d'un Johan Gloucestre, nadgairs abbe illoeqes, et d'autres ses nadgairs predecessours, a cause de quell nostre tressoverain seignur le roi ad priz en sa main mesme l'abbecie et toutz ses possessions et les comys en garder a certeins persones pur relevacion d'icelle maison et continuance de les divines illoeqes affairz, come par ses lettres patentz ent faitz piert pluis pleinement. Qe come William Bray clamant d'avoir de le lesse du dit Johan nadgairs abbe devant son cesser la ferme del manoir de Tregoinan et del esglise de Seint Keveran en le countee de Cornewaile, qeux sont parcell de la fundacion de la dit abbecie et de la value annuell de viij^{xx} marcz et les qeux ont este la grande partie de le vivre de les abbe et covent illoeqes ad occupit mesme le manoir et la rectorie du dit esglise par long temps ove fort maner et uncore occupie et les issues et profitz de mesmes les manoir et esglise le meen temps provenantz ove tiel force ad priz et uncore print et vers luy mesmes detient non duement et sanz title ovesqe plusours chartres et munimentz du dit maison nient voillant eux deliverer et auxi nient soeffrant les ditz abbe et covent ne null de eux ne les ditz gardeins nostre dit seignure le roi ne lour deputez rien des ditz manoir et rectorie medler ne \profit/ ent prendre, en contempt nostre seignur le roi et tresgrande meschief damage et arrerissement du dit maison. Plese voz, tresnobles et tresgracious seignures considerez les grandes meschief, ruine et poverte suisditz, de ordeigner remedie en ceste partie en resevacioun et salvacioun d'estat de mesme la masoun et susteinances de les divines illoeqes solonc la fundacion d'ycell affaire, pur Dieu et en oevre du charite.

Endorsed: Le xx jour de decembre anno nostro etc. septisme, presens en consail messurs les evesqe de Baath, le chancellor et gardein du Prive Seal, accordez est qe brief soit fait direct a William Bray deinz escrit d'estre devant le counsail nostre seignur le roy al la quinzeine de Seint Hiller prochien venir, sur peyne de xl li pur respoundre a ce que lui serra lors surmys touchant le matire dedeinz comprise.

1405. Following the promotion of the previous abbot, Tideman of Winchcombe, as bishop of Llandaff in 1393 there was a dispute over the abbacy between Richard Middleton (the petitioner) and John Gloucester which continued until at least 1413. This petition is one small episode in the struggle. The best guide to this dispute is in *Heads of Houses III*, 265–6, with many references. Those present in council were Henry Bowet, bishop of Bath and Wells 1401–7, Thomas Langley, then dean of York and chancellor, and Nicholas Bubwith, then archdeacon of Dorset and keeper of the privy seal. William Bray was granted ratification of his estate as vicar of St Keverne (Cornwall) in March 1405 (*CPR 1405–8*, p. 83). However, since one Thomas Bosfrawell was granted ratification of his estate as vicar of St Keverne on 22 January 1406 (*CPR 1405–8*, p. 92), it appears that judgement was granted in favour of the petitioners in this case.

117

Fountains, WRY (? 1427)
Cistercian
(SC 8/111/5525)

The abbot of Fountains petitions the king and Lords of the present parliament for a writ to the sheriff of Yorkshire to make a proclamation in Yorkshire and Lancashire that John Tunstall

and Robert Worsley be before the council to answer for their assaults on the abbot's tenants in Craven, taking their goods and chattels and destroying their houses, and threatening them so that none will return, to the abbot's great damage; and if they do not appear then it is requested that they be put out of the king's protection.
Endorsed on face: *By the chancellor, 25 November.*

A nostre soveraigne seignur le roy et a toutz lez auters seignurs espirituelx et temporelx de cest present parlement supplie humblement vostre povere oratour l'abbe de Fontayns qe come Johan Tunstall del counte de Lancastre, gentilman, Robert de Worseley del dit counte, gentilman, ... comons riottours au dit suppliaunt disconuz, arraiez a faire de guerre a le nombre de xxviij persones, ove force et armes, le xxiiij jour d'Octobre l'an du regne nostre seignur le roi q'ore est .... placez du dit suppliaunt appellez Overbordeley, Langerhouse, Tranehouse et a diversez auters measons, terrez et tenementz le dit suppliant en Cravene en le counte d'Everwyk pur ....[Thomas] Dyconsone, Johan Dene et auters tenauntz le dit suppliaunt illoeqes demurantz s'ils ussent este trovez et lez biens et chateux de mesmes lez tenauntz illoeqes trovez, c'estassavoir .... necessaries de houshold hors dez ditz maisons getterount, debruserount et tout outrement distruerount, as graundez damagez et arrerissement de mesmes lez tenauntz et lez .... saunz vesture sur eux ousterount, eux enchargeauntz sur peyne de lour vies lez ditz measons voider et uncqes en apres sur la terre ne tent le dit suppliaunt a demurer et a ceo parfourmer ils ......nt eux .... huyses et fenestres dez ditz measons debruserount et baterount en petitz peces, par cause dez queux ryottez, manacez et damagez lez ditz Thomas Kydde, Thomas .....esone, Thomas Dycon[sone] .... dit suppliant en Cravene suisdit lez terrez et tenementz du dit suppliant ount voidez et auters lez ditz terres et tenementz n'osent ocupier pur lez causez suisditz et pur doute de mort, issint qe le dit suppliaunt lez profitz dez d............. temps ad perduz et est verraysemblable d'aver trope graund perde et damage par celle enchesoun si gracioluse remedie par vous ne soit a luy purveu. Please a voz tresgraciousez seignurie, par autorite de cest present parlement .... un breif direct al viscount del counte d'Everwyk a fair proclamacions en dieux countes ou troys procheins a teners en mesme le counte d'Everwyk,apres le livere du dit breif qe lez ditz Johan Tunstall, Robert de Worseley .... appergent devaunt le counsell nostre seignur le \ roi/ a certein jour par le dit counsell a limiter pur y respoundre, sibien a nostre dit seignur le roy come au dit suppliaunt, dez riottez et trespassez avauntditz, et pur trover seurte de pease au dit [suppliaunt et sez] tenauntz et servauntz; et en cas q'ils ne veignent a mesme le jour apres lez ditz proclamacions faitz, adoncqes cestuy qe fait defaute soit mys hors de proteccion du roy, consideraunutz lez ditz Johan Tunstall, Robert de Worseley ... sount vacaboundez en lez countes de Lancastre et Everwyk suisditz, et n'ount terres, tenementz, bienz ne chateux parount ils puissent estre distreignez ou mesnes en respounce par cours del comone ley, et ceo pur Dieu [et en] oevere de charite.

Endorsed on face: Per cancellarium, xxv die Novembris.

? 1427. The petition is speculatively dated based on the dating attribution in the guard note, though no evidence to support this is given. This being the case, the petitioner is John Ripon, abbot from at least 1416 until 1435, although he and Roger Frank, a monk of Fountains, had been in dispute over the title since the death of Abbot Robert Burley in 1410. Brief biographical details of John Tunstall, who was MP for Westmorland in 1453–4, can be found in J. C. Wedgwood, *Biographies of the Members of the Commons House 1439–1509* (London, 1936), pp. 881–2. For other petitions from Fountains Abbey in the fifteenth century, see 'Monastic Chancery Proceedings (Yorkshire)', ed. J. S. Purvis, *Yorkshire Archæological Society* 88 (1934), nos 36–43. The right-hand side of this petition is damaged. For an earlier transcript, see no. 30 of PRO 31/7/117.

118

Vale Royal, Cheshire (1439–58)
Cistercian
(SC 8/145/7218)

Thomas, abbot of Vale Royal, petitions the Commons of parliament, stating that he owes annual suit for the church of Llanbadarn-fawr, and other possessions in Carmarthenshire and Cardiganshire, at the king's sessions, in person or by attorney, but that those holding the sessions often insist on him attending in person – which means a long journey from his monastery. Also, at the last sessions at Cardigan he and his men were assaulted by certain Welshmen, falsely imprisoned and indicted, and kept in prison until he had made fine to the king. He asks the Commons to ask the king to ordain, by the assent of the Lords, that in future abbots might be able to appear in these sessions by attorneys, without any fine or penalty for non-appearance being exacted. He also asks that if any presentment for felony or treason is made against the abbot at any other petty session or court, resulting in a warrant for arrest or distraint, this warrant should be returnable at the next great session of these courts, when open proclamation should be made of the indictment or presentment, so that the abbot can answer it at the next great session.
Endorsed on face: *Let it be sent to the Lords.*
Endorsed: *The king, with regard to the appointment of the attorney as specified in the petition, and the receiving of the same attorney as specified in the petition, agrees that it is to be as is desired, provided that the matter for which the attorney may be made or received does not extend to felony or to treason; and with regard to the proclamation made in the county courts of Carmarthenshire and Cardiganshire, the king wishes that before the abbot of Vale Royal, whoever he is, is outlawed, proclamation should be made in these shires, or one of them as the case requires, at three of the last full county courts before outlawry is pronounced. And with regard to the rest of the petition, the king will be advised.*

To the right wise and discrete comunes of this present parlement humbli bisetheth Thomas, abbot of the monastery of Val Riall in the counte of Chestre, the which is of the kynge's fundacion, that where he is seised of a ...... perpetuell as in right of the seide monastery of a church called Llanpidernbaur withe .... tenementis in þe shires of Kermerdyne and Kardigane in Southwales, for þe which he owith to do a sieut yerely in his propre persone, or by his attorney at his election, to the kynge's grete Cessiones þere to be holdene, and often tyme þe justices of the said .... record and admitte attorne for hym to do þat sieute, so that bi grete necessite he is full ofte compellyd to come in his propre persone to that Cessiones which is vij^{xx} myle and mor fro his seide hows, to his grete labour, charge and use .... the last grete Cessiones þere at Kardygane holdene þere were grete assautis and affrayes by nightis tyme made uppone hym and his servauntes and men of his counsell by certein Walsshmen, and þere by þaim they were putte in grete .... bette and sum of þam maymed and putte in grete orrible prisone. And more ovir, by a certain enquest taken bi þe othes of the saide Wallshmen þat so assautid and imprisoned hym, he was endited while he was in prisone of divers .... never gilty and kept still in prisone in to the tyme he agreed in þe same Cessione to pay to þe kyng at his grace C marc at certein daies here aftir to come. And ovir that he founde sieurte to pay to þe saide Walsshmen .... þay shold not procure no bodily harme nother other grevaunces to be done to hym ne to none of his servauntis lv marc, and in this wise here aftir and more hevily he, his successours and þaire servauntis et .... in this partye. Please it to youre wise discrecions, þe premisses considerid, to pray þe king oure soverain lord to graunt and ordeyne, bi the assent of the lordes espirituelx and temporelx at þis present parlement assemblid, and by auctorite .... successours, abbotes of the seide monastery, may appere bi þair attourne to be made by a lettre of attourne under the comune seal of the abbot and covent of the same hows for the tyme beyng, to do thaire sute to all þe Grete .... Kardygane aforeseide, and to make thaire claymes in the seide Cessiones of all libertees and fraunchises graunted or to be graunted to the seide abbot, his predecessours or eny of his successours, or bi the saide abbot and his predecessours ...... fully used .... and his successours may appere by þaire attourne made bi such warrant in the fourme aforesaid to alle enditmentis of trespas, and ther presentmentis and sieurte to be taken or hadde a yenst þaim or eny of thaym .... Cessiones ...... with ynne the shires of Kermerdyn' and Kardygan aforeseide, in the which enditmentis, presentmentis and sieurtis bi the comune lawe þey myght appere by attourne made by other suffisiaunt lawefull warrant and .... of þe same Cessiones and courtes for þe tyme beyng schall admitte and accept the same abbot and his successours to do the same sieut, and make þaire claymes, and to answere to all enditmentis, presentmentis .... made by suche warrant with out eny amercement, fyne, peyne, imposicion, defaut or condempnacion to be putte uppone þam or eny of tham for thaire none beyng or none apparaunce to or in the seide Cessiones .... peyne, imposicion, defaut or condempnacion be sette or awarded uppone thaym or eny of thayme for thaire none apparaunce that hit be voyde so that thay offre to appere bi thayre attourne in the fourme aboveseide. And .... presentmentis of felony or tresone to be taken ageynst the same abbot and his saide successours in eny Petit Cessione or other court thanne the Grete Cessione, to be holden in eny of the seide shires and places .... uppon .... awarded to take thaym by thaire bodyes or to distrayn thaym bi theire godes, that the same processe, write or warraunt be retournable at the next Grete Cessione to be holdon there next aftir the same processe .... Cessione opene proclamacion be made of the saide appel, enditment or presentment and of all matiers in þaym comprehendid. And more ovir, that the seide abbot and his successours uppone whom such appell, enditment or presentment .... to the same appell, enditmentis and presentmentis at the next Grete Cessions than next there to be holden. And that at the same Cession thanne processe lawefull to be awarded ayenst the same abbot and his successours .... appere nought. And yf eny processe uppone eny such appell, enditment or presentment ayenst the saide abbot or his successours taken in the same Petit Cessione or other court be hadde and process .... as aforeseide that thenne the same processe be voyde and none in lawe. And if eny such appell, enditment or presentment be hadde or taken ayenst þe saide abbot or his successours in any Grete Cessions .... be made in the same Cessions of the same appell, enditment or presentment, and þe first processe to be awarded to be retournable at the next Grete Cessione than next to be holden. And þen .... aftir the comune lawe to be awarded, and yf eny processe of suche appell, enditment or presentment be awarded or servyd in othir wise that hit be voyde and none in lawe. And this [for God and in way of charity].

Endorsed on face: Soit baille as seignurs.
Endorsed: The kyng will þat, as to ward þe article of makyng of attourne specified in þis peticion, and þe same attourne to be receyved in manere and fourme as it is rehersed in þe same, it be as it is desired, so þat þe matiere wherin attourne is or shal be so made and receyved be noþer felonie nor treson; and as toward þe proclamacione to be made in þe shiree of Kermarddyn and Cardygan, þe kyng will þat raither and affore þat þe abbot of Vall Riall, what som ever he be for tyme beyng, be outlawed, proclamacione be made in þe saide shires, or one of hem as þe case requires, atte thre of þe last full countees to be hade þere affore prononieng of such utlawrie. And as toward þe remnaunt of þis peticione, þe kyng will be avysed.

1439–58. Thomas Kirkham was abbot of Vale Royal from 1439 until c. 1472 (he died between 1472 and 1475). This petition probably dates to before 1458, when he was made bishop of Sodor and Man. It is most likely to have been presented at some point in the 1440s: a related petition was enrolled on the parliament roll in 1442 (*PROME*, parliament of 1442, item 13), and on 20 January 1448 an inspeximus and confirmation of a charter concerning the church of Llanbadarn-fawr was made (*CPR 1446–52*, p. 142). The right-hand edge of this petition is damaged. The mid-fifteenth century was a particularly turbulent time for Vale Royal: *VCH Cheshire*, III, 161–2.

119

Hampole, WRY (1450)
Cistercian nuns
(SC 8/117/5838)

The prioress (and convent) of Hampole petitions the Commons for a writ of summons against John Pilkington and Thomas, Gilbert and John Butterworth, his accomplices, who she claims invaded their house on 29 April 1450, abducted Elizabeth Clarell, and attacked and injured the prioress and a number of the nuns and other women living there. She states that this danger has dissuaded women from joining her house or other such nunneries. She asks that the sheriff be ordered to make a proclamation at Doncaster, summoning the attackers to appear before the king on 20 June next, and that all who do not appear be held convicted of the crime.
Endorsed on face: *Let it be sent to the Lords.*
This bill is thought reasonable.
Endorsed: *The king wishes that it be done as desired.*

To þe right discrete comons of þis present parlement mekely besechene youre povere oratrices and nonnes þe priorasse and convent of þe monestre of Hampull in Yorkshire þat where as diverse and weldisposed wymmen of goode name and fame as wydewes, maidens and oþer mo, for þe goode report and opinyone þat is in þe cuntre of þe vertuous conversacion and lyvyng þat long tyme hath bene and is in þe religious persones of þe seid monasterie have desired to sojourne in þe same, and among oþer, now late oone Elizabeth, late wife of Thomas Clarell, þe which Elizabeth so beyng in þe seid monasterie, oone John Pilkyngtone, \late/ of Pilkyngtonehall in þe counte of Lancastre, gentilman, Thomas Boterworth, Gilbert Boterworth and John Boterworth of þe same shire, yomen, arraied in guerrable wyse, þe xxix day of Aprill þe yere of þe regne of our sovereigne lord þe kyng þat now is xxviij, cam to þe seid monastre to take oute of þe same be force þe seid Elizabeth, as he so did, and in þe tyme þat he besied hym self in þe takyng of her, he and oþer þat he was accompanyed of not only sett handes of violence uppone þe seid priorasse and oþer nonnes, sojournantez and servauntez of þe seid place which to here power labored to latte hym of execution of his ungodly and unlawfull purpos, of which ladyes and wommen þat so labored to withstonde he grevously bett and wounded, and among oþer Dame Margret Herkyngtone, Dame Johanne Foljambe, Alice Roudone, Johanne Sibsone, Elyne Hyne, Cristian Bakehous, Margerie Lawe, Johanne Brigge, and dayly þretes youre seid suppliauntez to brenne þeir houses in grete offence and contempt of God, of his servauntez and in especiall of oure sovereigne lorde þe kyng and of his pees, so þat of less þenne þe grete and orrible offence done to God in Goddeshous and his place, and to þe kyng oure sovereigne lorde in þe persones of his oratrices and beadewommen, be notably and grevously chastised, it is like, þat God defend, to cause þat weldisposed wommen neyþer sall dare entre into religione nor dwell in swich places of religione. Plese it youre right grete and discrete wisdomes to considre the premisses and to pray þe kyng oure sovereigne lorde þat he, be th'avise and assent of his lordes espirituelx and temporelx in this present parlement assembled, and by autorite of þe same, graunt a wrat to be direct to þe sheriff of Yorkshire comaundyng hym, apone peyne of CC li, to do make proclamacion in þe towne of Doncastre in \þe seid counte of Yorke/ þat þe seid John Pilkyngton, Thomas Boterworth, Gilbert Boterworth and John Boterworth, and everiche of þayme in þaire proprie persons, appier before þe kyng in his Chauncerie þe xx day of Juine next comyng, þere to fynde sufficiaunt surte of pees unto þe seid prioress, alswell for here persones as for byrnyng of here places, and to all þe kyngs lege peple, and þere to answere of þe seid riout. And if thei appier and will not nawþer may such surety fynde, þat þen þei and everich of þayme þat refuseth so to doo be committed to þe presone of Flete in Londone, þere to abyde unto þe tyme þat such suerety as is a bove rehersyd be foundone. And if þei or any of þeyme at þe seid xx day make defaut, þat þen þei and evereich of þayme þat so mayeth defaut be atteynt of þe seid riout and trespas done unto þe seid priorasse, Dame Margret Herkyngtone, Dame Johanne Foliambe, Alice Roudone, Johanne Sibsone, Elyne Hyne, Cristian Bakehous, Margerie Lawe, Johanne Brigge. And þat þe chaunceler of Inglande for þe tyme beyng have power be þe autorite aboveseid to awarde and deme to þe seid priorasse, Dame Margret Herkyntone, Dame Johanne Foljambe and to þe seid Alice, Johanne, Elyne, Cristian, Margerie and Johanne damages and costages aftur his discressione, and þere uppone to award and make such writtes of execucion as sall be necessarie and behofefull in þis behalf to þe seid parties grevid, and ichoone of theyme, for þe love of God and be þe way of charite.

Endorsed on face: Soit baille as seignuris.

This bille is thought resonable.
Endorsed: Le roy le voet come il est desire.

1450. The attack took place on 29 April 1450, and the proclamation was to be made by '20 June next'. Given that parliament was in session at the time, and it would be three years before another was held, it would appear most likely that the petition was presented soon after the attack, to the final session of the 1449–50 parliament. Thus, the petitioner was Margaret Normanvile, prioress 1445–52, and the chancellor of England was John Kemp. Joan Foljambe was the daughter of Sir Thomas Foljambe and Margaret, eldest daughter of Sir John Loudham. Sir John Pilkington, of Pilkington Lancs., would later rise to great prominence under the Yorkists, serving as esquire and knight of the body in the period 1461–79, as well as chamberlain of the exchequer (1477–9). Apparently as a result of this petition, parliament passed a special act against Pilkington, who was subsequently pardoned on 19 June 1452: see J. C. Wedgwood, *Biographies of the Members of the Commons House 1439–1509* (London, 1936), pp. 684–5.

120

Leighs, Essex (? 1472–5)
Augustinian canons
(SC 8/85/4236)

The prior and canons of Leighs petition the king and Lords of parliament, stating that they and their predecessors were peacefully seised, by right of their church, of the manor of Dernford in Sweffling, Suffolk, until Michaelmas in the king's tenth year, when certain servants of Robert Wingfield, knight, justice of the peace in Suffolk, entered the manor with force and arms, claiming by colour of a forged enfeoffment made by Adam Hacon to Robert Wingfield that it had been given to Adam and his heirs in perpetuity, although Adam had title in the manor only for a term of years; and Robert continues to uphold this forged document, and to occupy the manor. And he had a canon who entered the manor arrested, and certain goods of the prior's seized, which he would not release without payment, and still has some of them. And although these matters have been sent to arbitration, Robert had the prior, the canon who had entered the manor and the farmer of the manor indicted in his sessions of entering Adam's house and robbing him. As the common law can give him no remedy, because of Robert's power in the area, they request a remedy from the king.

To oure most sovereygne lord the kyng and all his lordes spirituels and temporels of this present parlement be sechyth mekely your power bedemen the priour of the chyrche of Seint John Evaungeliste in Leyghes in the counte of Essex and the chanouns of the same place that where they and here predecessours have be pesebily sesed, as in the right of there seid chirche, from tyme of here first fundacion, of the maner of Derneford in Swyftlyng in the counte of Suff', wyth the appurtenauncez, till the feste of Seynt Michell the Archangel the yeer of your reigne the x[e], that oon John Burnegile, John Glemham, John Walle, Thomas Halle, John Styward, Richard Rysyngtone, Adam Hacone, John Knyghtys, John Ederyche, William Palmer and othir servauntz of Sir Roberd Wynkefeld, knyght, be commaundement of the same Sir Robert that tyme, and yette beyng justice of the pees in the seid counte of Suff', wyth force and armes, that is to seye, bowes, swerdes and bokelers, entred the seid maner pretendyng a tytle in the name of the seid Adam by colour of a feffement made by the seid Adam to the seid Sir

Robert and othir, the whych Adam contrefeted and forged a dede endented, by the whyche the seid priour and covent shulde have gevyne and graunted the seid maner to the seid Adam and to his heires for ever more there, as the seid Adam hadde never title nee ryght in the seid maner but for terme of certeyn yeeres; the whiche contrefeted and forged dede the seid Sir Robert supportyth and maynteneth, and his astat upon the same continueth and kepith, wyth all the issues and profites of the seid maner, on to uttyr hynderyng to the seid priour and covent. And also where be cause that Robert Colne, conchanone of the seid priour, wyth othir officers of the seid priour, be comaundement of the same priour, entred, ocupied and menured the seid maner after the seid entre, the said Sir Robert sente his meyne and servauntes, that is to seyn, Raubyn Betell, John Man, John Pottesford, John Assle, Robert Fissher, John Shefeld and othir to the numbre of xvi persones, wyth bowes, arwes, swerdes, bokelers and pollexes, to the seid maner, and there wyth owtyn warant thei arestyd the seid Robert Colne and v hors, wyth othir goodes and catall of the seid priour, to the valew of xx marcs, there fownden toke and ledde a wey, and the seid Sir Robert wolde lete no lyvere to be made of the seid hors, goodes and catall be your wryttes of replevyn, but them kepte under areste be xxj dayes till that the seid priour paied xviij s and fonde vj men bownden be ther symple obligacion to the seid Sir Robert m[l] x li for lyvere of the seid hors and for parcell of the seid goodes, and parcell of the seid goodes yette remaygne in the possessioun of the seid Sir Robert. And more over, where as all these seid wronges, extorcions and oppressiouns done to the seid priour and covent, be mediacion of goode persones, be th'assent and agrement of the seid Sir Robert, were putte in ordinaunce and awarde of Robert Crane and John Jakys, to the which the seid priour agreed, and all matiers and sutes to be continued duryng the seid tretes, in the mene tyme the seid Sir Robert, a forne hym selfe in the sessiouns of the peas, wrongfully dede do endyte the seid prior and the seid conchanon and oon Robert Deye, which hadde the seid maner in ferme of the seid priour and covent, of felonie, supposyng that the seid priour, conchanon and fermer shulde have entrede the hows of the seid Adam Hacon' wyth inne the seid maner and certeyn evydences and othir goodes of the seid Adam there felenously have stole, to the uttyr anyntisment of your seid bedemen lesse than they have your gracious eide in that partie. Please yt to your roiall majeste to consider these grete wronges and extorciones and the grete power, grete ledyng and rewle that the seid Sir Robert hath of jurouts in the seid counte of Suff', he beyng oon of your justicez of the peas in the same countee of Suff', of the which your comune lawe is no remedie to your seid bedemen be cause of ther grete poverte wyth owtyn your gracious eide, to do right ben hadde to your seid bedemen, for the love of Godde and in the weye of charite, consideryng that these seid grevauncez and oppressiouns ben done to your seid pore bedemen in a foreyne counte where as thei have no socour ne supportacioun, and all the lyfflode for your seid pore priour and his ix conchanons and all his howeshold as not clarly to the summe of an C marcs, so as thei be not of power in no wyse to remedie these grevaunces be the sutes of the comune lawe.

No endorsement

? 1472–5. Tentatively dated to the parliament of 1472–5, with reference to the mention of Michaelmas, 10 Edward IV (1470) and to Robert Wingfield, who was appointed justice of the peace in Suffolk in the commissions of July 1471, December 1473 and September

1473 (*CPR 1467–77*, p. 631). As a leading member of the East Anglian gentry and Yorkist establishment, Sir Robert Wingfield was a formidable opponent for the prior of Leighs. In 1471 he was described as a king's knight and in the period 1474–81 he was Controller of the Household. The petition was presented to a parliament (1472–5) at which Wingfield himself had been returned, as MP for Norfolk, by consent of the dukes of Norfolk and Suffolk, and at an election presided over by his brother, John, then sheriff of Norfolk and Suffolk. See J. C. Wedgwood, *Biographies of the Members of the Commons House 1439–1509* (London, 1936), pp. 956–7.

4.1 Towns

121

Clerkenwell, London (c. 1275–1300)
Augustinian canonesses
(SC 8/98/4858)

The prioress of Clerkenwell petitions the king for a remedy because the people of London trample down and destroy her corn and her meadows with their miracle-plays and wrestling-matches, so that she can get not profit from her lands, and can have no remedy against them at law.
Endorsed: *The constable has been ordered not to permit etc.*

A nostre seingur le reys prient la povre pryurresse de Clerkenwelle ke il voyle acun remedi purver et commaunder de ceo ke le gent de Lundres, par lur miracles et luces ke il font sovent, desolunt et destruent lur bles et lur prez, issint ke eles ne nunt point deprou ne aver ne purrunt si le reys de ceo ne ayt pyte, pur ceo ke il funt sauvage gent et nus ne poum pas a nus encuntre estere, ne par nule ley les poums cunforter, dunt pur Deu, sire, de nus aet pyte.

Endorsed: Precepit constabilium quod non permittat etc.

c. 1275–1300. The petitioner was probably Agnes of Marcy, prioress of Clerkenwell from at least 1283 until 1305. For comment on this celebrated petition see E. K. Chambers, *The Mediaeval Stage*, 2 vols (Oxford, 1903), II, chpt. xxi, and W. O. Hassall, 'Plays at Clerkenwell', *Modern Language Review* 33 (1938), 564–7.

122

Shrewsbury, Shropshire (? 1309)
Benedictine
(SC 8/240/11982)

The abbot and convent of Shrewsbury petition the king, stating that their founder, Earl Roger of Bellême, who came over with the Conqueror, granted them a fair at Lammas (1 August) to last for three days, and that this was confirmed by William the Conqueror, and has been by every king since. Now the burgesses of Shrewsbury are claiming a fair for three days at the feast St James (25 July), to ruin the monks' fair, and in support of this they have produced a charter which, however, they will not allow anyone to read. The monks request a remedy.

Nostre seignur le rey, qui Deu gard, mustre le abbe de Salopeburs e le covent que le Counte Roger de Belem, qui veint ove le Conquerur Rey William, funda la meson de moignes de Salopeburs e lur dona une feyre a la Goule de Aust duraint la veylle e le jur e leindemein, e la vaunt dist rey le conferma, e pus de rey en rey est conferme, ore sunt venuz les burgeys de meme la vile pur graver les dist moignes e destrure lur feyre si ount crie une feyre a meme la vile de Salopeburs a la feste de Seint Jake curront treis jors, en meme la que mustrerent une chartre en plein conte mes ne voleyint la chartre overri ne suffrer que ele fu luwe. Dunt, Sire, s'il vus plest, vus priunt les dist moignes, pur Deu e pur le alme vostre pere, qui Deus asoyle, de si com autre fundeur ne avowe n'unt for vus, ke vus voylez ordener remedie qui les dist moignes ne seint de vostre aumoigne deserite.
[In a different hand] Et, cher seynur, veylit entendre ke il unt une feyre sys semenes devant cel feir.

No endorsement

? 1309. This petition was made in response to a grant of Edward II, dated 5 June 1309, to the good men of Shrewsbury of a three-day fair at the feast of St James (25 July) (*CChR 1300–26*, p. 127) in lieu of their three-day fair at the feast of St Clement (23 November), first granted to them on 20 September 1267 by Henry III (*CChR 1257–1300*, p. 80). The petitioner is William of Muckley, abbot of Shrewsbury 1292–1333. Roger of Bellême is Roger of Montgomery, first earl of Shrewsbury (cr. 1074, d. 1094) and founder of the abbey in 1083, who may or may not have first granted the Lammas fair to the monks. This petition was probably enclosed with a chancery warrant dated 7 July 1309 ordering a remedy to the petitioners (*CCW 1244–1326*, p. 290). It was not until 1327 that the fair was moved to St Matthew's day (21 September): *CChR, 1327–41*, p. 6. See also **132** and Introduction, pp. xxxvi–xxxvii.

123

Holy Trinity (Christ Church), Canterbury, Kent (? c. 1315–31)

Benedictine
(SC 8/200/9996)

The prior of Holy Trinity, Canterbury, petitions the council for a remedy. He has been guarding the coast at great expense to his house, and is still guarding it, but the mayor and citizens of London have seized the small rent that he has in the city, challenging a quarter of it, because of various expenses and costs that they have had.

Al counseil nostre seignur le roi prie le priour de la Trinite de Canterbirs qe sicome il ad este sure la garde de la mere moult aforcement as grant custages de sa eglise, et unqore lui covent estre, et sur ceo le maire et les cyteyns de Loundres ount arestu la petite rente q'il ount en la dite cyte, chalengeant la quatre partie de la dite rente, pur diverses mises et custages q'ils ount fait en avant ces houres unqe ne firent contribucioun ovesqe eux, qe par voz avisementz remedie lui soit ordeine.

No endorsement

? c. 1315–31. The petitioner is Henry of Eastry, prior of Holy Trinity, Canterbury, from 1285 to 1331. From the hand, this petition would seem to date from the later part of this period.

124

Faversham, Kent (c. 1340–65)
Benedictine
(SC 8/227/11335)

The abbot of Faversham petitions the king for a writ so that he can pursue the people of Faversham to clean their streets of dung, pigs and rubbish and repair the roads so that people passing are able to go and carry without disturbance.

Plese a nostre seignur le roi graunter bref al abbe de Faversham, qe est seignur de mesme la ville, qe il chase les gentz de la dite ville de moundeir les rues en la ville de fym et de pors et trounkes, et q'ils reparaylent les dites chemyns issint qe les gentz passauns par yceles puissent aler et carier saunz deturbacione, et qe ceo soit faite sure sertayn payne.

No endorsement

c. 1340–65. If the tentative date, given on the basis of the hand, is correct, then the petitioner is either John *dictus* Ive, abbot 1325–56, or William of Maidstone, abbot 1356–70.

125

St Mary's, York (c. 1350)
Benedictine
SC 8/176/8780

The abbot and convent of Our Lady (St Mary's), York petition the king, requesting the final discussion of the debate between them and the mayor and the citizens of York concerning Bootham. The abbot and convent claim Bootham as their borough, and the mayor and citizens claim it as their suburb, and following an earlier debate, the matter was resolved in the abbot and convent's favour by an inquisition, but now the mayor and citizens again claim it as their suburb and have ousted the abbot and convent.

Plaise a nostre seignur le roi entendre qe la ou debat est par entre le abbe de Nostre Dame d'Everwyk et le meir et les citezeins de la cite d'Everwyk de la ville de Bouthome, la quele le dit abbe cleym come sa burgh et les ditz meir et citezeins la cleyment come lour suburbe, et autiel debat et en tiele manere en temps de vostre aiel feust mewe entre les parties avauntditz de la dite ville d... .... rien forprendre ou devision faire, et adonqes feust trove par solumpne enqueste de xxx des mienz vautz chivalers et servauntz del counte d'Everwyk, en queux les ditz abbe, meir et citezeins se mistrent qe la dite ville feust le burgh le abbe, et agarde feust qe la dite ville demurast le burgh le dit abbe et ses successours a toutz jours, et qe les ditz meir et citezeins ne lour heirs de cele temps apre... ne se entremellent de riens tochaunt le dit burgh, et qe les ditz meir et citezeins clamont la dite ville come lour suburbe nient contresteant .... et se afforcent de les oustez de lour droit avauntdit et de grant partie de lour abbeye par lour power et richesces. Par quei prient sa seignurie qe lui pleise prendre lour dit bosoigne a coer et q'ils ne soient oustez de lour droit encontre le juggement avaundit, et .... a son counseil q'ils passent hors du ville avuant qe final discussioun soit faite de la dite bosoigne, si qe le dit abbe et son covent puissent .... a lour dit abbeie de priere pur vous et les voz, et autres pur queux ils sount chargez et tenuz de priere.

No endorsement

c. 1350. On April 20 1350 the borough was taken into the king's protection and on 20 May 1350 a commission was issued to examine the rival claims to Bootham (*CPR 1348–50*, pp. 497, 584). The petitioner was therefore Thomas of Moulton, abbot 1331–59. Related petitions indicating the continued hostility towards the abbey by the city authorities in the early 1350s are SC 8/26/1286 and SC 8/162/8089. SC 8/178/8867 presents the arguments of the York citizens. In February 1351 Bootham was restored to the city following irregularities in the abbey's plea on the matter: *CCR, 1349–54*, p. 286. However, in November 1352 a special commission of oyer and terminer was granted at the request of the abbey, on complaint that the abbot and his men had been attached and tallaged in the borough against the tenor of their charters: *CPR 1350–4*, pp. 392–3. It was not until 1354 that 'final discussion' on the matter resulted in the royal council placing Bootham into the city's jurisdiction, on the understanding that the monks had immunity from arrest within its boundaries: *CPR 1354–8*, pp. 84–6. TNA C 49/7/25 is a council memorandum which details the abbey's complaints against York's civic officials: it was probably written as part of the adjudication process. For the long history of tension between St Mary's and the city, see *VCH City of York*, pp. 39–40, 68–9.

126

Abingdon, Berkshire (1368–9)
Benedictine
(SC 8/297/14842)

Memorandum that a writ was sent to the keepers of the peace in Oxfordshire and Berkshire, and to the sheriff of these counties, to go to Abingdon, summon the community and receive a security from them not to harm or molest the abbot and monks of Abingdon, or their men or servants, and to arrest and imprison all those who refuse to give such a security; and that as a result of this, the keepers of the peace in Berkshire and others did this on the Wednesday after Michaelmas last, and list the names of those who gave security, and the names of those who refused to do so.

Memorandum quod quoddam breve domini regis de Cancellaria directum fuit custodibus pacis ipsius regis in comitatibus Oxon' et Berk', necnon vicecomitibus comitatum predictorum, quod ad villam de Abyndon' personaliter accederent, et omnes et singulos homines ville predicte ac totam comunitatem eiusdem ville coram eis venire et ipsos ad inveniendum coram eis sufficientem securitatem, videlicet quemlibet eorum sub pena centum librarum et dictam comunitatem sub pena mille librarum, compelli facerent quod abbati et monachis abbatie Beate Marie de Abyndon', hominibus seu servientis suis, in personis, bonis aut aliis rebus seu possessionibus suis injuriam, dampnum, violenciam, molestiam, impedimentum aliquod seu gravamen non inferrent nec inferri procurent, et omnes illos qui huiusmodi securitatem coram eisdem custodibus pacis etc. invenire recusaverint arestari et prisone domini regis committi, et ipsos in prisona quousque hoc gracis facere voluverint detineri et salvo custodiri facerent; pretextu cuius brevis Edmundus de Chelerey et Johannes de Esbery, custodes pacis domini regis in comitatu Berk', una cum aliis fidelibus domini regis, accesserunt apud villam de Abyndon', die mercurii proximo post festum Sancti Michaelis ultimo preteritum, et ibidem venire fecerunt coram eis Walterum Bryan, Thomam Romesy, Ricardum Deyghe, Alanum Smyth, Johannem Lyford, Johannem Bache, Johannem Colnham juniorem, Eustachium Yonge et Willelmum Cholseye, qui singillatim invenerunt coram eisdem custodibus etc. sufficientem securitatem in forma supradicta, et eciam venire fecerunt coram eis tunc ibidem Thomam Thame seniorem, Ricardum Bate, Walterum Oxeburgh, Johannem Ledecoumbe, Johannem Aleyn, Ricardum Ferour, Robertum Chaloner, Robertum Glench, Johannem Hampton', Thomam Hasele, Henricum Tannere et Thomam Hakeborne qui coram eis sufficientem securitatem in forma predicta invenire omnino recusarunt, per quod iidem custodes pacis corpora eorum persone domini regis in custodia Rogeri de Cotesford, vicecomitis, commiserunt ibidem moratura quousque hoc gracis facere voluverint etc.

No endorsement

1368–9. The memorandum dates between 10 July 1368, when Edmund de Chelerey and John de Esbury were appointed to the peace commission for Berkshire (*CPR 1367–70*, p. 195), and 5 November 1369, when Roger of Cotesford's second term as sheriff of Oxfordshire and Berkshire came to an end. The abbot was Peter of Hanney, 1361–99. For discussion of this dispute, see G. Lambrick, 'The Impeachment of the Abbot of Abingdon in 1368', *EHR* 82 (1967), 250–76. See also **127** and Introduction, pp. xxxiv–xxxv. Further petitions relating to the dispute between the townsmen and abbey are: SC 8/21/1042, 88/4370, 88/4392, and 209/10412.

127

Abingdon, Berkshire (1368–9)
Benedictine
(SC 8/297/14843)

Petition to the chancellor, stating that Walter of Oxeburgh and John Ledecombe, cobblers, and others of Abingdon were asked to find security to keep the peace before Edmund Chelerey and his companions, justices of the peace in Oxfordshire and Berkshire, together with other malefactors from Abingdon, and that because of their rebellion and disobedience before these justices, they were thrown into prison in Oxford, from where they have now escaped, and are wandering with force and arms, boasting of their escape and threatening William of Shiltwode, William Catyn and other servants of the abbot of Abingdon. The petition asks that Chelerey might be ordered to make his record and to certify chancery of the names of the rebels, and that such a remedy might be ordained as to serve as an example to others.
Endorsed: *Abingdon.*

Au chanceller nostre seignur le roi soit moustrez qe come Wauter de Oxeburgh et Johan Ledecombe, soutores, ove autres meffesours de la ville de Abyndone, devant Esmond Chelreye et ses compaignons, justicz de la pees es les contees de Oxon' et de Berk', assignez par vertue de brief nostre seignur le roi as ditz justicz directe de les faire trover seurte de la pees pur lour rebealte et inobedience devant les ditz justicz, fourent commys en la gaole de Oxenford en garde du viscont de les savement garder en prisone tanqe nostre dit seignur le roi eust autrement de eux ordenez, les queux Wauter et Johan et autres sont eschapes hors de la dite prisone, sanz fyn faire ou seurte de la pees trover, et contre comandement des ditz justicz, et vont wacraunt ove force et armes, faisaunt lour bobauns de lour eschape et manaceant overtement de vie et de membre William de Shiltwode, clerk, et William Catyn et autres de servantz l'abbe de Abyndone, s'ils n'osont seurement nulle part aler pur doute de mort. Dont plese au dit chanceller comander au dit Esmon de faire son record et de certifier les nouns des ditz rebealx en la Chancellerie come le dit brief voet, et outre tiele remedie ordener qe autres ne pernont ensaumple par eux ne hardement de mal faire.

Endorsed: Abyndone.

1368–9. This petition, which mentions Oxeburgh's and Ledecombe's appearance before the justices, must have been presented some time after the events described in **126** (see note).

128

Hatfield Regis or Hatfield Broad Oak, Essex (1378)

Benedictine
(SC 8/215/10737)

The prior of Hatfield Regis, which is of the patronage of the earl of Oxford who is the king's ward, petitions the council for remedy against John Cok, vicar of Hatfield Regis, those endorsed on this bill and the greater part of the town of Hatfield, who came with arms to the priory on 7 June in the first year of Richard II (1378), assaulted the petitioner, monks and servants, knocked down most of the cloister and walls and opened all the doors of the priory, entered its church and caused such alarm that the prior and monks have left the priory for fear of their lives. The prior also requests that he and his monks can safely return to the priory.
Endorsed: *[List of the accused].*
A commission of oyer and terminer should be made of the trespass at the petitioner's suit, on the matter contained within, to John of Cavendish, Henry Percehay, Thomas Tirell and William of Wauton, or to three or two of them, provided that either Cavendish or Percehay are included.

A counseille nostre tresredoute seignur le roi moustre le priour de Hattefeld le Roi en le contee d'Essex, quele priori est de patronage le count d'Oxenford q'est deinz age et en la gard nostre seignur le roi, qe Johan Cok, vicar de Hattefeld susdit, et autres sur cest bille endoses, et la greindre partie de tout la comunaltie de la ville de Hattefeld avauntdit, par graunt malice entre eux, purpense viendront en la ville avauntdit a la dit priorie le vij[e] jour de Juyne l'an du regne le Roi Richard q'orest primer, ove graunt multitudie des gentes ove arkes et settes, bastons et plusours autres armes, et le dit priour et ses commoignes et servauntz en lour priorie avauntdit assaut, firont et graunt partie de lour cloistre et des mures, par queux le dit priorie jadis estoit enclose, ount abatuz, et les huys de la dit priorie ount deffermes, et en la esglise le dit priorie entreront, et tiele manere de fray devers lez ditz priour et ses moignes firont et puis ount continuz issint qe le dit priour et ses moignes sont departez d'illeoqes pur dout de lour mort. Par qei plese a vostre tresnoble seignurie ordeigner pur le dit priour q'il poet illeoqes ove ses moignes surement solonc la ley demurer, et outre de lui ordeigner remedie par la ley de la malice et tort avauntdit, en salvacioun du dit priorie et en oevre de charite.

Endorsed: Johan Angre, Johan Michecok, William Smart, Petre Smalhach', Johan Stakwode, Johan Sherman, Johan Thurgood, Johan[10] Shrubbe, William Bussh', Johan Piphele, William atte Water, Robert Pernull senior,[11] Robert Gilleson, Robert Shrubbe,[12] Thomas Taillour, William Ford, Johan Yve senior,[13] Thomas Dryver, Stephen Ryngdale, Johan Ferant, Johan Waryn,[14] Johan Whitebred, Petre Lambard, Johan Gull senior,[15] Geffrey Mose, William Frensh', William Shrubbe,[16] Johan Parmonter,[17] Johan Peyntour, Robert Wych', Henry Douneshed senior,[18] Roger Palmere, Johan Tortelof junior,[19] Thomas Chanterell', Johan Branktre, Johan Cook de Busshesend, Johan Peticru, Johan Malot senior,[20] Hugh Olyver, Robert Neuton', William Gulle, William filius,[21] Johannis Robert[22] de Brunshoo, Thomas Spirk, Richard Hutte, Richard fitz William Palmer, Robert Haukyn, Johan Londenys, Rauf Maskhall', Johan Speller, Johan Campe junior,[23] Robert Hope senior,[24] Robert Hope junior,[25] Johan Brond senior,[26] Johan Sorell', Johan Pekkere, Johan Banham, Thomas Coteller \Hattefeld Regis/, Johannes filius Johannis Angre de Halyngbury[27]

Soit fait commission de oier et terminer de trespas a la suite du suppliant et sur le matere deinz comprise, \c'estassavoir/ a Monsire Johan de Cavendissh, Monsire Henry Percehay, Monsire Thomas Tyrelle et Monsire William de Wautone, quatre, trois ou deux de eux, des queux le un des ditz Johan et Henry soit un.

1378. The petitioner is Thomas of Bradeleye, prior 1369–80. The earl of Oxford is Robert de Vere, who was 'almost of full age' on 4 July 1380 (*CCR 1377–81*, p. 402). On 21 July 1378 commissions of oyer and terminer were issued in accordance with the petition, naming Cok's companions, as recorded on the dorse of the petition (*CPR 1377–81*, pp. 303, 304–5). As the deletions testify, the names on the dorse were written in Anglo-Norman, and then amended in part into Latin. The prior made two further petitions to the crown (*CPR 1377–81*, pp. 526, 535). He also petitioned the bishop of London (TNA C 49/47/14, in 2 Richard II), William Courtenay, whose register has

10 *Scrub* deleted.
11 *Pernull l'eisne* deleted.
12 *Scrub* deleted.
13 *l'eisne* deleted.
14 *Wareyn* deleted.
15 *l'eisne* deleted.
16 *Scrub* deleted.
17 *Parmonter* deleted.
18 *Doneshed l'eisne* deleted.
19 *le puisne* deleted.
20 *l'eisne* deleted.
21 *filz* deleted.
22 *Robert* deleted.
23 *le puisne* deleted.
24 *l'eisne* deleted.
25 *le puisne* deleted.
26 *l'eisne* deleted.
27 *Gerson de Johan Panyot* deleted.

not survived. Following this dispute between priory and parishioners, the conventual church was separated from the parish church by a wall built across the western arch of the crossing. The conventual church continued in use until the Dissolution when it was demolished, but shortly after 1378 the parish church was extensively rebuilt: *VCH Essex*, VIII, 182 (no references), and F. W. Galpin, 'The History of the Church of Hatfield Regis or Broad Oak, with Some Account of the Priory Buildings', *Transactions of the Essex Archaeological Society*, new ser., 6 (1898), 327–45. For general discussion of the phenomenon of shared monastic-parochical churches (with a plan of Hatfield Regis), see M. R. V. Heale, 'Monastic-Parochial Churches in Late Medieval England', in *The Parish in Late Medieval England*, ed. C. Burgess and E. Duffy (Donnington, 2006), pp. 54–77. For a petition on a similar theme, see below, **207**.

129

Bury St Edmunds, Suffolk (1384)
Benedictine
(SC 8/199/9922)

The abbot and convent of Bury St Edmunds petition the king and council in parliament, stating that the people of Bury St Edmunds are delaying providing the security of perpetual peace demanded of them towards the king and towards the abbot and convent, after their late rebellion, and ask that an ordinance might be made for this in the present parliament. They ask that the recognisances might be made based on the lands held by the people of Bury at the time of the Lent parliament of 1383, as many of them have since alienated their lands.
They ask that Richard White, Thomas Lakforthe, John Ouseburn, John Toller, Roger Rose and Richard of Rougham, present in this parliament, be compelled to make the recognisances before they leave Salisbury.
They ask that fifty other people of Bury, nominated by the petitioners, be summoned to make the recognisances in chancery at the quinzaine of Trinity next, and that commissioners be appointed to come to Bury to take recognisances from the rest.
They also ask for remedy, and that sufficient punishment be ordained for those refusing to make these recognisances.
Endorsed: *Let it be known that the schedule attached to this bill was read in parliament and amended there in the manner shown in the same schedule, and that it was agreed that every single person in the town of Bury should find surety by recognisance to be made in chancery, both to the king and to the abbot and convent, according to the form of the schedule and the conditions therein: which conditions the abbot will grant on record for his part. Item, this bill was granted in parliament in all respects; and to counteract the malice of the alienation of lands, it was agreed that all recognisances shall bind them and their lands in Bury as if they were made on the Monday on which the said parliament of the sixth year was held. And it is agreed that the rebels shall be constrained to find this surety by the threat of the imprisonment of their bodies without bail, and if necessary by the seizure of their goods, chattels and tenements in Bury, notwithstanding the common course of the law of the land to the contrary.*

A nostre tresredoute seignour le roi et a tout son tressage conseil en cest parlement supplient treshumblement voz devoutz oratours abbe et covent de Bury Seint Esmon qe come les gentz de la ville de Bury, apres lours horribles mesprisiouns par eux attemptez en la derren riote des communes rebeaux encontre vostre roiale majestee et voz ditz oratours, et lour eglise q'est de vostre patronage, en salvacioun de lours vies se submistrient en haut et baas a la noble grace et ordenance de vous, nostre seignour le roy suisdit, come piert de record, et depuis ce il ad estee tressovent ordinee, grantee et establi par gracieus consent de vous, nostre seignour, et de autres seignours de vostre roialme, sibien en parlement tenuz a Westm' le lundy en la tierce simaigne de Quarresme l'an de vostre regne sisme, come en plusours autres voz nobles consails, qe les ditz gentz de Bury, a cause de lours mesfaitz et custumables rebellions encontre vostre corone et la dite eglise, dussent faire auxi suffisante seuretee de lour bon port envers vous et la dite esglise en tout temps avenir come meultz purroit estre devisee, et a ce estre obligez sibien a vous, nostre seignour, come a voz oratours abbe et covent desuisditz severalment, pur seuretee du pees perpetuele, devant q'ils eussent aucune chartre de pardoun, grace ou remissioun par voie quecomqe. Plese a vostre tresgracious seignourie, considerantz lours dites submissions a vostre roiale majestee ensi faitz, et coment les ditz gentz ne ont voluz tanqe en cea faire la dite seuretee en aucun manere, comebien qe par force de lour dite submissioun ce ad estee ordinee tressovent, et la manere d'icelle seurtee qe serroit une reconussance affaire en vostre Chancellerie lour ad este moustrez et profri en escript, [ore faire] bone ordinance en cest parlement, et comander estroitement qe les dites seurtees sanz pluis longe proloignement soient faitz et parfournys par toutz les gentz et [enhabitantz de] mesme la ville de Bury, et chescune singulere persone d'icelle, en manere et par fourme come y fuist declarree en especial par vostre grant consail tenuz [a Westm' a comencem]ent de Quarresme prochein passee. La manere et fourme de [quelle] seuretee ordeignee en vostre derrein grant consail est contenuz en une cedule an[nexe a ceste bille; faisan]tz nientmeins expresse protestacioun de adder ou oustier [de m]esme la cedule, solonc ce qe semblera reasonable en ceste parlement a [vostre tresgracious seignourie suisdite.] Outre ce, voz ditz oratours, abbe et covent, priont treshumblement, pur tant qe plusours des ditz gentz ore par tressutil engyn, et par voie de fraude, ont alienez lours [terres et tenementz a foreins g]entz et autres persones qi ne sont mie de la ville de Bury suisdite, al ent[ente] qe lour tenementz ne serroient mie chargez par les reconussances affaires; qe [lours dites reconussances] unqore affaires par ordenances et establissementz ent affaires en cest present parlement, emportent plenere vertue de lien et de obligacioun par re[conisance soi extenda]ntz sibien a toutz les terres et tenementz queux les ditz gentz avoient et tenoient come lours propres, et fuirient seises en ycelles; ou autrement autres ge[ntz a lour profit, le d]it lundy en la tierce simaigne de Quarresme avauntdit, come autres lours tenementz en la ville de Bury quecomqes, auxi avaunt come mesmes l[es reconussanc]es ferroient si celles eussent estee faitz duement en la chancellerie par mesmes les gentz de Bury a lundy desuisdit. Et ce par cause qe en ycelle vostre parlement especiale mensioun fuit faite de lours dites seurtees a trovers; come il appiert overtement par expresses paroles en la roule du dit parlement; et auxint par une especiale bille en mesme le parlement endossee, desicome fraude et deceyte ne deivent doner a eyde a nully par voie de reasoun.

Item, ils prient qe vj persones, c'estassaver Richard White, Thomas Lakforthe, Johan Osbern, Johan Tollere, Roger Rose \et/ Richard de Rougham, qi sont de les pluis sufficeantz persones du dite ville de Bury, et ore sont personelment en ceste ville de Novell Salesbury, facent les dites reconussances en manere et par fourme avauntditz, devaunt q'ils departient hors de ceste ville de Salesbury suisdite.

Item, qe cynqant autres persones de la dite ville de Bury, par nominacioun de

voz dites oratours, abbe et covent, soient appellez, et par vostre roiale majestee compellez, pur venir et faire les dites reconussances, en la Chancellerie suisdite a la quinszeine de la Trinitee prochein avenir, ou autre jour covenable et brief par voz oratours avauntditz a vostre noble consail si vous plest a limiter et nomer. Et qant a toutz \les/ autres persones enhabitantz en la dite ville, vous plese granter sufficeante poair et commissioun a ascune sufficeantz persones, qe vendront a certein brief terme personelment a la dite ville de Bury, as coustages de voz ditz oratours, pur prendre les dites reconussances en fourme et en manere suisditz, de toutz autres et de chescune singuliere persone enhabitantz ou enhabitante mesme la ville de Bury.
Item, voz ditz oratours priont treshumblement qe due remedie soit ordene en cest present parlement, pur chastier et arter sufficeantment les persones rebealx des ditz gentz, en cas qe ascuns de eux ne veullient obeier ne faire les dites reconussances en manere et fourme ordenez et establis, come ils deivent et sont tenuz de faire par force de lour submissioun et l'ordinance avauntditz, sibien c'estassaver par emprisonement de lours corps sanz meynprise en le cas, come autrement par seisine de lours terres, biens et chateaux. Et plese a vostre tresgracieuse seignourie grauntier et ordiner qe toutz cestes seurtees avauntdites soient trovez et executz sanz proloignement faire, et si hastiement come ils poent bonement: qar le proloignement qe unqore est et \qe/ ad estee tanqe encea, est \et ad este/ trop perillouse a voz oratours, abbe et covent desuisditz. Et si tost come les dites seuretees soient plenerement trovez par les ditz gentz, en manere et fourme come par vostre noble et gracieuse dignitee est ordinez, voz dites oratours, abbe et covent resceivantz des dites gentz v^{c} marcz, qe lour sont ordinez par vous et vostre consail pur lours grauntz perdes et damages, sont et serront delors et tantost prestz de faire tielle acquitance as dites gentz en le cas, come vous nostre seignour par avys de vostre consail lour avetz promys sur la faisance de lour fyn de ij^{m} marcz q'est de record.

Endorsed: Est assavoir qe la cedule annexe a ceste bille et de la quele ceste bille fat mencion lue en parlement, et illeoqes amende en partie et corrigee par manere come mesme la cedule purporte, estoit accordz illoeqes qe chescun singuler persone de la ville de Bury ferroit la seuretee par reconisance a faire en la Chancellerie, sibien au roy nostre seignour come a l'abbe et convent deinz escritz, par [fourme et] manere en toutes choses, et par les condicions comprises en mesme la cedule; les queles condicions l'abbe [de] Bury grantera et conoistra de record pur sa partie. Item, ceste bille est grantez et assentuz en ceste mesme parlement en toutz pointz; et especialment pur obver la malice conceuz parmy l'alianacion de lours tenementz en Bury puis le dit parlement tenuz l'an sisme: est assentuz et accordez qe toutes les reconisances quelles sont encores affaires et a resceivoires de ceulx de Bury par celle cause, et chescune d'ycelles, tiegne et tiegnent tiele force et vertu de reconisances en touz pointz, et lient eux et lours terres en Bury auxi avaunt del dit lundy quant le dit parlement l'an sisme estoit tenuz q'est ja passez, come elles ferroient si mesmes les reconisances qe sont issint affaires eussent este faites par mesmes les gentz de Bury al lundy avauntdit. Et enoultre \est/ assentuz qe \touz/ les rebeulx en le cas, si nulles ysoient, soient compuls par emprisonement de lours corps sanz mainprise, et s'il embusoigne par seisine de lours tenementz, biens et chateulx en Bury, \de faire la dite surtee/, par manere qe par ceste bille est demande, nientcontreesteant qe la comune cours du loy de la terre est encontre ceste grant et ordinance, les queux sont \ore/ faitz tantsoulement pur le bien de pees \maintenir desore/ en dit lieu, et salvetee de l'abbeye de Bury avauntdite, qe a diverses foitz devant ceste heure ad este mys a grant meschief \et destruccion/ par les gentz de Bury, qi sont lours propres tenantz trestoutz, et pur nulle autre cause.

1384. The petition was presented in the parliament held at Salisbury in April 1384. It concerns the rebellion of the townsmen against the abbey in 1381: R. S. Gottfried, *Bury St Edmunds and the Urban Crisis: 1290–1539* (Princeton, 1982), pp. 231–6. The petitioner was John of Timworth, abbot 1379–89 (*CPR 1377–81*, p. 418; *CPR 1389–92*, p. 45). On 1 September 1384 Thomas Lakforthe, John Ouseburn, John Toller and Richard Rougham were among the twenty-five men of Bury St Edmunds appointed to keep the peace in the town, with regard to certain people there who 'do all the damage they can … to the abbot and convent of Bury, against whom they have a grudge' (*CPR 1381–5*, p. 501). Around 1385 a number of petitions were presented on this subject: from the assessors complaining about people who should have been assessed moving to another county to avoid paying (SC 8/20/972); from the people of Bury complaining that the assessors had assessed themselves and their friends very favourably, laying heavier burdens on others, forcing them to leave town (SC 8/300/14953); and a complaint that a new assessor had taken bribes (SC 8/300/14981). A copy of this petition and its associated schedule was enrolled on the parliament roll (*PROME*, parliament of April 1384, item 19). The schedule, which is now missing, is incorrectly referenced as SC 8/255/9577 in *PROME*. See discussion in Introduction, pp. xxxv–xxxvi.

130

Westminster (1415–20)
Benedictine
(SC 8/188/9369)

The abbot and convent of Westminster petition the king for remedy. They state that while their tenants at Morden were holding a procession, William and John Yerd and others from Cheam attacked them, stealing their cross and banners, which they kept for a year, until they were returned following a request from the archbishop and delivered to Richard Harweden, the keeper of the town. However, the Yerds, together with Thomas Hayton, appeared at the church and ordered the tenants not to make any more processions, and at the same time carried off all the tenants' animals from their demesne.

Au roy nostre tresgracious et tressoverein seignur supplient humblement voz oratours l'abbe et convent de vostre esglise de Westm' qe come lour servauntz et tenauntz de la ville de Mortone furent alant en processioun le lundy en la semaigne appelle Rogacioun l'an de vostre regne second entour lour champes, solonc coe qe autres voz lieges fount de custome par my vostre roialme en mesme le temps, et un William Yerd et Johan, sone fitz, ovesqe disconuz et tenauntz de Cheyham, viendrent ove fort main et en lour ditz servauntz et tenauntz assaut firent, et lour croys et lour baners pristerent et emporterent, et par un an deteinerent, c'estassavoir tanqe al lundy en la semaigne de Rogacioun l'an de vostre regne tierce, a quel jour l'ercevesqe de Cauntirbirs envoia a dite ville de Cheyham pur les ditz baners et croys et eux a Daun Richard Harwedene, gardein del dit ville de Mordone, deliverast pur ent faire solonc lour auncien custume devaunt use, a quel jour le ditz William Yerd et Johan, sone fitz, et auxi un Thomas Haytone, par colour q'il est un des justices de pees mes come verray partie, venoient as mures de l'esglise du dite ville de Mordone, manassant a touz lour servantz et tenauntz avauntditz, et eux commandant du par le dit ercevesqe q'ils ne passerent la dite esglise pur null processioun faire, et en le mesme temps les ditz William Yerd, Johan, sone fitz, et Thomas Haytone touz les bestes des ditz servauntz et tenauntz sur lour demesne et sur lour comune appurtenaunt a vostre dite esglise ount chacez, pris et amesnez, et uncore les deteignent. Qe please a vostre tresgracious seignurie, en salvacioun del droit de vostre dite esglise, ordeiner graciouse remedie celle partie solonc vostre tressage discrecioun, pur Dieu et al reverence de Seint Edward et en oevre de charite.

No endorsement

1415–20. Morden (Surrey) was one of Westminster's smaller manors, B. Harvey, *Westminster Abbey and its Estates in the Middle Ages* (Oxford, 1977), pp. 435–6, and lies three miles north of Cheam, a parish in the immediate jurisdiction of the archbishops of Canterbury. William Yerd, for whose colourful career see *HC*, IV, 935–7, was MP for Surrey four times between 1413 and 1423, and in 1421 was appointed deputy constable of the Tower of London. This appointment 'was terminated abruptly' when five high-profile prisoners – one of them the lollard Thomas Payn – escaped, allegedly with Yerd's help. John Yerd was probably William's son. It is possible that Yerd's hostility to the procession arose from sympathy towards lollardy. Thomas Hayton, an esquire who had seen service in Wales with Prince Henry, was a justice of the peace in Surrey, commissioned, 1412, 1413, 1414, *CPR 1408–13*, p. 484; *CPR 1413–16*, p. 424. Archbishop Chichele's intervention in this case was not recorded in his register.

131

Bath, Somerset (c. 1418)
Benedictine
(SC 8/302/15089)

To the chancellor from the prior of Bath requesting a remedy as the mayor and people of the town have congregated in the town's churches, except the church of St James, and sound the bells of those churches day and night as they please, though the greater part of the churches are of the patronage of the prior and his convent, it being the custom that no bell be sounded between curfew and the ringing of the cathedral bells the next morning between Easter and the feast of the exaltation of the Cross. And this despite the king having ordered the mayor and other people to observe the customs in response to an earlier petition by the prior and convent.

A tresreverent pier en Dieu et tresgracious seignur le chaunceller d'Engleterre supplie treshumblement vostre povres chapellayn et oratour le priour del esglise cathedrale de Seint Pietre de Bathe, del patronage nostre soveraign seignur le roy et de fundacione de ses tresnobles progenitours, qe come le dit priour \et soun convent/ sount patronez del greindre partie de les esglises del ville avauntdite et du subbarbes d'icell, et teignount ascun des parsonages des esglises avauntditz en propre oeps, et ount jurisdiccione ordinarie de toutz les esglises avauntdite, et qe le dit priour et convent et toutz lour predecessours ount estes seisi en peisible possessione come de droit de lour esglise avauntdite de temps dount memorie ne cuert, de tiel usage et custume qe null campane en null esglyse deinz la dite ville ne subbarbes de ycell doit estre sonne en null jour ne noet apres coverfeu sonne en la dite esglise cathedrale tanqe al leve del dit convent en la dit esglise sonne ademayne, ne en le temps de estee apres la houre de noon parentre le jour de Pasqe et le feste del Exaltacione de la Seint Croyce tanqe al secunde houre apres ferme en le clok, salve qe les gentz de les ville et subbarbes avauntditz purroient et userent toner un campane en esglises, appelle *knollyng*, saunz autrement sonner en ascun guyse s'ils voudroient aler a lour matyns devaunt le dit leve del dit convent sonne, tanqe ore tarde qe nostre soveraign seignur le roy passe overe le meir en ceste tresgraciouse viage en sa terre de Normandie, qe Richard Wydecombe, mair de la ville et subbarbes avauntditz, Rauf Hunt, Walter Riche, Henri Bokerell, Johan Northfelk, Johan Wyttokysmede, Johan Mareys, Robert Drewe, Robert Phelippes, Thomas Kyngtone, Johan Heyne, Geoffrey Masone, ovesqe plusours autres des comunes et ceo la greindre partie de la ville et subbarbes avauntditz, ount confederees et de lour malveys covyns et assent ount sonne lour campanes en chescune esglise del ville et subbarbes avauntditz, forsqe l'esglise de Seint Jakes, chescun noet et jour a quele temps qe lour plese, a contrarie del dit custume et usage avauntdit, et auxi ount faitz comunez assembles et comunes coillettes et comunes burs entre eux pur mayntener lour tort et querele nient droiturel. Sur quoy le dit priour suya par peticione a nostre soveraign seignur le roy, esteant en sa terre de Normandie, pur eus avoir remedie et redresse, et nostre dit seignur le roy de sa treshabundante grace, voillant et desiraunt la dite esglise cathedrale de sa patronage aver et enjoier lour auncient custumes et usages, envoia ses tresgraciouses lettres al mair et as autres gentz del dite ville, eux expressement chargeant par ycell de cesser de tiel maner voluntarie governaunce come avaunt est dist, tanqe a soun revenir, ove l'aide de Dieu, en soun roialme d'Engleterre, come par la dite lettre pluys playnement appiere. Quex tresgraciouses lettres par le dit mayr receuz devaunt luy et les auters lieux et de eux entenduz, et les ditz mair et les autres avauntditz malfaisours a ycestz tresgraciouses lettres nient donantz regarde, mes a contrarie de ycell jour et noet usont et fount user et sonner lour campanes come ils firent devaunt qe les ditz lettres feurent peux resceax et plus, et ceo quant les ditz priour et convent sount en lour meillour repos, parissint qe les ditz priour et convent ne purrount estre ables ne disposes a faire et dire lour divinez services solonc lour reule et fundacione, au contempt de nostre soveraigne seignur le roy, grande damages del dit priour, final destruccione del esglise cathedrale suisdite, si due remedie par vous, tresgracious seignur, ent ne soit ordine, considerant, tresgracious seignur, le lever del dit convent a mye noet et qe l'esglise cathedrale est esteant pres lewe d'un parte et les esglises avauntditz si pres l'esglise cathedrale d'autre parte envyrount, qe le sonner de les campanes sonnez en les esglises del ville et subbarbes avauntditz sonnent pluys en l'esglise cathedral qe en les esglises ou ils sount sonnes. Qe plese a vostre tresgracious seignurie de considerer les grevaunces et diseases avauntditz, et sur ceo ordiner tiel remedie come serretz de vostre tresgracious discrecione avise, solonc droit et resone, pur Dieu et en oevre de charite.

No endorsement

c. 1418. It is likely that the previous petition referred to is SC 8/176/8781, in which the prior and convent of Bath request letters commanding the chancellor to make a commission to sufficient persons to enquire into the matter of the ringing of bells in the town. The commission was duly issued to examine the complaint on 30 August 1418 (*CPR 1416–22*, p. 205). For the signet letters issued by the king to the citizens of Bath ordering them to cease ringing their bells and to the chancellor ordering him to hold the commission, see J. L. Kirby, ed., *Calendar of Signet Letters of Henry IV and Henry V (1399–1422)* (London, 1978), nos 811 and 843. This present petition is unlikely to be too much later. Thus, the petitioner is John Tellesford, prior 1412–25, and the addressee is Thomas Langley, bishop of Durham and chancellor. The dispute began in 1408 when the mayor and corporation of the city first began to ring their bells before those of the monastery: *VCH Somerset*, II, 76. It was finally resolved in 1423 as a result of the mediation of Nicholas Bubwith, bishop of Bath and Wells: *Register of Nicholas Bubwith, Bishop of Bath and Wells, 1407–1424*, ed. Thomas Scott Holmes, Somerset Record Society, 29 (1914), II, 460–4, no. 1266. The bishop forbade bell-ringing before 6 a.m., at which time the bell of the town clock in St Mary at Stalls was to sound six strokes. Simple tolling was permitted on the hour until 7 p.m. in winter, 8 p.m. in summer, with a break between noon and 2 p.m. In return for these concessions the mayor and community of Bath were obliged to offer a candle of three pounds weight at the time of High Mass in the abbey church. See Introduction, p. xxxvii.

132

Shrewsbury, Shropshire (1423)
Benedictine
(SC 8/71/3550)

The abbot of Shrewsbury petitions the duke of Gloucester and the Lords Temporal and Spiritual in parliament for a commission out of chancery of oyer et terminer at his suit, of the injuries done to them by John Perle, bailiff of Shrewsbury, and others, who at the last fair held from the feast of St Peter ad Vincula came arrayed for war and took the profits which pertained to the abbot. He further requests writs to Perle and the others to appear before the chancellor and to find sufficient surety to keep the peace towards the abbot and all the king's lieges.
Endorsed: *It is ordered by the Lords in parliament held at Westminster on 20 [October] 1423 that the petition be sent to the king's council who, with the assent of the Lords, should have the power to hear and finally determine the matter comprised within the petition at their discretion; and that a writ be directed to the bailiffs of Shrewsbury and the commonalty to be before the council at Hilary next to answer the matters contained within the petition with all the relevant records of the town, with authority to do and receive what the council adjudges. And another writ is to be directed to Perle and the others to be before the council at the same time to answer for the same. And another writ is to be directed to the abbot and convent to send one or two members of their community with sufficient authority to sue their petition and present their evidence. And it was commanded by the chancellor in parliament to John Perle and Urien St Peter, burgesses of the town at that parliament, to keep the peace towards the abbot and convent under penalty of 1,000 marks, and it was ordered to William Pole, monk of the abbey, to keep the peace to the burgesses and commons of the town under the same penalty.*
Because Richard Lakyn, before the lords of the council, has attested that he is obliged to stand for the abbot and convent to the arbitration of the arbitors elected by the parties, and that it is the abbot's wish, the same bailiffs and burgesses and other people named above should be dismissed. Therefore they are quit and without a day.

A treshaut e puissant prince le duc de Gloucestre et as autres tresgracious seignurs espirituelx et temporelx assemblez en cest present parlement supplient humblement l'abbe del mynstre .... de Salop', q'est del patronage nostre tressoverayn seignur le roy, qe come il et ses predecessours, abbes de mesme le lieu, de temps dount memorie ne court ount euez annuelment une feire, sibien deinz mesme la ville de Salop' come en un lieu appelle Monkenfreyt joust mesme la ville de Salop', del heure des vespres en la veille de Seynt Pier l'advincula et par trois jours alors proscheyn ensuantz, ove toutz maners tolnus, profites et commoditees du dite feire provenauntz, et auxint ount euez .... temps toutes multre de toutz les molyns deinz mesme la ville esteantz. Et auxi le dit suppliant et toutz des tenauntz de Monkenforeyt de mesme le temps ount usez tiel liberte q'ils duissent estre quietz de checune tolnue .... la ville .... appaier, desqeux feire et tolnus, profitz et commoditees d'ecell provenauntz annuelment del heure des ditz vespres et troi jours alors proscheinz ensuantz, multre et liberte d'estre quietez et tolnue le dit ore abbe et sez prede[cessours] ....[sine le temps] de memorie ..... ount estez peseiblement seisez tanqe a la veille de Seynt Pier l'advincula darreyn passe q'un Johan Perle et Nicholas Shettone, alors baillifs du dite ville, et[28] ore un des .... de mesme la ville ove Johan Gamell, Johan Shettone, John Beget, William Forester et Johan Broun, aggregantz a eux plusours maeffaisours disconuz, armez et arraiez a feere de guerre en manere de novell insurreccioun, ove l'assent .... oettement de la c......... de dit ville a l'entent pur disheriter le dit ore abbe et ses successours del profit de feire avauntdit ove fort mayn encontere la peas nostre seignur le roy garderont les portes de mesme la ville et les ditz baillifs par l'assent de dit c.......... toutz de tolnous, comoditees et profites du dite feire en la veille de Seynt Pier l'advincula darrein passe et trois jours alors proschein ensuantz au dit ore abbe come en droit de sa dite esglise appurtenauntz al oeps des ditz baillifs et c..... de .... Et auxi ......tont et ne veillent soeffrer le dit suppliant avoir la multure suisdite ne d'estre quietez del tonue avauntdit come desuis est dit. Et outere ceo manasseront le dit ore abbe et toutz sez comoignes et auteres servauntz .... feurent sy hardy d'approchier les ditz portes pus outrer la dite ville pur prendre tolnus, commoditees ou profitz du dite feire queconqes deinz le temps suisdit de couper lour tetes et de arder, bater et finalment destroier la dite abbeie pur toutz jours .... quele manasse le dit abbe ne null de sez comoignes ne servauntz, les portes suisditz pur la dite ville entrer et les profitz du dite feire coiller pur doute de morte n'osoient approchier. Et auxint .... le dit or abbe .... ses rentes et profitz des terres et tenementz deinz la dite ville, sibien en frank almoigne donez par les foundours du dit abbie al predecessour du dite ore abbe come par auters puis la fundacioun pur divine service aff............... dit ore abbe et ses successours, s'il n'eit vostre gracious aide et socour en celle partie. Que please a vostre hautessez de considerer les premisses et sur ceo de graunter au dit suppliaunt un commissioun hors del Chauncerie .... par vous .... oier et terminer al suyte le dit suppliaunt toutz les trespasses, injuries et grevances a luy faitz en cell partie, et en le mesne temps de graunter briefs directz as ditz Johan, Nicholas, [Johan, Johan, Johan] William et Johan, sur certeyne peyne par vous alimiter, de apparer devaunt le chaunceller nostre dit seignur le roy de trover sufficeante seurte de peas al dit ore abbe et toutz les lieges nostre dit seignur le roy ou de purveyer au ....

28 The name *William Goure* has been deleted.

.... ceste partie solom vostrez hautessez discrecions, et ceo pur Dieu et en overe de charite, et pur l'amour de Seynte Wenefrede.

Endorsed: Acordez est par les seignours d'icest parlement, tenuz a Westm' le xx[e] jour de [Octobre] l'an du regne du Roy Henry le sisme puis le Conquest secunde, qe ceste peticioun baillez en mesme le parlement soit baille au conseil du roy, et ait mesme le conseil poair par assent des seignurs du dit parlement de les matires comprisez dedeinz la dite peticioun oier et finalment determiner selonc lour discrecioun; et qe un brief desuz le grande seal soit direct as baillifs de la ville de Salop' q'ils, ou l'un de eux ovec ascuns auters du dite ville par la comunaltee d'icelle a ceo assignera, soient devaunt le dit conseil a la xv[e] de Seint Hiller proschein avenir a respondre as certeins matirs compriz deinz mesme la peticioun, apporteantz ovec eux sufficeant poair pur eux et pur toute la comunaltee susdite desouz le comune seal du dite ville, ensemblement ove lour chartres, escriptz et auters lour evidences necessairs celle partie, et de faire outre et receiver ceo qe par le dit conseil lors serra agardez. Et qe un autre brief soit auxi direct a Johan Perle, Nicholas Shettone, Johan Gamell, Johan Shettone, John Beget, William Forester et Johan Broun dedeinz nomez q'ils en lour propres persones soient au dite xv[e] devaunt le dit conseil illoeqes a responder a les matirs envers eux par la dite peticioun surmys, et de faire etc. ut supra. Et soit auxi un autre brief direct a les abbe et covent de Salop' dedeinz nomez q'ils, par un ou deux de lour commoignes aientz sufficeant poair desouz lour comune seal, soient devaunt mesme le conseil au dit jour a pursuer lour dite peitcioun et de moustrer lour evidences et munimentz tochantz les dites maters. Et commande fuist par le chaunceller d'Engleterre en le dit parlement a Johan Perle et Urian Seintpier, burgeis du dite ville lors illoeqes esteantz et venuz au dit parlement comme burgeys de mesme la ville, q'ils et toutz les comunes d'icell ville gardent la pees envers les ditz abbe et covent et lour servantz et ministres, et riens ne facent a eux ne a null d'eux encontre la pees du roy en le mesne temps, sur peine de mill marcz alevere al oeps du roy s'ils viendrent au contrair. Et auxi commande fuist a Frere William Pole, un des commoignes du dit abbe, qe les ditz abbe et covent et lour servantz et ministres gardent la pees en le mesne temps envers les ditz burgeis et comunes sur la peine avauntdite.
Quia Ricardus Lakyn, miles, coram prefatis dominis de consilio ore tenus, est testificatus quod ipse est obligatus pro prefatis abbate et conventu ad standum arbitrio certorum arbitratorum inter eorum, et prefatos ballivos et burgenses electorum quodque voluntas prefati abbatis existit quod \tam/ iidem ballivi et burgenses quam prefate alie persone superius nominate dimittantur. Ideo consideratum est quod eant quieti sine die.

1423. The petition is dated to 1423 as the first response records that this was a petition presented at the Westminster parliament of October 1423. John Perle was MP for Shrewsbury in this assembly. The petitioner was Thomas Prestbury *alias* Shrewsbury, abbot 1399–1426. The left-hand side of this petition is partly illegible. See also **122**.

133

St Augustine's, Canterbury, Kent (c. 1426)
Benedictine
(SC 8/101/5040)

The abbot of St Augustine's, Canterbury petitions the duke of Bedford that he and his consort arbitrate a dispute between the abbot and certain merchants over a consignment of wine. He states that recently a ship loaded with various wines beached on lands appurtenant to the abbey (by tidal misfortune), which since time out of mind has not been covered in water, having right of wreck of the sea and everything appurtenant. The goods were saved by the petitioner with the help of many people and he salvaged thirty-nine tuns and one pipe, which he brought to the monastery, of which eight tuns were empty, two mixed with seawater and two delivered to the ship's master, and thus there remained twenty-seven tuns and one pipe that the petitioner still holds despite complaints from the wine-merchants. He asks that each party appoint two persons to decide all matters and assemble sufficient surety together to abide the said award and ordinance, on which each party should release their actions.
Endorsed on face: *By the duke of Bedford, 20 March.*

A treshaut trespuissant et tresdoubte seignour moun soveraigne seignour le duc de Bedford supplie treshumblement vostre pover chapelayn et devote oratour l'abbe del monstre de Saint Augstyne juxt Caunterbirs qe come ore tarde un nief charge ovesqe certeins vins, par infortunie de temps en le mere, fuist mys et rumpe sur lez terrez appurtenauntz al dit abbe, ou il abbe de temps dont memorie ne court ad ewe et aver doit lez wrekkys de mere et touz cez qe appurtent al wrek de mere, et auxi le moite de touz lez biens illeoqes esteantz en voie et point de perdicion et par luy ou ces servauntz savez. Et pur ceo l'avauntdit abbe veiant qe ces vins ne purroient en aucun maner estre savez saunz graunt aide de plusours gentz entour aultres fist sa diligence de aidre a saver aucun partie dez ditz vins, auxi qe il ad save xxxix toneux et j pipe de vin saunz pluis, les queux sont amesnez en soun manoir de Monstre, des queux viij toneux sont voidez, ij medlez ove lewe de mere, et ij deliverez al meistre del dit nief, et si reviendront illeoqes xxvij toneux et un pipe, des queux l'avauntdit suppliant tout temps fuist, et unqore est, prest de faire tout ceo qe raison ou equite vorront demandre as eaux qe clamount eaux estre merchanz dez vins avauntditz. Plaise a vostre trespuissant et tresgracious seignourie considerer lez premissez et qe rien dez ditz vins, forspris lez ditz xxxix toneux et j pipe, jamez devendrent al possessioun del dit abbe ne de aucun aultrez a soun use, et qe le dit suppliant, al reverence de vostre treshaut et tresgracious seignourie et a la plesance de sa soveraigne dame, vostre compaigne, est prest a deliverer a lez ditz merchanz lez ditz xxxix toneux et j pipe de vin, parissint qe lez ditz merchanz voilent parailement come voet le dit suppliant esteir a la garde et ordenaunce des deux personez par lez ditz merchaunz a eslire et deux aultriz estre esluz par le dit suppliant de toutz lez matiers suisditz, et trovez sufficiant suirte semblablement come ferra le dit suppliant dobbeit lez ditz agard et ordenaunce, et qe sur le dit relivere dez ditz vins et devaunt lez ditz suirtez faitz, lez ditz partiez relessent entrechaungeablement lez uns et lez aultrez toutz meners des accions personelx, et ceo pur Dieu et en eovre de charite.

Endorsed on face: Per ducem Bedford, xx die Marcii.

c. 1426. On 26 March 1426 a commission of oyer and terminer was ordered upon complaint by French merchants claiming that the abbot and others, 'arrayed in manner of war, arrested a certain ship, loaded with wines of Peytowe (Poitou) ... and with other merchandise, which ship touched at the said abbot's island of Tanet ... on Conception day last, claiming the ship and goods to belong to Spanish enemies of the king' (*CPR 1422–9*, p. 360). This may, or may not, refer to the events described in this petition. If it does, the petitioner is Marcellus Daundelyon, abbot of St Augustine's 1420–6. The petition is addressed to John of Lancaster, duke of Bedford, Protector of England during Henry VI's minority. His wife, the duchess of Bedford, was Anne of Burgundy (d. 1431).

134

Blyth, Nottinghamshire (1427)
Benedictine
(SC 8/84/4181)

The prior and convent of Blyth petition the duke of Gloucester and lords of the council for writs to Hugh Crecy the younger of Grove and many others to be before the duke and council at a certain day and to receive punishment at their discretion, and the prior and convent to have remedy and amends of the harm that they did to the prior and convent when they came armed with many others, destroying their closes and ditches, a grange and houses at Farworth at a place called Northland.

A treshault et trespuissant prince et moun tresgracious seignur le duc de Gloucestre et a les tressages seignurs du counseill nostre tressoverain seignur le roy supplient treshumblement voz povres oratours lez priour et covent del measoun de Nostre Dame de Blythe deinz le countee de Notyngham, q'est de la fundacioun de lez tresnobles progenitours nostre soverain seignur le roy et de sa patronage, qe come une Hugh Crecy le puisne de Grove, gentilman, Johan Letone de Sterope, Thomas Drewe de Sterope, Thomas Alvy de Sterope, Johan Coterell de Sterope, Johan Hancok de Sterope et Richard Theker de Sterope deinz le countee avauntdit, husbondmen, Johan Aubresone de Blythe, Johan Dove, cordewaner, Richard Barbour, Robert Palfreman, Elys Skynner, clerc, Johan Maunsfeld, wryght, Johan Skynner, skynner, Robert Skynner, skynner, Laurence Taillour, John Lytster, lytster, Thomas Barker, barker, William Candeler, Johan Dawebry, Richard Hale, William Haleday, preest, William Bryght, Thomas Bagley, draper de Blythe deinz le countee avauntdit, Richard Drewe de Hareworth de dit countee et William Estfeld de Thykyll, gentilman, ovesqe graunde noumbre dez gentz disconutz de lour affinite et assent, arraies affaire de guerre a le noumbre de CCCC persones, ove force et armes violentment et horriblement a graunt et terribles clamours et cries par manere de insurreccioun viendrent, le xxvij jour de Marche l'an de mesme le roy sisme a Farewath en un lieu appelle Northlound, q'est de severale soile du dit priour, et lez hayez, fossez et closez le dit priour illoesqes de toutz pars rumpirent, dejeterent et debrouserent, et un grange et place de dit priour illeosqes esteant et lez \mesons/ d'icell auncienement edifies, c'estassavoir cynks maisons, ove haches, gisarmis et auters instrumentz les postes et maeresme dez ditz maisons couperont et lez ditz mesons tunerent et debouterent tout outrement a le terre, par cause du quelle riotes, insurreccions, manaces et assautes lez ditz suppliantz n'osent pour doute de mort illoesqes demurer a lez divine service affaire, ne lez servantz de dit priour lez terres ne tenementz ne la occupacion al profit le dit priour pour doute de lour mortz n'osent ocupier, en graund arerisment de la povre estat des ditz suppliantz et final destrccioun de le priour suisdit, et a tresparillouse et tresmaveis example des auters tiels mesfaisours, si par voz tressages discrecions et ordinaunce ne soit en celle partie purveu de remede. Que please a vostre treshault et trespuissant seignurie et a tressage discrecion des seignurs avauntditz de considerer lez premisses, et ceo a la reverence de Dieu, et grauntier briefs severalment directz as ditz maffaisours d'estre devant vous a certein jour, checun sur certein peine par vous alimiter, d'estre examiner devant vous, et sur lour examinacion pour eux punier solonc voz tressages discrecions, parensi qe les ditz suppliantz purrount aver due remede et amendes dez grevauncez avauntditz, et ceo pour Dieu et en oevere de charite.

No endorsement

1427. On 16 June 1427 a commission was issued to arrest the malefactors and bring them before the king and council (*CPR 1422–9*, p. 466). The petitioner was John Gaynesburgh, prior 1421–30.

135

Plympton, Devon (c. 1439)
Augustinian canons
(SC 8/135/6740)

Robert, prior of Plympton and parson of its church, petitions the Commons of parliament for action against various misdoers of Plympton, led by John Silverbock, who, armed and arrayed for war, attacked the secular chapel in the priory grounds, dug up, and attacked the dead body of his late servant, Gerard Jonson, nine days after his burial, and threw it in a ditch in the church yard, performing mock rites over the body, including singing, a false offering, and the kissing of the hand, in derision of the church's custom. Meanwhile other misdoers of the same faction, also arrayed for war, lay in wait at the church doors to kill the prior or his men in case they came out and interrupted the others. Soon after the same misdoers came to the chapel and assaulted William Holdich, a canon of the priory, while he was saying mass. Also, when, as is the custom, the prior and canons processed to the chapel to pray for the king, his ancestors and the realm and to say mass on St Mark's day, the same misdoers barred the doors to the chapel so that they could not enter, forcing them to flee. They also threaten those who would buy the church's tithes, so that none dare buy them. This has so terrorised the priests that they dare not say the mass. He requests a writ of proclamation against the misdoers, namely Thomas Ashman, John Brown, Reynold Boway, William Brokyng, Thomas Wyoth atte Ford, John Whitehill, Henry Shirwyll, Walter Laury, John Sturt, Henry Robyn, John Littlejohn, Thomas Balard, John Lachebroke and the said John Silverbock, directed to the sheriff of Devon to proclaim that the misdoers appear in chancery on a certain day, on pain of £20, to be examined on the matter and, if found guilty, punished with imprisonment without bail.
Endorsed on face: *Let it be sent to the Lords.*
Endorsed: *Let it be done as he requests.*

To the full wyse and discrete comunes of the present parliament besechieth mekely Robert, priour of Plymptone in the counte of Devenshire, that wher the seid priour is parson of the church of Plymptone, and he and his predecessours of tyme that no m[an's mind runs to the] contrarie the same church have hold in propre use as in the right of the seid priorie, and all manere of sacramentes in a chapell sette in the church yerd of the seid priorie by a seculer prest depute by the seid priour and his predecessours allway to all the parisshens of t.................... have ministred, and wher on Gerard Jonson, a vertuose man of the seid parishe, be servaunt unto the seid priour late died and in the seid chapell was beried, ther come ix dayes aftur his berying to the seid chapell diverse mesdoers \with/ grete multitude of mysgoverned people ....ies of the same toune in grete noumbre, armed and arayed in maner of werr with bowes, arowes, swerdes, bokelers, jackes, paletes, gleyves, axles, daggairs and other defensible wepyns, at the malicious steryng and procuryng of on John Sylverboc of Plymptone, and for grete malice [that the]i hedde to the forseid priour thei ther maliciously and horribilly toke uppe the seid ded body out of his grave. And aftur the same dede body was so violently takyn uppe thei bette hit and leid opon hit with ther wepyns, and so horribly fared with hit that hit is not \ones.../ .... or declare. And then thei bere hit forth with a thre men song hevelowe, rumbelowe,[29] and threwe hit in to a myre with inne the seid church yerd, and made on of the seid misgoverned people to stond ther above to resceyve offuryng, holdyng his typette in hie hondes. And then all the riotouse people offred silver to hym and kyssed his hond, in dirisione of the blessed custome of the church, and then wente to the ale and drank hit. And all the tyme of this horrible dede doyng, a grete multitude of other mysdoers of ther covyne and assent, arayed in manere of werr, by the steryng of the seid John as hit is above seid, sette hem at the durres of the seid chapell to lye in awaite to have slayn the seid priour or his meygne, in case thei hadde come out of the seid priorie for to have letted or withstond the seid misgoverned people of ther maliciouse entente. And sone aftur that a chanon of the seid priore, callud William Holdich, come to the same chapell and as he was seying ther the parissh masse, the forseid misgoverned people, in manere of werr with sowdyours, atte steryng of the seid Johne as hit is afore seid, come in to the same chapell and ther made such affray and assaute opon the seid chanon that he myght not procede in his mass with out helpe of a nother prest, and nor he hedde kepped hym in the vestrarie of the same chapell aftur masse done he hedde be slayn. And over that wher, aftur the usage and custome of tyme out of mynd used fro yere to yere, the priour and chanons of the same priorie on Seint Mark day usyth with procession to come to the seid chapell to pray for the kyng oure soveraigne lord, his nobull progenitours and the prosperite of his realme, and to sey a masse in the seid chapell, ther come the forseid misgoverned people nowe late on Seint Mark day, arayed in forme and manere above seid, ayenst the lawe of our seid soveraigne lord, and shutte the durres of the forseid chapell in lettyng the priour and chanouns ther of ther devocion and vertuose custome, as hit is above seid, and hem wold not suffur the seid procession to use, but them ther of wyllfylly restreyned, so that they were fayn with all the menes that they couth to ascape in to ther priorie in savyng of ther lyves. And over that the seid misdoers, by the procuryng above seid, manasuth suche persons

29 *ME Dictionary* defines each word separately as 'a sailor's cry'. However in each citation the words are used together, and with the word 'songe'.

as wold bye the tithes of the seid churche so sore and in such wise that no man dar by hem, to the utturest hyndryng of the seid besecher withe oute your help and socour in this partie. Plesyth your wyse discretions to consider the horrible dedes above seid, thus done ayenst the lawe of Godde and of oure seid soveraigne lord, and ther opon to ordeyn, by autorite of this present parliament, that the seid besecher may have oute of the Chauncerie a writte of proclamacion ayenst the seid mysdoers, that is to sey, Thomas Asshman, John Brown, Reynold Boway, William Brokyng of Sporeham, Thomas Wyoth atte Ford, John Whitehill, Henry Shirwyll, Wauter Laury, John Sturt, Henry Robyn, John Lyttiljone, Thomas Balard, John Lachebroke and the forseid John Silverbok, that writte to be directe to the shireve of the same shire for the tyme beyng, hym comaundyng to proclame in the seid shire, that is to sey, at the next shire ther holden by the seid shirreve aftur the lyvere made to hym of the same writte, that the seid mysdoers severally in her own persones apper in the seid Chauncerie at a certeyn day, every persone of hem opon the payn of xx li, ther to be examyned of these premisses, and by the autorite that the seid chaunceler of Englond \for the tyme beyng/, and certeyn juges of the lawe by hym to be named, have power aftur ther discrescion to here, examyn and determyn all the seid wrongus and uche of hem, and severally to punyssh the seid mysdoers yf they be founde gilty ther of by her examinacion, or in eny other wise, and ther opon by the same autorite that the seid chauncelere and juges have power to committe the seid misdoers and uche of hem to prisone, ther to abyde with oute .... bayle or maynprise in to the tyme that they have made fyn withe the kyng and satisfied and contente the seid besecher for his costus and damages, such as shall be to hym awarded by the seid chauncellere and juges. And yif th............. hem make defaute and apper not in his own persone in the seid Chauncerie atte that day so to be specified in the seid writte, that then they or he that so maketh defaute stonde atteynte of the seid offences, and that the seid cha[uncellere and] juges have power aftur her discrecion to sette tax and assesse damages for the seid wronges and offences to the seid besecher, and that he ther opon may have ayenst the seid mysdoers that so happuth to be atteynte such .... execucion as he myght or shuld have ayenst them and they wer atteynte at his sewte by the cours of the comune lawe, for the love of Godde and the way of charite.

Endorsed on face: Soit baille as seignurs.
Endorsed: Soit fait come il est desire. Le chaunceller d'Engleterre appellant a luy deux justices de l'un bank et de l'autre.

c. 1439. In 1441 an agreement was reached between the prior and townsmen over the status of the church of St Mary's: *The Register of Edmund Lacy, Bishop of Exeter, 1420–1455*, ed. G. R. Dunstan, C&Y 62 (1967), III, 244–56. The petition is likely to have been presented in the last parliament before this, which met in November 1339. The petitioner is therefore Robert Boys, prior 1437–40. For more general discussion of relations between the priory and town, see A. D. Fizzard, *Plympton Priory: A House of Augustinian Canons in South-Western England in the Late Middle Ages* (Leiden, 2008), pp. 169–72. See also Introduction, pp. xxxvii–xxxviii.

4.2 Tenants

136

Bec Hellouin, Normandy, France (1331)
Benedictine
(SC 8/164/8157)

The abbot of Bec petitions the king and council that justices be assigned to enquire into the manner in which the villeins of Ogbourne hold their land, and by what services, because the same villeins, who are tallagable and owe him certain services and customs which are attached to their lands from time out of memory, will not give him rents, services or customs, to the great damage of the abbey and of the king in times of vacancy of the abbey.
Endorsed: *Because the matters contained in the petition are in impairment of the peace and affray of the people and also to the damage of the king and his heirs, certain men should be assigned to enquire into the matter, and into their resistance if any was made and into any other necessary points, and the inquest returned in chancery. And if they are villeins of the abbot and have made resistance, the abbot shall have the help of the king and his court to bring justice to his said villeins as their lord.*

A nostre seignur le roi et a soen conseil prie soen chapeleyn l'abbe de Bek Herlewyn qe come ses vileins de la ville de Okebourne, que soleient estre taillables chescun an a sa volunte et faire a lui certeynes services et coustumes qe a lour terres appendent du temps dont memorie ne court, tauncqe a un temps de treis auntz passez qe eux sont levez countre le dit abbe et ses maistres et ne voillent a lui faire rente, services ne coustumes ne autre attendaunce, quele chose, si ele soit soeffert, purra auxibien estre a grant damage nostre seignur le roi au temps de voidaunce del abbeye du Bek avantdit come a damage le dit abbe en autrez temps. E mesme celui abbe, pour doutez de mort de homme et por resistence q'il ad trove e entent trover en eux, ne les ose prendre ne justicer solonc la ley de la terre, ne il ne puet les ditz peisauntz enpleder nule part en la court le dit nostre seignur le roi, s'il ne les feist de fraunche condicioun, q'il plese a nostre seignur le roi et a son bon conseil assigner certeines justices d'enquere de lour estat, e de lour port, et de la manere coment eux soleyent lour terrez venir, e par queux serment. Et si eux troeffent par bone enqueste qe les ditz vileins soient de tiele condicioun come de suis est dist, qe adonqes les facent prendre, justicer et chastier solonc resoun et le ley de terre, issint qe le dit abbe puisse estre servi de ses rentes et services avauntditz, et le dit nostre seignur le roi en temps de voidaunce del abbeye avauntdit.

Endorsed: Por ceo qe les choses contenues en la peticion souvent en enblemissement de la pees et affray du poeple et auxint au damage du roi et de ses heirs en cas qe l'abbeie seit voide et les temporaltez \en sa main de sa ...../, seient certeines gentz assignez d'enquere des contenues en la peticion, et de leur porte, et de la resistence si nul ysoit faite, et de totes autres points necessaires et l'enquest retourne en Chauncellerie. Et si trove seit par ycele qe ils seient les villeins le dit abbe et eient fait resistence ou voillent faire donqes seit le dit abbe par le roi et sa court eide a justicer ses ditz villeins a faire ali ceo qe faire deveront come a leur seigneur.

1331. The resulting inquisition was held on 3 January 1332 and found that the men of Great and Little Ogbourne were villeins of the abbot of Bec Hellouin and had been paying yearly tallage for time out of mind, until three years previously when they forcibly resisted the abbot and his servants (*CIM 1307–49*, no. 1269). This was one episode in a long struggle of the tenants to secure their free status, which began before 1309 and continued intermittently until 1416. The tenants lost every time but 'failure did not discourage them' (M. Morgan, *The English Lands of the Abbey of Bec* (Oxford, 1946), p. 108). In 1327 there was widespread disorder in the south of England and, coincidently, the prior of Ogbourne died on 24 August and the lands were taken into the king's hands. The tenants refused cooperation with Richard de Beauseville, keeper of the temporalities, which led to this petition. The story continues in the following petitions (**137** and **138**). For background, comment, and further references see Morgan, *Lands of the Abbey of Bec*, pp. 106–8; also R. H. Hilton, 'Peasant Movements before 1381', *Economic History Review*, 2nd ser., 2 (1949), 117–36, repr. in *Essays in Economic History*, ed. E. Carus-Wilson, 3 vols (London, 1954–62), II, 73–90.

137

Bec Hellouin, Normandy, France (1332)
Benedictine
(SC 8/239/11950)

The abbot of Bec Hellouin petitions the king and council, stating that when the villeins of Ogbourne rose up against him and his ministers, refusing to perform the services and customs due from them, he was too afraid to seize them or to do justice on them, and petitioned the king to assign justices to inquire into their estate and their behaviour, and the manner in which they held their lands. The justices assigned by the king have now held their inquisition, and he asks the king to order the chancellor to ordain a suitable remedy according to its findings.

A nostre seignur le roi et a soen consail prie soen chapeleyn l'abbe de Beck Herlewyn qe come ses vilens de Okebourne fuissent nadgieres levez countre lui et ses ministres et ne vousisent a lui faire rentez, services ne coustumes ne autre attendaunce et mesme celui abbe, pur doute de mort de homme et pur resistence q'il ad trove et entent trover ne les osa prendre ne justicer pur les ditz services et coustumes, seur quoi autrefoiz pria a nostre dit seignur le roi assigner certeynes justices d'enquere de lour estat, et de lour port, et de la manere coment eux tiegnent et soleyent lour terres tenir, et nostre seignur le roi somonse eust assigne Sire Johan de Stonore, Sire Thomas de Luwe et William de Shareshull, ou deux de eux, to enquere des choses avantdites et de certefier la Chauncelerie de coe qe eus troverent en coe cas, les queux Sire Johan et William, par vertue du bref nostre seignur le roi a eux direct en la forme avauntdite, ont pris une enqueste et retourne en Chauncelerie, par quoi le dit abbe prie a nostre seignur le roi qe lui plest comaunder a son chaunceler q'il lui face ordener remedie covenable sour coe q'est trove par l'enqueste avaundite en Chauncelerie retourne come desuis est dit, auxibien pur l'estat et profuist nostre seignur le roi en temps de vacacionz del abbeye du Beck avaundit come du dit abbe en autre temps, et auxi come le roi de Fraunce autrefoiz a nostre dit seignur le roi pria par ses lettres.

No endorsement

1332. This petition, seeking remedy, followed the inquisition of 3 January 1332 in which the men of Ogbourne were found to be villeins of the abbot of Bec Hellouin and subject to tallage yearly (*CIM 1307–49*, no. 1269). The chancery warrant with which this petition was formerly enclosed is dated 28 January 1332 (no. 5198 of C 81/187). Various commissions of oyer and terminer were then issued in the dispute between the people of Ogbourne and the abbot of Bec, dated 18 May 1332 (*CPR 1330–4*, pp. 299, 347), 7 September 1333 (*CPR 1330–4*, p. 501) and 16 July 1334 (*CPR 1330–4*, p. 583). The king of France is Philip VI (1328–50). See also notes to **136** and **138**.

138

Bec Hellouin, Normandy, France (1334)
Benedictine
(SC 8/11/538)

Richard of Beausevall, proctor of the abbot of Bec Hellouin, petitions the king and council that the king order his chancellor to send a writ to Robert Selyman and Robert of Aston to stop their commission which was obtained by the villeins of the manor of Great Ogbourne concerning how the manor and church were granted to the abbey of Bec Hellouin, and what services and alms were made. Because the grant was made such a long time ago, there is no one alive who can know anything of it, and he is prepared to show the charter and confirmation when and where it pleases the council.
Endorsed: *He does not have any cause at all, nor does the petition advance anything by which the king ought to stop this commission.*

A nostre seignur le roi et a son consail prie Frere Richard de Beausevall, procuratour l'abbe de Bek [Herlewin en Engleterre, qe come Maud de Walyngford] dona les manoir et esglise de Grant Okebourne al abbe du Bek, tost apres le Conqueste, pur vestir les moignes [du dit lieu] du Bek, [en pure et] perpetuele aumoigne, par sa chartre, et lui et ses predecessours eient tenuz mesmes les manoir et esglise [puis son temps] en cea par la dite chartre et par confirmacioun des rois. Ore de novel, par procurement des vileins le dit abbe du dit manoir, est commissioun de soutz le grant sele issue hors de la Chauncelerie a Monsire Robert Selyman et Monsire Robert de Astone d'enquere coment les ditz manoir et esglise furent dones au dit abbe, et a queux services, et queles aumoignes faire, q'est [tout] countre resoun, depuis qe il les ad si longement tenuz, come desuis est dit, et ne puet sovenir a homme vivaunt de doun fait [si longe temps] passe. Qe lui plese commaunder a son chaunceler de faire bref as ditz Monsire Robert et Robert, de repeller la dite commissioun et [de surseer de] prendre l'enqueste suisdite, desicome il serra prest de mostrer les chartre et confirmacion avantdites ou et quant il plerra a nostre seignur le roi et a soun consail.

Endorsed: Il n'y ad mie cause en ceste peticion moter pur qoi le roi doit faire repeller cele commissioun.

1334. The petition is dated to the parliament of 1334 by its inclusion in a Hale manuscript containing petitions from this parliament (*RP*, II, 76, no. 17). The petitioner was appointed proctor-general in England by the abbot of Bec Hellouin on 15 October 1331 (*CPR 1330–4*, p. 184). For a letter by the same petitioner, see SC 8/346/E1394. Other petitions by the same petitioner are SC 8/11/537, SC 8/163/8137 and SC 8/305/15246.

Various commissions relating to the abbot's interests in Ogbourne can be found in the patent rolls (*CPR 1330–4*, pp. 299, 347, 501). The commission referred to in this petition may be the special commission of oyer and terminer issued to the inhabitants of Ogbourne in July 1334 (*CPR 1330–4*, p. 583), a response to their petition against the abbot of Bec (SC 8/63/3133). The right-hand side of the petition is badly damaged. Tentative readings have been taken from the Hale manuscript (*RP*, II, 76, no. 17). See also **136** and **137**.

139

Takeley, Essex (c. 1336)
Benedictine (alien)
(SC 8/296/14796)

To the chancellor from Andrew, prior of Takeley stating that, on the advice of Robert Farning, he expelled one Willliam Wychard of Takeley, bondsman, from a virgate of land in Takeley, for rebellion and withholding his customary services, which he did at the instigation of certain kinsmen of his in London. Wychard brought an oyer et terminer against the prior and his people, before John de Hildeslee and his companions at Stratford-le-Bow; and during this a great crowd of malefactors from London came to the prior's lodging, seeking to behead him, and he only just escaped by crossing the Thames in a boat to Kent. William's kin have also corrupted the inquiry through bribery; and strange people have come into the country asking about him and his people; and they have killed his steward. He asks that the case might be brought before the king so that he might have justice.

Endorsed: *[Deleted] The justices are to be ordered to have the record and process brought before the king.*

The justices are to be ordered that if the plea has been such as the petition claims, they are to send the record and process before the king, for the reasons contained in the same petition.

And the sheriff is to be ordered that if the prior finds security to appear before the king at the quinzaine of Easter next and to answer to the party, then he is to cease the exigent.

The keepers of the peace in Essex are also to be ordered that they are to do what belongs to their commission concerning those who killed the steward and brought about the other evils.

Au chaunceler nostre seignur le roy moustre et grevousement se pleynt Andreu, le povre priour de Takeleye, qe come il, par le cunseil et l'avisement de Robert Farnyng, eust ouste un William Wychard de Tackeleye, sun neyf, d'une verge de terre en Takelegh, quele il tynt de luy en vilenage, purceq'il fut rebel et retynt ses custages q'il \et ses auncestres/ soleit fere de tempe dount memorie ne court, par baudour d'asqune genz de sa parentes de Loundres, qe par reson veulent estre d'accele condicion queux le promistrent d'enfrancher, sur quel oster le dit Williem pora un oyr et terminer sur le dit priour et ses gentz, devant Mestre Johan de Hildeslee et ses cumpaignouns qe nadgeres sistrent a Stratford ate Bowe forqe treys leues de la cite de Loundres; en ces de la cite vyndrent a force et armes ove graunt multitude de mesfesours et le quistrent en son ostel demene pur lave decole, a quel temps il eschapa apeyne en son bat outre Tamise en Kent. Et ces qe furent de sun consel luyrent chesqun sa part apeyne ove la vie et a mesme le temps firent un nome en le bref venir par acord et pleder, et par une enqueste procure assistrent les damages a cink centz et xl marz, et donerent jour outre en mesme le leu, ore ice mardy apres demy quasreme, et quei pur doute qei sour lour argent ount acoily le viscompte devers eux, et procure un panel devant la meyn de leyntyme gentz,et done a eux a asqun xx s, a asqun xl s devant la meyn. Et estre ce pus les dit temps estranges gentz sunt venuz en le pays et se ont tenu en boys et privez passages en mucestes, demandantz apres le priour et ses genz de pastours souz boys, et ore ice judy en la seconde semayne de qasreme, un demy leu de sa mesoun a Takeleye ottiront sun seneschal qe solet sure ses busoynes, et unqore vont illees en boys et en autres paas getanz ly mesmes, et plusors de ses genz demandantz apres eux et la manere de lour estre et aler, par quoi, qe pur l'affray nageres a Stratford, qe pur la mort sun seneschal q'est si fresch, [qe] pur les manaces uncore fetz, qe pur l'amiste q'il ount du viscompte et ces qe ponent ses fedz et ses robes le ount refuse et wey.............. il net en ceste bosoygne et il ne put trover nul homine de court ne dels pays qe sache son droit qe ove luy ose ou voil................ pur riens q'il les put doner. Par quele meyntenance il issi destrut q'il ne poet vivre ne ad dont et s'il venist al leu san...................... qe seuent son droit, il serroit destrut et sa esglise desherite pur touz jours. Par quei il prie, pur Dieu, de pus qe vous estes chief .... de tute Engleterre et de la place q'est funtayne de remedie, q'il vous plese, en salvacion del estat de seynt esglise et de .... le parole devant nostre seygnur le roy en il puse dreit aver et con conseil mever.

Endorsed: [Deleted] Soit mande as justices q'il envoient record et proces devant le roi.
Soit mande as justices qe si un eit pledez come la peticion suggist, q'il envoient le record et proces par les cause contenuex en meisme la peticion devant le roi. Et sunt mande au viscont qe si le priour lui troesse seurete d'estre devant le roi a le quinzeyne de Pask procheyne avenir et de respoundre a la partie, adoncs surfeit del exigend.
Soit auxi mande as gardeyns de la pees en le countie d'Essex qe il faciet ce qe apent a lour commission endroit de ceux qi ont tuez le seneschal et purchacent les autres malx.

c. 1336. The petitioner was Andrew of Goue, prior, occurs 1320–40. The oyer and terminer was ordered against him on 20 July 1336 on Wychard's complaint (*CPR 1334–8*, p. 356), and an inquisition into the attack on the petitioner at Stratford-le-Bow was granted on the following 6 October (*CPR 1334–8*, p. 365). It was found by inquisition that Wychard was not a bondman of the manor of Takeley, and on 26 February 1339 the king ordered the justices to render judgement (*CCR 1339–41*, p. 103). On Thursday 24 June 1339, by a letter patent written in French at Canfield (Essex), William Wychard of Takeley acknowledged receipt from Brother Andrew prior of Takeley of twenty bolts [of cloth] and 20,000 [stalks] of linen (*vynt cheves et vynt myl de teale*), and the prior was quit. Sealed on a tag: the seal red, a lion with 'William Wychard' as legend. A fine impression. New College, Oxford, N.C. 13,120: T.C.268. For John Hildesley see *BRUO*, II, 933–4. The bottom right-hand corner of this petition is damaged.

140

Chertsey, Surrey (1377)
Benedictine
(SC 8/103/5106)

The abbot of Chertsey petitions the king and parliament for consideration of various matters and an order for a remedy. He shows how his abbey has manors appurtenant to its foundation by

the king's ancestors, and conjointly the tenants of Chobham, Frimley, Thorpe and Egham, held along with others of villein blood, and other bondsmen held at the petitioner's will, rendering each year rents, customary payments and services etc., as they were established, and more made since the foundation of the abbey by Frithewold and St Erkenwold in the year AD 722, and these rents, payments etc. have been held without interruption ever since until recently, when they were bought by malicious council, alliance and conspiracy by persons who acquired a patent called an exemplification, by which they supposed to have their freedom etc., which would destroy the abbey forever. When the petitioner by his officials wished to charge the tenants with their services (in winter as in summer), they were resisted and menaced with staves and other weapons, and threatened with the burning of the abbey and the killing of the monks. The petitioner then purchased a writ directed to the sheriff to distrain them and took distress by virtue of the said writ, and then they broke the said seizure on their own authority and threatened that if they did not have their way thousands of men in these lands would die.
Endorsed: *An answer is made to this petition among the general petitions of the Commons.*

A tresexcellent et tresredoute seignur nostre seignur le roi et a son noble counseil de parlement moustre et supplie humblement l'abbe de Certeseye en le countie de Surr', q'est del fundacion des progenitours nostre dit seignur le roi, qe come ils ont diverses manoirs appertinauntz a lour dit fundacion, entre queux les tenauntz de Chabeham, Fremele, Thorp, Egeham tiegnent lour tenure ascuns en vilenage de sang auncestrell et ascuns tiegnent par veige terre bonde al volente del dit abbe, paiant et rendant ent par an les rentz custumes et services duez et acustumez, sicome ils soloient et deveient faire puis la fundacion du dit abbeye, quel fust founde par Frithewold et Seint Erkenwolde, q'est a present translate en l'esglise cathedrale de Seint Poule de Londres, et cele fundacion du dit abbee fuist en l'an del incarnacion nostre seignur Jesu Crist DCCxxij, et mesmes les rentz, custumez et services ils ont bien faitz et lour auncestres, neifs et terretenantz, a volente avauntdit et sanz interrupcion, tanqe ore tarde q'ils ont purchace, par malveis counseil, aliaunce, confederacie de plusours de lour condicion des tenauntz des diverses seignurs, une patent appelle exemplificacion par quel ils bien supposent d'estre francz et de franc condicion, et q'ils ne deveient rien faire ne paier a lour seignur, mais tansoulement lour rentz et suite de court, sanz ascun altre custume ou service faire, le quel serroit destruction al dit abbeye a touz jours, et auxi anientisement del fundacion suisdit. Et si le dit abbe ne puisse avoir ses possessions, divine service ne puisse estre fait pur les progenitours nostre dit seignur le roi. Et quanqe le dit abbe, par ses ministres, voet avoir distreint ses tenantz suisditz pur faire lour services, sibien en yver com en estee et en Augst, ils par fort main ove lour alliaunce ont fait rescours et vegnent a force et armes, ove arrowes, bastones, gisarmes et autre armure, pur avoir tue les ministres du dit abbe et manacent pur ardre le dit abbeye et tuer les moignes en icelle. Et apres, pur cause de doute de lour malice, le dit abbe purchaceast un brief direct al vicunte de mesme le countie pur estre eidant a destreindre les ditz tenantz q'il fuist son office par son baillif erraunt, et il prist destresse pur vertue de dit brief, le quele fuist bien pres tue entre eux, et apres ils debruseront la dite areste de lour auctorite mesme and manacent overtement qe s'ils ne purront avoir lour purpos, qe mill des homes en ceste pais serront mortz. Quel vous pleise, pur Dieux et en oevre de charite, considerer les ditez matieres, mischiefs qe purront avener par les ditz causes si soit soeffre, et ent remedie ordiner solonc vostre noble excellent et graciouse discrecion.

Endorsed: A ceste peticion est responce faite en generaltes entre les comunes peticions.

1377. The petition was presented in the parliament of October 1377, where it informed the contents of a common petition and a subsequent statute: *PROME*, parliament of October 1377, item 88; *SR*, II, 2–3 (vi). On 18 May 1378 the resulting commission of oyer and terminer was appointed (*CPR 1377–81*, p. 251). The petitioner is John of Usk, abbot 1370–1400. Although the petition dates the abbey's foundation by St Erkenwald and Frithwald, subregulus of Surrey, to 722, other sources give different dates, including Capgrave's *Life of St Erkenwald* which dates the foundation to 630, the abbey's cartulary which dates it to 666 (*VCH Surrey*, II, 55 n. 1), and *The Chronicle of Florence of Worcester* which dates it to 756 (p. 25). The episode described here was the 'Great Rumour' of 1377; see R. Faith, 'The "Great Rumour" of 1377 and Peasant Ideology', in *The English Rising of 1381*, ed. R. H. Hilton and T. H. Aston (Cambridge, 1984), pp. 45, 53, 55, 57–8, 59, 73 and further references. For further discussion, see Introduction, pp. xxix–xxx. See also **210**.

141

Peterborough, Northamptonshire (c. 1381–2)

Benedictine
(SC 8/94/4698)

The abbot and convent of Peterborough petition the king and council that they be granted the correction of their tenants involved in the rebellion, or that another remedy is ordained so that the abbot and abbey are not destroyed and burnt by them in the future, and that no charter of pardon be granted to any of those indicted until they have made satisfaction for their rebellion. The rebels have been indicted before Lord Zouche by a commission of the king.

A nostre seignur le roi et a son bone counceil moustront vos chapeleyns l'abbe et covent de Bury Seynt Piere qe come plusurs de lour tenantz illoqes nadgairs al devery des rebelles demanderent del dit abbe et covent par bille endente diverse franchys, articlez et redresse encountre la comune lay par enbaudisment del venu des ditz rebelles, les qeux demandes vos ditz chapeleyns les ussent grantez encountre lour volunte, pur doute de morte et de arson si les tresreverent pier le evesqe de Norwych et le Seignur de la Zouche n'ussent venu, par la grace de Dieu, en le mesne temps, des qeux poyntz les ditz tenantz sont enditez devant le dit Seignur de la Zouche et ses compaignons par vostre comission. Plese a vostre tresdote seygnury real de granter al dit abbe la corection de ses ditz tenantz en cest mater, ou auterment d'ordeyner tiel remedy en cel case issint qe les ditz abbe et abbey, quel est del fundacion des vos tresnoblez progenitours, ne soyent destruytes et ars par tiels rebelles en temps a vener, et qe nule chartre de pardoun doit grantee a nule des ditz enditez devante q'ils ount fiat gree et satisfaccion as vos ditz chapellayns del rebellion et mespricion avanditz.

No endorsement

c. 1381–2. The petitioner is Henry of Overton, abbot 1361–91. The petition concerns the aftermath of the Peasants' Revolt, placing the petition in the latter half of 1381 or perhaps 1382, though the commission referred to may be one of those issued in early July 1381 (*CPR 1381–5*, p. 70). Lord Zouche is William la Zouche of Harringworth, justice of the peace for Northants. and Rutland following the Peasants' Revolt (*CPR 1381–5*, p. 64).

Henry Despenser was bishop of Norwich 1370–1406. An account of the suppression of the revolt in Peterborough by Despenser is given in *Knighton's Chronicle 1337–1396*, ed. G. H. Martin (Oxford, 1995), pp. 224–7. For a similar petition from the bishop and prior of Ely, see **63**. Further discussion of this case is in Introduction, p. xxx.

142

Ely, Cambridgeshire (? 1426)
Benedictine
(SC 8/164/8185)

The prior and convent of Ely petition the council for remedy against John Greenlaw, John Marsh, John James and John Cully of Haddenham. The king's progenitors were seised from time of memory of £250 10s ½d of recognisances of the free and customary tenants of the bishopric of Ely in times of vacancy of the same bishopric, which King Edward by his letters patent granted to the prior's predecessor and the convent forever, rendering to the king and his heirs £2000 every year that the bishopric is vacant. When the said prior wished to levy £8 from the customary tenants of Haddenham for the last vacancy, two hundred men came against him with force and arms on 28 April 1426, led by Greenlaw, Marsh, James and Cully, and rang the common bell of the vill, and when John Prior came to Haddenham bearing a letter from the duke of Exeter commanding Greenlaw to cease all riots, they imprisoned him for a day and night, took 6s 2d from his purse and treated him badly, so that the prior and his ministers will not come to Haddenham to levy the said £8, for fear of their lives.

A noble et tresage counseyll nostre sovereyn seignur le roi suppliount humblement voz povres oratoures et chapellynes le priour et covent d'Ely, qe suent sibien pur nostre seignur le roy come pur eux mesmes, qe come lez nobles progenitoures nostre soverayne seignur le roy fuerount seisy de tout temps dount memore ne court de CCl li x s obole de recognicions dez tenauntez frankes et custumarie de l'evescherie d'Ely checun temps de voidaunce de mesme l'evecherie, come plainement apeirt de record en l'Escheker nostre soverayne seignur le roy, et coment Edward, jadis roy d'Engleterre, progenitour a nostre seignur le roy qe ore est, par sez lettres patentez graunta al predecessour le dit ore priour et a le covent de mesme le lieu l'evescherie comander et toutz lez temporaltees de mesme l'evescherie, a avoir et tenir a eux et lour successours a checun voidaunce del dit evescherie a toutz joures, reddaunt ent a dit nadgairs Roy Edward et a sez heires checun an qe le dit evescherie serra voide MM li, come en lez ditz lettres patentez du dit nadgaires Roy Edward est continues plus apleyn. Et pur ceo qe le dit priour par cez ministres voillet leve et destreine pur viij li due au dit priour dez tenauntez custumares de Hadenham pur cest darrein voidaunce del dit evescherie, la Johan Grenelaue de Hadenham, Johan Merssh, Johan James, Johan Cully et plusours autres de mesme la ville disconyous a la somme de CC hommes, ove force et armes, c'estassavoir espees, bokeleres, arkes, cestes, gleynes et pichforkes, le xxviij jour d'Aprill l'an nostre seignur le Roy Henri qe ore est, qe Dieu garde, quart, a Hadenham avaundit en le counte de Cantebr', oriblement en countre la pees nostre seignur le roy, par le excitacion et comaundement du ditz Johan Grenelaue, Johan Merssh, Johan James et Johan Cully, soy liverount et lez comunes campanes de mesme la ville a hauk pulserount, et eu un Johan Priour, servaunt au dit priour d'Ely et portour d'un lettre de noble prince le duke

d'Excestre a dit Johan Grenelaue direct, luy comaundaunt de par le roy de cesser de toutz maneres ryotes et congregaciouns de pepil nostre seignur le roy, assaut firount, et luy a Hadenham avaundit pristerount, et par un jour et un noet illoqes imprisonerount, et vj s ij d de sa burse pristerount, et malement treterount, en taunt qe le dit priour ne ces ministres noiserount ne oisent venir a le dit ville de Hadenham pur lever les avaunditz viij li pur doute de lour mort, si noun due remedie soit purveu par vostrez sages discrecions cele parti. Que please a vostres tresages discrecions de considerer lez premisses, et veresemble disheriticion et prejudice qe puist avenir sibien a nostre soverayne seignur le roy come as ditz suppliauntz, et sur ceo de purveier covenable remedie au ditz suppliauntz, pur Dieu et en oevere de charite.
Pleges de prosecution: Johannes Rowe; Thomas Parsouns.

No endorsement

? 1426. The petitioner is Peter of Ely, prior 1425–c.1429. The duke of Exeter is Thomas Beaufort.

143

Combe, Warwickshire (1427)
Cistercian
(SC 8/25/1233)

The abbot of Combe petitions the king and Lords in parliament, stating that he had, by charters of the king's progenitors and by prescription, view of frankpledge in the vill of Wolvey of both his abbey's tenants and of Giles Astley and his tenants, until the view held at Easter last when Astley and his tenants withdrew from the view and were amerced and assessed according to the law. Astley and his men have assaulted the abbot's servants and tried to kill him and his servants. The abbot has a warrant from the justices of the peace of the county for the arrest of Astley and the others to find sureties to keep the peace, but the officers dare not execute the warrant. The abbot requests that he be granted a writ, by authority of parliament, under certain pain, directed to the sheriff of the county, ordering him to proclaim in the vill that Astley and the others should appear in chancery and make certain sureties to keep the peace under certain pain, and that the abbot and his servants be able to go about their affairs. If they fail to appear he requests that the chancellor issue another writ directed to the sheriff for them to be taken and put in the county gaol until they pay the fine and find sureties in the aforesaid form.
Endorsed on face: *To Lord Gloucester, 12 October.*
It should be sent to the Lords.
Endorsed: *For the notable causes within the petition, it is ordained by authority of parliament that proclamation be made in the vill of Wolvey that Giles Astley and the others appear before the king in chancery on 12 December next, each of them under £100, to find sufficient surety to keep the peace towards the abbot and other lieges of the king. The £100 is to be forfeit to the king from each of them if they do not appear, and another process is to be made against them in accordance with the wishes of the petition.*

Au roy nostre tressoveraigne seignur et a les seignurs espirituelx et temporelx de cest present parlement supplie humblement l'abbe del esglise de Nostre Dame de Combe en le countee de Warrwyk que come le dit abbe et sez predecessours, sibien par lez chartres dez progenitours nostre seignur le roy come par temps dont memorie ne court, et par allouaunce devaunt justices en Eire, ount ewe et use pesiblement deinz la ville de Wolvey deinz le dit countee vewe de francplegge et tout ceo q'a vewe de francplegge appartient, come de droit de lour dite esglise, sibien de lour propres tenauntz illeoqes resceantz come de Gyles Asteley, esquyer, et sez tenauntz et resceauntz illeoqes, et de lour auncestres et lour tenauntz illeoqes resceantz; tanqe ore tarde, a un viewe de francplegge tenuz illeoqes apres la Paske darrain passe par le seneschalle del dit abbe, qe le dit Gyles fist toutz sez tenauntz illeoqes resceauntz, eux retraier et absentier del dite viewe, par qi ils furent amerciez et apres affierez solonc ceo qe la ley demaunde. Le quell abbe apres, par un Bawdewyn Motley, esquyer, et soun servant, fist distreindre un dez ditz tenauntz del dit Gyles par sez avers pur soun amerciment, la quelle distresse mayntenaunt, al request del priour de Coventre, par le dit abbe fuist delivere al dit tenaunt, saunz ascune processe de ley ou damage de luy; et nient obstant la livere suisdit, mayntenant apres le dit Gyles et un Thomas Blankamy, soun servant, ymaginant pur destruer le dit abbe et sez servantz, et pur luy et sa esglise avauntdite dis.....er firent un George Astley, fitz le dit Gyles, et un Johan Tailour de Wolvey, tailour, et auters disconuz, eux araier ove force et armes a feere de guerre, et de gisser es diversees lieus en agaite del dit abbe et sez servantz, et en la dite ville de Wolvey al dit Bawdewyn soy mesmes illeoqes chevachant assaut firent, et sa mayn sinestre illeoqes ove force couperont, et diverses horribles plaies luy adonqes doneront, par ont il mayme pur toutz jours; et auxint lez ditz George et Thomas, et un William Asteley, auter dez fitz le dit Gyles, ove auters diverses persones disconuz, ailent de jour en auter en la dite ville, armes et arraiez a feere de guerre, a tuer le dit abbe et sez servauntz, par issint q'il est en dispere de sa vie, et pur luy mettre en si graund doute q'il enapres ne prendra ascune distresse pur ascun tiel amerciment, en desheritaunce del dit abbe et de sa esglise a toutz jours, s'il n'eit remedie en ycest parlement; et auxint nient contresteant qe les dit abbe ad ewe garantz des justices del pees de mesme le countee, d'avoir arestuz lez ditz Gyles, George, Thomas, William et Johan, a trover surete del pees, lez officers illoeqes n'oseront pur doute de lour vies executer les garantz avauntditz. Que please a nostre soveraigne seignur le roy et toutz seignurs espirituelx et temporelx de cest present parlement de grauntier un brief al dit abbe, par auctorite de parlement, sur certein peyne par vous a limitier, envers les ditz Gyles, George, Thomas, William et Johan, directz al viscounte del dit countee, q'il face proclamacion en la dite ville q'ils appargent en la Chauncery nostre seignur le roy et certeyn jour en le dit brief limite, de trover al dit abbe et toutz les liegez nostre dit seignur le roy sufficeant suerete de la pees, su certein peyne par vous a limitier envers lez ditz Gyles, George, Thomas, William et Johan, directz al vicounte deldit countee, q'il face proclamacioun en la dite ville q'ils appargent en la Chauncery nostre seignur le roy et certeyn jour en le dit brief limitez, et trove al dit abbe et toutz lez liegez nostre dit seignur le roy sufficient suerete de la peer ssur certeyn peyne par vous ent a limitier; parissint qe le dit abbe et sez servauntz puissent peisiblement alier entour lour affairs; et s'ils n'appargent my al jour del dit brief retourne en la dite Chauncery, q'ils forfacent a roy la dite peyne en le dit brief limitee, et \autre/ brief de *capias* par le chaunceller agarde, direct al dit vicounte, de eux prendre, et en la gaole nostre seignur le roy del dit countee mettre, tanqe ils eient paiez al roy le dit fyne, et auxint q'ils trovent seurete en la fourme avauntdeit, et qe celle suerete soit retourne arere par le vicounte en la dite Chauncerye.

Endorsed on face: Domino Glouc', xxij die Octobris.
Soit baille as seignurs.
Endorsed: Pur les notables causes dedeinz escriptz, ordinez est et assentuz par auctorite de cest parlement qe proclamacioun soit fait en la ville de Wolvey dedeinz especifiez qe Gyles Asteley, George Asteley, Thomas Blankamy, William Asteley et Johan Taillour, en ceste peticion nomez, appiergent devaunt le roi en sa Chauncellerie le xij jour de Decembre proschein avenir, chescun de eux sur peine de C li, a trover sufficeante seurtee de pais al abbe de Combe dedinz escript, et toutz auters lieges du roi. La quelle somme de C li ordinez est d'estre forfait au roi par checun des ditz Gyles, George, Thomas, William and Johan s'ils n'appiergent mye en la dite Chancerie al dit jour en la forme susdite; et qe enoutre, processe soit fait envers mesmes les Gyles, George, Thomas, William et Johan en manere et forme come il est desire par mesme la peticioun.

1427. On 13 December 1427 the sheriff of Warwickshire was ordered to arrest Astley and the others following their failure to appear in chancery (*CCR 1422–9*, p. 355). The identity of the petitioner is unknown. The prior of Coventry was Richard Crosby (1398–1437). Lord Gloucester is Humphrey of Lancaster, duke of Gloucester. An earlier edition of the petition is printed in *RP*, IV, 365–366, no. 6.

4.3 Inter-house strife

144

Bromholm, Norfolk (1305)
Cluniac
(SC 8/276/13761)

To the king from the prior and convent of Bromholm, who are of the king's patronage and subject to no religious house except insofar as they are of the profession, rule and order of the abbot of Cluny, requesting a writ ordering the priors of Lewes and Castle Acre to cease from their distraint of the petitioners, made at the abbot of Cluny's order on pain of excommunication of their monks, to pay 30s to an alien named Heymes to support a plea, which he is suing at the Court of Rome and elsewhere, to enter the priory of Thetford, which he claims of the abbot's gift, since they have never before aided other houses in tallages, contributions for the support of pleas or anything else.
Endorsed: *Because the priory is of the king's patronage, a writ of chancery should be sent to the priors of Lewes and Castle Acre prohibiting them from demanding anything etc. without consulting the king.*

Le priur e le covent de Bromholm, qe sunt del avowerie nostre seignur le roy, prient grace e remedie qe par la ou priur ne moigne \pot/ estre en la meson \ de Bromholm/ fors de lur eleccion e alur volente demeigne, ne nule rens ne funt de pension, ne de contribucion, ne de taliage, ne subjeccion, ne de vent a nule meson de religion fors entaunt qe heus sunt de la profession, e de la reule, e del ordre le abbe de Cluny, sicome yl pot estre trove apertement al Escheker par record, qe nostre seignur \le roy/ hi maunda, dunt sire Wiliam de Carletone prist l'en queste par bref nostre seignur le roy, le quel record fu lyvere al Escheker le an xxiiij terme de Seint Hillarie, par la venent les priurs de Lewes e de Chastelacre par maundement le abbe avaunt dit e destreinent par escomenger les moignes de Bromholm avant ditz a paeer xxx s a un Dauntz Heymes, alyen, a sustenaunce de un plai qe yl suet a la curt de Rome e aliours pur aver entre en la priurie de Theford, qe yl cleyme del doun le abbe avant dit. Dunt le priur e le covent de Bromholm prient bref a les priurs de Lewes e de Chastelacre qe heus cessent del execucion avant dite, de sicome unqes rens ne eiderent a autres mesons de taliages, de contribuciouns pur pletz sustenir, ne pur autres aventures qe unqes avant ces hures vindrent.

Endorsed: Quia prioratus est de advocacione regis, fiat breve de Cancellaria prioribus de Lewes et de Castellacre, per quod prohibeatur eis ne aliquid petant etc. rege inconsulto.

1305. The petitioner was William of Tuttington, prior, occurs 1304–13. Stephen of Sancto Romano was prior of Lewes (1302–7). The petition was enrolled on the parliament roll: *PROME*, Edward I, Roll 12, item 130 (126). On 12 January 1296 it was ordered that the priory should be restored to its prior and convent, since it was found by inquisition that the latter were Englishmen and not aliens (*CCR 1288–96*, p. 469).

145

Dunwich, Suffolk (1306)
Hospital
(SC 8/43/2112)

The chaplains and brothers of the chapel of Dunwich (Holy Trinity or Maison Dieu) petition the king, stating that one William Licequen, who served the chapel, stole a valuable cross and other relics from them, and carried them off to the abbey of St Osyth. They ask the king to make the abbot of St Osyth return the cross and relics.
Endorsed: *In chancery. By the chancellor.*

A nostre seignur le rey mustrent les chapeleyns e ses freres de sa chapelle de Donewiz ke la ou yl aveyont une preciouse croyz a ky graunt aport vynt dount yl aveyont tote lur sostenaunce, un Williame Licequen, ky servi la chapelle avauntdyte, cele croyz ou autre relikes pryst e enporta a le abbeye de Seynt Osith, et clokkes si rendy chanonye, dount yl ont perdu le aport e les offrendes ke ylokes seleyt \en/ venyr, par quey yl sont devenu poveres e mendinaunz, dount yl pryent lur segnur le rey ke yl volye de sa grace \fere/ ke le vaunt dyt abbe la vauntdyte croyz e les autres relikes ke si torcenousement furont enporte e en sa mesoun recetes a sa chapelle avauntdyte face restorrer.

Endorsed: In Cancelleria. Per cancellarium.

1306. On 4 November 1306 the king restored to Adam de Brome, master of the hospital of God's House, Dunwich, the stolen cross, returned to him by the abbot of St Osyth (*CCR 1302–7*, p. 423). The abbot of St Osyth was 'David' who occurs 1303–16. The hospital received letters of protection for a year 24 October 1304; on 30 May 1306 Adam de Brome, king's clerk, was appointed master for life in place of Robert de Sefeld, who was removed; on 3 June 1306 protection for the house was renewed for a year, *CPR 1301–7*, pp. 265, 438, 439. The successful result of this petition was perhaps due to Adam de Brome being a king's clerk, who later (1326) founded Oriel College, Oxford (*BRUO*, I, 274–5).

146

Elstow, Bedfordshire (c. 1307)
Benedictine (nuns)
(SC 8/202/10100)

The abbess of Elstow petitions the council for a remedy concerning a royal highway which she and her people have between Elstow and the king's town of Bedford. The master of the hospital of St Leonard's in Bedford purchased a writ, in the time of the late king, to inquire into what damage would come to the people of the country if he enclosed the highway; and the inquisition found that this would obstruct the nuns and their people. The matter was brought before the king and council at Carlisle, and, through the procurement of Walter of Molesworth, then sheriff of Bedfordshire, and the maintenance of Walter Langton, then treasurer of England, the then chancellor was instructed to give the brothers a charter to obstruct the highway; with the result that they have done so, with force and arms.
Endorsed: *She is to sue to the next parliament. But she is to have a writ of* venire facias *from chancery to have the master of St Leonard's appear there with the charter that he has concerning the contents of the petition, and to answer to this claim before the council there.*

Au conseil nostre seignour le roi prie l'abbesse de Elmestouwe pur lui e pur son gentz remedie, qe la ou lui e ses gentz aveient roial chemin adresces de la vile de Elmestouwe desqes a la vile le roi de Bedeford a marcher a pes, a cheval e a charette, la est venu le meestre de Seint Leonard e les freres de meimes le lu e unt purchace un bref le roi en tens nostre seignour le roie qi mort est, a queu dammage des genz du payis l'estopeure serreit se il eussent le roial chemin enclos, dount il aveient bref d'enqueste d'enquerre devaunt Sire Roger de Heghham e Sire Henri Spigornel, par quele enqueste il fu trovee si l'estoupement fu fait q'il serreit nusaunt a nuli, dount il fu trove q'il fu nusaunt a les dites dames e a lor genz de aler plus lointein d'une quarenteine, la quele enqueste fu retournee en Chauncelerie e la Chauncelerie mist l'enqueste devaunt le conseil le roi a Cardoil, e la devaunt le conseil l'enqueste veuwe e oyie a la sute des freres avauntditz. E pur ceo q'il fu trove par meisme l'enqueste q'il feust a nusaunce a l'abbesse e a ses genz, si fu l'enqueste regetee e la chartre le roi des freres destourber desqes a taunt qe meillour enqueste fu feete, e saunz aver regard a cele nusaunce qe fu trovee par procurement de Wauter de Molesworthe, adonqes vescount de Bedeford, e par la meintenaunce Wauter de Langetone, adonqes tresorer, fist comaunder au chaunceler qe adonqes estoit q'il seist la chartre le roi as ditz freres pur cel roial chemyn estouper, par force de quele chartre memes les freres du dit hospital a force e a armes de nuyt e de jour unt cel roial chemyn enclos. Pur quei la dite abbesse prie a nostre seignour le roi remedie desicome par l'enqueste fu trovee qe l'estoperurre serreit a nusaunce, par quei l'enqueste si regetee e les ditz freres unqes autre enqueste ne suirent puis mes per la chartre le roi pur Wauter de Molesworth e par Wauter de Langetone, adonqes tresorer, lor meintenours, unt estopee a force e a armes de nuyt e de jour, e unqore par memes la force detenent estopee, dount la dite abbesse au counseil nostre seignur le roi prie remedie.

Endorsed: Servatur ad \proximum/ parliamentum, set habeat breve de Cancellaria de venire facias ibidem magistrum[30] Sancti Leonardi cum carta quam habet de contentis in peticione, et ad respondum coram consilio ibidem ad suggestionem istam.

c. 1307. The petitioner was Clemence of Balliol, abbess 1294–1314. Robert Cuppe was master of St Leonard's, Bedford, 1294–1310. Walter of Molesworth was sheriff of Bedfordshire from November 1297 to October 1307, from May 1308 to October 1309, and from October 1312 to April 1313. In 34 Edward I (1305–6) the inquisition mentioned was held into whether the master and brothers could enclose the highway (C 143/62/17). On 21 June 1307 they were granted licence to enclose this highway, provided that they made another on their own land (*CPR 1301–7*, p. 531). From the mention of the late king, this petition clearly dates from early in Edward II's reign. Walter Langton was treasurer until 22 August 1307.

147

Bardney, Lincolnshire (? 1307–10)
Benedictine
(SC 8/31/1545)

The prior and convent of Bardney petition the king for a protection with the clause concerning pleas for their abbot, who is overseas, to last until Pentecost, as the prior of Sempringham and others have brought various writs against him, and plan to take him in some default in his absence; and if he were in the country he would have various muniments to help him, which cannot be acquired in his absence. They also ask the king to continue a general attorney until the aforesaid term.
The prior and convent of Bardney petition the king, stating that monks who have been excommunicated are trying to enter the monastery in the absence of the abbot, by a false suggestion and by the fault of Robert of Lacy, official of Canterbury and canon of their mother church of Lincoln, which will prevent them from conducting divine service as they ought. They request that the king order the official to do common justice to the abbot in the matter of his pleas which are before him between him and his monks, so that no harm comes to the abbey in the absence of the abbot. They also ask that the pleas between the abbot and his monks be determined in Court Christian.
Endorsed: *To the first: he is to have a protection without the clause.*
To the second: he is to have a letter to Master Robert of Lacy. For the rest, nothing is to be done.

A nostre seigneur le roi priont le priur et le covent de Bardnay qu'il voille graunter sa protections ove la clause des pletz pur lur abbe qui est outre meer, adurer jesqes a la Pentecost, par ceo qe le priur de Sempyngham et autres unt port sure ly divers brefs et ly quidont susprendre par ascun defaute en sa absence. Et si le abbe fust en pays, il trovereit plusurs munimentz parly as queus nul homme puit avoir avant sa venue. Et auxi qe nostre seigneur le roi voille cuntinuer un general attornetz adurer jesqes au terme avantditz.

A nostre seigneur le roi mustrent le priur et le covent de Bardnay qe les moygnes qui sunt escomanges pur lur commune seal et lur biens emportes et pur autres trespasses qu'il unt fet a la meson avantdit, des queus isint ateyntz en partye et en

30 *priorem* deleted and *magistrum* written above.

partye ateyntz serrunt voyllent entrer lur mesone en la absence le abbe par une fause sugestione et par favur de Mestre Robert de Lacy, official de Caunterbirs et chanun de la mere eglise de Nicol, et s'il aveigne qu'il entrent la mesone les moygnes qui iloqes sunt pur Dieu servir ne pount chaunter ne le service Dieu fere pur nostre seigneur le roi et pur ses auncestres ne pur nul autre ausi come eus deyveit pur la sentence avantdite. Dount il priunt pur Dieu a nostre seigneur le roi, desicome il unt nul autre suvereyn et mayntenur de leur mesone en la absence lur abbe, qu'il voille maunder al official avantdit qu'il face commun dreyt al dit abbe endreyt de ses plees que sunt devant ly entre ly et ses moignes, issink qe nul damage ne moleste aveigne a la mesone de Bardnay en la absence le abbe. Et outre ceo qe les plees soient terminez entre l'avantdit abbe et ses moygnes de divers trespasses en curte cristiene.

Endorsed: Ad primam: habeat proteccionem sine clausula.
Ad secundum: habeat litteram Magistro Roberto de Lascy. De aliis nichil fiat.

? 1307–10. These are two separate petitions sewn together. In each case the absent abbot is Robert of Wainfleet, who was elected in 1280, deposed in 1303, restored in 1311, and finally resigned in 1318. The requests probably date to 1307, when a simple protection until Whitsunday was granted to Robert, abbot of Bardney, who was staying overseas (*CPR 1301–7*, p. 495). In 1310 a similar protection until Whitsunday was granted to Robert of Wainfleet, 'who calls himself Abbot of Bardney', going to the court of Rome (*CPR 1307–13*, p. 277), but as the petitioners clearly state that their abbot is already overseas, a date of 1307 seems much more likely. The prior of Sempringham was John of Hamilton (1298–1324). For the outline of the bitter and long-running dispute between Wainfleet, other members of the house, and Bishop Dalderby see *Heads of Houses II*, 20–1. Wainfleet was deposed by Dalderby in 1303 but the case did not end until his resignation in 1318. See also TNA, Significations of Excommunication, C 85/1786/3, and D. F. Logan, *Runaway Religious in Medieval England, c. 1240–1540* (Cambridge, 1996), p. 186. The case features extensively in Dalderby's memoranda register (LAO, Lincoln Register III), and is further discussed in the Introduction, p. xl.

148

St Julian by St Albans, Hertfordshire (? c. 1309)

Hospital
(SC 8/142/7075)

The sick brothers of the hospital of St Julian by St Albans petition the king and council, stating that although their hospital was founded by one Geoffrey, abbot of St Albans, the present abbot is harrassing and oppressing them, and acting contrary to their charters and privileges in many ways. And now, because of certain claims on behalf of the estate of their house made by some of them before the abbot, he has ordered them to leave and to give him the keys to their chambers and common coffer; and because they would not do this, he has had Walter of Aylesbury, his brother Hugh, William of Windsor and others throw them out by force, break into their house and take their possessions; and the abbot has carried off their charters. They request upright men and loyal justices to inquire into the truth of these molestations, and of other things of which they will inform them, and to do full justice to them.
Endorsed: *The justices assigned to hear and take the assizes are to be assigned.*

Ces mustrons a nostre seignur le roy et a son conseil les povres freres malades del hospital de Seint Julian de hors la vile de Seint Auban ke la ou meimes il hospital est funde de un Gofre, jadis abbe de Seint Auban, predecessur meymes cesti abbe ke ore est, e feffe de luy e del covent de une porcione de terre la ou lur hospital est asis. Dunt nul se doit entremettre de denz meimes cel hospital fore ke eus e lur ministres les queus il voleit la mettre. Et ja de novel est cesti abbe ke ore est venuz en contre lur chartres e lur privileges, e lur fet grant tort e duresce en mult [demercieres] e lur mette sur mult de maneres de trespas ke unkes ne furent fet pense ne parle pur ous grever. E pur ceo ke les uns de eus alegerent devant le abbe pur lestat de lur mesone, il les comande voyder la mesone e rendre a luy les clefs de lur chambres e de lur comune cofre, de lur chartres e de lur propre biens demanda la veue. Et pur ceo ke eus ne li volaient ceste chose fere, il comande certyne genz engettre les hors de lur mesone, les queus mistrent main maliciousement en les avant diz freres e les engeterent hors de lur mesone a tort e sanz jugement, ceo est saver, Gauter de Aylesbire, Hue son frere, William de Wyndeshoure e autres, treis freres detenent de hors les queus alerent hors a lur comandement, e lur va e lur serures debriserent, e lur propres chateus pristrent e en porterent a la value de lx li et x s de plus, dunt il i avoit en une cofre xxxvj li et ix s le mone, et ix li de or, e quatre livres del perrus ke fust a les vant diz Wauter e Hue. E ja de novel, quant lez ministres le roy vindrent pur seeler cofres puis ke les freres furent enchacez dist lur fust li e il troveraient en viro cele cofre tresor al oes le roy, e vindrent e troverent cele cofre desclose e voyde sanz or e argent. E puis ke le vant dist abbe ad debrise la servire de la commune cofre de lur chartres e lur privileges[31], e lur chartres prist e en porta par la ou il veleit. Dunt les avant diz freres malades prient a nostre seignur le roy, pur Deu e pur les almes de ses auncestres, k'il lur voil granter prodes homes \e loaux/ justise asignez de enquerre la verite del avant diz torz e grevances en le avant dist hospital, e des autres choses les queus il lur frunt a saver a lur venue de si cum il sunt febles genz e mult malades ki ne prent ayllurs sute fere e ke il lur face plener dreyture pur Deu.

Endorsed: Assignantur justicii ad assisas audiendum capiendum assignati.

? c. 1309. On 17 June 1309 it was ordered that letters patent be made that nothing should be taken from the hospital while Walter de Langley was warden (*CCW 1244–1326*, p. 293). This probably relates to the dispute. If so, the petition dates to the interregnum between abbots John de Maryns 1302–9 and Hugh of Eversden 1309–27. Walter of Aylesbury was possibly the former royal justice of that name, though this cannot be proved (*VCH Herts.*, IV, 456 n. 4). The hospital's founder was Geoffrey de Gorron, abbot 1119–46.

149

Dover, Kent (1319)
Benedictine
(SC 8/145/7210)

The sub-prior and convent of Dover petition the king and council for remedy because, although by the terms of the charter of Henry II they are exempt from any jurisdiction except that of the archbishop of Canterbury, during the last vacancy, after the death of Robert of Winchelsey,

31 *E lur privileges* has been written a second time, and then deleted.

the prior of Holy Trinity (Canterbury) attempted to exercise jurisdiction over them. The prior complained to the king about this impairment of his crown and dignity, and the king sent a writ of prohibition to the prior of Holy Trinity. He ignored it, however, and excommunicated the prior and officers, put their churches under interdict, and sequestrated their goods and benefices. He then arranged for the new archbishop to put this sentence into execution, and now, during a vacancy in the priory, will not let the monks have their prior.

A nostre seignur le roi et a son conseil mustrent ces povres chapeleyns moignes suppriour et covent de sa eglise de Seint Martyn de Dovre qe come le Roi Henri Secund, progenitour nostre seignur le roi q'ore est, dona et granta et par sa chartre conferma a Dieu et al eglise de Caunterbirs, et a Tebaud adonqe ercevesqe, et a touz ses successours, la eglise de Seynt Martyn de Dovre ove les auncien provandres annexes a l'avauntdite eglise de Seynt Martyn, et meismes celui roi ordeina et par sa riale auctorite comanda qe ordre de moigne en la dite eglise de Seynt Martyn de Dovre par l'autorite Innocent, adonqe pape, et de dit Tebaud, adonqe ercevesqe, fust institucioun solonc la reule de Seynt Benet de cel hour en avaunt par durablement fust garde qe la dite eglise de Seynt Martyn remeyndreit en la meyn et la seignurye le dit ercevesqe et de ses successours, et qe les ditz moignes de Dovre fusent exemptes de chescune manere jurisdiccion ordinarie et especiale mes qe del ercevesqe tant soulement, et nul autre usunt dispositour ne ordeinour de temporaute ne des spirituaute mes qe soul ercevesqe, et qe en temps de vacacion del avantdite eglise de Caunterbirs totes choses fusent reservez al ercevesqe avenir, sicom piert plus pleynement par privileges de papes confermez. Et me qe la dite eglise de Seynt Martyn et les ditz moignes de meismes le leu faisent et sount issi exemptes, le priour de La Trinite de Canterbirs en la dreyne voidaunce apres la mort Robert de Wynchelse, adonqe ercevesqe, fist somoundre le priour de Dovre en le dit leu exempt, et lui defendre qe nul moigne en la priorie de Dovre fust resceu saunz assent et examinement du dit priour et le chapitle de la Trinite de Canterbirs, ne nul moigne de dit priorie de Dovre aillours q'en la dite eglise de Canterbirs fust profes, et taunt par la reson de la priourte come de les provandres apurtenantis en teu manere, come avant est dit, exemptz obedience demanda du dit priour et de les moygnes de Dovre, ovesqes autres charges grevouses meyns dreitureles. Et pur ceo qe le dit priour et le covent de Dovre ne poient ne volerent teux choses faire, qe sonereit emblemisement de la coroune et la dignite le roi et en prejudice des ercevesqes avenir, et en defesaunce de lour monimentz du roi et des papes a eux grantez, le dit priour de Dovre cestes grevances au roi et a son conseil moustra, et par nostre seignur le roi fust comande au dit priour de Dovre q'il ne feit chose qe trovast en prejudice au roi ou al ercevesqe avenir durant la vacacion, et defendu fust au dit priour de Caunterbirs par bref de prohibiccion nostre seignur le roi q'il fait rien en countre l'eglise et les dites moignes de Dovre, les queux nostre seignur le roi dist estre exemptz devers lui et devers chescun autre juge ordinarie; le dit priour de La Trinite de Canterbirs nule eaunt consideracion au premesses, cest asaver au comandement nostre seignur le roi, ne a lour monimentz de roi et de papes qe les fait de dit priour et d'en chapitle de Canterbirs, et de touz autres jugges ordinaries exemptz, le dit priour et les unes officers de la dite meson de Dovre escomenge, et les eglises et leur biens en teu manere exemptz entredit, et les frutz et benefitz sequestra, et les sentences par luy par mestre Hughe de Forsham, en cel partie soen commissari, par totes les plus solempn lues de la diocise de Canterburs, issi escomenge les fist pronuncier duraunt tote la vacacion del ercevesche, et a ceo ne voleit le dit priour de Canterbirs cesser qe en agreggement de plus grant male al avantdite meson de Dovre procura l'ercevesqe qe il \la/ sentence a eux done en temps de la vacacion en execion [*sic*] mandaste. Et ore a lour present voidaunce de lour priourte de Dovre, de la fest de Seynt Lucie dreyne passe tanqe a cest jour, ad les dites moignes de Dovre destourbe q'il ne peussent lour priour aver, solomc Dieu et reson, et procure l'ercevesqe, en countre chescune manere de droit, et en countre la forme et la volunte de lour primer foundour, et possession en et use de fine un moigne de la Trinite priour en la priourte de Dovre, come avant ces hours ount eu par la ordinaunce de ces predecessours, et est tenu par son serment et profession de ceo faire totes cestes choses par le dit priour de La Trinite sount faites et uncorez conteinuz, en grant blemisement de la coroune et en arerisement des aumoignes et des autres biens faitz pur nostre seignur le roi et ces auncestres, foundours de la dite meson de Dovre, et en prejudice del ercevesqe, et damage des avauntditz suppriour et covent de Dovre de mille marcs. Dount les avantditz suppriour et le covent de Dovre prient, pur Dieu et par seynte charite, qe remedi lour seit face.

No endorsement

1319. Prior Robert of Wetacre died in 1318. On 3 June 1319 the petitioner, Ralph of Walmer, subprior of Dover, was granted custody of the priory during pleasure as a result of this petition (*CPR 1317–21*, p. 339), until the appointment of the new prior, John of Sholden, in 1321. Walter Reynolds, who had succeeded Robert of Winchelsey as archbishop of Canterbury in 1318, was granted the advowson of the priory unconditionally in 1320, with the proviso that henceforth the prior was to be chosen from among the monks of the priory, and that in times of voidance, if the archbishopric was also void, the subprior would have custody of the priory (*CPR 1317–21*, p. 531). Holy Trinity, Canterbury, did not, however, give up their claims against the priory; and Archbishop Islip made an ordinance on 20 May 1350, confirmed by the king on 26 May, clarifying the complex relationship and obligations between the two religious houses (*CPR 1348–50*, pp. 508–9). Henry of Eastry was prior of Holy Trinity 1285–1331. This petition forms one of a number of related documents on this issue in SC 8 (8/82/4093; 128/6383 and 6387; 257/12847; 259/12911; 264/13198 and 13199; 267/13302; 278/13877). The dependent status of Dover Priory was also the subject of litigation at the Roman court in 1319–20: J. R. Wright, *The Church and the English Crown 1305–1334* (Toronto, 1980), p. 327.

150

London Dominicans (1348)
(SC 8/13/627)

The prior and Brother Arnold Lym of the London Dominicans petition the king and council, making three complaints and requesting remedy, or that the bishop of Winchester be ordered to summon the abbot, monks and the seculars, by whose oaths he can redress the complaints, and also take Lym into his special protection until the truth of the matter has been enquired into: (1) Although the pope and Adam, late bishop of Winchester, determined that Lym is a friar preacher and not a monk, the abbot and monks of Hyde have challenged this falsely and procured bulls that he ought to be restored to their order. They imprisoned him for nine years

and mistreated and tortured him so that he has not recovered his health. Thomas Haspal and others have cognisance of these matters.
(2) Whereas the provincial prior of the Dominicans barred the challenges to Lym, the abbot and monks of Hyde have procured certain people of their party to make false indictments against them so that they are ruined and are unable to have writs in chancery for their allies without making heavy fines.
(3) Also, John Blaunkchival and others at Westminster, in the presence of the king and his justices, took Lym and imprisoned him for five days and took from him his charter of protection from the king, money and other goods in his keeping. After this an agreement was made and closed by the oaths of Blaunkchival and others, but they have broken these and bribed the bishop of Winchester's clerks, to the damage of the friar and his order.
Endorsed: *If he wishes to sue at common law, he should have a writ of trespass upon his complaint; and the council will speak to the bishop to redress what has been done wrong as concerns him.*

A nostre seignur le roy et son conseil ses povres chapeleyns le priour des frers prechours a Londres et Frere Arnald Lym, son confrere, sa pleinount qe la qe nostre seint peir le apostoile et Adam, iadis evesqe de Wyncestr', avoient determine qe le dit Arnald estoit frere prechour et noun pas moigne, l'abbe et moignes de la Hyde ount chalenge le dit frere et chalengent faucement pur lur commoigne, et tous ces dis auns et plus ount enbesiles les bulles papals en quex le apostoile ordina certeigne forme par qe il deverit estre restore a son ordre, et en parnaunt a eux real pouer en lur abbe enprisonerount torceusement le dit frere noef auns, et ravirount de ly son habit, et desulerount son noen ...rs olur pees si quelibet qe en sink parties sa char est bloie, et serra tous les jours de sa vie. Et pur ceo qe il ne les voleit deliverer un instrument papal, necessarie a ly et son ordre, qex il avoit lie desuz son braihel, Dauns Johan Blaunkchival pressa si fort le dit frere Arnald par ces membres, qe a poy avoit perdu son sen. Et pur ceo qe son cri ne devererit estre oi en ces anguites, le dit moigne et altres ly mistrount frein en buche, et pus un altre torment trop horrible, c'est a savoir ungaunt plein de estreim envolupe en une touaile, le queil torment li fust lie a chefs si fort qe a poi avoit perdu sa vie. Par encheison de queil torment james ne recovera saunte de corps com il avoit en avaunt; et plusours altres tormentz ly firount qe il ne sofist ore destruire. De quex Thomas Haspaal, Willam Overtone, Johan Fide et altres bone gentz del pais ount bone conisaunce.

Item, pur ceo qe son priour provincial vint chalenge le dit Frere Arnald a son ordre, de forbarre le dit chalenge a totes accions pur le dit frere par sutiletes de lei de tere les avauntdites abbe et moignes unt procures certeigne gentz de lur covine de ly faucement endite, et tous ces parens, et autres amis seculers; quex par lur conspiracie, et nomeement Dauns Johan Blaunkchival, sount anientez et destrus, et ore ne porrount briefs avoir pur lur aliez en la chauncelrie sauns trop grevous fin faire, a quex ne porrount atteindre.
Item, le avauntdite Dauns Johan Blaunkchival et altres, en la sale et paleis de Weimostre, en presence le roy et ces justices, pristrount le dit frere Arnald et enprisonerount sink jours, et pristrount de li la chartre de protexion nostre dit seignur le roi, et un summe de argent et altres biens bailes a sa garde, et pus apres un acord fet, et ferme sovent pur ser:nent, le dit Johan Blaunkchival en presence le honurable baroun de Stafford et Sir Water de Westone et altres, les dites abbe et moignes, et nomeement Johan Blaunkchival, encountre lur serment

et covenaunt, diverces duresces suff...... dit frere, a perpetuel vilenie et damage del dit frere et son ordre, et destruccioun de ces parens et amis ......; quex mes qe le evezqe de Wyncestre, occupe en bosoignes le roy, eit comaunde ses clerks de justefier et au[tres] les dites clerks pur enpensiouns et livereisouns qex reteinount, plus meinteignount les dites errours qe a dount. Parqey al dites nostre seignur le roi et son conseil les dites povres freres et chapeleins suppliount d....ment, qe lur pleise de sa grace remedie ordiner, ou comaunder le evesqe de Wyncestre de faire venir .... moignes et seculers, par quex sermentez il porra conoystre et redresser les pleintes avauntdites et .... le dit Frere Arnald et sa cause en sa protexion especial jesqes il eit enquis la verite et .... die pur le de frere et son ordre.

Endorsed: S'il vuoille sywer a la comune ley, eit brief de trespas sur sa pleinte; et le cunsseil parlera al evesqe de redresser quant qe a lui attient ce qe ent est mispris.

1348. On 24 July 1347 Brother Lym was granted pardon for good service in the war with France (*CPR 1345–8*, p. 524). Thus, the pope and the late bishop of Winchester who determined his status as a friar were Clement VI (1342–52) and Adam Orleton, bishop of Winchester (1333–45). The abbot of Hyde was Walter of Fifehead (1319–62). Baron Stafford is Ralph Stafford, second Baron Stafford and, later, first earl of Stafford. For context, see J. Röhrkasten, *The Mendicant Houses of Medieval London, 1221–1539* (Münster, 2006), pp. 330–7. The bottom right-hand corner of the petition is missing. An earlier edition of this petition is in *RP*, II, 186–7, no. 47.

4.4 Internal conflict

151

Norwich, Norfolk (c. 1287–9)
Pied friars
(SC 8/47/2330)

Robert of Forensete, chaplain, formerly brother of the order of St Mary of Areno, London, petitions the king and council that although he and Simon of Tunstude were appointed keepers of the house of their order in Norwich, with the assent of the whole chapter, a certain Walter of Croxton, who calls himself the provincial prior of the order in England, came often to that house and carried off its goods and ornaments to the value of £40, and when they refused to stand this any more he declared them fugitives and excommunicates. When they appealed to the head of their order, and received letters from him in their support, and also papal letters concerning other injuries inflicted upon them by the provincial, Croxton came to a house where they were with other brothers of the order and with a great number of laymen, and carried them off to Cambridge, where he beat and wounded them and imprisoned them for forty days, where Simon died of hunger without confession. And Robert's friends could obtain no release for him through writs of the king, as the provincial had bribed the sheriff. He requests a remedy, as the provincial has enough money to make satisfaction for the injury and the trespass against the king, and asks that he be swiftly arrested, as he is planning a bolt-hole abroad.
Endorsed: *Before the bishops.*

Domino regi et eius consilio ex parte Roberti de Forensete, capellani, nuper fratris ordinis Beate Marie matris Cristi de Areno London', est ostensum quod cum idem Robertus et quidam frater Simon de Tunstude, laicus \eiusdem ordinis/, deputati fuissent custodes domus predicti ordinis apud Norwicum, de assensu totius capituli, et quidam frater Walterus de Croxton', qui se gerit pro priore provinciale eiusdem ordinis in Anglie, veniens multociens ad dictum domum de Norwico et asportabat bona et ornamenta eiusdem domus ad valenciam quadraginta librarum, propter quod predicti fratres increrabant ipsum provincialem et nellent amplius pati dilapidacioni predictorum bonorum. Idem provincialis asserens ipsos esse fugitivos et dicebat ipsos fore excomunicatos, et ipsos ita excomunicatos pappales denunciavit propter quod predicti fratres, scilicet Robertus et Simon, appellarunt coram majorem totius ordinis qui moratur in partibus transmarinis de illa sentencia tanquam ab iniqua et habuerunt litteras majoris eorum et inhibitionem suam ne amplius \idem provincialis/ procederet in causa predicta, et eciam habuerunt litteras papales de aliis injuriis eisdem fratribus per predictum provincialem illatis, videlicet, unam litteram domino Hugoni de Kendale et domino Phillipo de Wyleweby, qui constituti fuerunt judices per dominum papam ad audiendum causas predictorum fratrum, et habuerunt litteras de citando predictum provinciallem, et idem provincialis pertiens hoc venit ad quandam domum ubi predicti fratres hospitati fuerunt, cum multitudine virorum laicorum et cum aliis fratibus eiusdem ordinis, videlicet, Fratre Willelmo de Faukeman, Fratre Johanne de Cerbidesham et Fratre Johanne de Norwico, et predictos fratres, videlicet Robertum et Simonem, ibidem ceperunt et abduxerunt usque ad Cantebr', et ibi spoliaverunt ipsos de habitu eorum et de tonsura capitis, et ipsos ibidem in capitulo suo verberaverunt et vulneraverunt cum cultultis et aliis, et eciam ipsos imprisonaverunt per quadraginta dies, ita predictus Simon fame interiit et mortus fuit in carcere sine confessione, et predictus Robertus jacit quasi quoddam monstrum horribile et prope amisit manus et pedes nec potuerunt amici eius licet fuisset in seculari habitu aliquam deliberacionem habere de ipso per duo brevia domini regis omnes vicecomites comitatis predicti corruptus fuit de muneribus dicti provincialis. Et de hoc supplicat dictus Robertus remedium quia dictus provincialis satis habet satisfacere lesio et eciam domino rege de transgressione et proponit subterfugia querere in partibus transmarinis nisi cicius capietur.

Endorsed: Coram episcopis.

c. 1287–9. Norwich appears to have been the earliest of the three houses of this order in England, and was apparently established by the mid-1250s (1253 x 1256); the other houses were Westminster (1267), and Cambridge (1273). Despite the order's suppression by a decree of the Council of Lyons (1245), which disbanded mendicant orders founded after 1215, the Pied friars went unmolested, and in both England and France they received alms from Edward I. But the order withered away as its members died; Westminster ended in 1317, Cambridge after 1319: F. Andrews, *The Other Friars: The Carmelite, Augustinian, Sack and Pied Friars in the Middle Ages* (Woodbridge, 2006), pp. 224–30, esp. 227–9 and nn. Walter de Croxton was signified as apostate from the Norwich house on 1 May 1287; he allegedly stole charters, chalices and a large sum of money and church ornaments from the friary. On 1 September 1288 William de Norwich was signified as apostate from the Westminster house; he had stolen books and other goods and was wandering about London with two other renegades, Thomas de Wyke and Hugh de York. Professor Logan speculates that Croxton and Norwich were the same person: F. D. Logan, *Runaway Religious in Medieval England, c. 1240–1540* (Cambridge, 1996), p. 251 and nn. This petition probably dates from the middle or later years of the decade 1280–90. The papal judges-delegate Hugh de Kendal and Philip de Willoughby were both leading king's clerks; for Willoughby see T. F. Tout, *Chapters in the Administrative History of Mediaeval England*, 6 vols (Manchester, 1920–33), VI, 449 for references. Kendal's equally distinguished career can be constructed from the calendars of chancery rolls, and see also Robin R. Mundill, *England's Jewish Solution: Experiment and Expulsion, 1262–1290* (Cambridge, 1998), pp. 21, 105, 142, 257–8, 268.

152

St Mary Magdalene, Winchester, Hampshire (c. 1333)
Hospital
(SC 8/63/3115)

The brothers and sisters of the hospital of the Magdalene, Winchester, petition the king and council for remedy concerning the wrong done to them by the warden of the hospital, and the withdrawal of their livery. They ask that a suitable brother be assigned to conduct their business, and that a writ be granted to enquire of their master and especially his concubine, Juliana, wife of Thomas Gautron, since they are not able to be served of their livery except at her will.
Endorsed: *They should declare if the hospital is a foundation of the king or not, and if it is then they should sue in chancery, and let justice be done to them there.*

A nostre seignur le roi et a son conseil prient les povres fratres et soeres malades et autres del hospital de la Maudeleyne p.................. Seynt Giles de Wyncestre grace et remedie de la defaute a eux fete par mye lour gardeyn illoeqes, c'est assavoir de .... et de lour livereson q'est retret q'ils soloient avoir de droit et de aunciene usage et par certeyne ordinances des foundours .... meson et dont ils ne sont mye servi par encheson qe lour mestre ne voelt lour bosoignes ensure mes soeffre lour remed[ie] .... et parditz, qe il pleise a nostre seignur le roi et a son bon conseil, en oevre de charite, ordeyner qe ascun covenable fratre .... dite meson puisse sivre lour bosoignes q'ils ne moergent de feym, et ensement granter bref d'enquere de lour meistre et .... et nomement de sa conkubyne Juliane la femme Thomas Gautron, la quele il tient a sa volunte, et les autres freres .... del avantdit hospital ne pont estre servi de lour service forsqe a la volunte l'avantdit Juliane, dont il prient, pur Dieu, ... remedie.

Endorsed: Declare si hospital sont de la fundacion le roi ou ne mie, et s'il soit de la fundacion le roi, adonqes sue in Chauncellerie et la lui soit fait droit.

c. 1333. The right-hand edge of this petition is damaged. This dispute made no impact on the Winchester episcopal registers, but on 26 November 1333 an enquiry (held in the cathedral) into the hospital's condition took evidence from fifteen witnesses. It found that Bishop Henry de Blois (1129–71) gave the hospital £25 19s 4d a year from the episcopal treasury, and that his successors continued the practice; but that the hospital had no title for this payment and consequently the inmates suffered greatly during episcopal vacancies. After the deaths of bishops Sandale (1319) and Assier (1323), William Hamond, then master, incurred considerable expense – details were produced – in securing this payment through writs to the exchequer, and guardians of the see, *sede vacante*. From May 1333 Bishop John Stratford (1323–33) was taking steps to appropriate Wonston church (Hants.), which was in his patronage, to the hospital to secure its finances. But despite securing papal approval, and drawing up a form of appropriation, Stratford left the business uncompleted at his elevation to the see of Canterbury in late 1333. Wonston remained a rectory, but the hospital continued to receive £25 12s 4d p.a. from its revenues (paid through the Church Commissioners) into the twentieth century: *Chartulary of Winchester Cathedral*, ed. and trans. A. W. Goodman (Winchester, 1927), nos 183–4, 186, 419–23. The high number of vacancies in the see, five in the period 1304–33, greatly contributed to the hospital's problems.

153

Bindon, Dorset (c. 1330)
Cistercian
(SC 8/37/1829)

The abbot and convent of Bindon petition the king and council, showing that they are totally ruined, and that their seal has been stolen by thieves who have used it to forge blank charters of corrodies and pensions. They request that they be granted keepers with the power to defend them from such excesses.
Endorsed: *Let this bill be ordered into chancery, and the chancellor is to do what should be done.*

A nostre seigneur le roi et a son consail mostrent ses chapelayns l'abbee et le covent de Bynedon' qe come par leur election demeigne saunz fundacion de ses progenitours ou de lui leur est patroun et avoee purchacie, sicome il par sa chartre demeigne qe demeurt en sa tresorie par les ditz religious purchacie pleinment est contenuz, et il sont destruit et leur commun seal ravi et asportez par larouns, et puis par suyte de la Chancelerie debrise et pur nul tenuz, et de queu seal les ditz larons enfirent chartres blanches et escritz de corrodies, de robes et d'empensions et lettres, en destruccion pur touz jors \de/ la dite maisoun, si remedie qe les aneynte et destruie ne isoit ordene covenable. Pleise au roi et au consail doner gardeyns qi eyent poer a defendre la dite maison de tieus utray en ses demandes, en relevacion de ses almones e des moynes qe sont en \dispersion/.

Endorsed: Soit ceste bille mande en Chancellarie, et face la chanceller ceo q'il veit qe soite a faire par eure de charite.

c. 1330. This complaint concerns the actions of John of Mountacute (Montagu), as described in SC 8/239/11943 (**154**), and the petitioner is presumably Abbot William, Mountacute's successor, who occurs in Oct. 1331. Other related petitions in SC 8 are: 37/1830; 37/1831 (**155**); and 93/4613. For the misdeeds of John de Mountacute, who claimed to be abbot, see *CPR 1330–4*, pp. 89, 131, 142, 201, and *VCH Dorset*, II, 84–5. He was named as an apostate monk of the house some time before a writ for his arrest was issued, 22 March 1331, D. F. Logan, *Runaway Religious in Medieval England, c. 1240–1540* (Cambridge, 1996), p. 206.

154

Bindon, Dorset (1331)
Cistercian
(SC 8/239/11943)

The monks of Bindon petition the king and council, stating that they have been completely ruined by the machinations of the king's ministers and by a malevolent abbot, John of Mountacute, who has rightly been expelled. They ask that the gifts and grants made under their stolen common seal, between the feast of St Nicholas in the king's second year and the present, might be repealed, that they might be given some suitable remedy for their plundered goods, and that they might be discharged of liveries, pensions and robes for three years.

Pleyse a nostre seignur le roy e a son consayl qe com ses moignes chapelayns de Bynedone sont tout poveres par destruccion e mayntenement de ses uns ministres e d'un maveis abbe, Frere Johan de Montagu, qui a grant droit fust este e depose, sont destrut lour oor, argent, reliques, ornementz, liberarie, chaliz, bestaile e quantq'il eurent, e lour commun seal raux, par gentz armes byn a cync centz entrant a force deunt a damage de cync mile libres et de plus, et enprisonerunt atoure les uns moignes entre commun larons a Dorcestre, et par le dit commun seal ravi enfirent blanche chartres et aultres plusours e diverse dons come de terres, liversons e depensions, qu'il pur Deux voille repeller teuls dons e grantz puis la dite destruccio e commencement de cele ravyne, qe fust a la feste Seint Nicholas l'an de son regne second tantqe aores, e estre ceo grantier e ordener covenable remedye au dit tresgrant meschef de touz lour byenz despences, car sanz ses aydes graciouses il ne purront en nul temps relever e sont de tiout poer de ensivre lour bosoygnes ne aprofere les chanteryes e les aulmones com il soleent avant. E priont dovotement qe il seunt descharges des lyversons, de enpensyons e des robes par tres ans pur lour poverte avant dite, la qele seont byn lor gardens done par le roy, c'est asaver Monsire Hugh Courtenay e Monsire Hugh Poynz, e grant partye de aulme.

No endorsement

1331. John of Mountacute first occurs as abbot of Bindon on 29 October 1327. He was excommunicated on 12 January 1329 and, following commissions of oyer and terminers into acts against the abbey (*CPR 1330–4*, pp. 63, 131), a writ for his arrest was issued on 22 March 1331 (*CPR 1330–4*, p. 89). In April a writ of aid was issued for taking Mountacute back to Bindon (*CPR 1330–4*, p. 142). And in August individuals were appointed 'to retake and conduct to Bindon abbey to be chastised according to the rule of his order John de Monte Acuto, sometime abbot, who had escaped from the custody of William Trussel, to whom he had been delivered by the sheriffs of London when arrested by the king's mandate as an apostate' (*Heads of Houses II*, p. 263). The chancery warrant with which this petition was formerly enclosed is dated 17 December 1331 (no. 5074 of C 81/186). Related petitions are SC 8/37/1831 (below, **155**), SC 8/37/1830 and SC 8/37/1829 (above, **153**). Another petition from this house is SC 8/93/4613.

155

Bindon, Dorset (c. 1331)

Cistercian
(SC 8/37/1831)

The abbot of Bindon petitions the king and council that William of Stoke, coroner of Dorset, be removed from the office of steward of Bindon since he has revealed himself to be unsuitable by many actions, and another suitable person put in his place. John of Mountacute, monk of Bindon, ruined the house by Stoke's maintenance and made him his steward, and procured an appealer to accuse the monks who did not assent to him.

Endorsed: *He should sue to the chancellor.*

A nostre seigneur le roy et au consail mostre l'abbee de Bynedone qe come une Frere Johan de Montagu destrucist cele maison par mayntenance Willame de Stokes, coroner de Dors', et fust son senescal et fist et procurast un appellour fausement appeller moignes et freres qi n'estoient pas del assent du dite frere Johan, et a ceo prist de Frere Watier de la Suterie xl s, \lui/ surmettant q'il fust appellez pur avoir du seon queu Willame, par plusours enchesons, n'est pas covenable al office du coroner, pleise au roi et au consail ostier le del office et mettre un altre pluis covenable.

Endorsed: Sue au chaunceller.

c. 1331. It is not clear whether this petition precedes SC 8/37/1829 (**153**), but both petitions as well as SC 8/37/1830 and SC 8/239/11943 (**154**) are closely linked and were drafted within a short space of time: all concern the injury that John of Mountacute had done the house. The petitioner is Abbot William, occurring October 1331. A further related petition is SC 8/93/4613.

156

Repton, Derbyshire (1340–64)

Augustinian canons
(SC 8/175/8742)

The prior and convent of Repton petition the king that Robert Tebbe be arrested so that they can continue to serve God. He was one of their canons and was attainted of many heinous crimes for which lenient penance was enjoined on him, but he broke out of the house and became apostate. He has taken to secular clothes and he and his company threaten them and their property with malice and destruction.

A lour treshonerable seignur lige Sire Edward, par la grace de Dieu roi d'Engleterre et de Fraunce et seignur d'Irlaunde, les seons povres chapleyns le priour et covent de Repindone honurs et reverences come a lour seignur lige, Seignur, tresgraciouse a voustre graunde hautesce, plestil entendre qe Frere Robert Tebbe, un nouster chanoygne de Repindone del ordre Seint Austyne, fust atteint de plusours crimes in noustre comune chapitre qe trop hydouse serroyt adeheis rehercer, pur les queus crimes penaunce ease si fust enjoynt ne mie d'asset solonk la quantite de les crimes, la quele penaunce trop legere n'est unqore volu faire, maus sue est alee ore la tierce foith de muttauntre, et debruse nos mesouns et passe nos murs et va apostataunte, et chaunge son habitz et va en secle en habitz seculer, ove arche, setter et aultres armes manaceaunt ove sa compaignye nos corps a malmettre et tuer, et nos graunges et nos biens de mettre en flaumbe, a grande deshonur de nouster ordre et arerisement de nouster estat. Pur qoi, tresreverent seignur, plestil a voustre graunde seignurie comaunder a vouster bon conseil qe la malice le dit Robert apostat per voustre real poar soit arestu, qe vos ditz chapeleyns en quiete a Dieu pussoms servir, et pur vous et vos touz jours le plus affectuosement prior. En tesmoignaunce de quele chose a cestes nos lettres avouns mys noustre comun seal. Done en nouster chapitre a Repindone le secounde jour de Jun.

No endorsement

1340–64. The petition is speculatively dated to 1340–64 on the basis of the hand. The discussion of this petition in *VCH* suggests a date of c. 1364, since on 2 November of this year Robert Stretton, bishop of Coventry and Lichfield, was conducting a visitation at Repton when the whole community of the town, armed with swords, staves, bows and arrows, besieged and attacked the priory, until persuaded to disband by two neighbouring gentlemen. In consequence of this violation of the king's peace, the bishop excommunicated the community and its parish church (*VCH Derbyshire*, II, 61). The evidence connecting this event to Tebbe's threat against the priory, however, is completely circumstantial.

157

Abbotsbury, Dorset (1354)
Benedictine
(SC 8/210/10470)

Walter, abbot of Abbotsbury, petitions John, archbishop of York, that whereas the bishop of Winchester, having heard certain accusations made against the abbot by his convent, ordained that the abbot should have competent board and clothing, his accustomed chamber, the services of a squire and two grooms to attend to his horses, Robert of Fardon, prior of Abbotsbury, Henry Toller, John Bremore and William Hoke, monks, Walter Waleis, Thomas Cary and John Munden, by virtue of the king's commission, withdrew from him all the said privileges to which he was entitled, so that, insufficiently clad and with his shoes in holes, he had been compelled to proceed more than 18 miles on foot in order to execute his business. He requests that the ordinance made by the bishop of Winchester remain in effect and power, and that the monastery be exonerated from alienation.

Venerabli in Cristo patri ac domino suo domino Johanni, permissione Dei Ebor' archiepiscopo, supplicat humiliter et devote frater Walterus, abbas monasterii de Abbotesbury, Sarum diocesis, quod cum nuper inter abbatem predictum et suum conventum propter certas discordias inter eosdem ortas, ex mandato domini nostri regis Anglie et Francie illustris inter cetera, pro venerabilem patrem Wynton' episcopum fuerat ordinatum quod predictus abbas de bonis monasterii de Abbotesbury supradicti victum et vestimentum perciperet per corpore suo competenter et quod haberet cameram suam consuetam, honestum scutiferum camerarium, duos garcones ad custodiendum equos suos quos ipse dominus voluit eum habere, et premissa ordinavit eum habere debere dumtaxat sumptibus et expensis monasterii supradicti, quousque dictum monasterium ere alieno esset exitum quo tunc existebat gravatum. Super quid Robertus de Farndon', prior monasterii supradicti, Henricus Teyl[e]r, Johannes Bremore, Willelmus Hoke, commonachi, dominus Walterus Waleis, Thomas Cary et Johannes de Mundeyn, virtute cuiusdam commissionis domini nostri regis, ut asserunt, contra predictum abbatem per suos emulos notorios prece et precio in hac parte corruptos, fraudilenter et clandestine inquisierunt in magnam infamiam abbatis supradicti, ac subsequenter omnia premissa et presertim victum et vestitum et equos suos per venerabilem patrem antedictum ad usum predicti abbatis ordinata, sibi penitus inhumaniter subtraxerunt, adeo quod indecenter vestitus, suis calciamentis enormiter fractis, in suis negociis necessariis bene ad octodecim leucas aliquociens ad plus ad pedes incedere cogebatur predicti vero Robertus, Henricus, Johannes et Willelmus, conmonachi, dominus Walterus, Thomas et Johannes, virtute auctoritatis et colore commissionis et potestatis eis commissarum in hac parte, commonacho dicti abbatis scutifero eciam et camerario, sub pena incarceracionis inhibuerunt ne decetero in commutiam abbatis supradicti remanerent, dictum eciam monasterium absque aliqua causa racionabili in centum sexaginta libras argenti de novo onerarunt, staurum eciam omnium per mille et CCC oves diminuerunt, et octodecim saccos lane vendiderunt, et precium eorundem saccorum in volitatem monasterii quod sciatur minime coverterunt. Placeat paternitati vestre reverende caritatis intuitu predictam ordinacionem domini Wynton' debito mancipare effectum et potestatem predictorum Roberti, Henrici, Johannis et Willelmi, commonachorum, domini Walteri, Thome et Johannis, qui splendida et sumptuosa covinia extra monasterium frequenter faciunt de bonis monasterii refrenare velit quod bona monasterii non consumant, et idem monasterium ere alieno cuius exoneretur.

No endorsement

1354. The petitioner was Walter of Stokes, abbot 1348–54. The addressee is John Thoresby, archbishop of York (1352–73) and chancellor (1349–56). Great poverty afflicted Abbotsbury in the fourteenth century, partly as a result of Stokes's bad government of the house. On 1 December 1353 the abbey was granted protection as a result of the debts incurred by the petitioner, and Robert of Farendon and Henry Toller, monks of the house, Walter Waleys, Thomas Cary and John of Munden were appointed keepers of the abbey (*CPR 1350–4*, p. 536). In this petition Stokes complains of his ill-treatment at the hands of the custodians. The following petition (SC 8/210/10471) details the custodians' complaints, which were not groundless, as was found by the inquisition into this matter (SC 8/210/101475). Henry Toller became abbot of Abbotsbury following Stokes's death. William Edington (1345–66) is the bishop of Winchester. The entire case is summarised, and the related inquisition translated, in *CIM 1348–77*, no. 183. For a detailed discussion of these events, see *VCH Dorset*, II, 51, which estimates the total injury done to the abbey by Stokes at £855 10s 8d.

(SC 8/210/10471)

Robert of Farendon and Henry Toller, monks of Abbotsbury, Walter Waleys, clerk, Thomas Cary and John of Munden, keepers of Abbotsbury Abbey, petition the king and council for satisfaction against the abbot.

Al chaunceler et as autres seignurs du counseil nostre seignur le roy moustront leur suggitz Frere Robert de Farendone et Henri de Tolre, moigns de l'abbeie de Abbodesbury, Water Waleys, clerk, Thomas Cary et Johan de Mundene qe come la dite abbeie ove terres, rentes, possessiouns, biens et chateux a icele abbeie regardaunz par certeins enchesouns soit commise a garder as ditz Robert, Henri, Water, Thomas et Johan sour certene forme contenue en une commissioun a eux direct, et iceux gardeyns eient diligeaument sourveu et examine l'estat de la dite abbeie, la quele est par inordine governement de Water, abbe q'ore est, si diversement endamagie et par reconsaunces et obligacions et en altre manere chargie ..... notorie chose est es parties de Dors', et assez bien conue par sovernele demaunde des dettes susditz qe apoine purra estre relevee, et les gardeins susditz pur les dettes susditz qe atignent a la somme de cink centz et trente qatres livres meltz paier et l'abbe et le covent et les almoignes establitz sustenir soient assentuz, qe les avantditz abbe et moignes vivereient en commun en une mesoun covenable a ceo ordinee pur fals et excessifs despens avant ses houres iloeqs usez eschivre et autres choses eient ordinez a lour entent en amendement de l'estat de l'abbeie susdit, le dist abbe as ditz assent et ordinance contrariaunt entre les ditz moignes ne en esglise ne en la dite meson ne en refrettour forsqe releivent a sa volente ne vynt mes a sa chaumbre se fait servir et les viaundes a son poer degaste continuaunt son primer usage et en diverses parties du counte susdit et hors du counte a divers temps va wacraunt fesont aprovit de devers enchargaunt la mesoun susdite par obligacions et reconisaunces et fesaunt reles et aquitaunces et procuraunt a son poer diverses gentz de contrarier et unire as gardeins susditz et a l'abbeie susdite. Par qei les ditz gardeins supplient al consail susdite qe remedie seit \sour ceo ordine/ et qe l'evesqe de Sarum \ordinaire/ du lieu soit overtement chargie de faire amendement de ceo si avant come faire le donera ou purra en resonable manere issint qe la dite abbeie, la quele est de la fundacion nostre dit seignur le roi, ne soit finalment destrut.

No endorsement

1354. The bishop of Salisbury was Robert Wyvil (1330–75), who was involved in the case as the abbey's diocesan.

(SC 8/210/10472)

Letters patent of Edward III, dated at Westminster on 28 January 1354, appointing Walter Waleys, Thomas Cary and John of Munden to hold an inquiry into the wastage of Abbotsbury Abbey's goods. He committed the custody of the abbey to them, with all its lands, tenements, rents and possessions, having understood that the abbot had falsely sold and demised the abbey's possessions for his own benefit. Wishing to be more certain, he has assigned them, or two of them, to enquire by the oaths of good men of the region which lands, tenements, rents and possessions of the abbey have been alienated and demised, and which goods, chattels and stock have been sold and eloigned, and by whom, and to whom, and why, by which title, when, how and in what manner, and to inform him of their findings.

Edwardus, Dei gracia rex Anglie et Francie et dominus Hibernie, dilectis sibi Waltero Waleys, clerico, Thome Cary et Johanni de Munden', salutem. Cum nos nuper abbaciam de Abbotesbury in comitatu Dors' quam progenitorum nostrorum quondam regum Anglie fundatam existit cum terris, tenementis, redditibus et omnibus possessionibus et rebus aliis tam mobilibus quam immobilibus ad eam pertinentibus ceperimus in protectionem [et defensionem] nostram specialem et eam cum terris, tenementis, redditibus et omnibus aliis possessionibus et rebus predictis vobis sub certa forma commiserimus custodienda prout in commissione nostra predicta vobis sic facta plenius continetur, intellexerimus quod tam terre, temenentes, redditus et possessiones eiusdem abbatie diversis hominibus parcium illarum per abbatem dicti loci ad usum suum et commodum sub sigillo suo proprio et non ad utilitatem et .... eiusdem domus diversimode dimissa quam bona et catalla ac instaurum domus illius tam vivum quam mortuum diversis personis per eundem abbatem per collusiones ac fictas vendiciones et .... et ante tempus dicte commissionis nostre in hac parte facte vendita et elongata existunt in nostri contemptum et dedetus ac dicte abbatie depauperacionem et adnullacionem manifestam. Nos volumus .... vos plenius certiorari assignavimus vos et duos vestrum ad inquirendum per sacramentum proborum et legalium hominum comitatus predicti tam infra libertates quam extra, per quos rei veritas melius sciri poterit que et cuiusmodi terre, tenementa, redditus et possessiones dicte abbatie alienata et dimissa et que et cuiusmodi bona et catalla et instaurum eiusdem abbatie vendita et elongata existunt et per quos vel per quem, et cui vel quibus, et qua causa, quo titulo, quo tempore, qualiter et quo modo. Et ideo vobis mandamus quod ad certos dies et loca quos vos vel duo vestrum ad hoc provideritis diligentes super premisses et aliis articulis, circumstanciis ea tangentibus faceritis inquisiciones et eas distincte et aperte factas nobis sub sigillis vestris vel duorum vestrum tot et tales probos et legales homines de balliva sua tam infra libertates quam extra per quos rei veritas in premissis melius scire poterit et inquiri. In cuius rei testimonium has litteras nostras fieri fecimus patentes. Teste me ipso apud Westm' xxviij die Januarii anno regni nostri Anglie vicesimo octavo regni nostri Francie quintodecimo.

No endorsement

(SC 8/210/10473)

Writ of Edward III to John of Palton, sheriff of Dorset, dated 28 January 1354, to support the commissioners appointed under the letters patent at SC 8/210/10472.
Endorsed: *Note provided by the sheriff that the action taken is in the attached schedule.*

Edwardus, Dei gracia rex Anglie et Francie et dominus Hibernie, vicecomiti Dors' salutem. Cum per litteras nostras patentes assignaverimus dilectos nobis Walterum Waleys, clericum, Thomam Cary et Johannem de Munden' vel duos eorum ad inquirendum per sacramentum proborum et legalium hominum de comitate tuo, per quos rei veritas melius sciri poterit que et quiusmodi terre et tenementes, reditus et possessiones abbatie de Abbotesbury alienata et dimissa et que et cuiusmodi bona et catalla et instaurum eiusdem abbatie vendita et elongata existunt et per quos vel per quem et cuis vel quibus et ex qua causa, quo titulo, quo tempore, qualiter et quo modo, prout in litteris nostris predictis plenius continetur, tibi precipimus quod ad certos dies et loca quos iidem Walterus, Thomas et Johannes vel duo eorum tibi scire facias venire facias coram eis vel duobus eorum tot et tales probos et legales homines de balliva tua tam infra libertates quam extra, per quos rei veritas in premissis melius scire poterit et inquiri. Et habeas ibi hoc breve. Teste me ipso apud Westm' xxviij die Januarii anno regni nostri Anglie vicesimo octavo regni vero nostri Francie quintodecimo.

Endorsed: Execucio istius brevis patentis in precepto huic brevi consuito. Johannes de Palton', vicecomes.

John of Palton was sheriff of Dorset from February 1353 to 1 April 1355. The attached schedule mentioned in the endorsement is SC 8/210/10474 (below).

(SC 8/210/10474)

Instructions, dated at Litton Cheney on 10 March 1354, from Walter Waleys, clerk, Thomas Cary and John of Munden, assigned to inquire into the demised lands, tenements, rents and possessions of Abbotsbury Abbey and the sold and eloigned goods and chattels, to the sheriff of Dorset to empanel a jury of 24 free and lawful men to appear before them, or two of them, for an inquisition into which lands, tenements, rents, possessions, goods, chattels and stock of the abbey were sold and eloigned, by whom, to whom, why, by what title, when, how and in what way to the wastage of the goods of Abbotsbury Abbey.
Endorsed: *Return of jurors and their pledges.*

Walterus Waleys, clericus, Thomas de Cary et Johannes de Munden' ad inquirendum de terris, tenementis, redditibus et possessionibus abbacie de Abbodesbury dimissis et bonis et catellis venditis et elongatis in comitatu Dors' assignati, vicecomiti Dors' salutem. Et parte domini regi tibi mandamus quod venire facias coram nobis vel duobus nostrorum die veneris proximo post festum Anunciationis Beate Marie apud Dorcestr' xxiiij liberales et legales homines, tam milites quam alios, de visneto de Abbodesbury, Tolepudele, Heltone, Gravestone et Louke, tam infra libertates quam extra, ad inquirendum que et cuiusmodi terre et tenementes, redditus et possessiones, bona et catalla ac instaurum predicte abbatie vendita et elongata existunt, per quos vel per quem, cui vel quibus, et ex qua causa, quo titulo, quo tempore, qualiter et quo modo, et ad alia facienda que eis ibidem ex parte domini regis injugetur. Et habeatis ibi nomine dictorum xxiiij hominum quos sic venire feceris et hoc mandatur. Dat' apud Litton' die lune proximo ante festum Sancti Gregorii anno regni Regis Edwardi tercii post conqestum xxviij.

Endorsed: Jures: M. Johan de Wattone: Johan Pere; William Cobbe
M. Robert Basset: Henri Ware; Richard Gile
M. Drogun Bardolf: William Fort; Johan Dru
M. Johan Jerard: Adam Peny; Johan Grym
M. Thomas Thomelyn: William Lobb; Richard Baron
M. Walter Hamound: Robert Fort; Adam Birt
M. Johan Salesbury: Johan Bryd; Thomas Horn
M. Robert Haulder: Johan Holt; William Styl
M. Johan Askerswell: William Doo; Richard Hony
M. Edward Orveyn: Johan Fort; Richard Luffe
M. Henri Bonevyle: William Hey; Adam Bare
M. Johan atte Hacche: William Louk; Johan Hore
M. Johan Ekerdone: Henri Davy; Richard Padel
M. Alexander Watercombe: Johan Mollard; Adam Horn
M. Simon Spraklyng: Johan Goys; Robert Not
M. Robert le Brut: Richard Bote; Johan Page
M. William Bulstroude: Adam Fort; Richard Loue
M. Johan Caukete: Robert Oke; Adam Horn
M. Johan le Yonge: Michael Sule; Johan Joob
M. William le White: Johan Parker; Robert Smert
M. John le White: Adam Hort; William Bere
M. Thomas Bonvyle: Richard Page; Johan Hake

M. William de Frome: Johan Hauward; Thomas Lovesome
M. John Couk: Richard Neulard; Robert Bochard

(SC 8/210/10475)

Inquisition held at Dorchester on 28 March 1354 before Walter Waleys, clerk, Thomas Cary and John of Munden, by the oaths of John of Watton, Robert Basset, Thomas Thomelyn, Henry Boneville, Walter Hamond, John Salesbury, Robert Haulder, John Jerard, Drew Bardolf, John of Askerswell, Edward Orveyn and John at Hacche, who say on oath that Walter of Stoke, abbot of Abbotsbury sold a corrody to John of Secta for which he received £20 to his own use. Various complaints were made against the abbot. These included accusations that he granted keeping of land in Horerigge and Welfield worth 5 marks yearly to William of Bettiscombe, rent-free; he wrongly gave to John Albon, who had married the abbot's sister, land in Tolpuddle and Ramsbury for a very small price; he gave to Edward of Cerne a villein named Adam Horn; he gave to John Albon and John Stoke, the abbot's brother, the services of those who hold of the abbot in villeinage; he granted freedom to William Torcher, a villein of the monastery, for a price; he wrongly sold hundreds of sheep and pigs to various people, keeping the money gained from these sales for himself; he gave John Sene, monk of Glastonbury, a cup with a silver and gilt foot worth 10 marks; he remised £20 of a debt of £100 which Nicholas of Pontz, knight, owed for transgressions committed against the house; he gave Agnes of London various items belonging to the house; he [sold?] the manor of Holwell belonging to the office of chamberlain, keeping the money for himself; he sold to Nicholas of Frompton, ... and Walter le Deyere all trees of a certain type growing in the abbey's manors, keeping the money received for himself; he gave various animals to various people, to the great damage of the monastery; he gave swans to various people; he remitted to Richard Peverel an annual rent of 6s 4d owed to the monastery for a place called Cakerigg which was six years overdue; he paid 5 marks on behalf of William of Bettiscombe to John Crabbe's wife for damages done to the land which the abbot demised to him in Horigge, as is said above; he kept many expensive hunting dogs for himself and others and often hunted with others for up to five days, at the expense of the monastery; he kept an excessive household, at the expense of the monastery; and he often made excessive gifts, such as furred robes, to many people, religious and lay and women. After the abbey was committed to the custodians, the abbot gave John Albon a great mare worth 60s, and Henry Paneter an ox worth 1 mark, without consulting anyone. After the said commission, the abbot acquitted Walter Honey, villein of the monastery, of all rents and services due to the abbey when he was reeve at Abbotsbury, Portisham, Graston and Louke for over seven years, and he acquitted Ralph Daionfold, reeve of Hilton, for the three years he was reeve, and remitted to him all rents and services. The abbot granted freedom to John Hake, villein of the manor of Hilton. In witness of which the aforesaid jury have put their seals on this inquisition. The total damages done by the abbot is estimated at £855 16s 8d, not including his debts which amount to £534. Thus the total of damages and debts is £1389 16s 8d.

Inquisicio capta apud Dorcestr' die veneris proximo post festum Anunciacionis Beate Marie anno regni Regis Edwardi tercii a conquestu xxviij coram Waltero Waleys, clerico, Thome Cary et Johanne de Munden' virtute litterarum domini regis patencium huic inquisicioni consuitarum per sacramentum Johannis de Watton', Roberti Basset, Thome Thomelyn, Henrici Bonevyle, Walteri Hamond, Johannis Salesbury, Roberti Haulder, Johannis Jerard, Drogonis Bardolf, Johannis de Askerswell, Edwardi Orveyn et Johannis atte Hacche, qui dicunt per sacramentum suum quod Walterus de Stoke, abbas de Abbodesbury, sine assensu conventus sui et ante tempus quo dicta abbacia predictis Waltero, Thome et Johanni fuit per dominum regem commisse custodienda, vendidit et concessit, per scriptum sigillo suo proprio sigillatum, unum corrodium sive redditum annuum, unius robe de secta armigerorum, vij quartas frumenti, ij quartas avene, ij boves, ij porcos, vj bidentas pro lardario, ij carectas feni, ij carectas straminis et ij carectas focalium preciis communis annuatim vj li ix s. Et idem abbas recepit pro corrodio predicto xx li quos in proprios usus convertit.

Item, dicunt quod idem abbas, sine assensu conventus sui, ante tempus custodie predicte commisse concessit et dimisit, quatuor annis iam elapsis, Willelmo de Betescombe custodiam unius messuagii, unius carucate terre cum pertinenciis in Horerigge et unam virgatam terre in Welfeld, que valent per annum v marcas, habenda eidem Willelmo … dicta mesuagium et carucatam terre usque ad legitimam etatem heredis Johannis Crabbe et dictam virgatam terre ad totam vitam predicti Willelmi, absque aliquo redditu inde percipiendo et absque aliquot mer ….

Item, dicunt quod idem abbas, ante tempus custodie predicte, propria voluntate sua et sine assensu conventus sui, tradidit collusive et ficte triennum elapso Johanni Albon, qui sororem dicti abbatis disponsavit, … de Tolpudele et quedam alia terras et tenementa in Remmesbury, habenda ad vitam eiusdem Johannis pro minori precio que valent hodierum diebus pro terciam partem veri valorum eorumdem, et est prejudicium dicte … c s.

Item, dicunt quod idem abbas, ante tempus dicte custodie sic commisse, sine assensu conventus sui, dedit et concessit Edwardo de Cerne imperpetuum quendam Adam Horn, nativum, p … causa meriti precedente racione cuius doni dicti abbas et conventus bona et catalla dicti Ade ac servicium eiusdem et exitus sui amiserunt \ad dampnum x li./

Item, idem abbas ante tempus commissionis predicte, sine assensu conventus sui remittit Johanni Albon et Johanni Stoke, fratri dicti abbatis, omnia servicia de eorum tenementa que tenet de dicto abbate in villenagio ad terminum vite eorumdem ad dampnum dicti monasterii per annum C ….

Item, idem abbas, ante tempus commissionis predicte et sine assensu conventus sui, manumisit et quantum in eo fuit liberum fecit Willelmum Torcher, nativum monasterii predicti, et recepit de predicto Willelmo pro manumissione p… in proprios usus convertebat, ad dampnum dicti monasterii xl li, eo quod idem Willelmus habundans est in bonis et xl li pro concessione libertatis predicte voluit abbati et conventui dedisse … predicti.

Item, idem abbas, sine assensu conventus sui et ante tempus custodie predicte, vendidit collusive et ficte, quo precio nesciunt, Willelmo de Syggeston' Dxx multones … precii Liiij li, Magistro \Willelmo/ Hamme CC hogges precii xvj li xiij s viij d, Willelmo Torcher CCxxx multones precii xxiij li, Willelmo Russel et Nicholao Haiward CCxx multones precii … CCx multones precii xxj li, Johanni Clerico et Nicholao Newelere C multones precii x li, Johanni Gibelot xx multones precii xl s, Johanni, capellano de Pudele, L multones, xx oves matrices precii … Hilvyng xxx multones, xxx oves matrices precii vj li, Johanni Albon L oves matrices, xij bidentes pro lardario precii vj li, Johanni Wylemot xx multones precii xl s, custodibus ecclesie … precii xl s, Radulpho Gaite iiij^{xx} multones precii viij li. Et omnes denarios pro dictis animalibus sic venditis dictus abbas privatim

per se recepit et in proprios usus suos convertit, absque hoc quod aliquam denar' … domus devenerunt.
Item, idem abbas, propria temeritate sua, ante tempus custodie predicte, dedit fratri Johanni Sene, monacho Glaston', unum ciphum cum pede argentum et deauratum de valore x marcas … predicta ut tesaur eiusdem existenti causa meriti nulla precedente.
Item, idem abbas, propria voluntate sua, remisit xx li sterlingorum de debito C li quos quidam dicte domui solvere manuceperunt Nicholao de Pontz, milite, pro diversis trangressionibus dicto abbati et domui predicte per eundem Nicholaem illatis.
Item, idem abbas, propria voluntate sua, ante tempus commissionis predicte, dedit cuidam Agneti de Londone et absque aliquo racione nulla precedente, unum dossorium, iij blankets, iij tapeta, ij linthiamina, j pelvum cum lavatorio, j firmaculum, j par de bedes de coral' et argente de bonis ad officium camerarii spectantis et unum plate argente pondus trium librarum pro quadam cruce inde conficienda ordinata de bonis dicte domus, ad dampnum eiusdem x li.
Item, idem abbas, ante tempus comissione predicte, sine assensu conventus sui, dedit diversis proventis in … Withston' diversis personis, ad dampnum dicte domus xx li absque causa nulla racionabili precedente.
Item idem abbas, propria voluntate sua, cum aliquibus voluntati sue temerariis adherentis aud'… More prepositi manerium de Holewale ad officium camerarii spectantem, nulli monachi in monasterii nec aliquo alio de concilio eiusdem monasterii existenti ad auditum compoti supradicti et arreragii eiusdem prepositi … extendebat recepit et eosdem denarios in proprios usus suos convertebat.
Item idem abbas ante \tempus/ comissionis predicte, sine assensu conventus sui, dedit ficte et collusive Johanni de Glaunvyle omnia blada in manerio de Holewale, pro uno anno ultra semen et liberati famuli in eodem manerio de servientis existentis de valore x marcas.
Item idem abbas, ante tempus comissionis predicte, vendidit Nicholao de Fromptone de … Waltero le Deyere de Bruweton omnes arbores vocates notebymes ubicumque in omnibus maneriis dicte abbacie crescentes pro tintura facienda de corticibus arborum predictis. Et idem abbas recepit pro eisdem xxx … pro … arbores ad x li racionabili precio estimabantur, quos denarios sic receptos idem abbas in proprios usus convertebat.
Item, idem abbas, ante tempus commissionis predicte, propria voluntate sua, dedit Willelmo Melbury tria … pro pullanis habendis et nutriendis ordinata et exitus eorum trium annorum precii xx li, et unum equum precii xvj s, Henrico Shirard ij jumenta magna precii xl s, et unum pullanum masculum precii xx s, Galfrido Walisch …, Willelmo, monacho de Middelton, unum equum precii iiij li, Thome de Upton, clerico, unum equum precii xx s, Willelmo de Betescombe, unum equum precii xx s, Ricardo Bitesthorn unum equum precii xx s, Johanni Pont…, Roberto Coco unum equum precii demi marce, Thome de Neborght, militi, j bovum precii j marca, Willelmo de Sigeston iij vaccas precii xxx s, iij quarteriis frumenti precii xx s, iij quarteriis avene precii x s, j … feni precii iiij marcas, iij quarteriis frumenti, v porcas precii xl s, ad magnum dampnum monasterii predicti et absque causa rationabili vel aliquo merito precedente.
Item, idem abbas, ante tempus comissionis predicte, propria voluntate sua, dedit Willelmo Smale de comitatu Devon' ij cignos aerarios et v alios cignos precii Lx s, Willelmo Sigeston ij cignos aerarios precii ij marcas, et eidem Willelmo vij alios

cignos precii xxiij s iiij d, Rogero Walisch iij cignos precii x s, Ricardo Peverel iij … precii xxxvj s, Johanni Glaunvyle iiij cignos precii j marca, Mathie Ludeford iij cignos precii x s, et alios pluries cignos diversis personibus quorum nomina ignorantur absque causa racionabili vel aliquo merito precedente.

Item, idem abbas, ante tempus commissionis predicte, sine assensu conventus sui, remisit Ricardo Peverel quendam annuum redditum vj s iiij d dicto monasterio debitum de quodam loco Chakerigg vocato de vj annis elapsis, ad summam xxxviij s, sine causa racionabili vel aliquo merito precedente.

Item, idem abbas, ante tempus commissionis predicte, solvit v marcas, propria voluntate sua, pro Willelmo de Betescombe uxori Johannis Crabbe, quas recuperavit per breve de dote pro dampnum de tercia parte unius messuagii unius carucate terre in Horigge detenta per dictum Willelmum de Betescombe cui dictus abbas dicta messuagium et terram dimisit ut est supradictum.

Item, idem abbas, a diu ante tempus custodie predicte, tenuit canes venaticos sumptuosos, in numero excessivo, tam suos quam alienos, et convocavit diversas persones sepius diversis temporibus ad s… venient' cum magna multitudine canum venaticorum, et expenses circa eas apposuit onerosas et convivia per tres, quatuor vel quinque dies continue duratur personas dicto monasterio non … ad eadem frequenter invitando fecit, in magnum prejudicium monasterii et eiusdem manifestam depauperacionem.

Item, idem abbas voluntarie a diu tenuit excessivam familiam et otiosam tam … quam pluribus et circa sustentacionem eorumdem minus onerosas fecit expensas ad dampnum irrecuperabilem monasterii supradicti.

Item, idem abbas, propria voluntate sua, diversis annis fecit notorie excessivam liberatam et onerosam panni dando robas cum pelura et furura multis et variis personibus, tam clericis quam laicis, et mulieribus pro maxima parte extra comitatu Dors' de gentibus ubi dictus abbas nulla habuit terras nec tenementa ad numerum, videlicet quinquaginta robarum qui dicto monasterio proferunt nec prodesse possunt per quas expensas diversimode et incomode ut premittitur facere status dicti monasterii sit in ymo ponitur quod dificile \erit/ temporibus modernis illum aliquo modo relevare.

Item, idem abbas, post tempus quo dicta abbacia dictis custodibus fuit commissa custodienda dedit Johanni Albon unum magnum jumentum pro pullanos nutriendos ordinatos et unum pullanum precii lx s, et Henrico Panetre unum bovum precii j marca, conventus et custodibus supradictis inconsultis.

Item, idem abbas, post tempus commissionis predicte, sine assensu dictorum conventus et custodium fecit acquietancia sub sigillo suo proprio sigillata cuidam Waltero Hony, nativo dicti monasterii et terre nativam tenenti de eo quod idem Walterus fuit prepositus apud Abbodesbury, Portesham, Graveston' et Louke per septennium et amplius, nullo compoto de tempore predicto per eundem Walterum reddito, et omnia servicia de tenementis dicti Walteri debita et consueta remisit ad totam vitam dicti Walteri et ipsum Walterum quantum in eo fuit liberum fecit et idem abbas recepit de dicto Waltero pro dicto facto sigillando C s, ad dampnum dicti monasterii xl li.

Item, idem abbas, post tempus commissionis predicte, dicti conventus et custodies inconsulti fecit acquietancia sub sigillo suo proprio sigillato cuidam Radulpho Dainold, preposito de Helton' de eo quod fuit prepositus ibidem per triennium, nullo compoto per ipsum Radulphum inde reddito et eciam remisit eidem Radulpho omnia reddita et servicia de quod tenemento nativo debita

et consueta, quod idem Radulphus habuit ex concessione dicti abbatis, ad dampnum dicti monasterii L li.
Item, dictus abbas, sine assensu conventus sui et ante tempus custodie predicte, scripto sigillo suo proprio signato manumisit et quantum in eo fuit liberum fecit Johannem Hake, nativum manerii de Helton' et omnia servicia de tenemento quod idem Johannes tenuit in villenagio eidem Johanni remisit et relaxavit, ad dampnum dicti monasterii xx li.
In cuius rei testimonium predicti jurati huic inquisicioni sigilla sua apposuerunt. Et est summa dampnum suprascriptorum per dictum abbatem et suos adherentes factorum prout per dictos juratos verisimiliter estimatur DCCCLv li xvj s viij d ante diem huius inquisicionis capte, absque debitis in quibus idem abbas per obligaciones et recogniciones et alio modo diversimode se et dictum monasterium oneravit que ad summam Dxxxiiij li se extendunt. Et sic est summam dampnum et debitum supradictorum: MCCCiiij^{xx}ix li xvj s viij d.

No endorsement

On 20 June 1354 the guardianship of the temporalities of Abbotsbury abbey was committed to Walter Waleys and John Munden, following Stokes's resignation (*CFR 1347–56*, p. 398). On 18 June 1354 licence was granted to elect a new abbot, and two weeks later royal assent was given to the election of Henry Toller as the new abbot of Abbotsbury (*CPR 1354–8*, pp. 73, 77).

158

Hastings, Sussex (? c. 1360–80)
Augustinian canons
(SC 8/297/14846)

The prior of Hastings petitions the chancellor for a writ to arrest Thomas, a canon of Hastings who has fled the priory with certain of its documents and has become apostate, lying in wait for the prior and his servants with men at arms, archers and others, and to return him to the priory and to religion, delivering him to the prior or sub-prior.
Endorsed: *To my most honoured and reverend lord, my lord the chancellor.*

A chaunceller nostre seignur le roi supplie soun simple chapellain le priour de Hastynges qe come il y a un Thomas, soun chanoun de sa dite priorie, q'est ale hors de sa maisoun ovesqe certains munimentz et evidences de mesme la maisoun, encountre la volunte soun dit priour et encountre sa professioun, est devenu apostata et jettet en pays ove force de gentz armez, archiers et autres, en agaitant son dit priour et ses ministres, issint q'ils nosent aproscher lour manoirs en pays ne lour profit faire. Qe luy please de sa grace graunter brief de prendre le dit apostata et de lui remover a sa dite maisoun et religioun, et de fair la liveree du dit apostata a soun priour ou a soun suppriour, en oevre de charite.

Endorsed: A moun treshonure et tresreverent seignur monseignur le chaunceller.

? c. 1360–80. Tentatively dated on the basis of the hand.

159

St Giles-in-the-Fields, London (1391–1402)
Hospital
(SC 8/324/E617B)

To the king and the Lords of the present parliament from the lepers of the hospital of St Giles outside Holborn requesting remedy as the current master of the hospital, the abbot of St Mary Graces, has withdrawn the alms and hospitality that they are assigned and does not wish to receive further sick into the hospital to bring it up to its full total.

A nostre soveragne et tresredoute seignur le roy et al nobles et sages seignurs de cest present [parlement] suppliont humblement voz poveres oratours les lepres del hospital Seint Gyles dehors Holborne el countee de Midd' qe [come] .... fuist foundu en sustinance des lepres, ratifie et conferme par les progenitours nostre dit seignur le roy en affermance et encreas, de quele .... de la dite citee ount donez et divisez tenementz et rentz provenantz de la value de quatres vintz livres annueles pur resceyver et sustiner .... lepres deinz la citee de Loundres et les suburbes d'ycelle, et ceo par veue des gentz de la dite citee eslieuz par le mair illeoqes qi pur .... et purtant qe pur le gardein del dit hospital qe pur le temps estoit en le temps l'aiel nostre dit seignur le roy q'orest, les ditz lepres furent estrangez et ousteez del dit hospital, finale accord soy prist par avys du dit aiel et soun conseil parentre les mair et la comunaltee de la dite citee et le dit gardeyn, par endentures entre eux ent faitez, qe mesme le gardeyn et ses successours dussent resceyver perpetuelement xiiij lepres de le dite citee et les suburbes d'ycelle, et par presentement du dite maire et ses ditz bones gentz, et en cas qe le nombre ne purroit estre parfourne par lepres francs du dite citee de le parforner en le countee de Middilsex al presentement de mesme le mair, et de les trover viver, vesture, chausure, fouale, lumer, liter, herbage et autres necessaires, come en mesmes les endentures plus pleinement poet appayer, la ad l'abbe de Grace joust le Tour de Loundres, ore gardein del dit hospital, sustreit la dite almoigne et hospitalite et a present ne ad deinz le dit hospitale qe cynk de malades avauntditz et ne voet plusours resceyver, et outre ceo purposant a deshospitaliter, estranger et subduire deux del ditz cynkes lepres, et entre ceo ad sustret graunde partie del almoigne a eu approprie, dount ile priount[32] remedy, pur Dieu et en eovere de charite.

No endorsement

1391–1402. The hand suggests that this petition is of the early fifteenth century. In 1391 Richard II removed legal possession of St Giles's Hospital from the master of Burton Lazars and granted the hospital, advowson and lands in frankalmoin to the abbey of St Mary Graces on Tower Hill (*CPR 1396–9*, pp. 47–8; *VCH Middlesex*, I, 207). In 1402, as a result of legal proceedings instigated by the dispossessed master of Burton Lazars, the abbey of St Mary Graces' grant of St Giles Hospital was revoked and Burton Lazars was restored to legal possession (*VCH Middlesex*, I, 208). Thus the abbot of St Mary Graces was William Wardon who occurred c. 1360–1405, and as warden of St Giles 1391–1402 (*CPR 1401–5*, p. 120). This petition was apparently consulted in the eighteenth century, as there is an endorsement in a hand of that period.

32 The letters *red* have been deleted.

160

Stratford Langthorne, Essex, and St Mary Graces, London (1471)

Cistercian
(SC 8/195/9721)

Letter, dated 15 January 1471, to Henry VI from Hugh, abbot of Stratford Langthorne, and Thomas, abbot of St Mary Graces, confirmers and reformers of the Cistercian order, stating that Thomas Oliver, abbot of [Buckland, Devon], was legitimately convicted before them and stripped of his abbacy, and that this was confirmed by the general chapter at Cîteaux; and he was also excommunicated for his contumacy in refusing to obey their commands and those of the general chapter. William Bretayn has now been appointed abbot, but Thomas and his supporters are preventing and obstructing him from gaining possession of the monastery. They request a remedy from the king.

Excellentissimo in Cristo principi et domino, domino Henrico, dei gracia regi Anglie et Francie ac domino Hibernie: nos Hugo et Thomas, permissione divina ... Marie de Stratford et de Graciis juxta Turrim London', ordinis Cisterciensis, Londoniens' diocesis, conservatores et reformatores monasteriorum dicte ... Wallie, salutem in eo per quem reges regnant et principes dominantur. Vestre regie celsitudini tenore presencium intimamus et intimare volumus ... et conservator predictus unacum venerabili confratre nostro Johanne, abbate monasterii Beate Marie de Wardon' dicte ordinis, Lincoln' diocesis, adtunc co.... monasterii juxta Turrim Londoniarum predict', in judicio et judicialiter sedentes contra quendum Dompnum Thomam Oliver, monachum ac abbatem monasterii Beate M[arie de Buckland, Ex]onien' diocesis, se pretendentem legitime procedentes servatis que in ea parte de jure servandis eundem Dompnum Thomam propter sua gravia et enorma pecca[ta] ... malam conversacionem de et super quibus coram nobis legitime convictus extitit ipsius dignitate et prelacia abbaciale predicta per nostram finam diffinitiva ... promulgatam privaminus, deinde vero per reverendum patrem abbatem Cistercii et totum generalem capitulium apud Cistercium adtunc celebratum decreti... profertur per nos late ac ipsam sentenciam justam et validam et legitime latam fuisse et esse ac de jure subsistere et tenere debet. Idem quoque Dompnus Thomas contumacias manifestas in non parendo certis decretis et monicionibus per nos et abbatem Cistercii et generale capitulum ibidem celebratum legitime late et ... et capituli auctorite excommunicatus fuit ac pro excomunicato publice et solempniter denunciatus, ac sic stetit quasi per triennium ac stat in presenti annuo pert... matris ecclesie et regulas dicte ordinis nequiter contempnendo. Quodque dictus venerabilis confrater noster Johannes et nos Thomas de Ward... [conser]vatores et reformatores predicti, auctoritate qua fungebamur in ea parte jure devolucionis, venerabilem confratrem nostrum Dompnum Willielmum Bretay[n] ... [mo]nachum et prefatum ordinem expresse professum in abbatem futurum eiusdem monasterii adtunc solacio abbaciali destituto canonice preficimus et ordinamus ... [or]dinacio eiusdem abbatis erat per dictum abbatem Cistercii et capitulum generale ibidem celebratum canonice confirmata et roborata, ipse que dompnu[m] ... suam dignitatem et prelaciam abbacialem sic canonice assentam cum suis juribus et pertinenciis universis per nonnulla tempora possedit pacifi... gravaminum subscriptorum. Prefatus tamen Dompnus Thomas Oliver premissis non obstantibus unacum complicibus et fautoribus suis in subvers... Dompni Willelmi Bretayn', abbatis antedicti tempore malicie adinvicem confederati et colligati eundem Dompnum Willelmum, abbatem predictum, in ... mancipari procuravit, fecit et obtinuit prout injuste detruditur et mancipaturi in presenti. Sic que et alias idem Dompnus Thomas Oliver pref[atum Willelmum] Bretayn' abbatem predictum circa jus, titulum et possessionem sua premissa multipliciter et injuste molestavit, inquietavit et perturbavit ac ... perturbat in presenti ac impedivit et impedit quominus dictus Dompnus Willelmus Bretayn in spiritualibus et temporalibus dicti sui a... dignitate abbaciale gaudere ut deberet in animam dicti Dompni Thome Oliver gravem periculum ac prefati Dompni Willelmi Bretayn', ab[batem mo]nasterii sui predicti, dampnum nonmodicum dicte que ordinis contemptum et scandalum manifeste \regie celsitudini prelibate humiliter supplicantes ut in premissis provideatur de remedio in hac parte/. In quorum premissorum omnium et singulorum ...[Hu]go et Thomas, abbates ac conservatores et reformatores predicti, sigilla nostra presentibus apposuimus. Dat' in monasteriis nostris de ... quintodecimo die mensis Januarii anno domini millesimo quadringentesimo septuagesimo.

No endorsement

1471. Thomas Oliver became abbot of Buckland in 1464, but was deprived of his office in 1469 by the abbot of Quarr, who appointed William Breton as abbot, beginning a dispute over the abbacy. The petition appears to date to shortly after this event, the petitioners being Hugh Watford, who occurs as abbot of Stratford Langthorne from 1466 to 1490, and Thomas Bene, who occurs as abbot of St Mary Graces from 1458 to 1475. On 14 August 1469 justices of the peace were ordered to remove Oliver and others who held the abbey by force, and to put Breton into possession (*CPR 1467–77*, pp. 171–2). On 16 January 1471 a commission was ordered to arrest Thomas Oliver and bring him before the king and council, to release William Breton, imprisoned at Buckland by Oliver, and to bring him before the king and council to show his complaint (*CPR 1467–77*, p. 251). Thomas Oliver continues to occur as abbot until c. 1500. Further detailed discussion of this dispute, with references, can be found in *Heads of Houses III*, 275–6. The right-hand edge of the document is missing.

Part Five

PETITIONS FROM CORPORATE RELIGIOUS IDENTITIES

161

Cluniacs (1330)
(SC 8/159/7945)

The English monks of the order of Cluny petition the king and council:
(1) requesting amendment and remedy for the misgovernment of their houses.
(2) complaining that they are not visited by archbishops or bishops of the land.
(3) complaining that there are no elections, and those that are pastors are not clergy but money collectors who take their goods out of the land.
(4) complaining that if a monk speaks about the order and religion they are sent 100 leagues away on foot without expenses, so that none dare speak of the religion.
(5) complaining that they have to go overseas to be professed and get no expenses, and request that the prior of Lewes should be made an abbot to profess monks in this country so that they do not have to go abroad.
(6) complaining about having two nations in one house as they will never agree.
Endorsed: *The abbots and priors of the order who are of the king's patronage in England should be ordered to make hasty amendment of the things contained in the petition, so that the king does not have to do it in another manner. Concerning the abbots and priors who are of other patronage, let nothing be done.*

A nostre seygnur le rey e a son conseyl monstre plusurs [a]del[a] ordre de Cluny coment les mesuns sunt [a]malement[a] governe en spirituaute e en temperaute, en grant deshonur \de/ nostre [a]seygnour[a] le rey, e en grant damage des moynes e des mesuns, e de ce prient remedie. Premierement, en grant \damage/ de nostre seygnur le rey, e en disheritance de ses aucestres ke funderent les mesons, la ou dussunt estre karante moynes ou trente, ilnia sur la tierze partie, e [a]numement[a] a Montague e a Bermundesee e pertent, e de ce ke il dussent sustenir les moynes il donent grans douns pur mentenir lur errur e en portent les byns hors de la tere a dishonour de rey, e grant damage de mesons e des moynes.
Le secund mal: il ne sunt visite de Erceveke ne de eveke ne de nul de la [a]natiun[a] de la terre, a grant damage de mesuns e de moynes.
Le terz mal: il nia nul election, e ce est en contre la reule Seynt Benet, mes tel serra pastor ke ne set reyns de clergie mes queiller le argent e en porter sevent il byn hors de la terre.
Le quart mal: ke si un moyne parle de ordre ou de religiun, il serra maunde cent lewes hors e ape e apoy despenses, e purice le ordre de Cluny, en ale ahunte, e purice nul ne ose parler de religiun.
Le quint mal: est nous ne sumus vint profes en cete tere, e les aliens averunt despenses, e les Engleys faudrunt byn, e les virs sunt karaunte aunz en le ordre, avant ke il seyent profes, e les autres sunt jammes profes. Ce [a]fut[a] un des ordinances ordine en parlement pur le ordre de Cluny ke ky fut priur de Lewes dut

estre un abbe pur fere les moynes profes en lur tere de meyne, e oyr e determiner les pleyntes en lur tere, ke eus ne usunt mester de passer la mer e estre huny e pardu.
Le sime grant mal est ke le une naciun serrunt tuz mestres par heritage ne senent il ia si poy e ne facent il si malement e les autres tuz fugez ne facent il si byn, e ce est en contre la reule Seynt Benet. Les deus naciuns en une mesun ne sey acordement jammes Grant bounte serreyt de amender les grant damages ke attenent de ces maus.

Endorsed: Soit mande a les abbees et priours del dit ordre qe sont del patronage le roi en Engleterre, qil facent hastif amendement des choses contenues en ceste peticion, en peril_appertement issi qe le roi ne ad mester de metere la main en autre manere. Et quant [a–]as[–a] abbeis et priories qe sont de autre advoerie, nihil fiat.

[a–a] reading uncertain.

1330. This petition was printed by C. Reynerus, who found it in the Tower of London in an original bundle of petitions presented to the parliament at Winchester in March 1330. It was noted to be sixty-third in the bundle. C. Reynerus, *Apostolatus Benedictinorum in Anglia* (Douai, 1626), Appendix, pt III, no. lxviii, p. 148.

162

Cistercians (1299–1307)
(SC 8/265/13222)

To the king and council from the Cistercian abbots of England, executors of the late Queen Eleanor of Castile, requesting that the king release them from his demand that they give and grant him the Queen's Gold of 2000 marks taken since the time of her death.
Endorsed: *The council agreed that from the time the first queen died until the time of the new queen's marriage, there should be no levy of Queen's Gold, and if any was levied, it should be restored.*

A nostre seyngur le roy d'Engleterre e a son consail prient tutz ses abbes del ordre de Cisteus de sa terre qe pur ce ke les executurs Dame Alionore, jadis reyne e compayne nostre seygnur le roy, demandent de les avantditz abbes ...... son or de deus mil mars qe eus granterent e donerent a nostre seygnur le roy en noun de quintyme apres la mort la [dit] reyne, a ky alme Deus face verrey mercy, ke il de sa grace voille cele demande relesser, issint ke sa alme se........... plus especialment recomande en les messes, urisouns e en tutz les biens fetz del ordre.

Endorsed: Concordatus[33] est \per consilium/ quod a tempore quo alia regina decessa usque ad tempus quo nova regina desponsa fuit non levetur aurum ad opus earum pro finibus medio tempore factis, et si levas fuit, habeat inquirens super restitucione.

1299–1307. Eleanor of Castile died in November 1290. Edward remarried, to Margaret of France, in September 1299. 'Queen's Gold' was instituted by Queen Eleanor of Aquitaine (1122–1204) at the start of her reign as a way of establishing a degree of financial

33 *quod de* deleted.

independence for herself. By the thirteenth century it had become standardised as a levy of 10% on voluntary fines of 10 marks or more made to the king: T. F. Tout, *Chapters in the Administrative History of Medieval England*, 6 vols (1920–33), V, 264–7.

163

Cistercians (c. 1307)
(SC 8/321/E452)

To the king: an abbot on behalf of (himself and) the whole Cistercian order requesting that whereas in parliament at Westminster on 28 February 1305 Edward I ruled that no abbot, prior, master, warden or other religious of this realm could contribute any money to any other religious outside the realm on pain of grave punishment, mentioning especially abbots, priors and wardens of alien religious houses in his realm, which statute prevents Cistercian abbots from attending their general chapter and contributing to the necessary charges of the business of their order, that they may have the king's letters patent allowing them to attend the general chapter of their order and obey its statutes and ordinances as other abbots of their order do, and to contribute proportionately to any necessary charges ordained by the general chapter, notwithstanding the statute. They also ask for letters patent instructing all the king's officers and ministers to stop upholding and maintaining these declarations and ordinances towards them.

Regie magestati significat abbas Cistercii pro se et toto ordine Cistercii que inclite recordationis dominus Rex Edwardus, pater suus, die dominica post festum Sancti Mathei apostoli apud Westm' in parliamento suo anno regni sui xxxiij°, inter cetera statuit ne quis abbas, prior, magister, custos seu quis alius alicuius religionis sub potestate et jurisditione suo constitutus censum aliquem per superiores suos, abbates, priores, magistros, custodes religiosarum domorum vel locorum importum vel inter se ipsos aliqualiter ordinatum extra regnum suum et dominium sub nomine redditus, tallagii, aporte, impositionis cuiuscumque vel alio nomine escambii, venditionis, mutui vel alterique contractus quocumque nomine censeantur, per se vel per mercatores aut alios, clam vel palam arte vel ingenio deferat vel transmittat seu deferri faciat quocumque modo, nec etiam ad ...neas partes divertat causa visitationis vel colore alio quisitio ut sic bona et monasteriorum et domorum suarum extra regnum et dominium suum predictum abducat. Et si quis que dictum statutum venire presumpserit considerata qualitate delicti et regie prohibitionis pensato contemptu graviter puniatur. Preterea inhibuit dictus dominus rex in eodem statuto omnibus et singulis abbatibus, prioribus, cutodibus religiosarum domorum et locorum alienigenis quorum potestati, subjectioni et obediencie domus eorundem ordinum in regno et dominio suo existentes subduntur ne decetero tallagia, impositiones, aporta, contributiones seu alia quecumque onera aliquibus monasteriis, prioratibus seu aliis domibus religiosis eis subjectis imponant aut faciant aliqualiter assidere. Et hoc sub forefactura omnium que in potestate sua obtinent et forefacere \poterunt/ in futurum. Occasione cuius statuti contigit et posset contigere in futurum quod aliqui abbates dicti ordinis regni et dominii sui ad generale capitulum Cistercii temporibus quibus tenentur non venerunt nec venirent. Et illa que pro communibus, neccessitatibus seu negociis et oneribus totius ordinis Cistercii pro rata eos contingente in ipso generali capitulo sicut ceteris abbatibus aliorum regnorum et terrarum imposita fuerunt temporibus retroactis et in futurum imponentitur prestare, solvere, contribuere et portare, per se vel per alios, prout aliter si consuetum est ab antiquis temporibus et servatum obmiserunt, cessaverunt et forte obmitterent, cessarent seu desisterent in grave totius ordinis prejudicium et contemptum, et status unitatis religionis et obedientie detrimentum. Quare supplicat idem abbas nomine quo supra humiliter eidem regie magestati quatenus dignetur per suas patentes litteras declarare et ordinare quod, non obstante predicto statuto et prohibitionibus ac penis in eo contentis, abbates dicti ordinis et eorum quilibet regni et dominii sui possint libere et absque aliquo impedimento ire et accedere consuetis temporibus ad dictum capitulum generalem ut parere positur et obedire statutis et ordinationibus dicti capituli sicut et ceteri abbates ordinis universi. Et illa quod per ipsum capitulam generale decetero ipsis abbatibus et cuilibet eorumdem ratione communium expensarum, negociorum, neccessitatum seu onerum totius ordinis supradicti pro rata eos contingente sicut ceteris abbatibus aliorum regnorum et terrarum imponentur seu imposita fuerint libere et absque alicuius impedimento possint per se vel alium seu alios portare, mittere et de regno et dominio suo extrahere et solvere seu contribuere, prout in ipso generali capitulo fuerit ordinatum. Et nichilominus per alias suas patentes litteras mandare dignetur omnibus et singulis suis justiciis, constabulariis, ballivis, portuum custodibus et aliis eius ministris seu officiis quocumque nomine censeantur que predictam declarationes et ordinationes suas diligenter teneant et observent. Et quod nec ipsas declarationes et ordinationes in nullo veniant nec et aliquem venire permittant.

No endorsement

c. 1307. A Latin summary of an earlier petition by the same petitioners on this same matter was enrolled on the parliament roll of the parliament held in February 1305 (*Memoranda de Parliamento*, ed. F. W. Maitland (London, 1893) pp. 312–13, no. 485; and *PROME*, Edward I, Roll 12, item 573 (485)). This petition, however, clearly refers to events of the thirty-third year of the reign of Edward I (1304/5), who is described as the king's father, so it must date to Edward II's reign. On 4 October 1308 the release was ordered of several Cistercian abbots who had gone overseas without licence to attend the general chapter (*CCR 1307–13*, p. 79), and in 1309 permits were issued to eighteen heads of houses to attend the general chapter of that year (*CCR 1307–13*, p. 165). The petition links with the campaign of Edward I to prevent the export of English currency, which gained statutory authority in the parliament held at Carlisle in 1307: *PROME*, Vetus Codex, 19; *SR*, I, 150–2. This was a delayed response to a petition presented by the earls, barons and community of England in 1305 who complained about the tallages imposed by the abbot of Cîteaux on English Cistercian houses: *Memoranda de Parliamento*, pp. 313–14, no. 486; and *PROME*, Edward I, Roll 12, item 574 (486). From 1298 Edward specifically forbade Cistcercian abbots from attending their general chapter without special licence from the English crown: L. A. Desmond, 'The Statute of Carlisle and the Cistercians 1298–1369', in *Studies in Medieval Cistercian History Presented to Jeremiah F. O'Sullivan* (Shannon, 1971), pp. 138–62.

164

Knights Templars (Nov. 1308 – Spring 1310)
(SC 8/191/9530)

The master of the Temple petitions the king, making three requests:
(1) that he might be released on mainprise, and that he might have some of his brothers to keep him company, until the king orders their deliverance or his will, as he will become ill if he remains in the castle any longer.
(2) that the king make some ordinance concerning the chantries given to the Templars.
(3) for remedy concerning the pensions and other maintenance given by the Templars to various people.
Endorsed on face: *[To the second] The chantries and alms are to be maintained as they should be.*
[To the third] The allowances which have hitherto been granted by those who have power to grant them, for money, possessions or good service, to various people for term of life, are to be made according to the advice of the treasurer and of the king's council, when they have shown their titles; and to those to whom pensions are due, it is answered that when anyone comes forward to sue and show his title, he will be given a fitting response.

A nostre seignur le roy prie le meistre de Temple qu'il li vueille, pur Dieu, granter sa demoere en aucun lieu lyvest hors de chastel par bone meinprise, et peut partie des freres pur lui tenir cumpaignie ilueqes, ci la qe le roy eit comandez lur deliverance \ou sa voluntez/, car le dit meistre cherra tost en grant maladie si il demoere gueres en chastel.
Item, pur ce qe diverses terres, rentes et autres possessions sont donees as Templiers en Engleterre depar les ancestres nostre seignur le roy et autres prodeshommes de la terre, pur messes chanter en les chapelles de Temple pur le salut de lur almes et de lur ancestres et successors, prie le dit meistre qe le roy, pur Dieu, wueille ordiner de ce son pleisir pur si bone aumosne meintenir.
Item, come diverse gentz eient dona au Temple lur terres, rentes et autres biens, les uns pur avoir lur sustenance en Temple et les autres certaine liveree de viande et autres certeine enpension en deniers, et autres y az qui pur le bon service qu'il tut lur aage unt fait as Templers, unt certaines enpensions du Temple par bones chartres a nostre seignur le roy, prie le dit meistre qu'il de sa grace vueille pur les avantdites gentz comander remedy, si li pleist.

Endorsed on face: [To the second] Soient les chaunteries et les aumones meintenues solonc ce qe elles devient.
[To the third] Les livreisons qe sont grantez avant ces heures par ceux qu'il poer avoient de les granter, por deners ou pur possessions ou pur bon servise, a diverses gentz a terme de leur vies, soient faites selonc l'avisement du tresorer et du consail le roy, quant il auront moustrez lour titles; et de ceux a qui enpensions sont dues, respondu est qe quant nul vendra sivre et moustra son title, hom en ordenera tieu respons comme appent.

Nov. 1308 – Spring 1310. William de la More, the Master in England, was arrested on 9 January 1308 and imprisoned at Canterbury, but under comfortable conditions: he had many personal possessions and was allowed the company of two brethren. He was released on 27 May, but rearrested on 27 November 1308. It is not clear where he was then imprisoned until the summer of 1311 when he was sent to the Tower, where he died before February 1313. The plea for companions, and the reference to a castle, suggest that this petition dates from his second period of imprisonment, and probably fairly soon after his second arrest, for by the time of his examination before a provincial council in spring 1310 he could have had no hope of being released on mainprise: M. Barber, *The Trial of the Templars* (Cambridge, 1978), pp. 195–202.

165

Cistercians (1324–5)
(SC 8/8/359)

The community of the Cistercian order in England petition the king and council for remedy because, although they receive into their order people of every nation, provided that they are of good life and morals, the abbots of Ireland are refusing to admit Englishmen, but take only the Irish. The community requests that the Irish monks accept Englishmen of good life – as the English houses accept them.
Endorsed: *The justiciar of Ireland is ordered to command the said abbots to receive these people as they would others; and if not, he is to have them appear before him to show their reasons, and then inform the king of them.*
Before the great council.
For the community of the Cistercian order.

A nostre seingnur le roy et a son consail mustre la communaute del ordre de Cistens en Engletere qe par la ou eux receyvent en lour religion et de comun dreit deyvent receyvere genz de chekun nacion, issint qe eux seyent genz de bone faire, bone vie et bon conversacion, les abbes d'Irland ne velunt receyvere nul home entre eux qe est de la nacion d'Engletere fors tantsolement de lour nacion demeyne, en despisaunt nostre seingnur le rey et ces genz de sa tere d'Engletere. Par quey tut la comunaute del dit ordre en Engletere prie a nostre seingnur le rey, si luy pleise, q'il voile de ceo ordener remedie, issint qe la dit religion d'Irlande receyve entre eux le genz d'Engletere qe seient de bon conversacion si cum les gentz d'Engletere loux receyvent entre eux en Engletere.

Endorsed: Soit mande au justice Irlaunde qil face mander au ditz abbes qeux receyvere auxi bien un com autres; et qi ceo none, q'il les face venir devant li a moustrer leur resons, et puis certefie le roi de leur cause.
Coram magno consilio.
Pro comunitate ordinis de Cisteux.

1324–5. This petition probably belongs to 18 Edward II, although there is no indication that it was presented either at the non-parliamentary assembly of October 1324 or the parliament of June 1325 (*PROME*, Appendix of Unedited Petitions, 1307–37). It appears to be a duplicate, with only minor embellishments, of SC 8/8/360 which was probably presented at the same time (*RP*, I, 420, no. 14). The complaint was a product of the political and social situation in Ireland, where, from the later thirteenth century, the power of the Anglo-Norman lordship was failing. As law and order broke down ill-feeling between the two races grew more marked, the tension between the two nations being strongly manifest in religious communities, especially among the Franciscans and Cistercians. See K. Walsh, *A Fourteenth-Century Scholar and Primate: Richard FitzRalph in Oxford, Avignon and Armagh* (Oxford, 1981), pp. 4–15 and references, and J. A. Watt, *The Church and the Two Nations in Medieval Ireland* (Cambridge, 1970), pp. 173–83, 189–91.

166

Bury St Edmunds, Suffolk, and Holy Trinity, Norwich, Norfolk (c. 1362)
Benedictine
West Dereham, Norfolk
Premonstratensian canons
West Acre, Pentney and Wormegay, Norfolk
Augustinian canons
Shouldham, Norfolk
Gilbertine
(SC 8/211/10502)

The abbots of Bury St Edmunds and West Dereham, the priors of Norwich, West Acre, Shouldham, Pentney and Wormegay, Lord Bardolf and Lord Scales petition the king and council, complaining of the pressures on the communities of Wiggenhall, Watlington, South Lynn and Setchey in the Marshland in Norfolk as a result of the acquisition by John Wesenham of the whole of South Clenchwarton.
Endorsed: *Order of Wesensham and others to appear before the council.*

A nostre seignur le roi et a soen counseil priont ses devoutz chapeleyns les abbes de Burghe Seynt Esmond et de Derham, et les priours de Norwycz, Westacre, Shouldham, Pentenye et Wyrmegeye, le seignur Bardolf, le seignur de Scales, pur eaux et lour tenauntz et pur tote soen lege poeple des villes de Wygenale, Watlyngtone, Southe Lynne et Sechehythe en Mershland, qe come Johan de Wesenham eit purchace des diverses gentz tote le plus de la vill de Southclenchewartone, quele ville soleit garder et fair lez mures et fosses devers la myer pur lour quantite, sicome lez altres villes avantditz de mesme la paies sont chargiez, chescune de lour salvacioun saunz eide avoir nule ville d'autre, le dit Johan ad par feynt sugestioun purchace comissioun de la Chauncellery as certeyn gentz de son paiis pur fair les avantditz religiouses et seignours, lour tenantz et le dit poeple des villes avantditz contributoris et charges de la fesantz et meyntenantz des mures et fosses de Southclenchwartone avantdit, quele charge la dite ville de Southclenchewartone deveroit fair a tote tiemps ad fait, par l'ou \et/ issint sont les autres villes chargiez chesqune de sa gard alleours de deinz sa ville demesme. Qe plese a sa hautesse comander a soen counseill d'oier les resons des religiouses et seignours avantditz, et auxint de dit Johan de Wesenham et d'autres terre tenantz de Southclenchwarton' avantditz, q'ont jour a ore devant counseill par garnisement par brief nostre seignur le roi, et les ajugger par lour avys et descrecioun siqe le dit Johan par sa richesse et mestrie ne soit suffert d'aler a finale oppressioun et destruccioun de le dit poeple et des altres lieges nostre dit seignur le roi en celles parties, et eiant regard qe des religiouses et seignours avantditz, l'abbe de Burghe Seynt Esmond, le seignour Bardolf, le seignur de Scales teneient en chief de nostre seignur le roi grante quantite de lour terres en les villes de Wygenale, Watlyngtone, Southe Lenne et Sechhythe avantditz, queles terres si devenissent as meyns nostre seignur le roi par gard ou altre voie serreient chargiez en sa meyn, a grant descresse et damage de lui.

Endorsed: Soit Johan de Wesenham et les autres tenantz de Southclenchewartone garniz de venir devant le conseil a certein jour, et aussi les seignurs nomez en la bille et les tenantz des dites villes d'autre part garniz de venir a mesme le jour, et illoqes oiez lour resons d'une partie et d'autre, soit droit fait as parties.

c. 1362. On 16 February 1362 John Bardolf and Robert of Scales, with others, were named as commissioners *de walliis et fossatis* on the sea between South Clenchwarton and Wiggenhall (*CPR 1361–4*, p. 206); although Bardolf had been named on previous commissions (*CPR 1354–8*, pp. 385, 450), this was Scales's only appointment. It is thus likely that this petition dates to 1362. If this is the case, some of the petitioners can be identified as: John of Brinkley, abbot of Bury St Edmunds 1361–78; John of Weeting, occurring as abbot of West Dereham 1351–63; Nicholas of Hoo, prior of Norwich 1357–81; Peter Bysshop *alias* of Buckenham, prior of Pentney 1353–81; John Bardolf, third Lord Bardolf (d. 1363); Robert of Scales, third Baron Scales (d. 1369). The identities of the priors of West Acre, Shouldham and Wormegay are not known.

167

The Commons of Parliament (1376)
SC 8/293/14610

The Commons in parliament petition the king, asking that he consider how his ancestors founded many houses of religion in England which are subject to other houses overseas, and how French monks are sent to govern these English houses, who do not understand English people or the manners of the land, so that through their ignorance these houses are often badly governed; and their heads have always refused to appoint English monks to these houses. They ask the king to write to these heads, asking them to appoint deputies or vicars in England, and to present to the king and other lords English-born monks to govern these houses, so that they can be properly governed, especially as most of the monks in these houses are English, and quite capable of governing them.

Pleise a nostre seignur le roi de emendre coment ses progenitours ount foundez plusours maisons de religioun conventueles en Engleterre les [quelles] sount soget as autres maisons de par de la la meere, as queles maisons en Engleterre sount maundez moignes Fraunceis pur government des dites maisons, les queles ne ount conisaunce des gentz ne savont la maner de la terre, et pur lour ignoraunces les maisons sount moult empire et nounpas si bien governetz come bone serroit, et outre ceo les sovereignetz par de la ount euwe de deigne dont temps devaunt ses heures de presenter nulle moigne Engleis as dites maisons conventueles. Dount pleise a nostre dit seignur le roi de escrire et prier as sovereignes de par de la q'ils presentent ou facent vicaries ou deputes en Engleterre, q'ils purrent presenter a ly et as autres seignurs en semblable cas, moignes Engleis et qe ount este devant ses heures empiretz par les aliens pur la cause suisdit, et qe divine servise et almoignes et autres chargez apurtenantz regard sount Engleis et nounpas aliens et la plus graunt partie de eux auxi sachaunt et suffisant ou plus de governer en Engleterre nulle alien come la chose se moustre enfait.

No endorsement

1376. This petition follows closely the first part of a common petition on the parliament roll of 1376 (*PROME*, parliament of 1376, item 128 (LXIX)) and appears to represent a first version of the final enrolled version. In the first parliament of Richard II's reign, which met in October 1377, the Commons further petitioned for the expulsion of all alien religious (and others) for the duration of the war: *PROME*, parliament of October 1377, item 91 (L). For background, see A. K. McHardy, 'The Alien Priories and the Expulsion of Aliens from England in 1378', in *Church, Society and Politics*, ed. D. Baker, Studies in Church History, 12 (Oxford, 1975), pp. 133–41 and **92** above.

168

Chaplains, Abbots and Priors of England (? 1377)

(SC 8/102/5091)

The chaplains, abbots, priors and other men of religion petition the king for an ordinance in this present parliament preventing certain abuses that hinder their duty to God and the souls of the founders of their houses in peace, as the freedom of Holy Church demands, without wasting their goods in litigation. They complain that before this time many corrodies were granted to various men by false representation, to houses not held of the king nor established of his foundation, by which grants the poor religious are greatly impoverished and are unable to discharge such burdens without lengthy litigation, to their great and grievous cost and expense.

A lour tresexelent segniour le roi suplient ces povres chapleyns, abbes, priours et altres gentz de religioun qe come avaunt ces heurez pluisours corrodiez ount este grauntez as diverses gentz par faulx susgestioun en lour mesouns la oue les dit religious rienz ne tiegnent del roi ne sount de sa fundacioun, par quelx grauntz les ditz povrez religiouns sount grandment enpovres et anentiz et ne pount eux descharger de tielx chargez saunz longe sute faire par proces de ley et grandz et grevouses custagez et despencez pur la grand maintenaunce qe telx grauntez fount encountre eux, q'il pleise a sa tresgraciouse signurie, en ovre de charite, ordiner en cest presente parlement tielx remedie qe les ditz povrez religiouns ne soient issint par cel cause destrutz et q'ils puissent server Deux et les almez de lour foundeours en pees, com franchise de seint eglise demande, saunz gaster lour bienz entour tielx sutez nient resonablez.

No endorsement

? 1377. Dated on the guard, though there is no evidence to confirm this. The granting of corrodies in religious houses not of royal foundation and holding nothing of the crown, which is alleged in this petition, indicated the huge pressure facing the king to provide pensions to his servants. Fullest discussion of this is by J. H. Tillotson, 'Clerical Petitions 1350–1450', unpublished D.Phil. thesis, Australian National University (1969), pp. 33–41.

169

Dominicans (1378)

(SC 8/138/6869)

Thomas Rushook, prior provincial of the order of friars preachers in England, petitions the king and Lords of parliament that John Leicester, William Cambre and Peter Daniel be permitted, as proctors of the order of friars preachers, to lay certain matters before parliament concerning John Parys.

A nostre tresexcellent et tresredoute seignur le roy et as les tresages seignurs de son parlement supplient treshumblement voz devotez oratours Frere Thomas Rysshok, priour provinciale del ordre des Freres Prechours d'Engleterre, et toute le darrein chapitre provincialez del ordre et province avantditz, qe pleise as voz tresexcellent seignuries doner esconte a dit provinciale ou as ses procuratours, Frere Johan Leycestre, vicare de meisme l'ordre en Irland, Frere William Cambre, bacheler en devynite, et Frere Piers Daniell, pur vous moustrer certeines grevances, contemps et prejudicez qe sont faitez par une Frere Johan Parys encontre l'onour de vostre tresredoute seignur le roy et le roialme en defaute de nostre religioun en Engleterre ou devant voz deputez en excusacioun a vous de dit ordre de ces contemptez et prejudicez faitez par le dit Frere Johan Parys, pur l'amour de Dieu et conservacioun de nostre religioun.

No endorsement

1378. This petition arose from a dispute within the Dominican order between Thomas Rushook, provincial by 1373, and John Paris, who was vicar-general of the English province in 1378. In 1378 a dispute between Paris and Rushook (along with other officers of the order) led to Rushook's deposition by a general chapter of the order at Carcassonne, but on 10 November 1378, probably as a result of this petition, the crown permitted him to appeal to the pope. The case was heard by Cardinal Carracciolo, and on 25 August 1379 Rushook was restored to office by the new (Roman) pope Urban VI. Both Rushook and Paris subsequently had royal connections; Rushook became Richard II's confessor in spring 1379, and bishop, first of Llandaff (1383), then Chichester (1385): R. G. Davies, 'Rushook, Thomas (*d.*1393)', *ODNB*. Paris, whose main importance lay in the pursuit of heretics, preached before Richard at York in 1396: *BRUC*, 441–2. A Dominican of London, named 'Parris', was one of the jurors in the case against the heresy of John Wyclif in 1382 (J. Foxe et al., *History Acts and Monuments* (1570), p. 534).

170

Dominicans (1390)
(SC 8/132/6589)

The Dominicans of England petition the king and Lords in parliament that whereas they were founded to resist and destroy the heresies and errors of the church and to preach and inform the people of God of the law, to do which they must be of good living and a master of divinity, certain members of their order, apostates condemned to prison by the order, cross the sea to purchase the degree of master of divinity and other graces. They request that all the priors and convents of their order be commanded, on pain of forfeiture, not to deal with such apostates with such purchases or provisions as masters of divinity approved by examination of their order and of a university, and not to allow them to enjoy such graces, but to resist them.
Endorsed: *The king wills it for all the four mendicant orders and for all other religious.*

A tresexcellent et tresgracious seignur nostre seignur le roi et les treshonurables seignurs de cest present parlement suppliont humblement voz poveres chapelleins et oratours les freres precheurs d'Engleterre qe come le dit ordre fuist founduz a resister et destruer les heresizes et errours queux sourderent et puroient sourder counter la ley de seint esglise, et de precher et enfourmer le poeple de Dieu de la dite leye, as queles choses affair et accomplier sont pluis necessairs bone \vie/ et doctrine de divinite, en quele doctrine et auxi de lour conversacioun les ditz freres devaunt ces heures soleient estre et unqore serroient examinez et approvez, sibien entre lour mesmes come en universite, et ensy faitz maistres de divinite. Et ore est ensy qe ascuns de dit ordre en la dite leye nient approvez ne apris... apostatatz et ....rment vicious, et pur lour vices et trespasses ajuggez a prisoun par lour dit ordre, ont passez hors de roialme d'Engleterre as partes de dela et sont de jour en autre, et la ont purchaser et purchasont la ...... de meistre de divinite et autres graces exemptories pur estre desportez, honurez et favorez entre lour freres come un maistre de divinite, en anientisment de l'onour et supportacioun de seinte esglise et prejudice de le roialme et vileine et estlandre de lour ordre avauntdit. Plese a voz treshautes et tresgraciouses seignurs, pur l'onour de Dieu et de seinte esglise, profit du dit roialme et honeste de lour dit ordre, ordeigner et commandre toutz les priours et coventz des freres du dit ordre q'ils, sur forfaiture de tout ceo q'ils purront forfaire devers nostre seignur le roi, ne treitent entre eux nuls tiels apostotatz et vicious par colore de tiel purchase ou provisioun, ne soeffrent estre traite en honour, favour ou liberte come un maistre de divinite duement fait et approve par examinacioun de lour ordre et de universite, mes tantsoulement solonc ceo qe lour ordre, science et conversacioun demandent, et auxi q'ils en qanqe ils purront ne soeffrent nulles tielx apostatatz \et/ vicious enjoier entre eux autielx graces de exemptioun, mes les facent resister a lour pouir, pur Dieu et en eovere de charite.

Endorsed: Le roy le voet pur toutz les quatres ordres des mendynantz et pur touz autres religiouses.

1390. On 1 December 1390, in response to this petition, it was ordered 'that no such friar be admitted to the liberties, honours or favours accorded to doctors in theology, or allowed to enjoy the graces and exceptions so obtained' (*CPR 1388–92*, pp. 330–1).

171

Cistercians (1396)
(SC 8/332/15772)

To the chancellor from the president, diffinitors and abbots of the Cistercian order, having lately assembled at their general chapter in London, requesting the king's letters patent restoring John Holland, abbot of Dore, to his abbacy, since they and the pope have declared that he was wrongly ousted by Jordan of Biggleswade, a monk of St Mary Graces.

A tresreverent pier en Dieu et lour tresgracious seignur le chanceller d'Engleterre supplient humblement voz povres oratours les president, diffinitours et abbes del ordre de Cisteux, nadgairs assemblez en lour general chapitre tenuz en l'esglise de Grace joust la Tour de Londres, qe come Johan Holand, abbe de Nostre Dame de Dora del dit ordre, nadgairs par un Jordan de Bykeleswade, moigne del dit abbacie de Grace, estoit forciblement sanz ascun title ou droit espoilez de sa dite abbacie de Dora, et ore soit ensi qe le dit Johan, sibien par nostre tresseint pier le pape come par touz voz ditz suppliantz, ove pleine deliberacioun et comune assent de lour dit chapitre, par vertu des lettres de nostre dit tresseint pier et auxint solonc les auncientz privileges, ordinances et constitucions del dit ordre, soit restitut a la dite abbacie de Dora ove touz ses droitz et appurtenances come verai abbe et possessour d'icelle, et enoutre ordeine et pleinement en le dit chapitre declare qe le dit Jordan come intrusour, qe nul droit ou title ad ou unqes avoit en la dite abbacie de Dora ou en ascune parcelle d'icelle, soit ent voide et toutentrement ouste come resoun demande, qe plese a vostre tresgraciouse seignurie, a la reverence de Dieu, continuance et augmentacioun de divine service et greindre pees et quiete del dit abbe de Dora, vostre oratour, et a la priere de touz voz ditz oratours, les queles en pleine tesmoignance de la verite du dite matire a icestes ont mys lour comune seal, granter lettres patentes tantz et tiels come busoignera a touz lieges et ministris nostre seignur le roy celles parties, q'ils suffrent le dit Johan avoir, tenir et enjoier sa dite abbacie ove touz les droitz et profitz appurtenantz a icelle solonc le purport de sa restitucioun avantdite, et q'ils luy susteignent et mainteignent en sa possessioun, et touz les rebelx et contrariantz, si ascuns ysoient, refreignent et destourbent en tant come a lour affiert de droit et resoun, pur Dieu et en oevre de charite.

No endorsement

1396. On 26 September 1396 John Holland, abbot of Dore, was granted protection, 'having been dispossessed by armed force by Jordan Bikeleswade, monk of St Mary Graces, London, and subsequently restored by the Holy See and a second time spoiled by the malice of Jordan, when a chapter general of the order being held, and the president, triers and abbots pronounced in his favour as true abbot of Abbey Dore' (*CPR 1396–9*, p. 30). The dispute between Holland and Bikeleswade over possession of the abbey continued; by 8 October 1403 Bikeleswade was under arrest, having been indicted of certain felonies (*CPR 1401–5*, p. 438). For further references, see *Heads of Houses III*, 262. The chancellor was Thomas Arundel, archbishop of York. Boniface IX was pope.

172

Franciscans (1400)
(SC 8/194/9671)

The minister and brothers of the order of the Friars Minor in England petition the king, stating that the king had granted that the convent of Llanfaes in Wales, which had rebelled against him, should be punished bodily within the order. They ask that, as the rebels have scattered and Llanfaes is left desolate, with no-one to perform divine service, they might have permission to re-establish the convent with English and Welsh brothers, to be henceforth under the jurisdiction of the English. They also request a commission to inquire into whose hands the goods and chattels which were carried off from the convent have come, and to have them restored.

A nostre tresexcellent et tresredoute seignur le roi supplient humblement voz povres oratours les ministre et freres de l'ordre des menours de vostre roiaume d'Engleterre qe come nadgairs de vostre grace especiale grantastes qe les freres menours del convent de Lanvas en Gales, nadgairs rebels a vous, tresgracious seignur, serroient chastrez de leur corps deinz le dit ordre pur lour rebellion faire, qe please a vostre royale majestee avoir consideracion qe la dite mesoun de Lanvas est tout desolate, et divine service qe y soloit estre fait tout lessez, a cause qe mesmes ceux rebels sount disparplez et nul y n'ose demorer sanz licence de vous, tresgracious seignur, et sur ce de vostre grace especiale graunter as ditz ministres et freres q'ils lour covent de freres Engloys et Galoys y puissent avoir et tenir sicome il ad este devant ces heures, pur estre gouvernez desore en avant par les freres Engloys. Et enoutre de vostre habundante \grace granter/ commission les pluis sufficeantz en paiis d'enquerir de touz les biens et chateux qe feurent emportez de la dite meson, et les faire estre restorez en qui mains qu'ils soient trovez, en relevacion de la dite meson et en encresse et continuance de divine service y ancienement ordeiniez estre fait pur les almes des grantz et gentile du roiaume illeoqes ensevelez, pur Dieu et en oevre de charite.

No endorsement

1400. On 23 December 1400 the king ordered the chancellor to put the effect of this petition, which had been granted, into execution, without taking a fine for this (no. 2258 of C 81/605), enclosing this petition. On 28 January 1401 a commission was appointed to inquire into the seizure of the convent's goods (*CPR 1399–1401*, p. 418).

173

Abbots and Priors of England (1421)

(SC 8/24/1159)

The abbots and priors of England petition the Commons of parliament, complaining of the inconvenience and problems caused when the archbishops and bishops make them collectors of the tenths granted by the clergy to the king in places that are very distant from where they live. They ask the Commons to ask the king that it might be ordained in the present parliament by statute that no abbot or prior should in future be made a collector in any diocese, archdeaconry or county other than the one in which he lives; and if this does happen, that, if they complain to the treasurer and barons of the exchequer, the bishop who did this should answer to the king for the tenth, and a process should be started against him.

Endorsed on face: *It is to be delivered to my lord the archbishop of Canterbury. This bill is to be shown to the archbishop.*

Endorsed: *Be it remembered that this petition and its response are enrolled on the roll of the parliament held at Westminster on 2 May in the 9th year of the reign of King Henry, the fifth since the conquest.*

A les tresages comunez de cest present parliament suppliount toutz les abbes et les priours del roialme d'Engleterre qe come, par diverses convocaciouns faitz par lour tresreverentez pierez en Dieu l'erchevesqes du dit roialme devaunt ceoz hourez, eunte este grauntez diverses dismes a nostre sovereyne seignur le roy et a sez progenitours en supportacioun del bons governaunce et eide du dit roialme. Et lez ditz pierez en Dieu et altres evesqes ount faitz coilours des ditz dismes abbes et priours en plusours countez, diocisez, archidekenes en estraunge pays longement a eux, ou ils ne demurount mye et sount ascun foith fait par malice, et sur ceo distreintz par force des brefs nostre sovereyn seignur le roi issaunt de l'Escheqer de coiler les ditz dismes, et par cause q'ils sount travailez si longement a lour measons et en diverses diocesez, archedekenes et countez as grauntez costages d'eux anyentisment et enpoverisment dez ditz abbez et priours et de lour measons et ascun foith a lour destruccioun par cause qe lour servantz sont robbes et tues en estraunge pays. Que please a vous de supplier nostre dit sovereyn seignur le roy q'il poet estre ordeigne en cest present parliament par estatut qe nul archevesqe ne evesqe ordeigne nul abbe ne priour d'estre coilours dez dismes et subsidiez en temps avenir a grauntrerz par eux en altrez diocisez et archidekenez et countes qe ils sount demurauntz ou conversauntez, et si ascun archevesqe ou evesqe face le contrarie, et le abbe ou le priour issint fait veigne devaunt le tresorer et le barouns de l'Escheker en propre parsone ou par attourne, et allegge qe il est fait coilour en altre diocise ou archedekene ou counte q'il n'est mye demurant, q'adonqes nul bref issera hors de l'Escheker vers le ditz abbe ou priour de luy faire colier lez dismes mez l'evesqe qe li fist respondera a le roi dez dismez, et qe processe soit fait vers le archevesqe our evesqe qe luy noma a le roi pur coilour, et qe le dit abbe ou priour soit excuse.

Endorsed on face: Soit baille a monsire l'ercevesqe de Cantirbirs.
Soit celle bille moustre a l'erceveske.
Endorsed: Memorandum quod ista peticio et responsa eiusdem arrotulantur in rotulo parliamenti tenti apud Westm' secunda die Maii anno regni Regis Henrici quinti post conqestum nono.

1421. This petition was 'adopted' by the Commons in the parliament held at Westminster on 2 May 1421 and forwarded to Henry Chichele as archbishop of Canterbury. It was subsequently enrolled on the parliament roll with the following response: 'The king wills that no abbot or prior in the realm should henceforth be appointed by any archbishop or bishop to be a collector of any tenths or subsidies outside that county where he is living or resident. And this ordinance will last until the first parliament to be held after the return of our sovereign lord to England from overseas': *PROME*, parliament of May 1421, item 15. For the resulting legislation see *SR*, II, 208 (c. ix).

174

Augustinian canons (c. 1421)
(SC 8/24/1166)

The Augustinian canons petition the king, stating that they, alone of the religious orders, have no college or house where they can study at Oxford. The bishop of Exeter had been commanded by the king to look for a suitable site for one and found three messuages and four tofts for sale, outside the university walls near the monks of Durham. They ask the king to order the chancellor and treasurer to buy this land and give it to the Augustinians, without fine or fee being paid, for a house to be built at their own expense.

A roi nostre tressoverain seignur supplient treshumblement voz poveres et continuelx oratours les noirs chanons del ordre de Seint Austyn qe come certeine des ditz chanons sueront a vous ore tarde a Leycestre, reherceant coment toutz autres religiouses avoient a eux approprez places et colleges honestes et necessaries deinz vostre universite d'Oxenford, par grauntes, ordinances et licences de voz tresnobles progenitours, pur continuer lour studie illoeqes en les escoles, al encresce de science et vertue, al supportacioun de seinte esglise et la foie cristiene, forspris voz ditz oratours, queux sont desolatz de soil ou place deinz la dite universite pur eux edifier pur lour studie, en graunde anientisment de eux. Et sur ceo, tresgracious seignur, l'evesqe d'Excestre avoit en commandement depart vous \d'enquerer/ s'il fuist ascun lieu ou soil deinz la dite universite a vendre, quelle fuist competent pur faire une convenable place pur le studie des ditz suppliantz. Et sur cella le dit evesqe est enfourme qe sont trois mees et quatre toftes a vendre, assiz sur Candiche joust les moynes de Duresme, dehors les mures du dite universite, queux sont del value annuel de quatre marcz outre les reprises, et le soil des ditz mees et toftes est covenable de edifier autiel place pur les ditz suppliantz, come avaunt est dit, ovesqe ceo q'ils purront avoir vostre gracious seignurie et socour en ceste partie. Plese a vostre roial mageste, a la reverence de Dieu et nostre dame et de Seint Johan de Bridelyngton', qi jadis fuist du dit ordre, de commander voz chanceller et tresorer d'Engleterre q'ils achatent en vostre noun les mees et toftes suisditz de les possessours d'icelles, et qant ils ount les achatez, q'ils par vostre licence et grace especial purront doner les ditz mees et toftes solonc vostre advis et ordinance as ditz suppliantz et lour successours, ou a ascun de eux, a toutz jours, pur faire une mesoun competent pur lour studie, et de prier pur vous come pur lour foundour perpetuelment. Et ceo sanz fyn ou fee apaier a vostre oeps, l'estatuit des terres et tenementz a donerz a mort main fait a contrarie non obstant, pur Dieu et en oevre de charite. Considerant, tresgracious seignur, qe si les ditz suppliantz purront avoir par vostre gracious ordinance les ditz mees et toftes, ils vorront a lour costages ordeiner pur la edificacioun et novel constructioun du dite mesoun.

No endorsement.

c. 1421. The meeting of the Augustinian order at Leicester, described in the petition, was held in 1421, whereon this petition was made to the king. However, owing to Henry V's death in 1422, this plan came to nothing, and the Augustinian canons remained without a college until 1435, when Thomas Holden and Elizabeth, his wife, founded St Mary's College, giving the canons land in the parishes of St Michael at the Northgate and St Peter le Bailey and building a chapel (*VCH Oxfordshire*, II, 102). The bishop of Exeter was Edmund Lacey (1420–55). A calendar of this petition appears in L. Toulmin Smith, ed., 'Parliamentary Petitions Relating to Oxford', in *Collectanea*, ed. M. Burrows, Oxford Historical Society, 32 (1896), III, 153, no. 118. The results of the petition are described by R. B. Dobson, 'The Religious Orders, 1370–1540', in *The History of the University of Oxford, vol. II: Late Medieval Oxford*, ed. J. I. Catto and T. A. R. Evans (Oxford, 1992), p. 554 and nn. This petition is printed in *RP*, IV, 159, no. 4.

175

Carthusians (1423)
(SC 8/198/9898)

The priors and convents of the Carthusian order petition the king and Lords of parliament, stating that by the letters patent of the king's predecessors they have always been quit of tenths and fifteenths and other taxation until, in the time of the king's father, the treasurer and barons of the exchequer refused to allow them this liberty, on the grounds that the grants of taxation were made after the date of the letters patent; and, because of a difference of opinion among the barons on this, they currently enjoy a respite from these taxes. They ask the king and Lords to grant, by authority of parliament, that these letters patent should be good and effectual, both for the past and for the future.

Endorsed: *It was agreed and assented by the Lords in the parliament held at Westminster on 20 October in the second year of King Henry VI that a letter under the privy seal should be addressed to the treasurer and barons of the exchequer to cease from any process to be made against the said supplicants, and all others who have liberties, to be quit of tenths and fifteenths of the grant of the king's noble progenitors, until they have other commands from the king.*

A nostre tresredoute et tressoveraigne seignur le roy et au lez autres seignures espirituelx et temporelx de cest present parlement supplliount treshumblement voz poverez et contynuels oratours toutz les priours et coventz del ordre de Charthous deinz vostre royalme d'Engleterre qe come voz tresnobles progenitours, nadgairs roys d'Engleterre, par lour severalx lettres patentz ount grauntez as predecessours dez ditz suppliauntz et a lour successours severalment diversez libertees et fraunchisez, entre queux il est contenuz qe si les biens temporels ou esppirituels d'autres religiousez de la royalme d'Engleterre, par enchesoun d'ascuns grauntez par la comunalte du dit royalme ou par la clergie de mesme la royalme, dehors affairs serrount taxes, les propres biens et possessiouns de lours ditz predecessours et de lours successours par la cause de tielx grauntes ne soient taxes, ne rienz ent levez al ops du voz ditz tresnobles progenitours roys, ou de lours heirs, sicome en lez chartres et confirmacions ent fait est contenus plus au playne. Par force des quex grauntez les dit suppliauntz et lours predecessours ount estes quites et dischargez de toutz tielx dismes, quinsismes, aides, tallages, contribucions et autres customs qeconqes tanqe al temps del tresnoble seignur le roy vostre piere, qe Dieu assoille, en quel temps le tresorer et barouns de vostre Escheqer ne voloiont mye allower as ditz suppliauntz et a lours predecessours les ditz libertees et acquitaunces en droit des dismes, quinsismes, aides, tallages et contribucions grauntez a dit nadgars roy et sez tresnoblez progenitours avauntditz puis lez datez de les lettres patentz suisditz, a cause qe tielx grauntez des dismes, quinsismes, tallages, aides et contribucions furont faitz a voz ditz tresnobles progenitours puis la date de mesmez lez lettres; einz les allowancez de lours dit libertees et fraunchisez en cest partie, a cause de diversez opinions des barons d'Eschequer avauntdit, sount unqore pendauntz en respite en mesme l'Eschequer par l'encheson suisdit. Please a vostre tresgracious seignurie de considerer le povertee des ditz suppliauntz, et la bone et gracious volunte qe toutz voz tresnobles progenitours avoient a eux en lour temps, et qe les ditz suppliauntz sount exemptez a chescun convocacion de la clergie, et sur ceo, au reverence de Dieu, par autorite de cest present parlement, declarer et determiner qe les ditz lettres patentz soient effectuelx et vailables as ditz suppliantz et a lour successours solonc l'entent des grauntours d'icells, sibien pur temps passe come pur temps avenir a toutz jours, pur eux dischargez et acquiter de toutz tielx dismes, quinsismes, moitez des dismes et quinsismes et chescun autre quantite des dismes, quinsismes, taxes, tallages, aides, contribucions et imposicions devaunt sez heures grauntez ou en temps avenir agrauntiers, ceo qe les grauntez de tielx dismes, quinsismes, taxes, tallages, aides, contribucions et imposicions, ou ascun quantitee d'icells, furont faitz apres la date du ditz lettres patentz ou serront faitz en temps avenir, ou ceo qe les ditz dismes, moites et autres quantitees et parcels dez dismez nadgars grauntes par la clergie ensy la forme des grauntes d'icells sont levables des exemptez et nient exemptez et privilegies et nient privilegies, come desuis est dit. Et ceo qe les sommez particulers et totales d'icells ne sont expressez en cest peticion ou autre forme des grauntes des tielx dismez, moites et autres quanitites et parcels dez dismes par la clergie, et auxint dismes, quinsismes, moites et autres quantites et parcels dez dismez et quinsismes, aides, taxes, tallages, contribucions, customs, impositions et autres charges suisditz, par les leies de la royalme ou autre maner qeconqe fait ou affaire, ou ceo qe les ditz charters furont grauntez desouth diverses formes et variantz en ascunz poyntz ou la dit opinioun de voz ditz tresorer et barouns, ou autre opinioun qeonqe de les tresorer et barouns ou autres pur le temps esteauntz, moeve ou qe poet estre move en temps avenir donte difficulte .... en ley ou autre cause qeconqe prive en expresse a l'encountre ou derogation des charters et confirmacions discharge et relesse suisditz nient contristeauntz, pur amour de Dieu et oevre de charite.

Endorsed: Accordez est et assentuz par les seignurs en parlement tenuz a Westm' le xx jour d'Octobre l'an du regne le Roy Henry le Sisme seconde qe une lettre desouz le pryvee seal soit direct as tresorer et barons de l'Eschequer de ourseier de qeconqe processe affaire envers les ditz suppliantz, et toutz autres q'ount libertees, d'estre quite de dismez et quinszismes par les grauntes des nobles progenitours du roy, tanqe ils eient autrement en commandement depar le roy.

1423. This petition was presented, and answered, at the parliament held at Westminster in October 1423.

Part Six

PETITIONS AGAINST ABBOTS AND PRIORS

176

St Albans, Hertfordshire (? c. 1273)
Benedictine
(SC 8/202/10087)

William Mervyn of Sandridge petitions the king and council, stating that although he holds his lands as a free man, the abbot of St Albans is claiming that he is a villein and demanding from him services and customs that he ought not to perform. Because of this he impleaded the abbot in the court of the late King Henry III, in the 54th year of his reign, and the case has continued, amid theft, assault, imprisonment and attempted fraud on the abbot's part. He eventually had judgement in his favour, through the abbot's default, but now the abbot has expelled him again, and in the first year of the present king had his corn threshed and committed other outrages against him; and he can have no justice because of the abbot's position. He asks the king to have pity on him, his wife and children, and that this matter might come before him and his council.

Au tresnoble rey d'Engleterre e a son conseil se plente Willem Mervyn de Sandrugge ke de sicome il e ses ancestres tindrent lor tenemenz en memes la vile solum le costume del maner, k'est del aunciene demeine de la corone nostre seignur le rey tenanz par certein service, l'abbe de Seint Auban [en le mem] cel manere demanda a memes celi Willem autres costumes e services qe fere ne devoient e soloient el tens ke le maner fu en les meins des reis d'Engleterre, predecessors nostre seignor le rei \k'ore est/, par quoi memes celi Willem enpleida memes l'abbe qe ore est en le cort le Rei Henri, qe Deus assoille, l'an de son regne Liiij, devant Sire Martin de Litlebir' e ses compaignons, justices du banc a Westm', k'il ne lui demandast costumes ne services qe fere ne devoit ou ke ses ancestres fere ne soloient el tens ke le maner fu en le mein del predecessors nostre seignor le rois. L'abbe lui mist sus k'il estoit vilein e prist ses biens e ses avers prist a sa volunte e amena, e autres damages e grevances fist al des heriteson memes celi Willem e de sa femme e de ses enfanz, par quoi le Rei Henri, ke Deus assoille, fist l'abbe venir devant Sire Martin de Litlebir' e ses compaignons, donc justices du banc, a Westm' a respundre l'avantdit Willem del trespas avantdit. Et donc fu enjoint al abbe k'il seist delivrer a memes celi Willem ses avers e ses biens pendant le plai entrens en la court le Rei Edward, en sorqetot fu comande al viscount de Hertford ke pur la defaute memes celi abbe entrast sa franchise e les biens e les avers avantdiz seist delivrer e les tenist delivrer pendant le plai avantdit. Icel abbe ja le meins les biens e les avers encore detient e tantost apres ceo envoia ses genz a force e a armes a la meson le devantdit Willem en Sandrugge le prochien dimenche apres le decollacion Saint Johan l'an du regne le Rei Henri Lv. Le devantdit Willem les vit clost ses hus e ses fenestres e eus l'assaillirent \la maison/ e debriserent ses hus e ses fenestres, e celi Willem de denz la meson troverent e batirent, navrerent e malement treterent, e les genz memes celi Willem si batirent ausi k'il de hors meson troverent, e navrerent e malement treterent. Post, pristrent memes celi Willem e ses genz e les enprisonerent e un mois e j jor en prison detindrent encontre la pes. Et le penerent de jor e de noit pur poi deskes a la mort pur li fere reconoistre vilein konkes par nul comandement qe le Rei Henri porroit comand, ne ke ses amis porroient porchacer, ne par nule matiere de plevine ne poett estre delivre desqes atant ke memes celi abbe, par grant veidie e fraude pur celi Willem desoeivre e desheriter, purchaca un bref el nom Willem tant com il estoit en prisone, e rien de sa ne savoit, qe ala al viscount de Hertford, k'il trovast suffisante mein prise enteu manere, ke le devantdit Willem ne venist a certein jor ke done li fu en cel bref devant le Rei Henri, e provast solum lei de terre k'il fu franc e ses terres e ses tenemenz franchement deust tenir, k'il de cel jor enavant demorast le vilein l'abbe e totes ses terres e ses tenemenz sa vilein terre. Par cel bref fu le devantdit Willem delivre, issi k'il vint a cel jor ke done li fu devant Mestre Richard de Stanes, aidonc justice des plez le rei, e xxij chivalers e xv gentils homes, prist aprover sa franchise, e a cele prove plus plenement parfornir ont il purchace le bref le rey hors del Domesdai, ke tesmoine tot pleinement ke ses ancestres tindrent les avantdites terres et tenemenz franchement en la vile de Sandrugge. Al qel jor l'abbe memes fu en la cort le rei mes ne veut aparer, par ont ke pur sa defaute avant le devantdit Willem, jugement por li e le bref de jugement de Mestre Richard de Stanes e de ses compaignons al viscount de Hertford de mettre le en plenere seisine de totes ses terres e ses tenemenz avantdites. De quele seisine l'abbe de meintenant atort e sanz jugement autrefoiz lengeta e hors de sa seisine deskes a cel jor lui a detenu e encore detient in despit de la cort nostre seignor le rei e en cuntre commune dreiture del reaume; e en apert desheriteson del devantdit Willem e a force e encuntre la pes nostre seignor le rei ke ore est, l'an de son regne primerein, fist batre hors des granges le devantdit Willem ala montance de CC quaters de toz maners de ble e autrez damages e grevances a fet ala montance de CCC mars e plus, par ent ke memes celi Willem e sa femme \e ses enfanz/ ont toz jors pus este mendinanz e pain queranz, ne memes celi Willem a nul dreiturez ne poet atteindre por ses grant dous e por sa grant hautesce e pur ses grant poer, por quoi il prie a nostre seignor le rei, por Deu e por sa douce mere, qu'il eit pite e merci de lui, e k'il deigne regarder son desheriteson e sa grant poverte k'il e sa femme e ses enfanz ont soffert tant detens e encore est a soffrer si Deu e li ne prenge pite, e qe ceste chose pusse estre devant son cort termine, e devant vostre consail.

No endorsement

? c. 1273. From the mention of events of 54 Henry III and of 1 Edward I, this petition would seem to date from after 1273. It also names Richard of Staines as a former justice: he was chief justice of the King's Bench 1269–72, justice of the King's Bench 1272–74 and justice of Common Pleas 1274–76; he was dead by Michaelmas 1277. Thus, the abbot of St Albans concerned was Roger of Norton (1263–90). The reference to Martin Littlebury as presiding judge ties the hearing to the period from Hilary 1273, when he was probably appointed, to Easter 1274, the last term for which he was paid: Sainty, *Judges*, p. 6. Another contemporary petition from the same petitioner on this matter is SC 8/202/10086.

177

St Benet of Hulme, Norfolk (1275–1300)
Benedictine
(SC 8/69/3407)

Robert Rose petitions the king and council, stating, on the king's behalf, that the abbot of St Benet of Hulme and Denise of Munchensy are distraining the people of Flegg and all the neighbouring country for a heavy toll for the crossing at Bastwick, where the bridge has been broken by a storm at sea. He states that because this is common water and the road the king's high road, the king should be levying this toll – whereas they are levying it for their own use, and furthermore the burden is falling on the poor rather than the rich. He requests a remedy, and that this toll might be put to the repair of the bridge.

A nostre seyngur le rey a son conseyl mustre Robert Rose, pur le rey, de ceo ke le abbe de Seynt Beneyt e Dame Dionise de Montchensy destraunt les gens de Fleg e de tut le pays en viron par un grous truage ke il parnunt de mes les gens pur le passage de Bastwyk, la ou le pont est derumpu par la tempeste de la mer, desicom cele ewe est comune e tus jurs ad este, e haust chymyn le rey de tut pars, pur quey si nul en dust ren prendre ceo dust estre le royz, e ceo truage parnunt alur as demeizne e n'ent a redrescement du poynt, e tut de povers gens e ren de riches pur cel ke les riches ne dusent ren en parler e a bayer les povers de \en/ parler. De quel ceo il prie remedie pur le rey e pur tut le pays avant dit, e ke cele prise de ceo truage put returner aredrecement du pont.

No endorsement

1275–1300. Dated on the basis of the hand, in which case the abbot was Nicholas of Walsham (1275–1302). Denise of Munchensy was the widow (after 1255) of Warin of Munchensy of Norfolk. Bastwick (Norf.), although some six miles inland, lies on the River Thurne. Flegg is the low-lying district to the north-west of Great Yarmouth. 'Marine floods' were a feature of the last quarter of the thirteenth century (1275, 1279, 1282, 1288, 1292), C. E. Britton, *A Meteorological Chronology to A.D. 1450* (London, 1937), p. 177.

178

Binham, Norfolk (1278)
Benedictine (dependent)
(SC 8/237/11809)

Thomas Fitz Roger petitions the king and council, making various complaints against Robert, prior of Binham, Robert of Littlebury and Roger, his clerk: that the prior of Binham and his men have beaten him, stolen his livestock (which they still have) and prevented him from obtaining any profit from his land for four years and more; and that they have sued him maliciously in various courts and prevented him from obtaining justice, in association with Littlebury. He states that Littlebury has had him imprisoned, and that he and his clerk Roger have had him beaten – and he asks that this may be inquired into by a jury of poor and middling people. He also complains that they are withholding writs from him and delaying his case – and he asks that this too may be inquired into by a jury of poor and middling people, and by those who were present when he was incarcerated. He also states that they have tried to have him hanged because he complained about them. He asks that the truth of all this and other things too may

be inquired into, and that he might have some amendment of his estate, that his affairs might not perish for lack of justice, and that he might have his writs without paying a redemption.
Endorsed: *The poor men beg, for the love of God and the soul of the lord king, that ... you might be pleased to inquire of your office by twelve men, legitimately sworn and carefully examined, from every county of England, how poor men pleading at the Bench are defrauded of their business; and when they have been questioned and diligently examined, the truth about the collusions, deceptions and deceitful greed will be laid bare.*
He is to go to chancery.

Illustri regi Anglie et eius consilio excellentissimo, Thomas filius Rogeri graviter conqueritur [damaged ms] est que mee tristicia causa querele, conqueror de Roberto, priore de Binham, et de gentibus suis qui me male verberaverunt, sanguinem extraxerunt et alleria ceperunt, et adhuc detinent et me perturbabant. Ita quod de terris meis per quatriennium et amplius fructus percipere non potui, et hoc fecerunt predicte gentes per preceptum et procuracionem dicti prioris, impetravi brevia domini regis nichil mihi prodescunt. Item, predictus prior fecit me citari per tria diversa loca Anglie, scilicet apud Waltam coram conservatoribus abbatis Sancti Albani, et apud Huntingdon' coram suppriore et sacrista, et extra Bedeford apud ipsum locum. Ego tuli sibi prohibiciones domini regis et nichil voluit pro eis facere. Ego feci ipsum atachiari que venit contra prohibiciones quos predictus prior procuravit tam versus Robertum de Lytlebir' quod ego non potui in curia de Banco consequi justiciam.
Conqueror de domino Roberto de Lyttlebiri qui fecit me incarceri ut prostraret brevia mea. Conqueror de Roberto de Lyttlebiri qui \me/ procuravit verberari in capite de virgis clamatorum de Banco. Conqueror de Rogero, clerico dicti Roberti, qui verberavit me in capite et solitus est me et alios verberare quod ista sint vera inquiratur per mediocres et pauperes fideliter juratos, et per pares meos de eadem curia.
Conqueror de predicto Roberto et Rogero qui detinebant brevia mea judicialia de quindena Passce de octabis Sancte Trinitatis et adhuc detinent, et pro defectu brevium judicialium predicti dies periuntur, et dati sunt dies in octabis Sancti Michaelis per rotulos, ad huc sunt centum brevia judicialia facienda pro defectu redempcionis. Conqueror de \predictis/ Roberto et Rogero eo quod nec sine redempcione nec cum redempcione potui brevia mea judicialia optinere hoc precor quod inquiratur rei veritas per pares meos per mediocres et pauperes et per illos qui fuerunt presentes quando fui incarceratus sine judicio justiciariorum.
Conqueror de predictis Roberto et Rogero qui procurabant me suspendi que conquestus eram de populis apud Gloverniam occasione cuius suspensionis domini mei amittent negocia sua. Quare vobis supplico, pro amore Dei et anima patris domini regis, quatinus diligenter inquiratis reiveritatem de hiis etaliis, et quatinus reformacionem status mei mihi concedere dignemini, ne negocia dominorum meorum pro defaultum justicie pereantur et quod possim habere brevia mea judicialia sine redempcione pro amore salvatoris nostri.

Endorsed: Pauperes supplicant, pro amore Dei et pro anima domini regis, quatinus vos ex officio vestro per xij legitime juratos et diligenter examinatos, de quolibet comitatu Anglie, inquirere veliter quatres pauperes placitantes as Bancum defraudantur de negociis suis. Hiis itaque inquisitis et diligenter examinatis, patebit rei veritas de collusionibus et deceptionibus et fraudulentis capiditatibus.

Ideat Cancellaria.

1278. This petition has been identified as 'a reference to a complaint made against Robert of Littlebury, one of the senior clerks of the Common Bench, and his clerk Roger by a professional attorney of the court at this parliament' (*PROME*, parliament of Summer 1278, Introduction, n. 7). Robert of Waltham occurred as prior 1272–91.

179

Ware, Hertfordshire (c. 1286–92)
Benedictine (alien)
(SC 8/31/1504)

Emma of Arneburth petitions the king and council for a remedy because Richard, prior of Ware, and other malefactors broke into her husband's house at Moggerhanger by night, stole his goods, beat and ill-treated him, and took him away bound, so that she does not know where he is or if he is alive or dead. She is not powerful enough to sue these people.
Endorsed: *In chancery.*

A nostre seignur le roy e a seon conseil se pleint Emme de Arneburth de Richard, prior de Ware, Johan Aster, Willame Power, Johan de Haunebyry, Johan de Hyntes, Simon Fraunceys e Thomas Godhyne ke de nuyt a Mokeshanger, une vile del cunte de Bedeford, la meson Robert Arneburth, baron la avant diste Emme, debruserent e meyme celuy Robert roberent de ses chatels a la value de cent souz, s'ils batirent e playerent e malement le tresterent, e meyme celuy Robert meverint lye, ensi ke la avant diste Emme, sa femme, ne soit ou il est devenuz ne si il soit vif ou mort. Parunt ele requert a nostre seignur le roy e a soun conseil remedie key ele est povere e nunpussante de purseuere en forme de play vers le avant dist priur e les autres nomez.

Endorsed: In Cancellaria.

c. 1286–92. Dated notionally to the reign of Edward I on the basis of the hand. The only known Prior Richard of Ware during this period occurs in 1288 and 1290. His predecessor, Prior Fulk, last occurs in 1286, and his successor, Ralph le Graunt, became prior of Ware in 1292.

180

Dunstable, Bedfordshire (c. 1287)
Augustinian canons
(SC 8/277/13802)

William Norman of Dunstable petitions for a remedy because when William, prior of Dunstable had his view of frankpledge in Dunstable on St Barnabas day 1286, a man of Dunstable came and, out of hatred, presented that 20 years ago Norman had found £20 in a place called 'Pyneknol' between Barnet and London, 25 miles from the prior's franchise, which presentment was entered on the coroners' roll without any other indictment or inquisition. The prior was so angry with Norman that he ordered his bailiff, Thomas of Bolhurst, to enter his house on market day (the Wednesday before St John Baptist in the same year), take his merchandise and imprison him for the said presentment, contrary to the statute made in 1285, until he was

replevied by the king's writ by twelve pledges until the next Eyre. At the tourn of John of Vaus and his associates at Dunstable in 1287, Norman was again imprisoned and brought before them as a thief, and they took it amiss that he was wrongly brought before them on suspicion only, and when Roger Loveday accused him of finding this money and asked how he would acquit himself, he responded that he would swear on God and his country that he had found no money or other treasure, and the twelve jurors of the franchise acquitted him. And Norman has complained about this trespass to those assigned by the king, and the sheriff of Bedfordshire was ordered to cause the prior of Dunstable and Bolhurst to come, but when the prior came he claimed that he was not the king's minister, and that Norman should sue at the common law.
Endorsed on face: *[To the first] He should petition to the king, and it should be inquired into in the county, and determined there.*
[To the second] This thing he wills to be done as it can be awarded by law.
Endorsed: *Bedfordshire: Petition of William Norman of Dunstable concerning the prior of Dunstable.*
Response of the bailiff: The king should provide a magnate.
He should have a writ in chancery to complain in the county if he wishes ...

Willeme Norman de Dunstaple se \pleynt/ de Willeme, priur de Dunstaple, e Thomas de Bolhurst, qe en ca tens fu sun bailif, qe par la u le priur aveyt sa vuue de frauncplege en la ville de Dunstaple le jour de Seynt Barnabe le Apostle en l'an du rengne nostre seynur le Rey Edward quatorzyme, un poi apres sun passage utre mer, la vint un homme de meime la vile qe esteyt coruce e meyme cely Willeme Norman e pur hayne presenta qe yl dust aver trove \plus de xx auns passe/ vint livers de argent \en le haut chemin/ en un lu qe est apele Pyneknol entre la Barnet e la cyte de Loundres, vint e cink luwes hors de la fraunchise le priur, si qe ycel simple presentement de un homme fu entre en role de coroners tut saunz autre enditement u enqueste. Ne purqant Willeme ala avaunt tut empes avint qe le priur se corusa ver meyme cely Willem Norman e \si qe yl/ maunda Thomas de Bolhurst, son baylyf, par un jour de Marche al aviesun Willeme la u yl fu entur sa marchaundie, ce est asaver le megerdi precheyn devaunt la feste Seynt Johan le Baptist en meyme l'an avaunt dit, e la ly prist e amena en la priurie e ly emprisona pur le presentement avaunt dit, e ce countre le estatut nostre seynur le Rey Edward fet a Westm' en l'an de sun rengne trezyme qe unt qe nul homme ne seyt emprisune pur tel presentement[34] si yl ne soyt par enditement de xij jurez atut le meyns, e \sur/ cel enditement metent lur sels, e qe nul seynur ne veucunte ne baylyf de fraunchyse ne emprisune nul homme pur presentement sy il ne eyt tel garaunt, e il fu emprisune cuntre l'estatut pur presentement de un homme de autre part desicum yl fu replevisable yl ne[35] ly voleyent lesser par nule plevine desicum yl la tendit asez suffisaunce. Si la qe yl fust replevi par bref le rey e par xij meynpernurs, e ce jeqe a le eyre de justices ici qe cuntrere la venuwe de justices errauns Sire Johan de Vaus e se cumpaynus [*sic*] a Dunstaple l'an quinzyme a pres la Seynt Illeyre cy fu Willeme autre[36] feze pris e emprisone e a lur venuwe fut ameue de vaunt justices cum un larun, parunt qe le justices pretrent amal qe yl fu si vileynement ameue de vaunt ews pur tel suspeciun, e Sire Roger Loveday ly acupa de cel trovure de deners e coment yl

34 MS has *presentemaent* with the *a* expunged.
35 There follow five illegible letters, which have been scraped away, and expunged.
36 MS has *atre* with *a* expunged and *au* interlined above.

se vodreyt aquiter, e yl respundit e dyt qe yl se vodreyt mettre en Deu e en le pays saunz nule \homme/[37] refuser qe unqes nul argent \ne trova/ ne autre tresor, e la vindrent le xij jurez de la fraunchise e ly aquiterent tut utre par lur seremenz ke yl aveyent fez a Deu e au rey, e de ce se met yl sur \record de/ le roules de le Eyre.

E de ca trespaz Willem Norman mustur une pleynte a ceuws qe sunt asingnez de par le rey de oyer le pleyntes, e comaunde fut au veucunte de Bedeforde qe yl feyt vener le priur de Dunstaple e Thomas de Bolhurst, si qe vint le priur e alegga qe yl ne est une ministre le rey e meyntenaunt ly fut aluwe e comaunde qe yl alart a Deu, e que Willem ne dust purchacer par la commune ley, e de ceste chose pur Deu prie remedye si acune dise en ceu trespas, kar yl ne put ove ly pleder pur ce qe yl est taunt destrut e anenty par le priur e sun procurement e checun jour uncore ly e sa gent ly courent a taunt a le harel, qe si yl n'eyt remedye par tens yl ne avera ne sa femme ne sez enfauns dunt vivere.

Endorsed on face: [To the first] Et supplicat domino regi istud inquiratur in comitatu et terminetur ibidem.
[To the second] Ceste chose vuot yl mettre aveyr par quant qe put estre agarde par ley.
Endorsed: Bed': Peticio Willelmi Norman de Dunstaple super priorem de Dunstaple.
Responsum ballivi: Mangnatum provideat rex.
Habeat breve in Cancellaria ad placitandum in comitatu si veluerit ad utramque p....

c. 1287. William of Wederhore was prior 1280–1302. For another version of this petition see SC 8/274/13697, and for a related petition see SC 8/331/15666.

181

Tynemouth, Northumberland (1289–90)
Benedictine (dependent)
(SC 8/65/3212)

The burgesses of Newcastle upon Tyne petition the king's council, stating that the prior of Tynemouth is encouraging merchants to unload their ships at North Shields and to deal with him, depriving them of their customs and the king of his prises; and that he has also transformed North Shields from a collection of huts to shelter fishermen driven ashore by storms into a large town, forestalling Newcastle by brewing and baking to supply these merchants. They ask for a remedy to save their franchise, and, as the prior has impleaded them in Common Pleas, that judgement might not be given in this case without the king or his representative, as they fear the prior's influence.
Endorsed: *In chancery. He is to sue a writ for the king and the burgesses of Newcastle to have the prior of Tynemouth come to the next parliament after Easter.*
He is to have a writ according to the form of the petition.

Co mustrent au conseil nostre seygnur le rey les burgeys de Neuchastel sur Tyne ke la ou meymes ceus burgeys unt la vile a ferme de nostre seygnur le rey pur une certeyne summe de argent rendaunt par an, la vient le priour de Tynemuwe

37 The word *de* has been deleted.

e voet enfrauncher les marchaunz ke venent od lur marchaundises en le ewe de Tyne ke a ly vendent, e ne soffre ke il paent lur custume du eynz lur fet charger e descharger dedenz le ewe de Tyne en un lu ke hom apele les Schelez, e vendent a marchaunz payn e cerveyse e co ke mester lur est en deseritisoun nostre seygnur le rey e encountre sa fraunchise e en destruccioun de la vile avantdite, de sicom la custome de la vile est tiele ke nule nyf venaunt ov marchaundises ne poet attamer rien de denz le havene de Tyne de sa marchaundise vendre ou descharger ke il ne paye custume de kaunt ke il ad dedenz la neyf, la vent le priour avant dit e vout enfrauncher ceus marchaunz ke il ne payent custome com fere deyvunt solom les usages avant diz. Dunt memes cely priur enplede les burgeys au Baunk e de co ke la ou nostre seygnur le rey soleit aver ses prises, ceo est asaver de chescone navee de harang un cent de chescon batel venaunt od pesson a l'avauntdite vile j morue pur j dener e j cent de haddoke de chescon batel en la sesun pur vj deners, dunt le rey ne ad rien de chose k'est descharge en le lyu avant dite, et de co prient il remedie si ke la fraunchise nostre seygnur le rey ne seyt perie taunt com il sunt ses fermers ne le play par entre eus, e le priur avaunt dit ne passe mye en jogement saunz la presence nostre seygnur le rey ou la vostre ke son lyu tenez, purco ke il dutent le pays ke taunt est procure par le priur. E estre ceo, la ou soleyunt estre caseles al Sheles a herberger pestors venaunz delamer soulement pur tempeste la est ore leve une vile graunde aforestal de la vile avantdite, ou il bracent e furneent en destruccion de la vile avant dite, dunt la vile nostre seygnur le rey est enpire chescon an de dyz liveres.

Endorsed: In Cancellaria. Sequatur breve pro rege et burgensibus Novi Castri ad faciendum venire priorem de Tinemue ad proximum parliamentum post Pascha. Habeat breve secundum formam peticionis.

1289–90. This petition is dated to 1289–90 in *Ancient Petitions Relating to Northumberland*, ed. C. M. Fraser, Surtees Society, 171 (1961), pp. 232–4, no. 207. The complaint prompted a lengthy hearing in the parliament of Easter 1290. This left a record of proceedings on the parliament roll detailing the actions taken by the priory against the burgesses' interests (*PROME*, Edward I, Roll 1, item 23 (17)). It was noted that the priory had four ovens built to supply bread to the sailors, that it had established a market in Tynemouth in which fines for bread and ale were collected (apparently without licence), and that some monks had turned their hand to buying and selling untanned hides (they are described, perhaps with irony, as 'merchants'). The prior, Simon of Walden (c. 1280–94/5), attempted to hold proceedings up by claiming errors in the legal process, but ultimately he could not withstand the force of the burgesses' case, which skilfully argued that his actions deprived the king of valuable income in taxes and tolls. In 1292 judgement was finally passed against him. An earlier related petition from the prior of Tynemouth is SC 8/76/3799.

182

St Augustine's, Canterbury, Kent (c. 1301)

Benedictine
(SC 8/271/13529)

Letter of the mayor, bailiffs and community of the barony of Faversham to the king reciting the king's writ to them, dated 18 February 1301, asking them to make sure that those people of their town who have been attacking the abbot of St Augustine's, Canterbury, and his men, desist from this, and informing him in their turn of violent and murderous attacks on them by monks and other of the abbot's men. In particular they ask him to order what seems good to him with regard to the sixteen men captured by them in one attack.

Nobilissimo principi ac domino suo precunctis mortalibus diligendo et metuendo domino Edwardo, Dei gracia illustrissimo regi Anglie, domino Hibernie et duci Aquitanie simul in omnibus maior, ballivi et comunitas baronum de Faversham salutem. Et se ad omnia sibi beneplacita et precepta paratos usque ad divisionem corporis et anime Katerine domine nomine vestram clemenciam et dominacionem metuendam nobis precepisse in tenore subsequenti:

'Edwardus, Dei gracia rex Anglie, dominus Hybernie et dux Aquitanie, maiori et baillivis de Faversham salutem. Quia quidam de villa vestra predicta transgressiones quam plures et injurias ac eciam gravamina intolerabilia dilecto nobis in Cristo abbati Sancti Augustini Cantuar' et suis voluntarie et absque causa racionabili in eadem villa multipliciter intumberunt, et de die in diem inferre non desistant in ipsi abbatis et suorum dampnum non modicum et gravamen sicut ex querela sua accepimus. Nos dicti abbatis quietam in hac parte prospicere volentes, vobis mandamus quod omnes predictos transgressores ab huiusmodi injuriis et gravaminibus dicto abbati aut suis de cetero inferendis, quantum in vobis est, desistere faciatis esse pro defectu vestri clamor ad nos inde perveniat iteratus pro quo oporteat nos aliter ad hoc apponere manum. Teste me ipso apud Lincoln', xviij die Februarii anno regni nostri vicesimo nono.'

Cuius virtute mandati per manus Philippi le Clerk, attornati religiosi viri abbatis, memorati nobis exhibiti de nominibus dictorum transgressorum diligenter ab eodem duximus inquirendis ipso nobis respondente dominum suum antedictum de membris conquerendo unde nos pacem nostram proclamavimus firmiter inhibendo, ne quis comunitatis nostre sub omni eo quod forisfacere poterit dicto abbati suisve dampnum molestiam inferat vel gravamen. Super quo die mercurie proximo post festum Sancti Gregorii pape nunc preteritum, fratres Willielmus Hubert, Hugo de Berkyng', Ricardus Bertelot, Johannes Godchep, monachi domus, memorate Johannes de Bekles, Thomas Glomvile, Thomas Gillebert, Thomas Dagh, Nicholaus frater eius, Stephanus Pestor, ... domum cuiusdam Ricardi ate Welle infra libetatem nostram ingressi sunt, cuius corpus rapientes ipsum defunctum asserebant uxor eius nomine Margeria .... ipsos prosequitur dicens quod inter brachia sua virum suum interfecerunt memoratum una cum corpore catalla sua asportantes ma.................. nobisque ad clamorem confluentibus et pro pace nostra fovenda ipsos capere nolentibus ad rescursionem eorum occurrebant Johannes Gravene, Thomas et Richardus filii eius, Willemus le Taverner, Gilbertus frater eius, Willelmus de Cantuar' et alii homines incongniti, numero quatuor centum, qui vi et manu armata quamplurimos homines et feminas comunitatis nostre graviter vulnerantes quemdam Cristianum de Brenle interfectum reliquerunt comunitate sibi nostra plenius congregata tam pacis vestre transgressores quam felones predictos capere volentes ad personiam [*sic*] dicti abbatis apud Faversham fugierunt et inhibi ut in castro existentes ad pacem vestram quampluries rogati venire noluerunt quoquomodo. In crastino, autem, cum esset hora nona essemus que in prandio egressi sunt armati villam que nostram ingressi insultum fecerunt, in eandem balistis et arcubus sagittando unde ad nos huthesium pervenit iteratum nobisque eisdem resistentibus et cum clamore patrie tamquam felones et pacis vestre transgressores prosequentibus. Fugientes capti sunt sexdecim de isdem suos digne duximus incarcerandos vestram igitur excellentissimam dominacionem humiliter duximus deprecandam quatinus de eisdem precipiat vestra dominacio quod sibi viderit expedire manum nobis ulterius porrigendo adjutricem super minis homicidii et incensii que de die in diem patrium per abbatem predictum et alios sibi adherentes valeat et vigeat vestra excellens dominacio per tempora longa.

No endorsement

c. 1301. The letter contains the transcript of a writ of 18 February 1301, and commissions concerning the dispute were issued on 27 March 1301 (*CPR 1292–1301*, p. 626). This episode was part of a struggle between St Augustine's and the archbishops of Canterbury which had been simmering since the 1280s. It involved not only Thomas Findon, abbot of St Augustine's (1283–1310), and archbishops Pecham and Winchelsey, but also Edward I and Boniface VIII, and was ended only by Boniface's ruling in favour of the archbishops' rights in 1303. See *William Thorne's Chronicle of St Augustine's Abbey Canterbury*, trans. A. H. Davis (Oxford, 1934), pp. 334–84; R. Graham, 'The Conflict between Robert Winchelsey, Archbishop of Canterbury, and the Abbot and Monks of St Augustine's, Canterbury', *JEH* 1 (1950), 37–50; J. H. Denton, *Robert Winchelsey and the Crown 1294–1313* (Cambridge, 1980), pp. 180–3 and references. This case is also discussed in the Introduction, pp. xxxix–xl.

183

Ogbourne St George, Wiltshire (1304)
Benedictine (alien)
(SC 8/163/8111)

The people of the rape of Hastings (Sussex) petition the king and council that the king grant justices, the constable of Dover and coroners of the land to hear and determine their complaints against Theobald, prior of Ogbourne, and Walter of Rokesle, farmers of the prior of St Martin (Normandy), who claim to have right by gift of the count of Eu, forfeited all the aforesaid tenants' lands of ancient demesne contained in Domesday Book pertaining to the manor of Hooe (Sussex) and put the tenants in prison, and chased them with arms out of the county to Kent, beat and wounded them and demanded suits and services, so that their women and children were left hungry.

A nostre seigneur le rey e a son consail demoustrent ses tenans e sa gent del rap de Hastynges qe par la ou il teingnent totes leurs terres e tenemens, queis sont de anciene demeygne par certaignes services contenuz den le Domesday del Eschekere nostre seigneur le rey apurtenaunz au maner de Ho, de Ew de quel maner e de terres e de la seigneurie le rey est esteez saunz gree a lui fait, sont venuz le priour de Okeburne e Wauter de Rokesle, servient le priour de Saint Martin en Normandye, qi clayme [av]er dreit par le doun le cunte de Ew, pur forfyt totes ses terres e mettent en prison les povers tenaunz avantdiz, e les enchasent e deboutent de terre e de tenement, e apportent touz leur chateaus en contre la pees, e enchasent leur avers hors del conte tant al conte de Kent, e les ensuiwent a force \e/ as armes, e les batent e nauffrent tant qe a la mort, e leur destreinent e demandent de eaus suites e services qeus faire ne deyvent, e issint les deiverient q'il ne ossent demorer en le pays, dont eus e leur femmes e leurs enfanz morrunt de faym. E s'il font nul purchas a la Cancellerie le visconte n'el ensuit poynt. Par quey il prient a nostre seigneur le rey \e/ a son consail q'il leur grante justices, le conestable de Dovere e les coroners du pays de oyer e a terminer celes pleyntes, ou autre remedye mettre come lui \e son consail/ serra avys, q'il peussent en la pees Dieu e nostre seigneur le reys estre en leur pays e en leurs tenemens demorer tant qe nostre seigneur le rey plus ensoit certefiez en cele part, qar grantment tornera a son preu \cel trespas/, e a ceo se obligent meismes ceaus trente tenanz vye e menbre, e qe leur pleinte est verreye e grant besoigne leur fait ...... qar il ont este ensi demenez touz jours puis q'il ad este deu sa guerre, e sont si poveres q'il n'ount riens dont vivere ne il ne soi poont purchasier por poverte.

No endorsement

1304. On 26 August 1304 a commission of oyer and terminer was issued upon the complaint of six men of Hooe that the prior of St Martin aux Bois, Theobald, prior of Ogbourne, Walter of Rokesley and others broke into their houses, stole their goods, prevented them from cultivating and sowing their lands, and drove their beasts to unknown places so that they could not replevy them (*CPR 1301–7*, p. 285). The names of the supplicants are given as Richard of Chollond, William of Upton, Geoffrey le Palmer, John Attebrok, Roger Sprot and Richard Godewyn, all of Hooe. Theobald of Cambremer occurs as prior 1295–1306. For the lands of the priory of St Martin in Sussex, see D. Matthew, *The Norman Monasteries and their English Possessions* (Oxford, 1962), pp. 54–6, 67. For further comment see note to **136** above.

184

St Albans, Hertfordshire (1315)
Benedictine
(SC 8/170/8472)

The burgesses of St Albans petition the king and council for a remedy as the abbot of St Albans holds the town in chief of the king and owes the service of finding two burgesses to attend parliament, but this has recently been withdrawn, in contempt of the king and to the damage of the burgesses.
Endorsed on face: *Hertfordshire.*
Endorsed: *The rolls of chancery should be examined to see if the burgesses are summoned or not, and if so let justice be done to them.*

A nostre seignur le rei e a son conseil mustrent les burgeys de la ville de Seint Auban qe come l'abbe de Saint Auban tient la ville de Seint Auban en chief du rei e devient le service de trover deuz burgeys de la dite ville de venir a son parlement, ausi fraunchement com autres burgeys devient trover par toutz manere de services appendauns au rei, e nostre seignur le rei, piere nostre seignur le rei qu'ore est, touz temps fust seisi de mesme le service, e nostre seignur le rei qu'ore est tot soun temps ausi ad este seisi de cele venue, jekes a ore qe le dit abbe e son conseil unt taunt procure qe les ditz burgeys n'avoiunt mye garnicement de fere le service avandit. Par quei mesme le service est mauveisement retret en despit du rei e damage des burgeys avanditz pur eux mettre en autre servage qe fere ne dusent, dount il prient remedie.

Endorsed on face: Hertford.
Endorsed: Scrutentur rotuli de Cancellaria si temporibus progenitorum regis burgenses predicti solebant venire vel non, et tunc fiat eis super \hoc/ justicia, vocatis evocandis si necesse fuerit.

1315. This petition belongs to the parliament of January 1315 since it was written up in Latin in the parliament roll of this assembly (*PROME*, parliament of January 1315, item 233 (195)). The abbot at this time was Hugh of Eversden (1309–27). Representatives from St Albans had been summoned to parliament on several occasions at the end of Edward I's reign, but no returns were made. The matter is discussed by M. McKisack, *The Parliamentary Representation of the English Boroughs during the Middle Ages* (Oxford, 1932), pp. 10, 12, 136.

185

St James, Northampton, Northamptonshire (1315)
Augustinian canons
(SC 8/35/1711)

The free sokemen of Bozeat (Northants.) petition the king and council, stating that the abbot of St James, Northampton has claimed from them services which they should not perform. They complained about this and obtained a writ of monstraverunt, *but the abbot has ill-treated them in many ways as a result. They request the king's grace and aid in this matter, and a letter to the exchequer to search Domesday so that they might know how the land ought to be held, as a replacement for a letter previously granted to them which was stolen from their attorney. They also ask that the abbot be ordered to show his evidence for his claim. They ask the king's grace and aid to be maintained in their rightful estate, paying their proper annual rent as the charter of Domesday demands.*

A noster seignur le roy e a son consayl demoustrent e prient vostre lige francsokemen de Bosyate, membre de Thyngdene, qe Nichol, abbe de Seyn Jake de hors Norhamptone, lour demaunt autre services et autre coustumes qe le estat de lour tenure veuler, e qe nul houme az demaunde devaunt, pur quoi nus fesimes pleynte en vostre court issi quod nous aveymes le bref de moustraverunt qe fust maunde al abbe par nostre lige franksokeman, qe est apele Thomas en le Sebil.. wic [damaged ms.] de Bosyate, le \dit abbe/ comaunde mentenaunt en prisoner le dist Thomas, messager de vostre bref, e en prison le tint jeke Thomas le avoit graunte chartre de sang e de chatels, de femme e de enfaunz, de mebles e de noun mebles, quele chartre fust lu devaunt tute la paroche en le eglise de Bosyate, pur ceo qe Thomas ne devoit nyent coundire son fet q'il graunta par ensone de enprisounement, e sur cel maunda le dist abbe ces gens e fist engettre Thomas e sa femme e ses enfaunz, e mist autre gens estraunges en sa mesoun, e pus mande ces gens ov force e armes a touz les autres tenaunz qe ne voleient nyent graunter tel fait com le dist Thomas grante en prisoun, par quoi il prist touz lour bestes, ouvesqe lour autre chatels, e les en chassa e en abater fist par ces gens de meyne horse de cel fraunchise, e ore cleyme proprete de corps e de chatels e de quant q'il ount de queles il ne pusent nule deliveraunce avoir, q'il pusent vos dreitures ensure ne lour estat saunz voster grace e voster eyde plus longement meintener, e pur ceo qe nous fusums renduz a vous en tot noster homage le samedi devaunt le Asumpcioun Noster Dame en voster regne le nofyme, e vous nous reffutes en la vile de Seynt Alban de cel jour en avaunt de south voster protexioun. Par quoi nous vous prioums, si vus plest, qe vous nus voillez granter voster grace de voster lettre a Cheker de ensercher noster Domesday de Thyngdone en Neveslondhundr', issi qe nous pusoums saveir com bien de terre deit estre tenu par un service, e qe vous \voillez/ faire ensercher en qel lu del hundret la terre gist, e qe vous voillez graunter noster lettre \a nous/, la quele nous fust grante e done par voster comaundement devaunt de avoir en Cheker e en Chauncelrie a Haneper en serjauntie saunz rien doner, e qe nostre chartre pust estre delivers e a ferme, de quele lettre \Mestre Huwe le Carpenter, portour de ceste bille/, noster attorne, fust de robbe, e de quant q'il avoit e namiere pres a la mort \ver Loundres/ a pres le ure qe le dist abbe fust homage a torne par pleges a la pes, pur quele robberie nous sumus moult a rerys, chire sire, umblement en prioums qe voster grace de de [*sic*] une tele lettre, si vous plest, nous soit restore par voster comandement qe autrement nus serroums tot a nentys. E auxi nus vous prioums qe vous voillez fere le dist abbe demoustrer seo q'il az pur luy, par quoi il nous cleyme enperperte, e qe luy feffa, e a ky il est feffe, e de combian qe nus savoms bian qe roi e deserite de un de mi feo de chivaler del honur de Peverel, e de la rentez de .... verge terre, e de my de franc sokage membre de Thyngdene e fust done en le Esthalle. Auxi fait a remembrer de le fraunchises des queles nous avoms este feffes, e unquore sumes, de le queles fraunchises \cum vus dist devaunt/ le abbe de Seyn Jake de hors Norhamptone nous voileit coler, par la ou nule resoun a luy apent ne nule segnurie ne ..., mes qe par terme de cynquaunt anz, la qele terme e passe e x anz plus, e nul autre veir de droit mes qe roi. Nos frauncheses sount celes qe mentenantz com le enfaunt est nez e pust estre oy il est de age de avoir sa terre, e si \le/ pere soit mort, le enfaunt serra baile en la garde de sa mere, e quant il savera demander sa terres sa mere luy bailera e luy rendra a counte, e le enfauns delivert sa mere se douwarie fraunchement, e tendra cel dowarie del enfaunt e de nul autre segnur, e si talent a vigne al enfaunt il pust avendre sa terre par franc chartre auxi com frank houme pust faire, e il memes aler par le ou beal luy soit e en autre seignurie demorer, e issi avoums fait .... ensa pur quele terre l'en serra al Pentec' checun hyde demy mark de certeyn rente, e pur \ceo/ nous avochoums Domesday engardunt qe nous ne dusoums autre services faire des qels tenaunz le dist abbe cleyme proprete e neifte e de luy tenir en noun certein, auxi com en bondage, par quoi nous vous prioms de voster eide qe nous pussoums vostre droiture e noster estat en countre le dist abbe mentener, e a vous noster rente anuel rendre auxi com il fesoient de antiquite, e com la chartre de nostre Domesday demande.

Fet auxi a remembrer qe par le tens le Roy Edward e le Reigne Edith si fust la rente de vij verge de terre en la ville e en les chaunps de Bosyate, membre de Thyngdone, en ceste manere rendu, c'est a savoir en une bource de une maile de monie, la rente le lundy lendemeyn de Pent' a un aubeespyne qe este entre Wolastone e Stryxstone par oure de prime, et si les balifs le roi de cele fraunchise ne furent nyent prestez le pertours de la rente devoient aler en une mesoun qe est apele Frаunceis de Strixston, qe le meson ore est a Sire William de Deneford, e leser la la bource en teumoignaunce q'il usent este la a oure asigne e plus outre, e le dist tenaunz devoient aporter la rente a rerez a le roi le renderat a cele ...., e si aventure avynt qe les dit tenaunz ne furent nient prestes a oure certeyn, le bailifs le roi devoient venir a Bosyate e en seler lour huys, jeke la rente fust paie e deus deners \e maile/ outre pur lour dyner, les quels deus deners \e maile/ unquore sount coiles ov la rentez, del les quels deners nous fasoums chaunter pur le un dener une messe en noun de Seynt Espirit, e le trois mailes a eus qe coilent cele rente pur lour turnail, des queles fraunchises nous avoums bone chartre jeke le tens fare le lauedy e ele nus fist demoustrer nostre chartre, la quele chartre ele jetta .... e le fist arder.

No endorsement

1315. The privy seal warrant with which this petition was formerly enclosed is dated 30 October 1315 (no. 3530 of C 81/93). Nicholas of Flore was abbot 1300–34. The petition also mentions the homage done in the king's ninth year (1315/16).

186

Bradenstoke, Wiltshire (c. 1316–18)
Augustinian canons
(SC 8/279/13929)

Andrew, a convert, who was baptised at the age of two in the time of Henry III and ordered by his letter to Bradenstoke, where he remained during the lives of Henry III and Edward I, petitions Edward II for his letter so that his commands can be obeyed. After the king's coronation he was denied his maintenance, but upon his request the king restored it, and he remained at the priory for five years until the prior and convent refused to keep him. He requested the king's grace at Waltham and was granted a letter of privy seal, but they forced him to say, and they said, that he had taken silver and goblets from their cellar and sang mass as a Jew. For this indictment he was imprisoned in Salisbury, and the prior and convent asked and prayed the good people of the region to put him to death, but they knew it had been done falsely and out of hate, and released him as a good and loyal Christian and said so before John of Foxley, justice. When he was released he asked for the maintenance which Henry III had granted and Edward I confirmed but was told to go as a beggar since he meant nothing to the king and queen.

A mun seignur par la grace Deu Rey Edward vus cri merci e pri vostre grace, pur Deu, sy vus plest, pur l'amor vostre pere e vostre mere Elianore, de un convers qe ad nun Andreu, qe fust batize al age de ij anz en le tens le Rey Henri e mande par sa lettre a Bradenestok de aver ma sustinance, e la fu sustenu tote sa vie e la vie vostre pere Roy Edward, a pres vostre coroment fust de nye ma sustinance qe nule ne purra aver, cher seignur, jeo requis vostre grace de restitucion de ma sustinance, e vus me grantastes vostre lettre de vostre prive ceal a la grave prede Langhelee. Sunt passe cynk anz, e jeo le pora al prior e al covent il ne tyndrent ren de ceo mesme cel an jeo requis vostre grace a Waltham, vos me grantastes vostre lettre o prive cel pur l'alme vostre pere e vostre mere Elianore qe ren ne me valust mes pur ceo qe jeo auxi grace de aver vos lettres o vos prive ceals il me firent a diter, e disent, qe jeo avey de pesse le us de lur celer e anporte peces de argent e hanaps, e qe dusse aver chante messe ca un Judei, par mesme cel inditement jeo fu mis en la prisone de Salesbure, el prior el covent manderunt e prierunt a les bones genz del \paii/ qe il me dussent aver mys a la mort, mes les bones gens savent bent qe se fest pur haye e par fausine e me de livererunt cum leal e bon Cristien, e disent ben de \vant/ le justice qe fust a mesme le houre,

Syre Johan de Foxlee, qe se fust pur haye, e quant jeo fu delivres jeo demanda ma sustinance qe le Rey Henri me dona e granta e le Rey Edward confirma, e il me responderunt va tan begant ja pur rey e reyne n'averet tant ne qant. Cher seygnur, jeo vus pri, pur l'amor Deu, eetz pite de mei povre qe jeo ne perde la vie pur de faute de sustinance qe jeo fu veil e feble e ne pus travailler, pur Deu mon siegnur, jeo vus pri une lettre qe vos comandemenz pussunt estre tenuz.

No endorsement

c. 1316–18. It seems likely that the harsh treatment of Andrew was the result of the series of poor harvests which began in 1315: I. Kershaw, 'The Great Famine and Agrarian Crisis in England 1315–1322', *Past and Present* 59 (1973), 3–50. Sir John Foxley, an exchequer baron (1309–22), was a justice of oyer and terminer at Windsor in 1316: Sainty, *Judges*, p. 108; *The Register of Roger Martival, Bishop of Salisbury 1315–1330, Vol. III: Royal Writs*, ed. Susan Reynolds, C&Y, 59 (1965), no. 46.

187

Bermondsey, Surrey (1320)
Cluniac
(SC 8/39/1944)

Henry de Cliff and Adam de Brome, clerks, whom the king, considering the dilapidation and destruction of the goods of the priory of Bermondsey made by the prior and convent there, assigned to be keepers of the priory, petition the king, showing that when they first arrived at the priory they found that there was nothing to sustain the prior and 18 monks, the house was in great debt, and all their manors and houses, except Bermondsey and Waddon, and all their churches, which they should hold to their own use, were let at farm. The keepers have acted to reduce costs and to make arrangements for the prior and monks, but because the prior could not have his way he has accused the keepers of selling their growing corn below its value. They request that the chancellor, treasurer, Hugh Despenser and Robert of Baldock be charged to go to the priory and survey its estate, and also examine their acts, and that the house be taken into the king's hand.
Endorsed: *The chancellor and treasurer should ordain upon the contents of the petition what they consider ought to be done.*

A nostre seignur le roi mostrent ses clers Henri de Clif et Adam de Brom qe come nostre seignur le roi, entendant dilapicacion et destruction des biens de la priourte de Bermundeseye faites par le priour et le covent de meisme le lieu, assigna les ditz Henri et Adam gardeins de la dite priourte, les queux gardeins a lour primere venue ilokes, c'est assavoir le primer jour de Augst, ne troverent illosqes ble ne argent ne autre chose pur sustenaunce du priour et xviij moignes, et autant des liveresons saunz ministres necessaries qe amont a grant summe d'argent par la semaine, et a mesme le tenps il troverent la meson en dette par diverses reconissances faites par le priour qi ore est en M[l] CCC lxxiiij mars, et toutz lour maners, forspris Bermundeseye et Waddone, et totes leur eglises, qe eux soloint tenir en propre use, lesses a ferme, les unes a terme de vie et les unes a terme d'anz, et tuz l'argent pris avant main, et auxint quant qe eux poaint lever de lour fermes de Londres auxibien du tenps passe come des termes avenir tot despendu et gaste. Par qai les ditz gardeins troverent de lour deners demeine grant piece les custages pur les moignes et les autres avantditz, et fesoint redresser lour molins qe estoient auxi come abatuz a terre, et par la ou il fust acorde par le dit prior et les gardeins avantditz qe meisme le prior deveroit demorer en ascun certein lieu hors de la priorie privement pur esparnier mises et custages et il commencea ceo faire une piece ore est il returne en la priourie, et pur ceo q'il ne poet avoir sa volunte de faire outrageus despens come il soleit il va disant qe le ditz gardeins se sount malement porte en la dite garde et qe eux ount vendu les blez qe crusteront sur lour terre a Bermundeseye pur meins q'ils ne valeint la ou il furent venduz a la verrai value, et au tenps qe les ditz gardeins ne poaint autre chevisance faire pur la sustenance des moignes et autres avantditz ne rien navaient des biens \de la dite meson/ vount il poaint faire entrer les ditz blez. Par qai meismes les gardeins priont a nostre seignur le roi q'il lui pleise charger le chaunceler ou le tresorer, Monsire Hugh le Despenser ou Mestre Roberd de Baldok, d'aler a Bermundeseye en propre persone et surveer l'estat de la priourie, et de examiner auxint les faitz des ditz gardeins, et ordiner issint del estat de cele mesone qe vos avions ne se perdent, car, Sire, si vous ne preignez garde et mettez la maine certeinement, Sire, ele est en point d'estrer destruit et hom ne trovera dount sustener les moignes et les autres ministres.

Endorsed: Ordinent cancellarius et thesaurarius super contentis in peticione prout eis videbitur faciendum.

1320. The prior was Peter of St Laurence (1312–c.1321). The petitioners were appointed keepers of the priory on account of its debt on 17 June 1320 (*CPR 1317–21*, p. 457). The order was superseded on 26 October 1320, and the priory returned to the prior (*CPR 1317–21*, p. 512). Less than a month later two different keepers were appointed, before the goods of the priory were again restored to St Laurence on 1 October 1321 (*CPR 1317–21*, p. 529; *CPR 1318–23*, p. 403). The chancellor was John Salmon, bishop of Norwich, and the treasurer Walter Stapeldon, bishop of Exeter. For a discussion of these events, see *VCH Surrey*, II, 70–1. The petitioners were chancery clerks. For Adam de Brome, future founder of Oriel College, Oxford, see **145** above, and references. The very distinguished career of Master Henry de Cliff can be followed in T. F. Tout, *Chapters in the Administrative History of Mediaeval England*, 6 vols (Manchester, 1920–33), VI, 205; B. Wilkinson, *The Chancery under Edward III* (Manchester 1929), p. 233; and *BRUO*, I, 438–9.

188

Peterborough, Northamptonshire (1320)
Benedictine
(SC 8/77/3819)

Peter of Borle petitions Aymer of Valence, earl of Pembroke and keeper of England, for a remedy because in a plea concerning the taking of livestock between him and the abbot of Peterborough, he was awarded the animals by judgement of the court, but the abbot has refused to abide by this decision, and has stolen the animals with force and arms.

A son trescher seignur et treshonurable sire Aymer de Valence, counte de Pembr' e gardeyn d'Engelterre, Peres de Borle, son servant, se pleint qe par la ou mesmes cesti Peres pleda ove le abbe de Borugh Seint Pere devant Sire William de Bereford e ses compaignons en plee de pris des avers la par agard de la court e par juggement fust agarde au dit Peres le avers le abbe, issint qe les bestes demoroient ove le avant dit Peres tant qe le abbe s'ensist de aver hors sez bestes par brief de juggement e par comandement de nostre seignur le roi, mes l'abbe, en despit de roi, en defesant la ley, e force e armes manda voz gentz e lez dit bestes prist hors de la possession le avant dit Peres a totz. Et vous prie, pur Dieu, qe vous soiet en eide qe ceste chose soit redresse.

No endorsement

1320. Aymer de Valence was regent in the king's absence 19 June – 22 July 1320, *Handbook of British Chronology*, ed. E. B. Fryde, D. E. Greenway, S. Porter, and I. Roy, 3rd ed. (London, 1986), p. 39. The abbot was Godfrey of Crowland (1299–1321).

189

Hatfield Broad Oak or Hatfield Regis, Essex (? 1320)

Benedictine
(SC 8/88/4353)

John of Waltham, cook, who has long served first the king's father, and then his brothers, Thomas and Edmund, from the time when they first had a household of their own, and is now too old to work, petitions the king for his letters to the prior and convent of Hatfield Broad Oak (Hatfield Regis) to grant him a corrody there.
Endorsed: *He is to provide for himself elsewhere, as they are already charged by the king.*

A nostre seignur le roi prie son povre vallet Johan de Wautham, keu, qui longement servi nostre trescher seignur le roi vostre piere, qe Dieux assoille, et pus ad servi voz treschers freres, Thomas et Edmond, du temps qu'il tindrent primerement hostiel en cea, et ad despendu tut son temps d'enfaunce en lur services, parqoi, Sire, il est ore si vieuz et si travaillez q'il ne sei pust mesmes aider ne mes travailler, par quoi, trescher seignur, voillez avoir regard a Dieu et a charite et vous plese grauntir voz lettres au priour et au covent de Hatfeld Brodhok q'il voillent grauntir et doner au dit Johan sa gareson covenable pur son estat. Et de ceste chose, Sire, vous pregne pite qe le povre home ne chiete en poverte deshonuree en ses dreins jours.

Endorsed: Se purvoie aillours, car il sont chargez par le roi.

? 1320. A note at the start of this file, dated 5 May 1932, states that 'Nos 4351–4364 are copied in R.C. Transcripts I 156, and appear to form part of an original file of petitions to the parliament of Michaelmas 1320.' The king's father is Edward I, his brothers are Thomas of Brotherton, earl of Norfolk, and Edmund of Woodstock, earl of Kent. The identity of the prior of Hatfield Regis at this time is not known. Waltham's case was not untypical; a substantial proportion of the requests for a corrody were refused, and many crown servants had several disappointments before finally achieving 'the security of letters patent under the common seal of a house'. The period 1300–30 saw the crown fiercely exploiting and extending its rights to provide for its former servants: J. H. Tillotson, 'Pensions, Corrodies and Religious Houses: An Aspect of the Relations of Crown and Church in Early Fourteenth-Century England', *Journal of Religious History* 8 (1974), 127–43.

190

St Albans, (1327)
Benedictine
(SC 8/30/1483)

The burgesses and community of St Albans petition the king and council for a remedy because the abbot of St Albans and some of his monks have demanded from them certain indentures concerning an arbitration made in certain disputes between the abbey and the burgesses, and the king's charter of confirmation of these indentures, and are charging them with certain services contrary to their state of free burgage, which they have by these documents. They have refused to do as he wishes. The abbot, who is powerful enough to control the sheriff, coroner and justices, has moved against them, and has maliciously indicted them of various crimes and threatened them, in order to have the indentures and charter annulled, causing them to flee the town.
Endorsed: *Sir Roger Grey, justice, etc. is to be ordered to have brought into chancery the record and process held before them concerning the abbot and convent of St Albans and the people of the same town and this business.*

A nostre seignur le roi et a son consail moustrent et prient les soens poveres burgeys et la comunalte de la ville de Seint Alban qe come sur certeynes plez et debatez ascun temps meuz par entre l'abbe et le covent de Seint Alban d'une part et les soen burgeys et comunalte de mesme la ville d'autre part, acord final se prist de lour comun assent et par comunes amys entreventantz en la manere come plus plainement est compris en certeyns endentures sur ceo faites de lour comun assent et bone volunte en la presence Monsire Johan de Croumbewell, Monsire Henri de Gray, Monsire Robert Walkfare, Monsire Wauter de Nevyle, Robert de Kellesseie, Johan de Shardelowe, Thomas Bacoun, Thomas de Nichol et autres, apres queux pleez et debatz entre eux come avant est dit amyablement determinez et les avanditz burgeys suerent a nostre seignur le roi et a son consail, empriantz qe celes ditz endentures voleit confermer, sur quei l'avandit abbe vient en court devant nostre seignur le roi qe ore est, qe Dieu sauve, a Rammeseye \ et/ devant Sire Johan de Hothom, evesqe de Ely, adonqes chanceller nostre dit seignur le roi, ou \il/ coneusoit les dites endentures estre ses faitz et les faitz son covent, et de lour bone volunte as ditz burgeis estree faites grantant et voillant pur lui et son covent la chartre nostre seignur le roi de confermer ses touz les pointz compris en les dites endentures, sur quei nostre dit seignur le roi les conferma par sa chartre touz les ditz pointz, come prestz sont a moustrer par les dites chartre et endentures, apres queu tepms [*sic*] l'abbe de Seint Alban qe ore est et de ses moignes plusurs abbettantz sovent ount maundez a les avanditz burgeis et comunalte arendre a eux les avandites endentures et chartre nostre dit seignur le roi contre lour faitz demeigne, enfreynantz le avandit acord et accollier de eux chescune manere estat de franc burgage, de quel estat ils sont par lour faitz demeigne et par la chartre nostre dit seignur le roi. Et sur ceo la voleient charger le avanditz burgeis et comunalte contre comune lai affaire seute a ses molyns et acollier de eux lour mesmes molyns, et affaire autres servages come a charger chescun estan dedeinz la ville de un ferthyng, par la sameig[ne], et de plusurs autres servages encontre l'estat de franc burgeis, et par la reson qe les avanditz burgeis et comunalte ne voillent a eux rendre les avandites endentures et chartre ne entre en les servages susditz, le dit abbe en est moen envers les ditz burgeis et comunalte, et par son grant poer et roiale franchise q'il ad et use had viscont attrez a lui avol..... et coroner du soen remuable a sa volunte, et justices de ses foez, et de ses robes et autres ministres roials ove touz les autres plu avant del contee de Hertford, a graunt oppressioun du poeple et damage nostre seignur le roi, et ad procure maliciousement enditer par les soens et ses alliez les ditz burgeis et comunalte de roberies, homicides et des autres mauvettez, come plus plainement appiert par tiel enditement retourne devant nostre seignur le roi et par autre enditement fait ore tard a Hertford devant Sire Johan de Cauntebrigge, seneschal le dit abbe, overtement swy et procure par le dit abbe et ses ministres de conspiraciez, confederauciez, assegementz faites a sa abbeie et autres mauvettez faites a lui et a sa abbeie fesaunt assavoir, et les ditz enditours apertement par lui et ses moignes et autres de son consail qe les avandites endentures et autres se firent par manace des ditz burgeis et par poour d'estre tuez et ars, et ceste suggestioun fount ils par la cause les avandites chartre et endentures voider a touz jours, pur doute des que[ux] maliciouses enditementz et oppressiouns les ditz burgeis nostre seignur le roi et comunalte s'en sont sewys ore de Seint Alban requerant et la grace et l'aide [nostre seignur] le roi et son consail, a lour grant mescheif et damage et destruccioun si de ceo ne ayent remedie, et q'ils poessent a la pees et al acord le dit abbe par nostre seignur [le roi], sanz qe aide et seignurie a la pes le dist abbe ja n'attyndrent et le dit \abbe/ les maunde si les dite endentures et chartre ne voillent a lui rendre qe tant come ils .... remedie des choses et grevances susdites l'abbe et ses moignes ove lour consail ount parentre lour isseues si hautes q'ils passent se vaillant de lour terres .... chateux, et a tieles isseues encrestre plus hautes pur les tust outrement destrure, fount et procurent lour baillifs et ministres roials porter lour billes de divers trespas et d'autre mauvettez feintes, a quels seutes ils ount fait lour issues desresonables come desus est dit. Dont les avanditz burgeys et comunalte prient, pur Dieu, a nostre seignur le roi et a son consail remedie.

Endorsed: Soit maunde a Sire Roger de Grey, justice, etc. de fore venir en Chauncellerie le record et proces ewes devant eux tochantz l'abbe et covent de Seint Auban et les gentz de mesme la ville et ceste besoigne.

1327. The petition is most likely to have been presented to the parliament of January 1327, at the end of Edward II's reign, when the townsmen of St Albans had an opportunity to appeal to the new regime of Isabella and Mortimer against the abbey. It probably followed an earlier failed attempt to appeal directly to the abbot to grant them greater freedom and rights within the town: *Gesta abbatum monasteri sancti Albani*, ed. H. T. Riley, Rolls Series, 28, 3 vols (1867–9), II, 157–8. The abbot is therefore Hugh Eversden 1309–27. John Hothom, described in the petition as chancellor, held office 1318–20. Of the eight men before whom the previous agreement was made, two, Bacon and Shardlow, were future judges (Sainty, *Judges*, pp. 23, 24, 62,63, 65). But two more were politically active. Robert Walkfare was described as a kinsman and follower of Thomas, earl of Lancaster (*Gesta abbatum*, II, 131), was the earl of Hereford's steward (J. R. Maddicott, *Thomas of Lancaster 1307–1322* (Oxford, 1970), p. 263), and was a known opponent of the king whose lands were confiscated in 1322 (*CPR 1321–4*, pp. 18, 81, 179), while John Cromwell, formerly a staunch royalist, constable of the Tower and a royal banneret, was blacklisted by Edward II in 1321 (Maddicott, *Thomas of Lancaster*, pp. 78, 112, 211, 267, 299). It is plausible to suggest that the setting aside of this agreement followed the changed political situation after the defeat of the king's enemies at Boroughbridge in 1322. The petition provides a backdrop for the outbreak of rebellion in St Albans, and in other monastic boroughs, in 1326–7, for which see N. M. Trenholme, *The English Monastic Boroughs: A Study in Medieval History* (Columbia, 1927), pp. 31–7 and references.

191

Monks Kirby, Warwickshire (c. 1327)
Benedictine (alien)
(SC 8/7/303)

William, messenger of the sheriff of Warwickshire and Leicestershire, petitions the king and council, complaining that when he was appointed by the commission of the sheriff of Warwickshire and Leicestershire to commandeer horses and carts in those counties to send to Scotland, on the orders of Edward I, Peter, prior of Monks Kirby, John Pardieu of Kirby, Richard of Pailton, chaplain, William Davy of Kirby, Peter le Hayward, Adam Inge of Rugby and Robert son of William Woodward of Pailton came with force and arms, and on the king's highway called the Fosse, which runs between Warwickshire and Leicestershire, beat him and left him for dead, and took a cart of the prior's which he had seized. He requests justices, namely John Peche, John of Cave and John of Peyto, or two of them, to hear and determine this trespass.
Endorsed: *He is to sue at common law.*

A nostre seignur le roy et a soun counseil se pleint William le messager \le visounte de Warrewyk et de Leycestre/ de Daunz Piers, priour de Monkeskyrkeby, Johan Pardieu de Kyrkeby, Richard de Paylyntone, chapeleyn, William Davy de Kyrkeby, Piers le Hayward, Adam Inge de Rokesby et Robert le fitz William Wodeward de Paylintone, qe come il fust assigne par la commission le viscounte de Warrewyk et de Leycestre de prendre chivals et charettes en les dites countes de maunder en Escoce, come comaunde fust de par le roy, piere nostre seignur le roy qe ore est, qe mort est, qe Dieus assoille, les avantditz priour et les autres vindrent a force et armes en lehaut chemyn nostre seignur le roy q'est apele Fosse, q'est merch entre le counte de Warrewyk et de Leycestre, et le dit William assaylerent, batirent, naufrerent et malement treterent, et pur mort illoeqes lui lesserent, et un charette le dit priour, le quel il avoyt pris al oeps le roy pur son cariage par soun garaunt q'il avoyt, lui tolirent, en despit du roy de cent li et damage le dit William de lx li. Dount le dit William prie, pur Dieu, q'il pleyse a nostre seignur le roy graunter justices en le counte de Warrewyk de oyer et terminer cel trespas, c'est a saver Johan Peche, John de Cave et Johan de Peyto, ou dieus de eux.

Endorsed: Sequatur ad comunem legem.

c. 1327. One of a collection of petitions published on pages 387ff of *RP*, I, which all seem to date from around 1322. However, the petition dates the assault to the king's father's reign and the only recorded Prior Peter of Monks Kirby was Peter Franciscus, prior 1314–26. So the petition must date to the start of Edward III's reign. The attack on William might have occurred during preparations for Edward II's invasion of Scotland in the summer of 1322. Thus, the petitioner is the messenger of Thomas le Rous, sheriff of Warwickshire and Leicestershire October 1321 – October 1322. The 'justices', John Peche, John of Cave and John of Peyto, all appear to have been prominent officeholders and landowners of the midlands, active as commissioners of the peace and justices of oyer and terminer throughout the second half of Edward II's reign. Their careers can be constructed by reference to the printed chancery rolls. For an earlier edition of the original petition, see *RP*, I, 408, no. 127.

192

Coventry, Warwickshire (c. 1327–30)
Benedictine
(SC 8/152/7591)

The people of Warwickshire petition the king, making several requests for remedy for the following causes:
(1) The prior of Coventry has maintained false quarrels and impeded the law. They would like an enquiry into this matter.
(2) Richard of Napton, steward of the prior of Coventry, held land in Napton from Robert of Napton, and when he died Robert of Napton entered it, but by conspiracy the prior and John Chaloner brought and passed an assize of novel disseisin against him.
(3) By many threats and grievances and by false pleas the prior has disseised Agnes Baker and her son.
(4) The prior has extorted £20 from Richard Dalby of Coventry for maintaining Agnes Baker.
(5) The prior has ejected Robert of Chiltern from land that he did not wish to sell to the prior, and he can have no legal redress.
(6) The prior attaches the goods of any man who is bound in a debt to anyone in Coventry of the power of the prior, without process, and the goods cannot be recovered without first making satisfaction to the prior.
(7) The prior takes fines from many criminals and thieves and assizes to the king's prejudice, and releases some without judgement.
(8) The prior purchases lands in mortmain to the king's disinheritance because he retains the sheriffs and bailiffs.
Endorsed: *Concerning the first, this falls under the common ordinance concerning conspirators and other malefactors.*
Concerning the others, saving the last, they should sue in chancery, and have writs according to their case.
Concerning the last, let the chancellor be certified of the names of the seizers, and let writs be made in suitable form.

A nostre seignur le roi moustrent ses liges gentz del counte de Warwyk qe le priour de Coventre est comun enpernour e meyntenour de fause quereles e chaumpartour de tenementz pledables, issi qe nuyl dreit puyt estre trye pur sa confederacion de plusours gentz de pays qe sount a luy alyez e jurez defaire chose q'il enprent, dount nul homme du pays puyt dreit aver en sa querele endreiture meyntener la ou le dit priour enprent l'adverse partie, de quei les dites gentz priont a nostre seignur q'il voile de ceste chose faire remedie. E si ceo pleise a nostre seignur le roi de ordeiner certeines justices tens qe ne sount de la retenaunce le dit priour ne de sa alyaunce de ceste chose enquere par leles gentz du pays triez la verite de ceste chose serra trove, a graunt profyt de nostre seignur le roi e a sauvacion de plusours qe sount e serront desherites e anientyz par sa conspiracie e sa fause alyaunce, si nostre seignur le roi de sa grace ne face remede.

Com y pert par Sire Robert de Naptone, chivaler, qe par la ou un Richard de Naptone, seneschal le dit priour, tint du dit Sire Robert une charue de terre en Naptone, le quel Richard feust bastard e morust sanz heir de son corps, le dit Robert les tenemenz entre com en sa eschete, le dit priour fyst par sa conspiracie un Johan le Chaloner porter bref de novele disseisine vers le dit Robert, par vertue de une chartre la quele le priour fyst faire, e sur quei nule seisine feust lyvere en la vie le dit Richard, e fist l'assise passer countre le dit Robert, a grant damage e desheritaunce de luy.

Ensement y pert par diverse grevaunces et duresces qe le dit priour ad fait devers Agneys qe fuist la femme Robert le Pestour de Coventre e Henry son fyz, cest asavoir qe le dit priour les ditz Agneis e Henry, atort e countre ley de terre, \ad/ des[eisi] et par plee mu de fause quereles, les ditz Agneis e Henry unt par certeine gentz de lour counseil a Sire Johan de Hastinges baile, en priauntz q'il voile prier a nostre seignur le roi qe remedie lour seit faitz.

Ensement le dit priour surmyst un Richard Dalby de Coventre q'il meintent la dite Agneyse outre[a] ly, e si fort ly meva[a] par cele encheson q'il ly fist vint lyveres. Ensement y pert par un Robert de Chilterne de Coventre qe pur ceo q'il ont veleit vendre au dit priour une charue de terre la quele il coveita, il fist engeitre[a] le dit Robert issi qe unkes puis ne osa il purchacer par la ley ne sa terre aprocher.

Ensement si nul homme seit tenuz a autre en une dette qe seit de la vile de Coventre denz le power le priour, il fet attacher les bienz le dettour saunz autre proces de ley, issi qe le dettour ne puyt a ses biens aprocher tauntqe il fet gree au dit priour, e ceo pur chaumpartie de la dette avoir.

Ensement le dit priour prent fyns de cinsours de bourses e de autres barouns qe sount pris en la vile de Coventre sovent ove diverses felonies, e de brazours e pestours e forestalleres e de fauses mesures qe sount hors de assise del estandart d'Engleterre, les queuz le dit priour meyntent pur fin fete a luy, en prejudice de nostre seignur le roi e a graunt grevaunce de poeple.

Ensement un laroun ajugge de pendre en sa court fut delyveres saunz juggement avoir par assent del priour e ses bailifs.

Ensement le dit priour purchace terres e tenemenz en divers leuz e fet mettre ses cosins en les chartres de feoffementz, e il meysmes prert les profytz e ausi pur prent suys autri soil la ou sa terre est joynaunte, issi qe les tenemenz devenont en mort meyn, en desheritaunce nostre seignur le roi, ne le eschetour ne puyt cele chose trover pur ceo qe le priour retent ove ly viscountes e baylyfs qe sount de sa covyne e mettont en .... gentz de sa confederacion, par quey la verite ne puyt estre sue.

Endorsed: Quant al primer point, ce chiet souz la commune ordenance qe se fera de conspiratours et d'autres mesfesours.
Quant as autres, sauve le drein, suent en Chauncellerie a la commune ley et eient brefs solonc lour cas.
Et quant al derrein, soit le chaunceller certifiez des nouns des seissours, et soient faite brefs covenable forme.

a reading uncertain.

c. 1327–30. This petition sheds light on a long-running dispute between the prior and townsmen of Coventry. The conflict initially focussed on trading rights within the city and attempts by merchants in the 'Earl's Half' to hold a market independently from the prior. In 1323–4 the dispute became a *cause célèbre* when the townsmen were alleged to have employed a necromancer to countenance the deaths of the king and the Despensers, as well as the prior of Coventry and his supporters: see J. Röhrkasten, 'Conflict in a

Monastic Borough: Coventry in the Reign of Edward II', *Midland History* 18 (1993), 1–18. The dating of the petition is uncertain, though it seems doubtful that it was presented in the later stages of Edward II's reign, when the prior held favour with Edward II. John Chaloner, a wealthy Coventry merchant, was also amongst the defendants accused by the prior of conspiracy in 1323. On 24 July 1324 an order was given to the justices of the Bench and others not to molest or attack John Chaloner at the prior's suit as he was on the king's service and had not remained in England against his service as the prior alleged (*CCR 1323–7*, p. 203). Robert Napton occurs as a knight in 1330 and is known to have lived in the Coventry suburb of Spon in the 1330s and 1340s. Richard Dalby held property in Coventry in the 1330s. Robert Chiltern held property in the market place in 1314 and acted as a witness to one of the prior's property deals in 1320. Agnes Baker's husband, Henry Baker, was the prior's bailiff in the 1290s; her son took up the office in 1307. The evidence therefore suggests that the complaint was made early in Edward III's reign, when previous political and administrative affiliations had altered. Isabella, the queen mother, inherited the 'Earl's Half' of the city in 1330, so the petition might also have been drafted in light of new attitudes towards the prior which now prevailed at court. The petition is, in general, evidence for the vigorous programme of land acquisition implemented by the priory in the first half of the fourteenth century, for which see R. Goddard, *Lordship and Medieval Urbanisation: Coventry, 1043–1355* (Woodbridge, 2004), pp. 111–25. The prior of Coventry was either Henry of Leicester (1294–?1342) or Henry Irreys (occurs 1328), but these may be the same person: references to Prior 'Henry' continue until the next prior's appointment in 1342. For other petitions from the prior, see SC 8/159/7920 and 175/8746, and **30** above.[38]

193

Selby, WRY (1325)
Benedictine
(SC 8/197/9813)

Letter, dated 2 July 1325, to Edward II from the bishop of Lincoln, informing him that Richard of Garforth (Lincs.) who, falsely accused of a crime, had sought sanctuary in Lincoln cathedral, has been violently abducted from there and imprisoned in the abbot of Selby's prison at Selby, and that the abbot's bailiffs are refusing to deliver him. He asks the king to order the abbot and his bailiffs to return him.

Excellentissimo domino suo domino Edwardo, Dei gracia illustri regi Anglie, domino Hibernie et duci Aquitanie, Henricus, eiusdem permissione Lincoln' episcopus, salutem in eo per quem reges regnant et principes dominantur. Dominacioni vestre celsitudini patefacimus per presentes quod nonnulli presumptuosi viri se filios ecclesie sue matrici degeneres ostendentes Ricardum de Gerlethorp', qui, tamquam sibi constuis de crimine sibi falso forsan et maliciose inponito ad ecclesiam nostram cathedralem Lincoln' tam immunitatis et tuicionis ecclesiastice apertinende nuper confugerat, ab eadem ecclesia et eius cimiterio seu clauso contra immunitatem et libertatem eccliasticam per violenciam et vim armatam intractum perperam extraxerunt corpusque ipsius carceri abbatis de Seleby apud Seleby miserabiliter manciparunt. Quod quidem corpus ballivi dicti abbatis in

38 We wish to thank Dr Richard Goddard for generously supplying details about the backgrounds of the Coventry citizens named in this petition.

forma debita requisiti immunitati ecclesiastice a qua ut premittitur extractus est restituere ut accepimus pertinaciter contradicunt. Quocirca excellencie vestre attentius supplicamus quatinus . . abbatis et ballivis suis predictis dire velitis vestris in mandatis quod corpus dicti Ricardi immunitati ecclesiastice a qua ut predicitur extra.... restituant indilate valeat excellencia vestra regia in Cristo Jhesu per tempora diuturna. Dat' apud Hybury, sexto nonas Julii anno domini millesimo trescentesimo vicesimo quinto.

No endorsement

1325. The letter is from Henry Burghersh, bishop of Lincoln 1320–40. The abbot of Selby is John of Wistow II (1322–35). Richard of Gerlethorp almost certainly came from Garthorp, in the Isle of Axholme, north Lincolnshire, where Selby Abbey held property. This letter was not recorded among Burghersh's *memoranda.*

194

Sempringham, Lincolnshire (c. 1327)
Gilbertine
(SC 8/34/1671)

Roger of Birthorpe petitions the king and council, showing that there was a dispute between John of Camelton, prior of Sempringham, and himself for a prise to be taken by Birthorpe, who assembled Edmund Coleville, Geoffrey Luttrell, Guy Goband and many other great lords and good people of the country, and they came to the priory to treat with the prior concerning the business, but the prior had his gates closed and would not speak with them. After their departure the prior raised the hue and cry on Birthorpe, and by the maintenance of Hugh Despenser and his sisters, nuns of Sempringham, brought a writ of trespass against Birthorpe, and by the inquisition damages of 500 marks were awarded to the prior, though no trespass was made. By the prior's malice Birthorpe dared not reside in England and went to Ireland, and the prior had him outlawed, by which Henry of Beaumont seized Birthorpe's manor of Birthorpe as chief lord. Birthorpe requests that, since the king has granted him a charter of pardon, he may have restitution of his land and the attaint passed against him.
Endorsed: *Concerning the land, he should sue at the common law.*
And concerning the attaint, it is to be declared by the great council if it is their intent that the statute is to apply both to inquisitions taken before as to those taken after.

A nostre seignur le roi et a son counseaill moustre Roger de Birthorpe qe come une destaunce estoit meu par entre Johan de Cameltone, priour de Sempyngham, et le dit Roger pur une pryse d'avers qe le dit Roger fist prendre sur le dit priour, et pur bon acord entre eaux faire le dit Roger fist assembler Mounsire Edmound Colevyle, Mounsire Geffrey Luterel, Mounsire Guy Goband et plusours autres grantz seignurs et bones gentz du pays, et les mova ala priorie de Sempyngham pur treter ove le dit priour de la dite busoigne, et le dit priour apartenaunt leu vendu fist fermer ses portes et ne voleit ovesks eaux parler. Mes tauntost apres lour departyr se purpensa de manners compassement si fist decouper ses portes par ses gentz demeigne et fist lever hu et cry sur le dit Roger ove graunt sute tauntqe al maner de Birthorpe, et sur ceo, par l'avowerie et meyntenaunce Mounsire Hughe le Despenser et ses seors, dames en la dite priorie, porta bref de trespas oyer et terminer vers le dit Roger, et taunt fist par son faux compassement et procurement qe l'enqueste passa encountre le dit Roger as damages le priour de D marcz, la ou le dit Roger ne nul homme par luy nul trespas ne fyst. Et pur la grant malice le dit priour le dit Roger n'osa demorer en Engleterre mes passa en Irlaunde, et le dit priour ne voleit autre issue prendre mes siwy bref de prendre son corps et taunt siwy qe par sa continuacie fust utlaghe, par quele utlagherye Mounsire Henry de Beaumond seisy son maner de Birthrope, qe vaut xl li par an, auxi come chef seignur et l'ad tenu puys en cea en desheritaunce le dit Roger. Dount il prie, desicome nostre seignur le roi luy ad done sa chartre de pardoun et restituit a sa pees, q'il puysse aver restitucioun de sa tearre et la teynte sur l'enqueste qe passa fausement encountre lui.

Endorsed: Quant a la terre, sue a la comune lei.
Et quant al atteinte, soit declare par le grant conseil si \leur entencion soit qe/ l'estatut se estent auxibien as enquestes deillet prises come as enquestes qi sont a prendre.

c. 1327. The petition can be dated to c. 1327 by its reference to a statute about inquests (*SR*, I, 253 (vi)). This was legislation enacted by the regime of Isabella and Mortimer to allow writs of attaint to be obtained in oyer and terminer cases. John of Camelton, mentioned as prior, was in fact prior of Chicksands c. 1316–c. 1324; this was probably a scribal error for John of Hamilton, prior of Sempringham c. 1298–c. 1324. The incident that the petitioner refers to is likely to have taken place in 1312. In July 1312 a commission of oyer and terminer was granted to the prior of Sempringham on complaint that Birthorpe and others had attacked his men and carried away his goods: *CPR 1307–13*, pp. 530, 598. Later, in September, a commission of oyer and terminer was issued to investigate a counter-raid by the prior of Sempringham on Birthorpe: *CPR 1307–13*, p. 533. There are records of Birthorpe's appointment to hold pleas in the justiciary in Ireland in 1318 and 1320 (*CPR 1317–21*, pp. 193, 524). Geoffrey Luttrell, mentioned as one of Birthorpe's associates in the events of 1312, is the commissioner and patron of the famous illuminated manuscript, the Luttrell Psalter, for which see J. Coleman, 'New Evidence about Sir Geoffrey Luttrell's Raid on Sempringham Priory, 1312', *The British Library Journal* 25 (1999), 103–28 (this article also contains a full translation of the petition). There is no record that any of Hugh Despenser's (the younger) four sisters took the veil at Sempringham, but it is possible that two – Aline and Isabella – resided there temporalily between marriages in the 1310s. On the other hand, this may be a reference to the half-sisters of Hugh Despenser the elder, two of whom – Eleanor and Joan – were widows by this time. Sempringham continued to be closely associated with the Despensers. In January 1327 three of the younger Despenser's five daughters were forcibly placed into nunneries by Isabella and Mortimer, two months after their father had been executed: Eleanor Despenser was sent to Sempringham: *CCR 1323–37*, p. 624. She was in high status company: Gwenllian, daughter of Llywelyn ap Gruffudd, prince of Wales, spent over fifty years at Sempringham (c. 1283–1337): J. B. Smith, 'Llywelyn ap Gruffudd (*d.*1282)', *ODNB*. For a related petition see above, **85**.

195

Selby, WRY (? 1331–5)
Benedictine
(SC 8/46/2280)

Brother Thomas of Eyton petitions the king and council, stating that Thomas, earl of Lancaster, had obtained permission from the abbot of Selby for Brother Thomas to live in his household, which he did until he was made sub-prior of Tutbury, where he remained during the earl's lifetime; and then, at the king's request, the abbot and convent of Marmoutier appointed him as prior of Holy Trinity, York. However, as he was travelling to York to take up this post, the abbot of Selby's men seized him, took his horses, gear and treasure, and are still holding him in prison. He requests a remedy.
Endorsed: *It seems to the council that the king has nothing to do with the discipline of the abbot and his fellow-monk.*

A nostre seignur le roi et au soun counseil moustre Frere Thomas de Eytone qe come Sire Thomas, jadis noble counte de Lancastre, aveit purchace le coungee del abbe de Selleby qe le dit Sire Thomas feut demoraunt devers lui en soun hostiel et par aillours en il lui voleit assigner ou comaunder, par quel coungee le dit Frere Thomas feut demoraunt ove le dit counte taunqe il feut fait suppriour de la mesone de Tuttebury, et illeqes en cel office demora taunqe le dit counte de Lancastre resquist; et puis apres la mort le dit counte, a la requeste nostre seignour le roy qu'orest, l'abbe de Meremouster et soun covent graunta al dit Frere Thomas d'estre priour en la mesone de la Trinite de Everwik. Et apres \cel/ graunt \a lui/ grauntez et conferme par le dit abbe et soun covent, sicom le dit Frere Thomas feut en venaunt vers la ville de Everwik pur le dit office entrer, vignent les gentz le dit abbe de Selleby et luy pristrent en le chemyn, et ces chivaux et soun harneys et soun tresour amoverent ovesq'eux en le dit abbe de Selleby, isi l'emprisonerent saunz nulle manere d'enchesoun, et unqore luy deteignont en prisone. Dunt le dit Frere Thomas prie a nostre seignur le roy et soun counseil qe, pur Dieu et pur charite, sur ceo voillent ordeiner remedie.

Endorsed: Se semble au conseil qe le roi n'ad rien a faire de la discipline l'abbe et son commoigne.

? 1331–5. Thomas of Lancaster, earl of Lancaster, died in 1322. Although there is no reference to the appointment of Thomas of Eyton as prior of Holy Trinity, York, there is a gap for the years 1331–5; internal evidence would support this dating. Thus, the abbot of Selby is John of Wistow II (1322–35). Holy Trinity was an alien priory subject to the abbey of Marmoutier, near Tours.

196

Butley, Suffolk (1334)
Augustinian canons
(SC 8/171/8540)

Eleanor, widow of Guy Ferre, petitions the king and council for remedy as she holds the manor of Benhall by purchase by her late husband, with the reversion pertaining to the earl of Cornwall, and with this manor belongs the patronage of the priory of Butley with rights concerning the keeping of the priory during a vacancy, and to the election of priors, which have been ignored.

The canon chosen to be prior should be presented to her, and she should send to the bishop to receive the prior but she has been bypassed by Matthew of Pakenham, a canon of Butley, and held out of the priory by him and others. She cannot have a writ of quare impedit *against Pakenham naming him prior as the priory is vacant, and she cannot have a writ against men of religion without the name of the lord who is to be maintained.*
Endorsed: *She should sue at the common law.*

A nostre seignur le roi et a son consail moustre Alianore qe fust la femme Guy Ferre qe com ele soit tenaunt del maner de Benhale en le counte de Southfolk, par purchas fest a Guy Ferre, jadis son baron, et a luy et a les heirs Guy, son baron, et del quel maner la reversion est ore a son seignur le counte de Cornwaille, par reson de quel purchas del maner avauntdite appent a luy l'avowerie de la priorie de Buttele, et deit aver en temps qe la priorie est vacaunte de priour la garde de la priorie avauntdit. E quel houre et qant qe les chanouns par assent de lour chapitre averunt eslu un en priour, mesme celui ensi eslu serra maunde a luy a resceyvere en priour, et adonqe serra maunde par sa lettre al evesqe del lu tesmoignaunce qe ele ad un tel resceu a les temporaltes de la priourie, et par tiel manere serra resceu del evesqe. Dount par la ou la dite priorie fust voide par la mort Alisaundre de Stratford, le dreyn priour, par reson de quele vacacion de la dite priorie a la dite Alianore la garde de la dite priorie apendeit par le temps qe ele fust voide, ou serra voyde, solum ceo qe luy et ses feffeours, seignurs del maner avauntdit, ount este seisi del temps qe la dite priorie fust funde; un Matheu de Pakenham, chanun de la dite meson, qe fust par le covent de mesme cele priorie eslu en priour, et q'est resceu par le evesqe del leu, saunz ceo q'il fust maunde a la dite Alianore de estre resceu, ou rien a luy parler, et saunz ceo qe nul maundement avoit de luy al evesqe, et en tel manere fesount sei priour. Et mesme celuy Matheu, Frere Johan de Framelyngham, Frere Richard de Chiltenham, Frere Matheu de Gettone, conchanouns de la dite priorie, et William Testard et Johan de Badyngham, et autres desconutz, de tut le temps puys le mort le dit Alisaundre, priour, la dite Alianore de la dite priorie et de la garde avauntdite a force et armes ount hors tenu. Et le dit Mautheu le priorie com priour, saunz estre receu de luy par la manere susdite, \tent/. Sur quei la dite Alianore prie remedie, et pleise au conseil nostre seignur le roy aver regarde de cea qe ele ne put parter bref *quare impedit* de vers le dit Matheu de Pakenham, nomant luy priour, qe ceo serreit a supposer la priourie pleyne par priour, la ou ele est voide de dreit. Et qe nul bref ne put vers home de religion saunz nomer du soverayn est ... meyntenue.

Endorsed: Seuwe a la commune lei.

1334. The petition is dated to the parliament of 1334 by its inclusion in a Hale manuscript containing petitions from this parliament (*RP*, II, 85, no. 53). The earl of Cornwall at this time was John of Eltham. Alexander of Stratford was prior of Butley 1332–3, and Matthew of Pakenham 1333–53.

197

Newstead by Stamford, Lincolnshire (1338)
Augustinian canons
(SC 8/12/586)

The community and the sub-collectors of the vill of Ketton petition the king and council, showing that the prior of Newstead has been taxed and tallaged with the community of the vill for all manner of contributions and tallages for the tenements that he holds in the vill, as appears by the rolls of the sub-collectors. The prior has bribed the chief tax collectors to conceal his name in other taxes, and the prior alleges that the tenements are taxed with his spiritualities, to the great damage of the sub-collectors and to the charge of the community. They request that the king ordain a remedy for them for the concealment made by the chief tax collectors, which can be found by the rolls of the sub-collectors for this year and all years that the tax has been granted, and that the prior and convent were always taxed, and not assessed with their spiritualities. They request a writ to the treasurer and barons that they summon before them the prior, chief tax collectors and sub-collectors, and hear their reasons, and do justice, charging those that ought to be charged.
Endorsed: *The treasurer and barons of the exchequer are ordered to summon before them the tax collectors and sub-collectors of the vill and also the prior, and hear their reasons, and do justice.*

A nostre seignur le roi et son conseil mostrent la comune et les southtaxours de la ville de Ketene en le countee de Roteland qe come le priour del Novel Lieu juste Staunford ad este taxe et taille ove la comune de la dite ville, a toutes maners contribuciouns et taillages qe ount est faites puis la mort le Roi Henri encea, pur les tenementz q'il tent en la dite ville, sanz eslre [*sic*] desporte en nul temps, come apertement piert par les roulles des southtaxours de la dite ville, qe puis les temps encea ont este. Et purcoe qe les chiefs taxours del counte avantdit, par fin et fret a eaux fait par le dit priour, l'an sisme du regne nostre seignur le roi q'ore est, quaunt le tax del quinzisme dener a nostre seignur le roi estoit graunte primere, fust leve par les summes trovez sur les villes, dount nostre seignur le roi en semblable tax estoit servi, concelerent le noun le dit priour sanz retorner le ove les autres de la dite comune, le dit priour par sa sugescion fait devant le tresorer et barouns del Escheqier q'il est pur mesme les tenementz taxe ove l'espiritualte, et paie ses dimes pur yceles come pur chose espirituele, ad sui bref hors del dist Escheqier devers les southtaxours avantditz, et les ad mene en tiel prosces devant eaux qe les ditz barouns, purcoe q'ils ne trovent mie le noun le dit priour, ne nulle summe sur lui susrendu devant eaux par les chiefs taxours l'an sisme avantdite, ount mis les southtaxours avantditz agraunt raunson devers le dit priour, et charge a lever de la dite comune la summe mise sur le dit priour, en descharge de lui, a graunt damage d'eaux et en charge de la dite comune a touz jours, ou les dites southtaxours tenderont d'averrer, par touz les tax temporels et espirituels qe de cea en arere ount este, q'ils ount este tut temps taxez ove la comune come avant est dit, et qe les tenementz avantditz ne sont compris ne taxez ove lour espiritualte, et ils riens de coe ne poient estre oiz. Dount ils prient a nostre seignur le roi et son conseil q'ils voillent pur eaux tiele remedie ordiner, qe par le concelement qe les ditz chiefs taxours firent, quel apertement purra estre trove par les roulles les southtaxours avantditz de mesme l'an et de touz les aunz qe tax ad este graunte, queles ils ount endentez entre eaux de mesme le tax, solonc la fourme hors de la Chauncellerie as ditz taxours livere, ne tourne mie en avauntage le dit priour, ne en destres de nostre seignur le roi, ne en charge de la dite comune, desicome les ditz tenementz ne furent unqes en estente de lour espiritualte mes tut temps taxe, et le roi servi de ycele ove la comune de la dite ville. Par qi ils prient bref as ditz tresorer et barouns, q'ils apelent devant eaux le dit priour et les chiefs taxours avantditz, et auxi les southtaxours, et oiz les resouns entre eaux \pur le roi/, facent outre droit, et chargount ceaux qe deyvent estre chargez.

Endorsed: Soit mande as tresorer et barons de l'Escheker qe appellez devant \ eux/ les taxours et soutz taxours de la dite ville, et auxi le dit priour, et oyez lour resons, facent droit etc.

1338. The name of the prior of Newstead at this time is not known. For an earlier edition of this petition, see *RP*, II, 98, no. 3.

198

Wymondham, Norfolk (c. 1346)
Benedictine (dependent)
(SC 8/16/766)

Robert of Knapton and Thomas Bennet, sub-collectors of the ninth in Bedingham, petition the king and council, stating that they were forced to collect the ninth in Bedingham by the prior of Wymondham, John of Brunham, and their companions, chief collectors of the ninth in Norfolk, because they could not sell this duty, as so much of the town belongs to the prior of Walsingham that it brings in very little. They paid their true value, but when the account was re-audited, as John of Brunham had falsely informed the king that certain things should be assessed communally in each town, they were imprisoned, and their lands seized and goods sold to pay their arrears, with no regard had to the true value of the ninths. They ask that those holding the inquiry into the ninths be given a warrant to inquire into the true value of ninths collected by people commissioned to do this, and that what is in arrears of this sum should be levied as above, and no more. They also state that the sub-collectors in Brooke and Caistor St Edmund, where the abbot of Bury St Edmunds has his demesnes, are in a like case, and also request the same aid.
Endorsed: *This petition is to be sent by writ of chancery before the treasurer and barons of the exchequer, and when the account of the ninth in the aforesaid town has been examined, and information has been received from John of Houton and Edmund of Grimsby who have a commission to inquire into the ninths in the same counties, and the people of the town and others who should be called have been called, justice and reason should be done to the sub-collectors of the town.*

A nostre seignour le roi et a son counseil moustront Robert de Knaptone et Thomas Beneyt, suthcoillours de la ville de Bedyngham en le countee de Norff' de le noefvysme nadgers grauntee a nostre seignour le roi, qe par la ou la dite noefvysme poet a nuli estre vendue al tax del eglise, pur ceo qe le tax de la dite eglise s'estent a chescune chose taxable en la dite ville, de quele ville le priour de Walsyngham est parsone, et tient demeygnes illoeqes qe sont de dowarie del eglise, et auxint demeignes com seignour en partie de la dite ville, qe sont enpuryez et amortyez, qe curront en tax de la dite eglise qe amountont bien a la moyte de la dite villee, ou a plus, et pur queux demeygnes le dit priour paie ses dysmes a nostre seignour le roi entre ses espiritualtees. Et par cause qe le priour de Wymondham, Sire Johan de Brunham et lour compaignouns, chiefs coillours de la noefvysme en le dit countee, ne porreiont la dite noefvysme de la dite ville vendre a nully pur la petite value et par l'enchesoun suisdite, ils chacerent les avantditz Robert et Thomas par attachemenz et destresces d'estre coillours de la noefvysme en la dite ville, et de ceo les fesoient commissioun de coiller et de respoundre al roi de la value, et par force de cele commissioun ils coillerent la dite noefvysme countre lour voluntee, et paieront de chiefs coillours xxij marcz, qe amounte a la verroi value al pleyn. Et ore, par fauxe suggescioun faite par le dit Sire Johan de Brunham, un des chief coillours, a nostre seignour le roi, qe la noefvysme de treys choses, c'est assaver de garbe, tusoun et aignel, s'estent al tax communalment en chescune ville, priaunt recitacioun del acompte de la dite noefvysme, asaver mon com bien fuit arrere du tax en mayns des coillours de chescune ville, quel acompte rehercee, et les summes trovees, une commissioun issint a Sire Johan de Houtone et Sire Esmon de Grimesby, de faire venir lez coillours de la noefvysme de chescune ville, ou rien fuit arrere du tax devant eux, et de moustrer par acquitaunces et alters evidences com bien ils avoient paie, et si rien fuit arrere du tax de le faire lever par le viscount du countee, et ceo par enprisonement des corps des ditz coillours, seisine de lour terres et vente de lour chateux, sanz aver regard ou enquere de la verroie value des dites noefvysmes. Et issint sont les ditz povers hommes Robert et Thomas, qe contre lour voluntee furent faitz coillours et qe ont coille la noefvysme et le verroie value paie, pris et enprisonees pur le remeindrunt q'est arrere du dit tax, la ou ils ne poeient plus trover, coiller ne liver, qe n'y fuit en verite, ne par resoun de plus deyvent estre chargeez. Par qei ils priont a nostre dit seignour le roi et a son counseil qe, pur l'amour de Dieu et par seinte charite, et pur resoun faire a son povere poeple, qe les ditz enquerrours ou altres eient garraunt d'enquere de la verroie value dez noefvysmes coilles par gentz countre lour voluntee par commissioun, et nient vendues, et ceo qe trovez serra arrere de le verroie value soit levee en la fourme suisdite, et nient plus, ou altrement plusours suthcoillours en le dit countee serront faitz beggaunz pur touz jours saunz resoun ou descerte. Et auxint en mesme la manere tiel meschief est avenuz as povers gentz des villes de Brok and Castre Seint Esmon en mesme le countee, en queles villes l'abbe de Seint Esmond ad ses demeygnes, com parsone et seignour illoeqes, titles al office de la Chaumberie, qe riens ne pount aider a la dites noefvysme par la cause suisdite, des queles villes lez ditz suthcoillours priont aide en la fourme suisdite, pur Dieu et pur charite.

Endorsed: Soit ceste peticion mande par brief de la Chancellerie devant tresore et barons del Escheqier, et vewe l'accompt de la levee de la dite noefisme del ville susdite, et eu informacion ove Sire Johan de Houtone et Sire Esmon de Grymesby, qi avoient commission d'enquer des noefismes en mesme le countee, et appellez les gentz de mesme la ville et autres appellers celle partie, soit droit et reson fait as suthcoillours de la dite ville.

1346. On 6 August c.1346 a commission was issued to John of Houton and Edmund of Grimsby to investigate irregularities in the collection of the ninth, in accordance with the endorsement of this petition (*CPR 1345–8*, pp. 184–5). The prior of Wymondham at this time was Richard of Hethersett (1334–c.1347), the prior of Walsingham was Simon of Wyneton *alias* Storm (1335–49), and the abbot of Bury St Edmunds was William of Bernham (1335–61). The 'ninth' was a novel form of taxation granted in the parliament of March 1340. It entailed the levying of a ninth part of the total value of goods assessed, often by payment in kind (i.e. with wool, corn or lambs). For an earlier edition of this petition, see *RP*, II, 400–1, no. 124. Other petitions concerning the same ninth are SC 8/16/760 and SC 8/16/776.

199

Thame, Oxfordshire (1348)
Cistercian
(SC 8/13/622)

The community of the vill of Latchford in the parish of Haseley (Oxon.) petitions the king and council, showing that Henry Fynel, late parson of Haseley, established a perpetual chantry at Latchford to be served by a monk of the abbey of Thame for the souls of the earl of Cornwall and Hugh Despenser, for which lands were annexed to the abbey. The current abbot has ruined the chapel and stolen the charters and no man can go to law against him as he is a judge there. The commonalty request remedy as all the country knows that the chantry ought to have been made.
Endorsed: *They should sue at the common law, and also before the bishop if they wish.*

A nostre seignur le roi et a son bon conseil mustre la comune de la ville de Lacheford de la paroche de Haselee el countee de Oxenford qe come Sire Henri Fynel, jadys parsone de Hasele susdit, par licence le roi, ael a nostre seignur le roi q'or est, eit fait une chaunterie a Laccheford avantdit, d'estre fait par un moyne de l'abbee de Thame checun jour, perpetuelment adurer sanz nulle defaulte, pur quelle chaunterie mentenir et faire certeines terres et tenemenz sont annex a la dite abbee en la dite ville de Laccheford, pur les armes [*sic*] le counte de Cornwaill et de Monsire Hugh Despenser et pur lour heirs, et pur la dite comune de la ville de Laccheford. L'abbe de Thame q'ore est ad destruet la chapelle et embesiller les chartres ent faites, et detient et cesse la dite chaunterie faire, et de la ley ne poet homme avoir issue contre le dit abbe el dit countee tant est il bon assisour en pays. Par quei plese a nostre dit seignur le roi et a son bon conseil ent ordiner remedie en oevre de charite, car tut le pays bien sciet qe la dite chaunterie deveroit estre fait.

Endorsed: Sue a la comune lei, et devers l'evesque auxint s'il voille.

1348. The petition is dated to the parliament of 1348 by its inclusion in a Hale manuscript containing petitions from this parliament (*RP*, II, 184, no. 39). The chantry at Latchford was first built by the parson of Haseley in 1300 (*VCH Oxfordshire*, II, 84). The earl of Cornwall could be either Piers Gaveston (d. 1312) or John of Eltham (d. 1336). The abbot was John de Thame 1316–49.

200

Merton, Surrey (? 1348)
Augustinian canons
(SC 8/61/3007)

Tenants of the ancient demesne of the manor of Merton petition the king and council that they be able to recover the wrongs and grievances, and that the prior of Merton be made to come

before the king and show how he had ousted his tenants from their inheritance, and that right and remedy be ordained in their tenancy, and a protection granted to the tenants during their suit so that no one will harm them or their chattels, and that letters be sent to the justices of the Common Bench that the hour that the tenants make their case before them be favourable to them. King Harold gave the manor to the prior of Merton, and the tenants of the manor held their lands and tenements by certain customs and services according to the usages of the manor, until the prior and his canon, William of Kent, came by force and arms to the tenants' houses and took their charters and muniments, and later carried away their goods and chattels, which is contrary to Domesday Book. The prior has burnt and destroyed the tenements in the vill wrongfully and against the peace.
Endorsed: *They should pursue this at the common law*

A nostre seignur le roi et a soun counsail moustrent ses povres tenauntz del aunciene demesme dil manoir de Mertone en le counte de Surr' qe com le Roi Herald, jadys roi d'Engleterre, dona mesme le manoir ov les aportenaunces al priour de Mertone et a ses successoures, issint qe les tenauntz de mesme le manoir tiendrount lour terres et tenemenz par certeyns coustomes et servises solonc \les/ usages dil manoir, tanqe ore tard qe le priour qe ore est et Sire William de Kent, son conchanoun, vindrent a force et armes a les mesounes les avantdiz tenauntz et les cofres les avantditz tenauntz debroserent et lour chartres et lour monimnetz deynz lour dites cofres pristerent, et emporterent a tort et en countre la pees, et apres ceo les biens et les chateux les dites tenauntz deinz lur dites mesouns troves a la value de C li pristrent et emporterent, et les cleime pur lour neyvefs la ou qe trove est le revert en le livere de Domesday, et les constreynt de faire altres servises et coustomes qe faire ne doussent du droit, et les ad oustes de lour terres et lour tenemenz. Et xij tenemenz de mesme la ville ount ars et abatuz et de jour en altre sount en purpos de lez anyenter et destrure a tort et en countre la pees le roi. Dount plese a vostre tresnoble seignurie eyder et meyntener les dites povres tenauntz q'ils puissent avoir lour recoverer de les tortz grevauses, et faire venir le dit priour devant vous a moustrer coment il ad ouste ces tenauntz de lour heritage, par les queles ces predecessoures furent enffeffez par le Roi Herald, et sour ceo ordeyner droit et remedie en lour tenaunce, et q'il vous plese graunter un proteccioun pur les dites povres tenauntz duraunt lour seute qe nul homme les face mal ne moleste, damage de corps ne de chateux ...... et comaunder par voz gracLouses lettres a voz justices de Comune Bank qe a qele heure qe les dites povres tenauntz ount afaire devant eux, q'ils soient eydauntz et favorables a eux en mayntenance de vostre corune.

Endorsed: Pursuent a la comune ley.

? 1348. The chancery warrant with which this petition was probably enclosed is dated 10 April 1348 (no. 19425 in C 81/330). This being the case, the prior of Merton is William of Friston (1345–61).

201

Unknown (? 1381–2)
(SC 8/88/4389)

Petition to the king and Lords in parliament, stating that many abbots and priors of the abbeys and priories of the realm, and many masters and wardens of colleges and hospitals, have, for favour or profit, charged their houses with corrodies, pensions and other annual charges, to the impoverishment of the houses, the detriment of the divine service, alms and other works of charity for which they were founded, and the frustration of the purposes of their founders. It asks that a remedy might be ordained in the present parliament, that no abbot, prior, master or warden should burden his house with such a charge, or with any other unreasonable debt, without the permission of his bishop and his patron or founder, and if he should do so, that the letters for this might be considered null and void. It also asks that any such corrody or pension hitherto made might not be binding on the successor of the head of any house.

A tresexcellent et tresredoute seignur nostre seignur le roy et as tresnobles seignurs du parlement plese entendre qe comme les abbeies, priouries, colleges et hospitalx du roiaume furent ordeinez par les progenitours de nostre seignur le roi et autres seignurs et prelatz du roiaume pur certeine dyvyns almoignes et autres oevres de charite faire et sustenir a l'onour de Dieu, et pur les almes de leur foundours et de touz Cristiens, si est voir qe plusours abbees et priours des diz abbeies et priouries, et les mestres et gardeins des diz colleges et hospitalx, q'ont este et sont de jour en autre ont, ascuns pur favour, ascuns pur leur singuler profit, par vendicion et autrement chargez et de temps en temps chargent les diz abbeies, priouries, colleges et hospitalx de diverses corrodies, enpensions et autres annueles charges paront mesmes les abbeies, priouries, colleges et hospitalx sont enpoveritz et destruitz, et les dyvyns services et les almoignes et autres oevres de charite qe y deveroient estre faites ne l'ordenance et entent des diz foundours et de la fondacion des diz abbeies et autres mesons ny sont ne poent estre sustenuz. Sur quoi plese a vostre grande noblesse d'ordeigner en ce present parlement deue remede afin qe nul abbe, priour, convent, chapitre, mestre ne gardein d'ascuns abbeie, priourie, college ou hospital du royaume ne puisse desore en avant, sanz l'assent de son evesqe et de son foundour ou patron, charger soi ne sa meson ne les possessions d'icelle ne ses successours d'ascune corrodie, enpension ne d'autre charge annuele ne de nul autre debte nyent resonable en enpoverissement des mesons sernomez. Et si ascun le face qe touz les lettres et obligacions q'ils en feront soient tenuz pur nulles et de nulle value. Et q'il vous plese auxi ordeiner qe les successours ne soient tenuz apaier tielx corrodies et enpensions qe sont de eux demandez par tielx lettres et obligacions avant ces heures faites einz en soient deschargez en relevacion des dites mesons et en amendement des defautes et inconvenientz susditz.

No endorsement

? 1381–2. The guard of this petition dates it ? 1381–2. There is no evidence to confirm this, but on the basis of the hand the date seems plausible. For an earlier transcript, see no. 86 of PRO 31/7/108.

202

Coventry, Warwickshire (c. 1381)
Benedictine
(SC 8/75/3710)

Richard of Tysoe, parson of [Napton on the Hill] petitions the king and council, making two requests:

(1) He makes a complaint concerning a dispute between him and the prior of Coventry about the burial of a woman.
(2) He requests a remedy in an assize of novel disseisin falsely brought against him by the prior.

A tresredoute nostre seignur le rei et soun sage counseil de parlament moustre Richard de Tysho, parsone de la glise de [Napton], qe .... sepulture de corps et autres choses purtinans a sa esglise par le priour de Coventre et autres persones feust molestee, sur qeles .... la court de roine aveyt une sentence diffinitive un an passe et plus, et ore le dit priour novele mort come il dit .... q'est mort parochiene a dit esglise, et par voie de soun devys en sa testament estoit en la dite esglise enterrez .... demora et puys a tort vindrent plus qe trescens gens armes sodeynement a la dite esglise, et mesme la esglise ....runt et le corps de dit femme, sans processe et countre soun testament et la voluntee de dit Richard, hors de terre de la dite esglise .... charette le corps mutrunt, et hors de la dite vile par deux leux a la vile de Herdewyk, ou les .... de soun assent en un chanson, 'we hav hire, we hav hire,' amenerunt, nent countre esteant une .... pur le dit Richard en le countee de Warr' et a Coventre devant expressement publice, et nent contre esteant ....

Item, puys apres le dit priour purchassaa une assise de novele deseysyn pur une parcel de q'il feust de .... Richard et autres de .... parochiens feserunt mencion q'il feust desessy de soun franc tenement .... ces gens et a ces ....es, et queux debruserunt la dite esglise, et en countre queux le .... ounte baylee en presence des justises, et nent countre esteans ...us excepcions .... rassa et dit qe Richard Tysho et deux autres aveyent desesy le dit priour de soun franc tene[ment] .... de pres .... et armes, a damage de dit priour de ditz liveres, la ou le dit parcel ne valeyt qe xij ...... ou le dit priour .... de Naptone ne aveyt, et autres grevances le dit priour contre le dit Richard et a sa esglise .... en contempt de Dieu et de .... a dit nostre seignur le roi et a grant damage de ly. Sur qei le dit Richard supplie a dit nostre s[eignur le] roi et son sage conseill de.......................... remedie, pur Dieu et en overe de charitee, et pur le dreit de seynt esglise, et q'il .... suer ...... de passer .... son dreyt sur les grevances et violences avantditz, et a seynt esglise fetz, nent contr[e esteant] ..... dite assyse ....

No endorsement

c. 1381. A writ of *supersedeas* was issued to the justices on 6 September 1381, regarding the petitioner's suit against the attackers, who had sued a writ of *praemunire* against him in order to disrupt his case (*CCR 1381–5*, p. 86). On 20 November 1381 the king superseded all proceedings before him against Tysoe, particulary the writ of *praemunire*, since at the Northampton parliament (November 1380) the king's justices had found the cause to be spiritual (*CPR 1381–5*, p. 54). The prior of Coventry is William of Greneburgh (1361–90). The right-hand side of this petition is almost completely illegible. Other petitions from the same petitioner are SC 8/125/6214 (below, **203**) and SC 8/144/7159.

203

Coventry, Warwickshire (c. 1381)

Benedictine
(SC 8/125/6214)

Richard Tisho, parson of Napton on the Hill, petitions the king and council for a remedy in his dispute with the prior of Coventry. He states that the prior and others forced the exhumation of a body from his church, and committed other offences against him, but they argued that the matter was spiritual, and his suit against them was denied. The parties then made accords, and the king prohibited them from taking the case outside the realm, but the prior has now sued a case against him in the Roman Curia, contrary to the agreement, but he dare not challenge this in Rome due to the king's prohibition.

A nostre seignur le roi et soun sage counseil de parlement moustre Richard Tysho, parsoun de la glise de Naptone, qe come, pur exhumacion de un corps en la dite glise et autres choses featz en contempt de Dieu et seynt esglise, le priour de Coventre et autres gens sont denuncies escommongie, pur qele denunciacion est surmys en l'uyn et l'autre Banc le roi contre le dit Richard qe la dite seute est contre la regalie, qele seute en le parlement de Norhamptone feust trovee spirituel, sur qele chose le dit Richard feust dimys par patent, le qele patent le chanceler q'ore est ad prys de dit Richard et est suppos de repeller, et par entre le priour et Richard plusours acords furent prys, qe les debates entre eux du cet deyns la realme estre terminer, come apert en escript et par prohibicions le roi a l'uyn et l'autre partie envoies q'ils ne ducent rien hors de realme attempter, et nent contre esteantz les ditz prohibicions le dite priour ad pursuee contre le dit Richard en la court de Rome, la ou le dit Richard ne osa pursuer pur les prohibicions, a grant damage de ly. Sur qei a dite nostre seignur le rei et soun sage counseil de parlement supplie le dit Richard de commander le dit chanceler de fere restitucion de dit patent a rere, et qe declaracion soyt feat dewement de les bulles et processe de l'uyn et l'autre partie, et qele partie seyt trovee coupable q'il seyt puny selonc resoun a fyn qe le dit acord puyce estre tenens, ou qe le dit Richard puyce aver licence de pursure soun droit de seynt esglise, pur Dieu et en overe de charitee.

No endorsement

c. 1381. See **202** above. For an earlier transcript of this petition, see no. 77 of PRO 31/7/108.

204

Huntingdon, Huntingdonshire (? c. 1382)

Augustinian canons
(SC 8/143/7129)

John Tubbe, parson of Southoe, petitions the king and Lords of parliament, stating that because he refused certain agreements which were discussed between him and the prior of Huntingdon concerning the appropriation of the church of Southoe, as these could not take place without simony and without depriving him of his church, the prior and his people came to the parsonage and broke the doors down, but, because John's servants raised the hue and cry, people from the vill came and no damage was done. Nevertheless, the prior has made a false accusation to the chancellor that John and some tenants of the earl of Stafford broke into his buildings at the parsonage, attacked and wounded him and his men, killed one of his servants and stole his corn. He has had an oyer et terminer on this, and by misinformation John and the others have been fined. They ask that the matter might be re-examined by good people of the country who are in the present parliament, and if the prior's claim is found to be false, that the oyer et terminer might be annulled and a suitable remedy given them. And that in future no oyer et terminer should be granted without verifying the truth of the claim, as the statute demands.

A nostre tresdoute et tresexcellent seignur nostre seignur le roi et as noblez seignuris del parlement moustre Johan Tubbe, parsoun de la eglise de Southo, qe com certeignez covenantz fuerent enparlez parentre le priour de Huntyngdone et le dit Johan Tubbe couchant la propriacion de l'eglise de dit Southo, quels covenantz ne purront estre parfourniz sanz simonye et depryvance le dit Johan de sa dit eglise si refusa le dit Johan lez ditz covenantz parfournyr, sur ceo vient le dit priour et sez gentz de la ville pur estancher la fraye sanz ascun damage fait a dit priour ou a nulle de soens. Nientmeyns le dit priour feist suggestioun a le chaunceller nostre seignur le roi qe adonqes estoit qe le dit Johan Tubbe et diversez tenantz le count de Stafford, Monsire Robert Fereres, Walter Walssch, Simond de Burgh et Richard Hemyngford, entreront ove force et armez sez maesonz de dit parsonage et luy et sez gentz bateroun, naufreroun q'ils estoient en despoir de lour viez, et q'un Geffrey, son servant, illoqes tueroun, et qe le dit Johan et tenantz susditz sez bleez et dieux centz livers d'or et d'argent de lui malement pristeront et enporteront encountre la pees, depar quele suggestioun le dit priour avoit un oier et termyner sur lez ditez Johan et tenantz, si qe par male enformacion de dit priour un enquest condempna le dit Johan et tenantz susditz en iiij^{xx} et x li, quele suggestioun fuist faus par tut car le dit priour ad conuz qe lui mesmes ne nulle de soens n'avoit nulle male ne nulle molest. Si suppliont le dit Johan et tenantz susditz qe cest matere purra estre examyne et desclarre par bonz gentz de dit paiis qe ore sont en cest present parlement, et qe la suggestioun soit faus qe le dit oier et termyner soit anullez et covenable remedie soit ordeyne as touz povrez leigez nostre seignur le roi de tielx qe tiel faux suggestioun font, et qe nulle tiel cort ne soit maynteignuz encontre droit, ne nulle oyer et termyner soit grante desore enavant sanz ceo qe soit examyne qe la suggestioun soit veritable solonc la statue ent fait, pur Dieu et en oever de charite.

No endorsement

? c. 1382. The agreement for the appropriation of Southoe church with the annexed chapel of Hail Weston (Hailweston, Hunts.) was concluded at Lincoln 30 October 1380, and the priory's financial obligation to the bishop, a pension of 20 shillings a year, was dated 11 November 1380, LAO, Reg. 12 (Buckingham, Memoranda), ff. 216–216v. The most recent institution to the rectory was of John de Mulsho, clerk, on 14 March 1376, LAO Reg. 10 (Buckingham, Institutions I), f. 317. The first recorded institution to Southoe vicarage is in the register of John Chedworth (1452–71), Reg. 20, f. 309v. On 20 November 1381 a commission of oyer et terminer was issued on complaint of the prior of Huntingdon concerning an attack against him by the petitioner and others (*CPR 1381–5*, p. 82); this may be the oyer et terminer mentioned here. However, the details do not quite match, so this might relate to a different stage of the dispute. The prior was Henry of

Roxton (1375–1404). The earl of Stafford was Hugh Stafford (1372–86). For an earlier transcript of this petition, see no. 76 of PRO 31/7/108.

205

Walsingham, Norfolk (c. 1384)
Augustinian canons
(SC 8/277/13839)

Roger, son and heir of Edmund Mortimer, earl of March, a minor and the king's ward, petitions the king and Lords of parliament, recounting that his ancestors founded Walsingham Priory with its prior to be elected with the patron's permission and installed by the bishop, which right of patronage belongs to the king during his minority, but John, prior of Walsingham, purchased papal bulls naming him abbot and granting him power to govern the house as an abbey, whereon the king sent his writ of prohibition to the prior forbidding this and similar prohibitions to the canons of the house, to which the prior responded that he would do nothing to their prejudice or against law and custom, provided that he could use his bull with the canons obeying him as abbot. The petitioner requests that the king send a new writ of prohibition to the prior since the bull was granted on condition that it was not to the prejudice or damage of anyone, and at the petition of the prior and convent when the convent knew nothing about it, and the pope made him abbot without any election.
Endorsed: *He should sue in chancery to have the said prohibition*

A nostre tresredoute seignur le roi et as honurables seignurs du parlement moustre vostre liege Roger fitz et heir Esmon de Mortemer, nadgairs counte de la Marche, deinz age et en vostre garde esteant, qe come la priorie de chanoigns regulers de la meison de Nostre Dame de Walsyngham, en la diocise de Norwiz, est de la fundacioun des auncestres du dit Roger d'estre governe par un priour qi serroit esleu par congie du patroun, et l'eslit presente au dit patroun et acceptez, il serreit resceu del evesqe diocesan par les lettres de mesme le patroun tesmoignanz son assent a l'eleccioun et sur ceo enstallez et confermez par le dit diocesan sanz greindres coustages ou charges de la dite meison, de quele priorie le droit de foundour et patroun apartient a vostre hautesse par voie de garde durant le noun age du dit Roger, et quele priorie a tout temps ad estez governez par la manere susdyt puis le temps de la primer fundacioun d'ycelle, tanqe ore tarde qe Johan, priour de dite maisoun, machinant a defaire la volunte du primer foundour et la reulle de lour fundacioun, en prejudice de vous et desheriteson du dit Roger, par noun verroie suggestioun faite a le tresseint piere le pape, ad fait purchacer ses bulles par queles le dit seint piere luy ad fait abbe du dite maisoun et graunte poeir a luy et ses successours de governer la dite maisoun come abbe, parount par cause de tiele novellerie issint suffert grauntz meschiefs et charges importables dount homme n'est mys a pardoun purroient avenir al dit maisoun et overte desheritaunce au dit Roger, sur qoi nostre dit seignur le roi maunde son brief de prohibicioun al priour avaundite q'il ne usereit mye les bulles de le pestoile luy nomant abbe ne nulle execucioun de ses avaundites bulles excercereit en nulle manere, et sur mesme la forme et matire autre prohibicioun fuist direct as chanoigns de mesme la maisoun, et a chescun d'eux, en le plus districte manere qe le roi purroit et auxint south forfaiture de tout ceo q'ils purront forfaire devers le roi fust defenduz q'ils n'atemptereient rien qe fuist en prejudice de roi ou de dit Roger ou en enervacioun des leies, custumes, ordeignaunces et statuz de la reialme .... ou de la maisoun avaundite en nulle manere ne a mesme le priour come al abbe de l'avaundite maisoun altrement serroient obeissantz ou entendantz qe par lour fundacioun susdite durant l'avaundit Roger deinz age, sur qei apres fuist signifie par brief de consultacioun par meynz veritable suggescioun fait al counseill q'il ne fuist mye en prejudice du dit Roger ne en enervacioun des leies de roailme d'Engleterre ou de la fundacioun de l'avaundite maisoun, issint q'il purreit use ses bullez et a les avaunditz chanoigns q'ils purront estre obeissantz et entendantz a luy come al abbe non obstante l'avaundite prohibicioun. Qe pleise a vostre reale mageste considerer coment l'avaundite bulle fuist impetrer sur condicioun q'il ne fuist mye en prejudice n'en damage del diocesan de lieu ou d'autre persone quecumqe, et coment la dite bulle fuist impetrez encountre overte defence et prohibicioun de lour patroun, et coment graunt prejudice et damage purra avenir au roi durant le noun age l'eir le counte de la Marche et auxint al heir a soun plein age encountre la tenure de lour fundacioun et composicioun ent fait, et auxint considerer coment la bulle fait mencioun q'il fuist la peticioun del priour et covent en nulle de covent estre deux persones unqe ne dona assent ne rienz ne savoit d'ycelle, et coment la bulle fait mencioun qe l'avaundite maisoun est haboundantment dowez de posessions et en touz lours posessiouns ne sufficent de trover a ceux de la covent vivre et desture, et auxint coment le tresseintisme piere le pape luy fist abbe sanz eleccioun et ad commise administracioun de mesme l'abbey pleinerment, sibien en temporaltez come en spirtualtez, quel abbe ore ad fait de novelle un autre priour sanz ascun eleccioun usuelle, par quele bulle et les incident d'ycelle grauntz meschiefs et charges importables purront avenir al dite maisoun et desheritance al patroun avaundit, qe sur touz cestes causes novelle prohibicioun puisse estre direct al avaundit priour et autre as chanoigns, non obstante ascun cosultacioun [*sic*] precedent, et auxint qe nulle consultacioun issi durant le noun age del heir de la Marche susdit.

Endorsed: Pursue en la Chauncellerie pur le dit prohibicion avoir.

c. 1384. In March 1384 custody of the priory was given to the subprior, on behalf of the petitioner, because of contention between the subprior and John Snoring, prior of Walsingham 1374–1400, who was said to be wasteful of its revenues in his desire to secure the position of abbot (*CPR 1381–5*, p. 383). In 1389, during the dispute over the conversion of the priory into an abbey, Snoring was removed from office, but later restored. For further references see *Heads of Houses III*, 543–4 and *VCH Norfolk*, II, 395.

206

Castle Acre, Norfolk (1385)
Cluniac
(SC 8/88/4388)

Richard, earl of Arundel and Surrey, petitions the king and Lords of parliament, stating that one William of Warenne, still calling himself prior of Castle Acre after he had resigned his office into the hands of the prior of Lewes and a new prior had been appointed, made a second resignation into the hands of the pope, who then made a provision of the office of prior to him, and he bound the priory to pay a large sum of money for the first fruits of the priory. The pope's collectors are now collecting the revenues of the priory and have excommunicated the monks.

As the priory is of the patronage of the earl of Arundel, and William of Warenne was never lawfully in possession of it by the pope's provision, he asks for a writ to the papal collectors to cease from demanding this money.
Endorsed: *A prohibition should be made to the papal collector to cease utterly from making any levy, process or demand against the prior of Castle Acre, his fellow monks and their successors, or the said house, at any time in future for the first fruits or the sums mentioned in this petition.*

A nostre seignur le roy et as tresnobles seignurs de cest present parlement moustre Richard, counte d'Arrundell et de Surr', qe come un William de Garenne, nadgairs soi pretendaunt priour del priorie de Chastelacre, quel est del fundacion de dit counte et celle del priorie de Lewys, resigna le dit priorie de Chastelacre en les mayns de priour de Lewys, quel priour de Lewys la refuit come a luy apertenoit. Et puys fit un alore priour de Chastelacre, \quel/ continua peisible possesion toute sa vie et apres la resignacione avauntdite vivaunt le dit priour de Chastelacre, le dit William de Garenne fit une autre resignacione faux et feynte en les mayns nostre seint pier le pape, nient eiant regarde al resignacione quel il avoit fait adevaunt ne a la possessione quel le novel priour de Chastelacre avoit a cel oevre. Et puis nostre dit seint pier le pape a sa request luy fit provisione de dit priorie de Chastelacre, pur quel le dit William de Garenne obliga le dit priorie de Chastelacre a nostre seint pier le pape, apayer CCCC iiij^{xx} iiij li ix s ix d pur les primers fruitz de mesme le priorie de Chastelacre, par quele cause les fruxz, dymes et obvencions de le dit priorie sovent sount sequestrez par le collectour de nostre dit seint pier le pape en Engleterre, et le dit prior de Chastelacre et ses commoignes sovent [sou]nt excomyngiez, en graunt deterioracion et destruction du dit priorie de Chastelacre et impediment de divynez servicez et subruccione de [al]moyngnez et deserisoun de dit counte. Par qoy pleise a soun tresredoute seignur le roy et as seignurs de parlement, depuis qe le dit priorie de Chastelacre [est] de lay patronage et le dit William de Garenne nunqes en possession de la dit priorie par vertue de la provision de nostre dit tresseint [pier, et] ....aite ne nostre dit tresseint pier ne nulle de ses predecessours nunqes en possession des fruitz d'ascune esglise ou priorie de lay patronage .... envoier brief al collectour de nostre dit tresseint pier de tout outrement et fynelment sursere et cesser de la demaunde de les ....tz, en oevre de charite.

Endorsed: Soit prohibicion fait al collectour nostre seint p[ier] .... ou pur le temps serra de surserer et cesser outrement et finalment de faire ascune levee, process ou demaund envers le dit priour de Castelacre, ses commognes et lour successours, ou lour dite mesoun, en ascun temps avenire pur les primers fruitz ou summes dont ceste peticioun dedeinz fait mencioun.

1385. The petitioner, Richard (FitzAlan) earl of Arundel, was complaining about William de Warenne, illegitimate son of John de Warenne earl of Surrey (d. 1347). William was prior first of Monks Horton, Kent (occurs June 1335 – May 1339), then of Castle Acre, provided May 1342 x May 1343, occurs December 1361, January 1364. Further details of his colourful career can be found in *Heads of Houses II*, 224–5, 237. The prior of Lewes mentioned here was John of Janicuria (1344–c.1349). On 27 October 1385 the papal collector was prohibited from levying the sums mentioned in this petition, in accordance with the endorsement (*CCR 1385–9*, p. 87). The bottom left-hand corner of this petition is missing. For an earlier transcript of this petition, see no. 38 of PRO 31/7/109.

207

Dunstable, Bedfordshire (1392)
Augustinian canons
(SC 8/249/12418)

The burgesses of Dunstable petition the king for remedy since the king's progenitors granted the town many liberties and franchises at their foundation, but lately they have been disturbed by the prior and convent of Dunstable, at whose instigation the bishop compelled them to rebuild their church and to build an altar of the Trinity there, and recently officers of the prior and convent have removed the altar by night and broken a beautiful tabernacle with the image of the Trinity, and have defiled and removed images of St Peter and St Paul painted on the walls.

A tresexcellent, tresredoute et tresgracious seignur nostre seignur le roy moustrent voz povres liges et tenantz les burgeis de la ville de Dunstaple coment voz tresnobles progenitours doneront et granteront a les burgeis de la dite ville, a la primere fundacion d'ycelle, pluseurs libertees et franchisez, les queux ils useront et avoieront en quiete et en pees par plusours ans avant la \primer/ fundacion de la priorie de mesme la ville et depuis, tanqe ore tarde q'ils ont este forbarrez et destourbez de leur dites franchises en plusours pointz par le priour et covent qe ore est. Et outre ce, tresgracious seignur, la ou voz ditz tenantz, par procurement del dit priour et covent, feuront compellez par leur evesqe de faire et renoveller leur eglise, et firont en ycelle un auter de la Trinitee, la quel auter feut counue par le suffregan le dit evesqe, sibien par assent et coustages les ditz priour et covent come de voz tenantz susditz, ore tarde les ministres le dit priour ont debatuz et oustez le dit auter par noet, et debrusez un grant et beal tabernacle en quel feut mys la ymage de la Trinitee, et outre ce les ymages de Seint Pier et Paule queles estoient peyntez honestement seur les mures ils font defeulez, abrasez et ouster, a grant destourbance de divine service et desease et tort a voz tenantz avantditz. Plese a vostre tresgracious hautesse charger vostre tressage conseil de bien examiner et avoir consideracion a touz les pointz de les grevancez de voz ditz tenantz, et sur ce ordeigner due remede et justice, et endementiers charger les ditz priour et covent par voz tresgracious lettres de soeffrer voz ditz tenants estre en pees, tanqe vostre dit conseil eit fait et parfourne vostre commandement a ycelle, pur Dieu et en oevre de charitee.

No endorsement

1392. The chancery warrant with which this petition was formerly enclosed is dated 5 March 1392 (no. 7970 of C 81/532). A similar petition is SC 8/249/12418. The prior was Thomas Marescall (1351–1413), and the bishop was John Buckingham, bishop of Lincoln (1363–98). The petition presents a somewhat muddled picture of allegation and blame. In 1392 attempts were made to settle the dispute by arbitration, in which the prior agreed to keep the altar built by the parishioners, and the wall across the nave to which it was attached, but the church was formally to remain part of the priory, and would continue to be known as the church of St Peter, and not the church of Holy Trinity: *VCH, Bedfordshire*, III, 360 (and references). A year later the prior and canons of Dunstable presented a petition in which they asked the crown for permission to pursue their rights to the church and town of Dunstable in the royal and ecclesiastical courts: SC 8/183/9148. An agreement between Dunstable Priory and its lay neighbours was finally concluded on 21 May 1394, LAO, Reg. 12 (Buckingham, Memoranda, ff. 416–17). Bad feeling between the priory and the people of Dunstable had existed for some time, as was manifest during the Peasants' Revolt of 1381. See *Annales Monastici* vol. III, *Annales Prioratus de Dunstaplia, Annales Monstaerii de Bermundeseia*, ed. H. R. Luard (Rolls Series, 1388), pp. 415–19. For a petition on a similar theme, see **128**.

208

Thame, Oxfordshire (1392–3)
Cistercian
(SC 8/181/9041)

Richard Field, clerk, king's almoner, petitions the king that he summon the parties before the council and do right in his case against the abbot and monks of Thame regarding their disturbance of his rights as prebendary of Thame. He claims that the abbot has ignored agreements and orders on the matter and takes the profits of the prebend, while John Middleton and John Mussenden, two monks of Thame, dressed as lay men and attacked John Dymock, his official, at Albury (Oxon.) on 29 April 1392.

A nostre tresredoute et tresgracious seignur le roy moustre vostre humble clerc Richard de la Felde, vostre asmoigner, coment par la ou sur un querele moeve parentre l'abbe de Thame et le dit Richard, prevendrer de la prevende de Thame, a cause de certeins dismes et autres droitures regardantz a la dite prevende, dez queux le dit abbe ad nadgairs le dit Richard destourbez, assentuz estoit si bien depar le dit abbe come depar le dit Richard, a l'instance de Monsire Baudewyn Bereford, pur le bien de bon accorde en celle partie de lour submettre a bone et resonable traitee solonc l'avys dez conseilx d'ambedeux lez partiez, sur quoy le dit Richard, toutditz esteant prest a la dite traitee et peineblement se enclinant a la dit accord, et veullant purveier par toutz ses partiez a la bone seurtee touchaunt mesmes lez traitee et accord, pursua nadgairs a vostre hautesse au fyn d'avoir mandement par vos lettres desouz vostre signet au dit abbe pur faire droit et resoun au dit suppliant en la matiere suisdite, et qe rien ne serroit ettemptez de par le dit abbe pendant sa dite traitee countre l'accord desuisdite, lez queles lettres feurent grauntez au dit Richard et par un Roger Long, un de vos sergeantz as armes, depar vous au dit abbe presentees, et il a ceo nient eiant regard volentrerment et a tort a graund contempt de vous et de vostre dit mandement lez profitez de la dite prevende ad fait carier a sa mesoun. Et Danz Johan Miltone et Danz Johan Mussendene, sez commoignes, en seculers abitez jesauntz en agayte de Johan Dymmok, clerc official du dit Richard de sa jurisdiccion de sa dit prevende, lundy apres le fest Seint George l'an de vostre regne quinzisme a Aldebury en la countee d'Oxenford, et lui ont batuz et malement naufrez, et lez registres et autres munimentz regardantz a la dite jurisdiccion ardez countre la ley et vostre peex, a perpetuel arerissement de mesme la jurisdiccion et tresgraund anyentisment de diverses recuvires pendantz parentre partie et partie solonc la ley de seint esglise en la court de la jurisdiccion avantdite, et diverses autres grevauncez et disaises lez ditz abbe et moignes ont fait et de jour en autre unqore facent au dit suppliant contre l'accord desuisdite. Si please a vostre hautesse commander vostre conseill defaire venir, sibien les ditz abbe et moignes come le dit Richard, et oyez lez grevauncez de mesme celui Richard en la dite matere, et lez responses des ditz abbe et moignez en cell partie, d'ent faire droit parentre les partiez solonc la ley et come resoun et bone conscience luy requirent et demandent, pur Dieu et en oevre de charitee.

No endorsement

1392–3. The attack on Dymock occurred on 29 April 1392, and presumably the petition was presented at some point shortly thereafter. The petitioner was appointed to the prebend of Thame in February 1390, while orders to the constable of Rochester Castle to receive Middleton and Mussenden were issued on 19 May 1393 (*CPR 1391–6*, p. 64), probably following their detention in connection with this case. The identity of the abbot of Thame at this time is unknown. For further references to Richard Field's tenure of Thame prebend, 1390–1401, see Le Neve, *Fasti* I: *Lincoln Diocese*, comp. H. P. F. King (London, 1962), p. 116. For John Dymmok see *BRUO*, I, 617.

209

Ramsey, Huntingdonshire (1403)
Benedictine
(SC 8/232/11558)

Thomas Done of Exeter petitions the king that the abbot and the cellarer of Ramsey be summoned to answer for the wrongs that they did to him. While he was on his way to Boston he fell ill at Ramsey, and while he was ill the cellarer came and wished to buy one of his horses, and because he did not wish to sell, the abbot and cellarer had him imprisoned, and still detain his horses and goods to his great damage.

A tresredoute et tresgracious seignur le roy supplie treshumblement vostre povre lige Thomas Done d'Excestre qe come il font traveillant deinz vostre reialme parentre Excestre et Bostone pur chaunger diverses merchandises come merchant et merchant sovent font, et veignant vostre dit suppliant a Ramsey en le contee de Huntyndone ovesqe trois chivalx et deux pakkes des draps lanuz et autres merchandsise, et y mesme le suppliant font tenuz ove grande infirmies par deux jours issint q'il ne purroit travailler, deinz quel temps vient le selerer del abbei de Ramsey pur achater un de les chivalx susditz et celui veloit vendre solonc la volunte du dit selerer, pur quele enchesoun l'abbe de Ramsey et selerer maliciousement aresteront et grevousement emprisoneront vostre dit suppliant le dymenge prochein apres le fest de Pasqe darrein passe, en defaut q'il font un laroun, et pristront les chivalx, pakkes et merchandises susditz ovesqe sept nobles et cynk souldz d'argent en sa burs et un signet d'or pris de xxij s hors de son doige, et lui ensi emprisoneront jesqe al temps q'il avoit jour sur un livre q'il unqes ne pursueroit et ne reavoir null de les choses avauntdites, et quaunt le susdit suppliant ensi avoit jure, les ditz abbe et selerer luy lesseront aler et doneront a lui cynk souldz de sa propre monoie pur ses expens, issint qe vostre dit suppliant est tout outrement destruit pur la perde avantdit. Qe plese a vostre roiale majeste considerer la graund meschief et anientissement de vostre dit povre suppliant et de comander vostre chanceller de faire venir les ditz abbe et selerer devaunt vostre tressage conseil a un certein jour sur peine de C li pur respondre as choses qe a luy serront mys en cest cas, pur Dieu et en oevre de charitee.

No endorsement

1403. The abbot and cellarer were ordered to make restitution to the petitioner on 26 April 1403 (*CCR 1399–1402*, pp. 68–9; no. 3687 of C 81/619). The abbot in question is Thomas Butturwyk 1396–1419.

210

Chertsey, Surrey (1410)
Benedictine
(SC 8/144/7173)

The tenants of Thorp, Egham, Cobham and Chobham petition the king, stating that they were once tenants of the crown, but that since King Edgar gave their manors to the abbot and convent of Chertsey they have held of them by the same services by which they held of the crown. Now, however, the abbot is imposing tallages which they never used to pay, and is distraining them for non-payment. They request a remedy and an end to these tallages so that they are able to hold their lands and tenements as freely from the abbot as they did from the crown.

A nostre tresredoute, tresexcellent et tresgracious seignur le roy suppliont treshumblement vos poverez lieges les tenauntz dez manoirs de Thorpe, Egham, Coveham et Chabeham, jadys tenauntz inmediatez a vos tresnoblez predecessours, roys d'Engleterre, et a le corone, moustrantz coment un de vos ditz predecessours, le Roy Edgar come est suppose, dona les ditz manoirs ovesqe toutz lez appurtinauntz al abbe et le monasteire de Certeseye, a avoir et tenir al dit abbe et sez successours pur toutz jours, par vertue du quel doune les tenauntz des ditz manoirs deveigneront tenauntz a l'abbe du dit lieu pur tenir de luy auxi fraunchement come ils teignoient de la corone devaunt le dit doun, et lour terres et tenementz teigneront solonc la custume dez manoirs suisditz de l'abbe du dit lieu pur le temps esteant toutdys par mesmes lez services q'ils lez teigneront de la corone devaunt le doune avant dit saunz empeschement, tanqe ore tarde qe l'abbe q'ore est, et un ou deux de sez predecessours, ount de novel claymez et chalangez autres charges et services de les ditz tenauntz q'ils ne duissent faire nunqes firent a devaunt, c'estassaver mettaunt les ditz tenauntz a taillages chescun an a la volunte du dit abbe, disant q'ils poent tielx taillages lever de les ditz tenauntz quaunt plerra al dit abbe et sez successours, et pur noun paiement de les ditz taillages de novel demandez les ditz tenauntz sont distreignez et chacez par le dit abbe et sez ministers q'ils sont en point d'estre destrutz, contre la fourme de lour tenure et la volunte du dit donour, s'ils n'eient vostre graciouse socour en cell partie. Qe please a vostre roial mageste et graciouse seignurie consider qe plusours des ditz tenauntz sont francz de sanc et poent aliener et doner lour terres et tenementz, biens et chateux a qi lour plerra, et si le dit abbe purroit avoir sa volunte celle partie, il vorroit aver toutz lour biens quauntz luy plerroit par tielx novelle et torcinousez imposicions, et ordeigner remedy pur les ditz suppliantz qe tielx taillages torcenousement demandez ne soient levez de eux, meas q'ils poent tenir lour terres et tenementz auxi franchement del dit abbe come ils lez teigneront de la corone avauntdite devaunt le dit doun, pur Dieu et en oevere de charite.

No endorsement

1410. On 1 November 1410 a commission of oyer et terminer was issued, on the complaint that the tenants have withdrawn their services and leagued together to resist the abbot of Chertsey (*CPR 1408–13*, p. 310), seemingly in relation to this case. Thomas of Culverdone was abbot 1400–17. For a related petition see **140** and Introduction, pp. xxix–xxxii.

211

Waltham, Essex (c. 1413)
Augustinian canons
(SC 8/149/7449)

John Kemp and others named in the attached schedule, tenants of Waltham Holy Cross, petition the king, making various complaints about the abbot of Waltham, who is too powerful to be sued at common law. They ask the king that the abbot might be examined before him, or before such persons as the king should wish to assign, and that justice might be done. Their complaints follow:
(1) The abbot has increased the rent and services they owe for their land.
(2) The abbot now charges for pasture in Waltham forest, which was previously free.
(3) The abbot prevents them from cutting down, carrying away and selling the trees growing on their land, without his permission, contrary to their ancient rights.
(4) They sued to Henry IV on the above matters, and had a letter ordering the abbot to cease these oppressions and to come to an agreement with the tenants. A day was given them on the feast of St Bartholomew in the late king's 13th year, but the abbot lay in wait with armed men and seized and wounded several of the tenants, whose names are on a schedule attached to this petition, imprisoned them at Hertford and indicted them of murder, felony and other crimes.
(5) The abbot has imprisoned some of them to find surety of the peace, and has attacked and wounded them, and taken their livestock and chattels.
(6) The abbot threatens them with imprisonment and indictment, and also with death.
Endorsed: *Nazeing: John Kemp; Gilbert Simond; William Harry; Nicholas Simond; John Lambard, junior; William Maple; John Mott; John Thorp; William Gardener; John Harry; William Hayward; John Taylor; John Cademan; John Grove; John Knighton; Nicholas Webbe; John Orkesley; John Champ; Robert White; John Cornhull; Simon Wakerild; William Lovenoth; Simon Lovenoth; John Broke; Robert Brewer; John Baldwin; Henry Style; William Bullockherd; John Hendygome; Richard Warley; Thomas Warley; Richard Bullockherd; Nicholas Smaldon.*
Holyfield: John Tyler; John Milner; Walter Camp; Walter Hale; Walter Monigan; John Hay; John Greygoose; Richard Figg.
Upshire: Richard Green; John Briggs; John Frende; John Hegeman; Edmund Green; Thomas Butcher; William Shirey; John Walrey; William Green; John Green of Henkyns; William Bultell; and others, with consideration of five further bills.
John Beinys of Waltham; John Male; William Shirey; Richard Green; John Tailor of Nazeing; John Hendygome; Richard Warley; William Double.

A nostre tressauverain seignur le roy supplient humblement voz poeveres lieges tenants et orateurs Johan Kempe et autres, les nouns des queux sont en une cedule ay celle annexe contenuz demorants deinz la seignurie de Waltham Seyntcros, qe est auncien demesne et d'auncien temps ad este en les mains de voz tresnobles progenitours, et la quelle seignurie le ore abbe de Waltham suisdit ad par graunt en fait par voz tresnobles progenitours a ses predecessours, nadgairs abbes de mesme l'abbaie, a fee ferme, qe comme les dits supliants, lours auncestres et ceaux qe estat ils ont grant la seignurie suisdite fuist en les mains de voz dits tresnobles progenitours soloient et ont uses de temps dont memoire ne court et de droit deussent coupere, prendre, vendre, en carier et emporter les boais cressants enteur leurs terres appelles hegge rawes, sibien pour edifier leurs maisons, encloser leur hayes comme pour vendre a leur voulente, et aussi pour avoir commune de pasture comme de droit appendant a les tenements deinz le forest de Waltham, desquelles proufits de prendre de boais et pester de pasture prendre et avoir, et de diverse autres proufits, le dit abbe et autres de sa covyne et maintenaunce torcenousement destourbent les ditz supliants, et autres diverses extorciouns et injuries continuelment font a dits supliants, en final destruction de leur poeverez estats s'ils ne soient aidez par vostre tressauverain seignurie, quelles grevances et extorsions les dits suppliants ont prestes de moustrez en escript a vostre haulte presence. Plaise a vostre roiall magestie de vostre treshabundante grace considerer les premisses et qe les dits suppliants ne soient mye de poair pour suy a vostre commune ley envers le dit abbe de leurs grevances suisdites, par cause de son grand poair et maintenaunce, et sur ce d'envoie pour le dit abbe par voz gracieuses lettres d'estre devant vous hastifment pour estre examinez de les matieres suisdites en vostre roial presence, ou devant tielx persounes queux vous voillez assigne, et qe le dit abbe sur sa examinacion soit ensy justifie qe les dits supliants pourront avoir ceo qe droit et ley demandent in les matieres suisdites, a l'entent pour leur mettre en quiete et paix pour tousjours, pour Dieux etc.

Ceux sont les compleints des tenants del seignurie de Waltham Seyntcroys envers l'abbe de Waltham suisdit:

En primes, la ou les dits tenants, leurs auncestres et ceux qui estate ils ont de temps dont memoire ne court, et quant la seignurie feust en les mayns des progenitours nostre seignur le roy, ont eue et usee de paier pour checun acre de terre qu'ils tiegnent deinz la seignurie suisdit j d par an et de trouver un hom appelle un *kynge's bedrepe* pour un jour en temps d'Aeust checun an, ou a paier pour le dit hom iiij d, et aussi de trouver j carrue[39] appelle *kynge's benerth*[40] un jour checun an, ou a paier pour le dit carrue xij d, la le dit abbe outre les services avantdits cleyme pour checun acre de terre deinz la seignurie suisdit viij d apaier a luy, ou aultrement qu'ils deussent fimer, arer et seminer sa terre a lours costages propres a son commandment et a sa voulente.

Item, la ou les dits tenants ont eue et use del temps suisdit d'avoir leur commune de pasture as tous leurs bestes deinz la forest de Waltham suisdit fraunkement sanz rien en rendre a ascuny, la le dit abbe clayme pour checun porc iiij d par an, encontre l'auncien droit et coustume de leur tenure suisdite.

Item, la ou les dits tenants ont euez et useez de temps suisdit de couper, prendre, encarier, enporter et vendre les arbres sur leurs terres cressants deinz le seignurie suisdit frankement a leur voulente la, le dit abbe eux distourbe a co faire sanz sa licence, encontre les aunciens custumes de leur tenure suisdit.

Item, la ou les tenants pour les grevances avantdites sueront sibien a Henri nadgaires roy, pere nostre seignur le roy qu'ore est, pour estre remediez de les grevances avauntdits, tanqe ils avoient leurs lettres commaundants le dit abbe

39 In place of the deleted *carrow*.

40 Defined as 'the service which the tenant owed the landlord by plough and cart in Kent' in T. Wright, *Dictionary of Obsolete and Provincial English* (London, 1857), p. 198.

de surcesser de sa malice suisdite et de faire une final accorde parentre luy et les tenants suisdits de les grevances avantdites, par cause du quelle un jour feust pris et assise a Waltham suisdit, cestassaver en le feste de Seint Bartholomew l'an xiij[me] de dit nadgairs roy, au quel jour le dit abbe ove graund nombre de gents arraiez a faire de guerre giseront en agaite pour les dits tenants pour eulx prendre, tuer et mourdrer, et la pristeront diverses de les tenaunts suisdits, les noums des queux sont contenuz en une cedule a ycelle annex, et eux naufreint, bateront et malement treateront, et apres eux misteront en prison a Hertford en une gonge esteiants tanqe a demi jambe, et la eulx detiegnont tanqe il avoit eux endite, ascuns de mourdre, ascuns de felonye et ascuns d'insurreccion faite encontre le paix, a l'entent qu'ils y devoient comiser les servages et bondages avauntdites a dit abbe, en grand arrerissement ete destruccion d'eulx.

Item, apres les grevances avantdites as tenants suisdits par l'abbe suisdit faite, le dit abbe fist arrester diverses d'eulx pour trouver seurite de paix, et eux fist en parformer, et apres qu'ils avoient trouve seurete de paix par diverses temps, le dit abbe ove autres de sa covyne et assent, arraiez a faire de guerre, cest assaver ove arkes et seates et autres armeures, seteront et assault fisteront a diverses de dits tenants, et eulx manasseront, naufreront et malement treiteront, et pristeront torteneusement diverses de leurs bestes et chateux,al entent qu'ils deussent enfraindre leur seurete suisdite.

Item, le dit abbe manace de jour en autre les tenants suisdits pour eux enditer et enprisoner, et de jour en autre mete il en agaite diverses gents de sa covyne pour eulx tuer, ainsy qe a peyne ils n'osent mye suer a nostre seignur le roy par nulle voye ne ailler au large pour poursuer leur droit pour doubte d'estre tuez et mourdrez, par cause qu'ils ne vuellont devenir et comiser d'estre ses vilens et de faire les bondages avantdites, en grande arrerissement, anientisement et final destruccion d'eulx s'ils ne soient aidez et remediez de les mescheifs suisdites.

Endorsed: Nasing: Johan Kemp; Gilbert Simond; William Harry; Nicholas Simond; Johan Lambard, junior; William Maple; Johan Mott; Johan Thorp; William Gardener; Johan Harry; William Hayward; Johan Tayllour; Johan Cademan; Johan Grove; Johan Knyghtone; Nicholas Webbe; Johan Orkesley; Johan Champ; Robert White; Johan Cornhull; Simon Wakerild; William Lovenoth; Simon Lovenoth; Johan Broke; Robert Brewer; Johan Baldewyn; Henry Style; William Bullokherd; Johan Hedingome; Richard Warle; Thomas Warle; Richard Bullokherde; Nicholas Smaldone.
Halifeld: Johan Tyler; Johan Milnere; Walter Camp; Walter Hale; Walter Monigan; Johan Hay; Johan Greygoos; Richard Fygge.
Upschire: Richard Grene; Johan Brigges; Johan Frende; Johan Hegeman; Edmund Grene; Thomas Bocher; William Shirey; Johan Walrey; William Grene; Johan Grene de Henkyns; William Bulcell; et plus autre, ove le rerard de v billez la ente.
Johan Beinys de Waltham; Johan Male; William Sherey; Richard Grene; Johan Taillour de Nasyng; Johan Hendygome; Richard Warlowe; William Dowble.

c. 1413. From the mention of the feast of St Bartholomew, 13 Henry IV (24 August 1412), this petition would seem to date from the early years of the reign of Henry V. The object of the petitioners' complaint is William Harleton, abbot 1400–20. On 28 March 1411 pardons were issued to Richard Green and Thomas Butcher, two of the petitioners named in the endorsement, for conspiring to kill Abbot William, and for breaking and entering the abbey of Waltham Holy Cross with 200 men, assaulting the abbot, his servants and the sheriff of Essex, and breaking bridges so they could not escape (*CPR 1408–13*, p. 285). Similar pardons were also granted to Nicholas Webbe, John Green, Richard Warley, William Gardener, William Double, John Briggs and John Green, and others not included in this petition, for the same offence, which occurred as a result of the sheriff of Essex arresting Richard Green and others, at the abbot's suit, to find surety of good behaviour (*CPR 1408–13*, pp. 285–6). Tension between the abbey and its tenants evidently continued, as shown by the following petition (**212**) which was presented by William Bultell, named in this petition as an inhabitant of Upshire.

212

Waltham, Essex (c. 1423)
Augustinian canons
(SC 8/84/4186)

William Bultell of Waltham petitions the duke of Gloucester and the Lords in parliament for a remedy because the men of the abbot of Waltham came to his house and took livestock from his pasture for no reasonable cause. He is elderly and nearly blind and his wife permanently bedridden and they are utterly destroyed by this cruel extortion.
Endorsed: *Let the abbot of Waltham be charged to answer this petition.*

To you, ful high and mighti prince and ful gracious lord duke of Gloucetir, and to you, ful honurabil lordis atte this parlement assembled, sheweth and ful umbli besekith youre pore bedman William Bultell of Walteham that hou the abbot of Walteham sent his men to þe seid William's hous the Thursday next afore Seint Laurence's day last past, and there they toke and drofe awey out of þe same William's several pasture xij hede of nete and an hors, and hem their deliverid to þe same abbot, and he hath hem disposid at his oun wil wrongfulli and without ony cause resonabil, the which William is an old man and impotent and nigh blynd, and hys wyfe an agid woman and lyth continuelli bedrede, and nou have they no good to lyve bi, and bi that cruel extorcion aforseid they be uttirli destroied, but if þei [have remedie] bi your ful gracious lordshipes. Plese hit to your ful nobil lordship and wyse discrecions, atte reverence of almighti God, to have pitee on \þis/ your pore bedfolk and ordein remedie by your avise of þ'aforseid wrong so þat your pore bedfolk be not thus wrongfulli oppressid, and so bi malicius crueltie so destruied, for love of God and in dede of charitee.

Endorsed: Soit l'abbe de Waltham charge de respondre a la bille.

c. 1423. The petition has been speculatively dated to c. 1423 in accordance with the note on the guard linking this to a rebellion by the abbot's bond tenants at Waltham and elsewhere in 1423 (*CPR 1422–9*, p. 174). It must date to the 1420s since it is addressed to Humphrey of Lancaster, duke of Gloucester, who acted as Protector and Defender of England between 1422 and 1429, during the minority of Henry VI. The abbot is William of Hertford (1420–50). The petitioner was involved in an earlier challenge to the abbey's authority, see **211** above.

213

King's Langley, Hertfordshire (c. 1425–50)
Dominican
(SC 8/345/E1324)

The tenants of the town of King's Langley petition the king, complaining that the prior and his brothers have wounded them so they dare not go about their business, they should be enclosed but issue from a gate in their precinct, they neglect their parsonage, have taken their agriculture in hand and excluded the secular farmers, they pasture so many cattle on the common that it is bare, and the townspeople cannot common their cattle there, they carry weapons and make assaults upon the tenants going about their husbandry, they receive suspect people and women of ill repute, and they sue the townspeople at Westminster if they dare to make complaint, to their utter ruin. They request that letters of the privy seal be directed to the prior to appear personally before the king and council to answer such articles and causes that the tenants shall allege against him and others of his house, and to receive such direction as seems expedient so that the friars live according to their religion, and the tenants can live in peace without any vexation or trouble from the prior or anyone for him or in his name.
Endorsed: *Against the prior of Langley Regis.*

To the kyng our sovereign lord, pityously compleynen and shewen to your mooste noble highnes your poore tenauntes and dailly oratours of your town of Kynges Langley, wher amongest all other your said pore tenauntes and dailly oratours been grevously vexid and oppressid by the unlaufull meanes of Sir Robert Thomson, priour of the freres within Langley aforsaid and other his brethern, freres of the convent, thurgh his supportacion, contrary to your gracious peas and lawes, have bodily wounded dyvers of your pore tenauntes enhabitauntes within your said town, which been in parell of their lyves insomoch that for fere and drede of the said priour and of other his brethern they dare not goo abowte their bodily laboures and occupacions to get their livyng, for the said freres, contrary to their profescion and religion, have a certeyn gate made owte of their closure, which at their first fundacion was close and pulid, to th'entent they shuld kepe their reguler observaunce and divine service, which by the said priour and brethern is perusid, for their said gate openyth in to your highway which before was not seen untill now of late, nor the said religious men shuld meddill with catell nor husbondry, for all such seculer bysynes was in the handes of the fermour of the parsonage of the said freres, whiche parsonage the said religious men have suffred to fall down by cause they wolde have the husbondry and besynes in their own handes, and exclude the seculer fermoures whiche in tymes paste have had the occupacion and use of the same, aswell to the great hurtes and losses of the poore vicar and curate ther beyng incumbent as to your pore tenauntes for occupyeng their husbondry among theym, for the said freres dailly dryveth and rutteth furth at the said gate suche a multitude of catell in to the comon wode next unto their said gate that the said comon is made so bare that your pore tenauntes can not bryng up their catell nor lyve as they have doon tymes paste. Also the said freres often tymes have come furth at the said gate, and dailly doth, with wepons, and maketh assaultes upon your said tenauntes in their husbondry, and theym grevously betith and woundeth, and also owte of the said gate the same freres resorten to suspect persones and to myslyveng women of their bodyes, to the great displeasur of Almyghty God and great shame to the religion, and a perilous example to all your pore tenauntes. And bycause your said tenauntes spekith and replieth ayenst the said priour and his brethern of their inordinate demeanour the which is kept within your said town amongest theym, the said priour feynith and contrivith matieres and causes ayenst your said pore tenauntes, contrary to all right and conscience, and theym sueth at the lawe at Westmynster every terme, and witholdith from theym a great parte of their levyng, which by right and laudable custumme within your said town of tyme owte of mynd they have had, to their utterly undoyng. Wherfor pleise your gracious highnes of your rightwisnes to direct your gracious lettres of privy \seal/ unto the said priour, commandyng hym by the same personally to appere before your grace and counceill whersoyever your grace be within your realme of Englond, to make answer to suche articles and causes that your pore tenauntes shall allege ayenst hym and other of his brethern accordyng to right, and to set suche direction as shalbe seen moost expedient by your noble grace and counceill, so that the said freres may live accordyng to their religion, and your said pore \tenauntes/ to lyve in rest and peas withoute any further vexacion or trouble of the said prior or of any other for hym or in his name. And your said pore tenauntes shall dailly pray to God for the preservacion of your mooste gracious highnes.

Endorsed: Contra priorem de Langley Regis.

c. 1425–50. The petition is speculatively dated to c. 1425–50 on the basis of the hand, and also because the petition is in English. The hand might suggest a date early in this range.

214

Bushmead, Bedfordshire (c. 1433)
Augustinian canons
(SC 8/144/7172)

William Tristour, late of London, formerly saddler to Henry IV and Henry V, petitions the Commons of parliament, wishing, in order to found a chantry for their souls and his own, to give the advowson of the church of Tempsford, with appurtenances, to Bushmead Priory, and asks the Commons to request the king's permission for Richard Osbarne, William Caldewell and John Tanner, enfeoffed with this land and advowson to his use, to give it to the priory, and for the priory to receive it.
Endorsed on face: *Let it be sent to the Lords.*

To the right worshipfulle and discrete comunes of this present parlement, plese hit to yow to consider how William Tristour, late of Londone, sadiller alsewelle to Kyng Herry the forth, aielle to our souverayne lord, os to Kyng Herry the Vte, fader unto our sayd souverayne lord, who soules God assoille, purposyng alsewelle for the hele and merite of ther soules as for his awene, to yeve to the priour and the covent of the priorie of Bisshemede in the shire of Bedford and to ther successoures the advowesone of the chirch of Temmesford with th'appurtenantz in the sayd countee, forto have to hem and to here successours in propre use for evermore, and there one in his last wille declared unto Richard Oseberne, William Caldewelle and John Tanner, his feffez in the sayd advowesone, to do ther bisynesse in perfournyng of the sayd wille, for alsemuch as hit was noght done in his lyfe, to make request and prey to our sayd souverayne lord that he wille, by the advyse and assent of his lordes espirituelles and temporelles of this present parlement, of his hygh grace, graunte licence for hyme and for hys heires to the forsayd Richard Oseberne, William Caldewelle and John Tanner that they may yeve and graunte the sayd advowesone with th'appurtenantz, the which is noght holdene of our sayd souverayn lord, to Robert Techemerche, nowe priour of the sayd priorie, and his covent, and to ther successours for evermore, and also graunte licence for hyme and for his heires to the sayd priour and covent to receyve the forsayd advowesone with th'appurtenantz of the forsayd Richard, William Caldewelle and John, to have and holde to the sayd priour and covent and to here successours for evermore. And also that the sayd priour and covent and here successours possessione hadde of the sayd advowesone with th'appurtenantz, the forsayd chirch may appropre to hem and to here successours, and the sayd chirch so approprie may holde in here propre uses to heme and to here successours for evermore, the estatuit made of landes and tenementz noght to be putte to mort mayne ner noone other estatutes or ordinances made a contrarie noght withstandyng. And that with owtyne fyne or grete fee payng to the use of our sayde souverayne lord, atte the reverence of Almyghty God and in way of charitee, consideryng that the sayd priorie is noght of lyfelod yerly to the value of xl li, and also that hit is gretely charged of raparacion of the chirch of the sayd priorie and other howeses necessare therinne. And that for God and in way of charitee. Purveide algates þat the parsone or the incumbent of the saide chirche atte this tyme beyng be not hurt ne in no wyse harmed be this graunte.

Endorsed on face: Soit baille as seignuris.

c. 1433. On 8 July 1433 licence was granted for the feoffees to grant the advowson of the church of Tempsford to Robert Techemerche, called the late (?) prior, and the convent of Bushmead, in accordance with the petitioner's last will (*CPR 1429–36*, p. 296). This would seem to indicate that the petitioner was dead by this date, and so the petition must date to earlier. Although the dates for Techemerche's abbacy are unknown, the list of abbots in the Bushmead cartulary states that he ruled for thirty years (*Heads of Houses III*, 400). A similar petition from the same petitioner is SC 8/144/7169. For an earlier transcript of this petition, see no. 31 of PRO 31/7/118.

INDEX OF RELIGIOUS HOUSES

The Arabic numbers refer to the documents; the Roman numerals refer to page numbers in the Introduction.

KEY

A – Augustinian canons
B – Benedictine
Ba – Benedictine alien
Bd – Benedictine dependent
BC – Cluniac
C – Cistercian
CA – Carthusian
FA – Augustinian friars
FC – Carmelite
FD – Dominican
FF – Franciscan
FP – Pied friars
G – Gilbertine
Hosp. – Hospital
NA – Augustinian nuns
NB – Benedictine nuns
NC – Cistercian nuns
P – Premonstratensian canons

INDEX OF RELIGIOUS ORDERS

INDEX OF PEOPLE AND PLACES